MASTERS OF LENS AND LIGHT:

a checklist of major cinematographers and their feature films

by

WILLIAM DARBY

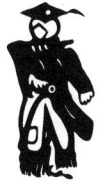

The Scarecrow Press, Inc.
Metuchen, N.J., & London
1991

9200005119

PN
1998
.D285
1991

British Library Cataloguing-in-Publication data available

Library of Congress Cataloging-in-Publication Data

Darby, William, 1942-
    Masters of lens and light : a checklist of major cinematographers
and their feature films / by William Darby.
        p.   cm.
    Includes bibliographical references and index.
    ISBN 0-8108-2454-X   (alk. paper)
    1. Motion pictures--Catalogs.   2. Cinematographers--Credits.   I.
Title.
PN1998.D285   1911
011'.37--dc20   91-20656

Dedicated to the memory of my mother

CONTENTS

v

ACKNOWLEDGMENTS

I would like to thank my brother-in-law, Thomas R. Panzenhagen, who, however unwittingly, triggered my initial interest in this subject. Claire Brandt and Heidi Brandt of Eddie Brandt's Saturday Matinee were most helpful in unearthing the illustrations that accompany the text.

Since any compilation of this size is likely to be incomplete despite the best of my intentions, I would welcome hearing from interested parties as to errors of omission or commission. It is hoped that the present list can be augmented and enlarged to provide an even better factual basis for this relatively neglected area of film scholarship.

I would, finally, like to dedicate the present work to the memory of my mother, Dorothy H. Darby (1919–1977), whose enthusiasm and capacities for painstaking genealogical research made her a model to emulate.

William Darby
Detroit, MI

This book sets forth the credits of more than seven
hundred cinematographers. These entries include only the
feature-length (at least 45 minutes) films of individuals who
are credited as principal or co-principal photographer on at
least five works. (I have made two exceptions to this rule by
including the entries for Edwin S. Porter and Ernest Schoedsack,
pioneer figures who deserve separate entries.) The greater
number of these cinematographers worked primarily in American
films, but I have also included notable figures from Great
Britain, France, Germany, Italy, Sweden, and the USSR. All
individual entries have been alphabetized and numbered for
ease of reference and Index retrieval. Each film title within
a particular cinematographer's filmography is also entered
alphabetically and accompanied by its year of release and some
production information: country of origin and major studio
affiliation. An asterisk (*) following a film title indicates that
more than one cinematographer was involved with the production.
I have used abbreviations for much of the production data
and the reader will find a key to them on page xxv.

A typical entry is as follows:

FRANK STANLEY

The Big Fix   1978   Univ.

Here the title is followed by the year of release and the name
of the studio which released the film (Universal). No country
of origin is included when the film comes from a major US or
international producer (e.g., Cannon, DeLaurentiis).

A more involved entry is as follows:

ERNEST STEWARD

Above Us the Waves   1955   GB--Rank/Rep.

Here, after the title and year of release, one finds the
country of origin (Great Britain) followed by the studios that
were involved with the film both in that country (Rank) and
in the United States (Republic). I have used dashes (--)
to separate countries from studios, even when the studio is
in that country. Slashes (/) separate countries, if a film
has been produced by various nations, or studios, when more
than one is involved, as in the second example above.

A lengthy miscellaneous section includes entries for
notable films that are not included among the works of major
cinematographers (e.g., American Graffiti) as well as cinematographers who have either not produced enough significant
work to be included in that group or emerged with major
credits only during the past two or three years. I have also
used this miscellaneous section to list significant foreign films,
particularly from Japan and the Soviet Union, that might be of
interest to an American audience. The format for this entire
section is slightly different in that all entries are listed alphabetically by title, followed by their production information
in parentheses, and then by the name(s) of the cinemato-
grapher(s) involved in the production. Once again, I have
used dashes to set off the country of origin from the studio;
and I have employed slashes to separate countries and/or
studios when there are more than one for an individual film.

A brief appendix follows. It lists all the Academy Award
nominees and winners (the latter in all capital letters) in cinematography since the Oscars began in 1928/29. In addition,
the cinematographic awards of the British Academy and the
American Society of Cinematographers are listed.

An index to all film titles completes the work. Most
titles are keyed to the entry number in the main body. Those
from the Miscellaneous section are keyed to page numbers.

BIBLIOGRAPHIC NOTE

Cinematography has never enjoyed the critical attention

that other facets of filmmaking (direction, acting, even music) have received. Indeed, many of its leading figures remain outside the pale of even the most encyclopedic of references or, if included in such works, are represented by only their more notable credits. One searches in vain for any mention of such prolific B cameramen as Harry Neumann or Ernest Miller; and even seemingly more significant figures, such as David Abel, are often omitted from the better-known reference books.

There are, of course, numerous technical studies of cinematography and filmmaking. John Alton's Painting with Light (1949) and Frederick Young's The Work of the Motion Picture Cameraman (1972) are simply two of many that detail numerous technical problems and solutions for the beginner. Young's book does have the advantage of talking briefly about his early career in British films. G. W. "Billy" Bitzer's autobiography, His Story (1973), is useful for its details on early equipment and methods; however, Bitzer is circumspect about the personalities with whom he worked and the book runs out of energy from about its midpoint. Karl Brown's Adventures with D. W. Griffith, a project that was encouraged by film historian Kevin Brownlow, is much more readable. Brown not only chronicles his own growing pains within the Griffith organization but also talks about the major personalities, the director and Bitzer, as well as a host of others with whom he worked. Joseph Walker's The Light on Her Face (1984) offers the recollections of a cinematographer who worked long and well for such diverse personalities as Harry Cohn and Frank Capra. Again, personal anecdotes dominate. Nestor Almendros' A Man with a Camera (1982) presents a view of international filmmaking by a cinematographer who has worked extensively in both Europe and the United States. Almendros concentrates on the individual films and the technical problems that they presented.

For anyone concerned with understanding the studio system within which so many cinematographers worked, David Bordwell, Janet Staiger, and Kristin Thompson's The Classical Hollywood Cinema (1985) is a must. Scholarly in tone and presentation, this work details the stylistic, technical, and business shifts that occurred in Hollywood from the silent era to approximately 1960.

There are three significant collections of interviews

with notable cinematographers that represent, perhaps, the best introductions to the field. Charles Higham's <u>Hollywood Cameramen</u> (1970) includes a critical/historical introduction and discussions with Leon Shamroy, Lee Garmes, William Daniels, James Wong Howe, Stanley Cortez, Karl Struss, and Arthur Miller. The tone of most of these conversations is informal and just a bit nostalgic, given the subjects' ages. Higham does include filmographies for each of his subjects.

Leonard Maltin's <u>The Art of the Cinematographer</u> (1971) contains the most extensive and insightful introduction to the history of cinematography. His interviews are with Arthur Miller, Hal Mohr, Harold Rosson, Lucien Ballard, and Conrad Hall, so that a much wider chronological spectrum is present than in Higham. Maltin also supplies filmographies for his principal subjects. The only weakness of his work is that it initially appeared nearly twenty years ago.

Dennis Schaeffer and Larry Salvato's <u>Masters of Light</u> (1984) continues the interview tradition, albeit with cinematographers who have gained prominence after 1960. Their book contains interviews with Nestor Almendros, John A. Alonzo, John Bailey, Bill Butler, Michael Chapman, William Fraker, Conrad Hall, Laszlo Kovacs, Owen Roizman, Vittorio Storaro, Mario Tosi, Haskell Wexler, Billy Williams, Gordon Willis, and Vilmos Zsigmond. For anyone concerned with how cinematographers work within the less structured world of contemporary filmmaking, these conversations will prove enlightening; at times, however, the authors and their subjects become a bit too technical for the average reader.

Probably the best ongoing publication in the field of cinematography is <u>American Cinematographer</u>, the monthly magazine of the American Society of Cinematographers. This publication began in 1919 and has featured articles on technical and personal accomplishments almost from its beginning. A particularly interesting issue is the 50th anniversary number (January 1969), which focuses on the history of cinematography and traces both technical and stylistic developments within the profession. Given its breadth of coverage--a typical issue includes a detailed study of the production of a famous earlier film, a brief description of the newest publications in the film world, articles on contemporary movies and their cinematographers, and comments on VCR issues of notable current and older films--<u>American Cinematographer</u> is one of the outstanding journals in film history and criticism.

In compiling individual cinematographers' credits the following works have proved invaluable:

Variety Film Reviews, 1907-1984. 18 volumes. New York: Garland, 1983-1986.

Variety (1985 to present)

Hansen, Patricia King, and Alan Gevinson, eds. The American Film Institute Catalog of Motion Pictures in the United States, 1911-1920. Berkeley: University of California Press, 1988.

Munden, Kenneth W., ed. The American Film Institute Catalog of Motion Pictures, 1921-1930. New York: Bowker, 1971.

Nash, Jay Robert, and Stanley Ralph Ross. The Motion Picture Guide. 14 volumes. Chicago and Evanston: Cinebooks, 1985-1989.

Halliwell, Leslie. Halliwell's Film and Video Guide, 6th ed. New York: Scribner's, 1987.

Krafsur, Richard P. The American Film Institute Catalog of Motion Pictures, 1961-1970. New York: Bowker, 1976.

INTRODUCTION

Motion picture production requires the collaboration of various specialists. Actors, directors, writers, musicians, designers, and editors all have pivotal roles at various stages of the process by which a story idea is converted into an on-screen reality. Clearly, cinematographers, who are responsible for designing the lighting and camera movements that will be filmed, play a major part in this process. Their talents should include artistic, scientific, and business expertise since they have to coordinate the demands of directors, equipment, and schedules. Cinematographers have to think like an artist in setting up shots for dramatic emphases and coherence; they have to be aware of the interplay between sources of light and the capacities of their cameras; and they have to supervise a work crew as well as deal with other technical specialists.

The cinematographer's varied roles have long been noted by commentators and by practitioners themselves. The title of John Alton's technical study of cinematography, Painting with Light (1949), suggests the duality of art and science involved; while long-time, celebrated British cinematographer Frederick Young has wisely insisted that his craft is "where the imagination meets the reality of the film process."[1] One needs only to extend Young's "reality" to include time and cost constraints in commercial filmmaking to appreciate the various kinds of expertise that any cinematographer should possess. While such business realities are constants, the decisive working relationship for any cinematographer is with the director. In essence, the latter's wishes are the commands which the cinematographer must try to obey, or at least to fulfill as well as possible. There have been numerous ongoing collaborations between cinematographers and directors--arrangements that underline the importance of this working relationship to successful filmmaking. During its heyday the studio system often supplied such production continuities as a matter of logistics. However, more independent working relationships, such as those between Robert Burks and Alfred Hitchcock, Allen Daviau and Steven Spielberg, and (on the international scene) between Eduard Tissé and Sergei Eisenstein, have contributed significantly to popular and critical cinematic successes.

One of the more notable of recent working partnerships between cinematographer and director is that of Nestor Almendros and François Truffaut. In an introduction to Almendros' A Man with a Camera (1982), Truffaut sets forth his ideas of what constitutes good motion picture photography. According to the noted New Wave director, the cinematographer's primary tasks include the "prevention of ugliness," the "purification" of the image so as to render apparent its emotional force, the plausible presentation of pre-twentieth-century settings when they are called for, and the manipulation of light sources, most particularly the sun.[2] To these essentially aesthetic prescriptions Almendros later sagely adds that any cinematographer needs to understand the laws of optics. However, he also concludes: "Once a few basic rules have been learned, the job is not very complicated, especially with an assistant to take care of focusing, measuring distances, and looking into the mechanics of the camera."[3]

The highly specialized craft that Almendros and other contemporaries practice has evolved from humbler circumstances. In the beginning, the cinematographer, or the cameraman, as he was more apt to be called, was the principal producer of the completed work. Edwin Porter, celebrated for The Great Train Robbery (1903), was producer, director, and photographer for that work and many others. G. W. "Billy" Bitzer filmed more than three hundred short features between 1899 and 1908. While Porter remained primarily interested in the technical aspects of photography, Bitzer moved on, through his association with D. W. Griffith, to become a pioneer in cinematography. The emergence of the director and then the producer as major decision-makers in filmmaking placed the camera operator in a new, subordinate role--one that enabled concentration on the intricacies of lighting and shot design. By 1920 Bitzer had demonstrated mastery of both soft (or impressionistic) and hard (or exact) photography in Griffith

productions for which style was consciously determined by artistic demands. Griffith's breakthrough into longer productions
also necessitated the systematic recording of individual camera
shots, a task that fell to the young and willing Karl Brown,
whose clipboard notes became a staple practice of film production thereafter.

Brown, who finagled a job with Griffith, worked along
with Bitzer on such productions as Birth of a Nation (1915)
and Intolerance (1916). Looking back many years later,
Brown felt that Bitzer's artistry resided primarily in his sense
of composition abetted by his judgments about exposures and
lighting.[4] Bitzer himself emphasized, however, that he and
his cohorts "often learned new tricks through our mistakes."[5]
At the same time, Bitzer was also acutely aware of the technical
realities within which he worked. He was operating a hand-
cranked camera for much of his career, so that speed control,
with all its consequences for film exposure, was a matter of
personal judgment and dexterity. Focusing had often to be
set up before a scene and could not be significantly altered
once actual shooting had begun. Bitzer also had to work initially with a camera that weighed close to a ton; and, to a
significant extent, the making of an epic like Birth of a Nation
was facilitated by the development of lighter equipment (i.e.,
the Pathe lightweight camera). While his contributions to filmmaking techniques included the development of the close-up,
the iris "in and out" technique, and the shading of the lens
in order to photograph directly into the sun, Bitzer gradually
became a subordinate figure within the Griffith studio. Indeed, by his own admission, he lived in semi-retirement from
1920 until his death in 1944.

Bitzer also served as a personal inspiration and guide
to later cinematographers, and in this role he again foresha-
dowed future practices. In addition to Karl Brown, who went
on to become a major cinematographer in the 1920s, Bitzer (and
Griffith) also encouraged such talents as Oliver Marsh and
Joseph Walker. Indeed, the apprenticeship Karl Brown served
with Bitzer, one in which he moved up from custodial to independent photographic assignments, would be typical of much
subsequent Hollywood practice. Brown also worked for other
early movie cameramen, such as Alfred Gosden, Marcel Le
Picard, and Victor Scheurich; while Marsh and Walker, who
went on to become mainstays in the cinematography depart-
ments at MGM and Columbia, respectively, began by doing odd

jobs for Bitzer and others. In the later 1920s, Walker himself
was aided by Milton Krasner and Robert Planck, who served
as his camera operators before moving up to be major cinematographers themselves. James Wong Howe worked in various
capacities for Alvin Wyckoff (Cecil B. DeMille's principal cameraman through 1923), Henry Kotani, and Bert Glennon. Stanley
Cortez, who achieved fame with his work on The Magnificent
Ambersons (1942), also started with Wyckoff and did stints
with Karl Struss, George Barnes, Charles Rosher, Charles
Schoenbaum, Hal Mohr, Joseph August, and Arthur Miller
during the 1920s and 1930s. Gregg Toland gained entrance
to the profession through serving an apprenticeship with George
Barnes, one in which the younger man gradually became a co-
photographer with his older colleague. Even in the 1960s one
finds John A. Alonzo working as an operator for James Wong
Howe; and Conrad Hall working for such luminaries as Ernest
Haller, Robert Surtees, Ted McCord, Hal Mohr, and Burnett
Guffey--who, in turn, earlier worked for Leon Shamroy who,
as we have seen, apprenticed with Joseph Walker.

The advent of television in the 1950s changed this apprenticeship system somewhat by providing an alternative field
in which fledgling cinematographers could learn their craft.
Bill Butler and Owen Roizman began their careers in this medium doing commercials, as did noted British cinematographer
Billy Williams. Haskell Wexler produced independent films
before his emergence as a major Hollywood cinematographer in
the 1960s.[6] The decline of the studio system also enabled
photographers from other backgrounds to become involved as
cinematographers. Thus, university graduates Conrad Hall
and William Fraker (both from the University of Southern
California) came to enjoy notable assignments; and emigrants
like Laszlo Kovacs and Vilmos Zsigmond (both from Hungary)
gradually emerged from B to A status. In the current international framework of movie production, it is hardly surprising
to find a figure such as the Italian-born Mario Tosi working
consistently on American films and his more renowned countryman, Vittorio Storaro, employed on such prestigious epics as
Apocalypse Now (1979) and Reds (1981). Hollywood has, of
course, never been reluctant to use foreign talent as can be
seen in the career of Karl Freund, who had worked with F.
W. Murnau in Germany in the 1920s before coming to California
in the early 1930s. Freund's subsequent credits include some
very stylish assignments (Dracula, 1931, and The Mummy,
1932, which he directed with Charles Stumar as his

cinematographer), some standard studio products (South of St. Louis, 1949, and Bright Leaf, 1950, at Warner Bros.), and some television work (on I Love Lucy).

Like so many other film technicians during the 1930s, 1940s, and early 1950s, cinematographers adapted to the studio system, often working for extended periods while under contract to one or another organization. If some individuals moved from studio to studio, others stayed in one place and came to personify the photographic styles associated with their particular employer's products. George Folsey and Joseph Ruttenberg did so at MGM, while Tony Guadio and Sol Polito came to define the look of Warner Bros. Joseph Walker and Burnett Guffey were the most notable major cinematographers at Columbia; John Seitz and Victor Milner stood out at Paramount; Joseph Valentine and Russell Metty handled most of Universal's more prestigious assignments; Charles Clarke and Leon Shamroy were stalwarts at Twentieth Century-Fox. Even the lesser studios had their own cinematographers, with RKO being well served by Nicholas Musuraca, Republic by Reggie Lanning and Jack Marta, and (most notably) Goldwyn by the celebrated Gregg Toland until his early death in 1948.

These studio cinematographers and their more independent colleagues had to deal with various stylistic and technological changes during Hollywood's heyday. The employment of a second camera before 1920 added a greater fluidity to film-making while further necessitating a more specialized role for the cinematographer. For many observers movie photography reached its zenith during the 1920s, especially in the opulent looking Sunrise (1927), which featured a collaboration between cinematographers Charles Rosher and Karl Struss and emigré director F. W. Murnau. Rosher's development of the suspended camera, the increased use of the camera boom, and the introduction of panchromatic film stocks throughout the 1920s, all served to provide an ever greater freedom of movement and contrast in the art of movie photography. However, the advent of the sound film with The Jazz Singer (1927) brought a temporary end to these freedoms as multi-camera shooting from stationary positions became necessary for recording clarity. The weight of contemporary cameras and the noises of their operation also served as obstacles to fluid photography. Only the development of lighter and quieter equipment enabled cinematographers to regain the photographic sophistication of the 1920s in the early 1930s. Incandescent lighting came to replace the older arc lights which, according to William Daniels, often smoked.[7] The zoom lens supplied an in-camera capacity for movement, while more sophisticated tracking methods supplied further renewed artistic freedom. This latter inventiveness probably reached a peak when James Wong Howe went on roller skates to photograph some of the fight sequences in Body and Soul (1947).

The 1930s and 1940s have also been singled out as the "best" period in movie photography.[8] The advent of viable technicolor film gradually led to more productions being rendered in that format. Initially, certain cinematographers, most notably W. Howard Greene and Ray Rennahan, specialized in the newer technicolor processes and were often hired as advisors and co-photographers on major studio productions. However, by the mid-1940s technicolor had become a standard option understood by virtually all cinematographers. This development was symbolized by the division of the Academy Awards for cinematography into black-and-white and color categories in 1939, a distinction that was observed until 1966. Deep focus photography became a rage with the release of Citizen Kane in 1941. While cinematographer Gregg Toland's contributions to this powerful film are many, his technical inventiveness has probably been exaggerated. Deep focus photography had been used and understood before Citizen Kane; the apparent innovation of including ceilings in interior shots can be seen in Stagecoach (1939), a film Welles claimed he studied as a preparation for his own work. Many of the stunning technical effects were the work of the largely uncredited Vernon Walker, who contrived to make often small sets seem vast indeed.[9] In the late 1940s Hollywood experienced another stylistic shift, motivated in part by the neo-realistic filmmakers of post-World War II Italy. A documentary look was created in such films as The House on 92nd Street (1945), Call Northside 777 (1947), and, most notably, The Naked City (1948), for which William Daniels won an Oscar. This downbeat visual emphasis nicely complemented the film noir tendencies and mood so apparent in Hollywood films after 1945.

While television supplied a training ground for many young cinematographers, its immediate impact on Hollywood was much less happy. The studios, faced with declining attendance figures, decided that new photographic processes, ones that used larger screen dimensions than television could hope

to supply, were the answer to their woes. These new processes, which included Cinerama, CinemaScope, Todd A-O,
and VistaVision (as well as the even shorter-lived 3-D),
were not welcomed by contemporary cinematographers, who
were appalled by the new dimensions and the visual distor-
tions that often accompanied these wide-screen novelties.
Lee Garmes seemingly spoke for nearly all his colleagues years
later when he declared: "I found working CinemaScope a
horror. Shallow focus, very wide angles, everyone lining up,
awful."[10] Fortunately, Hollywood's craze for gigantic-sized
screens and stories came to an end by the early 1960s. In
France this same period witnessed the emergence of a new
cinematic style that utilized hand-held cameras and natural
light sources to create more intimate and more "immediate"
looking films (e.g., A Bout de Souffle, 1959). These in-
novations would be incorporated into American cinematography
throughout the turbulent 1960s.

During that decade and the 1970s, the increasing re-
laxation of censorship standards and the demise of the studio
system made for less structured modes of production in which
cinematographers were employed on a much more random basis
than heretofore. Technology and enhanced special effects,
as can be seen in the Star Wars series, increasingly came to
stand for more than photographic style or panache. Indeed,
many newer films stylistically resemble television shows in their
excessive use of close-ups which create feelings of claustro-
phobia much at odds with the more spacious, artistic, and
relaxed compositions of the past. Paradoxically, if the modern
cinematographer commands a much greater technical repertoire
than his predecessors, all too often this enhanced capacity
is dissipated on rudimentary visual designs.

A major source of critical debate among practicing cinematographers has always been the subject of light and how it
should be employed. Different cinematographers have emphasized different lighting schemes with emphases running between
extreme stylization and extreme realism. John Seitz was an
early advocate of the use of the "north light" so often associated with the paintings of Rembrandt. Lee Garmes' lighting
for Morocco (1930) has been widely praised for its chiaroscuro
effects. James Wong Howe was a lifelong advocate of realistic
light sources that could be justified as coming from somewhere
in nature. Stanley Cortez consistently strived to manipulate
light along more impressionistic lines and even insisted that

color photography should not be "naturalistic" in order to best utilize the symbolism of various shades and hues.[11] Cortez's practice is, of course, belied by such newer realistic color films as The Wild Bunch, where director Sam Peckinpah's revisionistic plot emphases are visually reinforced by starkly "realistic" photography. Long-time Hollywood cinematographer William Daniels proved himself capable in many visual styles; indeed, he went from the flattering (and often gauze-enhanced) photography of Greta Garbo at MGM in the 1930s to the harsher, documentary style of The Naked City in the 1940s and to the widescreen effects of Strategic Air Command in the 1950s. Daniels probably defined the cinematographer's role best when, in discussing lighting, he insisted that he always varied his work "considerably according to the story."[12] In a popular medium like motion pictures such pragmatism is undoubtedly the ultimate wisdom.

NOTES

1. Frederick Young and Paul Petzold, The Work of the Motion Picture Cameraman (New York: Communications Arts Books, 1972), p. 23.

2. Nestor Almendros, A Man with a Camera, Trans. Rachel Phillips Belash (New York: Farrar, Straus, Giroux, 1982), vii.

3. Almendros, p. 4.

4. Karl Brown, Adventures with D. W. Griffith (New York: Farrar, Straus, Giroux, 1973), p. 50.

5. G. W. Bitzer, G. W. Bitzer: His Story (New York: Farrar, Straus, Giroux, 1973), p. 4.

6. Career backgrounds for newer cinematographers can be gleaned from the interviews in Dennis Shaefer and Larry Salvato, Masters of Light: Conversations with Contemporary Cinematographers (Berkeley: University of California Press, 1984). The older cinematographers' career backgrounds can be found in the interviews contained in Charles Higham, Hollywood Cameramen: Sources of Light (Bloomington: Indiana University Press, 1970), and Leonard Maltin, The Art of the Cinematographer:

A Survey and Interviews with Five Masters (New York: Dover Publications, 1971).

7. Higham, p. 66.

8. Higham, p. 13.

9. David Bordwell, Janet Staiger, and Kristin Thompson, The Classical Hollywood Cinema: Film Style and Modes of Production to 1960 (New York: Columbia University Press, 1985), pp. 348-349.

10. Higham, p. 54.

11. Higham, p. 98.

12. Higham, p. 57.

KEY TO ABBREVIATIONS

*	Two or more cinematographers involved with production
AA	Allied Artists
ABC	American Broadcasting Company
AE	Avco Embassy
AFT	American Film Theatre
AIP	American International Pictures
Alg.	Algeria
Arg.	Argentina
Aus.	Australia
Aust.	Austria
Belg.	Belgium
Bio.	Biograph
Braz.	Brazil
Bulg.	Bulgaria
BV	Buena Vista
Can.	Canada
CBS	Columbia Broadcasting System
Col.	Columbia Pictures
Czech.	Czechoslovakia
DeL.	DeLaurentiis Entertainment Group
Den.	Denmark
Dis.	Disney (includes Buena Vista)
Eal.	Ealing Studios
EL	Eagle-Lion
Emb.	Embassy Pictures
EMI	EMI Productions
FBO	Film Booking Offices of America
Fin.	Finland
FN	First National

Fox	Fox Productions
Fr.	France
GB	Great Britain
Ger.	Germany
GN	Grand National
Gold.	Samuel Goldwyn Productions
Ham.	Hammer Films
HBO	Home Box Office
Hem.	Hemdale
HgKg.	Hong Kong
Holl.	Netherlands
Hung.	Hungary
Ice.	Iceland
Ire.	Ireland
Isr.	Israel
It.	Italy
Jap.	Japan
Lip.	Lippert Pictures
Lor.	Lorimar Productions
Lux.	Luxembourg
Metro.	Metro
Metro.-Gold.	Metro-Goldwyn
Mex.	Mexico
MGM	Metro-Goldwyn-Mayer
MGM-UA	Metro-Goldwyn-Mayer/United Artists
Mon.	Monogram
NBC	National Broadcasting Company
NG	National General
Nig.	Nigeria
Nor.	Norway
NZ	New Zealand
Par.	Paramount
PDC	Producers Distributing Corporation
Pol.	Poland
Port.	Portugal
PRC	Producers Releasing Corporation
Rep.	Republic Pictures
RKO	Radio-Keith-Orpheum Pictures
Rom.	Romania
Rus.	Russia
S.Afr.	South Africa
Selz.	Selznick Films/Selznick International
Sp.	Spain
Swed.	Sweden
Switz.	Switzerland

TC	Twentieth-Century
TCF	Twentieth-Century-Fox
Touch.	Touchstone Pictures
Tri-S.	Tri-Star
Tun.	Tunisia
UA	United Artists
UFA	Deutsche Universum-Film AG
UN	United Nations
Univ.	Universal (and Universal International)
US	Minor Studios and Independent Producers
USSR	Union of Soviet Socialist Republics
Vita.	Vitagraph
WB	Warner Bros.
Yugo.	Yugoslavia

1. DAVID ABEL

The Affairs of Susan	1945	Par.
Ann Vickers	1933	RKO
The Awful Truth	1929	Pathe
Babbitt	1924	WB
Bachelor Bait	1934	RKO
The Barefoot Boy	1923	US
Beau Brummel	1924	WB
The Black Diamond Express	1927	WB
Bunker Bean	1935	RKO
The Buster	1923	Fox
Case of the Curious Bride	1935	WB
The Caveman	1926	WB
Compromise	1925	WB
Courage	1921	FN
Craig's Wife	1928	Pathe
Crime of the Century	1933	Par.
Criminal Lawyer	1937	RKO
The Crusader	1922	Fox
The Dark Swan	1924	WB
A Daughter of Two Worlds	1920	FN
Dearie	1927	WB
Don't Tell the Wife	1927	WB
The First Auto	1927	WB
Follow the Boys	1944	Univ.
Follow the Fleet	1936	RKO
The Forbidden Woman	1927	Pathe
The Gay Divorcee	1934	RKO
Geraldine	1929	Pathe
The Grand Parade	1930	Pathe
The Great Night	1922	Fox
Grumpy	1930	Par.
The Heart of Wetona	1919	US
Her Private Affair *	1929	Pathe
Hips, Hips, Hooray	1934	RKO

His Jazz Bride	1926	WB
The Honeymoon Express	1926	WB
How Baxter Butted In	1925	WB
The Hun Within	1918	Par.
I Dream Too Much	1935	RKO
The Isle of Conquest	1919	US
Ladies of the Big House	1931	Par.
Lady of the Dugout	1918	US
Little Miss Smiles	1922	Fox
A Lost Lady	1924	WB
Lovebound	1923	Fox
The Lover of Camille	1924	WB
Madame Butterfly	1932	Par.
Maggie Pepper	1919	Par.
Make Way for a Lady	1936	RKO
The Men of Zanzibar	1922	Fox
Merrily We Go to Hell	1932	Par.
Midnight Madness	1928	Pathe
Miracle Man	1932	Par.
Mixed Faces	1922	Fox
Money to Burn	1922	Fox
My Official Wife *	1926	WB
Ned McCobb's Daughter	1929	Pathe
The New Moon	1919	US
Noisy Neighbors	1929	Pathe
A Notorious Gentleman	1935	Univ.
Phantom President	1932	Par.
The Primitive Lover	1922	FN
The Probation Wife	1919	US
The Racketeer	1929	Pathe
Recompense	1925	WB
Rich Man's Folly	1931	Par.
Rose of the World	1925	WB
The Santa Fe Trail	1930	Par.
Scandal Sheet	1931	Par.
A Self-Made Man	1922	Fox
Seven Sinners	1925	WB
Shall We Dance?	1937	RKO
She Loves and Lies	1920	US
Show Folks	1928	Pathe
A Sister of Six	1916	US
Sky Bride *	1932	Par.
The Splendid Sinner	1918	Gold.
Square Shoulders	1929	Pathe
Stand and Deliver	1928	Pathe
Swing High	1930	Pathe
Swing Time	1936	RKO
Tenth Avenue	1928	Pathe
Thais	1917	Gold.
This Man Is Mine	1934	RKO
Three Weeks in Paris	1925	WB

Unseen Forces	1920	FN
The Virtuous Sin	1930	Par.
The Way of a Woman	1919	US
What Every Girl Should Know	1927	WB
Where Is My Wandering Boy Tonight	1922	US
The Woman Gives	1920	FN

2. WILLIAM S. ADAMS

The Air Patrol	1928	Univ.
The Blood Barrier	1920	Pathe
Born to the Saddle	1929	Univ.
The Christian	1914	Vita.
The Cloud Dodger	1928	Univ.
Destiny's Isle	1922	US
East Lynne	1921	US
From Headquarters	1919	Vita.
Forbidden Valley	1920	Pathe
Grit Wins	1929	Univ.
The House of the Tolling Bells	1920	Pathe
Man and His Woman	1920	Pathe
The Moonshine Trail	1919	Pathe
My Husband's Other Wife	1919	Pathe
The Painted World	1919	Vita.
Passers-By	1920	Pathe
The Phantom Flyer	1928	Univ.
Respectable by Proxy	1920	Pathe
Shadows of the Past	1919	Vita.
Sky-High Saunders	1927	Univ.
Sky Skidder	1929	Univ.
The Smiling Terror	1929	Univ.
Three Miles Up	1927	Univ.
Tides of Passion	1925	Vita.
Tricks	1925	US
Two Women	1919	Vita.
Won in the Clouds	1928	Univ.

3. PHILIPPE AGOSTINI (1910-   )

Angels of the Streets	1950	Fr.
Les Anges du Peche	1943	Fr.
Camille	1953	Fr.
Castles in Spain	1954	Fr./Sp.
The Country I Come From	1956	Fr.
Les Dames du Bois de Boulogne	1964	Fr.
Les Derniers Vacances	1947	Fr.
Doors of Night	1946	Fr.
Douce	1943	Fr.
Gates of the Night	1950	Fr.

If Paris Were Told to Us	1956	Fr.
Jour Se Leve *	1939	Fr.
Julie de Carneilhan	1950	Fr.
Paris Palace Hotel	1956	Fr./It.
Le Plaisir	1952	Fr.
Rififi	1955	Fr.
Son Copain	1951	Fr./Can.
Summer Storm	1950	Fr.
Sylia and the Ghost	1944	Fr.
Their Last Night	1953	Fr.
Three Make a Pair	1957	Fr.

4. LLOYD AHERN (?-1983)

The Brasher Doubloon	1946	TCF
Cry of the City *	1948	TCF
Father Was a Fullback	1949	TCF
For Heaven's Sake	1950	TCF
Gorilla at Large	1954	TCF
Hot Rods to Hell	1967	MGM
The Klansman *	1974	Par.
The Looters	1955	Univ.
Love Nest	1951	TCF
Love That Brute	1950	TCF
Mr. Belvedere Goes to College	1949	TCF
O. Henry's Full House	1952	TCF
Princess of the Nile	1954	TCF
The Sand Castle	1961	US
The Silver Whip	1953	TCF

5. MAC AHLBERG

The Cats	1969	Swed.
Chained Heat	1983	US
Daughter: I a Woman III	1970	Den.
Deepstar Six	1989	TRI-S.
Dolls	1987	US
Eliminators	1986	US
Future Cop	1985	US
Ghost Town	1988	US
Hell Night	1981	US
The Horror Show	1989	MGM/UA
House	1986	US
House II: The Second Story	1987	US
I, a Nobleman	1968	Den./Swed.
I, a Woman	1966	Den./Swed.
I, a Woman II	1968	Den./Swed.
Meridian	1990	US
Metalstorm: The Destruction of Jared Syn	1983	Univ.

My Tutor	1983	US
Nocturna	1984	US
Parasite	1982	Emb.
Prime Risk	1985	US
Prison	1988	US
Re-Animator	1985	US
Robot Jox	1990	US
The Seduction	1982	AE
A Time in the Sun	1970	Swed.
Young Warriors	1983	Cannon
Zone Troopers	1986	US

6. JOHN ALCOTT (1931-1986)

Barry Lyndon	1975	GB--WB
The Beastmaster	1982	MGM-UA
A Clockwork Orange	1971	GB--WB
Disappearance	1977	GB/Can.
Fort Apache: The Bronx	1980	US
Greystoke: The Legend of Tarzan	1984	GB--WB
Little Malcolm	1974	GB
March or Die	1977	GB
Miracles	1987	Cannon/Orion
No Way Out	1987	Orion
Overlord	1975	GB
The Shining	1980	GB--WB
Terror Train *	1980	Can.
Under Fire	1983	Orion
Vice Squad	1982	AE
White Water Summer	1987	Col.
Who Is Killing the Great Chefs of Europe?	1978	WB

7. G. R. ALDO (1902-1953)

Heaven Over the Marshes	1949	It.
Indiscretion of an American Wife	1954	It.--Selz.
Miracle in Milan	1951	It.
Otello	1951	It.
La Provinciale	1953	It.--WB
Singing Taxi Driver	1953	It.
La Terra Trema	1948	It.
Three Forbidden Stories	1952	It.--WB
Tomorrow is Another Day	1951	It.

8. HENRI ALEKAN (1909-   )

Accursed	1947	Fr.

Les Amants de Verone	1948	Fr.
Anna Karenina	1947	GB
Austerlitz	1959	Fr./It./Yugo.
La Bataille du Rail	1945	Fr.
The Beautiful Prisoner	1983	Fr.
Beauty and the Beast	1946	Fr.
Berlin, Jerusalem	1989	Fr./Isr.
Best Part	1956	Fr./It.--Col.
Black Tights	1962	Fr.
La Bourgeois Gentilhomme	1958	Fr.
Case of Dr. Laurent	1958	Fr.
Christmas Tree	1969	Fr./It.
Damned	1947	Fr.
Encounter	1952	It./US
Figures in a Landscape	1970	GB
Five Miles to Midnight	1962	Fr./It.
Forbidden Fruit	1952	Fr.
Front	1982	Fr.
Gun Wound	1984	Fr./Ger.
Heroes Are Tired	1955	Fr.
Julietta	1953	Fr.--Col.
Juliette ou La Clef des Songes	1957	Fr.
Lady L	1965	Fr./It.
La Marie au Port	1950	Fr.
Marriage of Figaro	1963	Fr.
Mayerling	1968	Fr./GB
My Apple	1950	Fr.
One, Two, Three, Four!	1960	Fr.
Other Christopher	1963	Cuba
Paris Is Always Paris	1952	Fr./It.
Les Parisiennes *	1962	Fr.
Poppy Is Also a Flower	1966	U.N.
Princess of Cleves	1961	Fr.
Provisional Liberty	1958	Fr./Czech.
Red Sun	1971	Fr./It.
Roman Holiday *	1953	Par.
Une Si Jolie Petite Plague	1949	Fr.
Sky Over Berlin	1987	Fr./Ger.
State of Things	1983	US
A Stone in the Mouth	1983	Fr.
Strange Love Affair	1985	Fr.
Stranger on the Prowl	1952	UA
Tales of Paris *	1962	Fr./It.
Territory	1983	Port./US
Topkapi	1964	UA
Triple Cross	1967	GB--WB
Trout	1982	Fr.
Twelve Hours by the Clock	1959	Fr./Ger.
Voyage to America	1951	Fr.
Zoe	1954	Fr.

9. PAUL ALLEN (1886-1956)

Arizona Days	1928	US
Arizona Speed	1928	US
Captain Cowboy	1929	US
Cheyenne Trails	1928	US
Crashin' Through	1924	US
Down to the Sea in Ships *	1922	US
Fangs of Fate	1925	US
Fighters of the Saddle	1929	US
Happy Warrior	1925	Vita.
Isle of Vanishing Men	1924	US
Law of the Mounted	1928	US
Lonesome Trail	1930	US
Lovin' Fool	1926	US
Mystery Rider	1928	US
On the Divide	1928	US
Outlaws of the Sea	1923	US
Riders of the Storm	1929	US
Sky's the Limit	1925	US
Texas Tommy	1928	US
Torrent *	1924	US
Virgin *	1924	US
West of Santa Fe	1928	US
Western Trails	1926	US

10. NESTOR ALMENDROS

Bed and Board	1970	Fr.
The Blue Lagoon	1980	Col.
Cambio de Sexo	1976	Sp.
Carrot Top	1973	Fr.
Claire's Knee	1970	Fr.--Col.
Cockfighter	1974	US
La Collectionneuse	1966	Fr.
Confidentially Yours	1983	Fr.
Days of Heaven	1978	Par.
L'Enfant Sauvage	1969	Fr.--UA
Entire Days in the Trees	1976	Fr.
Finally Sunday	1983	Fr.
Goin' South	1978	Par.
Green Room	1978	Fr.--UA
Heartburn	1986	Par.
Improper Conduct	1984	Fr.
Kramer vs. Kramer	1979	Col.
The Last Metro	1980	Fr.
Life Before Him	1977	Fr.
Love on the Run	1978	Fr.
Love, the Afternoon	1972	Fr.

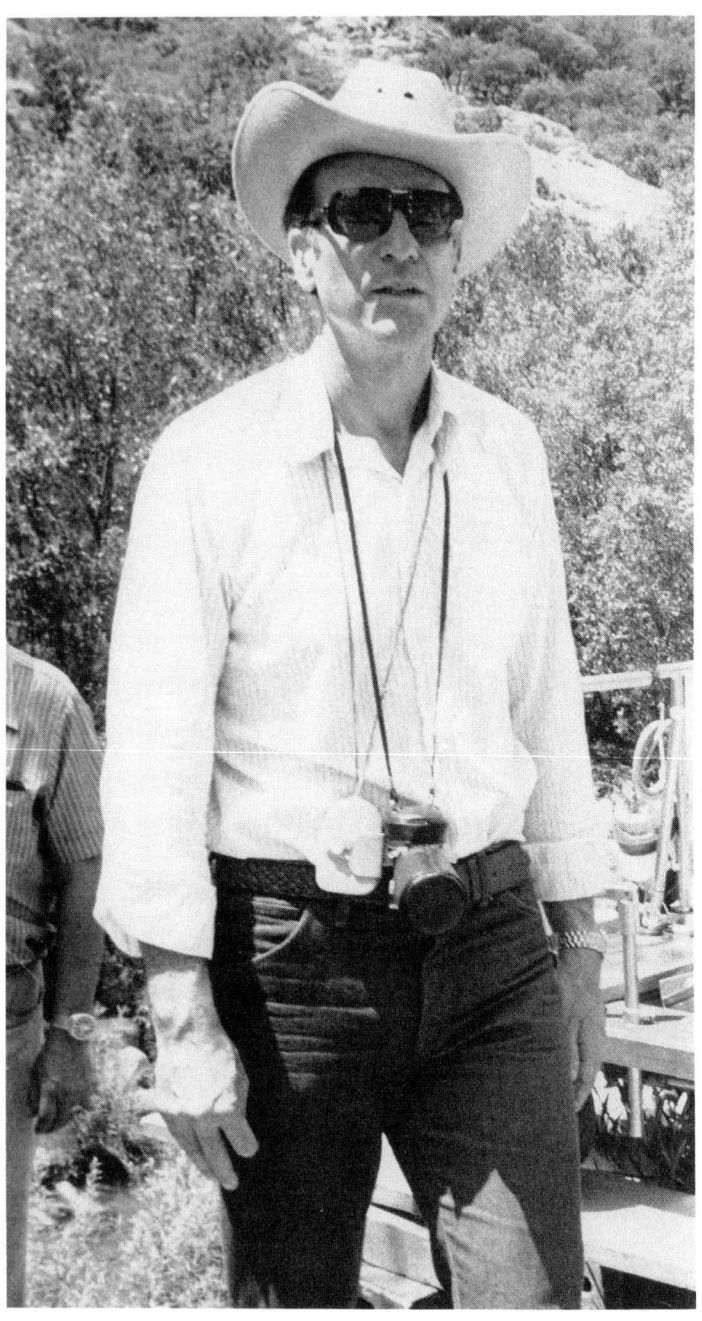

Nestor Almendros on location with <u>Days of Heaven</u> (1978).

Ma Nuit Chez Maude	1969	Fr.
Man Who Loved Women	1977	Fr.
Marquise of O	1976	Fr./Ger.
Mistress	1976	Fr.
More	1969	Lux.
Mouth Agape	1974	Fr.
My Little Loves	1975	Fr.
Nadine	1987	Tri-S.
New York Stories *	1989	BV/Touch.
Pauline at the Beach	1983	Fr.
Perceval Le Gallois	1978	Fr.
Places in the Heart	1984	Tri-S.
Rare Bird	1973	Fr.
Six in Paris *	1968	Fr.
Sophie's Choice	1982	Univ.
Still of the Night	1982	MGM
The Story of Adele H	1975	Fr.
Two English Girls and the Continent	1971	Fr.
Valley	1972	Fr.
Wild Racers	1968	AIP
Women in the Sun	1974	Fr.

11. JOHN A. ALONZO

Back Roads	1981	CBS
Bad News Bears	1976	Par.
Beyond Reason	1985	US
Black Sunday	1977	Par.
Bloody Mama	1969	AIP
Blue Thunder	1983	Col.
Casey's Shadow	1978	Col.
The Cheap Detective	1978	Col.
Chinatown	1974	Par.
Conrack	1974	TCF
Cross Creek	1983	EMI
Farewell My Lovely	1975	AE
The Fortune	1975	Col.
Get to Know Your Rabbit	1972	WB
The Guardian	1990	Univ.
Harold and Maude	1971	Par.
Hit!	1973	Par.
I Will, I Will, for Now	1975	US
Internal Affairs	1990	Par.
Jo Jo Dancer, Your Life Is Calling	1986	Col.
Lady Sings the Blues	1972	Par.
The Naked Ape	1973	Univ.
Navy Seals	1990	Orion
Norma Rae	1979	TCF
Nothing in Common	1986	Tri-S.
Once Is Not Enough	1975	Par.

Out of Control	1985	US
Overboard	1987	MGM-UA
Pete 'n Tillie	1972	Univ.
Physical Evidence	1989	Col.
Real Men	1987	MGM-UA
Scarface	1983	Univ.
Sounder	1972	TCF
Steel Magnolias	1989	Tri-S.
Tom Horn	1979	WB
Vanishing Point	1971	TCF
Which Way Is Up?	1977	Univ.
Zorro the Gay Blade	1981	US

12. JOHN A. ALTON (1901-   )

Affairs of Geraldine	1946	Rep.
Amazing Dr. X	1948	EL
An American in Paris *	1951	MGM
Apache War Smoke	1952	MGM
Atlantic City	1944	Rep.
Battle Circus	1952	MGM
The Big Combo	1955	AA
The Black Book	1949	EL
Border Incident	1949	MGM
The Brothers Karamazov	1958	MGM
Bury Me Dead	1947	EL
Canon City	1948	EL
Captain China	1949	Par.
The Carter Case	1942	Rep.
The Catered Affair	1956	MGM
Cattle Queen of Montana	1954	RKO
Count the Hours	1942	RKO
The Crooked Way	1949	UA
Designing Woman	1957	MGM
Devil's Doorway	1949	MGM
Dr. Christian Meets the Women	1940	RKO
Driftwood	1947	Rep.
Duffy of San Quentin	1953	AA
Elmer Gantry	1960	UA
Enemy of Women	1944	Mon.
Escape to Burma	1955	RKO
Father of the Bride	1950	MGM
Father's Little Dividend	1951	MGM
Forced Landing	1941	Par.
Ghost Goes Wild	1947	Rep.
Girls of the Big House	1945	Rep.
Grounds for Marriage	1950	MGM
A Guy Could Change	1945	Rep.
He Walked by Night	1948	EL
Hit Parade of 1947	1947	Rep.

I, the Jury	1953	UA
Ice Capades Review	1942	Rep.
It's a Big Country *	1952	MGM
Johnny Doughboy	1943	Rep.
Lady and the Monster	1944	Rep.
Lake Placid Serenade	1944	Rep.
Lonelyhearts	1958	UA
Love, Honor and Goodbye	1945	Rep.
The Madonna's Secret	1946	Rep.
Melody for Three	1941	RKO
Moonlight Masquerade	1942	Rep.
Murder in the Music Hall *	1946	Rep.
Mystery Street	1950	MGM
One Exciting Week	1946	Rep.
Pardon My Stripes	1942	Rep.
Passion	1954	RKO
Pearl of the South Pacific	1955	RKO
The People Against O'Hara	1951	MGM
Power Dive	1941	Par.
Pretender	1947	Rep.
Raw Deal	1948	EL
Red Stallion in the Rockies	1949	EL
Remedy for Riches	1940	RKO
The Scar	1948	EL
Silver Lode	1954	RKO
Slightly Scarlet	1956	RKO
Steel Cage	1954	UA
Storm Over Lisbon	1944	Rep.
The Sultan's Daughter	1944	Mon.
T Men	1948	EL
Take the High Ground	1953	MGM
Talk about a Stranger	1952	MGM
Tea and Sympathy	1956	MGM
The Teahouse of the August Moon	1956	MGM
Tennessee's Partner	1955	RKO
Three Faces West	1940	Rep.
The Trespasser	1947	Rep.
12 to the Moon	1960	Col.
Washington Story	1952	MGM
Winter Wonderland	1947	Rep.
Witness to Murder	1954	UA
Wyoming	1947	Rep.

13. M. A. ANDERSON

The Adorable Cheat	1928	US
August Week-End	1936	US
Beauty Parlor	1932	US
Below the Deadline	1929	US
Below the Deadline	1936	US

Betty Co-Ed	1946	Col.
Border Feud	1947	PRC
The Bridge of Sighs	1936	US
Brilliant Marriage	1936	US
By Appointment Only	1933	US
Circumstantial Evidence	1929	US
Circumstantial Evidence	1936	US
Condemned to Live	1935	US
Confessions of a Wife *	1928	US
Crashing Through *	1928	US
Cross-Examination	1932	US
Cross Streets	1934	US
The Curtain Falls	1935	US
Dance, Girl, Dance	1933	US
The Dark Hour	1936	US
Death from a Distance	1935	US
Delinquent Parents	1938	US
Easy Money	1936	US
Fagasa	1928	US
False Pretenses	1935	US
Fifteen Wives	1934	US
Forbidden Company	1932	US
Forbidden Grass	1928	US
Fugitive Road	1934	US
The Ghost Walks	1934	US
Girl Who Came Back	1935	US
Green Eyes	1934	US
Grief Street	1931	US
Happiness COD	1935	US
Hitch Hike to Heaven	1936	US
House of Secrets	1937	US
House of Shame	1928	US
In Love With Life	1934	US
Jazz Cinderella	1930	US
Just Off Broadway	1929	US
The King Murder	1932	US
Ladies in Love	1930	US
The Lady in Scarlet	1936	US
Lady Luck	1936	US
Last Dance	1930	US
The Last Ride	1932	Univ.
Little Red Schoolhouse	1936	US
Lotus Lady	1930	US
A Man of Sentiment	1933	US
The Midnight Special	1930	US
Missing Girls	1936	US
Murder at Glen Athol	1936	US
Murder on the Campus	1934	US
Notorious But Nice	1934	US
One in a Million	1935	US
The Peacock Fan	1929	US

Port of Lost Dreams	1935	US
Public Opinion	1935	US
Rainbow Over Broadway	1933	US
Ring Around the Moon	1936	US
A Shot in the Dark	1935	US
Silent Sentinel	1929	US
The Sky Rider	1928	US
Slightly Married	1933	US
Society Fever	1935	US
Sons of Steel	1935	US
South of Panama	1928	US
Stolen Sweets	1934	US
Symphony of Living	1935	US
Tango	1936	US
Three of a Kind	1936	US
Twin Husbands	1934	US
Women Don't Tell	1933	US
The World Accuses	1935	US

14. LUCIEN ANDRIOT

Almighty Dollar	1916	US
Almost Human	1927	Pathe
Always in Trouble	1938	TCF
And Then There Were None	1945	US
The Animal Kingdom *	1932	RKO
Anne of Green Gables	1934	RKO
The Arizona Wildcat	1939	TCF
Bachelor Brides	1926	US
Before Dawn	1933	RKO
Big Town Girl	1937	TCF
The Big Trail *	1930	Fox
Bondage	1933	Fox
Borderline	1950	Univ.
Boy Friend	1930	TCF
Bucking the Barrier	1923	Fox
A Butterfly on the Wheel	1915	US
Cafe Metropole	1937	TCF
Camille	1915	US
Camille	1917	Fox
Captain Fly-by-Night	1922	US
Captain Hurricane	1935	RKO
The Case Against Mrs. Ames	1936	Par.
Charlie Chan at the Opera	1936	TCF
Charter Pilot	1940	TCF
Chasing Yesterday	1935	RKO
Christina	1929	Fox
City of Chance	1946	TCF
Cock of the Air	1932	US
Code of the West	1925	Par.

A Connecticut Yankee in King Arthur's Court	1921	Fox
The Corpse Came COD	1947	Col.
Daddy Longlegs	1931	Fox
Dance Hall	1942	TCF
The Dangerous Flirt	1924	US
Daytime Wives	1923	US
The Diary of a Chambermaid	1946	UA
Dishonored Lady	1947	US
Don't Bet on Women	1931	Fox
Earthbound	1940	TCF
East of Broadway	1924	US
The Face in the Moonlight	1915	US
Feast of Life	1916	US
A Fool There Was	1922	Fox
The Gay Desperado	1936	UA
Gigolo	1926	US
The Girl From Avenue A	1940	TCF
The Glory Brigade	1953	TCF
The Golden Calf	1930	Fox
Golden Hoofs	1941	TCF
Grand Old Girl	1935	RKO
The Hairy Ape	1944	UA
Hallelujah, I'm a Bum	1933	UA
Happy Days	1930	Fox
Help Wanted--Male!	1920	Pathe
High School	1940	TCF
His Family Tree	1936	RKO
Home Town Story	1951	MGM
Hooray for Love	1935	RKO
I'll Give a Million	1938	TCF
I'll Take Romance	1937	Col.
The Imposter	1915	US
In the Palace of the King	1923	Gold.
International Settlement	1938	TCF
Intrigue	1947	UA
Jitterbugs	1943	TCF
Johnny One-Eye *	1950	UA
Just Off Broadway	1942	TCF
The Lady Escapes	1937	TCF
The Lady in Question	1940	Col.
Lady Luck	1946	RKO
Lafayette, We Come! *	1918	US
The Last Trail	1921	Fox
Let 'Er Go Gallagher	1928	Pathe
The Life of Vergie Winters	1934	RKO
Light of Western Stars	1925	Par.
Lone Star Ranger	1942	TCF
Love, Laugh and Live	1929	Fox
Loves of Carmen	1927	Fox
The Loves of Edgar Allan Poe	1942	TCF

Lucky Cisco Kid	1940	TCF
The Mad Martindales	1942	TCF
The Man Who Came Back	1924	Fox
The Man Who Lost Himself	1920	Selz.
Manila Calling	1942	TCF
The Marked Woman	1914	US
The Million Dollar Dollies	1918	US
Mr. Moto in Danger Island	1939	TCF
Mr. Moto's Gamble	1938	TCF
M'Liss	1915	US
A Modern Othello	1917	Selz.
Monte Cristo	1922	Fox
Moon Over Her Shoulder	1941	TCF
Nellie, the Beautiful Cloak Model	1924	Gold.
New Orleans	1947	US
Oh, Boy!	1919	Pathe
On the Avenue	1937	TCF
On the Sunny Side	1942	TCF
Outpost in Morocco	1949	UA
Over My Dead Body	1942	TCF
Pack Up Your Troubles	1939	TCF
Paris After Dark	1943	TCF
Penthouse	1933	MGM
A Poor Little Rich Girl *	1917	US
The Price	1915	US
The Pride of the Clan *	1917	US
The Primal Law	1921	Fox
Protea I	1913	Fr.
The Ragged Heiress	1922	Fox
Red Dice	1926	US
The Return of Peter Grimm	1935	RKO
Ride on Vaquero	1941	TCF
Riders of the Purple Sage	1941	TCF
The Right to Lie	1919	Pathe
Right to Romance	1933	RKO
The River Pirate	1928	Fox
Rough Shod	1922	Fox
Secret Agent of Japan	1942	TCF
Shame	1921	Fox
A Ship Comes In	1928	Pathe
The Silent Master	1917	Selz.
The Southerner	1945	UA
Stop, Look and Love	1939	TCF
Straight Is the Way	1934	MGM
The Strange Woman	1946	UA
The Sullivans	1944	TCF
Thanks for Everything *	1938	TCF
That Girl Montana	1921	Pathe
They Came to Blow Up America	1943	TCF
The Thundering Herd	1925	Par.
Topaze	1933	RKO

Traffic in Hearts	1924	Col.
Trooper O'Neil	1922	Fox
Two Alone	1934	RKO
The Valiant *	1929	Fox
La Vie de Boheme	1916	US
The Virtuous Model	1919	Pathe
Volcano	1926	Par.
West of Chicago	1922	Fox
Westward Passage	1932	RKO
When Love Comes	1922	US
While New York Sleeps	1938	TCF
White Gold	1927	US
Why Trust Your Husband?	1921	Fox
Women of All Nations	1931	Fox
Yes	1915	Fox
You Can't Have Everything	1937	TCF
Zigomar	1911	Fr.

15. RICHARD ANGST (1905-   )

Aren't We Wonderful?	1959	Ger.
Axel Munthe, Doctor of San Michele	1962	Fr./Ger./It.
Black Abbot	1962	Ger.
The Burning Street	1933	Ger. --Univ.
Das Indische Grabmal	1958	Ger.
De Sade	1969	Ger./It.--AIP
The Dirty Game	1966	Fr./Ger./It. --AIP
Executioners	1961	Ger.
Fight for Rome--Part I	1969	Ger./Rom.
The Good Soldier Schweik	1963	Ger.
Gripsholm Castle	1964	Ger.
Heidi	1968	Aust.--WB
Herrliche Zeiten im Spessart	1967	Ger.
Hit Parade	1954	Ger.
Hocuspocus	1966	Ger.
Ingrid--Story of a Model	1955	Ger.
Journey to the Lost City	1960	Ger.
A Kingdom for a Horse	1949	Holl.
The Last Man	1956	Ger.
Liselotte von der Pfalz	1967	Ger.
The Phantom of Soho	1967	Ger.
Praetorius	1965	Ger.
Rheinsberg	1967	Ger.
The Ski Chase	1938	Aust.
SOS Iceberg *	1933	Ger.
Spessart Inn	1961	Ger.
Storm Over Tibet *	1951	Ger.
Storms Over the Mont Blanc *	1931	Ger.
Three Men in the Snow	1955	Aust.

Tiger of Eschnapur	1959	Ger.
Two Humans	1931	Ger.
The Wedding Trip	1969	Ger.--Col.
The White Hell of Pitz-Palu	1952	Ger.
White Intoxication	1931	Ger.

16.   ART ARLING (1906-   )

Belles on Their Toes	1952	TCF
Boys' Night Out	1962	MGM
Call Me Mister	1951	TCF
Captain From Castile *	1947	TCF
The Farmer Takes a Wife	1953	TCF
Flood Tide	1958	Univ.
Glass Slipper	1954	MGM
The Great American Pastime	1956	MGM
The Homestretch	1947	TCF
The I Don't Care Girl	1953	TCF
I'll Cry Tomorrow	1955	MGM
Kathy O	1958	Univ.
The Kettles on Old MacDonald's Farm	1957	Univ.
Love Me or Leave Me	1955	MGM
Lover Come Back	1961	Univ.
Man in the Shadow	1957	Univ.
Meet Me After the Show	1951	TCF
Mother Is a Freshman	1948	TCF
My Six Loves	1963	Par.
The Notorious Landlady	1962	Col.
Once Before I Die	1966	US
Once Upon a Horse	1958	Univ.
Pillow Talk	1959	Univ.
Ransom	1955	MGM
Red Garters	1954	Par.
The Secret Invasion	1964	UA
Ski Party	1965	AIP
The Story of Ruth	1960	TCF
Strait-Jacket	1963	Col.
Swinging Along	1962	TCF
Take a Giant Step	1959	UA
Tammy and the Bachelor	1957	Univ.
This Happy Feeling	1958	Univ.
Three For the Show	1955	Col.
Wabash Avenue	1950	TCF
When the Girls Take Over	1962	US
You're My Everything	1949	TCF

17.   JOHN ARNOLD (1889-1964)

Aladdin's Other Lamp	1917	Metro.

Along Came Ruth	1924	MGM
The Auction Block	1925	MGM
The Barricade	1917	Metro.
The Beauty Prize	1924	MGM
Becky	1927	MGM
The Big Parade	1925	MGM
Blackmail	1920	Metro.
Blue Jeans	1917	Metro.
Breakers Ahead *	1918	Metro.
Bright Lights	1925	MGM
The Broadway Melody	1929	MGM
The Cardboard Lover	1928	MGM
A Chorus Girl's Romance	1920	Metro.
Crinoline and Romance	1923	Metro.
Dance Madness *	1925	MGM
Dangerous to Men	1920	Metro.
Don't Doubt Your Husband	1924	MGM
False Evidence	1919	Metro.
Fire Brigade	1926	MGM
The Five Dollar Baby	1922	Metro.
Flower of the Dusk	1918	Metro.
The Fog	1923	Metro.
The Fourteenth Lover	1922	Metro.
The Garden of Eden	1928	UA
Glass Houses	1922	Metro.
The Gold Cure	1919	Metro.
The Heart Bandit	1924	Metro.
Heaven on Earth	1927	MGM
Her Fatal Millions	1923	Metro.
His Father's Son	1917	Metro.
Hollywood Revue of 1929 *	1929	MGM
Home Stuff	1921	Metro.
In Search of a Thrill	1923	Metro.
June Madness	1922	Metro.
Lady Barnacle	1917	Metro.
Life's Darn Funny	1921	Metro.
Love in the Dark	1922	Metro.
Love's Blindness *	1926	MGM
The Match-Breaker	1921	Metro.
The Microbe	1919	Metro.
Mr. Wu	1927	MGM
A Noise in Newboro	1923	Metro.
The Off-Shore Pirate	1921	Metro.
The Only Road	1918	Metro.
Opportunity	1918	Metro.
Paris	1926	MGM
The Parisian Tigress	1919	Metro.
Please Get Married	1919	Metro.
Proud Flesh	1925	MGM
Puppets of Fate	1921	Metro.
Revelation	1924	MGM

Riders of the Night	1918	Metro.
Rose-Marie	1928	MGM
Rouged Lips	1923	Metro.
Satan Junior	1919	Metro.
Seeing's Believing	1922	Metro.
The Show	1926	MGM
Show People	1928	MGM
Sinners in Silk	1924	MGM
So This Is Marriage	1924	MGM
The Social Code	1923	Metro.
Some Bride	1919	Metro.
Springtime	1914	US
Sun-Up	1925	MGM
There Are No Villains	1921	Metro.
They Like 'Em Rough	1922	Metro.
Threads of Fate	1917	Metro.
The Understanding Heart	1927	MGM
Very Truly Yours	1922	Fox
The Way of a Girl	1925	MGM
Weaver of Dreams	1918	Metro.
Wife of the Centaur	1924	MGM
The Willow Tree	1920	Metro.
The Wind	1928	MGM
The Winding Trail	1918	Metro.

18. JEROME ASH

Babes on Swing Street	1944	Univ.
The Cat Creeps *	1930	Univ.
City Limits	1934	Mon.
The Climax	1930	Univ.
The Cohens and Kellys in Hollywood	1945	Univ.
Crimson Canary	1945	Univ.
Desperate Trails	1939	Univ.
Don't Get Personal	1942	Univ.
The Drake Case	1929	Univ.
East Is West	1930	Univ.
Easy to Look At	1945	Univ.
Enemy Agent	1940	Univ.
Ex-Bad Boy	1931	Univ.
Fangs of Destiny	1927	Univ.
The Four-Footed Ranger	1928	Univ.
Framed	1940	Univ.
Gals Incorporated	1943	Univ.
Graft	1931	Univ.
Hi, Good-Lookin'	1944	Univ.
Hit the Road	1941	Univ.
I Can't Escape	1934	US
I'll Remember April	1945	Univ.
I'll Tell the World	1934	Univ.

In Society *	1944	Univ.
Jungle Jim	1937	Univ.
King of Jazz *	1930	Univ.
Law and Order	1940	Univ.
Legion of Lost Flyers	1939	Univ.
Mad Doctor of Market Street	1942	Univ.
Many a Slip	1931	Univ.
Mighty Treve	1937	Univ.
Modern Love	1929	Univ.
Moon Over Las Vegas	1944	Univ.
Moonlight in Vermont	1943	Univ.
Oklahoma Frontier	1939	Univ.
Pillow of Death	1945	Univ.
Pirates of the Skies	1939	Univ.
Ragtime Cowboy Joe	1940	Univ.
Reckless Age	1944	Univ.
River Gang	1945	Univ.
Road Agent	1941	Univ.
Shakedown *	1929	Univ.
Shannons of Broadway	1929	Univ.
She Gets Her Man	1945	Univ.
Sing a Jingle	1943	Univ.
Sing Another Chorus	1941	Univ.
South of Dixie	1944	Univ.
South to Karanga	1940	Univ.
Stagecoach Buckaroo	1942	Univ.
The Strange Death of Adolf Hitler	1943	Univ.
Swingtime Johnny	1943	Univ.
Tonight at Twelve	1929	Univ.
Tropic Fury	1939	Univ.
Trouble at Midnight	1937	Univ.
Undertow	1930	Univ.
Unexpected Father	1932	Univ.
West of Carson City	1940	Univ.
What's Cookin'?	1942	Univ.
When Love Is Young	1937	Univ.

19. MONROE ASKINS

Blood of Dracula	1958	AIP
The House on Skull Mountain	1974	TCF
The Human Duplicators	1965	US
Napoleon and Samantha	1972	Dis.
Sorority Girl	1957	AIP
This Rebel Breed	1960	WB
Thunder Alley	1967	AIP

20. JOSEPH AUGUST (1890–1947)

After the Dance	1935	Col.

All That Money Can Buy	1941	RKO
Among the Missing	1934	Col.
The Ancient Mariner	1925	Fox
The Apostle of Vengeance	1916	US
Arabian Love	1922	Fox
The Aryan	1916	US
As the Devil Commands	1933	Col.
The Bargain	1914	US
The Beloved Rogue	1927	UA
Between Men	1916	US
Big Dan	1923	Fox
The Black Camel *	1932	Fox
Black Moon	1934	Col.
Blue Blazes Rawden	1918	US
The Border Wireless	1918	US
Branding Broadway	1918	US
The Brat	1931	Fox
Breed of Men	1919	US
A California Romance	1922	Fox
The Captain Hates the Sea	1934	Col.
Charlie Chan's Chance	1932	Fox
Civilization *	1916	US
Civilization's Child	1916	US
Cocktail Hour	1933	Col.
The Cold Deck	1917	US
Come to My House	1927	Fox
The Cradle of Courage	1920	Par.
Cupid's Fireman	1923	Fox
Dante's Inferno	1924	Fox
The Dawn Maker	1916	US
The Defense Rests	1934	Col.
The Desert Man	1917	US
The Devil's Devil's Double	1916	US
The Disciple	1915	US
Don't Marry	1928	Fox
8 Bells	1935	Col.
An Even Break	1917	US
Every Saturday Night	1936	TCF
The Farmer's Daughter	1928	Fox
Fifty Roads to Town	1937	TCF
Fig Leaves	1926	Fox
The Fighting Heart	1925	Fox
The Flying Horseman	1926	Fox
The Folly of Vanity *	1924	Fox
Golden Rule Kate	1917	US
Good-By Girls!	1923	Fox
Grand Jury	1936	RKO
Greater Than a Crown	1925	Fox
Gun Law	1938	RKO
The Gunfighter	1917	US
Gunga Din	1939	RKO

Heartbreak	1931	Fox
Hell's Hinges	1916	US
Honor Bound	1928	Fox
Honor First	1922	Fox
The Hunchback of Notre Dame	1939	RKO
I'll Love You Always	1935	Col.
The Informer	1935	RKO
John Petticoats	1919	Par.
The Last Act	1916	US
Lightnin'	1925	Fox
The Love Gambler	1923	Fox
Madness of Youth	1923	Fox
Man of Conquest	1939	Rep.
Man Trouble	1930	Fox
Man Who Won	1923	Fox
Man's Castle	1933	Col.
Mary of Scotland	1936	RKO
Master of Men	1933	Col.
Melody Ranch	1940	Rep.
Men Without Women	1930	Fox
The Money Corral	1919	US
Music for Madame *	1937	RKO
Mystery Ranch	1932	Fox
The Narrow Trail	1917	US
No Greater Glory	1934	Col.
No More Orchids	1933	Col.
Not a Drum Was Heard	1924	Fox
Nurse Edith Cavell *	1939	RKO
O'Malley of the Mounted	1921	Par.
On Our Merry Way *	1948	UA
On Your Back	1930	Fox
The Patriot	1916	US
The Plough and the Stars	1936	RKO
The Poppy Girl's Husband	1919	US
Portrait of Jennie	1948	Selz.
The Primal Lure	1916	US
Quick Millions	1931	Fox
The Regenerates	1917	US
The Return of "Draw" Egan	1916	US
The Road to Glory	1926	Fox
St. Elmo	1923	Fox
The Saint in New York	1938	RKO
Salute	1929	Fox
Sand *	1920	Par.
Sea Devils	1937	RKO
Seas Beneath	1931	Fox
Selfish Yates	1918	Fox
Shark Monroe	1918	US
The Silent Man	1917	US
Soft Living	1928	Fox
The Soldier and the Lady	1937	RKO

The Square Deal Man	1917	US
Square Deal Sanderson	1919	US
Strong Boy	1929	Fox
Super Sleuth *	1937	RKO
Sylvia Scarlett	1935	RKO
The Temple of Venus	1923	Fox
The Testing Block	1920	Par.
That's My Boy	1932	Col.
There Goes My Girl	1937	RKO
They Were Expendable	1945	MGM
This Marriage Business	1938	RKO
Three Word Brand	1921	Par.
The Tiger Man	1918	US
The Toll Gate	1920	Par.
Travelin' On	1921	Par.
Truthful Tulliver	1923	Fox
Tumbleweeds	1925	UA
Twentieth Century	1934	Col.
Two Arabian Knights *	1924	UA
Up the River	1930	Fox
The Vagabond Trail	1924	Fox
Vanity Street	1932	Col.
Very Confidential	1927	Fox
Wagon Tracks	1919	US
The Whistle	1921	Par.
White Oak	1921	Par.
The Whole Town's Talking	1935	Col.
Wolf Lowry	1917	US

21. GORDON AVIL (?-1970)

Beachhead	1953	UA
Big House USA	1954	UA
Billy the Kid	1930	MGM
The Black Sleep	1956	UA
Canyon Crossroads	1955	UA
The Champ	1931	MGM
Christmas Eve	1947	US
Convict Stage	1965	TCF
Deadly Duo	1962	UA
Desert Sands	1955	UA
Don't Knock the Twist	1962	Col.
Fort Courageous	1965	TCF
Fort Yuma	1955	UA
Git	1965	Emb.
Hallelujah!	1929	MGM
King Dinosaur	1955	Lip.
On Our Merry Way *	1948	UA
The Outlaw's Daughter	1954	TCF
Rebel in Town	1956	UA

Shield for Murder	1954	UA
Teenage Millionaire	1961	UA
Ten Who Dared	1960	Dis.
13 Frightened Girls	1963	Col.
Twist Around the Clock	1961	Col.
The Underwater City	1962	Col.
War Paint	1953	UA
War Party	1965	TCF
The Wild Westerners	1962	Col.
The Yellow Tomahawk	1954	UA

22. JOHN G. AVILDSEN (1937?-)

Cry Uncle	1971	US
Guess What We Learned in School Today?	1970	US
Joe	1970	Cannon
Okay Bill	1971	US
Out of It	1969	UA
The Stoolie	1972	US
Turn On to Love	1969	US

23. JEAN BACHELET (1894-   )

Les Bas-Fonds	1936	Fr.
Bouni Sees Paris	1954	Fr.
Le Crime de M. Lange	1935	Fr.
Compliments of Mr. Flow *	1941	Fr.
Le Gros Bill	1949	Fr.
I Did It Three Times	1952	Fr.
The Life of an Honest Man	1953	Fr.
Love Always Love	1952	Fr.
Mlle. Desiree	1948	Fr.
Mains Sales	1951	Fr.
Moutonnet *	1936	Fr.
Nana *	1926	Fr.
Pasteur	1936	Fr.
La Petite Marchande d'Allumettes	1928	Fr.
Le Poison	1952	Fr.
Portrait of Innocence	1948	Fr.
Rare Bird	1935	Fr.
Le Regle de Jeu *	1939	Fr.
Remounting the Champs Elysees *	1938	Fr.
Soiled Hands	1951	Fr.
Street Singer *	1938	Fr.
Three on a Honeymoon *	1933	Fr.
Us Kids	1941	Fr.

24. JEAN BADAL (1927-   )

Adventure Starts Here	1965	Swed.
The Assassins of Order	1971	Fr.
Ballad for a Hoodlum	1963	Fr.
Be So Till Death	1960	Fr.
Behold a Pale Horse	1964	Col.
Blondy	1976	Fr.
Ciao, You Guys	1979	Fr.
Education Sentimentale	1962	Fr.--UFA
Foul Play	1961	Fr.--TCF
Goodbye Emanuelle	1978	Fr.
Green Heart	1966	Fr.
Le Guepiot	1981	Fr.
Gypsy Law	1963	Fr.
A King Without Distractions	1963	Fr.
The Last Leap	1970	Fr.
A Little Sun in Cold Winter	1971	Fr.
Love in Question	1978	Fr.
Mass in C Minor	1990	Fr.
Midnight Meeting	1962	Fr.
One Must Live Dangerously	1975	Fr.--TCF
The Other One	1967	Fr.
Parade *	1983	Fr.
Playtime *	1968	Fr.
Private Projection	1973	Fr.
Promise at Dawn	1970	Fr./US
Serious as Pleasure	1975	Fr.
Vagabond Humor *	1971	Fr.
Verdict	1974	Fr.--Col.-WB
Very Curious Girl	1970	Fr.
What's New Pussycat?	1965	Fr.

25. JACOB BADARACCO

Across the Deadline *	1925	US
After Midnight	1921	Selz.
Bucking the Tiger	1921	Selz.
Butterfly Range	1922	US
Coax Me	1919	US
The Devil's Bowl	1923	US
Headin' Through	1924	US
The Heart of a Texan *	1922	US
Huntin' Trouble	1924	US
The Inn of the Blue Moon *	1918	US
The King of Kings *	1927	Pathe
The Loser's End	1924	US
Love's Law	1918	US
Love's Masquerade	1922	Selz.
Lure of Gold	1922	US

Miss Crusoe	1919	US
Not Built for Runnin'	1924	US
Nothing But Lies	1920	Metro.
Nothing But the Truth	1920	Metro.
The Office Scandal	1929	Pathe
Out of the Chorus	1921	US
The Poison Pen	1919	US
Rangeland	1922	US
The Secret of the Pueblo *	1923	US
Shadows of the Sea	1922	Selz.
The Shield of Silence	1925	US
South of the Northern Lights *	1922	US
The Steel King	1919	US
Table Top Ranch	1922	US
Tangled Trails	1921	US
The Trail of the Cigarette	1920	US
Turkish Delight	1927	Pathe
The Very Idea	1920	Metro.
West of the Pecos	1922	US
Woman of Lies	1919	US

26. HANANIA BAER

Again Forever	1985	Cannon
Always	1985	US
American Ninja	1985	Cannon
Assassination	1987	Cannon
Bad Guys	1986	US
Breakin'	1984	Cannon--MGM-UA
Choices	1981	US
Diving In	1990	US
Dracula Sucks	1980	US
Eating	1990	US
Echoes	1983	US
Elvira, Mistress of the Dark	1988	US
Fellow Travelers	1984	Isr.
Masters of the Universe	1987	Cannon
New Year's Day *	1989	US
Ninja III-The Domination	1984	Cannon
Seven Hours to Judgment	1988	US
Someone to Love	1987	US

27. KING BAGGOT

Beatlemania	1981	US
Cheech and Chong's Next Movie	1980	Univ.
Dr. Detroit	1983	Univ.
Dream a Little Dream	1989	US

Fast Walking	1982	US
Gotcha!	1985	Univ.
The Hand	1981	Orion--WB
High Encounters of the Ultimate Kind	1982	Cannon--Univ.
Little Vegas	1990	US
Second Thoughts	1983	Univ.
Some Kind of Hero	1982	Par.
Tough Guys	1986	Touch.
Vice Versa	1988	Col.

28. BEN BAIL

Across the Deadline *	1925	US
Are All Men Alike?	1920	Metro.
Dangerous Little Demon	1922	Univ.
Discontented Wives	1921	US
Hills of Missing Men	1922	US
King's Creek Law	1923	US
Kissed	1922	Univ.
The Perfect Alibi	1924	US
The Ruse of the Rattler	1921	US
The Sage Hen	1921	Pathe
The Strongest	1920	Fox

29. JOHN BAILEY

The Accidental Tourist	1988	WB
American Gigolo	1980	Par.
The Big Chill	1983	Col.
Boulevard Nights	1979	WB
Brighton Beach Memoirs	1986	Univ.
Cat People	1982	RKO--Univ.
Continental Divide	1981	Univ.
Crossroads	1986	Col.
Honky Tonk Freeway	1981	Univ.
Legacy	1975	US
Light of Day	1987	Tri-S.
Mafu Cage	1978	US
Mishima	1985	WB
My Blue Heaven	1990	WB
Ordinary People	1980	Par.
The Pope of Greenwich Village	1984	MGM-UA
Racing With the Moon	1984	Par.
Silverado	1985	Col.
Swimming to Cambodia	1987	US
That Championship Season	1982	Cannon
Tough Guys Don't Dance	1987	Cannon
Vibes	1988	Col.
Without a Trace	1983	TCF

30. BRYDON BAKER

Aquasex *	1964	US
Ballad of a Gunfighter	1964	US
Cattle Empire	1958	TCF
Copper Sky	1957	TCF
Escape From Red Rock	1958	TCF
From Hell It Came	1957	AA
Frontier Days	1935	US
The Mermaids of Tiburon	1962	US
Phantom From 10,000 Fathoms	1956	US
Return of the Fly	1959	TCF
Ride a Violent Mile	1957	TCF
Ring of Terror	1962	US
Scandal Incorporated	1956	Rep.
Snowfire	1958	AA
Spacemaster X-7	1958	TCF
The Storm Rider	1957	TCF
Taffy and the Jungle Hunter	1965	AA
20,000 Eyes	1961	TCF
Valley of the Dragons	1961	Col.
The Wetback Hound	1956	Dis.

31. FRIEND C. BAKER

Broken Commandments	1919	Fox
The Call of the Soul	1919	Fox
Chasing Rainbows	1919	Fox
Fighting for Gold	1919	Fox
Flame of Youth	1920	Fox
Girl of My Heart	1920	Fox
The Gray Dawn *	1922	US
Hell Roarin' Reform	1919	Fox
Her American Husband	1918	US
Kultur	1918	Fox
The Long Chance	1915	Univ.
Love Never Dies	1916	US
Merely Mary Ann	1920	Fox
The Rebellious Bride	1919	Fox
The Sneak	1919	Fox
Thieves	1919	Fox
Two Moons	1920	Fox
While the Devil Laughs	1921	Fox

32. IAN BAKER

Barbarosa	1982	Univ.
The Chant of Jimmie Blacksmith	1978	Aus.
The Clinic	1983	Aus.

A Cry in the Dark	1988	WB
The Devil's Playground	1976	Aus.
Everybody Wins	1990	Orion
Iceman	1984	Univ.
Plenty	1985	TCF
The Punisher	1990	US
Roxanne	1987	Col.
The Russia House	1990	MGM/UA

33. SILVANO BALBONI

The Acquittal	1923	Univ.
Alias Mary Flynn	1925	US
Broadway Daddies	1928	Col.
The Fire Patrol	1924	US
Forbidden Cargo	1925	US
Kipps	1921	GB
Lady Robinhood	1925	US
Midnight Molly	1925	US
Shifting Sands	1923	US
Silk Stocking Sal	1924	US
Smooth as Satin	1925	US

34. BERT BALDRIDGE

Beyond All Odds	1926	US
The Candy Kid *	1928	US
A Daughter of Luxury	1922	Par.
Fair Week	1924	Par.
The Hour of Reckoning	1927	US
The Lone Chance	1924	Fox
Racing Hearts	1923	Par.
Romance Ranch	1924	Fox
Secret Menace	1932	US
Soiled *	1924	US
Thundering Speed	1926	US
Wages of Conscience	1927	US
Walloping Kid	1926	US
Wings *	1927	Par.

35. ROBERT BALDWIN

Basket Case 2	1990	US
The Bounty Hunter	1989	US
The Exterminator	1980	US
Frankenhooker	1990	US
Let's Scare Jessica to Death	1971	Par.

The New Life Style	1970	Ger.
Nightmare Weekend	1986	Fr./GB/US
Refuge	1981	US
The Soldier	1982	Emb.
Stigma	1972	US
Vietnam Texas	1990	US
Zombie Island Massacre	1984	US

36. LUCIEN BALLARD (1904-1988)

Al Capone	1959	AA
Anna Lucasta	1958	UA
The Ballad of Cable Hogue	1970	WB
Band of Angels	1957	WB
Berlin Express	1948	RKO
Blind Alley	1939	Col.
Boeing-Boeing	1965	Par.
Bomber's Moon	1943	TCF
The Bramble Bush	1960	WB
Breakheart Pass	1975	UA
Breakout	1975	Col.
Buchanan Rides Alone	1958	Col.
The Caretakers	1963	UA
City of Fear	1958	Col.
Coast Guard	1939	Col.
Craig's Wife	1936	Col.
Crime and Punishment	1935	Col.
Dear Brigette	1965	TCF
The Desert Rats	1953	TCF
Desire in the Dust	1960	TCF
The Devil Is a Woman	1935	Par.
Devil's Playground	1937	Col.
Diplomatic Courier	1952	TCF
Don't Bother to Knock	1952	TCF
Drum	1976	US
An Eye for an Eye	1966	US
The Final Hour	1936	Col.
Fixed Bayonets	1951	TCF
Flight to Fame	1938	Col.
The Getaway	1972	US
Girls Can Play	1937	Col.
Highway Patrol	1938	Col.
Holy Matrimony	1943	TCF
Hour of the Gun	1967	UA
The House on Telegraph Hill	1951	TCF
How Sweet It Is!	1968	WB
I Married a Woman	1956	RKO
I Promise to Pay	1937	Col.
Inferno	1953	TCF
Junior Bonner	1972	US

The Killer Is Loose	1956	UA
The Killing	1956	UA
The King and Four Queens	1956	UA
A Kiss Before Dying	1956	UA
Lady Ice	1973	US
Let Us Live	1937	Col.
Life Begins With Love	1937	Col.
The Lone Wolf in Paris	1938	Col.
The Lodger	1944	TCF
The Magnificent Matador	1955	US
Marines Let's Go!	1961	TCF
Murder by Contract	1958	Col.
Nevada Smith	1966	Avco
New Faces	1954	US
The New Interns	1964	Col.
Night Song	1947	RKO
Night Without Sleep	1952	TCF
O. Henry's Full House *	1952	TCF
Orchestra Wives	1942	TCF
Outside These Walls	1939	Col.
The Parent Trap	1961	Des.
The Party	1968	UA
Pay or Die!	1960	AA
Penitentiary	1938	Col.
Prince Valiant	1954	TCF
The Proud Ones	1956	TCF
Rabbit Test	1978	AE
Racketeers in Exile	1937	Col.
The Raid	1954	TCF
Return of the Texan	1952	TCF
Tide the High Country	1962	MGM
Rio Grande	1938	Col.
The Rise and Fall of Legs Diamond	1960	WB
Roustabout	1964	US
St. Ives	1976	WB
Seven Cities of Gold	1955	TCF
The Shadow	1937	Col.
The Sons of Katie Elder	1965	Par.
Squadron of Honor	1937	Col.
Susan Slade	1961	WB
Sweet and Low Down	1944	TCF
Take Her, She's Mine	1963	TCF
Temptation	1946	Univ.
Texas Stampede	1939	Col.
This Love of Ours	1945	Univ.
Thomasine and Bushrod	1974	Col.
Three the Hard Way	1974	AA
The Thundering West	1939	Col.
A Time for Dying	1971	US
Tonight We Raid Calais	1943	TCF
True Grit	1969	Par.

The Undying Monster	1943	TCF
The Unholy Wife	1957	RKO
The Villain Still Pursued Her	1940	RKO
Wall of Noise	1963	WB
What's the Matter With Helen?	1971	US
Whispering Ghosts	1942	TCF
White Feather	1955	TCF
The Wild Bunch	1969	WB
Wild Geese Calling	1941	TCF
Wild Penny	1967	Par.
Wives and Lovers	1963	Par.

37. MICHAEL BALLHAUS

Adolf and Marlene	1977	Ger.
After Hours	1985	WB
The Autograph	1984	Fr./Ger.
Baby, It's You	1983	Par.
Baja Oklahoma	1985	HBO
Beware of a Saintly Whore	1972	Ger.
Big and Little	1980	Ger.
The Bitter Tears of Petra von Kant	1972	Ger.
Broadcast News	1987	TCF
Chetan, Indian Boy	1973	Ger.
Chinese Roulette	1976	Ger.
The Color of Money	1986	Dis.
Consequence	1977	Ger.
Dear Mr. Wonderful	1982	Ger./US
Despair	1978	Ger.
Dirty Rotten Scoundrels	1988	Orion
Edith's Diary	1983	Ger.
The Fabulous Baker Boys	1989	TCF
The First Polka	1979	Ger.
Fox	1975	Ger.
Friends and Husbands	1983	Ger.
German Spring	1980	Aust./Ger./ Switz.
Germany in Autumn *	1978	Ger.
The Glass Menagerie	1987	US
Goodfellas	1990	WB
The House of Carroll Street	1988	Orion
How to Make It in the Movies	1981	Ger.
Kaleidoscope	1979	Ger.
A Labor of Love	1983	Fr./Ger.
The Last Temptation of Christ	1988	Univ.
Looping	1981	Ger.
The Magic Mountain	1982	Fr./Ger./It.
Malou	1981	Ger.
The Marriage of Maria Braun	1978	Ger.
Martha	1974	Ger.

Might Makes Right	1975	Ger.
Old Enough	1984	Orion
Postcards From the Edge	1990	Col.
Reckless	1984	MGM-UA
Sand	1971	Ger.
Satan's Brew	1976	Ger.
Summer Guests	1976	Ger.
Trilogy of Wiedersehns	1979	Ger.
Under the Cherry Moon	1986	WB
The Uprising	1981	Ger.
We-Two	1970	Ger.
Whity	1971	Ger.
Willie and the Chinese Cat	1977	Aust./Ger.
Working Girl	1988	TCF

38. LIONEL BANES

Against the Wind *	1947	GB--Eal.
The Captive Heart *	1946	GB--Eal.
Fiend Without a Face	1957	GB
Grip of a Strangler	1958	GB
I Only Asked	1958	GB--Ham.
The Magnet	1950	GB--Eal.
The Night My Number Came Up	1954	GB--Eal.
No Road Back	1957	GB
Passport to Pimlico	1949	GB--Eal.
That Woman Opposite	1957	GB
They Were Ten	1960	Isr.
Train of Events *	1949	GB--Eal.
Valley of Song	1953	GB

39. LEONIDA BARBONI

After the Fox	1966	GB/It--UA
And the Wild Women *	1958	It.
Angela	1955	It.--TCF
Bambole *	1965	It.--Col.
Bandit of Tacca del Lupo	1952	It.
Bad Street	1961	It.
Bora Bora	1968	Fr./It.
The Captive City	1963	It.--Par.
Corruption	1963	It.
Countersex *	1964	Fr./It.
A Difficult Life	1962	It.
Disorder	1962	Fr./It.
Divorce Italian Style	1961	It.
El Greco	1964	Fr./It.--TCF
The Facts of Murder	1965	It.
Fame and the Devil	1950	It.

Fathers and Sons	1957	It.
Filumena Marturano	1952	It.
The Five Man Army	1969	It.--MGM
The Great Hope	1954	It.
Hell in the City	1959	It.
The Hunchback of Rome *	1963	It.
Il Nomme della Laga	1949	It.
Jealousy	1953	It.
The Lady of the Lake	1965	It.
Man of Straw	1958	It.
A Midsummer Holiday	1950	It.
Neapolitans in Milan	1953	It.
One Night of Fame	1950	It.
The Passionate Thief	1963	It.--Emb.
La Presidentessa	1952	It.
Queens *	1968	Fr./It.
Railroad Man *	1956	It.
Red Shirts-Anita Garibaldi	1952	Fr./It.
The Road to Hope	1950	It.
Run With the Devil	1963	Fr./It.
The Sex of Angels	1969	Ger./It.
La Traviata	1968	It.
The Verona Trail	1963	It.
A Very Handy Man	1966	Fr./It.
Via Margutta	1960	It.
La Viaccia	1961	It.
The Witch	1969	It.

40. ANDRE BARLATIER

Adam and Evil	1927	MGM
The Argyle Case	1917	Selz.
The Baby Cyclone	1928	MGM
Barriers Burned Away	1925	US
Beau Broadway	1929	MGM
The Belle of New York	1919	US
The Black Butterfly	1916	Metro.
Break the News to Mother	1919	US
The Bugle Call	1927	MGM
The Burglar	1917	US
Cecilia of the Pink Roses	1918	US
Cheaper to Marry	1925	MGM
A Dangerous Adventure *	1922	WB
A Daughter of the Gods *	1916	Fox
The Destroying Angel	1923	US
Devil's Island	1926	US
Earthbound	1920	Gold.
Exclusive Rights	1926	US
Exit Smiling	1926	MGM
The Flying Dutchman	1923	US

Going the Limit	1926	US
Half-a-Dollar Bill	1924	Metro.
Her Honor the Governor	1926	US
The Kentuckians	1921	Par.
Lady of the Night	1925	MGM
The Little Girl Next Door	1923	US
The Miracle Makers	1923	US
Neptune's Daughter	1914	Univ.
On Ze Boulevard	1927	MGM
Out of the Storm	1920	Gold.
The Painted Flapper	1924	US
The Passion Song	1928	US
The Primrose Path	1925	US
Redhead	1941	Mon.
A Regular Girl	1919	US
A Single Man	1929	MGM
The Snob	1924	MGM
Spangles	1926	Univ.
Tea for Three	1927	MGM
Two Can Play	1926	US
Without Limit	1921	Metro.
Your Wife and Mine	1927	US

41. GEORGE BARNES (1893-1953)

Alice Adams	1923	US
The Awakening	1928	UA
The Beautiful Gambler	1921	Univ.
The Bells of St. Mary's	1945	RKO
Black Legion	1936	WB
Blondie of the Follies	1932	MGM
The Boy With Green Hair	1948	RKO
Broadway	1942	Univ.
Broadway Bad	1933	Fox
Broadway Gondolier	1935	WB
The Bronze Bell	1921	Par.
Bulldog Drummond *	1929	Gold.
Cain and Mabel	1936	WB
Colleen *	1936	WB
Condemned *	1930	Gold.
Conquering the Woman	1922	US
Dames *	1934	WB
Dangerous Hours	1920	Par.
Dark Angel	1925	FN
Desire	1923	Metro.
The Devil Dancer *	1927	UA
The Devil to Pay *	1930	Gold.
Devil's Island	1939	WB
Dusk to Dawn	1922	US
The Eagle *	1925	UA

The Emperor Waltz	1948	Par.
Ever Since Eve	1937	WB
The False Road	1920	Par.
The File on Thelma Jordan	1949	Par.
Five and Ten	1931	MGM
Flirtation Walk *	1934	WB
Footlight Parade	1933	WB
Force of Evil	1948	MGM
Free, Blonde and 21	1940	TCF
Frenchman's Creek *	1944	Par.
From This Day Forward	1946	RKO
Gambling Lady	1934	WB
Girl From Avenue A *	1940	TCF
Girls on Probation *	1937	WB
Gold Diggers in Paris *	1938	WB
Gold Diggers of 1935	1935	FN
Good Sam	1948	US
Goodbye Again	1933	WB
The Greatest Show on Earth *	1952	Par.
The Greeks Had a Word for Them	1932	UA
Hairpins	1920	Par.
Haunted Bedroom	1919	Par.
Havana Windows	1933	FN
He Was Her Man	1934	WB
The Heart Line	1921	US
Her Husband's Friend	1920	Par.
Here Comes the Groom	1951	Par.
Hollywood Hotel *	1937	WB
Hudson's Bay	1940	TCF
I Live for Love	1935	WB
In Caliente *	1935	WB
The Irish in Us	1935	WB
It Comes Up Love	1942	Univ.
Jane Eyre *	1943	TCF
Janice Meredith *	1924	Metro.-Gold.
Jesse James	1939	TCF
Just For You	1952	Par.
Kansas City Princess	1934	WB
Ladies in Retirement	1941	Col.
A Lady's Morals	1930	MGM
The Law of Men	1919	Par.
Let's Dance	1950	Par.
Little Boy Lost	1953	Par.
Love, Honor and Behave	1938	WB
Mademoiselle Modiste	1926	FN
The Magic Flame	1927	UA
Marked Woman	1937	WB
Maryland *	1940	TCF
Meet John Doe	1941	US-WB
Mr. Lucky	1943	RKO
Mr. Music	1950	Par.

Mourning Becomes Electra	1947	RKO
The Night of Love *	1927	UA
Nightmare	1942	Univ.
No Minor Vices	1948	MGM
None But the Lonely Heart *	1944	RKO
One Heavenly Night	1931	Gold.
Once Upon a Honeymoon	1942	RKO
Opened Shutters	1921	Univ.
Our Dancing Daughters	1928	MGM
Our Neighbors-The Carters	1939	Par.
Parole Fixer	1940	Par.
Partners Three	1919	Par.
Peg 'O My Heart	1922	Metro.
Peg 'O My Heart	1933	MGM
Polly of the Circus	1932	MGM
Raffles *	1930	Gold.
The Real Adventure	1922	US
Rebecca	1940	Selz.
Remember the Day	1941	TCF
The Rescue	1929	UA
The Return of Frank James *	1940	TCF
Riding High *	1950	Par.
Rings on Her Fingers	1942	TCF
Road to Bali	1952	Par.
Sadie Thompson *	1928	TCF
Samson and Delilah	1949	Par.
Sherlock Holmes	1932	UA
Sinbad the Sailor	1947	Par.
The Singing Kid	1936	WB
Sister Kenny	1946	RKO
Smarty	1934	WB
Society Girl	1932	Fox
Somebody Loves Me	1952	Par.
Something to Live For	1952	Par.
The Son of the Sheik	1926	UA
The Spanish Main	1945	RKO
Spellbound	1945	Selz.
Stanley and Livingstone	1938	TCF
Stars Over Broadway	1935	WB
Stepping Out	1919	Par.
Street Scene	1931	Gold.
The Teaser	1925	Univ.
That Uncertain Feeling	1941	UA
This Is Heaven *	1928	Gold.
Tracks	1922	US
Travelling Saleslady	1935	WB
The Trespasser *	1929	UA
Two Lovers	1928	Gold.-UA
The Unholy Garden *	1931	Gold.
Unholy Partners	1941	MGM
Variety Show *	1937	WB

Venus of Venice	1927	FN
The Virtuous Thief	1919	Par.
The War of the Worlds	1952	Par.
The Wet Parade	1932	MGM
What a Widow!	1930	US
What Every Woman Learns	1919	Par.
The Winning of Barbara Worth *	1926	UA
Woman in the Suitcase	1920	Par.
Woman Wake Up!	1922	US
Yolanda *	1924	Metro.-Gold.
Zander the Great	1925	Metro.-Gold.

42. FRANKLYN BARRETT

Australia's Peril	1917	Aus.
The Breaking of the Drought	1920	Aus.
The Enemy Within	1918	Aus.
A Girl of the Bush	1916	Aus.
The Joan of Arc of Loos	1916	Aus.
Know Thy Child	1921	Aus.
The Lure of the Bush	1918	Aus.
The Mutiny on the Bounty	1916	Aus.
The Pioneers	1916	Aus.
A Rough Passage	1922	Aus.
A Romance of the Burke and Willis Expedition	1918	Aus.

43. ANDRZES BARTKOWIAK

Daniel	1983	Par.
Deadly Hero	1976	US
Deathtrap	1982	WB
Family Business	1989	TRI-S.
The Morning After	1986	TCF
Nuts	1987	WB
Power	1986	TCF
Prince of the City	1981	Orion-WB
Prizzi's Honor	1985	TCF
Q & A	1990	TRI-S.
Terms of Endearment	1983	Par.
Twins	1988	Univ.
The Verdict	1982	TCF

44. MARIO BAVA

Adventures of Giacomo Casanova	1955	Fr./It.
Antonio di Padua	1949	It.
Before the Fact-The Ecology of a Crime	1971	It.

Black Sunday	1961	It.--AIP
Blood and Black Lace	1965	It.--AA
Caltiki	1959	It.--AA
Carnage	1971	It.
Christmas at Camp 119 *	1948	It.
City at Night	1957	It.
Cops and Robbers	1952	It.
The Day the Sky Exploded	1961	Fr./It.
The Devil's Commandment	1956	It.
Erik the Conqueror *	1963	Fr./It.--AIP
Esther and the King	1960	It.--TCF
Evil Eye	1962	It.--AIP
The Giant of Marathon	1960	It.--MGM
Hatchet for the Honeymoon	1969	It./Sp.
Her Favorite Husband	1950	It.
Hercules	1957	It.--WB
Hercules and the Queen of Lydia	1959	Fr./It.
Hercules in the Haunted World	1964	It.
Hercules Unchained	1959	Fr./It.--WB
I Vampiri	1957	It.
Labors of Hercules	1958	It.
Mad About Opera	1950	It.
Miss Italia	1950	It.
Le Morte Viene Dalla Spazio	1958	It.
Nero's Mistress	1962	It.
This Wine of Love	1948	It.
Villa Borghese	1954	It.
What!	1965	It.
White Warrior	1961	It.

45. WILLIAM BECKWAY

Bab the Fixer	1917	US
Betty Be Good	1917	US
A Bit of Kindling	1917	US
Checkmate	1917	US
Comrade John	1915	Pathe
Fighting Playboy	1937	US
Man's Desire	1919	US
Old Lady 31	1920	Metro.
Secret Patrol *	1936	Col.
Stampede *	1936	Col.
Sunny Jane	1917	US
Told at the Twilight	1917	US
Twin Kiddies	1917	US
What Price Vengeance? *	1936	US
The Wildcat	1917	US
Woman Against the World *	1938	Col.

46. PAUL BEESON

An American Dream	1988	GB
Africa-Texas Style!	1967	Par.
Against the Wind	1947	GB--Eal.
Attack on the Iron Coast	1967	UA
Ballet Gayane	1978	US
Candleshoe	1977	Dis.
Crescendo	1969	GB--Ham.
The Cruel Sea *	1952	GB--Eal.
Die, Monster, Die	1965	AIP
Dr. Syn-Alias the Scarecrow	1962	Dis.
Dunkirk	1958	GB--Eal.
Escape From the Dark	1976	Dis.
The Feminine Touch	1950	GB--Eal.
Greyfriars Bobby	1960	Dis.
The Happy Thieves	1962	UA
Hawk the Slayer	1980	GB
Hell Boats	1970	UA
In Search of the Castaways	1961	Dis.
Indiana Jones and the Last Crusade *	1989	Par.
Jane and the Lost City	1987	GB
Jane Eyre	1971	GB
Kidnapped	1959	Dis.
Kidnapped	1971	GB
The Lost Continent	1968	GB--Ham.
The Moon Spinners	1964	Dis.
Moon Zero Two	1969	GB--Ham.
Mosquito Squadron	1968	UA
The Mutations	1974	Col.-WB
Nearly a Nasty Accident	1961	GB
Not With My Wife You Don't!	1966	WB
Nowhere to Go	1958	GB--Eal.
One of Our Dinosaurs Is Missing	1975	Dis.
Out of the Clouds	1954	GB--Eal.
The Scapegoat	1959	MGM
Season of Passion	1961	UA
The Shiralee	1957	GB--Eal.-MGM
Silver Dream Racer	1980	GB
The Spaceman and King Arthur	1979	Dis.
Spare the Rod	1961	GB
Starcrash *	1979	US
Submarine X-1	1967	UA
Taste of Excitement	1968	GB
Tarzan Goes to India	1962	MGM
The Three Loves of Thomasina	1963	Dis.
To Sir, With Love	1967	Col.
Train of Events *	1949	GB--Eal.
The Unidentified Flying Oddball	1979	GB--Dis.
Under Capricorn *	1949	GB--WB
A Warm December	1972	GB

West of Zanzibar	1954	GB--Eal.
Where No Vultures Fly *	1951	GB--Eal.
The Wolves of Willoughby Chase	1990	GB

47. FRIEDL BEHN-GRUND (1906-   )

The Affair Blum *	1949	Ger.
All Night Through	1959	Ger.
Alraune	1952	Ger.
Barberina	1932	Ger.
Black-White-Red Four Poster	1963	Ger.
Buddenbrooks	1962	Ger.
The Confessions of the Swindler		
Felix Krull	1957	Ger.
Council of the Gods	1950	Ger.
Crook's Honor	1966	Ger.
Dancer of Sansoucci	1932	Ger.--UFA
The Divine Jette	1937	Ger.
Eight Girls in a Boat	1932	Ger.
The Empress and I	1933	Ger.--UFA
The Forester's Daughter	1952	Ger.
I by Day, You by Night	1933	Ger.--UFA
Karamazov	1931	Ger.
Louisa, Queen of Prussia	1931	Ger.
The Man Who Sold Himself	1959	Ger.
Maria Theresa	1952	Ger.
Marriage in the Shadows *	1948	Ger.
Matrimonial Agent Aurora	1962	Ger.
Melody of Love	1932	Ger.
The Murderer	1931	Ger.--UFA
Murderers Are Amongst Us	1947	Ger.
My Heart Calls You	1934	Ger.
Police Raid	1948	Ger.
The Pride of the Third Company	1932	Ger.
Promise Me Nothing	1937	Ger.
The Puppet *	1931	Ger.
The Restless Night	1964	Ger.
Retreat on Rhine *	1933	Ger.
A Tale of Five Women *	1962	GB--UA
Trapeze *	1932	Ger.
Truxa	1937	Ger.
24 Hours Out of the Life of a		
Woman *	1931	Ger.
Zappenstreich am Rhein *	1930	Ger.

48. GEORGES BENOIT

The Bad Lands *	1925	US
The Baker's Wife *	1939	Fr.

Beyond the Border *	1925	US
Blue Blood and Red	1916	Fox
Carmen *	1915	Fox
Charge of the Gauchos *	1928	US
The Danger Girl	1926	US
The Derelict	1917	Fox
The Dice Woman *	1927	US
La Femme du Boulanger *	1938	Fr.
Forbidden Waters	1926	US
Heart of Paris *	1938	Fr.
The Honor System	1917	Fox
Idle Hands	1920	US
Jewels of Desire	1927	US
The Little 'Fraid Lady	1920	US
Live and Let Live	1921	US
A Lover's Oath	1925	US
The Man From Red Gulch	1925	US
No Control	1927	US
Omar the Tentmaker	1922	FN
Pals in Paradise	1926	US
The Prairie Pirate	1925	US
Regeneration	1915	Fox
The Scarlet Letter	1917	Fox
The Scarlet West *	1925	FN
The Serpent	1916	Fox
The Speeding Venus	1926	US
Stealers	1920	US
Stop Flirting	1925	US
Temptations of a Shop Girl	1927	US
The Texas Trail	1925	US
Trilby	1923	TN
The Wagon Show	1928	FN
Wandering Daughters	1923	FN
Welcome Stranger	1924	US
West of Broadway	1926	US
What's a Life Worth?	1921	US
The Wonder Man	1920	US

49. RUDOLF BERGQUIST

After His Own Heart	1919	Metro.
Billions	1920	Metro.
The Brass Check	1918	Metro.
Camille	1921	Metro.
Don't Write Letters	1922	Metro.
Extravagance	1921	Metro.
The Four Flusher	1919	Metro.
Full of Pep	1919	Metro.
Garments of Truth	1921	Metro.
The Girl From Montmartre	1926	FN

A Girl in Every Port *	1928	Fox
The Great Romance	1919	Metro.
The Heart of a Child	1920	Metro.
Heart of a Siren	1925	FN
His Bonded Wife	1918	Metro.
The Hunch	1921	Metro.
I Can Explain	1922	Metro.
In His Brother's Place	1919	Metro.
Little Eva Ascends	1922	Metro.
Madame Peacock	1920	Metro.
Marriage	1927	Fox
One Increasing Purpose	1927	Fox
One Night in Rome	1924	MGM
Painted People	1924	FN
A Pair of Cupids	1918	Metro.
Passion Fruit	1921	Metro.
The Play Girl	1928	Fox
Potash and Perlmutter	1923	FN
Quincy Adams Sawyer	1922	Metro.
Red Lights	1923	Gold.
Red, White and Blue Blood	1918	Metro.
Romeo and Juliet	1916	Metro.
Sandy	1926	Fox
Shadows of Suspicion	1919	Metro.
The Shooting of Dan McGrew	1924	Metro.
Silk Legs	1927	Fox
Social Quicksands	1918	Metro.
Square Crooks	1928	Fox
Stronger Than Death	1920	Metro.
Under Suspicion	1918	Metro.
The Voice of Conscience	1917	Metro.
The Way of the Strong	1919	Metro.
The White Monkey	1925	FN
The White Sister	1915	US
With Neatness and Dispatch	1918	Metro.
Womanpower	1926	Fox
Your Friend and Mine	1923	Metro.

50. RAY BINGER

The Goldfish	1924	FN
Her Night of Romance *	1924	FN
Men of the North	1930	MGM
Private Lives	1931	MGM
Strike Me Pink *	1936	UA
Wild Justice	1925	UA
Women Love Diamonds	1927	MGM

51. JOSEPH BIROC (1903-   )

Airplane!	1980	Par.
Airplane II: The Sequel	1982	Par.
All the Marbles	1981	MGM
Amazing Colossal Man	1957	AIP
Appointment in Honduras	1953	RKO
Attack!	1956	UA
The Bat	1959	AA
Bengazi	1955	RKO
Beyond the Poseidon Adventure	1979	WB
The Black Whip	1956	TCF
Blazing Saddles	1974	WB
Born Reckless	1959	WB
Bullet for a Badman	1964	Univ.
Bwana Devil	1952	UA
Bye Bye Birdie	1963	Col.
Cahill, U.S. Marshal	1973	WB
China Gate	1957	TCF
The Choirboys	1978	Lor.
Confessions of an Opium Eater	1962	US
Convicts Four	1962	AA
Cry Danger	1951	RKO
The Detective	1968	TCF
The Devil at Four O'Clock	1961	Col.
Donovan's Brain	1953	UA
Down Three Dark Streets	1954	UA
The Duchess and the Dirtwater Fox	1976	TCF
Emperor of the North Pole	1973	TCF
Enter Laughing	1967	Col.
Escape From the Planet of the Apes	1971	TCF
The FBI Story	1958	WB
Fitzwilly	1967	UA
The Flight of the Phoenix	1965	TCF
Forty Guns	1957	TCF
The Garment Jungle	1957	Col.
Ghost Town	1956	UA
The Glass Wall	1953	Col.
Gold of the Seven Saints	1961	WB
The Grissom Gang	1971	US
Gunfight at Comanche Creek	1963	AA
Hammett *	1982	Orion
Hitler	1961	US
Home Before Dark	1958	WB
Hush Hush Sweet Charlotte	1964	TCF
Hustle	1975	Par.
I Saw What You Did	1965	Univ.
Ice Palace	1960	WB
It's a Wonderful Life *	1946	RKO
Johnny Allegro	1949	Col.
The Killer That Stalked New York	1950	Col.

The Killing of Sister George	1969	US
Kitten with a Whip	1964	Univ.
Lady in Cement	1968	TCF
The Legend of Lylah Clare	1968	MGM
Loan Shark	1952	Lip.
The Longest Yard	1974	Par.
Magic Town	1947	US
Mrs. Mike	1949	US
Mrs. Pollifax-Spy	1970	UA
Nightmare	1956	UA
On Our Merry Way	1948	UA
Operation Eichmann	1961	AA
The Organization	1971	UA
Promises! Promises!	1963	US
Quincannon Frontier Scout	1956	UA
Red Planet Mars	1952	UA
The Ride Back	1957	UA
Ride the Wild Surf	1964	Col.
Roughshod	1949	RKO
Run of the Arrow	1956	US
The Russians Are Coming, the Russians Are Coming	1966	UA
Sail a Crooked Ship	1961	Col.
The Swinger	1966	Par.
The Tall Texan	1953	Lip.
Tension at Table Rock	1956	RKO
Thirteen Ghosts	1960	Col.
To Trap a Spy	1965	MGM
Tony Rome	1967	TCF
Too Late the Hero	1969	US
The Towering Inferno *	1974	TCF
Toys in the Attic	1963	UA
The Twonky	1953	UA
Ulzana's Raid	1972	Univ.
Under the Yum Yum Tree	1963	Col.
Underwater Warrior *	1958	MGM
The Unknown Terror	1957	TCF
Verboten!	1958	Col.
Vice Squad	1953	UA
Viva Las Vegas	1964	MGM
Warning Shot	1966	Par.
Whatever Happened to Aunt Alice?	1969	US
Who's Minding the Mint?	1967	Col.
Without Warning	1952	UA
World for Ransom	1954	AA
The Young Lovers	1964	MGM

52. G. W. (BILLY) BITZER (1872-1944)

America *	1924	UA

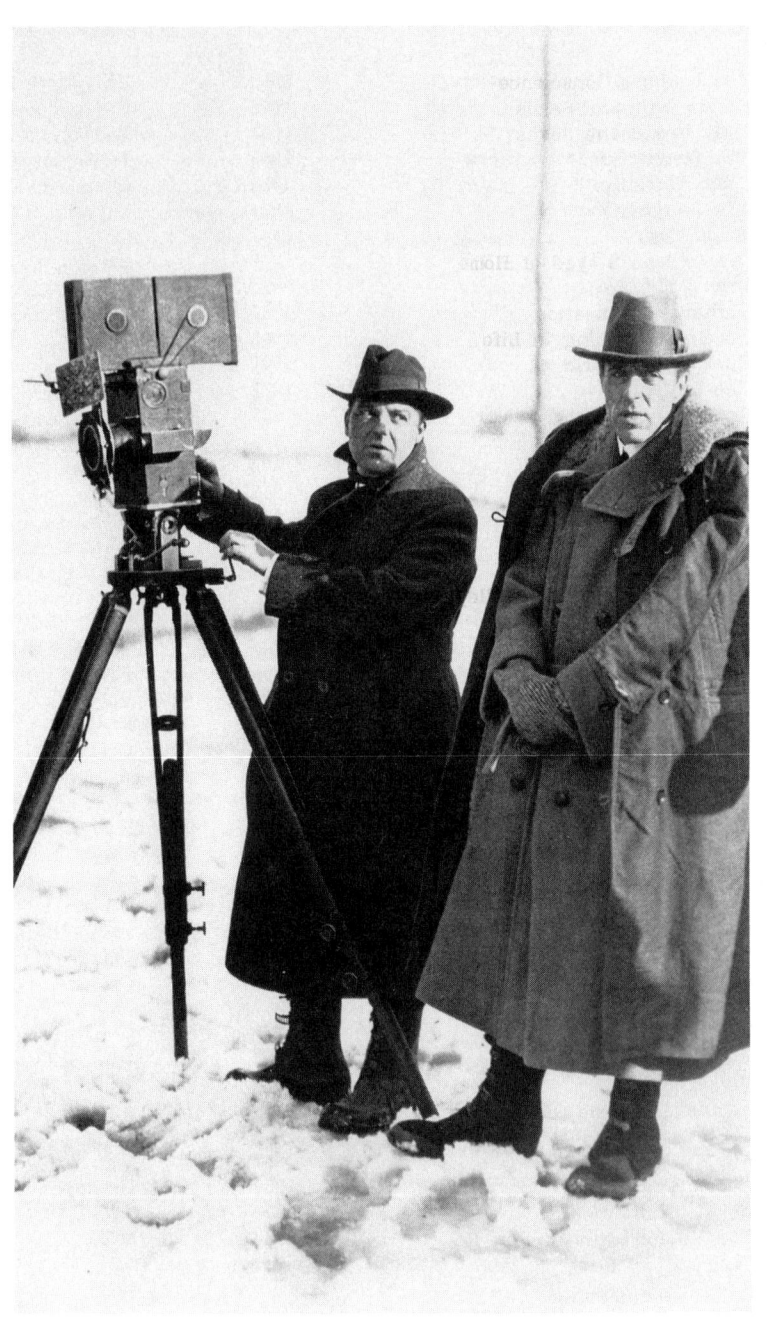

G. W. "Billy" Bitzer (left) with D. W. Griffith.

The Avenging Conscience	1914	US
The Battle of the Sexes	1914	US
The Battle of the Sexes	1928	US
Birth of a Nation *	1915	US
Broken Blossoms *	1919	UA
Drums of Love *	1928	UA
The Escape	1914	US
The Girl Who Stayed at Home	1919	US
The Great Love	1918	US
The Greatest Question	1920	FN
The Greatest Thing in Life	1918	US
Hearts of the World *	1918	US
Hotel Variety *	1933	US
Home Sweet Home	1914	US
The Idol Dancer	1920	FN
Intolerance *	1916	US
Judith of Bethulia	1914	US
Lady of the Pavements *	1929	UA
The Midnight Girl *	1925	US
Orphans of the Storm *	1921	UA
The Romance of Happy Valley	1919	US
Scarlet Days	1919	Par.
Sure Fire Flint *	1922	US
True Heart Susie	1919	US
Way Down East *	1920	US
The White Rose *	1923	UA

53. LOUIS C. BITZER

Coincidence	1921	Metro.
Face in the Dark	1918	Gold.
King Tut-Ankh-Amen's Eighth Wife	1923	US
Romance	1920	UA
Suspence	1919	US

54. JACQUES BIZEUIL

Charge It	1921	US
A Daughter of the Old South	1918	Par.
The Deep Purple	1920	US
Eyes of the Soul	1919	Par.
Man of Glengarry	1923	US
The Marriage Price	1919	US
The Mystery of the Yellow Room	1919	US
The New York Idea	1920	US
Out of the Shadow	1919	Par.
Paid in Full	1919	Par.
A Pasteboard Clown	1922	US
Under the Greenwood Tree	1918	US
A Woman's Woman	1922	US

55. PETER BIZIOU

Another Country	1984	GB
Bugsy Malone *	1976	GB--Rank/ TCF
Life of Brian	1979	GB
Mississippi Burning	1988	Orion
9½ Weeks	1986	MGM-UA
Our Cissy	1974	GB--EMI
Pink Floyd The Wall	1982	GB--MGM
Rosencrantz and Guildenstern Are Dead	1990	GB
Secret World	1969	Fr.--TCF
Time Bandits	1981	GB
A World Apart	1988	GB

56. WILLIAM J. BLACK

The Cowardly Way	1915	US
Five Thousand an Hour	1918	Metro.
His Wife's Money	1920	Selz.
A Man's Home	1921	Selz..
Out of the Snows	1920	Selz.
Sealed Hearts	1919	Selz.
Success	1923	Metro.
Tropical Love	1921	US
Virtuous Men	1919	US
Wet Gold *	1921	Gold.

57. RALF BODE

The Accused	1988	Par.
The Big Town	1987	Col.
Coal Miner's Daughter	1980	Univ.
Cousins	1989	Par.
Critical Condition	1987	Par.
Distant Thunder	1988	Can.--Par.
Dressed to Kill	1980	US
Foreplay *	1975	US
Gorky Park	1983	Orion
A Little Sex	1982	Univ.
The President's Women	1981	US
Raggedy Man	1981	Univ.
Rich Kids	1979	UA
S.O.S.	1975	US
Saturday Night Fever	1978	Par.
Slow Dancing in the Big City	1978	UA
Somebody Killed Her Husband *	1978	Col.
Stoolie	1974	US
There Is No 13	1974	US

Uncle Buck	1989	Univ.
Violets Are Blue	1986	Col.
The Whoopie Boys	1986	Par.

58. JEAN BOFFETY

Act of the Heart	1970	Can.
Angel's Leap	1971	Fr.
The Angry Man	1979	Can./Fr.
Are You Polly Magoo?	1966	Fr.
As Long as You're Healthy	1966	Fr.
Les Aventuriers	1967	Fr.
A Bad Son	1980	Fr.
The Big Shots	1972	Fr.
A Bite of Living	1982	Fr.
Bolero	1982	Fr.
A Butterfly on the Shoulder *	1978	Fr.
By Design	1981	Can.
Cesar and Rosalie	1972	Fr.--Orion/ Par.
The Chinese in Paris	1974	Fr.
Death of a Killer	1964	Fr.
Died on a Rainy Sunday	1986	Fr.
Dizengoff 99	1979	Isr.
Dog Day	1984	Fr.
Don't Bite, We Love You	1976	Fr.
Edith and Marcel	1983	Fr.
Eliza's Horoscope *	1975	Can.
Everybody He Is Nice, Everybody He Is Beautiful	1972	Fr.
Garcon!	1983	Fr.
The Good Life	1963	Fr.
The Great Love	1969	Fr.--TCF
Ho	1968	Fr.
In the Midst of Life	1963	Fr.
The Ins and the Outs	1981	Fr.
Je T'Aime, Je T'Aime	1967	Fr./Swed. --TCF
Journey	1972	Can.
The Lacemaker	1977	Fr.
The Last Adventure	1968	Fr./It.
A Little, A Lot, Passionately	1971	Fr.
Live at Night	1968	Fr.
Mad Enough to Kill	1975	Fr.--TCF
Mado	1976	Fr.
Marked Eyes	1964	Fr.
Me, I Want to Have Dough	1973	Fr.--UA
A New World	1966	Fr./It.--UA
Pastures of Disorder *	1966	Fr./Greece

Place by the Sea	1988	Fr.
The Porcelain Anniversary	1975	Fr.--TCF
Quintet	1979	Fr.
The Red Sweater	1979	Fr.
Rights of Man	1960	Fr.
Rise Up Spy *	1982	Fr.
Rum Boulevard	1971	Fr.
A Simple Story	1978	Fr.
The Troubles of Alfred	1972	Fr.
Vincent, Francois, Paul ... and the Others	1974	Fr.
Wise Guys	1969	Fr./It.
With the Lives of Others	1966	Fr./It.
Yo Yo	1967	Fr.
Yoho	1965	Fr.--WB
A Young World	1966	Fr./It.
Zita	1968	Fr.

59. HASKELL BOGGS

As Young as We Are	1958	Par.
The Bellboy	1960	Par.
Cinderfella	1960	Par.
The Delicate Delinquent	1956	Par.
Don't Give Up the Ship	1959	Par.
Fear Strikes Out	1957	Par.
The Geisha Boy	1958	Par.
Hear Me Good	1957	Par.
I Married a Monster From Outer Space	1958	Par.
The Leather Saint	1955	Par.
Red Line 7000 *	1965	Par.
Rock a Bye Baby	1958	Par.
St. Louis Blues	1958	Par.
Short Cut to Hell	1957	Par.
Teacher's Pet	1958	Par.
Young Fury	1965	Par.

60. LAMAR BOREN

Around the World Under the Sea	1966	MGM
Brewster McCloud *	1970	MGM
Clarence, the Cross-Eyed Lion	1965	MGM
Flipper *	1963	MGM
Flipper's New Adventure	1964	MGM
Namu, the Killer Whale	1966	UA
The Old Man and the Sea *	1958	WB
Rhino! *	1964	MGM
September Storm *	1960	TCF
Underwater Warrior *	1958	MGM
Zebra in the Kitchen	1965	MGM

61. OSMOND BORRADAILE (1898-   )

Bonnie Prince Charlie *	1948	GB
Drums *	1938	UA
Elephant Boy	1937	GB--Korda
The Four Feathers *	1939	GB--Korda
I Was a Male War Bride *	1949	TCF
The Lion Has Wings *	1939	GB--Korda/UA
The Overlanders	1946	GB--Eal.
Saints and Sinners *	1948	GB
Scott of the Antarctic *	1948	GB--Eal.
Storm Over the Nile *	1955	GB
The Thief of Bagdad *	1940	GB--Korda

62. JEAN BOURGOIN (1913-   )

Les Assasins du Dimanche	1956	Fr.
Before the Deluge	1953	Fr.
The Black File	1955	Fr.
Black Orpheus	1958	Braz./Fr./It.
The Cavalryman	1956	Fr./It.
The Counterfeit Traitor	1962	Par.
Crazy Show	1950	Fr.
Dedee d'Anvers	1948	Fr.
Follow That Man	1953	Fr.
Germinal	1963	Fr.
Gigot	1962	TCF
A Girl for the Summer	1960	Fr.
Goha	1953	Tun.
Hans the Sailor	1949	Fr.
The Hotshots	1968	Fr.
The House on the Dune	1952	Fr.
Impossible on Saturday	1966	Fr./Isr.
It Happened at the Inn	1943	Fr.--MGM
It Happened in Paris	1953	Fr.
Justice est Faite	1950	Fr.
Life Is Ours	1936	Fr.
The Longest Day *	1962	TCF
Maneges	1950	Fr.
La Marseillaise	1938	Fr.
Mr. Arkadian	1955	Fr./GB/Sp.
A Mistress for the Summer	1964	Fr./It.
Mon Oncle	1956	Fr.
Nous Sommes Tous Les Assassins	1952	Fr.
Une Partie de Campagne *	1936	Fr.
Ragpicker of Emmaus	1955	Fr.
The Real Guilty	1951	Fr.
The Red Room	1973	Belg./Fr.
The Riding School	1950	Fr.
Shadow and Light	1951	Fr.

The Solitary Conquerors	1952	Fr.
Watch Out, La Tour	1958	Fr.
Ways of Love *	1950	Fr./It.
Who?	1970	Fr./It.

63. RUSSELL BOYD

Almost an Angel	1990	Par.
Backroads	1981	Aus.
Between Wars	1974	Aus.
Blood Oath	1990	Aus.
Break of Day	1977	Aus.
Burke and Willis	1985	Aus.
Chain Reaction	1980	Aus.
"Crocodile" Dundee	1986	Aus.--Par.
Crocodile Dundee II	1988	Par.
Dawn	1979	Aus.
The Dragon Flies	1975	Aus.--TCF
Gallipoli	1981	Aus.--Par.
High Tide	1987	Aus.
In Country	1989	WB
Just Out of Reach	1979	Aus.
The Last Wave	1977	Aus.
The Man From Hong Kong	1975	TCF
Matchless	1974	Aus.
Maybe This Time	1981	Aus.
Mrs. Soffel	1984	MGM-UA
Phar Lap	1984	Aus.--TCF
Picnic at Hanging Rock	1975	Aus.
The Rescue	1988	Dis./Touch.
The Singer and the Dancer	1977	Aus.
A Soldier's Story	1984	Col.
Stanley	1984	Aus.
Summer of Secrets	1976	Aus.
Tender Mercies	1983	EMI/Univ.
The Year of Living Dangerously	1982	Aus.--MGM

64. CHARLES BOYLE (1893-1968)

After the Fog	1929	US
Anchors Aweigh! *	1945	MGM
Apache Drums	1951	Univ.
The Battle at Apache Pass	1952	Univ.
Behind the Front	1926	Par.
Beyond the Blue Horizon *	1942	Par.
The Cimarron Kid	1952	Univ.
City Beneath the Sea	1953	Univ.
Clancy's Kosher Wedding	1927	US
Column South	1953	Univ.

Davy Crockett	1955	Dis.
Follow Thru *	1930	Par.
Frontier Gal *	1945	Univ.
The Great Locomotive Chase	1956	Dis.
Gunsmoke	1953	Univ.
Horizons West	1952	Univ.
In Old California	1929	US
Johnny Tremain	1957	Dis.
The Lady From Texas	1951	Univ.
The Little Adventuress	1927	US
Mamba	1930	US
Mark of the Renegade	1951	Univ.
Old Ironsides *	1926	Par.
Old Yeller	1957	Dis.
Ranger of the North	1927	US
A Regular Fellow	1925	Par.
The Riding Renegade	1928	US
The Runaway	1926	Par.
Saddle Tramp	1950	Univ.
The Stand at Apache River	1953	Univ.
Steel Town	1952	Univ.
Tillie's Punctured Romance	1928	Par.
Tomahawk	1951	Univ.
Uneasy Payments	1927	US
Untamed Frontier	1952	Univ.
We're in the Navy Now	1926	Par.
Westward Ho the Wagons!	1956	Dis.

65. JOHN W. BOYLE

The Adventurer	1920	Fox
The Bridge of San Luis Rey	1944	UA
Broadway Fever	1929	US
Burma Convoy	1941	Univ.
Carson City	1952	WB
Cattle Raiders	1938	Col.
Cleopatra *	1917	Fox
Curley	1947	US
Danger Lights *	1930	RKO
A Dangerous Adventure *	1922	WB
Dark Sands	1938	GB
Destination Unknown	1942	Univ.
The Devil's Pipeline	1940	Univ.
Double Date	1941	Univ.
Drag Harlan	1920	Fox
Excuse Me	1925	MGM
The Fabulous Joe	1946	US
The Fall of a Nation	1916	US
The Far Cry	1926	FN
Flying Cadets	1941	Univ.

Forbidden Music	1936	GB
Gallant Bess	1946	MGM
The Gentleman From Arizona	1940	Mon.
Give Us Wings	1940	Univ.
The Golden Gift	1922	Metro.
Good Morning, Judge	1945	Univ.
The Good-Bye Kiss	1928	FN
The Greater Glory *	1926	FN
Greater Love Hath No Man *	1915	Metro.
Gridiron Flash	1935	RKO
Half Way to Shanghai	1942	Univ.
He's My Guy	1943	Univ.
Heart Strings	1920	Fox
Her Great Match	1915	Metro.
Her Second Chance	1926	FN
Here Comes Trouble	1948	US
Hero for a Day	1939	Univ.
Hi, Buddy	1943	Univ.
If I Were King	1920	Fox
Jack London	1942	UA
The Joyous Troublemakers	1920	Fox
Jukebox Jennie	1942	Univ.
Keep Your Seats Please	1936	GB
The Keeper of the Bees	1925	US
Kid From Kansas	1941	Univ.
Labernum Grove	1936	GB
The Last of the Duanes	1919	Fox
The Lone Star Ranger	1919	Fox
Love in Jalisco	1943	Mex.
Marked Woman	1937	FN
Mickey	1948	EL
Midnight Daddies	1930	US
Midshipman Easy	1935	GB
Miss Nobody	1926	FN
Mississippi Gambler	1942	Univ.
Mr. Dynamite	1941	Univ.
Mutiny in the Arctic	1941	Univ.
Mutiny on the Blackhawk	1939	Univ.
My Madonna	1915	Metro.
Mystery of the White Room	1939	Univ.
Northwest Stampede	1948	EL
The Orphan	1920	Fox
Outlaws of the Prairie	1938	Col.
The Perfect Sap	1927	FN
Queen of Hearts	1936	GB
The Queen of Sheba	1921	Fox
The Restless Breed	1957	TCF
Ride 'Em Cowboy	1941	Univ.
Salome *	1919	Fox
The She Devil *	1918	Fox
The Siren's Song	1919	Fox

Six Lessons From Madame La Zonga	1941	Univ.
Skyscraper	1928	US
The Skywayman *	1920	Fox
Slave of Desire	1923	Gold.
Society Smugglers	1939	Univ.
Song of the Open Road	1944	UA
The Soul of Buddha	1918	Fox
The Spirit of Youth	1929	US
Strangers All	1935	RKO
Strictly in the Groove	1942	Univ.
The Sundown Rider	1933	Col.
There's One Born Every Minute	1942	Univ.
Topsy and Eva	1927	UA
Tropical Nights *	1928	US
Unseen Enemy	1942	Univ.
When a Woman Sins	1918	Fox
When Men Desire	1919	Fox
When My Ship Comes In	1919	US
Where Did You Get That Girl?	1941	Univ.
Who Killed Doc Robin?	1948	US
Wild Oranges	1924	Gold.
The Wings of the Morning	1919	Fox
Wolves of the Night	1919	Fox
A Woman There Was	1919	Fox

66. WILLIAM BRADFORD

Adventures of Gallant Bess	1948	EL
Along the Navaho Trail	1945	Rep.
Apache Country	1952	Col.
The Arizona Cowboy	1950	Rep.
Barbed Wire	1952	Col
Behind City Lights	1945	Rep.
Beyond the Purple Hills	1950	Col.
The Big Sombrero	1949	Col.
The Blazing Sun	1950	Col.
Call of the South Seas	1944	Rep.
Carson City Cyclone	1943	Rep.
Carson City Raiders	1948	Rep.
Chicago Kid	1945	Rep.
Cow Town	1950	Col.
The Cowboy and the Indians	1949	Col.
Don't Fence Me In	1945	Rep.
End of the Road	1944	Rep.
Exposed	1947	Rep.
False Faces	1943	Rep.
The Fighting Seabees	1944	Rep.
Fugitive From Sonora	1943	Rep.
Gay Blades	1946	Rep.
Gene Autry and the Mounties	1951	Col.

Goldtown Ghost Raiders	1948	Rep.
Grissly's Millions	1945	Rep.
Heldorado	1946	Rep.
Hills of Utah	1951	Col.
Home in Oklahoma	1946	Rep.
In Old Los Angeles	1948	Rep.
Indian Territory	1950	Col.
The Invisible Informer	1946	Rep.
Jamboree	1944	Rep.
Last of the Pony Riders	1953	Col.
Last Round-Up	1947	Col.
Loaded Pistols	1949	Col.
Man From Music Mountain	1943	Rep.
Man From Oklahoma	1945	Rep.
Mantrap	1943	Rep.
Marshal of Cripple Creek	1947	Rep.
Mule Train	1950	Col.
My Pal Trigger	1946	Rep.
Mystery Broadcast	1943	Rep.
Night Stage to Galveston	1952	Col.
Night Train to Memphis	1946	Rep.
Old West	1952	Col.
On the Isle of Samoa	1950	Col.
On Top of Old Smoky	1953	Col.
Pack Trail	1953	Col.
Paris Model	1953	Col.
Passkey to Danger	1946	Rep.
The Phantom Speaks	1945	Rep.
Port Sinister	1953	RKO
Return to Treasure Island	1954	UA
Riders in the Sky	1949	Col.
Riders of the Whistling Pines	1949	Col.
Rim of the Canyon	1949	Col.
Robin Hood of Texas	1947	Rep.
Roll On Texas Moon	1946	Rep.
Saginaw Trail	1953	Col.
The San Antonio Kid	1944	Rep.
San Fernando Valley	1944	Rep.
Santa Fe Saddlemates	1945	Rep.
Scotland Yard Investigator *	1945	Rep.
Secrets of Scotland Yard	1944	Rep.
Silent Partner	1944	Rep.
Silver Canyon	1951	Col.
The Sombrero Kid	1942	Rep.
Sons of New Mexico	1949	Col.
Sunset in El Dorado	1945	Rep.
Texans Never Cry	1951	Col.
Thoroughbreds	1945	Rep.
Three's a Crowd	1945	Rep.
Top Banana	1953	UA
Trail to San Antone	1947	Rep.

Twilight on the Rio Grande	1947	Rep.
Under Nevada Skies	1946	Rep.
Utah	1945	Rep.
Valley of Fire	1951	Col.
Wagon Team	1952	Col.
Whirlwind	1951	Col.
Winning of the West	1953	Col.

67. OTTO BRAUTIGAN

Big Town Ideas	1921	Fox
The Blushing Bride	1921	Fox
Duds	1920	Gold.
Elope If You Must	1922	Fox
The Flight of the Duchess	1916	US
Hicksville to Broadway	1921	Fox
Little Miss Hawkshaw	1921	Fox
Maid of the West	1921	Fox
Milestones	1920	Gold.
Partners of Fate *	1921	Fox
The Tomboy	1921	Fox
The Triumph of Venus	1918	US
Vanity Fair	1915	Edison
Whatever She Wants	1921	Fox

68. ELWOOD (WOODY) BREDELL

The Adventures of Don Juan	1949	WB
The Amazing Mrs. Holliday	1943	Univ.
Argentine Nights	1940	Univ.
The Beautiful Cheat	1945	Univ.
Behind the Mike	1937	Univ.
The Big Guy	1939	Univ.
Big Town Czar	1939	Univ.
Black Friday	1940	Univ.
Butch Minds the Baby	1942	Univ.
Call a Messenger	1938	Univ.
Can't Help Singing *	1944	Univ.
Christmas Holiday	1944	Univ.
Code of the Street	1939	Univ.
Cowboy in Manhattan	1943	Univ.
Danger on Wheels	1940	Univ.
Dark Streets of Cairo	1940	Univ.
Double Alibi	1940	Univ.
Escape From Hong Kong	1942	Univ.
Ex-Champ	1939	Univ.
Female Jungle	1956	US
Follow the Band	1943	Univ.
Forbidden Valley	1938	Univ.

Freshman Year	1938	Univ.
Gangs of Chicago	1940	Rep.
The Ghost of Frankenstein *	1942	Univ.
Hellzapoppin	1942	Univ.
Hers to Hold	1943	Univ.
His Butler's Sister	1943	Univ.
Hold That Ghost *	1941	Univ.
Honeymoon Deferred	1940	Univ.
Horror Island	1941	Univ.
How's About It	1943	Univ.
I Can't Give You Anything But Love, Baby	1940	Univ.
I'm Nobody's Sweetheart Now	1940	Univ.
The Inspector General	1949	WB
The Invisible Woman	1941	Univ.
Journey Into Light	1951	TCF
The Killers	1946	Univ.
La Conga Nights	1940	Univ.
Lady on a Train	1945	Univ.
Little Tough Guy	1938	Univ.
Ma, He's Making Eyes at Me	1940	Univ.
Man Made Monster	1940	Univ.
Mob Town	1941	Univ.
The Mummy's Hand	1940	Univ.
The Mystery of Marie Roget	1942	Univ.
Phantom Lady	1944	Univ.
Private Buckaroo	1942	Univ.
Reckless Living	1938	Univ.
Romance on the High Seas	1948	WB
Sandy Gets Her Man	1940	Univ.
Secrets of a Nurse	1938	Univ.
Sherlock Holmes and the Voice of Terror	1942	Univ.
Smooth as Silk	1946	Univ.
Snowbound *	1927	US
So's Your Uncle *	1943	Univ.
South of Tahiti	1941	Univ.
Spirit of Culver	1939	Univ.
The Strange Affair of Uncle Harry *	1945	Univ.
The Strange Case of Dr. X	1942	Univ.
Strange Faces	1938	Univ.
Swing It Soldier	1941	Univ.
Swing, Sister, Swing	1938	Univ.
Swing That Cheer	1938	Univ.
Tangier	1946	Univ.
That Night With You *	1945	Univ.
That's My Story	1937	Univ.
Tight Shoes	1941	Univ.
Two Bright Boys	1939	Univ.
The Unsuspected	1947	WB
Westbound Limited	1937	Univ.
You're Not So Tough	1940	Univ.

69. JULES BRENNER

Dillinger	1973	AIP
Johnny Got His Gun	1971	US
The Last Word	1979	US
1969	1988	US
Outlaw Blues	1977	WB

70. MILTON BRIDENBECKER

The Clean-Up Man *	1928	Univ.
Desert Dust	1927	Univ.
Greased Lightning	1928	Univ.
Straight Shootin'	1927	Univ.
Thunder Riders	1928	Univ.

71. NORBERT BRODINE (1897-1970)

The Affair of Susan	1935	Univ.
Almost a Husband	1919	Gold.
Always Tomorrow	1934	Univ.
Bachelor's Affairs	1932	Fox
Beast of the City	1932	MGM
Black Oxen	1924	FN
A Blind Bargain	1922	Gold.
Boomerang	1947	TCF
Brass	1923	WB
Brass Knuckles	1927	WB
Broadway to Hollywood *	1933	MGM
The Bullfighters	1944	TCF
Captain Caution	1940	US
Captain Fury	1939	US
The Clown	1927	Col.
Counsellor at Law	1933	Univ.
The Dancing Masters	1943	TCF
The Death Kiss	1932	US
Deluge	1933	RKO
The Desert Fox	1951	TCF
The Divorcee	1930	MGM
Dr. Gillespie's Criminal Case	1943	MGM
Dollars and Sense	1920	Gold.
Don Juan Quilligan	1945	TCF
Don't Get Personal	1936	Univ.
Dulcy	1923	FN
The Eagle of the Sea	1926	Par.
East of Java	1935	Univ.
Five & Ten Cent Annie	1928	WB
Five Fingers	1952	TCF
The Foolish Virgin	1924	Col.

The Frogmen	1951	TCF
Going Some	1920	Gold.
The Good Fairy	1935	Univ.
Grand Larceny	1922	Gold.
The Great Accident	1920	Gold.
The Grim Comedian	1921	Gold.
The Guardsman	1931	MGM
Her Husband's Secret	1925	FN
Her Private Affair *	1929	Pathe
Holiday	1930	Pathe
The House on 92nd Street	1945	TCF
The Housekeeper's Daughter	1939	US
The Human Side	1934	Univ.
I Was a Male War Bride *	1949	TCF
The Invisible Power	1921	Gold.
Kiss of Death	1947	TCF
Lady For a Night	1941	Rep.
Lady Tubbs	1935	Univ.
Let Us Be Gay	1930	MGM
Libeled Lady	1936	MGM
The Lion and the Mouse	1928	WB
Little Man, What Now?	1934	Univ.
Look Your Best	1923	Gold.
Madame Spy	1934	Univ.
Made On Broadway	1933	MGM
The Man From Lost River	1921	Gold.
Merrily We Live	1938	US
Model Wife	1941	Univ.
Night Court	1932	MGM
Nobody's Baby	1937	MGM
Nobody's Fool	1936	Univ.
Of Mice and Men	1939	US
Officer 666	1920	Gold.
One Exciting Adventure	1935	Univ.
One Million BC	1940	US
One-Round Hogan	1927	WB
Pagan Lady *	1931	Col.
Paris at Midnight *	1926	US
Paris Bound *	1929	Pathe
Pay As You Enter	1928	WB
Pick a Star	1937	MGM
Pleasure Mad *	1923	Metro.
Poor Girls	1927	Col.
Princess O'Hara	1935	Univ.
Rebound	1931	Pathe/RKO
Remembrance	1922	Gold.
A Reno Divorce	1927	WB
Rich Men's Sons	1927	Col.
Rich People	1929	Pathe
Right Cross	1950	MGM
Road Show	1941	US

The Romantic Age	1927	Col.
The Sea Hawk	1924	FN
Sentimental Journey	1946	TCF
She Gets Her Man	1935	Univ.
The Silent Watcher	1924	FN
The Sin Flood	1922	Gold.
Sing Sing Nights	1935	Mon.
Sitting Pretty	1948	TCF
Somewhere in the Night	1946	TCF
The Splendid Road	1925	FN
Stop Thief	1920	Gold.
Swiss Miss	1938	MGM/US
A Tale of Two Worlds	1921	Gold.
There Goes My Heart	1938	US
Thieves' Highway	1949	TCF
13 Rue Madeline	1946	TCF
This Thing Called Love	1929	Pathe
Toby's Bow	1919	Gold.
Topper	1937	MGM/US
Topper Returns	1941	US
Topper Takes a Trip	1939	US
Turn Back the Hours	1928	US
Turnabout	1940	US
Unashamed	1932	MGM
Uptown New York	1933	US
The Voice From the Minaret *	1923	FN
What Fools Men	1925	FN
Whistling in the Dark	1933	MGM
Wild Girl	1932	Fox
Winds of Chance	1925	FN
The Wise Guy	1926	FN

72. H. LYMAN BROENING (1892-1983)

Abraham Lincoln *	1924	FN
American Pluck	1925	US
Bab's Matinee Idol	1917	Par.
Being Respectable	1924	WB
The Better Half	1918	US
A Broken Doll *	1921	US
California or Bust	1927	US
Chelsea 7750	1913	FP
The Conspiracy	1914	Par.
The County Chairman	1914	Par.
Cyclone Cavalier	1925	US
Dancing Days	1926	US
Dancing Girl	1915	Par.
The Dark Star	1919	Par.
David Harum	1915	Par.
The Death Dance	1918	US

The Devil's Masterpiece	1927	US
Drusilla With a Million	1925	US
Fighting Fate	1925	US
Getting Mary Married	1919	US
Helene of the North	1915	Par.
Her Father Said No	1924	US
Hook and Ladder No. 9	1927	US
In the Bishop's Carriage	1913	FP
Kindred of the Dust *	1922	FN
Leah Kleschna	1914	FP
The Lighthouse by the Sea	1924	WB
The Little Irish Girl *	1926	WB
Lost Paradise *	1914	Par.
The Luck of the Irish *	1920	US
Man-Woman-Marriage	1921	FN
Marta of the Lowlands	1914	Par.
May Blossom	1915	Par.
The Mysterious Miss Terry	1917	Par.
A Perfect Crime	1921	US
Pretty Sister of Jose	1915	FP
The Rainbow Princess	1916	FP
Rose of the Tenements	1926	US
Salvation Jane	1927	US
The Scoffer	1920	FN
Silks and Satins	1916	FP
Snow White	1916	Par.
Soldiers of Fortune *	1919	US
The Spirit of Lafayette	1919	US
Still Waters	1915	FP
This Woman	1924	WB
Truthful Sex *	1926	Col.
Wandering Footsteps	1925	US
Wildflowers	1914	Par.

73. ROBERT BRONNER (1906-1969)

Ask Any Girl	1959	MGM
Don't Go Near the Water	1957	MGM
Gidget Goes Hawaiian	1961	Col.
Gidget Goes to Rome	1963	Col.
The Horizontal Lieutenant	1962	MGM
It Started With a Kiss	1949	MGM
It's Always Fair Weather	1955	MGM
Jailhouse Rock	1957	MGM
The Mating Game	1959	MGM
Meet Me in Las Vegas	1956	MGM
The Opposite Sex	1956	MGM
Party Girl	1958	MGM
Please Don't Eat the Daisies	1960	MGM
Pocketful of Miracles	1961	UA

Quick Let's Get Married	1965	US
Seven Faces of Dr. Lao	1964	MGM
The Sheepman	1958	MGM
Silk Stockings	1957	MGM
Ten Thousand Bedrooms	1956	MGM
The Tunnel of Love	1958	MGM
Where the Boys Are	1960	MGM

74. JOSEPH BROTHERTON

Against All Odds	1924	Fox
Angel Child	1918	US
The Beautiful Liar	1921	FN
The Body Punch	1929	Univ.
The Boomerang *	1919	US
Chastity *	1923	FN
Code of the Yukon	1919	US
The Crimson Canyon	1928	Univ.
The Desert Outlaw	1924	Fox
The Grail	1923	Fox
Her Social Value	1921	FN
Heroes and Husbands	1922	FN
The Infidel	1922	FN
The Law That Divides	1919	US
The Lonely Road	1923	FN
The Long Lane's Turning *	1919	US
Melody Lane	1929	FN
Midnight Rose	1928	Univ.
Money! Money! Money!	1923	FN
My Lady's Latchkey	1921	FN
The Notorious Miss Lisle	1920	FN
Pagan Passions	1924	Selz.
Passion's Playground	1920	FN
Refuge *	1923	FN
The Ridin' Demon	1929	Univ.
The Scarlet Lily	1923	FN
Silks and Saddles	1929	Univ.
Stranger Than Fiction	1921	FN
Tarzan the Fearless *	1933	US
Times Have Changed	1923	Fox
Trust Your Wife	1921	FN
Western Luck	1924	Fox
When Odds Are Even	1923	Fox
White Shoulders	1922	FN
Winner Takes All *	1924	Fox
The Woman Conquers	1922	FN
The Woman's Side	1922	FN

75. JAMES S. BROWN, JR.

Avenging Fangs	1927	Pathe/US
The Big Bluff	1933	US
Case of the Baby Sitter	1947	US
Catch-as-Catch-Can	1927	US
Cheating Blondes	1933	US
A Close Call for Ellery Queen	1942	Col.
The College Boob	1926	US
The Counterfeiters	1948	TCF
Crime Doctor	1943	Col.
The Crime Doctor's Strangest Case	1943	Col.
Crime, Inc.	1945	PRC
Crime Takes a Holiday	1938	Col.
Dancing Man	1934	US
Dangerous Intruder	1945	PRC
Daniel Boone Thru the Wilderness	1926	US
A Desperate Chance for Eldery Queen	1942	Col.
The Devil Bat's Daughter	1946	PRC
Down Grade	1927	US
Dragnet	1947	US
Ellery Queen Master Detective	1940	Col.
Ellery Queen and the Murder Ring	1941	Col.
Ellery Queen and the Perfect Crime	1941	Col.
Ellery Queen's Penthouse Murder	1941	Col.
Enemy Agent Against Ellery Queen	1942	Col.
Fangs of Justice	1926	US
Flight into Nowhere	1938	Col.
Flying High	1926	US
Frontiers of '49	1939	Col.
Fugitive at Large	1939	Col.
Fugitive From a Prison Camp	1940	Col.
Fugitive Sheriff	1936	Col.
Gas House Kids in Hollywood	1947	EL
The Great Flamarion	1945	Rep.
The Great Plane Robbery	1940	Col.
The Great Swindle	1941	Col.
Hard Boiled Mahoney	1947	Mon.
Harvest Melody	1943	PRC
The Hat-Box Mystery	1947	Lip.
Her Forgotten Past	1933	US
Heroes of the Range	1936	Col.
Hidden Power	1939	Col.
In Early Arizona	1938	Col.
The Kid Sister	1945	PRC
Killer at Large	1947	PRC
The Law Comes to Texas	1939	Col.
Law of the Range	1937	Col.
Lone Star Pioneers	1939	Col.
Making the Headlines	1938	Col.
The Man Who Walked Alone	1945	PRC

The Missing Corpse	1945	PRC
Mr. Hex	1946	Mon.
Night Alarm	1935	US
No Place for a Lady	1943	Col.
North of Nome	1937	Col.
One Chance in a Million	1917	US
Outlaw of the Orient	1937	Col.
Outside the 3-Mile Limit	1940	Col.
Passport to Alcatraz	1940	Col.
Phantom Gold	1938	Col.
Phantom of 42nd Street	1945	PRC
Pioneer Trail	1938	Col.
The Prairie	1947	US
Ranger Courage	1937	Col.
The Rangers Step In	1937	Col.
Reckless Roads	1935	US
Reformatory	1938	Col.
Rio Grande Ranger	1937	Col.
Roaring Timber	1937	Col.
Rolling Caravans	1938	Col.
The Scarlet Letter	1934	US
Sea Devils	1931	US
Secret Sinners	1933	US
Shadows in the Night	1944	Col.
Shadows of the Orient	1937	Mon.
She Had to Choose	1934	US
The Snarl of Hate	1927	US
Spuds *	1927	Pathe
Stage to Mesa City	1948	PRC
Stagecoach Days	1938	Col.
Stop, Look and Listen *	1926	Pathe
The Strange Case of Dr. Meade	1939	Col.
Tornado Range	1948	PRC
The Trap	1947	Mon.
Trapped by G-Men	1937	Col.
Trapped in the Sky	1939	Col.
Under Suspicion	1937	Col.
The Unknown Ranger	1936	Col.
The Vanishing Frontier	1932	Par.
Western Frontier *	1935	Col.
What's Your Racket?	1934	US
Where Trails Begin	1927	US
Whispering Enemies	1939	Col.
The Whistler	1944	Col.
Winning Wallop	1926	US
Zamba	1949	EL

76. JOHN (JACK) W. BROWN

Ace of the Saddle	1919	Univ.

Action	1921	Univ.
Ashamed of Parents	1921	WB
Average Woman *	1924	US
Bare Fists	1919	Univ.
The Broken Melody	1920	US
Bucking Broadway	1918	Univ.
Bullet-Proof *	1920	Univ.
The Capitol	1920	US
Changing of the Northwest	1922	Selz.
The Daughter Pays	1920	Selz.
The Deciding Kiss	1918	US
The Flapper	1920	Selz.
Fool and His Money *	1920	Selz.
The Forbidden Trail	1923	US
A Gun-Fightin' Gentleman	1919	Univ.
Lend Me Your Husband *	1924	US
A Marked Man	1917	Univ.
Marked Men	1920	Univ.
Mind the Paint Girl	1919	FN
The Miracle of Life	1915	US
The Outcasts of Poker Flat	1919	Univ.
The Police Patrol *	1925	US
The Point of View	1920	Selz.
The Prince of Avenue A	1920	Univ.
The Quest	1915	US
Restless Wives	1924	US
Rider of the Law	1919	Univ.
Riders of Vengeance	1919	Univ.
Roped	1919	Univ.
Sitting Bull at the 'Spirit Lake Massacre'	1927	US
Society Snobs	1921	Selz.
Someone Must Pay	1919	US
The Spitfire *	1924	US
Thieves' Gold	1918	Univ.
Three Mounted Men	1918	Univ.
Three O'Clock in the Morning	1918	Univ.
Tiger True	1921	Univ.
Trifling With Honor	1923	Univ.
The Undercurrent	1919	US
Virtuous Wives	1919	FN
Which Woman?	1918	US
Why Girls Leave Home	1921	WB
Wild Women	1918	Univ.
Youth for Sale	1924	US

77. KARL BROWN

The Avenging Conscience *	1914	US
Beggar on Horseback	1925	Par.

Birth of a Nation *	1915	US
Brewster's Millions	1921	Par.
Broken Blossoms *	1919	UA
The City of Masks	1920	Par.
The City That Never Sleeps	1924	Par.
The Covered Wagon	1923	Par.
Crazy to Marry	1921	Par.
The Dictator	1922	Par.
The Dollar-a-Year Man	1921	Par.
The Enemy Sex	1924	Par.
The Fighting Coward	1924	Par.
The Fourteenth Man	1920	Par.
The Garden of Weeds	1924	Par.
The Goose Hangs High	1925	Par.
Hollywood	1923	Par.
Intolerance *	1916	US
Is Matrimony a Failure?	1922	Par.
The Life of the Party	1920	Par.
Mannequin	1926	Par.
Marry Me	1925	Par.
Merton of the Movies	1924	Par.
The Old Homestead	1922	Par.
One Glorious Day	1922	Par.
The Pony Express	1925	Par.
Ruggles of Red Gap	1923	Par.
Thirty Days	1922	Par.
To the Ladies	1923	Par.
The Traveling Salesman	1921	Par.
Welcome Home	1925	Par.

78. FAYTE BROWNE

Across the Badlands	1950	Col.
Arizona *	1941	Col.
Bandits of El Dorado	1951	Col.
Frontier Outpost	1950	Col.
The Hawk of Wild River	1952	Col.
Hoedown	1950	Col.
Horsemen of the Sierras	1949	Col.
Jungle Jim in the Forbidden Land	1952	Col.
The Kid From Amarillo	1951	Col.
The Kid From Broken Gun	1952	Col.
Laramie Mountains	1952	Col.
Lightning Guns	1950	Col.
Outcast of Black Mesa	1950	Col.
Pecos River	1951	Col.
Prairie Round-Up	1951	Col.
Renegades of the Sage	1950	Col.
Ridin' the Outlaw Trail	1951	Col.
The Rough Tough West	1952	Col.

Smoky Canyon	1952	Col.
Snake River Desperadoes	1951	Col.
South of Death Valley	1950	Col.
Streets of Ghost Town	1950	Col.
Texas Dynamo	1950	Col.

79. JOSEPH BRUN

Edge of the City	1957	MGM
Explosion	1970	Can.
Fat Spy	1966	US
Flipper *	1963	MGM
Girl of the Night	1960	WB
The Joe Louis Story	1953	UA
The Last Mile	1959	UA
Love at Night	1961	Fr.
Martin Luther	1953	US
Middle of the Night	1959	Col.
Odds Against Tomorrow	1959	UA
Slaves	1969	US
That Darn Kid	1956	US
300 Year Weekend	1971	ABC
Thunder in Carolina	1960	US
Trilogy *	1969	AA
Walk East on Beacon	1952	Col.
The Whistle at Eaton Falls	1951	Col.
Who Killed Teddy Bear?	1965	US
Wind Across the Everglades	1958	WB

80. LEONCE-HENRI BUREL (1892-   )

Abused Confidence	1938	Fr.
As Others See Us	1948	Fr.
Crainqueville	1922	Fr.
Crossroads *	1938	Fr.
Deo Gratias	1963	Fr.
Diary of a Country Priest	1950	Fr.
Dragnet Night	1931	Fr.
The Dying Swan *	1938	Fr.
Education of a Prince	1938	Fr.--Par.
L'Equipage	1928	Fr.
Fanatics	1958	Fr.
Friends Through Thick and Thin	1967	Fr.
Gooseflesh	1963	Fr.
Highway Pickup	1965	Fr./It.
I Accuse	1919	Fr.
L'Image	1924	Fr.
Life in a Song	1951	Fr.
Love in Morocco	1933	Fr.

A Man and His Wife	1939	Fr.
A Man Escaped	1956	Fr.
The Man From the Niger	1940	Fr.
Marrianne of My Youth	1955	Fr./Ger.
Mater Dolorosa	1917	Fr.
Michael Strogoff	1925	Fr.
My Childish Father	1953	Fr.
My Mother Is a Miss	1939	Fr.
Mystery of the Yellow Room *	1931	Fr.
Napoleon *	1927	Fr.--Metro-Gold
Ne Le Criez pas sur Les Toits	1942	Fr.
One Night on the Beach	1961	Fr.
Other Side of Paradise	1954	Fr.
Pantalaskas	1960	Fr.
Parade of Lost Time	1948	Fr.
Pickpocket	1959	Fr.
Rita	1950	Fr.
La Rone *	1923	Fr.
La Route Napoleon	1953	Fr.
Secrets d'Alcove	1954	Fr./It.
Spice of Life	1954	Fr.
Strange Desire of Mr. Bard	1954	Fr.
The Swallow and the Titmouse	1920	Fr.
Tenth Symphony	1918	Fr.
Thank Heaven for Small Favors	1965	Fr.
That Night	1958	Fr.
Trial of Joan of Arc	1962	Fr.
The Turh About Bebe Donge	1952	Fr.
Visage d'Enfants	1924	Fr.
The Whole Town Accuses	1956	Fr.
You Get It!	1956	Fr./It.
Zone of Death	1917	Fr.

81. ROBERT BURKS (1910-1968)

Beyond the Forest	1949	WB
The Birds	1963	Univ.
The Black Orchid	1958	Par.
The Boy From Oklahoma	1953	WB
But Not for Me	1959	Par.
Close to My Heart	1951	WB
Come Fill the Cup	1951	WB
A Covenant With Death	1966	WB
The Desert Song	1953	WB
Dial M for Murder	1954	WB
The Enforcer	1950	US
Escape in the Desert	1945	WB
The Fountainhead	1949	WB
The Glass Menagerie	1950	WB

The Great Imposter	1961	Univ.
Hondo *	1954	WB/US
I Confess	1953	WB
A Kiss in the Dark	1949	WB
Make Your Own Bed	1944	WB
The Man Who Knew Too Much	1956	Par.
Mara Maru	1952	WB
Marnie	1964	Univ.
The Music Man	1962	WB
North by Northwest	1959	MGM
Once a Thief	1965	MGM
A Patch of Blue	1966	MGM
The Pleasure of His Company	1961	Par.
Pride of the Marines *	1945	WB
The Rat Race	1960	Par.
Rear Window	1954	Par.
Room for One More	1952	WB
So This Is Love	1953	WB
The Spirit of St. Louis	1957	WB
Strangers on a Train	1951	WB
Task Force *	1949	WB
To Catch a Thief	1955	Par.
To the Victor	1948	WB
Tomorrow Is Another Day	1951	WB
The Trouble With Harry	1955	Par.
The Vagabond King	1956	Par.
Vertigo	1958	Par.
Waterhole No. Three	1967	Par.
The Wrong Man	1957	WB

82. STEPHEN H. BURUM

Arthur 2: On the Rocks	1988	WB
The Bride	1985	Col.
Casualties of War	1989	Col.
Death Valley	1982	Univ.
8 Million Ways to Die	1986	Tri-S.
The Entity	1983	TCF
The Escape Artist	1982	Orion
Nutcracker: The Motion Picture	1986	US
The Outsiders	1983	WB
Pacific High	1980	US
Rumble Fish	1983	Univ.
St. Elmo's Fire	1985	Col.
Something Wicked This Way Comes	1983	Dis.
The Untouchables	1987	Par.
The War of the Roses	1989	TCF
Uncommon Valor	1983	Par.
Wild Gypsies	1969	US

83. DICK BUSH

All the Way Up	1970	GB
Blood on Satan's Claw	1970	GB
Curse of the Pink Panther	1983	MGM-UA
Dracula AD 1972	1972	GB--Ham.
Falling in Love Again *	1980	US
The Fan	1981	Par.
The Hound of the Baskervilles *	1978	GB
In Celebration	1974	AFT
The Journey of Natty Gann	1985	Dis.
The Lair of the White Worm	1988	GB
Laughter in the Dark	1969	UA
The Legacy *	1979	Col./EMI/WB
Little Monsters	1989	MGM/UA
Mahler	1974	GB
One Trick Pony	1980	WB
Our Miss Fred	1972	EMI/MGM
Phase IV	1974	GB--Par.
Savage Messiah	1972	EMI/MGM
Sorcerer *	1977	Par./Univ.
Staying Together	1989	GB
Take a Girl Like You	1970	GB--Col.
Tommy *	1975	GB
Toomorrow	1970	GB
Trail of the Pink Panther	1982	MGM-UA
Twins of Evil	1971	GB--Ham.
Victor, Victoria	1982	GB
When Dinosaurs Ruled the Earth	1969	GB--Ham.

84. BILL BUTLER

Adam's Woman	1972	Aus.--WB
Alex and the Gypsy	1976	TCF
Beer	1986	Orion
Big Trouble	1986	Col.
Biloxi Blues	1988	Univ.
The Bingo Long Traveling All-Stars and Motor Kings	1976	Univ.
Can't Stop the Music	1980	EMI
Capricorn One	1978	US
Child's Play	1988	MGM-UA
The Conversation	1974	Par.
Damien: Omen Two	1978	TCF
The Deathmaster	1973	AIP
Demon Seed	1977	MGM
Drive, He Said	1970	Col.
Fearless Frank	1969	AIP
Graffiti Bridge	1990	WB
Grease	1978	Par.

Hickey and Boggs	1972	UA
Ice Castles	1978	Col.
It's My Turn	1980	Col.
Jaws	1975	Univ.
Lipstick *	1976	Par.
The Manchu Eagle Murder Caper		
Mystery	1975	UA
Melinda	1972	MGM
Night the Lights Went Out in Georgia *	1981	AE
The Rain People	1969	WB
Rocky II	1979	UA
Rocky III	1982	UA
Rocky IV	1985	MGM-UA
The Sting 2	1983	Univ.
Stripes	1981	Col.
Uncle Joe Shannon	1978	UA
Wildfire	1988	US

85. MICHAEL BUTLER

Cannonball Run	1980	US
Charley Varrick	1973	Univ.
Harry and Tonto	1974	TCF
Jaws 2 *	1978	Univ.
Megaforce	1982	TCF
The Missouri Breaks	1976	UA
92 in the Shade	1975	UA
A Small Circle of Friends	1980	UA
Smoky and the Bandit II	1980	Univ.
Telefon	1977	MGM
Wanda Nevada	1979	UA

86. BOBBY BYRNE

Blue Collar	1978	Univ.
Bull Durham	1988	Orion
California Dreaming	1979	AIP
The End	1978	UA
First Love	1977	Par.
Going Berserk	1983	Univ.
Head Over Heels in Love	1979	UA
Hooper	1978	WB
The Lemon Sisters	1989	US
Paternity	1981	Par.
Sixteen Candles	1984	Univ.
Smokey and the Bandit	1977	Univ.
Stealing Home	1988	WB
Things Are Tough All Over	1982	Col.
Those Lips, Those Eyes	1980	UA

The Villain	1979	Col.
Walk Proud	1979	Univ.

87. A. A. CADWELL

Clothes	1920	Metro
Fine Feathers	1921	Metro.
God's Law and Man's	1917	Metro.
The Inner Man	1922	US
Laughing Bill Hyde	1918	Gold.
Madonnas and Men	1920	US
A Royal Family	1915	Col./Metro.
Salomy Jane *	1914	US
A Scream in the Night *	1919	US
The Sunbeam	1916	Metro.
Three Black Eyes	1919	US
Too Fat to Fight	1918	Gold.
A Wife by Proxy	1917	Metro.
Women's Business	1920	US

88. DAVID CALCAGNI

The Auction Block	1917	Gold.
The Devil's Daughter	1915	Fox
High Pockets	1919	Gold.
A Misfit Earl	1919	Gold.
Oh Johnny	1919	Gold.
The Road Called Straight	1919	Gold.
Sandy Burke of the U-Bar-U	1919	Gold.
Speedy Meade	1919	Gold.

89. DUKE CALLAGHAN

Conan the Barbarian	1981	DeL.
Jeremiah Johnson	1972	WB
The Last Hard Men	1976	TCF
The Scalphunters *	1968	UA
The Take	1974	Col.
The Yakuza *	1975	WB

90. BERT CANN

Bell Boy 13	1923	FN
Boy Crazy	1922	US
Chickens	1921	Par.
Eden and Return	1921	US
The Foolish Age	1921	US

The Home Stretch	1921	Par.
The Jailbird	1920	Par.
Let's Be Fashionable	1920	Par.
Mary's Ankle	1920	Par.
One a Minute	1921	Par.
Passing Thru	1921	Par.
The Rookie's Return	1921	Par.
Second Hand Rose	1922	Univ.
23½ Hours Leave	1919	Par.

91. JACK CARDIFF (1914-   )

The African Queen	1951	GB
As You Like It *	1936	GB--TCF
Avalanche Express	1979	TCF
The Awakening	1980	EMI/Orion
The Barefoot Contessa	1954	UA
Behind the Iron Mask	1977	US
The Big Money	1956	GB--Rank
Black Narcissus	1946	GB
The Black Rose	1950	TCF
The Brave One	1956	US
Caesar and Cleopatra *	1945	GB--Rank
Cat's Eye	1985	MGM-UA
Conan the Destroyer	1984	DeL.
Crossed Swords	1954	It.
Death on the Nile	1978	EMI
The Dogs of War	1980	UA
Fanny	1960	WB
The Fifth Musketeer	1978	Aust.
The Four Feathers *	1939	GB--Korda
Ghost Story	1981	Univ.
Girl on a Motorcycle *	1968	Fr./GB
The Great Mr. Handel *	1942	GB--Rank
It Started in Paradise	1952	GB
Legend of the Lost	1957	UA
The Life and Times of Colonel Blimp *	1943	GB
The Magic Box	1951	GB
Man, a Woman and a Bank	1979	Can.
The Master of Ballantrae	1953	WB
A Matter of Life and Death	1946	GB
Million Dollar Mystery	1987	US
Pandora and the Flying Dutchman	1950	GB
The Prince and the Pauper	1977	US
The Prince and the Showgirl	1957	GB--WB
Rambo: First Blood Part II	1985	Tri-S.
The Red Shoes	1948	GB
Ride a Wild Pony	1975	Dis.
Scalawag	1973	US
Scandalous!	1984	GB

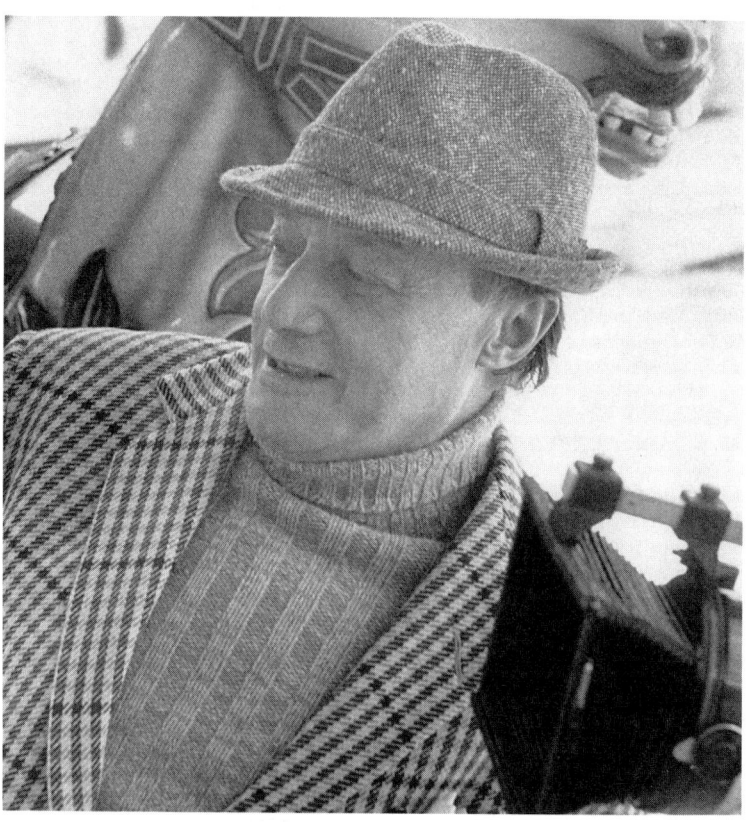

Jack Cardiff (ca. 1972).

Scott of the Antarctic *	1948	GB
Tai-Pan	1986	US
Under Capricorn *	1949	GB
The Vikings	1958	UA
War and Peace *	1956	It./US--DeL.
Western Approaches	1944	GB
The Wicked Lady	1983	GB--Cannon
Wings of the Morning *	1937	GB--TCF

92. HERBERT O. CARLETON

The Bigger Man	1915	Metro.
The Call of Her People	1917	Metro.
Fighting Bob	1915	Metro.
The High Road	1915	Metro.
A Magdalene of the Hills	1917	Metro.
My Own United States	1918	US
One Million Dollars	1915	Metro.
The Power of Decision	1917	Metro.
The Right of Way	1915	Metro.
Satan Sanderson	1915	Metro.
The Three of Us	1914	US

93. CARLO CARLINI

The Big Gundown	1968	Col.
Death Rides a Horse	1969	It.--UA
Everybody Go Home	1962	Fr./It.--DeL.
General Della Rovere	1959	Fr./It.
Gran Varieta	1955	It.
Hercules and the Captive Women	1963	Fr./It.
It Happened in Rome *	1959	It.--Rank
It Was Night in Rome	1982	It.
Italian Postcards	1987	It.
The Last Rebel	1971	Col.
Lobster for Breakfast	1983	It.
Of Wayward Love	1964	Ger./It.
Requiem for a Secret Agent	1966	It.
Siege of Syracuse	1962	Fr./It.--Par.
Son of the Red Corsair	1963	It.
Sons of Satan	1969	Fr./Ger./It. --WB
I Vitelloni	1956	Fr./It.
The Warrior Empress	1961	Fr./It.--Col.
You're On Your Own	1959	It.

94. ROY CARPENTER

As a Man Desires	1925	FN

Flowing Gold *	1924	FN
The Knockout	1925	FN
The Making of O'Malley	1925	FN
Men of Steel	1926	FN
The Unguarded Hour	1925	FN

95. ELLIS CARTER (1907-1964)

Arrow in the Dust	1954	AA
The Barefoot Mailman	1951	Col.
Big Town After Dark	1947	Par.
Big Town Scandal	1948	Par.
The Black Dakotas	1954	Col.
The Blonde Bandit	1950	Rep.
Caged Fury	1948	Par.
Captain John Smith and Pocahontas	1953	UA
Curse of the Undead	1959	Univ.
Damn Citizen	1958	Univ.
A Day of Fury	1956	Univ.
Deadly Mantis	1957	Univ.
Diary of a Madman	1962	UA
Disaster	1948	Par.
Dynamite	1948	Par.
El Paso	1949	Par.
The Fiercest Heart	1962	TCF
Gunmen of Abilene	1950	Rep.
Havana Rose	1951	Rep.
He Rides Tall	1964	Univ.
Hills of Oklahoma	1950	Rep.
Hootenanny Hoot	1963	MGM
The Human Jungle	1954	AA
The Incredible Shrinking Man	1957	Univ.
Indian Uprising	1951	Col.
Kissin' Cousins	1964	MGM
The Land Unknown	1957	Univ.
The Leech Woman	1960	Univ.
Lonely Hearts Bandits	1950	Rep.
The Magic Carpet	1951	Col.
Mr. Reckless	1948	Par.
The Mole People	1956	Univ.
The Monolith Monsters	1957	Univ.
Night of the Quarter Moon	1959	MGM
The Old Frontier	1950	Rep.
Oregon Passage	1958	AA
Outlaw Women	1952	US
Pirates of Tortuga	1961	TCF
Prisoners in Petticoats	1950	Rep.
Purple Gang	1960	AA
Rainbow 'Round My Shoulder	1952	Col.
Ranger of Cherokee Strip	1949	Rep.

The River Changes	1956	WB
Running Wild	1955	Univ.
Second Time Around	1961	TCF
Seven Ways From Sundown	1960	Univ.
Shaggy	1948	Par.
Showdown	1963	Univ.
Slim Carter	1959	Univ.
Sound Off	1952	Col.
Special Agent	1949	Par.
Speed to Spare	1948	Par.
The Texas Rangers	1951	Col.
Thief of Damascus	1952	Col.
Twice Told Tales	1963	UA
Unmasked	1950	Rep.
The Vanishing Westerner	1950	Rep.
Waterfront at Midnight	1948	Par.
The Wizard of Baghdad	1960	TCF

96. DARREL CATHCART

Carnival Magic	1982	US
Final Exam	1981	AE
Living Legend	1980	US
Rare Breed	1984	US
Seabo	1977	US
Wolfman	1979	US

97. CHRISTOPHER CHALLIS (1919-   )

Angels One Five	1952	GB
Arabesque	1966	Univ.
Battle of the River Platte	1956	GB
Blind Date	1959	GB
The Boy Who Turned Yellow	1972	GB
The Captain's Table	1958	GB
Catch Me a Spy	1971	GB
Chitty Chitty Bang Bang	1968	UA
Damn the Defiant!	1962	Col.
A Dandy in Aspic	1968	Col.
The Deep *	1977	Col.
The Elusive Pimpernel	1950	GB
The End of the River	1947	GB
Evil Under the Sun	1982	GB--EMI
Fire Over Africa	1954	GB
Five Golden Hours	1960	GB /IT.--Col.
The Flame and the Flesh	1954	MGM
Flame in the Streets	1961	GB
Floods of Fear	1958	GB
Follow Me	1971	GB

Footsteps in the Fog	1955	GB--Col.
Force Ten from Navarone	1978	GB--Col.
Genevieve	1954	GB
Gone to Earth	1948	GB--Selz.
The Grass Is Greener	1960	GB
Ill Met by Moonlight	1956	GB
The Incredible Sarah	1976	GB
Kaleidoscope	1966	GB--WB
The Little Prince	1974	Par.
The Long Ships	1963	GB/Yugo.-- Col.
Mary Queen of Scots	1971	GB--Univ.
Miracle in Soho	1957	GB
The Mirror Crack'd	1980	GB--EMI
Mr. Quilp	1975	GB
Never Let Go	1960	GB
Oh Rosalinda!	1955	GB
The Private Life of Sherlock Holmes	1970	GB--UA
Quentin Durward	1955	GB--MGM
Raising a Riot	1955	GB
Return From the Ashes	1965	GB--UA
The Riddle of the Sands	1978	GB
Rooney	1958	GB
S.O.S. Titanic	1980	Col./EMI/WB
Saadia	1953	MGM
Secrets	1984	GB/US
A Shot in the Dark	1964	UA
Sink the Bismarck	1960	GB--TCF
The Small Back Room	1949	GB
The Spanish Gardener	1956	GB
Staircase	1969	Fr.--TCF
Steaming	1985	GB--Col.
The Story of Gilbert and Sullivan	1953	GB
Surprise Package	1960	GB--Col.
The Tales of Hoffman	1951	GB
Those Magnificent Men in Their Flying Machines	1965	GB--TCF
Top Secret!	1984	Par.
Twenty-Four Hours of a Woman's Life	1952	GB
Two for the Road	1966	GB--TCF
The Victors	1963	GB--Col.
Villain	1971	GB--EMI
Windom's Way	1957	GB

98. MARC CHAMPION

Angela	1977	Can.
Breaking Point	1976	TCF
Out of the Blue	1980	US
Samuel Lount!	1986	Can.
Why Shoot the Teacher?	1976	Can.

99. MICHAEL CHAPMAN

Dead Men Don't Wear Plaid	1982	Univ.
Fingers	1977	US
The Front	1976	Col.
Ghostbusters II	1989	Col.
Hardcore	1979	Col.
Invasion of the Body Snatchers	1978	UA
Kindergarten Cop	1990	Univ.
The Last Detail	1973	Col.
The Lost Boys	1987	WB
Man With Two Brains	1983	WB
The Next Man	1976	US
Personal Best	1982	WB
Quick Change	1990	WB
Raging Bull	1980	UA
Scrooged	1988	Par.
Shoot to Kill	1988	Dis.
Taxi Driver	1976	Col.
The Wanderers	1979	US
The White Dawn	1974	Par.

100. RICHARD CIUPKA

Atlantic City	1981	Can./Fr.
Blood of Others	1984	Can.
Dirty Tricks	1981	AE
Hold-Up	1985	Can/Fr.
Joy *	1983	Can./Fr.
Melanie	1982	Can.
The Terry Fox Story	1983	TCF
Tigress	1985	Can.
Yesterday	1980	Can.

101. DANIEL CLARK

The Air Circus	1928	Fox
Angel's Holiday	1937	TCF
Arabia	1922	Fox
The Arizona Wildcat	1927	Fox
Back to Nature	1936	TCF
The Best Bad Man	1925	Fox
The Black Camel *	1931	Fox
The Bronco Twister	1927	Fox
The Canyon of Light	1926	Fox
Catch My Smoke	1923	Fox
Champagne Charlie	1936	TCF
Change of Heart	1938	TCF
Charlie Chan at Monte Carlo	1937	TCF

Charlie Chan at the Circus	1936	TCF
Charlie Chan at the Olympics	1937	TCF
Charlie Chan in Egypt	1935	Fox
Checkers	1937	TCF
The Circus Ace	1927	Fox
Country Doctor *	1936	TCF
Daredevil's Reward	1928	Fox
The Deadwood Coach	1925	Fox
Destry Rides Again	1932	Univ.
Dick Turpin	1925	Fox
Do and Dare	1922	Fox
Educating Father	1936	TCF
The Everlasting Whisper	1925	Fox
Eyes of the Forest	1924	Fox
The Fighting Streak	1922	Fox
Five of a Kind *	1938	TCF
For Big Stakes	1922	Fox
The Fourth Horseman	1932	Univ.
The Great K & A Train Robbery	1926	Fox
Hardboiled	1926	Fox
Harmony at Home	1930	Fox
The Heart Busters	1924	Fox
Hello Cheyenne	1928	Fox
Hidden Gold	1932	Univ.
The Holy Terror	1937	TCF
Horseman of the Plains	1928	Fox
Human Cargo	1936	TCF
Just Tony	1922	Fox
Ladies Love Danger	1935	Fox
Ladies to Board	1924	Fox
Last of the Duanes	1924	Fox
Last of the Duanes	1930	Fox
The Last Trail	1927	Fox
The Lone Star Ranger	1923	Fox
The Lone Star Ranger	1930	Fox
Lucky Horseshoe	1925	Fox
My Own Pal	1926	Fox
My Pal the King	1932	Univ.
No Man's Gold	1926	Fox
North of Hudson Bay	1924	Fox
Oh, You Tony!	1924	Fox
Outlaws of the Red River	1927	Fox
Painted Post	1928	Fox
Pepper	1936	TCF
The Rainbow Trail	1925	Fox
Rainbow Trail	1932	Fox
Red Wine	1929	Fox
Reunion	1936	TCF
The Rider of Death Valley	1932	Univ.
Riders of the Purple Sage	1925	Fox
Romance Land	1923	Fox

Rough Romance	1930	Fox
Silk Hat Kid	1935	Fox
Silver Valley	1927	Fox
Sing and Be Happy	1937	TCF
Smoky	1937	Fox
Soft Boiled	1923	Fox
Song of the Saddle	1936	WB
Step Lively Jeeves!	1937	TCF
Stepping Fast	1923	Fox
Straightaway	1934	Col.
Terror Trail	1933	Univ.
Texas Bad Man	1932	Univ.
This Is Life	1935	Fox
Three Jumps Ahead	1923	Fox
Tony Runs Wild	1926	Fox
The Trouble Shooter	1924	Fox
Tumbling River	1927	Fox
Up and Going *	1922	Fox
Why Leave Home?	1929	Fox
The Yankee Senor	1926	Fox

102. CHARLES G. CLARKE (1899-1983)

Accent on Love	1941	TCF
The All-American Chump	1936	MGM
The Barbarian and the Geisha	1958	TCF
The Big Lift	1949	TCF
Black Widow	1954	TCF
The Bride Wore Crutches	1941	TCF
Cadet Girl	1941	TCF
Captain From Castile *	1947	TCF
Careful, Soft Shoulders	1942	TCF
Carousel	1956	TCF
The Casino Murder Case	1935	MGM
The Cat and the Fiddle	1933	MGM
Charlie Chan in Honolulu	1938	TCF
City of Bad Men	1953	TCF
The Cowboy and the Blonde	1941	TCF
The Dawn of a Tomorrow	1924	Par.
Dead Men Tell	1941	TCF
Destination Gobi	1953	TCF
Evelyn Prentice	1934	MGM
The Exalted Flapper	1929	Fox
Flaming Barriers	1924	Par.
Flaming Star	1960	TCF
For Beauty's Sake	1941	TCF
Four Sons *	1928	Fox
Friendly Enemies	1925	US
Frontier Marshal	1939	TCF
The Garden Murder Case	1936	MGM

A Gentleman at Heart	1942	TCF
Girls Demand Excitement	1931	Fox
Going Crooked	1926	Fox
Golden Girl	1951	TCF
Green Grass of Wyoming	1948	TCF
Guadalcanal Diary	1943	TCF
The Half Breed	1922	FN
Ham and Eggs at the Front	1927	WB
Hello Frisco Hello *	1943	TCF
Holiday for Lovers	1959	TCF
Hot Pepper	1933	Fox
The Hound Dog Man	1959	TCF
The Hunters	1958	TCF
I'll Get By	1950	TCF
Iron Curtain	1948	TCF
It Happened in Flatbush	1942	TCF
Junior Miss	1945	TCF
Kangaroo	1952	TCF
Ladies of Washington	1944	TCF
Last of the Duanes	1941	TCF
The Light That Failed	1923	Par.
Madison Avenue	1961	TCF
The Man in the Gray Flannel Suit	1956	TCF
Man of the People	1937	MGM
Margie	1946	TCF
Marry the Boss's Daughter	1941	TCF
Masquerade	1929	Fox
Miracle on 34th Street *	1947	TCF
Mr. Moto Takes a Vacation	1939	TCF
Molly and Me	1945	TCF
Moonlight Murder	1936	MGM
Murder Among Friends	1941	TCF
Night People	1954	TCF
Nix on Dames	1929	Fox
Not Quite Decent	1929	Fox
Oh for a Man!	1930	Fox
Oh Men! Oh Women!	1957	TCF
One Minute to Play	1926	US
Pardon Our Nerve	1939	TCF
The Perfect Gentleman	1935	MGM
The Perfect Snob	1942	TCF
Plastered in Paris	1928	Fox
Prince of Players	1955	TCF
A Private's Affair	1959	TCF
Pursuit	1935	MGM
A Racing Romeo	1927	US
Red Dance *	1928	Fox
Red Skies of Montana	1952	TCF
Return to Payton Place	1961	TCF
The Return of the Cisco Kid	1939	TCF
Riley the Cop	1928	Fox

Rocking Moon *	1926	US
Safety in Numbers	1938	TCF
Sand	1949	TCF
Sandra	1924	FN
Second Hand Wife	1933	Fox
Shadow of a Doubt	1935	MGM
Sharp Shooters	1928	Fox
Sin Sister *	1929	Fox
Singed	1927	Fox
Slattery's Hurricane	1949	TCF
Smoky	1946	TCF
So This Is London	1930	Fox
Song of Kentucky	1929	Fox
The Sound and the Fury	1959	TCF
Stand In	1937	US
Stars and Stripes Forever	1952	TCF
Stopover Tokyo	1957	TCF
Street of Memories	1940	TCF
Suddenly	1954	UA
Tampico	1944	TCF
Tarzan and His Mate *	1934	MGM
Temple Tower	1930	Fox
That Wonderful Urge	1948	TCF
These Thousand Hills	1958	TCF
The Thirteenth Chair	1937	MGM
Three Brave Men	1956	TCF
Through Different Eyes	1943	TCF
Thunder in the Valley	1947	TCF
Thunderhead, Son of Flicka	1945	TCF
Tiger Love	1924	Par.
Time to Kill	1942	TCF
Too Busy to Work	1932	Fox
Top of the World	1925	Par.
Trouble for Two	1936	MGM
Under Cover of Night	1937	MGM
Upstream	1927	Fox
The Veiled Woman	1929	Fox
Violent Saturday	1955	TCF
The Virgin Queen	1955	TCF
Viva Cisco Kid	1940	TCF
Viva Villa *	1934	MGM
The Wayward Bus	1957	TCF
Whispering Smith	1926	US
The Winning Ticket	1935	MGM
Without Mercy	1925	US
Woman Wanted	1935	MGM
Words and Music *	1929	Fox
Yesterday's Heroes	1940	TCF
Young as You Feel	1940	TCF

103. DAL CLAWSON

Another Scandal	1924	US
Back to God's Country *	1919	FN
Bonds of Honor	1919	US
Captain Courtesy	1915	Par.
Civilization *	1916	US
The Conqueror	1917	Fox
Corsican Brothers *	1920	US
The Courageous Coward	1919	US
The Dumb Girl of Portici	1916	Univ.
Eve in Exile	1919	Pathe
For Husbands Only	1918	US
Forbidden *	1919	Univ.
A Heart in Pawn	1919	US
Hypocrites *	1915	Par.
It's No Laughing Matter	1915	Par.
The Lone Wolf *	1924	US
Love at First Sight	1930	US
The Love Kiss *	1930	US
The Marriage Chance	1922	US
Mary Regan	1919	FN
The Merchant of Venice	1914	Univ.
Miami	1924	US
A Midnight Romance	1919	FN
The Oath	1921	FN
The Red Red Heart	1918	US
The Rosary *	1915	US
Rose O' the Sea	1922	FN
Scandal	1915	Univ.
The Slaver	1927	US
Sunshine Molly	1915	Par.
Syncopation *	1929	RKO
The Temple of Dusk	1918	US
What Do Men Want?	1921	US
The Woman He Married	1922	FN
World's a Stage *	1922	US
The Yankee Girl	1915	Par.

104. GEORGE CLEMENS

Arizona Mahoney	1936	Par.
Big Brown Eyes	1936	Par.
Clarence	1937	Par.
Desert Gold	1936	Par.
Girl of the Ozarks	1936	Par.
Hideaway Girl	1937	Par.
Hollywood Blvd. *	1936	Par.
Klondike Annie	1936	Par.
The Return of Sophie Lang	1936	Par.
She's No Lady	1937	Par.
Wives Never Know	1936	Par.

105. ROBERT E. CLINE

The Ace of Clubs	1926	US
Aces Wild	1937	Col.
Am I Guilty?	1940	US
Arizona Gunfighter	1937	Rep.
The Black Raven	1943	PRC
Blazing Frontier	1944	PRC
Boss of the Rawhide	1944	PRC
Boys of the City	1940	Mon.
Buffalo Bill Rides Again	1947	US
Cattle Stampede	1943	PRC
Colorado Kid	1938	Rep.
The Contender	1944	PRC
Crossed Signals	1926	US
Death Rides the Plains	1943	PRC
Devil Dogs	1928	US
Devil Riders	1944	PRC
The Drifter	1944	PRC
Dugan of the Dugouts	1928	FN
The Duke Is Tops	1938	US
Durango Valley Raiders	1938	Rep.
Feud Maker	1938	Rep.
Fighting Pioneers	1935	US
Frontier Outlaws	1944	PRC
Fugitive Valley	1941	Mon.
Ghost and the Guest	1943	PRC
Ghost Town	1936	US
Hearts of Men	1928	US
Heroes of the Alamo	1938	Col.
I Accuse My Parents	1945	PRC
The Idaho Kid	1936	US
The Kid's Last Ride	1941	Mon.
Land of the Fighting Men	1938	Mon.
Law of the Lash	1947	PRC
Law of the Saddle	1944	PRC
Lone Star Law Men	1942	Mon.
Men of the Plains	1936	GN
Men on Her Mind	1944	PRC
Monster Maker	1944	PRC
Moonlight on the Range	1937	US
Nabonga	1944	PRC
Now We'll Be Happy	1939	Cuba
Obey Your Husband	1928	US
Painted Trail	1928	US
Paroled--To Die	1938	Rep.
Peggy of the Secret Service	1925	US
Prairie Badmen	1946	PRC
Pride of the Army	1942	Mon.
Pride of the Bowery	1941	Mon.
Queen of the Chorus	1928	US
Raiders of Red Gap	1944	PRC

Range Beyond the Blue	1947	PRC
The Rangers Take Over	1943	PRC
Red Blood	1926	US
Ridin' the Lone Trail	1937	Rep.
Riding to Fame *	1927	US
The Saddle King	1929	US
Saddle Mountain Roundup	1941	Mon.
Secrets of a Co-Ed	1943	PRC
Seven Doors to Death	1944	PRC
Shake Hands With Murder	1944	PRC
Texas to Bataan	1942	Mon.
That Gang of Mine *	1941	Mon.
Thunder in the Desert	1938	Rep.
Thundergod	1928	US
Thundering Gun Slingers	1944	PRC
Thundering Thompson	1929	US
Thundertown	1946	PRC
Toll of the Desert	1935	US
Tonto Basin Outlaws	1941	Mon.
Top Sergeant Mulligan	1928	US
Trail of the Silver Spurs	1941	Mon.
Trail Riders	1928	US
Trailin' Back	1928	US
Tumbledown Ranch in Arizona	1941	Mon.
Two Fisted Justice	1943	Mon.
The Underdog	1943	PRC
Underground Rustlers	1942	Mon.
Wagon Trail	1935	US
Waterfront	1944	PRC
West of Nevada	1936	US
West of Singapore *	1933	Mon.
Western Cyclone	1943	PRC
Wild Country	1947	PRC
Wild Horse Rustlers	1943	PRC
Wild Mustang	1935	US
Wolves of the Range	1944	PRC
Wrangler's Roost	1941	Mon.

106. WILFRID CLINE

The Adventures of Tom Sawyer *	1938	Selz.
Ain't Misbehavin'	1955	Univ.
Aloma of the South Seas *	1941	Par.
April in Paris	1952	WB
April Love	1957	TCF
Battle of the Coral Sea	1959	Col.
Because They're Young	1960	Col.
Bugles in the Afternoon	1952	US
By the Light of the Silvery Moon	1953	WB
Calamity Jane	1953	WB
Captains of the Clouds *	1942	WB

Colt 45	1950	WB
The Command	1954	WB
The Daughter of Rosie O'Grady	1950	WB
The Devil's Pit *	1930	Univ.
Dino	1957	AA
Face of a Fugitive	1959	Col.
Fiesta *	1947	MGM
Fighter Squadron *	1948	WB
The First Texan	1956	AA
From Hell to Texas	1958	TCF
The Giant Gila Monster	1959	US
Glory	1955	RKO
Gone With the Wind *	1939	MGM/Selz.
Happy Go Lucky *	1943	Par.
Hidden Fear	1957	UA
The Indian Fighter	1955	UA
It's a Great Feeling	1949	WB
The Killer Shrews	1959	US
The Last Wagon	1956	TCF
Law of the North *	1932	Mon.
Lucky Me	1954	WB
Lullaby of Broadway	1951	WB
Mardi Gras	1958	TCF
Navy Wife	1956	AA
One Sunday Afternoon *	1948	WB
Painting the Clouds With Sunshine	1951	WB
Raton Pass	1951	WB
The Second Greatest Sex	1955	Univ.
She's Working Her Way Through College	1952	WB
The Story of Seabiscuit	1949	WB
The Story of Will Rogers	1950	WB
Sugarfoot	1951	WB
Tall Man Riding	1955	WB
The Tall Stranger	1957	AA
Task Force *	1949	WB
Tea for Two	1950	WB
Ten Wanted Men	1955	Col.
The Tingler	1959	Col.

107. GHISLAIN CLOQUET (1928-1981)

Un Amour de Poche	1958	Fr.
At the Meeting With Joyous Death	1973	Fr.--UA
Au Hazard Balthazar	1966	Fr.
Belle	1973	Belg./Fr.
La Belle Americaine	1961	Fr.
Bells Without Joy	1962	Fr.
Benjamin	1966	Ger.
Big Risk	1963	Fr.

The Butcher, the Star and the Orphan *	1975	Fr.
Consider All Risks	1960	Fr.
Donkey Skin	1970	Fr.
Edifying and Joyous Story of Colinot the Skirt Puller-Upper	193	Fr.--WB
Faustine and the Beautiful Summer	1972	Fr.
The Fire Within	1964	Fr./It.
Four Friends	1981	US
Gentle Woman	1969	Fr.--Par.
Good Luck on the Marriage	1968	Fr.
The Hole	1959	Fr.
The Honors of War	1961	Fr.
The House of the Bories	1970	Fr.
I Sent a Letter to My Love	1981	Fr.
Love and Death	1975	UA
The Maddening Flame	1963	Fr.
A Man Called La Rocca	1961	Fr.
The Man Who Had His Hair Cut Short	1966	Belg.
Marry Me! Marry Me!	1969	Fr.
Meeting in Bray	1971	Belg./Fr.
Mickey One	1965	Col.
Monsieur Albert	1976	Fr.
Mouchette	1967	Fr.
Nathalie Granger	1972	Fr.
Night and Fog	1955	Fr.
Night Watch	1964	Fr./It.
Nude in His Pocket	1962	Fr.
One Night ... a Train	1968	Belg./Fr.--TCF
Say It With Flowers	1974	Fr.
Stadium Nuts	1972	Fr.
Tess *	1979	Fr./GB--Col.
Thumbs Up!	1972	Fr.
Le Trou	1960	Fr.
Vest Pocket Love	1958	Fr.
The Wonderful Age	1959	Fr.
The Young Girls of Rochefort	1967	Fr.--WB

108. WILLIAM CLOTHIER (1903-   )

The Alamo	1960	UA
Bandolero!	1968	TCF
Big Jake	1971	NG
Blood Alley	1955	WB
Bombers B-52	1957	WB
Cheyenne Autumn	1964	WB
The Cheyenne Social Club	1970	NG
China Doll	1959	US
Chisum	1970	WB

The Comancheros	1961	TCF
Confidence Girl	1952	UA
Darby's Rangers	1957	WB
The Deadly Companions	1961	WB
The Devil's Brigade	1968	UA
A Distant Trumpet	1964	WB
Donovan's Reef	1963	Par.
Dragoon Wells Massacre	1957	AA
El 113 *	1936	Sp.
Escort West	1959	UA
Firecreek	1968	WB
For You I Die	1947	US
Fort Dobbs	1957	WB
Gangbusters	1955	US
Goodbye My Lady *	1956	WB
Gun the Man Down	1957	UA
Hellfighters	1969	Univ.
The High and the Mighty	1954	WB
The Horse Soldiers	1959	UA
Killers From Space	1954	RKO
Lafayette Escadrille	1957	WB
McLintock!	1963	UA
Man in the Vault	1956	RKO
The Man Who Shot Liberty Valance	1962	Par.
Once a Thief	1950	UA
Phantom From Space	1953	UA
The Rare Breed	1966	Univ.
Ring of Fire	1961	MGM
Rio Lobo	1970	US
The Sea Chase	1955	WB
Seven Men From Now	1956	WB
Shenandoah	1965	Univ.
Sincerely Yours	1955	WB
Sofia	1948	US
Stagecoach	1966	TCF
Tomboy and the Champ	1961	Univ.
Track of the Cat	1954	WB
The Train Robbers	1973	WB
The Undefeated	1969	TCF
The War Wagon	1967	Univ.
Way Way Out	1966	TCF
The Way West	1967	UA
Wings *	1929	Par.

109. EDWARD COLMAN

The Absent-Minded Professor	1961	Dis.
The Adventures of Bullwhip Griffin	1967	Dis.
The Ambushers *	1967	Col.
Babes in Toyland	1961	Dis.

Big Red	1962	Dis.
Black Patch	1957	WB
Blackbeard's Ghost	1967	Dis.
The DI	1957	WB
Dragnet	1954	US
The Gnome Mobile	1967	Dis.
The Happiest Millionaire	1967	Dis.
The Love Bug	1968	Dis.
Mary Poppins	1964	Dis.
The Misadventures of Merlin Jones	1963	Dis.
The Monkey's Uncle	1965	Dis.
Savage Sam	1962	Dis.
The Shaggy Dog	1959	Dis.
Son of Flubber	1963	Dis.
That Darn Cat!	1965	Dis.
--30--	1959	WB
Those Calloways	1964	Dis.
The Ugly Daschund	1965	Dis.
Walk a Crooked Mile *	1949	Col.

110. JAMES A CONTNER

Cruising	1980	Lor./UA
Eddie Macon's Run	1983	Univ.
Heat	1987	US
Jaws 3-D	1983	Univ.
Let's Get Harry	1987	Tri-S.
Monkey Shines	1988	Orion
Nighthawks	1981	Univ.
So Fine	1981	WB
Times Square	1980	US
Tough Enough	1983	TCF
Where the Boys Are	1984	Tri-S.

111. CLYDE COOK

All Wrong *	1919	Pathe
The Deceiver	1920	US
A Double-Dyed Deceiver	1920	Gold.
The Girl of Lost Lake	1916	US
The Greater Law	1917	US
Humdrum Brown	1918	US
Love's Pay Day	1918	US
The Man Who Had Everything	1920	Gold.
Mutiny	1917	US
Mystic Faces	1918	US
The Show-Down	1917	US
Southern Justice	1917	US
Up or Down	1917	US
Wife or Country	1919	US

112.   DENYS COOP (1920-1981)

And Now the Screaming Starts	1974	GB--Rank/TC
Arrivederci, Baby!	1966	GB--Par.
Asylum	1972	GB--Par.
Billy Liar!	1963	GB
The Birthday Party	1968	GB
Brittania Mews *	1948	GB--TCF
Bunny Lake Is Missing	1965	GB--Col.
The Darwin Adventure *	1971	GB--TCF
The Double Man	1968	GB
The Executioner	1970	GB--Col.
The Girl on the Boat	1961	GB--UA
An Ideal Husband	1948	GB--Korda
Inserts	1975	GB--UA
A Kind of Loving	1962	GB
King and Country	1964	GB
The Little Ark *	1971	NG
The Mind Benders	1963	GB
My Side of the Mountain	1969	Par.
One Way Pendulum	1964	GB--UA
Rosebud	1975	UA
Ten Rillington Place	1970	GB--Col.
That Dangerous Age *	1949	GB
This Sporting Life	1963	GB
Traitor's Gate	1965	GB
Vault of Horror	1973	GB--Rank/TC

113.   HARRY COOPER

Avenging Shadow 8	1928	Pathe
Danger Trail	1928	US
The Law's Lash	1928	Pathe
Marlie the Killer	1928	Pathe
The Outlaw Express	1926	Pathe
Where Trails Begin *	1927	US

114.   WILKIE COOPER (1911-   )

Abandon Ship!	1957	GB--Col.
The Admirable Crichton	1957	GB
The Adventures of Sadie	1955	GB
The Adventuress	1946	GB
The Amorous Prawn	1962	GB
The Big Blockade *	1942	GB--Eal./UA
Call of the Blood	1948	GB
Captain Boycott	1947	GB
Champagne Charlie	1944	GB
Conquest of the Air *	1936	GB--Korda/U.

Dance Little Lady	1954	GB
Desert Patrol	1962	GB--Univ.
East of Sudan	1964	GB--Col.
The End of the Affair	1954	GB--Col.
Fiddlers Three	1944	GB
The Foreman Went to France	1942	GB--UA
Geordie	1955	GB
Green for Danger	1946	GB
The Halfway House	1944	GB
Hammerhead *	1968	GB/Col.
The Hasty Heart	1949	GB--WB
Hot Money Girl	1962	GB
The Hundred Hour Hunt	1952	GB
I Aim at the Stars	1960	Col.
Intimate Relations	1953	GB
It's a Wonderful World	1956	GB
Jason and the Argonauts	1963	GB--Col.
Lady Godiva Rides Again	1951	GB
Land Raiders	1969	Col.
Landfall	1949	GB
London Belongs to Me *	1948	GB
The Long Dark Hall	1951	GB
Man in the Middle	1963	GB
Man on the Run *	1949	GB
Maniac	1962	GB--Ham.
Mine Own Executioner	1947	GB
The Mouse on the Moon	1963	GB--UA
My Learned Friend	1943	GB
Mysterious Island	1961	GB--Col.
Notorious Gentleman	1945	GB--Rank/ Univ.
One Million Years BC	1966	GB--Ham.
The Pickwick Papers	1952	GB
Please Sir!	1971	GB
Port Afrique	1956	GB--Col.
Portrait of Allison	1955	GB
Run Wild, Run Free	1969	GB--Col.
SOS Pacific	1959	GB
Sea Devils	1953	GB--RKO
Sea of Sand	1958	GB
Seven Thunders	1957	GB
The Seventh Voyage of Sinbad	1958	Col.
Ships With Wings *	1942	GB--Eal./Univ.
The Siege of the Saxons *	1963	GB--Col.
Silent Dust *	1949	GB
Subway in the Sky	1959	GB
Svengali	1954	GB
They Who Dare	1954	GB
The 3 Worlds of Gulliver	1960	GB--Col.
Time Gentlemen, Please!	1952	GB
Treasure of San Teresa	1959	GB

Trunk Crime *	1939	GB
Two Left Feet	1963	GB
Undercover	1943	GB
The Valiant *	1961	GB--UA
Web of Evidence	1959	GB
Went the Day Well?	1942	GB--Eal./UA
What Every Woman Wants	1954	GB
The Whole Truth	1958	GB--Col.

115. JOHN COQUILLON

Absolution	1978	GB
The Amateur	1982	TCF
The Body Stealers	1970	GB
The Changeling	1979	Can.
Clockwise	1986	GB--Cannon/ Univ.
Cross of Iron	1976	Ger./GB-- EMI
Cry of the Banshee	1970	GB--AIP
Curse of the Crimson Altar	1968	GB--AIP
Echoes of a Summer	1975	Can./US
Egghead's Robot	1970	GB
Final Assignment	1980	Can.
The Four Feathers	1978	GB
Going Undercover	1988	GB
Hyper Sapien: People From Another Star	1986	US
The Impersonator	1961	GB
Inside Out	1975	Ger./GB--WB
Mr. Patman	1980	Can.
The National Health	1973	GB--Col.
The Oblong Box	1969	GB--AIP
The Osterman Weekend	1983	TCF
Pat Garrett and Billy the Kid	1973	MGM
Praying Mantis	1982	GB
Rentadick	1972	GB
Scream and Scream Again	1969	GB--AIP
Straw Dogs	1971	GB
The Thirty-Nine Steps	1978	GB
Triple Echo *	1972	GB
The Wars	1983	Can.
The Wilby Conspiracy	1975	GB--UA
Witchfinder General	1968	GB
Wuthering Heights	1970	GB--AIP

116. CHARLES CORRELL

Fast Break	1979	Col.

In God We Trust	1980	Univ.
Moving Violation	1976	TCF
National Lampoon's Animal House	1978	Univ.
Nice Dreams	1981	Col.
Revenge of the Nerds II: Nerds in Paradise	1987	TCF
Star Trek III: The Search for Spock	1984	Par.

117. STANLEY CORTEZ (1908-   )

Abbott and Costello Meet Captain Kidd	1952	WB
The Admiral Was a Lady	1950	WB
Alias the Deacon	1940	Univ.
The Angry Red Planet	1959	AIP
Armored Car	1937	Univ.
Back Street	1961	Univ.
Badlands of Dakota	1941	Univ.
The Basketball Fix	1951	US
The Black Cat	1941	Univ.
Black Tuesday	1954	UA
Blue	1968	Par.
Bombay Clipper	1941	Univ.
The Bridge at Remagen	1968	UA
Danger on the Air	1938	Univ.
A Dangerous Game	1941	Univ.
The Diamond Queen	1953	WB
Dinosaurs	1960	Univ.
Dragon's Gold	1954	UA
Exposed	1938	Univ.
Flesh and Fantasy *	1943	Univ.
For Love or Money	1939	Univ.
The Forgotten Woman	1939	Univ.
Fort Defiance	1951	UA
Four Days Wonder	1936	Univ.
The Ghost in the Invisible Bikini	1966	AIP
Hawaiian Nights	1939	Univ.
Lady in the Morgue	1938	Univ.
The Last Express	1938	Univ.
Laugh It Off	1939	Univ.
The Leatherpushers	1940	Univ.
The Madmen of Mandoras	1963	US
The Magnificent Ambersons	1942	RKO
Man From Del Rio	1956	UA
Man on the Eiffel Tower	1948	US
Margie	1940	Univ.
Meet the Wildcat	1940	Univ.
Models, Inc.	1952	US
Moonlight in Hawaii	1941	Univ.
The Naked Kiss	1964	AA

The Navy vs. Night Monsters	1965	US
The Neanderthal Man	1953	UA
The Night of the Hunter	1955	UA
Nightmare in the Sun	1963	US
Personal Secretary	1938	Univ.
The Powers Girl	1942	UA
Riders to the Stars	1954	UA
Risky Business	1939	Univ.
San Antonio Rose	1941	Univ.
Sealed Lips	1941	Univ.
Secret Beyond the Door	1948	Univ.
Shark River	1953	UA
Shock Corridor	1963	US
Since You Went Away *	1944	Selz.
Smart Woman	1948	Mon.
Smash-Up: The Story of a Woman	1947	Univ.
Stronghold	1952	Lip.
They Asked for It	1939	Univ.
The Three Faces of Eve	1957	TCF
Thunder in the Sun	1958	US
Top Secret Affair	1956	WB
The Underworld Story	1950	UA
Vice Raid	1959	UA
The Wildcatter	1937	Univ.
Young Dillinger	1964	US

118. FRANK COTNER

Battling Bunyon	1925	US
The Demon Rider	1925	US
The Fighting Cub *	1925	US
The Haunted Range	1926	US
Never Too Late	1925	US
The Old Code *	1928	US
The Phantom Rider	1929	US
The Rattler	1925	US
Western Hearts	1921	US
Wings *	1927	Par.

119. CURT COURANT (1895-   )

La Bete Humaine	1938	Fr.
Betrayal	1939	Fr.
Broken Blossoms	1936	GB
The Burning Heart	1930	Ger.
Daybreak *	1939	Fr.
Die Frau im Mond *	1929	Ger.
From Mayerling to Sarejevo	1940	Fr.
Hideout in the Alps *	1938	GB

House of the Maltese	1938	Fr.
The Iron Duke	1934	GB
It Happened in Athens	1961	TCF
The Life of Nina Petrovna	1937	Fr.
Lights of Paris *	1938	Fr.
Louise	1939	Fr.
The Man in the Mirror	1936	GB
The Man Who Knew Too Much	1934	GB
The Man Who Murdered	1931	Ger.--UA
Me and Marlborough	1935	GB
Monsieur Verdoux *	1947	UA
My Cousin From Warsaw	1931	Ger.
Orloft and Tarakanova	1938	Fr./It.
The Passing of the Third Floor Back	1935	GB
Perfect Understanding	1933	GB--UA
Princess Tarakanova	1938	Fr./It.
The Puppet *	1931	Ger.
The Puritan	1938	Fr.
Rasputin	1932	Ger.
Secrets of the Orient	1932	Ger.--UFA
She Knew What She Wanted	1936	GB
A Son From America	1932	Fr.
Spy of Napoleon	1936	GB
This One or None	1932	Ger.
Who Takes Love Seriously?	1931	Ger.

120. RAOUL COUTARD (1924-   )

A Bout de Souffle	1959	Fr.
The Adults	1961	Fr.
Alphaville	1965	Fr.
And Satan Calls the Turns	1962	Fr.
Are You Engaged to a Greek Sailor or an Airplane Pilot?	1970	Fr.
The Army Game	1963	Fr.
L'Aveu	1970	Fr.
Band of Outsiders	1966	Fr.
Bethune: The Making of a Hero	1990	Can./China/Fr.
The Bride Wore Black	1967	Fr./It.--UA
Burning Beds	1988	Ger.
Les Carabiniers	1968	Fr./It.
Chinese White	1988	Fr.
La Chinoise	1968	Fr.
The Confessions	1970	Fr.
Contempt	1964	Fr./It.
The Crab Drum	1977	Fr.
Crazy Pete	1965	Fr.
Dangerous Moves	1985	Fr.
The Dark Room of Damocles	1963	Holl.
The Defector	1966	Fr./Ger.--WB

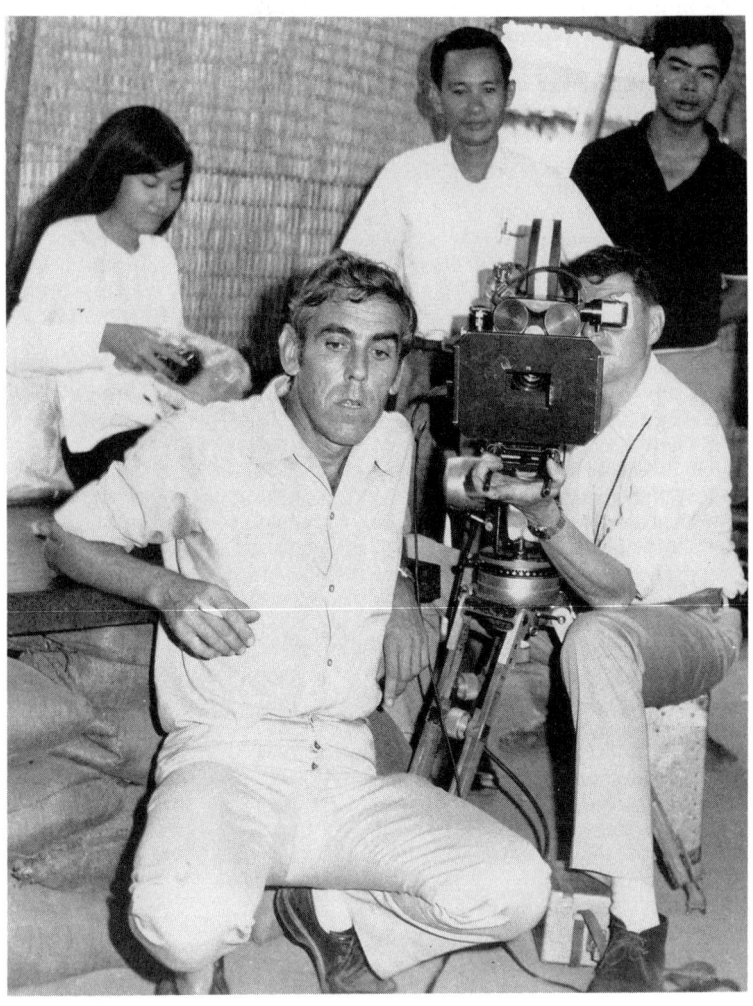

Raoul Coutard (left of camera; ca. 1970).

The Devil's Pass	1959	Fr.--TCF
The Doll	1962	Fr.
Embassy	1972	GB
First Name Carmen	1984	Fr./Switz.
The Five-Leaf Clover	1972	Fr.
Fuegos	1987	Fr.
Gang of Outsiders	1964	Fr.--Col.
A Hail Fellow Well Met	1964	Fr.--TCF
Hail! Mafia	1966	Fr./It.
L'Horizon	1967	Fr.
The Hostage Gang	1973	Fr.
Hoa Binh	1971	Fr.
Island Fishermen	1959	Fr.
It's Freezing in Hell	1990	Fr.
The Jerusalem File *	1971	Isr.--MGM
Jules et Jim	1961	Fr.
Let Sleeping Cops Lie	1989	Fr.
Liberty Riding High	1970	Fr.
Like a Pot of Strawberries	1974	Fr.
The Little Soldier	1963	Fr.
Live Her Life	1960	Fr.
Lola	1960	Fr.
Love Is Twenty Years Old *	1962	Fr./It./Jap.
Made in U.S.A.	1966	Fr.
Male Companion	1966	Fr.
The Married Woman	1964	Fr.
Max My Love	1986	Fr.
The Most Gentle Confessions	1971	Fr.--MGM
My Life to Live	1963	Fr.
Pain in the Neck	1973	Fr.
Passion	1983	Fr./Switz.--UA
Pierrot Le Feu	1968	Fr./It.
Platoon 317	1965	Fr.
Portuguese Vacation	1963	Fr.
La Poupee	1962	Fr.
The Sad Sack	1961	Fr.
The Sailor From Gibraltar	1967	GB
Salt on the Skin	1985	Fr.
Shoot the Piano Player	1960	Fr.
The Soft Skin	1964	Fr.
The Southern Star	1968	Fr./GB
Summer Chronicle *	1961	Fr.
Thick Skinned	1989	Fr
Time Out for Love	1963	Fr./It.
Two or Three Things I Know About Her	1967	Fr.
Weekend	1968	Fr./It.
A Woman Is Always a Woman	1964	Fr./It.
Z	1968	Alg./Fr.

121. JOHN J. COX

Adventure in Blackmail	1943	GB--MGM
The Adventures of Tartu	1943	GB--MGM
Alias John Preston	1956	GB
Almost a Honeymoon	1930	GB
Arms and the Man *	1932	GB
Babes in Bagdad	1952	US
Back Room Boy	1942	GB
The Big Money	1956	GB--Rank
Blackmail	1929	GB
Blighty	1927	GB
Broken Journey	1948	GB
Champagne	1928	GB
Charley's Big-Hearted Aunt	1940	GB
Cottage To Let	1941	GB
Crackerjack	1938	GB
The Cure for Love	1949	GB
Devil Girl From Mars	1954	GB
Dr. Syn	1937	GB
The Dominant Sex *	1937	GB
The Farmer's Wife	1928	GB
The Ghost Train	1941	GB
A Girl Must Live	1939	GB
Girl Thief *	1934	GB
Heart's Desire	1935	GB
Hi Gang	1941	GB--Rank
Holiday Camp	1947	GB
How He Lied to Her Husband	1930	GB
Idol of Paris	1948	GB
Inspector Hornleigh Goes to It	1940	GB--TCF
Inspector Hornleigh on Vacation	1939	GB--TCF
Jumping for Joy	1955	GB--Rank
Juno and the Paycock	1930	GB
Just My Luck	1957	GB--Rank
The Lady Vanishes	1938	GB
The Love Habit	1931	GB
Madonna of the Seven Moons	1944	GB
The Magic Bow	1946	GB
Man of the Moment	1955	GB
Man Who Changed His Mind	1936	GB
The Manxman	1929	GB
The Middle Watch *	1930	GB
Millions Like Us	1943	GB
Mimi	1935	GB
Mr. Drake's Duck *	1950	GB
Murder	1930	GB
Music Hath Charms *	1935	GB
Neutral Port	1940	GB
Number Seventeen	1932	GB
Okay for Sound	1937	GB

Once Upon a Dream *	1948	GB--Rank
One Good Turn	1954	GB
Owd Bob	1938	GB
Red Wagon	1934	GB
Rich and Strange *	1931	
Ring	1927	GB
A Romance of Wastdale	1921	GB
Second Best Bed	1938	BD
The Skin Game	1932	GB
The Square Peg	1958	GB--Rank
Strange Boarders	1938	GB
They Came By Night	1939	GB--TCF
They Were Sisters	1945	GB
Traveller's Joy	1949	GB--Rank
Two Thousand Women	1944	GB
Up in the World	1956	GB--Rank
Waterloo Road *	1945	GB
We Dive at Dawn	1943	GB
The Wicked Lady	1945	GB
Windbag the Sailor	1936	GB
A Woman Alone	1936	GB
You Made Me Love You	1933	GB

121a. VINCENT COX

Any Man's Death	1990	US
Creatures the World Forgot	1971	GB
Deadly Passion	1985	S.Afr.
The Demon	1981	S.Afr.
Killer Force	1975	Ire./Switz.
Rage to Kill	1989	US
Space Mutiny	1989	US
Wild Creatures	1968	S.Afr.

122. JAMES CRABBE (?-1989)

Agent for H.A.R.M.	1966	Univ.
The Baltimore Bullet	1980	AE
The China Syndrome	1979	Col.
The Entertainer	1975	US
For Keeps	1987	Tri-S.
The Formula	1980	MGM
Happy New Year	1987	Col.
How to Beat the High Cost of Living	1980	US
The Karate Kid	1983	Col.
Karate Kid Part II	1986	Col.
Like Father, Like Son	1961	US
Lost Flight	1970	Univ.

Night Shift	1982	WB
Players	1979	Par.
The Proper Time	1959	US
Rhinoceros	1973	AFT
Rocky	1976	UA
Save the Tiger	1972	Par.
Sextette	1978	US
Thank God It's Friday	1978	Col.
W W and the Dixie Dancekings	1975	TCF
The Young Sinner *	1965	US
Zigzag	1970	MGM

123. ARTHUR CRABTREE (1900-   )

Alf's Button Afloat	1938	GB
Bank Holiday	1938	GB
Convict 99	1938	GB
Dear Octopus	1943	GB
Everybody Dance	1936	GB
Fanny By Gaslight	1944	GB
For Freedom	1940	GB
The Frozen Limits	1939	GB
Gasbags	1940	GB
Good Morning Boys	1937	GB
Hey! Hey! USA	1938	GB
I Thank You	1941	GB
King Arthur Was a Gentleman	1942	GB
Kipps	1941	GB
The Love Test	1935	GB
The Man in Grey	1943	GB
Much Too Shy	1942	GB--Col.
Oh Mr. Porter	1937	GB
Old Bones of the River	1938	GB
Once a Crook	1941	GB--TCF
Out of the Blue *	1931	GB
Pot Luck *	1936	GB
South American George	1941	GB--Col.
Uncensored	1942	GB
Waterloo Road *	1944	GB
Where's That Fire?	1939	GB--TCF

124. JORDAN CRONENWETH

Altered States	1980	WB
Best Friends	1982	WB
Brewster McCloud *	1970	MGM
Citizens Band	1977	Par.
Count Your Bullets	1972	US
Cutter and Bone	1981	UA

The Front Page	1974	Univ.
Gable and Lombard	1976	Univ.
Gardens of Stone	1987	Tri-S.
Just Between Friends	1986	Orion
The Nickel Ride	1974	TCF
Peggy Sue Got Married	1986	Tri-S.
Play It as It Lays	1972	Univ.
Rolling Thunder	1977	AIP
State of Grace	1990	Orion
Trilogy *	1969	AA
Zandy's Bride	1974	WB

125. EDWARD CRONJAGER (1904-1960)

Ann Vickers *	1933	RKO
Beneath the Twelve-Mile Reef	1953	TCF
Best of the Badmen	1951	RKO
Bloodhounds of Broadway	1952	TCF
Canyon Passage	1946	Univ.
The Capture	1950	RKO
The Chicken Wagon Family	1939	TCF
Cimarron	1931	RKO
Colonel Effingham's Raid	1946	TCF
The Conquerors	1932	RKO
Countess of Monte Cristo	1948	Univ.
Desert Fury *	1947	Par.
The Devil's Partner	1958	US
Diplomaniacs	1933	RKO
Do You Love Me?	1946	TCF
Don't Trust Your Husband	1948	UA
Down to Their Last Yacht	1934	RKO
Easy Come, Easy Go	1928	Par.
Escape	1939	TCF
Everything Happens at Night	1939	TCF
Fast Company	1929	Par.
Fashions in Love	1929	Par.
Friendly Enemies	1942	UA
The Gang's All Here	1943	TCF
Gateway	1938	TCF
The Gay Caballero	1940	TCF
The Gay Defender	1927	Par.
Girl in 313	1940	TCF
Girl Trouble	1942	TCF
The Gorilla	1939	TCF
He Knew Women	1930	RKO
Heaven Can Wait	1943	TCF
Heaven With a Barbed Wire Fence	1939	TCF
Hell's Highway	1932	RKO
Home in Indiana	1944	TCF
Honeymoon	1947	RKO

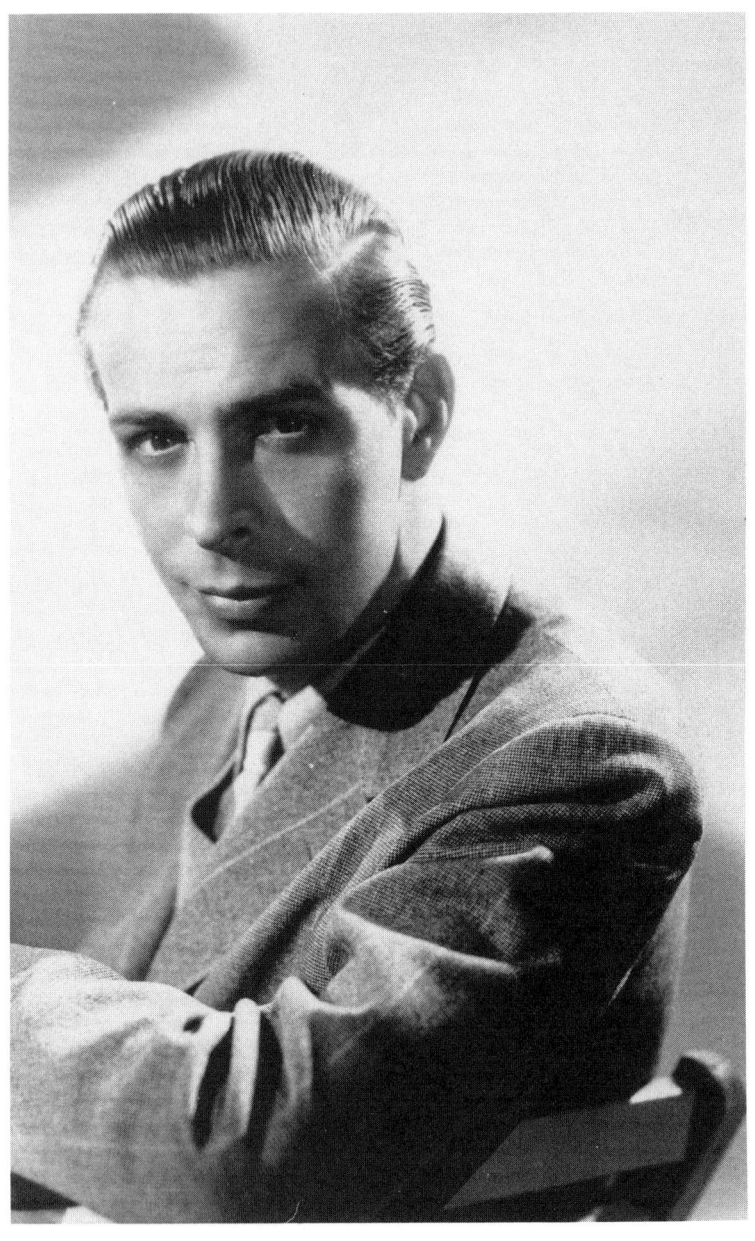

Edward Cronjager

House by the River	1950	Rep.
I Wake Up Screaming	1941	TCF
I Was an Adventuress *	1940	TCF
I'd Climb the Highest Mountain	1951	TCF
If I Were Free	1934	RKO
In Person	1935	RKO
Island in the Sky	1938	TCF
Jalna	1935	RKO
Just Married	1928	Par.
Keep Smiling	1938	TCF
Kentucky Kernels	1935	RKO
Knockabout Reilly	1927	Par.
Let's Get Married	1926	Par.
Life Begins at Eight Thirty	1942	TCF
Lightning Strikes Twice	1935	RKO
The Lost Squadron *	1932	RKO
The Love Doctor	1929	Par.
Lovin' the Ladies	1930	RKO
Lure of the Wilderness	1952	TCF
Man Power	1927	Par.
Margin for Error	1943	TCF
Moran of the Marines	1928	Par.
Nancy Steele Is Missing *	1937	TCF
The Nitwits	1935	RKO
No Marriage Ties	1933	RKO
Nob Hill	1945	TCF
Nothing But the Truth	1929	Par.
On Our Merry Way *	1948	UA
One in a Million	1937	TCF
Paradise for Two	1927	Par.
The Pied Piper	1942	TCF
Powder River	1953	TCF
Professional Sweetheart	1933	RKO
The Public Defender	1931	RKO
The Quarterback	1926	Par.
Rascals	1938	TCF
Redskin *	1929	Par.
Relentless	1948	Col.
Rise and Shine	1941	TCF
Roar of the Dragon	1932	RKO
Roberta	1935	RKO
Say It Again	1926	Par.
Secret Service	1931	RKO
Seven Keys to Baldpate	1929	RKO
Shanghai Bound	1927	Par.
Shooting Straight	1930	RKO
Siege at Red River	1954	TCF
Special Investigator	1936	RKO
Spitfire	1934	RKO
Sporting Goods	1938	Par.

Strictly Dynamite	1934	RKO
Sun Valley Serenade	1941	TCF
Sweepings	1933	RKO
The Texas Rangers	1936	Par.
Thin Ice *	1937	TCF
Three Married Men	1936	Par.
The Threat	1960	WB
To the Shores of Tripoli	1942	TCF
Too Busy to Work	1932	Fox
Treasure of the Golden Condor	1952	TCF
Two Tickets to Broadway *	1951	RKO
A Very Young Lady	1941	TCF
The Virginian *	1929	Par.
Wake Up and Live	1937	TCF
Warming Up	1928	Par.
Western Union	1941	TCF
What a Night!	1928	Par.
Wheel of Life	1929	Par.
Wife, Doctor and Nurse	1937	TCF
Winner Take All	1939	TCF
Womanhandled	1925	Par.
Yellow Dust	1936	RKO
Young Donovan's Kid	1931	RKO
Young People	1940	TCF
Youth Will Be Served	1940	TCF

126. HENRY CRONJAGER

Ace of Aces	1933	RKO
Back Home and Broke	1922	Par.
The Caillaux Case	1918	Fox
Clothes Make the Pirate *	1925	FN
The Combat	1916	Vita.
The Confidence Man	1924	Par.
Corporal Kate	1926	US
Daddy Long Legs *	1919	FN
The Deemster	1917	US
Don't Ever Marry *	1920	FN
Fifty-Fifty	1925	US
Fighting Love	1927	US
Fog Bound	1923	Par.
For France	1917	Vita.
The Great White Way *	1924	Gold.
The Heart Thief	1927	US
His Buddy's Wife	1925	US
Just Around the Corner	1921	Par.
Linda *	1929	US
Lord Chumley	1914	US
The Love Light *	1921	UA
Moral Suicide	1918	US

The Ninety and Nine	1916	Vita.
Old Loves and New	1926	FN
Party Girl *	1930	US
The Purple Highway *	1923	Par.
The Rejuvenation of Aunt Mary	1914	US
The River's End *	1920	FN
The Road to Ruin	1928	US
The Seventh Day	1922	FN
Sinners in Heaven	1924	Par.
Sonny	1922	FN
Three Men and a Girl	1919	Par.
Three Miles Out	1924	US
Tol'able David	1921	FN
Unguarded Women	1924	Par.
The Warfare of the Flesh	1917	US

127. JULES CRONJAGER (1872-1934)

Alias Mary Smith	1932	US
Anybody's Blonde	1931	US
Behind Stone Walls	1932	US
The Beloved Imposter	1918	Vita.
Cheap Kisses	1924	US
China Slaver	1929	US
Chivalrous Charley	1921	Selz.
Clay Dollars	1921	Selz.
Collegiate	1926	US
The Coward	1927	US
The Dancer of the Nile	1923	US
Docks of San Francisco	1932	US
Dynamite Denny	1932	US
Easy Millions	1933	US
Evidence *	1922	Selz.
First Aid	1931	US
Fortune's Child	1919	Vita.
Gilded Lies	1921	Selz.
The Gingham Girl	1927	US
The Girl Woman *	1919	Vita.
Girls Who Dare	1929	US
Greater Than Fame	1920	Selz.
Handcuffs or Kisses	1921	Selz.
Hell's Headquarters	1932	US
Hellbent for Frisco	1931	US
Her Mad Night	1932	US
Her Splendid Folly *	1933	US
Home Struck	1927	US
Is Life Worth Living?	1921	Selz.
Is That Nice?	1926	US
Isle of Retribution *	1926	US
John Smith	1922	Selz.

Justice Takes a Holiday	1933	US
The Kid From Arizona	1931	US
The King of the Turf	1926	US
Ladies Beware	1927	US
The Last Door	1921	Selz.
The Little Wild Girl	1928	US
Love Is an Awful Thing	1922	Selz.
The Man of Stone	1921	Selz.
Manhattan Madness	1926	US
Marooned Hearts	1920	Selz.
The Mating	1918	Vita.
Midnight Morals	1932	US
The Midnight Warning	1933	US
Miss Dulcie From Dixie	1919	Vita.
Modern Matrimony	1923	Selz.
Must We Marry?	1928	US
Neck and Neck	1931	US
Night Beat	1932	US
No Living Witness	1932	US
A Nymph of the Foothills	1918	Vita.
Old Age Handicap	1928	US
One Week of Love	1922	Selz.
The Pinch Hitter	1925	US
The Plunderer	1924	Fox
A Poor Girl's Romance	1926	US
The Prophet's Paradise	1922	Selz.
Reckless Youth *	1922	Selz.
Reported Missing	1922	Selz.
Shadow of the East	1924	Fox
Shadows of the Sea *	1922	Selz.
Sin's Payday	1932	US
The Sky Spider	1931	US
Soul of the Slums	1931	US
A Stitch in Time	1919	Vita.
The Storm Daughter	1924	Univ.
Tangled Destinies	1932	US
Too Many Crooks	1919	Vita.
The Wonderful Chance	1920	Selz.
Worlds Apart	1921	Selz.
Yours to Command	1927	US
Youthful Folly	1920	Selz.

128. FLOYD CROSBY (1899-1985)

Apache Woman	1955	US
The Arousers	1973	US
Attack of the Crab Monsters	1957	AA
Beach Blanket Bingo	1965	AIP
Bikini Beach	1964	AIP
Black Zoo	1962	AA

Blood and Steel	1959	TCF
The Brave Bulls *	1951	Col.
The Broken Land	1962	TCF
Carnival Rock	1957	US
Cold Wind in August	1960	US
The Comedy of Terrors	1963	AIP
The Cool Ones	1967	WB
Crime and Punishment USA	1958	AA
The Cry Baby Killer	1958	AA
The Explosive Generation	1961	UA
Fast and the Furious	1954	US
The Fight for Life	1940	US
Fireball 500	1966	AIP
The Firebrand	1962	TCF
Five Guns West	1955	US
Freckles	1960	TCF
The Gambler Wore a Gun	1961	UA
Hand of Death	1962	TCF
The Haunted Palace	1963	AIP
Hell's Horizon	1955	Col.
The High Powered Rifle	1960	TCF
High Noon	1952	UA
Hot Rod Gang	1948	AIP
House of Usher	1960	AIP
How to Stuff a Wild Bikini	1965	AIP
I, Mobster	1958	TCF
Indian Paint	1964	US
The Little Shepherd of Kingdom Come	1961	TCF
Machine Gun Kelly	1958	AIP
Man Crazy	1954	TCF
Man in the Dark	1953	Col.
Miracle of the Hills	1959	TCF
Monster From the Ocean Floor	1954	Lip.
My Father's House	1947	Pale.
Mystery Lake	1953	US
Naked Paradise	1957	AIP
The Naked Street	1955	UA
Night Tide *	1961	AIP
Pajama Party	1964	AIP
The Pit and the Pendulum	1961	AIP
Premature Burial	1961	AIP
The Purple Hills	1961	TCF
Raiders From Beneath the Sea	1965	TCF
The Raven	1963	AIP
Reform School Girl	1957	AIP
Ride Out for Revenge	1957	UA
Rock All Night	1957	AIP
The Rookie	1959	TCF
Salach Shabati	1964	Isr.
Sallah	1965	Isr.
Sergeant Deadhead	1965	AIP

Seven Women From Hell	1961	TCF
Sex and the College Girl	1970	US
Shack Out on 101	1955	AA
She Gods of Shark Reef	1958	AIP
The Snow Creature	1954	UA
The Steel Lady	1953	UA
Stormy the Thoroughbred *	1954	Dis.
Suicide Battalion	1958	AIP
Tabu	1931	Par.
Tales of Terror	1962	AIP
Teenage Caveman	1958	AIP
Teenage Doll	1957	AA
Terror at Black Falls	1962	US
Twelve Hours to Kill	1960	TCF
The Two Little Bears	1961	TCF
Walk Tall	1960	TCF
War of the Satellites	1958	AA
Wolf Larsen	1958	AA
Woman Hunt	1962	TCF
The Wonderful Country *	1959	UA
X-The Man with X-Ray Eyes	1963	AIP
The Yellow Canary	1963	TCF
The Young Racers	1963	AIP

129. ERIC CROSS

Beyond the Curtain	1960	GB--Rank
Chance of a Lifetime	1950	GB
Crossup	1955	GB
The Dark Man	1950	GB
Don't Take It to Heart	1944	GB
Escapade	1955	GB
The Flemish Farm	1943	GB
Fun at St. Fanny's	1956	GB
High Tide at Noon	1957	GB--Rank
High Terrace	1947	GB--AA/RKO
I'll Get You	1952	GB--Lip.
In the Wake of a Stranger	1959	GB
The Little Kidnappers	1953	GB--Rank
Make Up *	1937	GB
Mystery of the Marie Celeste *	1935	GB
The One That Got Away	1957	GB--Rank
Private's Progress	1956	GB
Quiet Weekend	1946	GB
Ships With Wings *	1941	GB--Eal.
Song of Freedom *	1936	GB
Sons of the Sea	1939	GB
Sporting Love	1936	GB
The Stranger In Between	1952	GB--Univ.
Tawny Pipit *	1944	GB

| Three Men in a Boat | 1956 | GB |
| Tiger Bay | 1959 | GB--Rank |

130. DEAN CUNDEY

Angels Brigade	1981	US
Back to the Future	1985	Univ.
Back to the Future, Part II	1989	Univ.
Back to the Future III	1990	Univ.
Bare Knuckles	1978	US
Big Business	1988	Dis./Touch.
Big Trouble in Little China	1986	TCF
Charge of the Model Ts	1979	US
D. C. Cab *	1983	Univ.
Escape From New York	1981	AE
The Fog	1979	AE
Galaxina	1980	US
Halloween	1978	US
Halloween Two	1981	Univ.
Halloween III: Season of the Witch	1982	Univ.
Ilse, Harem Keeper of the Oil Sheiks *	1976	US
Project X	1987	TCF
Psycho II	1983	Univ.
Road House	1989	MGM/UA
Rock n Roll High School	1979	US
Roller Boogie	1979	UA
Romancing the Stone	1984	TCF
Separate Ways	1983	US
The Thing	1982	Univ.
Warning Sign	1985	TCF
Where the Red Fern Grows	1974	US
Who Framed Roger Rabbit	1988	Dis./Touch.
Without Warning	1980	US

130a. STEFAN CZAPSKY

Child's Play 2	1990	Univ.
Edward Scissorhands	1990	Par.
Fear, Anxiety and Depression	1989	US
Flashback	1990	Par.
Last Exit to Brooklyn	1989	US
On the Edge	1986	US
Sons	1989	US
Vampire's Kiss	1988	US

131. STEPHEN DADE (1909-   )

| The Angry Hills | 1959 | MGM |

Appointment in London	1952	GB
The Bad Lord Byron *	1948	GB--Rank
The Bay of St. Michel	1963	GB--Rank
Bluebeard's Ten Honeymoons	1960	GB
The Brothers	1947	GB
Caravan	1946	GB
Christopher Columbus	1949	GB--Rank
Coast of Skeletons	1965	GB
The Crooked Road	1964	GB/Yugo.
The Dancing Years	1949	GB
Danny Boy	1941	GB
Dateline Diamonds	1965	GB
Dear Murderer	1946	GB
Doctor Blood's Coffin	1960	GB--UA
Don't Ever Leave Me *	1949	GB--Rank
Double Bunk	1961	GB
The Flesh Is Weak	1957	GB
Get Cracking	1942	GB--Col.
Get On With It	1961	GB
Good Time Girl	1948	GB--Rank
Knights of the Round Table *	1953	GB--MGM
The Late Edwina Black	1951	GB
The Man Who Finally Died	1962	GB
The Night Caller	1965	GB
A Place of One's Own	1944	GB
A Question of Adultery	1958	GB
The Root of All Evil	1946	GB
The Sea Shall Not Have Them	1954	GB
The Snake Woman	1961	GB
Snowbound	1948	GB
A Terrible Beauty	1960	GB--UA
Three On a Spree	1961	GB--UA
The Viking Queen	1967	GB--Ham./WB
The Vulture	1967	GB
We'll Meet Again	1942	GB--Col.
Zulu	1964	GB--Par.

132. MASSIMO DALLAMANO

Constantine and the Cross	1962	It.--Emb.
The Cossacks	1960	It.--Univ.
Desert Desperadoes	1959	It.--RKO
A Fistful of Dollars	1964	Ger./It./Sp. --UA
For a Few Dollars More	1967	Ger./It./Sp. --UA
Girl Game	1968	Braz./Fr./It.
Gringo	1963	It./Sp.
Herod the Great	1960	It.--AA
Love and Larceny	1963	Fr./It.

Mystery of the Black Jungle	1955	Rep.
The Nights of Lucretia Borgia	1960	It.--Col.
Pontius Pilate	1967	Fr./It.
Queen of the Nile	1964	It.

133. WILLIAM DANIELS (1895-1970)

Abandoned	1949	Univ.
Actress	1928	MGM
All the Fine Young Cannibals	1960	MGM
Altars of Desire	1927	MGM
Another Thin Man *	1939	MGM
Anna Christie	1930	MGM
Anna Karenina	1935	MGM
As You Desire Me	1931	MGM
Assault on a Queen	1966	Par.
Away All Boats! *	1956	Univ.
Back Street	1941	Univ.
Bardelys the Magnificent	1926	MGM
Barretts of Wimpole Street	1934	MGM
Beg, Borrow or Steal	1937	MGM
Benny Goodman Story	1955	Univ.
The Boob	1926	MGM
Bright Victory	1951	Univ.
Bringing Up Father	1928	MGM
Broadway Melody of 1938	1937	MGM
Broadway to Hollywood	1933	MGM
Brute Force	1947	Univ.
Camille	1936	MGM
Can Can	1960	TCF
Captain Salvation	1927	MGM
Cat on a Hot Tin Roof	1958	MGM
Christopher Bean	1933	MGM
Come Blow Your Horn	1962	Par.
Come September	1961	Univ.
Dance Madness *	1926	MGM
Deported	1950	Univ.
Design for Scandal *	1941	MGM
Dinner at Eight	1933	MGM
Dr. Kildare's Victory	1942	MGM
Double Wedding	1937	MGM
Dramatic School	1938	MGM
Dream of Love *	1928	MGM
Family Honeymoon	1948	Univ.
The Far Country	1955	Univ.
Flesh and the Devil	1926	MGM
Foolish Wives *	1922	MGM
For Me and My Gal	1942	MGM
For the Love of Mary	1948	Univ.
Forbidden	1953	Univ.

Foxfire	1955	Univ.
A Free Soul	1931	MGM
The Gal Who Took the West	1949	Univ.
Girl Crazy *	1943	MGM
The Glenn Miller Story	1954	Univ.
Glory Alley	1942	MGM
Grand Hotel	1932	MGM
Great Meadow *	1931	MGM
Greed *	1925	MGM
Harvey	1950	Univ.
Helen's Babies *	1924	US
A Hole in the Head	1949	UA
How the West Was Won *	1962	MGM
Idiot's Delight	1939	MGM
Illegal Entry	1949	Univ.
The Impossible Years	1968	MGM
In Like Flint	1967	TCF
Inspiration	1930	MGM
Interlude	1957	Univ.
Istanbul	1956	Univ.
Jumbo	1962	MGM
Keeper of the Flame	1942	MGM
The Kiss	1929	MGM
Lady of Chance *	1928	MGM
The Lady Pays Off	1951	Univ.
The Last Gangster	1937	MGM
The Last of Mrs. Cheyney	1929	MGM
The Latest From Paris	1928	MGM
The Life of Riley	1949	Univ.
Love	1927	MGM
Lovers Courageous	1932	MGM
Lured	1947	Univ.
The Maltese Bippy	1969	MGM
Marie Antoinette	1938	MGM
Marlowe	1969	MGM
Marriage on the Rocks	1965	WB
Mata Hari	1932	MGM
The Merry Widow *	1925	MGM
Merry-Go-Round *	1923	Univ.
Money Talks	1926	MGM
Montana Moon	1930	MGM
Monte Carlo	1926	MGM
The Mortal Storm	1940	MGM
Move	1970	TCF
My Man Godfrey	1957	Univ.
The Mysterious Lady	1928	MGM
The Naked City	1948	Univ.
Naughty Marietta	1935	MGM
Never So Few	1949	MGM
Never Wave At a WAC	1942	US
New Moon	1940	MGM

Night Passage	1957	Univ.
Ninotchka	1939	MGM
Ocean's Eleven	1960	WB
Olympia	1930	MGM
On Ze Boulevard	1927	MGM
The Painted Veil	1934	MGM
Pat and Mike	1952	MGM
Personal Property	1937	MGM
Plymouth Adventure	1952	MGM
The Prize	1963	MGM
Queen Christina	1933	MGM
Rasputin and the Empress	1932	MGM
Rendezvous	1935	MGM
Robin and the Seven Hoods	1964	WB
Romance	1930	MGM
Romeo and Juliet	1936	MGM
Rose Marie	1936	MGM
Shadow of the Thin Man	1941	MGM
The Shop Around the Corner	1940	MGM
The Shrike	1955	Univ.
Six Bridges to Cross	1955	Univ.
Skyscraper Souls	1932	MGM
So Ends Our Night	1941	UA
Some Came Running	1959	MGM
The Stranger's Return	1933	MGM
Strangers May Kiss	1931	MGM
Strategic Air Command	1955	Par.
Strictly Unconventional *	1930	MGM
Stronger Than Desire	1939	MGM
Susan Lenox, Her Rise and Fall	1931	MGM
Telling the World	1928	MGM
The Temptress *	1928	MGM
Their Own Desire	1929	MGM
They Met in Bombay	1941	MGM
Three Loves Has Nancy	1938	MGM
Thunder Bay	1953	Univ.
Thunder on the Hill	1951	Univ.
Tillie the Toiler	1927	MGM
The Torrent	1926	MGM
Trial of Mary Dugan	1929	MGM
The Unguarded Moment	1956	Univ.
Valley of the Dolls	1967	TCF
Voice in the Mirror	1958	Univ.
Von Ryan's Express *	1965	TCF
War Arrow	1953	Univ.
When in Rome	1952	MGM
The White Sister	1933	MGM
Wild Orchids	1929	MGM
Winchester '73	1950	Univ.
Wise Girls	1929	MGM

Woman in Hiding	1949	Univ.
A Woman of Affairs	1928	MGM
Women and Gold	1925	US

134. ALLEN DAVEY

Bavu	1923	Univ.
The Blue Bonnet	1920	US
The Bullet Mark	1928	Pathe
Durand of the Bad Lands	1925	Fox
Eyes Right!	1926	US
Fighting Jack	1926	US
Fools and Riches	1923	Univ.
The Girl Who Ran Wild	1922	Univ.
Gold and the Girl	1925	Fox
The Heart Specialist	1922	Par.
Hearts and Spurs	1925	Fox
The Last Man on Earth	1924	Fox
A Man of Nerve	1925	US
Railroaded	1923	Univ.
Sawdust	1923	Univ.
The Shadow *	1921	US
South of Suva	1922	Par.
Tillie	1922	Par.
Timber Wolf	1925	Fox
Typhoon *	1940	Par.

135. ALLEN DAVIAU

Avalon	1990	Tri-S.
The Color Purple	1985	WB
E.T.	1982	Univ.
Empire of the Sun	1987	WB
Harry and the Hendersons	1987	Univ.
Harry Tracy-Desperado	1983	US
Indiana Jones and the Temple of		
Doom	1984	Par.
Twilight Zone-The Movie	1983	WB

136. CHARLES J. DAVIS

Broadway After Midnight	1927	US
Broadway Bubble *	1920	Vita.
Captain Swift	1920	Vita.
The Girl of Today	1918	Vita.
Lilies of the Streets *	1925	US
The Masked Dancer *	1924	US
Police Patrol *	1925	US

The Road to London	1921	US
The Single Track	1921	Vita.
Slaves of Pride *	1920	Vita.
The Sporting Duchess *	1920	Vita.
The Truth About Women *	1924	US
The Whisper Market	1920	Vita.

137. HARRY DAVIS

Dangerous Friends	1926	US
Dangerously Yours	1937	TCF
Devil's Dice	1926	US
Lightning Reporter	1926	US
The Mad Dancer	1925	US
One Wild Night	1938	TCF
Runaway Girls	1928	Col.
Unknown Treasures	1926	US

138. BERT DAWLEY

As a Man Lives	1923	US
Broadway Broke	1923	Selz.
The Harvest Moon	1920	US
Has the World Gone Mad? *	1923	US
Lady of the Lake	1930	US
The Silent Barrier *	1920	US
A Virgin Paradise *	1921	Fox
Who Are My Parents?	1922	Fox

139. ROGER DEAKINS

Air America	1990	Tri-S.
Another Time, Another Place	1983	GB
Cruel Passion	1978	GB
Defence of the Realm	1985	GB--Rank/WB
The Innocent	1985	GB
The Kitchen Toto	1987	GB
The Long Walk Home	1990	US
Mountains of the Moon	1990	Tri-S.
Nineteen Eighty-Four	1984	GB
Pascali's Island	1988	GB
Personal Services	1987	GB
Return to Waterloo	1985	GB
Shadey	1985	GB
Sid and Nancy	1986	GB
Stormy Monday	1988	GB
White Mischief	1987	Col.

140. FAXON DEAN

All Soul's Eve	1921	US
Baby Mine	1928	MGM
Braveheart	1925	US
Breed of the Border	1933	Mon.
The Call of the North	1921	Par.
Coming Through	1925	Par.
The Copperhead	1920	Par.
The Countess Charming	1917	Par.
The Cowboy and the Lady	1922	Par.
A Cumberland Romance	1920	US
The Diamond Trail	1933	Mon.
Don't Call Me Little Girl	1921	US
The False Alarm	1926	Col
Fast Life	1929	FN
The Fighting Chance	1920	Par.
Fools of Fashion *	1926	US
The Frontier of the Stars	1921	Par.
A Gentleman of Leisure	1923	Par.
The Guilty One	1924	Par.
Her Own Money	1922	Par.
Her Winning Way	1921	Par.
The Invisible Bond	1920	Par.
Jazzland *	1928	US
The Little Clown	1921	US
Little Johnny Jones	1929	FN
The Look Out Girl *	1928	US
Lord Jim	1925	Par.
Lost in Transit	1917	Par.
Making a Man	1922	Par.
The Man Unconquerable	1922	Par.
Moonlight and Honeysuckle	1921	US
North of the Rio Grande	1922	Par.
The Olympic Hero	1928	US
One Year Later *	1933	US
Romance of a Rogue *	1928	US
Sixty Cents an Hour	1923	Par.
The Sporting Lover *	1926	FN
Stephen Steps Out	1923	Par.
The Stranger *	1924	Par.
Texas Pioneers	1932	Mon.
The Tiger's Claw	1923	Par.
Tongues of Flame	1924	Par.
The Tragedy of Youth	1928	US
Trailing North	1933	Mon.
While Satan Sleeps	1922	Par.
Wings *	1929	Par.

141. JAN DE BONT

All the Right Moves	1983	TCF
Bert Rigby, You're a Fool	1989	WB
Black Rain	1989	Par.
Blue Movie	1971	Ger./Holl.
The Clan of the Cave Bear	1986	WB
Cujo	1983	WB
Dakota *	1974	Holl.
Die Hard	1988	TCF
The Family	1974	Holl.
Flatliners	1990	Col.
Flesh and Blood	1985	Orion
The Fourth Man	1983	Holl.
The Hunt for Red October	1990	Par.
I'm Dancing As Fast As I Can	1982	Par.
The Jewel of the Nile	1985	TCF
Joao	1972	Holl.
Keetje Tippee	1975	Holl.
Leonard Part 6	1987	Col.
Max Havelaar	1967	Holl.
Memoirs of a Streetwalker	1971	Holl.
Paranoia	1967	Holl.
Private Lessons	1981	US
Roar	1981	US
Ruthless People	1986	Touch.
Turkish Delight	1973	Holl.
White Slave	1969	Holl.
Who's That Girl?	1987	WB

142. HENRI DECAE (1915-   )

An Almost Perfect Affair	1979	Par.
Les Amants	1958	Fr.
Le Beau Serge	1958	Fr.
The Beautiful Prisoner	1983	Fr.
The Black Tulip	1964	Fr.
Bob Le Flambeur	1956	Fr.
Bobby Deerfield	1977	Col.
Les Bonnes Femmes	1960	Fr.
The Boys From Brazil	1978	TCF
Broad Daylight	1960	Fr.
Castle Keep	1969	Col.
Circle of Love	1965	Fr.
Le Clan des Siciliens	1968	Fr.--TCF
The Comedians	1967	MGM
Cop or Hood *	1979	Fr.
Les Cousins	1958	Fr.
The Day and the Hour	1964	Fr./It.--MGM
Death of a Corrupt Man	1977	Fr.

Delusions of Grandeur	1971	Fr.
Diabolically Yours	1968	Fr.
Don Juan *	1973	Fr.
Double Twist	1949	Fr.
Les Enfants Terribles	1950	Fr.
Exposed	1983	MGM-UA
The Felines	1964	Fr.--MGM
Focal Point	1977	Fr.--Col./WB
The Four Hundred Blows	1958	Fr.
Frantic	1961	Fr.
The Godson	1972	Fr./It.
The Good Girls	1960	Fr.
The Grignolo	1980	Fr.
Hello Goodbye	1970	TCF
Hotel Paradiso	1966	GB--MGM
Inspector Blunder	1980	Fr.
Is This Really Reasonable?	1981	Fr.
Isabelle and Lust	1975	Belg./Fr.
The Island	1980	Univ.
The Jerk	1965	Fr./It.
Jo	1971	Fr.--MGM
Joy House	1964	Fr.--MGM
The Joy of Living	1961	Fr.
Leda	1961	Fr.
Leon Morin, Priest	1961	Fr.
Lift to the Scaffold	1958	Fr.
Light at the Edge of the World	1971	Licht./Sp.--NG
Magnet of Doom	1963	Fr.
The Mad Adventures of Rabbi Jacob	1974	Fr.
The Mustard Is in My Nose	1974	Fr.
Night of the Generals	1967	Fr.--Col.
The Onion Chase	1975	Fr.
The Only Game in Town	1969	TCF
Operation Daybreak	1975	Czech./GB--WB
Private Life	1962	Fr.
The Professional	1981	Fr.
Purple Noon	1961	Fr.
The Red Circle	1970	Fr.
The Right to Love	1972	Fr.--TCF
La Ronde	1964	Fr.
Seven Capital Sins *	1963	Fr./It.--Emb.
Seven Nights in Japan	1976	Fr./GB--EMI/Par.
Le Silence de La Mer	1949	Fr.
The Sucker	1966	Fr./It.
Sundays and Cybele	1962	Fr.--Col.
Sundays at Villa d'Aubray	1962	Fr.
Sweet and Sour	1964	Fr./It.
These Sorcerers Are Mad	1978	Fr.

The Thief of Paris	1967	Fr./It.
Two People	1973	Univ.
The Umbrella Coup	1980	Fr.
The Vengeance of the Winged Serpent	1984	Fr.
The Verdict	1959	Fr.
A Very Private Affair	1962	Fr./It.--MGM
Viva Maria!	1965	Fr.
Warning, One Woman May Be Hiding Another	1983	Fr.
Web of Passion	1961	Fr.
Weekend at Zuydcoote	1964	Fr.
Weekend at Dunkir	1966	Fr./It.--TCF
Witness in the City	1959	Fr.

143. ROBERT DEGRASSE (1900-1971)

Adventure in Baltimore	1949	RKO
Alice Adams	1935	RKO
The Bachelor and the Bobbysoxer *	1947	RKO
Bachelor Mother	1939	RKO
Badman's Territory	1946	RKO
Beyond London Lights	1928	US
The Body Snatcher	1945	RKO
Bodyguard	1948	RKO
Born to Kill	1947	RKO
Break of Hearts	1935	RKO
Breed of the Sunsets	1928	US
Canyon of the Fools *	1923	US
Carefree	1938	RKO
Chatterbox	1936	RKO
Chicago Calling	1951	UA
The Clay Pigeon	1949	RKO
Crack Up	1946	RKO
Crashin' Thru *	1923	US
A Dangerous Profession	1949	RKO
A Date With The Falcon	1941	RKO
Desert Driven *	1923	US
Desperate Trails *	1921	Univ.
Double Dynamite	1951	RKO
Fangs of the Wild	1928	US
Father Takes a Wife	1941	RKO
Fifth Avenue Girl	1939	RKO
The First Legion	1951	US
Flame of the Barbary Coast	1945	Rep.
Follow Me Quietly	1949	RKO
Footlight Fever	1941	RKO
Forever and a Day *	1943	RKO
Freckles	1935	RKO
Fury of the Wild	1929	RKO
Genius at Work *	1946	RKO

George White's Scandals *	1945	RKO
Good Men and True *	1923	US
Having a Wonderful Time	1938	RKO
Higher and Higher	1943	RKO
Highways By Night	1942	RKO
Home of the Brave	1949	US
The Iron Major	1943	RKO
The Judge Steps Out	1947	RKO
Kick Back *	1922	US
A Kiss for Corliss	1949	UA
Kitty Foyle	1940	RKO
Lady of Burlesque	1943	US
Law of Fear	1928	US
The Leopard Man	1943	RKO
Lightning Speed	1928	US
Love On a Bet	1936	RKO
Lucky Partners	1940	RKO
Make Mine Laughs *	1949	RKO
Marry Me Again	1953	RKO
The Mayor of 44th Street	1942	RKO
The Men	1940	US
The Miracle of the Bells	1948	US
M'Liss	1936	RKO
My Favorite Spy	1942	RKO
The One Man Dog	1929	RKO
The Outcasts of Poker Flat	1937	RKO
Pittsburgh	1942	Univ.
Quality Street	1937	RKO
Riverboat Rhythm	1946	RKO
Seven Days Leave	1942	RKO
Seven Keys to Baldpate	1935	RKO
Seven Miles From Alcatraz	1942	RKO
Show Business *	1944	RKO
The Sign of Four *	1932	GB
Stage Door	1937	RKO
Step Lively	1944	RKO
Story of Vernon and Irene Castle	1939	RKO
The Swift Shadow	1927	US
Tall in the Saddle	1944	RKO
Three Pals	1926	US
Thundergate *	1923	FN
Tracked	1928	US
Unexpected Uncle	1941	RKO
Vigil in the Night	1940	RKO
Vivacious Lady	1938	RKO
Wanted! Jane Turner	1936	RKO
The Witness Chair	1936	RKO
A Woman Rebels	1936	RKO

144. TOM DEL RUTH

Cross My Heart	1987	Univ.
Death Wish II	1982	US
Get Crazy	1983	Emb.
Look Who's Talking	1989	Tri-S.
Look Who's Talking Too	1990	Tri-S.
Motel Hell	1980	UA
Quicksilver	1986	Col.
The Running Man	1987	Tri-S.
Satisfaction	1988	TCF
Stand By Me	1986	Col.
Underground Aces	1981	US

145. TONINO DELLI COLLI (1923-   )

Accatone!	1961	It.
Bad Birds, Good Birds	1966	It.
The Beach House	1980	It.
The Beautiful Swindlers *	1967	Fr./It./Jap./ Holl.
Blood Feud	1979	It.
The Camp Followers	1965	Fr./It./Yugo.
Canterbury Tales	1971	It.--UA
China Is Near	1968	It.
City of Pain	1949	It.
Cometogether	1971	It.--AA
The Day of the Owl	1968	It.
The Dead Woman's Hand	1949	It.
Deaf Smith and Johnny Ears	1972	It.--MGM
Dear Michael	1976	It.
Dear Papa	1979	It.
The Decameron	1970	It.--UA
Donatella	1958	It.
The Executioner	1965	It./Sp.
Extraconjugal *	1965	It.
Federico Fellini's Intervista	1987	It.
Female Times Three	1957	It.
First Love	1979	It.--UA
The Forbidden Room	1977	Fr./It.--UA
Fugitive Lady	1951	It.
The Future Is Woman	1984	Fr./Ger./It.
Ghost of Love	1981	Fr./Ger./It.
Ghosts Italian Style	1967	Fr./It.--MGM
Ginger and Fred	1986	Fr./Ger./It.-- MGM-UA
The Good, the Bad and the Ugly	1966	It./Sp.--UA
Gospel According to Saint Matthew	1964	Fr./It.
Grandma Sabella	1957	It.
The Hawks and the Sparrows *	1967	It.

Help Me Dream	1981	It.
Homo Eroticus	1971	It.
Hot-Blooded Paolo	1973	It.
How Low Can You Fall?	1974	It.
I'm Photogenic	1980	Fr./It.--UA
Island of Procida	1952	It.
Lacombe, Lucien	1974	Fr.
Last Man on Earth	1964	It.
Love in Four Dimensions *	1965	Fr./It.
Lovers and Liars	1980	It.
Mafia	1969	Fr./It.
Mamma Roma	1962	It.
Man of the Year	1973	It.
The Master Touch	1975	Ger./It.--WB
Morgan the Pirate *	1961	Fr./It.--MGM
Name of the Rose	1986	TCF
The New Angels	1962	It.
No Roses for OSS	1968	Fr.
Not On Your Life	1965	It.
Once Upon a Time in America	1984	WB
One Night at Dinner	1969	It.
Pigsty *	1969	Fr./It.
Pilgrimage	1971	It.
Poor But Handsome	1957	It.
Poor Girl, Pretty Girl	1958	It.
The Purple Taxi	1977	Fr./Ire./It.
Pussycat, Pussycat, I Love You	1970	UA
Revenge	1979	It.
Rogopag *	1963	It/US
Roguish Stories	1973	It.
The Sack of Rome	1953	It.
Salo or the 120 Days of Sodom	1975	It.--UA
Seven Beauties	1975	It.
The Seven Hills of Rome *	1957	MGM
Spirits of the Dead *	1969	It.
Study of Love	1964	It.
Sunday Lovers	1980	Fr./It.--UA
The Swordsman of Siena	1962	It.--MGM
Tales of Mystery and Imagination *	1968	Fr./It.
Tales of Ordinary Madness	1983	It.
Thief of Baghdad	1961	It.--MGM
Toto in Color	1952	It.
Travels With Anita	1979	It.--UA
Trenchcoat	1983	Dis.
Venial Sin	1974	It.
A Very Handy Man	1966	Fr./It.
Viva Italia	1978	It.
The Voice of the Moon	1990	Fr./It.
The Woman From Africa	1990	Fr./Ger./It.
The World at Night	1960	It.

146. AUSTIN DEMPSTER

Bedazzled	1967	GB--TCF
Into the Blue	1950	GB
The Lady With a Lamp	1951	GB
The Little Ark *	1971	US
The Looking Glass War	1969	GB--Col.
Loot	1970	GB
Maytime in Mayfair *	1949	GB
Otley	1968	GB--Col.
A Severed Head	1970	GB--Col.
Tales of Beatrix Potter	1971	GB--EMI
A Touch of Class	1973	GB--Avco

147. ERNEST (HAP) DEPEW

Anne Against the World	1929	US
Better Days *	1927	US
Black Pearl	1928	US
Black Tears	1927	US
Boy of the Streets	1927	US
Branded Man	1928	US
Breezy Bill	1930	US
Bride of the Desert	1929	US
Brothers	1929	US
Casey Jones	1927	US
Code of the West	1929	US
Cold Steel *	1921	US
Devil's Chaplin	1929	US
Devil's Tower	1928	US
Divine Singer	1928	US
Duty's Reward *	1927	US
The Fighting Terror	1929	US
Fra Diavolo *	1933	MGM
A Gentleman Preferred	1928	US
Gun-Hand Harrison	1927	US
Gypsy of the North	1928	US
The Invaders	1929	US
Isle of Lost Men	1928	US
The Last Roundup	1929	US
Law and the Man	1928	US
A Light in the Window	1927	US
Lightnin' Shot	1928	US
The Lone Horseman	1929	US
Man From Headquarters	1928	US
The Man From Nevada	1929	US
The Man From Nowhere	1930	US
Million Dollar Mystery	1927	US
Modern Daughters	1927	US
My Home Town	1928	US

Mystery Valley	1928	US
Near the Rainbow's End	1930	US
'Neath Western Skies	1929	US
The Oklahoma Kid	1929	US
On the Stroke of Twelve	1927	US
The Parting of the Trails	1930	US
Pioneers of the West	1929	US
Prince of the Plains	1927	US
Riders of the Rio Grande	1929	US
Ridin' Luck	1927	US
Shanghai Rose	1929	US
Ships of the Night	1928	US
Should a Girl Marry?	1928	US
Silent Trail *	1929	US
Sisters of Eve	1928	US
Some Mother's Boy	1929	US
Two Sisters	1929	US
Wanderer of the West	1927	US
When Dreams Come True	1929	US
Wild Born	1927	US
You Can't Beat the Law	1928	US

148. PASQUALE DESANTIS

Aquarium	1988	It.
L'Argent	1984	Fr./Switz.
The Assassination of Trotsky	1972	Fr./It.
Bizet's Carmen	1984	Fr./It.
Conversation Piece	1974	Fr./It.
The Context	1976	It.--UA
The Damned	1969	Ger./It.--WB
Death in Venice	1971	Fr./It.--WB
The Devil, Probably	1977	Fr.
Eboli	1980	It.
The Enrico Mattei Affair	1972	It.
The Great Day	1977	Can./It.
Guernica	1972	It.
Harem	1985	It.
Illustrious Corpses	1975	It.
The Immortal Bachelor	1980	It.
The Innocent	1976	It.
Just Another War	1970	It./Yugo.
Lancelot of the Lake	1975	Fr.
Listen, Let's Make Love	1969	Fr./It.
Midnight Pleasures	1975	It.
Misunderstood	1984	MGM-UA
The Moment of Truth	1965	It./Sp.
More Than a Miracle	1967	Fr./It.--MGM
Nene	1977	It.

A Place for Lovers	1969	Fr./It.--MGM
Re: Lucky Luciano	1974	Fr./It.
Rigoletto	1987	Ger.
Romeo and Juliet	1968	GB/It.--Par.
Salome	1986	It.
Sheena	1984	Col.
A Special Day	1977	Can./It.
The Terrace	1980	It.--UA
Three Brothers	1982	It.
To Forget Palermo	1990	Fr./It.

149. CALEB DESCHANEL

Being There	1979	Lor.
The Black Stallion	1979	UA
More American Graffiti	1979	Univ.
The Natural	1984	Tri-S.
The Right Stuff	1983	WB
A Woman Under the Influence	1974	US

150. SANDRO D'EVA

The Big Fix	1988	It.
I Won the New Year's Lottery	1990	It.
In the Name of the Italian People	1971	It.
James Tont, Operation D.U.E.	1966	It.
James Tont, Operation U.N.O.	1965	It.
Let's Talk About Women	1964	Fr./It.
Life Is Tough, Eh Providence?	1972	Fr./Ger./It.
Matchless	1967	It.--UA
Normal Young Man	1969	It.
Nude Odyssey	1962	Fr./It.
One Million Dollars	1965	It.--Col.
The Reunion	1963	It.
School of Wives: Part II	1987	It.
Seducers	1970	It.
The Slave	1973	It.
Stories on the Sand *	1963	It.
Street Corner Kids	1982	It.
Success	1963	Fr./It.
The Tiger and the Pussycat	1967	It.--Emb.
Torture Me, But Kill Me With Kisses	1968	It.
Us Real Men	1987	It.

151. CLYDE DE VINNA (1892-1953)

Adele	1919	US
The Adventurer	1928	MGM

Ah, Wilderness	1935	MGM
All Wrong *	1919	Pathe
The Bad Man	1940	MGM
Bad Man of Brimstone	1937	MGM
Barnacle Bill	1941	MGM
Ben-Hur *	1925	MGM
Bird of Paradise *	1932	RKO
Blackmail	1939	MGM
Bridal Suite	1939	MGM
The Bugle Sounds	1941	MGM
California	1927	MGM
The Captive God	1916	US
The Caribbean Mystery	1945	TCF
The Cheater Reformed	1921	Fox
Civilization *	1916	US
A Corner in Colleens	1916	US
Crimson Gold *	1923	US
Cupid Forecloses	1919	Vita.
Face of the World	1921	US
Fast Company	1938	MGM
The Flame of the Yukon	1917	US
Foreign Devils	1927	MGM
The Frontiersman	1927	MGM
Girl Downstairs	1938	MGM
The Good Old Soak	1937	MGM
The Great Meadow *	1931	MGM
The Heart of Rachel	1918	US
Jackass Mail	1942	MGM
The Jungle	1952	US
Last of the Pagans	1936	MGM
The Law of the Range	1928	MGM
Leave It to Me	1920	Fox
The Lincoln Highwayman	1920	Fox
The Little Boss	1919	Vita.
Lost and Found on a South Sea Island *	1923	Gold
Madame Who?	1917	US
The Man in Blue	1925	Univ.
The Man Who Dared	1920	Fox
Of Human Hearts	1938	MGM
Old Hutch	1936	MGM
Over the Garden Wall	1919	Vita.
The Pagan	1929	MGM
Patriotism	1918	US
The People vs. Dr. Kildare	1941	MGM
Phantom Raiders	1940	MGM
Playthings of Passion	1919	US
Politics	1931	MGM
Rose o' Paradise	1918	US
The Sawdust Ring *	1917	US
The Skywayman *	1920	Fox

Spoilers of the West	1927	MGM
Sporting Youth	1924	Univ.
Sword of the Avenger	1948	EL
Tarzan and His Mate *	1934	MGM
Tarzan the Ape Man *	1932	MGM
Tarzan's Secret Treasure	1941	MGM
They All Came Out *	1939	MGM
Trader Horn	1930	MGM
Treasure Island *	1934	MGM
Twenty Mule Team	1940	MGM
The Victor	1923	Univ.
War Paint	1926	MGM
West Point of the Air *	1935	MGM
Where Is the West?	1923	Univ.
Whistling in Dixie	1942	MGM
White Shadows in the South Seas *	1928	MGM
Whither Thou Goest	1917	US
Wickedness Preferred	1928	MGM
The Wild Party	1923	Univ.
Wild Winship's Widow	1917	US
Winners of the Wilderness	1927	MGM
The Wolf Woman	1916	US
Wyoming	1928	MGM
Wyoming	1940	MGM
A Yankee Princess	1919	Vita.
Yellow Men and Gold	1922	Gold.

152. NORMAN DE VOL

The Big Diamond Robbery	1929	FBO/RKO
The Drifter	1929	FBO/RKO
King Cowboy	1928	FBO
Outlawed	1929	FBO
Son of the Golden West	1928	FBO

153. JAMES DIAMOND

Bare Knees	1928	US
Broadway Gold	1923	US
Broken Hearts of Broadway	1923	US
Broken Laws	1924	US
The City	1926	Fox
Daring Love *	1924	US
Death in the Sky *	1937	US
The Drums of Jeopardy	1923	US
Flying Luck	1927	Pathe
Glenister of the Mounted	1926	US
Her Splendid Folly *	1933	US
Horse Shoes	1927	Pathe

If Marriage Fails	1925	US
Jane Eyre	1921	US
Journey's End	1921	US
Keep Smiling *	1925	US
The Man From Guntown	1935	US
Married People	1922	US
A Million to One	1938	US
Night Rider	1932	US
Notoriety	1922	US
Other Women's Clothes	1922	US
The Outlaw Deputy	1935	US
Percy	1925	Pathe/US
A Perfect Gentleman	1928	Pathe
The Prairie Wife	1925	Metro.-Gold.
Red Kimono	1925	US
Risky Business	1926	US
The Shining Adventure	1925	US
Sucker Money *	1933	US
Texas Tornado	1934	US
They Never Come Back	1932	US
Vanity Fair	1923	Gold
White Pants Willie	1927	FN
Your Best Friend *	1922	WB

153a. ERNEST DICKERSON

Almacita di Desolata	1986	Holl.
Ava & Gabriel	1990	Curacao
The Brother From Another Planet	1984	US
Def by Temptation	1990	US
Do the Right Thing	1989	Univ.
Enemy Territory	1987	US
Krush Groove	1985	WB
The Laser Man	1988	HgKg.
Mo' Better Blues	1990	Univ.
Raw	1987	US
School Daze	1988	Col.
She's Gotta Have It	1986	US
Vampires *	1988	US

154. DESMOND DICKINSON (1902-   )

Action of the Tiger	1957	GB--MGM
The Alphabet Murders	1965	GB--MGM
The Arsenal Stadium Mystery	1939	GB
Baby Love	1968	GB--Avco
Berserk!	1967	GB--Bol.
Beyond the Fog	1981	GB
The Black Tent	1956	GB--Rank

Bloodsucker	1970	GB
The Browning Version	1951	GB
Burke and Hare	1971	GB--UA
Cairo	1963	GB--MGM
Carrington VC	1954	GB
City of Beautiful Nonsense	1935	GB
City of the Dead	1960	GB
Crooks and Coronets	1969	GB--WB
Decline and Fall ... of a Bird Watcher	1968	GB
Dick Turpin	1933	GB
Encore	1951	GB
The Face That Launched a Thousand Ships	1954	GB
The Fiend	1972	GB
Fire Down Below	1957	GB--Col.
Foxhold in Cairo	1960	GB
Frightened City	1961	GB
Gentlemen Marry Brunettes	1955	UA
Hamlet	1948	GB--Rank
The Hands of Orlac	1960	Fr./GB
The History of Mr. Polly	1949	GB
Horror on Snape Island	1971	GB--EMI/MGM
Horrors of the Black Museum	1959	GB
Hungry Hill	1946	GB
The Importance of Being Earnest	1952	GB--Rank
Intent to Kill	1958	GB--TCF
Konga	1961	GB
The Last Man to Hang?	1956	GB
Madness of the Heart *	1949	GB
The Man Between	1953	GB
Man From Nowhere	1976	GB
Mary Had a Little	1961	GB
Meet Me Tonight	1952	GB--Rank
Meet Mr. Lucifer	1953	GB--Eal.
Men of Two Worlds *	1946	GB
Moment of Danger	1960	GB
Morning Departure	1950	GB--Rank
Murder Ahoy	1964	GB--MGM
Murder Most Foul	1964	GB--MGM
The Net	1953	GB--Rank
Nobody Ordered Love	1972	GB
Orders To Kill	1958	GB
La Passenger Clandestine	1958	Aus./Fr.
The Rocking Horse Winner	1949	GB--Rank
Sophie's Place	1970	WB
A Study in Terror	1965	GB
Thursday's Child	1942	GB
Trog	1970	GB--WB
Two and Two Make Six *	1961	GB
Who Slew Autien Roo?	1972	GB--AIP
The Woman in Question	1949	GB

155. GORDON DINES (1911-   )

The Blue Lamp	1950	Can.
Bomb in the High Street	1961	GB
Bread	1971	GB
The Challenge	1948	GB
The Challenge	1960	GB
Circle of Deception	1960	GB--TCF
The Colditz Story	1954	GB
Come On George *	1939	GB
The Crowded Day	1954	GB
Dreams Come True *	1936	GB
The Cruel Sea *	1952	GB--Eal.
Frieda	1947	GB--Eal.
The Gentle Gunman	1952	GB
I See Ice	1938	GB
It Takes a Thief	1960	GB
It's in the Air *	1938	GB
Keep Fit *	1937	GB
The Lady is a Square	1958	GB
Let George Do It *	1940	GB--Eal.
Let's Be Famous *	1939	GB--Eal.
The Long Arm	1956	GB--Eal.
The Maggie	1953	GB--Eal.
The Man Who Wouldn't Talk	1957	GB
The Navy Lark	1959	GB
Nicholas Nickleby	1947	GB--Eal.
Penny Paradise *	1938	GB
The Phantom Strikes *	1939	GB
Pool of London	1950	GB--Eal.
The Secret People	1951	GB--Eal.
The Ship That Died of Shame	1955	GB--Eal.
The Siege at Pinchgut	1959	GB--Eal.
These Dangerous Years	1957	GB
Train of Events *	1949	GB--Eal.
Turned Out Nice Again	1941	GB
Wonderful Things	1958	GB
Yangtse Incident *	1957	GB

156. CARLO DI PALMA (1925-   )

Alice	1990	Orion
The Appointment	1969	MGM
The Black Stallion Returns	1983	MGM-UA
Blow Up	1966	GB
Chastity Belt	1969	It.--WB
Gabriella	1984	MGM-UA
The Girl With a Pistol	1968	It.--Par.
Hannah and Her Sisters	1986	Orion
Help Me, My Love	1969	It.

I Love You, I Love You Not	1979	It.--US
I Married You for Fun	1969	It.
Identification of a Woman	1983	It.
The Lady Killer of Rome	1965	Fr./It.
Love in Four Dimensions *	1965	Fr./It.
A Man's Tragedy	1981	It.--WB
A Matter of Honor *	1966	Fr./It.
The Motive Was Jealousy	1970	It./Sp.--WB
The Naked Hours	1964	It.
Nini Tirabuscle	1971	It.
Off Beat	1986	Dis.
Omicron	1963	It.--Par.
Pacifist	1961	Fr./Ger./It.
Paris, My Love	1962	It.
Pigeon Shoot	1961	It.
The Pizza Triangle	1960	It./Sp.--WB
Radio Days	1987	Orion
Red Desert	1964	Fr./It.
The Scarlet Woman	1969	Fr.
The Secret of My Success	1987	Univ.
September	1987	Orion
Terror-Creatures From the Grave	1967	It.--US
3 Fables of Love *	1963	Fr./It./Sp.
Three Faces of a Woman *	1965	It.
A Very Handy Man *	1966	Fr./It.

157. GEORGE DISKANT (1907-1965)

Bandits of Corsica	1953	UA
Banjo	1947	RKO
Between Midnight and Dawn	1950	Col.
Beware My Lovely	1952	RKO
The Bigamist	1953	US
David Harding, Counterspy	1950	Col.
Davy Crockett, Indian Scout *	1950	UA
Desperate	1947	RKO
Dick Tracy vs. Cueball	1946	RKO
Every Girl Should Be Married	1948	RKO
Face to Face	1952	RKO
Guns of Hate	1948	RKO
Kansas City Confidential	1952	UA
Law of the Badlands	1950	RKO
Masked Raiders	1949	RKO
The Narrow Margin	1952	RKO
On Dangerous Ground	1951	RKO
Port of New York	1949	EL
The Racket	1951	RKO
Riff Raff	1947	RKO
Sealed Cargo	1951	RKO
Storm Over Tibet *	1951	Col.

They Live By Night	1948	RKO
The Traveling Saleswoman	1949	Col.
Vacation in Reno	1946	RKO
A Woman's Secret	1949	RKO

158. GIOVANNI (GIANNI) DIVENANZO (1920-1966)

Abandoned	1954	It.
Le Amiche	1955	It.
And Suddenly It's Murder	1960	It.
Bachelor	1956	It.
Bebo's Girl	1964	It.
The Challenge	1958	It./Sp.
Chronicle for Poor Lovers	1954	It.
The Dauphins	1960	It.
Disbanded	1955	It.
Eclipse	1962	Fr./It.
Eight and a Half	1963	It.--Emb.
Eva	1962	Fr./It.--Rank
Girls of San Frediano	1955	It.
Il Grido	1957	It.--US
Hands of the City	1963	It.--WB
High Infidelity *	1965	Fr./It.
The Honey Pot	1966	GB--UA
Juliet of the Spirits	1965	Fr./Ger./It.
Kiss the Other Sheik *	1968	Fr./It.--MGM
The Lizards	1963	It.
Love in the City	1954	It.
Magliari	1959	It.
Moment of Truth	1965	It./Sp.
My Wife's Enemy	1967	It.
La Notte	1960	It.
Paranoia *	1966	Fr./It.
Persons Unknown	1958	It.
Rascal-Fifi	1958	Fr./It.
Salvatore Giuliano	1961	It.
South Wind	1960	It.
The Tenth Victim	1965	Fr./It.--Emb.
Time of Indifference	1965	Fr./It.
To Defend My Love	1956	Fr./It.
Venetian Honeymoon	1959	Fr.
When Angels Don't Fly	1956	It.
Woman Is a Wonderful Thing *	1964	Fr./It.

159. JACK DRAPER (1900-1962)

Across the Plains	1928	US
The Bullfighter and the Lady	1950	Rep.
Call Me Bad	1962	Mex.

Daniel Boone, Trail Blazer	1957	Rep.
800 Leagues Down the Amazon	1959	Mex.
El Canto de La Sirena	1948	Mex.
Forbidden Trails	1928	US
I, Sinner	1960	Mex.
Mexican Eyes	1916	Mex.
Midnight on the Barbary Coast	1929	US
A Mother's Sin	1962	Mex.
Mystery in Mexico	1948	RKO
Plunder of the Sun	1953	WB
Robbers' Roost	1955	UA
Simitrio	1961	Mex.
Tarzan and the Mermaids *	1948	RKO
Texas Flash	1928	US
Thrill Chaser	1928	US
To Each His Life	1960	Mex.
Two Disobedient Sons	1962	Mex.
Way Down on El Rancho Grande	1949	Mex.
Where the West Begins	1928	US

160. LAUREN DRAPER

I'm a Real Mexican	1943	Mex.
Pony Express Rider	1926	US
Ranger's Oath	1928	US
Riders of Vengeance	1928	US
Secrets of the Range	1928	US
The Texas Bearcat	1925	US
Throwing Lead	1928	US
Trails of Treachery	1928	US
Twin Six O'Brien	1926	US
When Children Leave Home	1943	Mex.

161. JOSEPH DU BRAY

Alimony *	1924	US
The Awful Truth	1925	US
Backstage *	1927	US
Beauty Shoppers *	1927	US
The Beloved Cheater	1920	US
Blow Your Horn	1923	US
The Broken Gate *	1927	US
Butterfly Man	1920	US
The Call of Home	1922	US
Can a Woman Love Twice? *	1923	US
Cheaters *	1927	US
The Clutching Hand	1915	US
The Enchanted Island *	1927	US
The Hidden Way	1926	US

Husband Hunters *	1927	US
If I Were Queen	1922	US
Kismet *	1920	US
The Man of the Forest	1921	US
Occasionally Yours	1920	US
Perils of Pauline	1914	US
The Princess from Hoboken	1927	US
Redheads Preferred	1926	US
The Remittance Woman	1922	US
Silent Years	1921	US
Snowbound *	1927	US
The Understudy	1922	US
Untamed Youth *	1924	US
Up and At 'Em	1922	US
A Wife's Awakening	1921	US
Wild Geese *	1927	US

162. EDWIN DU PAR (1890-1961)

The Better 'Ole *	1926	WB
The Bounty Hunter	1954	WB
Breakthrough	1950	WB
The Country Kid	1923	WB
A Dog of the Regiment	1927	WB
The Eddie Cantor Story	1953	WB
The Fortune Hunter	1927	WB
From the Earth to the Moon	1958	US
George Washington, Jr.	1923	WB
Giant *	1956	WB
Hero of the Big Snows	1926	WB
Heroes of the Street	1922	WB
I Was a Communist for the FBI	1951	WB
If I Were Single	1927	WB
Inside the Walls of Folsom Prison	1951	WB
Lights of New York	1928	WB
The Lion and the Horse	1952	WB
Little Church Around the Corner *	1923	WB
The Lone Ranger	1955	WB
The Love Hour	1925	Vita.
Main Street *	1923	WB
The Miracle of Our Lady of Fatima	1952	WB
The Night Cry *	1926	WB
Paris Follies of 1956	1955	AA
The Queen of the Night Clubs	1929	WB
A Race for Life	1928	WB
The Redeemer	1965	Sp.--US
Ring of Fear	1954	WB
The Royal Box *	1929	WB
The Sap	1926	WB
She's Back on Broadway	1953	WB

Ship of Souls	1925	US
Springfield Rifle	1952	WB
The System	1953	WB
The Tanks Are Coming	1951	WB
Target Zero	1955	WB
Tracked By the Police	1927	WB
White Flannels	1927	WB

163. MAX DUPONT

Blind Youth	1920	US
Caught Cheating	1931	US
Extravagance	1930	US
Galloping Fish	1924	FN
A Gentleman of Quality	1919	Vita.
Heroes of the Street *	1922	WB
His Forgotten Wife *	1924	US
His People	1925	Univ.
Hot Curves	1930	US
Judgment of the Storm *	1924	US
Just a Wife	1920	US
The Last Hour	1923	US
Love Never Dies	1921	US
A Man of Action	1923	FN
Mr. Robinson Crusoe	1932	UA
Morals for Women	1931	US
Once and Forever *	1927	US
Paradise Island	1930	US
A Rogue's Romance	1919	Vita.
The Speed Classic *	1928	US
Streets of Shanghai *	1927	US
The Third Alarm	1930	US
The Thoroughbred	1930	US
Three Must-Get-Theres *	1922	US
The White Sin	1924	US
Who Am I?	1921	Selz.
Winning With Wits	1922	Fox
The Wolf	1919	Vita.
The Yankee Consul	1924	US

164. ELMER DYER

Air Force *	1943	WB
Branded *	1931	Col.
Buffalo Bill in Tomahawk Territory	1952	UA
Cattle Queen	1951	UA
Clipped Wings	1938	US
Code of the Northwest	1926	US
Daughter of the Tong	1939	US

Dirigible *	1931	Col.
Flying Deuces *	1939	US
Gallant Journey *	1946	Col.
The Great Air Robbery *	1920	Univ.
The Hot Angel *	1958	Par.
Korea Patrol	1951	EL
Lightning Strikes West	1940	US
The Lone Wagon	1923	US
Mile a Minute Morgan	1924	US
Night Flight *	1933	MGM
Only Angels Have Wings *	1939	Col.
Special Agent K-7	1937	US
Spring Affair *	1960	US
Timber Fury	1950	EL
Two-Gun Troubadour *	1938	US
The Web of the Law	1923	US
West Point of the Air *	1935	MGM
Wings of the Navy *	1939	WB
The Winner's Circle	1948	TCF

165. EDWARD EARLE

The Blind Love	1920	US
A Dangerous Affair	1919	US
The Great Divide	1915	US
The Heart of a Gypsy	1919	US
Lahoma	1920	Pathe
Love, Honor and ?	1919	US
Sherry	1920	Pathe
Sun-Up	1919	US
Thunderbolt of Fate	1919	US
A Woman's Experience	1918	US
You Are Guilty	1923	US

166. ARTHUR EDESON (1891-1970)

Across the Pacific	1942	WB
All Quiet on the Western Front	1930	Univ.
Baby Mine	1917	Gold.
The Bat	1926	UA
The Better Wife	1919	US
The Big Brain	1933	RKO
The Big Trail *	1930	Fox
Bought and Paid For	1916	US
Casablanca	1942	WB
Castle on the Hudson	1940	WB
Ceiling Zero	1935	WB
Cheating Cheaters	1919	US
China Clipper	1936	WB

The Cockeyed World	1929	Fox
The Conspirators	1944	WB
Cowboy From Brooklyn	1938	WB
Deep Purple	1915	US
Devil Dogs of the Air	1935	WB
Dinky	1935	WB
Doctors' Wives	1931	Fox
The Dollar Mark	1914	US
The Drop Kick *	1927	FN
Each Dawn I Die	1939	WB
Extravagance	1930	US
Eyes of Youth	1919	US
Fast Companions	1932	Univ.
The Fighting O'Flynn	1949	Univ.
Flesh	1932	MGM
The Footloose Heiress	1937	WB
For the Soul of Rafael	1920	US
The Forbidden Woman	1920	US
A Gentleman of Quality	1919	Vita.
The Gilded Cage	1916	US
Girls Gone Wild *	1929	Fox
Go-Getter	1937	WB
Gold Diggers of 1937	1937	WB
Golden Arrow	1936	WB
Good Women	1921	US
Gorilla	1927	FN
Hearts in Exile	1915	US
Her Sister From Paris	1925	FN
Here Comes the Navy	1934	WB
His Double Life	1933	Par.
Hot Money	1936	WB
Hush	1921	US
Impatient Maiden	1932	Univ.
In Old Arizona	1929	Fox
Inez From Hollywood	1924	FN
International Squadron	1941	WB
Invisible Man	1933	Univ.
Jack Spurlock, Prodigal	1918	Fox
Joe Palooka	1934	UA
Just Another Blonde	1926	FN
The Kid Comes Back	1937	WB
Kid Nightingale	1939	WB
Kisses for Breakfast	1941	WB
Lady With Red Hair	1940	WB
Last Mile	1932	US
The Life of Jimmy Dolan	1933	WB
The Lost World	1925	FN
The Male Animal	1942	WB
The Maltese Falcon	1941	WB
The Man Who Came Back	1930	Fox
The Mask of Dimitrios	1944	WB

The Master Hand	1915	US
Maybe It's Love	1935	WB
McFadden's Flats	1927	FN
Me, Gangster	1928	Fox
Midchannel	1920	US
Mr. Chump	1938	WB
Mr. Dodd Takes the Air	1937	WB
Morals for Women	1931	US
Mutiny on the Bounty	1935	MGM
My Wild Irish Rose *	1947	WB
Nancy Drew Reporter	1939	WB
Nearly Married	1917	Gold.
Never Say Goodbye	1946	WB
No Place to Go	1939	WB
Nobody Lives Forever	1946	WB
The Old Dark House	1932	Univ.
One Way Street	1925	FN
Partners Again	1926	UA
The Patent Leather Kid *	1927	FN
Racket Busters	1938	WB
The Road Through the Dark	1918	US
Robin Hood	1922	UA
Romance of the Rio Grande	1929	Fox
Satan Met a Lady	1936	WB
The Savage Woman	1918	US
Sergeant York	1941	WB
Shine On Harvest Moon	1944	WB
Stallion Road	1947	WB
Stella Dallas	1925	UA
Strangers of the Evening	1932	US
Submarine D-1	1937	WB
Subway Sadie	1926	FN
Sweepstakes Winner	1939	WB
Sweet Daddies	1926	FN
Swing Your Lady	1937	WB
The Talker	1925	FN
Thank Your Lucky Stars	1943	WB
They Drive By Night	1940	WB
They Won't Forget *	1937	WB
A Thief in the Dark	1928	Fox
The Thief of Bagdad	1924	UA
Those We Love	1932	US
The Three Musketeers	1921	UA
Three Strangers	1946	WB
The Time, the Place and the Girl *	1946	WB
Tugboat Annie Sails Again	1940	WB
Two Guys From Milwaukee	1946	WB
Two Guys From Texas *	1948	WB
Waking Up the Town *	1925	UA
Waterloo Bridge	1931	Univ
While the Patient Sleeps	1935	WB

Wings of the Navy *	1939	WB
Worldly Madonna	1922	US

167. FREDERICK ELMES

Allan Quatermain and the Lost City of Gold *	1987	Cannon
Aria *	1987	GB--US
Blue Velvet	1986	DeL.
Breakfast in Bed	1978	US
Cold Dog Soup	1990	Aus.
Eraserhead	1978	US
Permanent Record	1988	Par.
River's Edge	1987	Hem.
Valley Girl	1983	US
Wild at Heart	1990	US

168. BASIL EMMOTT

Atlantic Ferry	1941	GB--WB
Battle of the V 1	1958	GB
Be My Guest	1965	GB
The Break	1962	GB
The Co-Optimists	1929	GB
The Curse of the Fly	1965	GB
Dangerous Medicine	1938	GB--WB
Educating Evans	1936	GB--WB
The Enemy General	1960	Col.
Flying Fortress *	1942	GB--WB
A Gentleman's Gentleman	1939	GB--WB
George and Margaret	1940	GB--WB
Get Off My Foot	1935	GB--WB
The Good Old Days	1939	GB--WB
The Great Armoured Car Swindle	1963	GB
The Green Buddha	1954	GB--Rep.
Hoots Mon	1939	GB--WB
I Was Monty's Double	1958	GB
Joe Macbeth	1955	GB--Col.
The Lodger *	1932	GB
The Long Haul	1957	GB
Man in the Dark	1965	GB--Univ.
The Man From Morocco	1944	GB
Man of the Moment *	1935	GB--WB
Master of Bankdam *	1947	GB
The Midas Touch	1940	GB--WB
Miss London, Ltd.	1943	GB
The Missing Rembrandt *	1932	GB
Mr. Cohen Takes a Walk	1936	GB--WB
Murder at Monte Carlo	1934	GB--WB

Murder Can Be Deadly	1963	GB
Mystery of the Rose Villa *	1930	GB
The Nursemaid Who Disappeared	1939	GB--WB
The Peterville Diamond	1942	GB--WB
The Prime Minister	1940	GB--WB
The Return of Carol Deane	1938	GB--WB
The Return of Mr. Moto	1965	GB
The Seventh Survivor *	1941	GB
Sing and Swing	1964	GB
Spin a Dark Web	1956	GB--Col.
Strongroom	1961	GB
That's the Ticket	1940	GB--WB
They Drive By Night	1938	GB--WB
This Was Paris	1941	GB--WB
Time Flies	1944	GB
To What Red Hell	1929	GB
Tomorrow at Ten	1962	GB
Town on Trial	1956	GB--Col.
Twelve Good Men	1936	GB--WB
Two for Danger	1940	GB--WB
Walk a Tightrope	1964	GB
Wicked As They Come	1956	GB--Col.
You Live and Learn	1937	GB--WB
Young, Willing and Eager	1967	GB

169. ROY ESLICK

Bantam Cowboy	1928	FBO
The Fightin' Redhead	1928	FBO
The Little Buckaroo	1928	FBO
The Pinto Kid	1928	FBO
The Trail of Courage	1928	FBO
Wizard of the Saddle	1928	FBO

170. MAX FABIAN

Don't	1925	MGM
The Dust Flower	1922	Gold.
The Exquisite Sinner	1926	MGM
Frisco Sally Levy	1927	MGM
His Back Against the Wall	1922	Gold.
Honeymoon	1928	MGM
In Old Kentucky	1927	MGM
Lovers?	1927	MGM
Shadows of the Night	1928	MGM
The Thirteenth Hour	1927	MGM

171. GEOFFREY FAITHFULL

Bobbikins	1959	GB--TCF
Calling Paul Temple	1948	GB
Comin' Thro' the Rye	1923	GB
Corridors of Blood	1958	GB
Danger Point	1971	GB
Devil's Harbour	1954	GB
Escape by Night	1963	GB
First Man into Space	1958	GB
Girl Who Couldn't Quite	1950	GB
Golden Disc	1958	GB
The Green Helmet	1961	GB--MGM
Headline	1943	GB--Eal.
Her First Affaire	1932	GB
Hindle Wakes	1952	GB
Honeymoon Deferred	1951	GB
Invasion Quartet	1961	GB--MGM
Kill or Cure	1962	GB--MGM
Kill Me Tomorrow	1957	GB
Kiss the Bride Goodbye	1944	GB
Ladies Who Do	1963	GB
The Last Hour	1930	GB
Life in Emergency Ward 10	1959	GB
Master Spy	1963	GB
The Murder Game	1965	GB
Murder She Said	1961	GB--MGM
The Mystery of the Marie Celeste *	1935	GB
Offbeat	1960	GB
On the Beat	1962	GB--Rank
Operation Snatch	1962	GB
Panic	1963	GB
River Beat	1954	GB
The Scarlet Thread	1950	GB
77 Park Lane *	1931	GB
Somewhere in England	1940	GB
Space Flight IC-1	1965	GB
Stormy Crossing	1958	GB
Story of Shirley Yorke	1948	GB
The Terrornauts	1967	GB--AE
Trouble Ahead	1934	GB
Two-Way Stretch	1960	GB
Variety Jubilee	1942	GB
Village of Daughters	1961	GB--MGM
Village of the Damned	1960	GB--MGM
When You Come Home	1947	GB
The World Owes Me a Living *	1944	GB

172. DANIEL FAPP (1900-   )

All the Young Men	1960	Col.

And Now Tomorrow	1944	Par.
Anything Can Happen	1952	Par.
Artists and Models	1955	Par.
Bachelor Flat	1961	TCF
The Birds and the Bees	1956	Par.
Bride of Vengeance	1948	Par.
The Caddy	1953	Par.
Darling, How Could You?	1951	Par.
Desire Under the Elms	1958	Par.
The Devil's Hairpin	1957	Par.
Double Trouble	1967	MGM
Dream Girl	1947	Par.
Easy Come, Easy Go	1947	Par.
The Far Horizons	1955	Par.
Five Card Stud	1968	Par.
The Five Pennies	1959	Par.
Fun in Acapulco	1963	Par.
The Girls of Pleasure Island	1953	Par.
Glamour Boy	1941	Par.
Golden Earrings	1947	Par.
The Great Escape	1963	UA
Hazard	1948	Par.
Henry Aldrich Boy Scout	1944	Par.
Henry Aldrich Gets Glamour	1942	Par.
Henry Aldrich Haunts a House	1943	Par.
Henry Aldrich Plays Cupid	1944	Par.
Henry and Dizzy	1942	Par.
Hold That Blonde *	1945	Par.
Hollywood or Bust	1956	Par.
Ice Station Zebra	1968	MGM
I'll Take Sweden	1965	UA
The Joker Is Wild	1957	Par.
Jumping Jacks	1952	Par.
Kings Go Forth	1958	UA
Kitty	1945	Par.
Knock on Wood	1954	Par.
Lady Bodyguard	1943	Par.
The Lemon Drop Kid	1951	Par.
Let's Make Love	1960	TCF
Li'l Abner	1959	Par.
Living It Up	1954	Par.
Lord Love a Duck	1966	UA
Marooned	1969	Col.
Money From Home	1954	Par.
Move Over Darling	1963	TCF
My Heart Belongs to Daddy	1942	Par.
A New Kind of Love	1963	Par.
No Man of Her Own	1949	Par.
On the Beach *	1959	UA
One Two Three	1961	UA
Our Man Flint	1965	TCF

Pardners	1956	Par.
The Pigeon That Took Rome	1962	Par.
The Pleasure Seekers	1964	TCF
Priorities On Parade	1942	Par.
Red, Hot and Blue	1949	Par.
The Redhead and the Cowboy	1950	Par.
Run for Cover	1955	Par.
Sailor Beware	1952	Par.
Send Me No Flowers	1964	Univ.
Song of Surrender	1949	Par.
Sorrowful Jones	1949	Par.
Spinout	1966	MGM
The Stooge	1951	Par.
Suddenly It's Spring	1947	Par.
Sweet November	1968	WB
To Each His Own	1946	Par.
The Trap	1958	Par.
True to the Army	1942	Par.
Union Station	1950	Par.
The Unsinkable Molly Brown	1964	MGM
West Side Story	1961	UA
World Premiere	1940	Par.

173. VINCENT FARRAR

Beauty on Parade	1950	Col.
Behind That Curtain *	1929	Fox
Best Man Wins	1948	Col.
Blondie Hits the Jackpot	1949	Col.
Blondie in the Dough	1947	Col.
Blondie's Anniversary	1947	Col.
Blondie's Big Deal	1949	Col.
Blondie's Hero	1950	Col.
Blondie's Holiday	1947	Col.
Blondie's Reward	1948	Col.
Blondie's Secret	1948	Col.
Boston Blackie's Chinese Venture	1949	Col.
Crime Doctor's Diary	1949	Col.
Down Missouri Way	1946	PRC
For the Love of Rusty	1947	Col.
The Gentleman From Nowhere	1948	Col.
Holiday in Havana	1949	Col.
I Surrender Dear	1948	Col.
It Had To Be You *	1946	Col.
Last of the Buccaneers	1950	Col.
Mary Ryan Detective	1949	Col.
My Dog Rusty	1948	Col.
The Palomino	1950	Col.
Queen of Burlesque	1946	PRC
The Red Dragon	1945	Mon.

Rookie Fireman	1950	Col.
Rusty Leads the Way	1948	Col.
The Shanghai Cobra	1945	Mon.
Song of Idaho	1948	Col.
Stork Bites Man	1947	US
Triple Threat	1948	Col.
When You're Smiling	1950	Col.

174. MIKE FASH

Betrayal	1983	GB--TCF
Brittania Hospital	1982	GB--EMI/Univ
Red Monarch	1983	GB
Success Is the Best Revenge	1984	GB
The Whales of August	1987	US

175. JOCKEY FEINDEL

Accomplice	1946	PRC
Bluebeard *	1944	PRC
Day the World Ended	1956	US
The French Key	1946	Rep.
The Great Mike	1944	PRC
Studs Lonigan *	1960	UA

176. JOAO FERNANDES

Big Score	1983	US
Braddock: Missing in Action III	1988	Cannon
Delta Force 2: The Colombian		
Connection	1990	Cannon
Friday the Thirteenth, Final Chapter	1984	Par.
Hollywood Vice Squad	1986	US
Human Experiments	1980	US
Invasion USA	1985	Cannon
It's Not My Body	1970	US
Kirilian Witness	1981	US
Land of No Return	1981	US
Nesting	1981	US
Red Scorpion	1989	US
The Spy Who Came	1969	US
That's Adequate	1989	US

177. GABRIEL FIGUEROA (1907-   )

Anxiety	1954	Mex.
Basket of Mexican Tales	1956	Mex.

Believe in God	1943	Mex.
Beyond All Limits	1961	Mex.
The Big Cube	1969	WB
The Children of Sanchez	1978	Mex.--US
La Cucaracha	1961	Mex.
Un Dia con El Diablo	1945	Mex.
El	1952	Mex.
Enamorada	1949	Mex.
The Empty Star	1962	Mex.
The Exterminating Angel	1962	Mex.
The Fever Rises in El Pao	1960	Mex.
Flor de Mayo	1959	Mex.
The Fugitive	1947	RKO
Girl in Love	1947	Mex.
Hell's Kitchen	1952	Mex.
The Hidden One	1956	Mex.
Hidden River	1950	Mex.
Impatient Heart	1960	Mex.
The Important Man	1961	Mex.
Interval	1973	Mex.--AE
Juanna Gallo	1961	Mex.
Kelly's Heroes	1970	Yugo.--MGM
Life Changes	1976	Mex.
Little Angel	1961	Mex.
Little Love of My Life	1952	Mex.
Macario	1961	Mex.
Maclovia	1948	Mex.
Maria Candelaria	1943	Mex.
Mr. Photographer	1953	Mex.
My Merry Widow	1942	Mex.
Nazarin	1958	Mex.
The Night of the Iguana	1964	MGM
Les Olvidados	1951	Mex.
Once Upon a Soundrel	1973	US
The Paper Man	1963	Mex.
The Pearl	1948	Mex.--RKO
Pedro Paramo	1966	Mex.
Portrait of Maria	1946	Mex.--MGM
Presage	1974	Mex.
Pueblerina	1949	Mex.
The Rebellion of the Hanged	1954	Mex.--UA
St. Simeon of the Desert	1965	Mex.
Soledad's Shawl	1952	Mex.
Sonatas *	1959	Mex.
Special Delivery	1964	Mex.
Straying Rooster	1952	Mex.
Tarzan and the Mermaids *	1948	RKO
The Three Musketeers	1942	Mex.
Three on the Great Ranch	1936	Mex.
The Torch	1950	EL
Town Tale	1949	Mex.

Two Mules for Sister Sarah *	1969	Univ.
Under the Volcano	1984	Univ.
The Weaver of Miracles	1962	Mex.
The White Rose	1972	Mex.

178. WILLIAM E. FILDEW

The Absentee	1915	US
Almost Married	1919	Metro.
The Blazing Trail	1921	Univ.
Blue Streak McCoy	1920	Univ.
Broad Daylight	1922	Univ.
Castles in the Air	1919	Metro.
The Danger Game	1918	Gold.
A Daughter of the Sioux	1925	US
The Day of Faith	1923	Gold.
Double Trouble	1915	US
Drifting	1923	Univ.
Enoch Arden	1915	US
The Failure	1915	US
Flirting with Fate	1916	US
Fools' Highway	1924	Univ.
The Fox	1921	Univ.
God's Outlaw	1919	Metro.
Heart of the Sunset	1918	Gold.
Her Inspiration	1919	Metro.
In for Thirty Days	1919	Metro.
The Island of Intrigue	1919	Metro.
The Lamb	1915	US
The Lost Horse	1915	US
The Magnificent Brute	1921	Univ.
The Martyrs of the Alamo	1915	US
Miss Robinson Crusoe	1917	Metro.
No Woman Knows	1921	Univ.
Oh Mary Be Careful	1921	Gold.
Outside the Law	1921	Univ.
Paid Back *	1922	Univ.
A Parisian Scandal	1921	Univ.
Peggy Does Her Darndest	1919	Metro.
The Petal on the Current	1919	Univ.
The Reckless Age	1924	Univ.
Reggie Mixes In	1916	US
The Return of Mary	1918	Metro.
The Self-Made Wife	1923	Univ.
Society Secrets	1921	Univ.
The Testing of Mildred Vane	1918	Metro.
Under Two Flags	1922	Univ.
The Virgin of Stamboul	1920	Univ.
White Tiger	1923	Univ.
The Wise Kid	1922	Univ.
The Wreck	1927	Col.

179. GERALD PERRY FINNERMAN

Barquero!	1970	UA
Brother John	1970	Col.
Buffalo Gun	1961	US
Littlest Hobo	1958	AA
The Lost Man	1969	Univ.
Nightmares *	1983	Univ.
Smorgasbord	1983	WB
Ssssssss	1973	Univ.
Tender Flesh	1976	WB
That Man Bolt	1973	Univ.
They Call Me Mister Tibbs	1970	UA

180. HARRY FISCHBECK

Aloma of the South Seas	1926	Par.
Backbone	1923	Gold.
The Big Broadcast of 1938	1937	Par.
Big Executive	1933	Par.
Border Flight	1936	Par.
Bulldog Drummond's Peril	1938	Par.
Cabaret	1927	Par.
The Canary Murder Case	1929	Par.
Cobra *	1925	Par.
The Crime Nobody Saw	1937	Par.
The Curse of Drink	1922	US
Dangerous Curves	1929	Par.
A Dangerous Woman	1929	Par.
The Devil	1921	Pathe
The Devil's Holiday	1930	Par.
Disbarred	1931	Par.
Disraeli	1921	UA
A Doctor's Diary	1937	Par.
Double Door	1934	Par.
The Eagle and the Hawk	1933	Par.
Evenings for Sale	1932	Par.
The Fleet's In	1928	Par.
The Gang Buster	1931	Par.
Grand Jury Secrets	1939	Par.
The Green Goddess	1923	Gold.
Her Bodyguard *	1933	Par.
Her Code of Honor	1919	US
Her Wedding Night	1930	Par.
The Hidden Code	1920	US
His Tiger Lady	1928	Par.
Honeymoon Hate	1927	Par.
The Humming Bird	1924	Par.
Illusion	1929	Par.
John Meade's Woman	1937	Par.

The Jungle Princess	1936	Par.
King of Alcatraz	1938	Par.
King of Gamblers	1937	Par.
Ladies Love Brutes	1930	Par.
Lady and Gent	1932	Par.
The Last Train From Madrid	1937	Par.
Life's Shop Window	1914	US
Limehouse Blues	1935	Par.
Love and Learn	1928	Par.
Man From Beyond *	1922	US
The Man From Wyoming	1930	Par.
Man Who Played God	1922	UA
Manhattan Cocktail	1928	Par.
Mark of the Beast	1923	US
Million Dollar Legs	1939	Par.
Millions in the Air	1935	Par.
Monsieur Beaucaire	1924	Par.
My American Wife	1936	Par.
The Mysterious Dr. Fu Manchu	1929	Par.
Mystery Sea Raider *	1940	Par.
A Night of Mystery	1928	Par.
A Night of Mystery	1937	Par.
No More Women	1934	Par.
Nobody	1921	US
Now and Forever	1934	Par.
Only the Brave	1930	Par.
Paramount On Parade	1930	Par.
Parole Fixer *	1940	Par.
Persons In Hiding	1939	Par.
Prison Farm	1938	Par.
The Ruling Passion	1922	UA
A Sainted Devil	1924	Par.
Sally of the Sawdust *	1925	UA
The Saturday Night Kid	1929	Par.
The Search for Beauty	1934	Par.
The Secret Hour	1928	Par.
Serenade	1927	Par.
The Sorrows of Satan *	1926	Par.
The Spoilers	1930	Par.
Stolen Harmony	1935	Par.
The Street of Sin *	1928	Par.
Suspicious Wives	1921	US
Television Spy	1939	Par.
Terror Abroad	1933	Par.
"That Royle Girl" *	1925	Par.
This Way, Please	1937	Par.
Three Cheers for Love	1936	Par.
Timothy's Quest	1936	Par.
The Trumpet Blows	1934	Par.
$20 a Week	1924	Selz.
Two-Fisted	1935	Par.

Unmarried	1939	Par.
White Woman	1933	Par.
Woman's Man	1920	US
World At Her Feet	1927	Par.

181. GUNNAR FISCHER (1910-   )

Aunt Green, Aunt Brown and Aunt Lilac	1948	Swed.
Black Palm Tree	1968	Swed.
Bom, the Sailor	1949	Swed.
The Boy in the Tree	1962	Swed.
The Castle Is Swinging	1959	Swed.
The Devil's Eye	1960	Swed.
Don't Give Up	1948	Swed.
The End of Day	1958	Swed.
The Face	1958	Swed.
491	1964	Swed.
Hamnstad	1948	Swed.
Harbor City	1948	Swed.
Made in Sweden	1969	Swed.
The Magician	1959	Swed.
Ola and Julie	1967	Swed.
Port of Call	1963	Swed.
The Rainbow Dilemma	1958	Swed.
Secrets of Women	1961	Swed.
The Seventh Seal	1957	Swed.
Short Is the Summer	1968	Swed.
Smiles of a Summer Night	1955	Swed.
Soldier's Reminder	1947	Swed.
Sr	1956	Swed.
Summer Interlude *	1950	Swed.
Summer Play	1951	Swed.
Summer With Monika	1952	Swed.
Thirst	1950	Swed.
Towards Joy	1971	Swed.
Two Living, One Dead	1964	GB/Swed.
Wild Strawberries	1957	Swed.
Women Waiting	1958	Swed.

182. GERRY FISHER (1926-   )

Accident	1967	GB
Aces High *	1976	GB--EMI
Adventure of Sherlock Holmes' Smarter Brother	1975	GB--TCF
Amazing Mr. Blunden	1972	GB
Amsterdam Affair	1968	GB
Bequest to the Nation	1973	GB--Univ.

Better Late Than Never *	1983	WB
Black Rainbow	1989	GB
Blind Terror	1971	GB--Col.
Brannigan	1975	GB--UA
Butley	1973	GB--US
Dead Bang	1989	WB
A Doll's House	1973	Fr./GB
Don Giovanni	1979	Fr./Ger./It.
The Exorcist III	1990	TCF
Fedora	1978	Fr./Ger.
The Fourth War	1990	US
The Go-Between	1970	GB--EMI
Hamlet	1969	GB--Col.
Highlander	1986	TCF
The Holcroft Covenant	1985	GB--Col./EMI
		WB
Interlude	1968	GB--Col.
The Island of Dr. Moreau	1977	AIP
Juggernaut	1974	GB--UA
The Last Remake of Beau Geste	1977	Univ.
Lovesick	1983	WB/US
Macho Callahan	1970	Avco
Malpertius	1972	Belg./Fr.
Man and the Snake	1972	GB
Man in the Wilderness	1971	WB
Man On Fire	1987	Tri-S.
The Mikado	1967	GB
Mr. Klein	1976	Fr./It.
Ned Kelly	1970	GB--UA
The Ninth Configuration	1980	Lor.
The Offence	1972	GB--UA
Roads of the South	1978	Fr.
The Romantic Englishwoman	1975	GB
Running On Empty	1988	WB
The Sea Gull	1968	GB--WB
Sebastian	1968	GB--Par.
Secret Ceremony	1969	GB--Univ.
S*P*Y*S	1974	GB
Twinkle Twinkle "Killer" Kane	1980	US
Victory	1981	Lor.
Wise Blood	1980	US
Wolfen *	1981	WB
Words To Say It	1983	Fr.

183. ROSS FISHER

After the Ball	1924	US
All Around Frying Pan	1925	US
The Bandit's Baby	1925	US
The Danger Point	1922	US

The Dangerous Coward	1924	Mon.
Desert Blossoms	1921	Fox
The Devil's Saddle	1927	FN
Don Mike	1927	US
Easy Money	1925	US
Fantasma Del Convento	1934	Mex.
The Fear Fighter	1925	US
The Fighting Sap	1924	Mon.
Galloping Gallagher	1924	Mon.
Geared to Go	1924	US
Girl in the Taxi	1921	FN
Going Up	1923	US
The Greatest Menace	1923	US
Hands Across the Border	1926	US
Honeymoon Flats	1928	Univ.
In the Name of the Law	1922	US
It Can Be Done	1929	Univ.
Keeping Up With Lizzie	1921	US
The Lamb and the Lion *	1919	US
Lavender and Old Lace	1921	US
Les Miserables	1944	Mex.
Lightning Romance	1924	US
Lone Hand Saunders	1926	US
Lotus Blossom	1921	US
Love Call	1919	US
The Mailman	1923	US
The Mask of Lopez	1924	Mon.
North of Nevada	1924	Mon.
On Your Toes	1927	Univ.
One Mad Kiss *	1930	Fox
One Man in a Million	1921	US
Passion's Pathway	1924	US
Phantom Express	1932	US
Prisoners of Love *	1921	Gold.
The Red Raiders	1927	FN
A Regular Scout	1926	US
Ridin' the Wind	1925	Mon.
Robes of Sin	1924	US
The Royal American	1927	US
The Shield of Honor	1927	Univ.
The Silent Stranger	1924	Mon.
The Snob Buster	1925	US
The Spirit of the U.S.A. *	1924	US
Sunset Derby	1927	FN
That Devil Quemado	1925	US
Thundering Hoofs	1924	Mon.
The Tough Guy	1926	US
Twin Beds	1920	FN
Two-Gun Man *	1926	US
The Veiled Woman	1922	US
Westbound Limited	1923	US

The Wild Bull's Lair	1925	US
Youth Gamble	1925	US

184. VICTOR FLEMING (1883-1949)

The Americano	1917	US
American Aristocracy	1916	US
Betty of Greystone	1916	US
Down to Earth	1917	US
The Good Bad-Man	1916	US
The Habit of Happiness	1916	US
The Half Breed	1916	US
His Majesty the American *	1919	UA
His Picture in the Papers *	1916	US
In Again-Out Again	1917	US
The Man From Painted Post *	1917	US
Manhattan Madness	1916	US
A Modern Musketeer *	1918	US
Mystery of the Leaping Fish *	1916	US
Reaching for the Moon *	1917	US
Wild and Wooly	1917	US

185. GEORGE FOLSEY (1900-1988)

Adam's Rib	1949	MGM
All the Brothers Were Valiant	1953	MGM
American Beauty	1927	FN
Andy Hardy's Double Life *	1942	MGM
Animal Crackers	1930	Par.
The Animal Kingdom *	1932	RKO
Applause	1929	Par.
Arsene Lupin Returns	1938	MGM
The Balcony	1963	US
The Big Broadcast	1932	Par.
The Big Hangover	1950	MGM
The Big Pond	1930	Par.
Born Rich	1924	FN
The Bride Wore Red	1937	MGM
The Bright Shawl	1923	FN
The Butter and Egg Man	1928	FN
The Case of Becky	1921	Par.
Cash McCall	1959	WB
Chained	1934	MGM
The Cheat	1931	Par.
The Clock	1945	MGM
The Cobweb	1955	MGM
The Cocoanuts	1929	Par.
Count Your Blessings *	1959	MGM
Dangerous Nan McGrew	1930	Par.

Deep In My Heart	1954	MGM
Dr. Gillespie's New Assistant	1942	MGM
Dr. Kildare's Wedding Day	1942	MGM
The Education of Elizabeth	1921	Par.
The Enchanted Cottage	1924	FN
Executive Suite	1954	MGM
Fast and Loose	1939	MGM
The Fastest Gun Alive	1956	MGM
The Fear Market	1920	US
The Fighting Blade	1923	FN
Forbidden Planet	1956	MGM
Forsaking All Others *	1934	MGM
Free and Easy *	1941	MGM
The Frisky Mrs. Johnson	1920	Par.
Game Chicken	1922	Par.
Gentlemen of the Press	1929	Par.
Glorifying the American Girl	1929	Par.
Going Hollywood	1933	MGM
The Gorgeous Hussy	1936	MGM
Grand Central Murder	1942	MGM
The Great Sinner	1949	MGM
The Great Ziegfeld *	1936	MGM
Green Dolphin Street	1947	MGM
The Green Years	1946	MGM
A Guy Named Joe *	1944	MGM
The Half-Way Girl	1925	FN
The Harvey Girls *	1946	MGM
A Heart to Let	1921	US
Hearts Divided	1936	WB
Her Wild Oat	1927	FN
The High Cost of Loving	1958	MGM
His Bridal Night *	1919	US
Hit the Deck	1955	MGM
Hold That Kiss	1938	MGM
The Hole in the Wall	1929	Par.
Honor Among Lovers	1931	Par.
House of Numbers	1957	MGM
I Live My Life	1935	MGM
I Passed for White	1960	AA
If Winter Comes	1948	MGM
Imitation General	1958	MGM
Kind Lady	1935	MGM
Ladies at Play	1926	FN
Lady Be Good	1928	FN
Lady Be Good *	1941	MGM
Lady of the Tropics	1939	MGM
The Last of Mrs. Cheyney	1937	MGM
The Laughing Lady	1929	Par.
Laughter	1930	Par.
The Law and the Lady	1951	MGM
The Letter	1929	Par.

A Life of Her Own	1950	MGM
Lovely to Look At	1952	MGM
Malaya	1949	MGM
The Man With a Cloak	1951	MGM
Mannequin	1937	MGM
Married Bachelor	1941	MGM
Meet Me in St. Louis	1944	MGM
Men in White	1934	MGM
Men Must Fight	1933	MGM
Men of the Fighting Lady	1954	MGM
Misleading Lady	1932	Par.
Million Dollar Mermaid	1952	MGM
Mr. Imperium	1951	MGM
My Sin	1931	Par.
Nancy From Nowhere	1922	Par.
Naughty But Nice	1927	FN
The Necessary Evil	1925	FN
Night Into Morning	1951	MGM
No Place to Go	1927	FN
Operator 13	1933	MGM
Orchids and Ermine	1927	FN
Page Miss Glory	1935	WB
Panama Hattie	1942	MGM
The Power and the Prize	1956	MGM
The Price of Possession	1921	Par.
Radio-Mania	1923	US
Reckless	1935	MGM
Remember?	1939	MGM
Reunion in Vienna	1933	MGM
Rio Rita	1942	MGM
Room and Board	1921	Par.
The Royal Family of Broadway	1930	Par.
Saddle the Wind	1958	MGM
The Savage	1926	FN
Scarlet Saint	1925	FN
The Secret Heart	1946	MGM
See You in Jail	1927	FN
Seven Brides for Seven Brothers	1954	MGM
Seven Sweethearts	1942	MGM
Shadow in the Sky	1951	MGM
Sheltered Daughters	1921	US
The Shining Hour	1938	MGM
Sinners	1920	US
Slim Shoulders	1922	US
The Smiling Lieutenant	1931	Par.
Society Lawyer	1939	MGM
Stage Mother	1939	MGM
State of the Union	1948	MGM
Stolen Heaven	1931	Par.
The Stolen Kiss	1926	US
Storm at Daybreak	1932	MGM

Take Me Out to the Ball Game	1949	MGM
Tennessee Champ	1954	MGM
These Wilder Years	1956	MGM
Third Finger Left Hand	1940	MGM
Thousands Cheer	1943	MGM
Three Hearts for Julia	1943	MGM
Till the Clouds Roll By *	1946	MGM
Tip On a Dead Jockey	1957	MGM
Too Much Money	1926	FN
Torpedo Run	1958	MGM
Trial of Mary Dugan	1941	MGM
Twenty-One	1923	FN
Two Girls on Broadway	1940	MGM
Vengeance Valley	1951	MGM
What's Wrong With the Women?	1922	US
White Cliffs of Dover	1944	MGM
Ziegfeld Follies *	1944	MGM

186. HARRY FORBES

Big Time or Bust	1934	US
Dangerous Waters	1936	Univ.
Daring Daughters	1933	US
Death Goes North	1939	US
Federal Agent	1936	Rep.
Fury and the Woman	1937	US
Headleys at Home	1939	US
The Important Witness	1933	US
Keep Going	1926	US
The Little Terror	1917	US
Marrying Widows	1934	US
The Raggedy Queen	1917	US
Riley of the Rainbow Division	1928	US
Sins of the Children *	1918	US
Tarnished Reputations *	1920	Pathe
Thunder Over Texas	1934	US
Together	1918	US
The Victory of Virtue	1915	US
What Price Crime?	1935	US
What Price Vengeance? *	1937	US
Woman Against the World *	1938	Col.

187. WILLIAM C. FOSTER

American Methods	1917	Fox
The Blindness of Divorce	1918	Fox
The Corsican Brothers *	1920	US
The Heart of a Lion	1918	Fox
Les Miserables	1918	Fox

The Man Hunter	1919	Fox
The Man Who Turned White	1919	US
Oliver Twist, Jr.	1921	Fox
The Price of Silence	1917	Fox
The Rainbow Trail	1918	Fox
Riders of the Purple Sage	1918	Fox
The Silver Horde	1920	Gold.
Sins of Her Parent	1916	Fox
A Tale of Two Cities	1917	Fox
To Please One Woman	1920	Par.
Too Wise Wives	1921	Par.
True Blue	1918	Fox
What's Worth While	1921	Par.
When Dawn Came	1920	US
A Woman of Pleasure	1919	Pathe

188. HARRY FOWLER

Crooked Alley	1923	Univ.
The Cub Reporter	1922	US
The Freeze Out	1921	Univ.
Hearts Up!	1920	Univ.
Her Sacrifice *	1926	US
"If Only" Jim	1921	Univ.
Men in the Raw *	1923	Univ.
Shadows of the North	1923	Univ.
Sundown Slim	1920	Univ.
Taking Chances	1922	US
Tarzan of the Apes *	1918	US
Tipped Off	1923	US
The Unknown	1921	US
The Wallop	1921	Univ.
West Is West	1920	Univ.
Wildcat Jordan	1922	US

189. WILLIAM A. FRAKER (1923-   )

Aloha Bobby and Rose	1975	WB
American Hot Wax	1978	Par.
Baby Boom	1987	MGM-UA
The Best Little Whorehouse in Texas	1982	Univ./RKO
Bullitt	1968	WB
Burglar	1987	WB
Chances Are	1989	Tri-S.
Coonskin	1975	US
The Day of the Dolphin	1973	AE
Divine Madness	1980	Ladd/WB
Dusty and Sweets McGee	1971	WB
Exorcist II; The Heretic	1977	WB

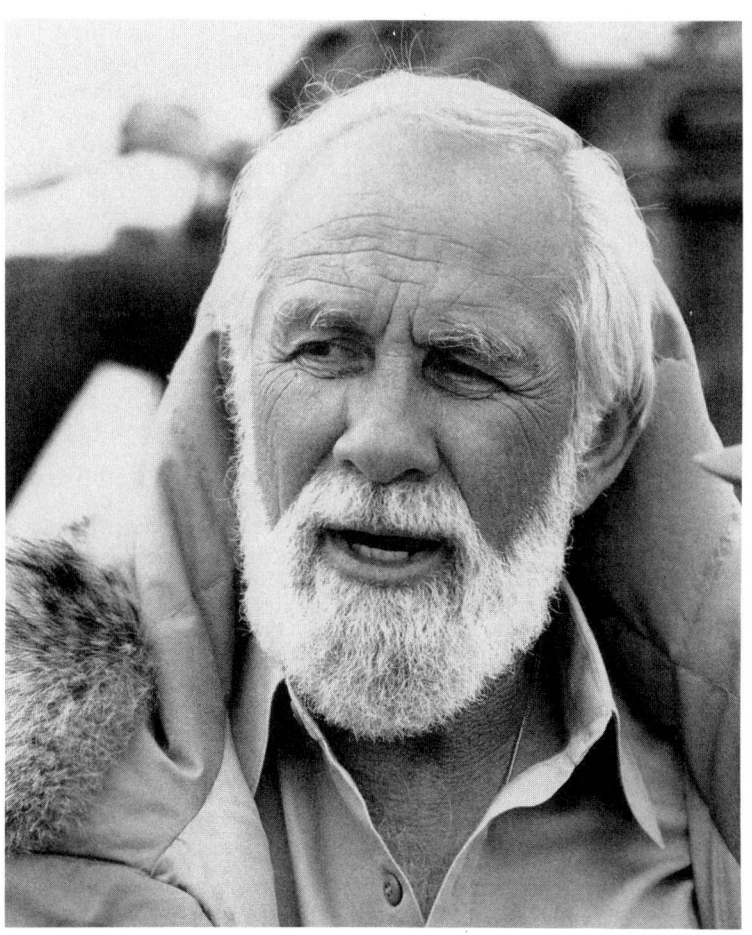

William A. Fraker (ca. 1981).

Fever Pitch	1985	MGM-UA
The Fox	1967	WB
The Freshman	1990	Tri-S.
Games	1967	Univ.
Gator	1976	UA
Heaven Can Wait	1978	Par.
The Hollywood Knights	1980	Col.
An Innocent Man	1989	BV
The Killer Inside Me	1976	WB
Lipstick *	1976	Par.
Looking for Mr. Goodbar	1977	Par.
Murphy's Romance	1985	Col.
1941	1979	Col./Univ.
Old Boyfriends	1979	AE
Paint Your Wagon	1969	Par.
The President's Analyst	1967	Par.
Rosemary's Baby	1968	Par.
Sharky's Machine	1981	Orion/WB
Spacecamp	1986	TCF
War Games	1983	MGM-UA

190.   FREDDIE FRANCIS (1917-   )

Battle of the Sexes	1960	GB
Brenda Starr	1989	US
Clara's Heart	1988	WB
Code Name: Emerald	1985	MGM-UA/NBC
Elephant Man	1980	EMI
The French Lieutenant's Woman	1981	GB--UA
The Golden Salamander *	1949	GB
Glory	1989	Tri-S.
Her Alibi	1989	WB
A Hill in Korea	1956	GB
The Innocents	1961	GB--TCF
Memed My Hawk	1984	GB
Never Take Sweets From a Stranger	1960	GB--Col.
Next to No Time	1958	GB
Night Must Fall	1964	GB--MGM
Room at the Top	1958	GB
Saturday Night and Sunday Morning	1960	GB
The Small Back Room *	1949	GB
Time Without Pity	1957	GB
Virgin Island	1958	GB

191.   ELLSWORTH FREDERICKS

At Gunpoint	1955	AA
The Bob Mathias Story	1954	AA
Buckskin Lady	1957	UA

Canyon River	1956	AA
Charro!	1969	NG
Dial Red O	1955	AA
Dig That Uranium	1956	AA
Escape From Zahrain	1961	Par.
Eye of the Cat *	1969	Univ.
Friendly Persuasion	1956	AA
High Time	1960	TCF
Hold Back the Night	1956	AA
Invasion of the Body Snatchers	1956	AA
Joy in the Morning	1956	MGM
The Last Challenge	1967	MGM
Last of the Badmen	1957	AA
The Light in the Forest	1958	Dis.
Maracaibo	1958	Par.
Mr. Buddwing	1966	MGM
The Pad and How to Use It	1966	Univ.
Picture Mommy Dead	1966	Emb.
The Power	1967	MGM
Sanctuary	1960	TCF
Sayonara	1957	WB
Seven Angry Men	1955	AA
Seven Days In May	1964	Par.
Shotgun	1955	AA
So Big	1953	WB
The Stripper	1963	TCF
Sudden Danger	1955	AA
Tall Story	1960	WB
Trooper Hook	1957	UA
Where Were You When the Lights Went Out?	1968	MGM
Wild River	1960	TCF
With Six You Get Egg Roll *	1968	NG
World Without End	1956	AA

192. HENRY FREULICH

Adventure in Manhattan	1936	Col.
Adventures in Silverado	1948	Col.
Air Hawks	1935	Col.
Ambush at Tomahawk Gap	1953	Col.
And So They Were Married	1935	Col.
Atlantic Convoy	1943	Col.
Battle of Rogue River	1954	Col.
Behind the Evidence	1935	Col.
Beware of Blondie *	1950	Col.
Black Eagle	1948	Col.
Blondie	1938	Col.
Blondie Brings Up Baby	1939	Col.
Blondie For Victory	1942	Col.

Blondie Goes Latin	1941	Col.
Blondie Goes to College	1942	Col.
Blondie Has Servant Trouble	1940	Col.
Blondie in Society	1941	Col.
Blondie Meets the Boss	1939	Col.
Blondie On a Budget	1940	Col.
Blondie Plays Cupid	1940	Col.
Blondie Takes a Vacation	1939	Col.
Blondie's Blessed Event	1942	Col.
Bodyhold *	1949	Col.
Bonanza Town	1951	Col.
The Boogie Man Will Get You	1942	Col.
Boston Blackie Goes Hollywood	1942	Col.
Bunco Squad	1950	RKO
Cannibal Attack	1954	Col.
Charge of the Lancers	1953	Col.
Chicago Syndicate	1955	Col.
Chinatown at Midnight	1949	Col.
Come Closer, Folks	1936	Col.
Conquest of Cochise	1953	Col.
Corky of Gasoline Alley	1951	Col.
Counsel for Crime	1937	Col.
The Crooked Web	1955	Col.
Cyclone Fury	1951	Col.
The Devil's Henchmen	1949	Col.
The Devil's Mask	1946	Col.
Don't Gamble With Love	1936	Col.
Duel on the Mississippi	1955	Col.
El Alamein	1953	Col.
First Offenders	1939	Col.
Five Little Peppers	1939	Col.
Five Little Peppers and How They Grew	1939	Col.
Flame of Calcutta *	1953	Col.
Footlights and Fools *	1929	FN
Fort Savage Raiders	1951	Col.
Girls' School	1950	Col.
Go West, Young Lady	1940	Col.
Good Day for a Hanging	1959	Col.
Good Girls Go to Paris	1939	Col.
Grand Exit	1935	Col.
The Gun That Won the West	1955	Col.
The Hard Man	1957	Col.
He Laughed Last	1956	Col.
Hell-Ship Morgan	1936	Col.
Hello God *	1951	It.--US
The Houston Story	1956	Col.
I Am the Law	1938	Col.
Inside Detroit	1955	Col.
The Iroquois Trail	1950	UA
It Came From Beneath the Sea	1955	Col.
It's All Yours	1938	Col.

It's Great To Be Young	1946	Col.
Jack McCall, Desperado	1952	Col.
Junction City	1952	Col.
Jungle Man-Eaters	1954	Col.
Kazan	1949	Col.
The Lady and the Bandit	1951	Col.
Lady From Nowhere	1936	Col.
Last Train From Bombay	1952	Col.
Law of the Barbary Coast	1949	Col.
The Law vs. Billy the Kid	1954	Col.
The League of Frightened Men	1937	Col.
Leather Gloves	1948	Col.
Let's Get Married	1937	Col.
The Little Adventuress	1938	Col.
Lone Wolf in London	1947	Col.
Lone Wolf Meets a Lady	1940	Col.
Lone Wolf Returns	1935	Col.
Lone Wolf Strikes	1940	Col.
Make Believe Ballroom	1949	Col.
Masterson of Kansas	1955	Col.
Meet Nero Wolfe	1936	Col.
Meet the Stewarts	1942	Col.
Men of the Night	1934	Col.
The Miami Story	1954	Col.
Montana Territory	1952	Col.
More Than a Secretary	1936	Col.
Murder in Greenwich Village	1937	Col.
My True Story	1951	Col.
The Nebraskan	1953	Col.
New Orleans Uncensored	1955	Col.
No Time To Be Young	1957	Col.
Not Wanted	1949	US
Okinawa	1952	Col.
One Way Ticket	1935	Col.
Over-Exposed	1956	Col.
The Pathfinder	1953	Col.
Personality Kid	1946	Col.
The Phantom Stagecoach	1957	Col.
Pirates of Tripoli	1953	Col.
Prison Warden	1949	Col.
Prisoners of the Casbah	1953	Col.
Reprisal!	1956	Col.
Return to Warbow	1958	Col.
Rusty Saves a Life	1949	Col.
Rusty's Birthday	1949	Col.
The Saracen Blade	1954	Col.
The Secret of St. Ives	1949	Col.
Seminole Uprising	1955	Col.
Serpent of the Nile	1953	Col.
Shakedown	1936	Col.
She Knew All the Answers	1941	Col.

Shut My Big Mouth	1942	Col.
Siren of Bagdad	1953	Col.
Slaves of Babylon	1953	Col.
Smiling Irish Eyes *	1929	FN
Son of Dr. Jekyll	1951	Col.
Song of India	1949	Col.
Sport of Kings	1947	Col.
Talk About a Lady	1946	Col.
Tarawa Beachhead	1958	Col.
Target Hong Kong	1952	Col.
The Tender Years	1947	TCF
Teen-Age Crime Wave	1955	Col.
That's Gratitude	1934	Col.
There's Always a Woman	1938	Col.
Thunderhoof	1948	Col.
Tillie the Toiler	1941	Col.
27th Day	1957	Col.
Under the Gun	1950	Univ.
The Unknown	1946	Col.
Unknown Woman	1935	Col.
Unknown World *	1951	Lip.
The Vicious Years	1950	US
When G Men Step In	1938	Col.
White Squaw	1956	Col.
Who Killed Gail Preston?	1938	Col.
Woman From Tangier	1947	Col.
Women of Glamour *	1937	Col.

193. KARL FREUND (1890-1969)

Air Mail	1932	Univ.
Back Street	1932	Univ.
Bad Sister	1931	Univ.
Balalaika *	1939	MGM
Barricade	1939	TCF
Blossoms in the Dust *	1941	MGM
The Boudoir Diplomat	1930	Univ.
Der Brennende Acker *	1922	Ger.
Bright Leaf	1950	WB
The Chocolate Soldier	1941	MGM
Conquest	1937	MGM
Cry Havoc	1943	MGM
Dangerous Partners	1945	MGM
The Decision of Christopher Blake	1948	WB
Dracula	1931	Univ.
DuBarry Was a Lady	1943	MGM
Faust *	1924	Ger.
Florian	1940	MGM
Golden Boy *	1939	Col.
Golem *	1920	Ger.

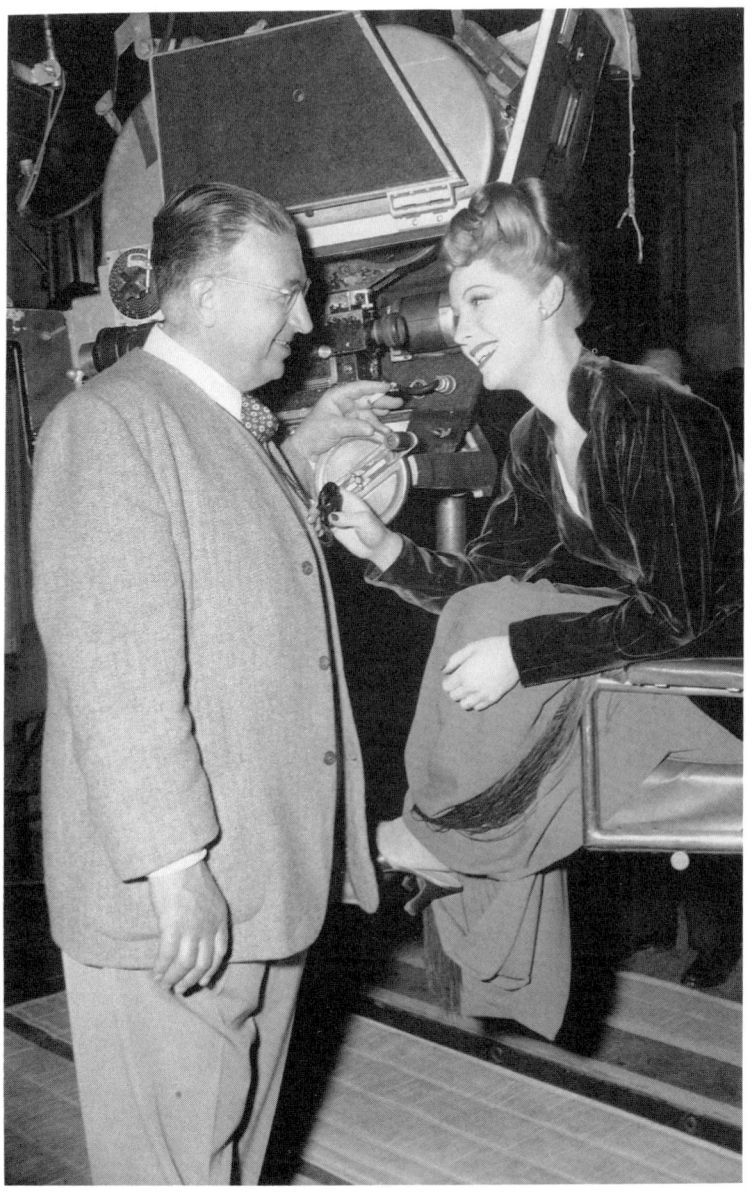

Karl Freund with Signe Hasso on the Set of <u>Dangerous Partners</u> (1945).

The Good Earth	1937	MGM
Green Hell	1940	Univ.
A Guy Named Joe *	1944	MGM
Keeping Company	1940	MGM
Key Largo	1948	WB
The Kiss Before the Mirror	1933	Univ.
The Last Laugh	1925	Ger.--UFA
Letter for Evie	1945	MGM
Man Proof	1938	MGM
Metropolis *	1927	Ger.--UFA
Missing Daughters	1939	Col.
Montana	1950	WB
Murders in the Rue Morgue	1932	Univ.
Parnell	1937	MGM
Personal Maid	1931	Par.
Port of Seven Seas	1938	MGM
Pride and Prejudice	1940	MGM
Rose of Washington Square	1939	TCF
Scandal for Sale	1932	Univ.
The Seventh Cross	1944	MGM
Sleeping Partners	1930	Par.
South of St. Louis	1948	WB
Die Spinnen *	1919	Ger.
Tail Spin	1938	TCF
Tartuffe	1925	Ger.
That Hagen GIrl	1947	WB
Thin Man Goes Home	1944	MGM
This Time For Keeps	1947	MGM
Two Smart People	1946	MGM
Undercurrent	1946	MGM
Up for Murder	1931	Univ.
Variety	1926	Ger.--UFA
Verlorene Moral	1921	Ger.
Wallflower	1948	WB
The War Against Mrs. Hadley	1942	MGM
We Who Are Young	1940	MGM
Without Love	1945	MGM
A Yank at Eton	1942	MGM

194. ABE FRIED (1898-1930)

Bertha, the Sewing Machine Girl	1926	Fox
The Brute	1927	WB
The Country Beyond	1926	Fox
The Good-Bad Wife	1921	US
His Forgotten Wife	1924	US
Man and Woman	1920	US
The Man From Hell's River	1922	US
The Midnight Kiss	1926	Fox
The Phantom Express *	1925	US

Rustling for Cupid	1926	Fox
The Silent Guardian	1926	US
The Tents of Allah *	1923	US
With This Ring	1925	US
The Woman Who Fooled Herself *	1922	US
Wreckage *	1925	US

195.   CLAUDE FRIESE-GREENE

Banana Ridge	1941	GB
Black Limelight	1938	GB
Drake of England	1935	GB
East of Piccadilly	1940	GB
Elstree Calling	1930	GB
The Farmer's Wife	1940	GB
The Flying Fool	1931	GB
The Gang's All Here	1939	GB
Give Her a Ring *	1934	GB
Great Mr. Handel *	1942	GB--Rank
The Greenwood Tree	1930	GB
Gypsy Melody	1936	GB
Hard Steel	1942	GB
House of Mystery	1939	GB
I Give My Heart	1935	GB
Jane Steps Out	1938	GB
Just Like a Woman	1938	GB
Loose Ends	1930	GB
Love Storm	1931	GB
Loves of Madame DuBarry	1938	GB
The Middle Watch *	1930	GB
Murder in Soho	1939	GB
Music Hath Charms *	1935	GB
My Wife's Family	1931	GB
No Monkey Business	1935	GB
The Old Curiosity Shop	1934	GB
On Approval	1943	GB
Our Fighting Navy	1937	GB
Public Nuisance No. 1	1936	GB
Saint in London	1939	RKO
Star of the Circus	1938	GB
Uneasy Virtue	1931	GB
The Yellow Mask	1930	GB
Young Woodley	1929	GB

196.   RICHARD FRYER

America *	1914	US
Bucking the Truth	1926	Univ.
The Clean Up	1923	Univ.

For You My Boy	1923	US
Forbidden Love *	1921	US
His Daughter Pays	1918	US
Legally Dead	1923	Univ.
The Miracle of Money	1920	Pathe
Swing It Sailor	1937	GN

197. TAK FUJIMOTO

Backfire	1987	US
Badlands *	1973	Col.
Blackout	1985	US
Bootleggers	1974	US
Borderline	1980	US
Cannonball	1976	US
Chatter-Box	1977	AIP
Crazy Mama *	1975	US
Death Race 2000	1975	US
Dr. Black and Mr. Hyde	1976	US
Ferris Bueller's Day Off	1986	Orion
Heart Like a Wheel *	1984	TCF/US
Last Embrace	1979	UA
Married to the Mob	1988	Orion
Melvin and Howard	1980	Univ.
Miami Blues	1990	Orion
My Main Man From Stoney Island	1981	US
Pretty in Pink	1986	Par.
Remember My Name	1978	US
Something Wild	1986	Orion
Stony Island	1978	US
Sweet Hearts Dance	1988	Tri-S.
Swing Shift	1984	WB
The Watts Monster	1979	US
Where The Buffalo Roam	1980	Univ.

198. JOHN P. FULTON

The Eyes of the World *	1930	US
Frontier Gal *	1945	Univ.
Hell Harbor *	1930	UA
In Society *	1944	Univ.
The Invisible Ray *	1936	Univ.
The Man I Marry *	1936	Univ.
The Merry Monahans *	1944	Univ.
Murder in the Blue Room	1944	Univ.
San Diego I Love You *	1944	Univ.
She Goes to War *	1929	US
Sutter's Gold *	1936	Univ.

199. JACK FUQUA

Ace of Cactus Range	1924	US
Before the White Man Came *	1920	US
Compassion	1927	US
King of the Herd	1927	US
The Love Pirate	1923	US
Peaceful Peters	1922	US
Phantom Justice	1924	US
Souls Aflame	1928	US

200. URS FURRER

Been Down So Long It Looks Like Up to Me	1971	Par.
Birch Interval	1976	US
Desperate Characters	1971	US
Playground	1965	US
The Seven-Ups	1973	TCF
Shaft	1971	MGM
Shaft's Big Score	1972	MGM
The Sidelong Glances of a Pigeon Kicker	1970	MGM
Sounder: * Part 2	1976	ABC
What Do You Say to a Naked Lady?	1970	UA
Where the Lilies Bloom	1974	UA

201. ALFRED GANDOLFI

After Five	1915	Par.
Bringing Up Betty	1919	US
Conceit	1921	Selz.
A Divorce of Convenience	1921	Selz.
The Grouch	1918	US
The Little Gypsy	1915	Fox
The Little Intruder	1919	US
Me and Captain Kidd	1919	US
The Oakdale Affair	1919	US
The Roughneck	1919	US
The Squaw Man	1914	FP
Thunderbolt	1919	FN
Trail of the Law	1924	US
The Viking *	1930	MGM
The Woman God Sent *	1920	Selz.

202. GLEN GANO

The Chorus Lady	1924	US

Flashing Fangs *	1926	US
Gold Fever *	1952	Mon.
A Guy, a Gal and a Pal	1945	Col.
The Isle of Retribution *	1926	US
The Silent Call *	1921	FN

203. FRANK GARBUTT

Experimental Marriage	1919	US
The Gypsy Trail	1918	Par.
Her Country First	1918	Par.
The Home Town Girl	1919	Par.
Huckleberry Finn	1920	Par.
An Innocent Adventuress	1919	Par.
Louisiana	1919	Par.
Mile a Minute Kendall	1918	Par.
Mirandy Smiles	1918	Par.
Poor Boob	1919	Par.
The Third Kiss	1919	Par.
Up the Road With Sallie	1918	US
You Never Saw Such a Girl	1919	Par.

204. LEE GARMES (1898-1978)

Abdulla the Great	1956	Egypt/GB
Actors and Sin	1953	UA
Adventures of a Young Man	1962	TCF
An American Tragedy	1931	Par.
Angels Over Broadway	1940	Col.
The Big Boodle	1957	UA
The Big Fisherman	1959	US
A Big Hand for the Little Lady	1966	WB
The Bottom of the Bottle	1956	TCF
Bright Lights	1930	WB
Call Her Savage	1932	Par.
The Captive City	1951	UA
The Carnival Girl	1926	US
Caught!	1948	US
China Girl	1943	TCF
City Streets	1931	Par.
Confessions of a Co-Ed	1931	Par.
Conquest of the Air *	1937	GB
Crack O' Dawn	1925	US
Crime Without Passion	1934	Par.
D-Day: The Sixth of June	1956	TCF
The Desperate Hours	1955	Par.
Detective Story	1951	Par.
Dishonored	1931	Par.
Disraeli	1929	WB

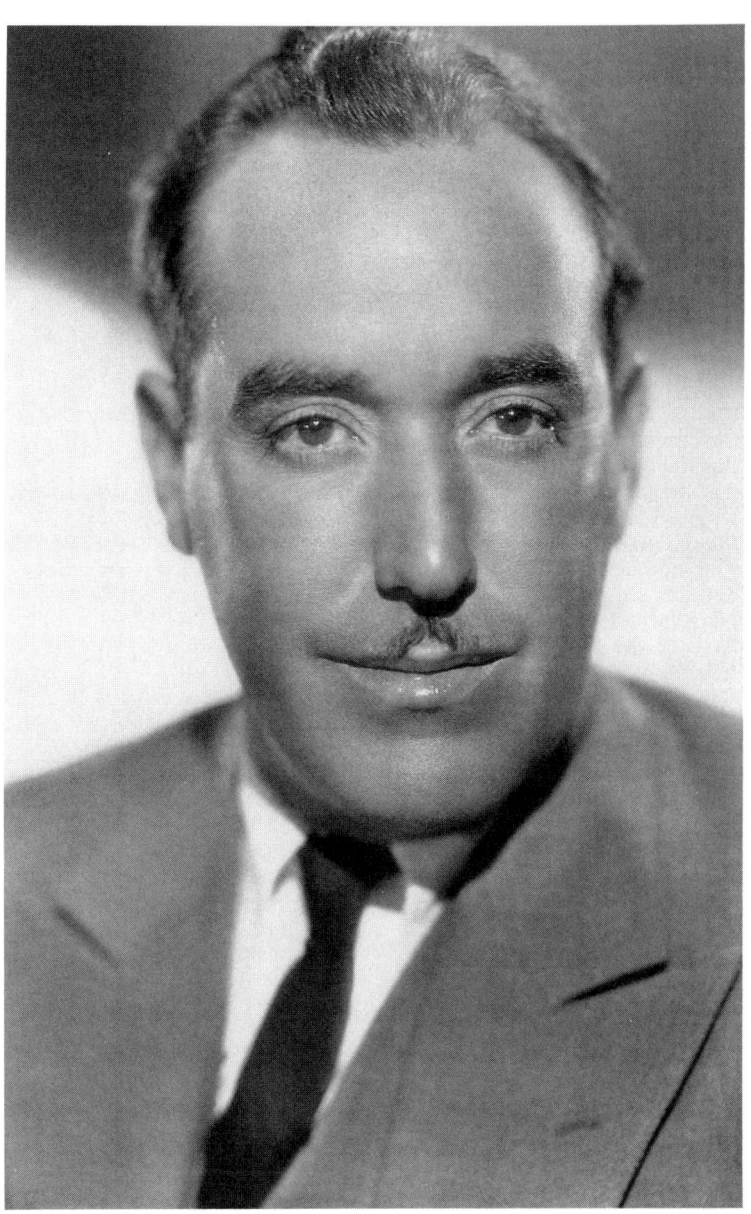

Lee Garmes (ca. 1931).

Dreaming Lips *	1937	GB
Duel in the Sun *	1946	Selz.
Face in the Sky	1933	Fox
Fighting Caravans *	1931	Par.
The Fighting Kentuckian	1949	Rep.
Find Your Man	1924	WB
Flight for Freedom	1943	RKO
Footlight Serenade	1942	TCF
Forever and a Day *	1943	RKO
The Garden of Allah *	1927	MGM
George White's Scandals *	1934	Fox
Goat Getter	1925	US
Gone With the Wind *	1939	MGM/Selz.
Grand Duchess and the Waiter	1926	Par.
The Great Divide	1929	FN
Guest in the House	1944	US
Hannah Lee	1953	US
Happy Anniversary	1959	UA
His Captive Woman	1929	WB
The Hope Chest *	1918	Par.
How to Save a Marriage and Ruin Your Life	1968	Col.
I Am Suzanne	1933	Fox
I'll Get Him Yet *	1919	Par.
The Jungle Book *	1942	Korda/UA
Keep Smiling *	1925	US
Lady in a Cage	1964	US
Land of the Pharaohs *	1955	WB
Lilies of the Field	1930	FN
The Little Shepherd of Kingdom Come	1928	FN
Love and the Devil	1929	FN
Love Letters	1945	Par.
The Love Mart	1927	FN
The Lusty Men	1952	RKO
Lydia	1941	GB--Korda
The Man with the Gun	1955	UA
Misty *	1961	TCF
Morocco	1930	Par.
My Foolish Heart	1949	Gold.
My Friend Irma Goes West	1950	Par.
My Lips Betray	1933	Fox
Never Love a Stranger	1958	AA
Nightmare Alley	1947	TCF
None Shall Escape	1944	Col.
Once In a Blue Moon	1936	Par.
The Other Tomorrow	1930	WB
Our Very Own	1950	Gold.
The Palm Beach Girl	1926	Par.
The Paradine Case	1947	Selz.
Paris Underground	1945	UA
The Popular Sin	1926	Par.

Prisoners	1929	FN/WB
Private Life of Helen of Troy *	1927	FN
Rose of the Golden West	1927	FN
Roseanna McCoy	1949	Gold.
Saturday's Hero	1951	Col.
Say It With Songs	1929	WB
Scarface *	1932	UA
The Scoundrel	1935	Par.
The Searching Wind	1946	Par.
The Secret Life of Walter Mitty	1947	Gold.
Shanghai Express	1932	Par.
Shanghai Madness	1933	Fox
The Sharkfighters	1956	UA
The Show Off	1926	Par.
Since You Went Away *	1944	Selz.
Smiling Through	1932	MGM
A Social Celebrity	1926	Par.
Song of the Flame	1930	FN/WB
The Specter of the Rose	1946	Rep.
Spring Is Here	1930	FN
Strange Interlude	1932	MGM
That's My Boy	1951	Par.
Thunder in the East	1951	Par.
Waterfront	1928	FN
Whoopee! *	1930	Gold.
The Yellow Lily	1928	FN
The Young Widow	1946	UA
Zoo in Budapest	1933	Fox

205. FREDERICK GATELY (1909-1988)

Badlands of Montana	1957	TCF
Harpoon	1948	US
I Bury the Living	1957	UA
The Naked Dawn	1956	Univ.
The Naked Hills	1956	AA
Tank Battalion	1958	AIP
Wicked Wicked	1973	MGM

206. MARCELLO GATTI

An American Wife *	1965	It.
The Anonymous Venetian	1970	It.--AA
The Assassin of Rome	1973	It.--Col.
The Battle of Algiers	1967	Alg./It.
The Black Belly of the Tarantula	1972	It.--MGM
Break Up	1978	It.
Burn!	1968	UA
Che?	1973	Fr./Ger./It.

Chronicle of the Years of Fire	1975	It.
Deceptions	1986	It.
The First Time on the Grass	1975	It.
Four Days in Naples	1962	It.--MGM
La Fuga	1966	It.--TCF
Love Factory	1969	It.
Massacre in Rome	1973	It.--NG
Moses	1976	GB/It.--AE
Ogro	1979	Fr./It./Sp.
The Penthouse	1963	It.--WB
The Protagonist	1968	It.
Run for Your Wife	1966	Fr./It.--AA
The Salamander	1983	GB/It.--US
Sierra Maestra	1969	It.
So Long Gulliver	1971	It.
The Strange Night	1967	It.
Summer Frenzy	1964	Fr./It.
Tall Women	1967	It.
Three Tigers Against Three Tigers *	1977	It.
What? *	1973	Fr./It.
What Did Stalin Do to Women?	1969	It.

207. EUGENE GAUDIO

The Brat	1919	Metro.
Eye for Eye	1918	Metro.
The House of Mirth	1918	Metro.
Kitty Kelly MD	1919	US
Life's Twist	1920	US
The Luck of Geraldine Laird	1920	US
The Man Who Stayed Home	1919	Metro.
The Red Lantern	1919	Metro.
The Shell Game	1918	Metro.
Social Hypocrites	1918	Metro.
Toys of Fate	1918	Metro.
20,000 Leagues Under the Sea *	1916	Univ.
The Uplifters	1919	Metro.
The White Terror	1915	Univ.

208. TONY GAUDIO (1885-1951)

Adam and Eva *	1923	Par.
The Adventures of Robin Hood *	1938	WB
An Affair of the Follies	1927	FN
Affectionately Yours	1941	WB
The Amazing Dr. Clitterhouse	1938	WB
Anthony Adverse	1936	WB
Another Dawn	1937	WB
Ashes of Vengeance	1923	FN

The Avenging Trail	1918	Metro.
Background to Danger	1943	WB
The Bandit of Sherwood Forest *	1946	Col.
Beckoning Roads	1920	US
Big Tremaine	1916	Metro.
The Blonde Saint	1926	FN
Blondie Johnson	1933	WB
Bordertown	1935	WB
Broadway Bill	1918	Metro.
Brother Orchid	1940	WB
Case of the Lucky Legs	1935	WB
Classmates	1914	US
The Constant Nymph	1943	WB
Corvette K-225	1943	Univ.
The Dawn Patrol	1938	WB
Days of Glory	1944	RKO
Declasse	1925	FN
Dr. Socrates	1935	WB
The Dragon Murder Case	1934	WB
East Is West	1922	FN
The Eternal Flame	1922	FN
Ex-Lady	1933	WB
Experiment Perilous	1944	RKO
The Fighting Shepherdess	1920	FN
The Fighting 69th	1940	WB
Fog Over Frisco	1934	WB
The Forbidden Thing	1920	US
Front Page Woman	1933	WB
Garden of the Moon	1938	WB
The Gaucho	1928	UA
The Gay Deceiver *	1926	MGM
General Crack	1930	WB
Go Into Your Dance *	1935	WB
God's Country and the Women	1936	WB
Graustark	1925	FN
The Great Lie	1941	WB
Happiness Ahead	1934	FN
The Haunted Pajamas	1917	Metro.
Hell's Angels *	1930	US
The Hidden Children	1917	Metro.
The Hidden Spring	1917	Metro.
High Sierra	1941	WB
Husbands and Lovers	1924	FN
I'll Be Seeing You	1944	Selz.
I've Always Loved You	1946	Rep.
In Old Kentucky	1920	FN
In Wrong	1919	FN
Th Inferior Sex	1920	FN
Juarez	1938	WB
Kid Galahad	1937	WB
The King and the Chorus Girl	1937	WB

Kismet *	1920	US
Knute Rockne, All American	1940	WB
Ladies Must Live	1933	WB
The Lady	1925	FN
Lady Killer	1933	WB
The Landloper	1918	Metro.
Larceny, Inc.	1942	WB
Lend Me Your Name	1918	Metro.
The Letter	1940	WB
The Life of Emile Zola	1937	WB
Little Big Shot	1935	WB
Little Caesar	1930	WB
Love From a Stranger	1947	EL
A Man of Honor	1919	Metro.
The Man Who Came to Dinner	1941	WB
The Man With Two Faces	1934	WB
Mandalay	1934	WB
The Mask of Fu Manchu	1932	MGM
The Masked Rider	1916	Metro.
Mister 44	1916	Metro.
Navy Blues	1941	WB
The Notorious Lady	1927	FN
Oil For the Lamps of China	1935	WB
The Old Maid	1939	FN/WB
On With the Show	1929	WB
The Only Woman	1924	FN
The Other Woman	1921	US
Out of the Fog	1919	Metro.
Pals First	1918	Metro.
Paradise Garden	1917	Metro.
Pidgin Island	1916	Metro.
Pilgrims of the Night	1921	US
Private Detective 62	1933	FN/WB
The Promise	1917	Metro.
The Racket	1928	Par.
The Red Pony	1949	Rep.
The River of Romance	1916	Metro.
Secrets	1924	FN
Shattered Idols	1922	FN
She Goes to War *	1929	UA
The Silk Express	1933	WB
The Sin of Martha Queed	1921	US
The Sisters	1938	WB
Sky Devils	1931	US
The Song of Love	1923	FN
A Song to Remember	1945	Col.
The Square Deceiver	1917	Metro.
The Story of Louis Pasteur	1936	WB
Swell Guy	1946	Univ.
The Temptress *	1926	MGM
Ten Dollar Raise	1921	US

That's My Man	1946	Rep.
Tiger Rose	1929	WB
Tiger Shark	1932	WB
Till We Meet Again	1939	WB
Torchy Blaine in Panama	1938	WB
Two Arabian Knights *	1927	UA
Under Handicap	1917	Metro.
The Unpardonable Sin	1919	US
Upstage	1926	MGM
Upperworld	1934	WB
The Voice From the Minaret *	1923	FN
Voltaire	1933	WB
We Are Not Alone	1939	WB
Whispering Devils	1920	US
The White Angel	1935	WB
The White Cockatoo	1935	WB
Wings for the Eagle	1942	WB
Within the Law	1923	FN
The Woman He Loved	1922	US
The Woman in Black	1914	Bio.
The World Changes	1933	WB
You Can't Escape Forever *	1942	WB

209. ROBERTO GERARDI

Arturo's Island	1962	It.--MGM
Bambole *	1965	It.--Col.
La Calda Vita	1967	It.
The Condemned of Altona	1962	TCF
Countersex *	1964	Fr./It.
The Defeated Victor	1959	It.
Detective Belli	1970	It.
Dick Smart 2/007	1966	It.
Drop Dead, My Love	1968	It.
Empty Canvas	1964	Fr./It.--Emb.
End of the Game *	1976	Ger./It.--TCF
Faustina	1968	It.
Fiasco in Milan	1963	Fr./It.
The Great War *	1959	Fr./It.
In Love, Every Pleasure Has Its Pain	1972	It./Yugo.
Lady Caliph	1971	Fr./It.
Ligabue	1978	It.
Madame	1961	Fr./It./Sp.
Mademoiselle Di Maupin	1966	Fr./It./Sp./ Yugo.
A Maiden for a Prince	1967	Fr./It.
Marriage Italian Style	1964	Fr./It.--Emb.
The Master and Margarita	1972	It./Yugo.
Murder on the Bridge	1975	Ger./It.--TCF
Mussolini: Last Days	1974	It.--Par.

A Rather Complicated Girl	1969	It.
Rita	1963	Fr./It.
This Kind of Love	1973	It.
3 Nights of Love *	1969	It.
Unexpected	1961	Fr./It.
Violent Breed	1985	It.
The Warm Life	1964	Fr./It.
The Wind's Anger	1971	It.

210. HENRY GERRARD

Along Came Youth	1930	Par.
Beggars of Life	1928	Par.
Blind Adventure	1933	RKO
Doomsday	1928	Par.
Dude Ranch	1931	Par.
Fighting Caravans *	1931	Par.
Follow Thru *	1930	Par.
The Fountain	1934	RKO
The Greene Murder Case	1929	Par.
His Private Life	1928	Par.
Honey	1930	Par.
Interference	1929	Par.
Ladies of the Mob	1928	Par.
The Little Minister	1934	RKO
Little Women	1933	RKO
The Magnificent Flirt	1928	Par.
The Man I Love	1929	Par.
Man of Two Worlds	1934	RKO
The Most Dangerous Game	1932	RKO
Of Human Bondage	1934	RKO
The Phantom of Crestwood	1932	RKO
Playboy of Paris	1930	Par.
Safety in Numbers	1930	Par.
Shootin' Irons	1927	Par.
Success at Any Price	1934	RKO
Thunderbolt	1929	Par.
The Vagabond King	1930	Par.
Wives Beware	1933	GB
Woman Trap	1929	Par.

211. MERRITT B. GERSTAD

Alias Jimmy Valentine	1928	MGM
As Good As Married	1937	Univ.
Beloved	1934	Univ.
A Certain Young Man	1928	MGM
Circus Rookies	1928	MGM
Conflict	1945	WB

Dangerous Innocence *	1925	MGM
The Daring Young Man	1935	Fox
Daybreak	1931	MGM
Devil-May-Care	1929	MGM
Eternally Yours	1939	US
Flying High	1931	MGM
Forbidden Hours	1928	MGM
Freaks	1932	MGM
The Galloping Ace	1924	Univ.
Gentleman's Fate	1931	MGM
Girls' Dormitory	1936	TCF
Goldie Gets Along	1933	RKO
The Great Lover	1931	MGM
Guilty Hands	1931	MGM
High Speed	1924	Univ.
The House Across the Bay	1940	US
I'm From Missouri	1939	Par.
The Ice Flood	1926	Univ.
Imitation of Life	1934	Univ.
A Lady to Love	1930	MGM
London After Midnight	1927	MGM
The Luckiest Girl in the World	1936	Univ.
The Mad Whirl	1925	Univ.
The Magnificent Brute	1936	Univ.
The Man From Wyoming	1924	Univ.
The Man Who Reclaimed His Head	1934	Univ.
A Man's Man	1929	MGM
Mockery	1927	MGM
Navy Blues	1929	MGM
Never The Twain Shall Meet	1931	MGM
A Night at the Opera	1935	MGM
Night World	1932	Univ.
Only Yesterday	1933	Univ.
Orchids to You	1935	Fox
Our Blushing Brides	1930	MGM
Payment Deferred	1932	MGM
Phantom Horseman	1924	Univ.
The Poor Simp *	1920	Selz.
Rhapsody in Blue *	1945	WB
The Road to Mandalay	1926	MGM
Seventh Heaven	1937	TCF
She Married an Artist	1938	Col.
Slightly Honorable	1940	UA
Social Register	1934	Col.
Strike Me Pink *	1936	Gold.
Tessie	1925	US
The Thirteenth Chair	1929	MGM
Those Three French Girls	1930	MGM
Tide of Empire	1929	MGM
Tom, Dick and Harry	1940	RKO
Under Oath	1922	Selz.

The Unknown	1927	MGM
Watch On the Rhine *	1943	WB
West of Broadway	1932	MGM
Winter Carnival	1939	UA
Wonder of Women	1929	MGM

212. HARRY W. GERSTED

Ali Baba and the Forty Thieves *	1918	Fox
Back to Yellow Jacket	1922	US
The Blue Bandanna	1919	US
The Broadway Cowboy	1920	Pathe
Chain Lightning	1922	US
The Danger Zone	1918	Fox
Fightin' Mad	1921	Metro.
Gambling In Souls	1919	Fox
The Girl With No Regrets	1919	Fox
The Innocent Cheat	1921	US
Jack and the Beanstalk *	1917	Fox
Legion of the Condemned	1928	Par.
The Parish Priest	1921	US
The Prince and Betty	1919	Pathe
The Rosary	1915	US
A Sage Brush Hamlet	1919	US
Salome *	1919	Fox
The Spoilers	1914	US
Women Men Love	1921	US

213. MAURY GERTSMAN

The All-American	1952	Univ.
Are You With It?	1948	Univ.
Back to God's Country	1953	Univ.
Behind the High Wall	1956	Univ.
Bengal Brigade	1954	Univ.
Blonde Alibi	1946	Univ.
Born To Be Loved	1959	Univ.
The Brute Man	1946	PRC
Cage of Evil	1960	UA
Cattle Drive	1951	Univ.
City Across the River	1949	Univ.
Commanche Territory	1950	Univ.
The Creature Walks Among Us *	1956	Univ.
Cuban Pete	1946	Univ.
Danger Woman	1946	Univ.
Double Crossbones	1950	Univ.
Dressed to Kill	1946	Univ.
Everything But the Truth	1956	Univ.
Five Guns to Tombstone	1961	UA

The Four Skulls of Jonathan Drake	1959	UA
Frenchie	1950	Univ.
Frontier Uprising	1961	UA
The Glass Web	1954	Univ.
The Golden Blade	1953	Univ.
The Great Sioux Uprising	1953	Univ.
Gun Duel in Durango	1957	UA
Gun Town	1946	Univ.
Gunfight in Abilene	1967	Univ.
Gunfighters of Abilen	1960	UA
House of Horrors	1946	Univ.
How To Make a Monster	1958	AIP
Inside Job	1946	Univ.
Inside the Mafia	1959	UA
Invisible Invaders	1959	UA
It Grows On Trees	1942	Univ.
I've Lived Before	1956	Univ.
Johnny Stool Pigeon	1949	Univ.
Jungle Captive *	1945	Univ.
Just Across the Street	1952	Univ.
Kelly and Me	1956	Univ.
The Lone Hand	1953	Univ.
Louisa	1950	Univ.
Ma and Pa Kettle	1949	Univ.
Ma and Pa Kettle at the Fair *	1952	Univ.
Meet Danny Wilson	1951	Univ.
Meet Me at the Fair	1952	Univ.
Monkey On My Back	1957	UA
Never Say Goodbye	1955	Univ.
One Desire	1955	Univ.
One Way Street	1950	Univ.
Pier 5, Havana	1959	UA
Police Dog Story	1961	UA
Rachel and the Stranger	1948	RKO
Rails Into Laramie	1954	Univ.
Raw Edge	1956	Univ.
Red Ball Express	1952	Univ.
Reunion in Reno	1951	Univ.
Riot in Juvenile Prison	1959	UA
Rogues' Regiment	1948	Univ.
She-Wolf of London	1946	Univ.
Singapore	1947	Univ.
Six Black Horses	1962	Univ.
Smuggler's Island	1951	Univ.
So This Is Paris	1955	Univ.
Son of Ali Baba	1952	Univ.
Song of the Sarong	1945	Univ.
South Sea Sinner	1950	Univ.
The Spoilers	1955	Univ.
Strange Confession	1945	Univ.
Tanganyika	1954	Univ.

Target Unknown	1951	Univ.
Terror oy Night	1946	Univ.
Three Came To Kill	1960	UA
Timbuktu	1959	US
Time Out of Mind	1947	Univ.
To Hell and Back	1955	Univ.
A Wave, a WAC and a Marine	1944	Mon.
World in My Corner	1955	Univ.
You Never Can Tell	1951	Univ.

214. EDWARD GHELLER

Bonds of Love	1919	Gold.
Broken Mask *	1928	US
The Cheerleader	1928	US
The Craving	1918	US
The Greater Profit	1921	US
Hearts and Spangles	1926	US
The Loves of Letty	1920	Gold.
My Old Dutch	1926	Univ.
One Week of Life	1919	Gold.
The Paliser Case	1920	Gold.
The Peace of Roaring River	1919	Gold.
The Salvation Hunters	1925	UA
The Unfoldment *	1922	US
The Woman On the Index	1920	Gold.

215. GERALD GIBBS

Alice in Wonderland *	1949	Fr./GB
At the Stroke of Nine	1957	GB
Black 13	1953	GB
Blue Murder at St. Trinian's	1957	GB
The Boys	1962	GB--Col.
Cover Girl Killer	1959	GB
Curse of the Voodoo	1965	GB
The Devil Doll	1963	GB
The Devil's Agent	1962	GB
Faithful City	1952	Isr.--RKO
Fortune Is a Woman	1957	GB--Col.
The Great British Train Robbery *	1966	Ger.
The Green Man	1956	GB
Hill 24 Doesn't Answer	1955	Isr.
Hostile Witness	1968	GB--UA
The Intimate Stranger	1956	GB
A Jolly Bad Fellow	1964	GB
The Leather Boys	1963	GB
Left, Right and Centre	1959	GB
Loyal Heart *	1946	GB

The Man Upstairs	1958	GB
No Orchids for Miss Blandish	1948	GB
Pardon My French	1951	UA
A Prize of Arms *	1962	GB
Pure Hell of St. Trinian's	1961	GB
Quatermass II	1957	GB
The Safecracker	1958	GB--MGM
The Second Mrs. Tanqueray	1952	GB
Station Six Sahara	1962	GB
Too Young to Love	1959	GB
The Webster Boy	1961	GB
Welcome Mr. Washington *	1944	GB
Whisky Galore *	1948	GB--Eal.
The World Owes Me a Living *	1944	GB
X the Unknown	1956	GB--Ham.
Your Witness	1950	GB--WB

216. AL GILKS (1892-1970)

The Air Mail	1925	Par.
An American in Paris *	1951	MGM
Ancient Highway	1925	Par.
And Sudden Death	1936	Par.
Beyond the Rocks	1922	Par.
The Big Killing	1928	Par.
The Blind Goddess	1926	Par.
Bluebeard's 8th Wife	1923	Par.
Bluff	1924	Par.
Bright Road	1953	MGM
Calling Dr. Kildare *	1939	MGM
The City Sparrow	1920	Par.
The Dancin' Fool	1920	Par.
Dancing Co-Ed	1939	MGM
Don't Tell Them Everything	1921	Par.
Double Speed	1920	Par.
The Enchanted Hill	1926	Par.
Excuse My Dust	1920	Par.
Excuse My Dust	1951	MGM
The Female	1924	Par.
Fiesta *	1941	MGM
Figures Don't Lie	1927	Par.
The First Kiss	1928	Par.
Get Your Man	1927	Par.
The Great Moment	1921	Par.
Halfway to Heaven	1929	Par.
Hell and High Water	1933	Par.
Her Beloved Villain	1920	US
Her Gilded Cage	1922	Par.
Her Husband's Trademark	1922	Par.
His Children's Children	1923	Par.

The Impossible Mrs. Bellew	1922	Par.
Jealousy	1929	Par.
Kibitzer	1930	Par.
Little Miss Marker	1934	Par.
Man on the Flying Trapeze	1935	Par.
Midshipman Jack	1933	RKO
The Milky Way	1936	Par.
Miss Fane's Baby Is Stolen	1934	Par.
My American Wife	1922	Par.
The Next Corner	1924	Par.
North of 36	1924	Par.
The Notorious Sophie Lang	1934	Par.
Old Ironsides *	1926	Par.
The Painted Hills *	1951	MGM
Peck's Bad Boy *	1921	FN
People Will Talk	1935	Par.
Prodigal Daughters	1923	Par.
Red Hair	1928	Par.
Riding On Air	1937	RKO
Ruggles of Red Gap	1935	Par.
Secret of Dr. Kildare	1939	MGM
Sick Abed	1920	Par.
Sins of Roxanne *	1920	Par.
The Snob	1921	US
Straight From the Shoulder	1936	Par.
Sweetie	1929	Par.
A Tailor Made Man	1931	MGM
Ten Modern Commandments	1927	Par.
These Glamour Girls	1939	MGM
Two Weeks With Love	1950	MGM
Under the Lash	1921	Par.
Vendetta *	1950	MGM
What's Your Hurry?	1920	Par.
Wife Savers *	1928	Par.
You're Telling Me	1934	Par.

217. CHARLES GILSON

Conductor 1492	1924	WB
The Crackerjack	1925	US
The Dead Line	1920	Fox
Dynamite Allen	1921	Fox
The Early Bird *	1925	US
Greed	1917	US
Jan of the Big Snows *	1922	US
Johnny Ring and the Captain's Sword *	1921	US
Little Johnny Jones	1923	WB
Luck *	1923	US
A Manhattan Knight	1920	Fox
Number 17	1920	Fox

The Plunger	1920	Fox
Rainbow Riley *	1926	FN
The Ramparts We Watch *	1940	RKO
The Speed Spook *	1924	US
The Star Spangled Banner	1917	US
Wrath	1917	US

218. IRVING GLASSBERG

Arctic Manhunt	1949	Univ.
Backlash	1956	Univ.
Bend of the River	1952	Univ.
The Big Beat	1958	Univ.
Black Bart	1948	Univ.
The Black Castle	1952	Univ.
The Black Shield of Falworth	1954	Univ.
Border River	1953	Univ.
Calamity Jane and Sam Bass	1949	Univ.
Captain Lightfoot	1955	Univ.
Casbah	1948	Univ.
Cave of Outlaws	1951	Univ.
Day of the Bad Men	1957	Univ.
Duel at Silver Creek	1952	Univ.
The Fat Man	1950	Univ.
Feudin', Fussin' and A-Fightin'	1948	Univ.
Flesh and Fury	1952	Univ.
Four Girls in Town	1956	Univ.
Francis	1950	Univ.
Francis Goes to the Races	1951	Univ.
Francis Joins the WACs	1954	Univ.
Here Come the Nelsons	1951	Univ.
I Was a Shoplifter	1950	Univ.
Joe Butterfly	1957	Univ.
Kansas Raiders	1951	Univ.
The Lady Takes a Flyer	1958	Univ.
Larceny	1948	Univ.
The Lawless Breed	1952	Univ.
Mississippi Gambler	1953	Univ.
Outside the Law	1956	Univ.
Outside the Wall	1950	Univ.
The Price of Fear	1956	Univ.
The Prince Who Was a Thief	1951	Univ.
The Purple Mask	1955	Univ.
The Rabbit Trap	1959	UA
The Rawhide Years	1956	Univ.
Red Canyon	1949	Univ.
Ride Clear of Diablo	1954	Univ.
River Lady	1948	Univ.
Sally and St. Anne	1952	Univ.
Shakedown	1950	Univ.

Showdown at Abilene	1956	Univ.
Spy Hunt	1950	Univ.
Story of Molly X	1949	Univ.
The Strange Door	1951	Univ.
Sword in the Desert	1949	Univ.
The Tarnished Angels	1957	Univ.
Twilight for the Gods	1958	Univ.
Undertow	1949	Univ.
Walking My Baby Back Home	1953	Univ.
The Web	1947	Univ.
Yes Sir, That's My Baby	1949	Univ.

219. HONE GLENDINNING

The Case of the Frightened Lady	1940	US
The Chinese Bungalow *	1939	GB
Crimes at the Dark House	1940	GB
The Flying Eye	1955	GB
Forbidden	1949	GB
John Wesley *	1954	GB
Merry Comes to Town	1937	GB
Midnight Episode	1950	GB--Col.
Noose	1948	GB
Sexton Blake and the Hooded Terror	1938	GB
The Shop at Sly Corner	1947	GB

220. PIERRE-WILLIAM GLENN

Avalanche	1978	US
Boy Soldier	1981	Fr.
Children of Chaos	1989	Fr.
Choice of Arms	1981	Fr.
Coup de Touchon	1981	Fr.
La Cousin Jules *	1973	Fr.
Coverup	1983	Fr.
Day for Night	1973	Fr.--Col./WB
Deathwatch	1980	Fr./Ger.
A Dry White Season *	1989	MGM/UA
L'Etoile du Nord	1982	Fr.
Exterior Night	1980	Fr.
The Eyes Closed	1972	Fr.
France Incorporated	1974	Fr.
Get Your Diploma First	1979	Fr.
Group Portrait With Lady	1977	Ger.
The Honeymoon Trip	1976	Fr.--TCF
Jean's Wife *	1973	Fr.
The Judge and the Assassin	1976	Fr.
Let Joy Reign Supreme	1975	Fr.
Like a Boomerang	1976	Fr.--TCF

A Little Romance	1979	Fr.
Loulou *	1980	Fr.
La Mort en Direct	1979	Fr.
The Murdered Young Girl	1974	Fr.
Night Patrol	1984	Fr.
One-Way Ticket	1971	Fr.
Out One Spectre	1974	Fr.
Paulina Is Leaving *	1969	Fr.
Prize of Peril	1983	Fr.
The Red Orchestra	1989	Fr./It.
Rise Up Spy *	1982	Fr.
Serie Noire	1982	Fr.
The Shock	1982	Fr.
Shot Pattern	1982	Fr.
Small Change	1976	Fr.
Spending Money	1976	Fr.
State of Things	1973	Fr.
Street of No Return	1989	Fr./Port.
Such a Gorgeous Kid Like Me	1973	Fr.--Col.
The Swindle	1980	Fr.
The Threat	1977	Can./Fr.
Thriller Story	1979	Fr.
Violated Love	1977	Fr.
The Watchmaker of St. Paul	1973	Fr.
A Week's Vacation	1980	Fr.
Where Did Tom Go?	1971	Fr.
You Can't Hold Back Spring	1971	Fr.

221. BERT GLENNON (1895-1967)

About Face	1952	WB
Alice in Wonderland *	1933	Par.
Are Parents People?	1925	Par.
Bad Boy	1935	Fox
Barbed Wire	1927	Par.
The Big Trees	1952	WB
Blonde Venus	1932	Par.
Burning Sands	1922	Par.
Can This Be Dixie?	1936	TCF
Changing Husbands	1924	Par.
Cheated Love	1921	Univ.
Christopher Strong	1933	RKO
The City Gone Wild	1927	Par.
Copacabana	1947	UA
Crime Wave	1954	WB
Crown of Lies	1926	Par.
The Dangerous Moment	1921	Univ.
A Daughter of the Law	1921	Univ.
Davy Crockett and the River Pirates	1956	Dis.
Desert Song	1943	WB

Desperate Journey	1942	WB
Destination Tokyo	1943	WB
Dimples	1936	TCF
Dive Bomber *	1941	WB
Domestic Relations	1922	FN
Drums Along the Mohawk	1939	TCF
Ebb Tide	1922	Par.
Eyes of the World	1917	US
Flower of Night	1925	Par.
Gabriel Over the White House	1933	MGM
Ginger	1935	Fox
Good and Naughty	1926	Par.
Grand Canary	1934	Fox
Grounds for Divorce	1925	Par.
Half Angel	1936	TCF
Half Naked Truth	1932	RKO
Hell in the Heavens	1934	Fox
Hotel Imperial	1927	Par.
House of Wax	1953	WB
The Howards of Virginia	1940	Col.
The Hurricane	1937	Gold.
Java Head	1923	Par.
Java Head *	1934	GB
Juke Girl	1942	WB
The Kentucky Colonel *	1920	US
Kidnapped *	1938	TCF
The Kiss	1921	Univ.
Lad: A Dog	1962	WB
The Last Command	1928	Par.
Little Miss Nobody	1936	TCF
Lloyds of London	1936	TCF
Lottery Lover	1935	Fox
The Mad Magician	1954	Col.
The Man Behind the Gun	1952	WB
The Man From Galveston	1964	WB
Melody Cruise	1933	RKO
Mission to Moscow	1943	WB
Mr. District Attorney	1946	Col.
Moonlight Follies	1921	Univ.
The Moonlighter	1953	WB
Morning Glory	1933	RKO
Nobody's Fool	1921	Univ.
One More Tomorrow	1946	WB
One Night in Lisbon	1941	Par.
Open All Night	1924	Par.
Operation Pacific	1950	WB
Our Town	1940	US
The Patriot	1928	Par.
The Prisoner of Shark Island	1936	TCF
Ramona *	1916	US
The Red House	1947	UA

The Red Light	1949	UA
The Reluctant Dragon *	1941	Dis.
Riding Shotgun	1954	WB
Rio Grande *	1950	Rep.
Ruthless	1948	EL
Salomy Jane	1923	Par.
San Antonio	1945	WB
The Scarlet Empress	1934	Par.
The Sea Hornet	1951	Rep.
Sergeant Rutledge	1960	WB
Shadow of a Woman	1946	WB
She Was a Lady	1934	Fox
Show Them No Mercy	1935	Fox
Stagecoach *	1939	UA
The Street of Sin *	1928	Par.
Susannah of the Mounties	1939	TCF
Swanee River	1939	TCF
The Ten Commandments *	1923	Par.
They Died With Their Boots On	1941	WB
This Is the Army *	1943	WB
Thunder in the Night	1935	Fox
Thunder Over the Plains	1953	WB
Tomorrow's Love	1925	Par.
The Torrent *	1921	Univ.
Triumph	1924	Par.
Underworld	1927	Par.
The Very Thought of You	1944	WB
Virginia *	1941	Par.
Wagonmaster *	1940	RKO
We're All Gamblers	1927	Par.
Wild Horse Mesa	1925	Par.
Woman of the World	1925	Par.
The Woman On Trial	1927	Par.
The Woman Who Walked Alone	1922	Par.
Worldly Goods	1924	Par.
You Can't Fool Your Wife	1923	Par.
Young Mr. Lincoln	1939	TCF

222. RICHARD GLOUNER

Another Chance	1988	US
Christina	1974	Can.
Devil's Eight	1968	AIP
The Dunwich Horror	1970	AIP
Enforcer	1976	WB
Glory Boy	1971	US
Gong Show Movie	1980	Univ.
The Gumball Rally	1976	WB
Hot Child in the City	1987	US
How Did a Nice Girl Like You Get Into This Business?	1970	Ger.

Making It	1971	TCF
Man With Bogart's Face	1980	TCF
Payday	1972	US
The Soul of Nigger Charlie	1973	Par.
Summertree	1971	Col.

223. DAVID W. GOBBETT

The Amateur Gentleman	1926	FN
The Big Show	1926	US
The Master Cracksman	1926	US
Ransom's Folly	1926	FN
The White Black Sheep	1926	FN
Winds of the Pampas	1927	US

224. STEPHEN GOLDBLATT

Breaking Glass	1980	Par.
Everybody's All-American	1988	WB
Hunger *	1983	MGM-UA
Lethal Weapon	1987	WB
Lethal Weapon 2	1989	WB
Outland	1981	WB
The Return of the Soldier	1981	GB--TCF
Young Sherlock Holmes	1985	Par.

225. FRANK B. GOOD (1884-1939)

Aladdin and the Wonderful Lamp	1917	Fox
Ali Baba and the Forty Thieves *	1918	Fox
Bar Nothin'	1921	Fox
The Border Patrolman	1936	TCF
A Boy of Flanders	1924	Metro.-Gold.
Bucking the Line	1921	Fox
The California Mail	1929	FN
Carolyn of the Corners	1919	Pathe
Cheyenne	1929	FN
The Children in the House	1916	US
Circus Days	1923	FN
The Cowboy Millionaire	1935	Fox
The Cyclone	1920	Fox
Daddy *	1923	FN
Daniel Boone	1936	RKO
Desert Love	1920	Fox
The Dixie Merchant	1926	Fox
The Dude Ranger	1934	Fox
An Enemy of Men	1925	Col.
Fan Fan *	1918	Fox

Flame of the Desert *	1919	Gold.
Fleetwing	1928	Fox
Get Your Man	1921	Fox
The Gilded Butterfly	1926	Fox
A Girl in Bohemia	1919	Fox
The Glorious Trail	1928	FN
Going Straight	1916	US
The Great Alone	1922	US
Gretchen, the Greenhorn	1916	US
Hard Rock Harrigan	1935	Fox
Isle of Fury	1936	WB
Jack and the Beanstalk *	1917	Fox
Johnny Get Your Hair Cut	1927	MGM
The Lawless Legion	1929	FN
Let Kathy Do It	1916	US
Lights of the Desert	1922	Fox
Little Robinson Crusoe *	1924	Metro.-Gold.
A Little Sister of Everybody	1918	Pathe
The Little School Ma'am	1916	US
Long Live the King	1923	Metro.
The Love That Dares	1919	Fox
Martha's Vindication	1916	US
The Merry-Go-Round	1919	Fox
The Mine With the Iron Door	1936	Col.
The New Teacher	1922	Fox
O'Malley of the Mounted	1936	TCF
Old Clothes	1925	Metro.-Gold.
The One-Man Trail	1921	Fox
Park Avenue Lodger	1937	RKO
Peck's Bad Boy	1934	Fox
Prairie Trails	1920	Fox
The Rag Man *	1925	Metro.-Gold.
Riding With Death	1921	Fox
The Road Demon *	1921	Fox
Road to Hollywood	1947	US
Rose of the West	1919	Fox
Smiles	1919	Fox
Smiles Are Trumps	1922	Fox
Straight From the Shoulder	1921	Fox
The Terror	1920	Fox
Three Gold Coins	1920	Fox
Thunder Mountain	1935	Fox
To a Finish	1921	Fox
Treasure Island	1917	Fox
The Untamed	1920	Fox
The Unwritten Law	1925	Col.
The Web of Chance	1919	Fox
When a Man's a Man	1935	Fox
When Fate Decides	1919	Fox
Whispering Smith Speaks	1935	Fox
Windjammer	1937	RKO

The Wise Wife	1927	Pathe
The Wizard	1927	Fox
The Wizard of Oz *	1925	US
The Woman and the Puppet *	1920	Gold.

226. PLINY GOODFRIEND

Fast Bullets	1936	US
Gay and Devilish	1922	US
Love Trader *	1936	US
Old Dad	1920	FN
Riding On	1937	US
The Silver Trail	1937	US
Skull and Crown	1937	US
The Woman in His House	1920	FN
Yankee Madness	1924	US

227. ALFRED GOSDEN (1873-1941)

All Dolled Up	1921	Univ.
Brazen Beauty	1918	US
The Breath of the Gods	1920	Univ.
Burnt Wings	1920	Univ.
The Call of the Klondike	1926	US
The Canvas Kisser	1925	US
Don Quixote	1916	US
Everything But the Truth	1920	Univ.
The Exquisite Thief	1919	Univ.
False Friends	1926	US
Fixed By George	1920	Univ.
Fort Frayne	1926	US
The Game's Up	1919	US
The Girl in the Rain	1920	Univ.
Going the Limit	1925	US
Her Own Story	1926	US
La La Lucille	1920	Univ.
The Mad Marriage	1921	Univ.
Melodies	1926	US
Old Hartwell's Club	1918	US
The Painted Lady	1924	Fox
Pretty Smooth	1919	Univ.
Princess of Virtue	1917	US
Set Free	1918	US
A Shocking Night	1921	Univ.
The Spitfire of Seville	1919	Univ.
Tonio, Son of the Sierras	1925	US
The Trembling Hour	1919	Univ.
Warrior Gap	1925	US
The Wicked Darling	1919	Univ.
The Woman Under Cover	1919	Univ.

228. ARTHUR GRANT

The Abominable Snowman	1957	GB--Ham.
The Agitator	1945	GB
Angel Who Pawned Her Harp	1954	GB
Background	1953	GB
The Beauty Jungle	1964	GB--Rank
Blood From the Mummy's Tomb	1971	GB--Ham.
The Blue Peter	1955	GB
The Brave Don't Cry	1952	GB
Candles at Nine *	1944	GB
Captain Clegg	1962	GB--Ham./Univ.
Carry On Admiral	1957	GB
Cash on Demand	1963	GB--Col.
A Challenge for Robin Hood	1967	GB--Ham.
Cone of Silence	1960	GB
Conflict of Wings	1953	GB
Count Five and Die	1957	GB--TCF
Curse of the Werewolf	1961	GB--Ham./ Univ.
The Damned	1961	GB--Col./Ham.
Danger Within	1958	GB
Demons of the Mind	1972	GB--EMI/MGM
The Devil Rides Out	1967	GB--Ham.
The Dragon of Pendragon Castle	1950	GB
Dracula Has Risen From the Grave	1968	GB--Ham.
Dry Rot	1956	GB
Eighty Thousand Suspects	1963	GB--Rank
The End of the Road	1954	GB
The Extra Day	1956	GB
Fear in the Night	1972	GB--Ham.
Frankenstein Created Woman	1966	GB--Ham./WB
Frankenstein Must Be Destroyed	1969	GB--Ham./WB
Friends and Neighbors	1959	GB
The Glass Mountain *	1949	GB
Heaven Is Round the Corner *	1943	GB
Hell Is a City	1959	GB--Ham.
Jigsaw	1962	GB
John and Julie	1955	GB
Judgment Deferred	1951	GB
Laxdale Hall	1952	GB
Loyal Heart *	1946	GB
Make Mine a Million	1959	GB
Master of Bankdam *	1947	GB
Medal for the General *	1944	GB
Miss Robin Hood	1952	GB
The Mummy's Shroud	1966	GB--Ham.
Not Wanted On Voyage	1947	GB
The Old Dark House	1962	GB--Col.
Orders Are Orders	1954	GB
Paranoiac	1963	GB--Ham.

Passport to China	1960	GB--Col./Ham.
Phantom of the Opera	1962	GB--Ham./Univ.
Pirates of Blood River	1961	GB--Ham.
The Plague of the Zombies	1965	GB--Ham.
Quatermass and the Pit	1967	GB--Ham.
Ramsbottom Rides Again	1956	GB
The Reptile	1966	GB--Ham.
Shadow of the Cat	1961	GB--Univ.
Son of Robin Hood	1958	GB--TCF
The Stranglers of Bombay	1959	GB--Col./Ham.
Taste the Blood of Dracula	1969	GB--Ham.
Terror of the Tongs	1960	GB--Ham.
They're a Weird Mob	1966	Aus.
The Tomb of Ligeia	1964	GB--AIP
A Touch of the Sun	1956	GB
The Unstoppable Man	1960	GB
Up the Creek	1958	GB
We'll Smile Again *	1942	GB
When We are Married *	1942	GB
Where the Spies Are	1965	GB--MGM
The Witches	1966	GB--Ham.
Yesterday's Enemy	1959	GB--Col./Ham.

229. FRED LEROY GRANVILLE

Divorce Trap	1919	Fox
Loot	1919	Univ.
Once to Every Woman	1920	Univ.
Rough Riding Romance	1919	Fox
Talk of the Town	1918	Univ.

230. GARY GRAVER

The Affairs of Aphrodite	1970	US
The Attic	1980	US
B.O.R.N.	1989	US
Blood Mania *	1970	US
Blood of Frankenstein *	1970	US
The Clones	1973	US
Commando Squad	1987	US
Deathsport	1978	US
Deep Space	1988	US
Diamond Stud	1970	US
Dracula vs. Frankenstein *	1971	Sp.
Erika's Hot Summer	1970	US
F for Fake	1976	US
The Fabulous Bastard From Chicago	1969	US
The Glove	1981	US
Grand Theft Auto *	1977	US

Hard on the Trail	1969	US
The Hard Road	1970	US
Hell's Bloody Angels *	1970	US
Hollywood High Part II	1981	US
Jaded	1989	US
Jessie's Girls	1976	US
L. A. Bounty	1989	US
Moon in Scorpio	1987	US
Moonshine County Express	1977	US
Mortuary	1983	US
Party Camp	1987	US
The Phantom Empire	1989	US
Sandra, the Making of a Woman	1970	US
Satan's Sadist	1969	US
Smokey Bites the Dust	1981	US
Sunnyside	1979	AIP
Sunset Cove	1978	US
They're Playing With Fire	1984	US
The Toolbox Murders	1978	US
Trick or Treats	1982	US
Twisted Nightmare *	1988	US

231. KING GRAY (1886-1938)

The Amazing Wife	1919	Univ.
Cheating Herself	1919	Fox
The College Orphan	1915	Univ.
Cowardice Court *	1919	Fox
The Double O	1921	US
The Feud Woman	1926	US
Flames *	1926	US
The Flashlight	1917	US
Flattery *	1925	US
Fools of Fortune	1922	US
Forgive and Forget	1923	Col.
The Gambling Fool	1925	US
The Ghetto Shamrock	1926	US
The Heart of Humanity *	1919	US
The Love Gamble *	1925	US
The Midlanders	1920	US
Midnight Faces	1926	US
More To Be Pitied Than Scorned *	1922	US
Paid In Advance	1919	Univ.
Peggy Puts It Over	1921	Vita.
The Piper's Price	1917	US
The Price of Silence	1916	US
The Rescue	1917	US
Solitary Sin	1919	US
Speed *	1925	US
Speed Crazed	1926	US

Temptation	1923	US
Under the Rouge *	1925	US
The Vanity Pool	1918	Univ.
West of the Rockies *	1931	US
White Fang *	1925	US
Wreckage *	1925	US
Yankee Go-Getter	1921	US

232. GUY GREEN (1913-   )

Adam and Evelyn	1949	GB--Rank
The Beggar's Opera	1952	GB
Blanche Fury *	1948	GB
Captain Horatio Hornblower RN	1951	GB--WB
Carnival	1946	GB--Rank
The Dark Avenger	1955	GB--AA
Decameron Nights	1952	GB
For Better For Worse	1954	GB
Great Expectations	1946	GB--Rank
The Hour of Thirteen	1952	GB--MGM
I Am a Camera	1955	GB
Madeline	1950	GB--Rank/Univ.
Night Without Stars	1951	GB
Oliver Twist	1948	GB--Rank/UA
The Passionate Friends *	1948	GB
Rob Roy the Highland Rogue	1953	GB--Dis.
Spellbound *	1940	GB
Story of Robin Hood and His Merrie Men	1952	GB--Dis.
Take My Life	1947	GB
The Way Ahead	1944	GB

232a. JACK N. GREEN

Bird	1988	WB
The Dead Pool	1988	WB
Heartbreak Ridge	1986	WB
Like Father, Like Son	1987	Tri-S.
Pink Cadillac	1989	WB
Rage for Glory	1989	US
The Rookie	1990	WB
Volunteers *	1985	Tri-S.
White Hunter, Black Heart	1990	WB

233. ADAM GREENBERG

Alien Nation	1988	TCF
The Ambassador	1984	Cannon

Belfer	1979	Isr.
The Big Red One	1980	UA
Daughters Daughters	1973	Isr.
Diamonds	1975	Isr.--US/AE
Ghost	1990	Par.
Going Steady	1979	Ger./Isr.
The House on Cherlouche Street	1973	Isr.
I Love You Rosa	1973	Isr.
I Was Born in Jerusalem	1971	Isr.
Iron Eagle	1986	Tri-S.
It's a Funny World *	1978	Isr.
Jocks	1987	US
La Bamba	1987	Col.
The Ladies Club	1986	US
The Last American Virgin	1983	Cannon
Lemon Popsicle	1978	Isr.
Love Hurts	1990	US
Madron *	1970	Isr.--US
My Michael	1975	Isr.
Near Dark	1987	US
Once Bitten	1985	US
Operation Thunderbolt	1977	Isr.
Over the Brooklyn Bridge	1984	Cannon/MGM-UA
Paradise	1982	Emb.
The Passover Plot	1976	Isr.--US
Peeping Toms	1973	Isr.
Private Popsicle	1983	Isr.
Private Resort	1985	Tri-S.
Safari 3000	1982	MGM-UA
Spellbinder	1988	MGM-UA
Take 2	1972	Isr.--UA
10 to Midnight	1983	Cannon
Teen Mothers	1980	Cannon
Three Men and a Baby	1987	Touch.
Three Men and a Little Lady	1990	Touch.
Turner & Hooch	1989	BV/Touch.
The Uranium Conspiracy	1978	Isr.
A Walk on the Moon	1987	US
War and Love	1985	Cannon
Wisdom	1986	TCF
Worth Winning	1989	TCF

234. ROBBIE GREENBERG

Creator	1985	Univ.
Far North	1988	US
The Milagro Beanfield War	1988	Univ.
Night Warning	1983	US
Sweet Dreams	1985	Tri-S.
Time Walker	1982	US
Youngblood	1978	AIP

235. MAX GREENE (MUTZ GREENBAUM)

Brothers in Law	1957	GB
Bulldog Jack	1934	GB
Car of Dreams	1935	GB
Carleton Browne of the FO	1958	GB
Chu Chin Chow	1934	GB
Climbing High	1938	GB
The Constant Nymph	1933	GB
The Courtnays of Curzon Street	1947	GB
Derby Day	1952	GB
Elizabeth of Ladymead	1948	GB
An Englishman's Home *	1939	GB--UA
Escape to Danger	1943	GB--RKO
Evensong	1934	GB
Forester's Daughter *	1931	Ger.
A Gentleman of Paris	1931	GB
Great Yearning	1930	Ger.
The Green Cockatoo	1937	GB--TCF
The Guvnor	1935	GB
Hatter's Castle	1941	GB--Par.
Heavens Above!	1963	GB
Hotel Reserve	1944	GB--RKO
I Live in Grosvenor Square	1945	GB
I'm All Right Jack	1959	GB
It's a Boy	1933	GB
Keep Smiling	1938	GB--TCF
King's Rhapsody	1955	GB
Lady Jane Grey	1936	GB
Lady With a Lamp	1951	GB
Laughing Annie	1953	GB--Rep.
Lilacs in the Spring	1954	GB--Rep.
Love On Wheels	1932	GB
Lucky Jim	1957	GB
Man in the Dinghy	1951	GB
Maytime in Mayfair *	1949	GB
The Midshipmaid	1932	GB
The Moonraker	1958	GB
My Teenage Daughter	1956	GB
Night and the City	1950	GB--TCF
1914	1931	Ger.
Non Stop New York	1937	GB
Odette	1950	GB
Office Girl	1932	GB
Old Iron	1939	GB
Only on the Rhine *	1931	Ger.
Pastor Hall	1940	GB
Piccadilly Incident	1946	GB
Pimpernel Smith	1941	GB
Princess Charming	1934	GB
Return of the Scarlet Pimpernel	1937	GB--Korda

The Risk	1961	GB
Sailing Along	1938	GB
The Secret Ways	1961	Univ.
Seven Sinners	1936	GB
77 Park Lane *	1931	GB--UA
Ships With Wings *	1941	GB
So Evil My Love	1948	Par.
Sparrows Can't Sing	1962	GB
Spring in Park Lane *	1948	GB
Squadron Leader X	1942	GB--RKO
Storm in a Teacup *	1937	GB--Korda
Strangers on Honeymoon	1936	GB
Suspect	1960	GB
There Ain't No Justice	1939	GB
They Flew Alone	1941	GB--RKO
This England	1941	GB
Thunder Rock	1942	GB
Trent's Last Case	1952	GB
Trouble in the Glen	1954	GB--Rep.
Tudor Rose	1936	GB
Two Humans *	1931	Ger.
Under Your Hat	1940	GB
Wanted For Murder	1946	GB
We're Going To Be Rich	1938	GB--TCF
Yellow Canary	1943	GB--RKO

236. W. HOWARD GREENE

The Adventures of Robin Hood *	1938	WB
Al Jennings of Oklahoma	1950	Col.
Ali Baba and the Forty Thieves *	1944	Univ.
Arabian Nights *	1942	Univ.
Blossoms in the Dust *	1941	MGM
The Brigand	1952	Col.
Can't Help Singing *	1944	Univ.
The Climax *	1944	Univ.
Cobra Woman *	1944	Univ.
The Garden of Allah *	1936	Selz.
Gun Belt	1953	UA
Gypsy Wild Cat *	1944	Univ.
High Lonesome	1950	EL
The Jungle Book *	1942	Korda/UA
Men With Wings	1938	Par.
Northwest Mounted Police *	1940	Par.
Nothing Sacred	1937	Selz.
Phantom of the Opera *	1943	Univ.
Pirates of Monterey *	1947	Univ.
Quebec	1951	Par.
Raiders of the Seven Seas	1953	UA
Salome Where She Danced *	1945	Univ.
Salute to the Marines *	1943	MGM

Shepherd of the Hills *	1941	Par.
Slave Girl *	1947	Univ.
A Star Is Born	1937	Selz.
The Trail of the Lonesome Pine *	1936	Par.
Untamed *	1940	Par.
The Violent Men *	1955	Col.
When Worlds Collide *	1951	Par.

237. JACK GREENHALGH

Adventure Island	1947	Par.
Adventures of Casanova	1948	EL
Anything for a Thrill	1937	US
Apology for Murder	1945	PRC
Ambush Trail	1946	PRC
Avalanche	1946	PRC
Bad Boy	1939	US
Beasts of Berlin	1939	PDC
Big Show-Off	1945	Rep.
Billy the Kid in Texas	1940	PRC
Billy the Kid Trapped	1942	PRC
Billy the Kid Wanted	1941	PRC
Billy the Kid's Fighting Pals	1941	PRC
Billy the Kid's Range War	1941	PRC
Billy the Kid's Roundup	1942	PRC
Blonde for a Day	1946	PRC
Border Badmen	1945	PRC
Border Caballero	1936	US
Border Phantom	1937	Rep.
Broadway Big Shot	1942	PRC
Buried Alive	1940	US
Code of the Rangers	1938	Mon.
Dakota Lil	1950	TCF
Dangerous Lady	1941	PRC
Dangerous Zone	1951	Lip.
Danny Boy	1946	US
Dead Men Walk	1943	PRC
Desperate Cargo	1941	PRC
Emergency Landing	1941	PRC
Everyman's Law	1936	US
FBI Girl	1951	Lip.
Fear In the Night	1947	Par.
Fighting Frontier	1943	RKO
Fighting Mad	1939	Mon.
The Fighting Texan	1937	US
Fingerprints Don't Lie	1951	Lip.
The Flying Serpent	1945	PRC
Frontier Crusader	1940	PRC
Frontier Scout	1938	GN
G. I. Jane	1951	Lip.

Galloping Dynamite	1937	US
Gentlemen With Guns	1946	PRC
Ghost Patrol	1936	US
Girls in Chains *	1943	PRC
Gun Code	1940	PRC
Heartaches	1947	PRC
High Conquest	1947	Mon.
High Hat	1938	US
His Brother's Ghost	1945	PRC
Hitler's Madmen *	1943	MGM/PRC
Hold That Woman	1940	PRC
Hollywood Barn Dance	1947	US
I Cover the Big Town	1947	Par.
I Take This Oath	1940	PRC
The Invisible Killer	1940	PRC
Jungle Flight	1947	Par.
Kentucky Jubilee	1951	Lip.
The Kid Rides Again	1943	PRC
King of the Sierras	1938	GN
The Lady Confesses	1945	PRC
Larceny in Her Heart	1946	PRC
Law and Order	1942	PRC
Lawless Land	1937	Rep.
Leave It to the Marines	1951	Lip.
Lightning Raiders	1946	PRC
The Lone Rider Ambushed	1941	PRC
The Lone Rider Crosses the Rio Grande	1941	PRC
The Lone Rider in Ghost Town	1941	PRC
Lost Continent	1951	Lip.
The Mad Monster	1942	PRC
Marked Men	1940	PRC
Mask of the Dragon	1951	Lip.
Miraculous Journey	1948	US
Mr. Washington Goes to Town	1941	US
Money Madness	1948	US
Murder Is My Business	1946	PRC
My Son the Hero *	1943	PRC
Mystic Circle Murder	1939	US
Navajo Kid	1945	PRC
New Mexico *	1951	UA
Outlaws of the Rio Grande	1941	PRC
Phantom Ranger	1938	Mon.
Pier 23	1951	Lip.
Prairie Rustlers	1946	PRC
Prisoner of Japan	1942	PRC
Racing Blood *	1938	US
Reefer Madness	1939	US
Riders of Black Mountain	1941	PRC
Roarin' Guns	1936	US
Roaring Six Guns	1937	US

Robot Monster	1953	US
Rogue of the Range	1937	US
Rogue River	1951	EL
Rough Ridin' Rhythm	1938	US
Satan's Cradle	1949	UA
Savage Drums	1951	Lip.
Secrets of a Model	1940	US
Seven Were Saved	1947	Par.
Sheriff of Sage Valley	1942	PRC
Sing While You're Able	1937	US
Six Gun Man	1946	PRC
16 Fathoms Deep	1948	Mon.
Sky High	1952	Lip.
Slaughter Trail	1952	RKO
Smoking Guns	1942	PRC
Stagecoach Outlaws	1945	PRC
State Department File 649	1949	US
Strange Mrs. Crane	1948	EL
Strange Voyage	1945	PRC
Sunset Legion *	1928	Par.
Swing It Professor	1938	US
The Sword of Monte Cristo	1951	TCF
Terrors on Horseback	1946	PRC
The Texas Marshal	1941	PRC
Thanks for Listening	1937	US
Three Desperate Men	1951	Lip.
Three On a Ticket	1947	PRC
Timber War	1936	US
Tomorrow We Live	1942	PRC
Too Many Winners	1947	PRC
Torture Ship	1939	PDC
Tough to Handle	1937	US
Trails of the Wild	1935	US
The Traitor	1936	US
Trigger Pals	1939	GN
Two-Gun Man *	1926	US
Valley of Vengeance	1944	PRC
West of Rainbow's End	1938	Mon.
Where the West Begins	1938	Mon.
Whistling Bullets	1937	US
White Pongo	1945	PRC
Wild Weed	1949	US
Yes Sir, Mr. Bones	1951	Lip.
Youth Aflame	1945	US

237a. DAVID GRIBBLE

Cadillac Man	1990	Orion
The F. J. Holden	1977	Aus.
Fast Talking	1986	US

Monkey Grip	1983	Aus.
Off Limits	1988	TCF
Private Collection	1972	Aus.
Tap	1989	Tri-S.

238. WALTER GRIFFEN

Baffled	1924	US
Barriers of the Law	1925	US
The Boomerang *	1919	US
Border Intrigue	1925	US
Border Justice	1925	US
City of Purple Dreams	1928	US
Cold Nerve	1925	US
Crossed Trails	1924	US
Cruise of the Hellion	1927	US
Dame Chance	1926	US
Danger Patrol	1928	US
A Desperate Adventure	1924	US
Flashing Spurs	1924	US
The Girl of My Dreams	1918	US
God's Great Wilderness	1927	US
The Golden Snare	1921	FN
The Heart of Broadway	1928	US
Hearts and Masks	1921	US
Heroes in Blue	1927	US
Jack O' Hearts	1926	US
Lost Limited	1927	US
Man in the Shadow	1926	US
A Midnight Adventure	1928	US
Modern Husbands	1919	US
Nomads of the North	1920	FN
Outwitted	1925	US
Peril of the Rail	1926	US
Phantom of the Turf	1928	US
Rapids *	1922	US
Riding Romance	1926	US
Rose of the Bowery	1927	US
Sweet Sixteen	1928	US
Then Came the Woman	1926	US
Trigger Finger	1924	US
A Two Fisted Tenderfoot	1924	US
Western Vengeance	1924	US
The Wheel of Destiny	1927	US
The Whipping Boss	1924	Mon.

239. LOYAL GRIGGS (1907?-1978)

| Banning | 1967 | Univ. |

Blueprint for Robbery	1960	Par.
The Bridges at Toko-ri	1954	Par.
The Buccaneer	1958	Par.
Bunny O'Hare *	1971	AIP
The Buster Keaton Story	1947	Par.
Crosswinds	1951	Par.
Elephant Walk	1954	Par.
GI Blues	1960	Par.
Girls! Girls! Girls!	1962	US
Greatest Story Ever Told *	1965	UA
The Hangman	1959	Par.
Hot Spell	1958	Par.
Hurry Sundown *	1967	Par.
In Enemy Country	1968	Univ.
In Harm's Way	1965	Par.
The Jayhawkers	1959	Par.
The Last Outpost	1951	Par.
Love in a Goldfish Bowl	1961	Par.
Mantrap	1961	Par.
The Night of the Grizzly *	1966	Par.
P. J.	1967	Univ.
Papa's Delicate Condition	1963	Par.
Passage West	1951	Par.
The Sad Sack	1957	Par.
Shane	1953	Par.
The Slender Thread	1966	Par.
The Ten Commandments	1956	Par.
That Certain Feeling	1956	Par.
Three Ring Circus	1954	Par.
Three Violent People	1956	Par.
...Tick, Tick, Tick...	1969	MGM
Tickle Me	1965	AA
The Tin Star	1957	Par.
Tonka	1958	Dis.
Visit to a Small Planet	1959	Par.
Walk Like a Dragon	1960	Par.
We're No Angels	1954	Par.
White Christmas	1954	Par.
The Young Warrior	1967	Univ.

240. MARCEL GRIGNON

A Tout Couer a Tokyo pour OSS 117	1966	Fr.
Adventures of Captain Fabian	1951	Rep.
America Seen by a Frenchman	1960	Fr.
Auguste	1961	Fr.
The Beast *	1975	Fr.
A Big Boss	1952	Fr.
The Big Vacation	1967	Fr.
A Blonde Like That!	1963	Fr.

Cadet-Rouselle	1954	Fr.
Cage of Women	1950	Fr.
Call Me Mathilde	1970	Fr.--Col.
Captain Fracasse	1961	Fr.
Danger Is a Woman	1952	Fr.
The Day of Glory	1976	Fr.
Fantomas	1966	Fr./It.
The Fixer	1968	MGM
Furia a Bahia pour OSS 117	1965	Fr.
La Garconne	1957	Fr.
La Gendarme et Les Extraterristes	1978	Fr.
The Gendarme Gets Married	1968	Fr.
Greed in the Sun	1965	Fr./It.--MGM
A Hand to Cut Off	1974	Fr.
The Happiest of Men	1953	Fr.
Hibernators	1969	Fr.
Horace 62	1962	Fr.
The Hunchback	1960	Fr.
Impossible Is Not French	1974	Fr.
L'Ingenue Libertine	1950	Fr.
Is Paris Burning?	1965	Fr.--Par.
Kolka, My Friend	1961	Fr.
Les Liaisons Dangereuses	1961	Fr./It.
The Little Zouave	1950	Fr.
Madron *	1970	Isr.--US
Massacre in Lace	1952	Fr.
Meeting in the Forest	1972	Fr.
Minn, the Simple Wanton	1950	Fr.
Miracle of the Wolves	1961	Fr.
Mitson	1957	Fr.
A Murder Is a Murder	1972	Fr.
My Husband's Marvelous	1953	Fr.
The Mysteries of Paris	1962	Fr.
Now Where Did the Seventh Company Get To?	1974	Fr.
OSS 117-Mission for a Killer	1966	Fr./It.--Emb.
100,000 Dollars in the Sun	1964	Fr.
Operation Lady Marlene	1975	Fr.
Une Parisienne	1958	Fr./It.--UA
The Perfectionist	1952	Fr.
Pioneers	1960	Braz./Fr.
The Postman Goes to War	1967	Fr.
Prey for the Shadows	1961	Fr.
Quai des Blondes	1954	Fr.
Raids On the City	1958	Fr.
Rapture	1965	TCF
Roman Rhythm	1963	Fr.
Rue de L'Estrapade	1953	Fr.
School for Coquettes	1958	Fr.
Le Secret du Chevalier d'Eon	1960	Fr.
The Seventh Company Has Been Found	1975	Fr.

The Seventh Company Outdoors	1977	Fr.
Shaft in Africa	1973	MGM
A Simple Case of Money	1952	Fr.
The Sorceress	1956	Fr.
Sorcery	1962	Fr.
Stew in the Caribbean	1967	Fr.
The Strangers	1969	Fr./Ger./It.
Taxi for Tobruk	1961	Fr./Ger./Sp.
The Three Musketeers	1953	Fr.
The Unknown From Hong Kong	1963	Fr.
Vice and Virtue	1965	Fr./It.--MGM
When the Child Appears	1956	Fr.
Where the Truth Lies	1962	Fr.--Par.
Work's Freedom	1960	Fr.
The Yokel	1960	Fr.

241. ENNIO GUARNIERI

Anyone Can Play	1967	It.
Arabella	1969	It.--Univ.
Ash Wednesday	1973	Par.
Bambole *	1965	It.--Col.
Be Sick ... It's Free	1968	It.
Il...Bel Paese	1978	It.
Better a Widow	1969	It.--Univ.
Bottleneck	1979	Fr./Ger./It./ Sp.
Brief Vacation	1975	It.
Brother Sun, Sister Moon	1972	GB/It.--Par.
Camille 2000	1969	Fr.
The Cassandra Crossing	1976	GB--AE
I Castrati	1964	Fr./It.
Cat	1978	It.--UA
Child of the Night	1978	Fr./It.
The Conjugal Bed	1963	It.--Emb.
Countersex *	1964	Fr./It.
Dancers	1987	It.
The Days Are Numbered	1962	It.
Down the Ancient Staircase	1977	It.--TCF
Drama of the Rich	1974	Fr./It.
End of the Game	1976	Ger./It.--TCF
Francesco *	1989	Ger./It.
Fun Is Beautiful	1980	It.
The Garden of the Finzi-Continis	1970	Ger./It.
Ginger and Fred *	1986	Fr./Ger./It.-- MGM-UA
The Girl and the General	1967	Fr./It.--MGM
The Girl Who Couldn't Say No	1969	It.--TCF
High Infidelity *	1965	Fr./It.
Hitler-the Last Ten Days	1973	GB/It.--Par.

Holiday	1973	It.
L'Ingorgo	1981	Fr.
The Inheritance	1976	It.
Lover, Wife	1977	It.
Luciano	1963	It.
Made in Italy	1967	Fr./It.
Marta	1971	It./Sp.
Medea	1970	Fr./Ger./It.
Metello	1970	It.
Moscow Farewell	1987	It.
Murder on the Bridge	1975	Ger./It.--TCF
The Persian Lamb Coat	1980	It.
The Queen Bee	1963	It.
Queens *	1968	Fr./It.--Col.
The Sea	1962	It.
A Sentimental Attempt	1963	Fr./It.
Seven Golden Men	1965	Fr./It./Sp.-- WB
Seven Golden Men Strike Again	1966	It.
She and He	1969	It.
Story of Piera	1983	It.
Talcum Powder	1982	It.
Tenderly	1969	It.
La Traviata	1982	Univ.
The Trip	1974	It.
The True Story of Camille	1981	Fr./It.
The Visitor	1980	It.
The Voyage	1973	It.
We'll Call Him Andrea	1972	It.
White Voices	1965	Fr./It.
Wifemistress	1979	It.
Wings of the Dove	1981	Fr./It.
Zapped by a Strange Destiny in a Blue August Sea	1975	It.

242. BURNETT GUFFEY (1905-1983)

All the King's Men	1949	Col.
The Ambushers *	1967	Col.
And Baby Makes Three	1950	Col.
Assignment Paris *	1952	Col.
Bamboo Prison	1955	Col.
Battle Stations	1956	Col.
Birdman of Alcatraz	1961	UA
Blonde from Brooklyn	1945	Col.
Bonnie and Clyde	1967	WB
The Brothers Rico	1957	Col.
A Close Call for Boston Blackie	1946	Col.
Convicted	1950	Col.
Count Three and Pray	1955	Col.

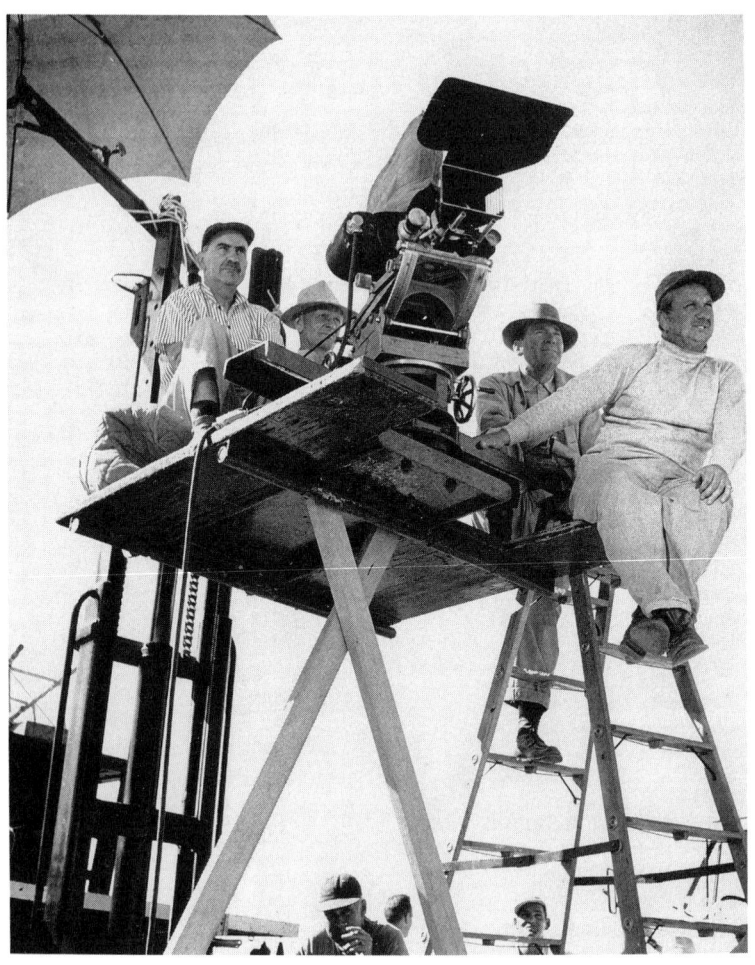

Burnett Guffey (far left) at work on <u>The Violent Men</u> (1955).

Cry for Happy	1961	Col.
Decision at Sundown	1957	Col.
Eadie Was a Lady	1945	Col.
Edge of Eternity	1959	Col.
Emergency Wedding	1950	Col.
Eve Knew Her Apples	1945	Col.
The Family Secret	1951	Col.
Father Is a Bachelor	1950	Col.
The Fighting Guardsman	1945	Col.
Flight From Ashiya *	1963	UA
Framed	1947	Col.
From Here to Eternity	1953	Col.
The Gallant Blade *	1948	Col.
Gallant Journey *	1946	Col.
Gidget	1959	Col.
The Girl of the Limberlost	1945	Col.
Good Neighbor Sam	1964	Col.
The Great White Hope	1970	TCF
Halls of Anger	1969	UA
The Harder They Fall	1956	Col.
Hell to Eternity	1960	AA
Homicidal	1961	Col.
How to Succeed in Business Without Really Trying	1967	UA
Human Desire	1954	Col.
I Love a Mystery	1945	Col.
In a Lonely Place	1950	Col.
Johnny O'Clock	1946	Col.
Kid Galahad	1962	UA
King Rat	1965	Col.
Knock On Any Door	1949	Col.
The Last Posse	1953	Col.
The Learning Tree	1969	WB
Let No Man Write My Epitaph	1960	Col.
The Madwoman of Chaillot *	1969	GB--WB
Me and the Colonel	1958	Col.
Meet Me On Broadway	1946	Col.
Mr. Sardonicus	1961	Col.
The Mountain Road	1960	Col.
My Name Is Julia Ross	1945	Col.
Night Editor *	1946	Col.
Nightfall	1956	Col.
The Notorious Lone Wolf	1946	Col.
Private Hell 36	1954	US
The Reckless Moment	1949	Col.
Sailor's Holiday	1944	Col.
Scandal Sheet	1952	Col.
Screaming Mimi	1958	Col.
Sign of the Ram	1948	Col.
The Silencers	1966	Col.
Sirocco	1951	Col.

The Sniper	1952	Col.
So Dark the Night	1946	Col.
Some Kind of a Nut *	1969	UA
Soul of a Monster	1944	Col.
The Split	1968	MGM
The Steagle	1971	AE
Storm Center	1956	Col.
The Strange One	1957	Col.
Suppose They Gave a War and Nobody Came?	1969	US
They Came to Cordura	1959	Col.
Three Stripes in the Sun	1955	Col.
Tight Spot	1955	Col.
To the Ends of the Earth	1948	Col.
The True Story of Lynn Stuart	1958	Col.
Two of a Kind	1951	Col.
U Boat Prisoner	1944	Col.
Undercover Man	1949	Col.
The Unwritten Code	1944	Col.
The Violent Men *	1955	Col.
Where It's At	1969	UA

243. RENE GUISSART

The Adventures of Carol	1917	US
Ben-Hur *	1925	MGM
The Breaking Point	1921	US
The Butterfly Girl	1921	Pathe
Fighting Odds	1917	Gold.
Harriet and the Piper	1920	FN
Hate Ship	1930	GB--FN
Honey	1931	Par.
Little Women	1919	Par.
Love and Hate	1916	Fox
The Lying Truth	1922	US
My Lady's Garter	1920	Par.
Paddy, the Next Best Thing	1923	GB
The Recoil	1924	Gold.
Sister Against Sister	1917	Fox
Sowing the Wind	1921	FN
Stolen Orders *	1918	US
Treasure Island	1920	Par.
Unwelcome Mother	1916	Fox
Victory	1919	Par.
The Volunteer	1918	US
Wanted-A Mother	1918	US
While Paris Sleeps	1923	US
Woman *	1919	Par.
The Yellow Taifun	1920	FN

244. DAVID GURFINKEL

America 3000	1986	Cannon
The Apple	1980	Ger.--Cannon
Appointment With Death	1988	Cannon
Aunt Clara	1977	Isr.
Avia's Summer	1988	Cannon
The Cop	1971	Isr.
The Delta Force	1986	Cannon
Don't Ever Ask Me If I Love	1978	Isr.
Emperor's New Clothes	1987	Cannon
Enter the Ninja	1981	Cannon
Escape to the Sun	1972	Fr./Ger./Isr.
Every Bastard a King	1970	Isr.
Fifty-Fifty	1971	Isr.
Fish, Football and Girls	1969	Isr.
The Fox in the Chicken Coop	1978	Isr.
Hamshin	1982	Isr.
Highway Queen	1971	Isr.
A Hole in the Moon	1965	Isr.
Hor Balevana	1965	Isr.
Iris	1968	Isr.
Katz and Karasso	1972	Isr.
Kazablan	1973	Isr.--MGM-UA
Laura Adler's Last Love Affair	1990	Isr.
Lover	1986	Cannon
The Magician of Lublin	1979	Ger./Isr.-- Cannon
A Man Called Sarge	1990	Cannon
Marriage: Tel Aviv Style	1979	Isr.
Mata Hari	1985	Cannon
Mute Love	1982	Isr.
My Mother, the General	1979	Isr.
Naked Face	1984	Cannon/MGM- UA
Not Mine to Love	1969	Isr.
Over the Top	1987	WB
Rage and Glory	1984	Isr.
Rappin'	1985	Cannon
Revenge of the Ninja	1983	MGM-UA
The Rooster	1971	Isr.
Rumpelstiltskin	1987	Cannon
Sahara *	1984	MGM-UA
Salsa	1988	Cannon
Siege	1969	Isr.
Sleeping Beauty	1987	Cannon
Take Off	1970	Isr.
A Thousand Little Kisses	1981	Isr.
Three Days and a Child	1967	Isr.
Worlds Apart	1980	Isr.--US

245. CARL GUTHRIE

All I Desire	1953	Univ.
Always Together	1947	WB
April Showers	1948	WB
Backfire	1949	WB
Barricade	1949	WB
Battle Flame	1959	AA
The Beast of Budapest	1958	AA
Bedtime for Bonzo	1951	Univ.
The Big Punch	1948	WB
Bonzo Goes to College	1952	Univ.
Bop Girl Goes Calypso	1957	UA
Caged	1950	WB
Christmas in Connecticut	1945	WB
Cry Wolf	1947	WB
The Dalton Girls	1957	UA
Dawn at Socorro	1954	Univ.
Death in Small Doses	1957	AA
Dondi	1960	AA
Embraceable You	1948	WB
Everything's Ducky	1961	Col.
Finders Keepers	1952	Univ.
Five Minutes to Live	1961	US
Flaxy Martin	1948	WB
Fort Bowie	1958	UA
Fort Massacre	1958	UA
Francis Covers the Big Town	1953	Univ.
Francis Goes to West Point	1952	Univ.
Francis in the Navy	1955	Univ.
Frankenstein '70	1958	AA
The George Raft Story	1961	AA
The Girl From Jones Beach	1949	WB
The Girl in the Kremlin	1957	Univ.
Girls in the Night	1953	Univ.
Gunfight at Dodge City	1959	AA
Hell Bound	1957	UA
Her Kind of Man	1946	WB
Highway 301	1950	WB
Hollywood Story	1951	Univ.
Hot News	1953	Mon.
Hotel Berlin	1945	WB
House on Haunted Hill	1958	AA
In Our Time	1944	WB
Iron Man	1951	Univ.
Jail Busters	1955	AA
Janie	1944	WB
Janie Gets Married	1946	WB
The Jazz Singer	1953	WB
Johnny Dark	1954	Univ.
Joy Ride	1958	AA

King of the Roaring Twenties	1961	WB
King of the Wild Stallions	1959	AA
Kiss of Fire	1955	Univ.
Lady Godiva	1955	Univ.
The Lively Set	1964	Univ.
Long John Silver	1951	Aus.
Ma and Pa Kettle at Home	1954	Univ.
Macabre	1958	AA
Oklahoman	1957	AA
One Last Fling	1949	WB
Playgirl	1954	Univ.
Private Eyes	1953	AA
Quantez	1957	Univ.
The Raiders	1952	Univ.
Ready For the People	1964	WB
Sergeants Three *	1961	UA
Shootout at Medicine Bend	1957	WB
Storm Warning	1950	WB
Summer Love *	1958	Univ.
The Tattered Dress	1957	Univ.
This Side of the Law	1950	WB
Three Sailors and a Girl	1953	WB
Too Much, Too Soon *	1958	WB
Too Young to Know	1945	WB
Twenty Plus Two	1962	AA
Undercover Girl	1950	Univ.
Untamed Youth	1957	WB
Up Periscope	1959	WB
Violent Road	1958	WB
Woman in White	1948	WB
X-15	1962	UA
Yankee Pasha	1954	Univ.
Yellowstone Kelly	1959	WB

246. JACQUES HAITKIN

The Ambulance	1990	US
Angel of H.E.A.T.	1983	US
Cage	1989	US
Cherry 2000	1988	Orion
Galaxy of Terror	1981	US
The Hidden	1987	US
Hot Tomorrows	1978	AFT
House Where Evil Dwells	1982	MGM-UA
The Imagemaker	1986	US
Last Plane Out	1983	US
Lucky Stiff	1989	US
Making the Grade	1984	Cannon/MGM-UA
My Demon Lover	1987	US

A Nightmare on Elm Street 2	1985	US
The Private Eyes	1981	US
The Prize Fighter	1979	Tri-S.
Quiet Cool	1986	US
St. Helens	1981	US
Shocker	1989	Univ.
They Went That-a-Way and That-a-Way	1978	US

247. CONRAD HALL (1926-   )

Black Widow	1987	TCF
Butch Cassidy and the Sundance Kid	1969	TCF
Catch My Soul	1974	US
Cool Hand Luke	1967	WB
The Day of the Locust	1975	Par.
Edge of Fury *	1958	UA
Electra Glide in Blue	1973	UA
Fat City	1972	Col.
The Happy Ending	1969	UA
Harper	1966	WB
Hell in the Pacific	1969	US
In Cold Blood	1967	Col.
Incubus	1965	US
Marathon Man	1976	Par.
The Professionals	1966	Col.
Running Target	1956	UA
Saboteur, Code Name Morituri	1965	TCF
Smile	1975	US
Tell Them Willie Boy Is Here	1969	Univ.
Tequila Sunrise	1988	WB
Trilogy *	1969	AA
Wild Seed	1965	Univ.

248. HARRY HALLENBERGER

Arizona *	1950	Col.
Forlorn River	1937	Par.
Louisiana Purchase *	1941	Par.
Night Work	1939	Par.
Riding High *	1943	Par.
Special Delivery	1927	Par.
The Virginian	1946	Par.

249. ERNEST HALLER (1896-1970)

Age of Indiscretion	1935	MGM
All This and Heaven Too	1940	WB
Always Leave Them Laughing	1949	WB
Any Woman *	1925	Par.

Armored Command	1961	AA
Back From the Dead	1957	TCF
Blues in the Night	1941	WB
Boy and the Pirates	1960	UA
The Bride Came C.O.D.	1941	WB
British Agent	1935	WB
Broadway Nights	1927	FN
Brother Rat	1938	WB
Call It a Day	1937	WB
The Captain's Kid	1936	WB
Carnival Story	1954	US
Chain Lightning	1950	WB
Chances	1931	WB
Chivato	1961	US
The Come On	1956	AA
Convoy	1927	FN
The Crash	1932	FN
The Cruel Tower	1956	AA
Dakota Incident	1956	Rep.
Dallas	1950	WB
Dance Magic	1927	FN
The Dancer of Paris	1926	FN
Dangerous	1935	WB
Dark Streets	1929	FN
Dark Victory	1939	WB
The Dawn Patrol	1930	WB
Dead Men Tell No Tales	1920	Vita.
Dead Ringer	1964	WB
Deception	1946	WB
Desirable	1934	WB
Devotion	1944	WB
The Discarded Woman *	1920	US
The Doughgirls	1944	WB
Drag	1929	FN/WB
Easy to Love	1934	WB
The Emperor Jones	1933	UA
Empty Hearts	1924	US
Escapade	1935	MGM
Fear No More	1961	US
The Finger Points	1931	WB
The Firebird	1934	WB
The Flame and the Arrow	1950	WB
Footsteps in the Dark	1941	WB
For the Love of Mike	1927	FN
Four Daughters	1938	WB
Four's a Crowd	1938	WB
French Dressing	1927	FN
George Washington Slept Here	1942	WB
Gilded Lily	1921	Par.
Girl in the Glass Cage	1929	FN/WB
Girls about Town	1931	Par.

God's Little Acre	1959	US
Gone With the Wind *	1939	MGM/Selz.
The Great Deception	1926	FN
The Great Garrick	1937	WB
The Great O'Malley	1937	WB
Hair Trigger Baxter *	1926	US
Harold Teen	1928	FN
Hell on Devil's Island	1957	TCF
Hell's Five Hours	1958	AA
Homeward Bound	1928	Par.
Honeymoon for Three	1941	WB
House of Horror *	1929	FN/WB
The House on 56th Street	1933	WB
Humoresque	1947	WB
In This Our Life	1942	WB
The Inner Voice	1920	US
International House	1932	Par.
Invisible Stripes	1940	WB
The Iron Trail	1921	UA
It All Came True	1940	WB
Jezebel	1938	WB
Jim Thorpe-All American	1951	WB
Journal of a Crime	1934	WB
The Key	1934	WB
King of the Jungle	1933	Par.
The Lash	1930	FN
Lilies of the Field	1963	UA
Mad Hour	1928	FN
Magic Fire	1956	Rep.
Man of the West	1958	UA
Manpower	1941	WB
Married Too Young	1962	US
Mary Jane's Pa	1935	FN/WB
Men in War	1957	US
Mildred Pierce	1945	WB
Millie	1931	RKO
The Miracle	1959	WB
Mr. Skeffington	1944	WB
Monsoon	1953	UA
Mothers of Men	1920	Selz.
Mountain Justice	1937	WB
Murders in the Zoo	1933	Par.
My Dream Is Yours	1949	WB
My Girl Tisa	1948	US
Naughty Baby	1929	FN
The Ne'er-Do-Well *	1923	Par.
Neglected Wives	1920	US
The New Commandment *	1925	FN
Night After Night	1932	Par.
No Time for Comedy	1940	WB
A Notorious Affair	1930	FN/WB

On Moonlight Bay	1951	WB
One Night at Susie's	1930	FN/WB
Out of the Ruins	1928	FN
Parisian Nights	1925	US
Petticoat Fever	1936	MGM
Pied Piper Malone	1924	Par.
Plunder Road	1957	TCF
Pressure Point	1962	UA
Prince of Tempters	1926	FN
Princess O'Rourke	1943	WB
Public Enemy's Wife	1935	WB
Rebel Without a Cause	1955	WB
The Reckless Lady	1926	FN
The Restless Ones	1965	US
Rhapsody in Blue *	1945	WB
The Rich Are Always With Us	1932	WB
The Road to Arcady	1922	US
The Roaring Twenties	1939	WB
Rough Ridin'	1924	US
Salvation Nell	1921	FN
Saratoga Trunk	1943	WB
Scarlet Dawn	1932	WB
The Secret Bride	1935	WB
Son of the Gods	1930	FN
Speed Crazy	1939	AA
Stacked Cards	1926	US
Strange Intruder	1957	AA
Street of Women	1932	WB
Such a Little Queen	1921	US
Sunny	1930	WB
Ten Cents a Dance *	1931	Col.
That Certain Woman	1937	WB
The Third Voice	1959	TCF
Three Blondes in His Life	1961	US
Three Keys	1925	US
Trumpet Island *	1920	Vita.
24 Hours	1931	Par.
The Unfaithful	1947	WB
The Verdict	1946	WB
Voice of Bugle Ann	1936	MGM
Weary River	1929	FN/WB
Wedding Rings	1929	FN/WB
Whatever Happened to Baby Jane?	1962	WB
Wheel of Chance	1928	FN
The Whip Woman	1928	FN
Wife Against Wife	1921	FN
The Wilderness Woman	1926	FN
Winter Meeting	1948	WB
Wolves of the Rail *	1918	US
Woman From Monte Carlo	1932	WB
Woman-Proof	1923	Par.

| The Young Don't Cry | 1957 | Col. |
| Young Nowheres | 1929 | FN/WB |

250. SOL HALPRIN (1902-1977)

Cowboy Kid	1928	Fox
Double Cross-Roads *	1930	Fox
The Girl-Shy Cowboy	1928	Fox
Married in Hollywood *	1929	Fox
Taking a Chance	1928	Fox
Wild West Romance	1928	Fox

251. WILLY HAMEISTER

Backstairs *	1921	Ger.
Cabinet of Dr. Caligari	1920	Ger.
Genuine	1920	Ger.
Die Marquise von Pompadour	1931	Ger.
No Ceremony Without Meyer *	1932	Ger.
Suzanne Cleans Up *	1931	Ger.

252. PETER HANNAN

Brimstone and Treacle	1982	UA
Club Paradise	1986	WB
Dance With a Stranger	1985	US
A Dangerous Summer	1982	Aus.
Eskimo Nell	1975	GB
Flame	1975	GB
Full Circle	1976	GB
Half Moon Street	1986	TCF
How to Get Ahead in Advertising	1989	WB
A Handful of Dust	1988	GB
Insignificance	1985	US
The Lonely Passion of Judith Hearne	1987	GB
The Missionary	1982	Col.
Monty Python's The Meaning of Life	1983	Univ.
Moon Over the Alley	1980	GB
Not Without My Daughter	1990	MGM
The Stud	1978	GB
Turtle Diary	1985	GB

253. RUSSELL HARLAN (1903-1974)

American Empire	1942	UA
Bad Men of Tombstone	1949	AA
Bar 20	1943	UA

Bar 20 Justice	1938	Par.
The Big Sky	1952	RKO
The Blackboard Jungle	1955	MGM
Border Patrol	1943	UA
Border Vigilantes	1941	Par.
Cassidy of Bar 20	1938	Par.
Cherokee Strip	1940	Par.
Colt Comrades	1943	UA
Darling Lili *	1970	Par.
Dear Heart	1964	WB
Doomed Caravan	1941	Par.
False Colors	1943	UA
Forty Thieves	1944	UA
Four Faces West	1948	UA
The Frontiersman	1938	Par.
A Gathering of Eagles	1962	Univ.
The Great Race *	1965	WB
Gun Crazy	1950	US
Hatari!	1962	Par.
Hawaii	1966	UA
Heart of Arizona	1938	Par.
Heritage of the Desert	1939	Par.
Hidden Gold	1940	Par.
Hopalong Rides Again	1937	Par.
Hoppy Serves a Writ	1943	UA
In Old Colorado	1941	Par.
In Old Mexico	1938	Par.
The Kangaroo Kid	1950	Aus.--US
The Kansan	1943	UA
King Creole	1958	Par.
Knights of the Range	1940	Par.
Land of the Pharaohs *	1955	WB
The Last Hunt	1955	MGM
Law of the Pampas	1939	Par.
The Leather Burners	1943	UA
The Light of Western Stars	1940	Par.
The Llano Kid	1939	Par.
Lost Canyon	1943	UA
Lumberjack	1944	UA
Lust for Life *	1956	MGM
The Man Who Cheated Himself	1950	TCF
Man's Favorite Sport?	1963	Univ.
The Mysterious Rider	1938	Par.
Mystery Man	1944	UA
North of the Rio Grande	1937	Par.
Operation Petticoat	1959	Univ.
Outlaws of the Desert	1941	Par.
The Parson of Panamint	1941	Par.
Partners of the Plains	1938	Par.
Pirates on Horseback	1941	Par.
Pollyanna	1960	Dis.

Pride of the West	1938	Par.
Quick Before It Melts	1964	MGM
Ramrod *	1947	UA
Range War	1939	Par.
Red River	1948	UA
Renegade Trail	1939	Par.
Riders of the Deadline	1943	UA
Riders of the Timberline	1941	Par.
The Ring	1952	US
Rio Bravo	1959	WB
Riot in Cell Block Eleven	1954	AA
The Round Up	1941	Par.
Ruby Gentry	1952	US
Run Silent, Run Deep	1958	UA
Rustlers Valley	1937	Par.
Santa Fe Marshal	1940	Par.
Secrets of the Wasteland	1941	Par.
The Showdown	1940	Par.
Silver on the Sage	1939	Par.
Silver Queen	1942	UA
Something of Value	1957	MGM
Southside 1-1000	1950	AA/Mon.
The Spiral Road	1962	Univ.
Stagecoach War	1940	Par.
Stick to Your Guns	1941	Par.
Sunrise at Campobello	1960	WB
Sunset Trail	1939	Par.
Tarzan and the Slave Girl	1950	RKO
Tarzan's Desert Mystery *	1943	RKO
Texas Masquerade	1944	UA
Texas Trail	1937	Par.
The Thing	1951	RKO
This Could Be the Night	1957	MGM
Three Men From Texas	1940	Par.
To Kill a Mockingbird	1962	Univ.
Tobruk	1967	Univ.
Tombstone: The Town Too Tough to Die	1942	Par.
Twilight on the Trail	1941	Par.
Undercover Man	1942	UA
A Walk in the Sun	1945	US
Wings *	1929	Par.
Witness for the Prosecution	1957	UA
The Woman of the Town	1943	UA

254. HARRY B. HARRIS

Band Wagon	1939	GB
Captain Macklin	1915	US
Destiny	1919	Univ.

Her Boy	1918	Metro.
Her Shattered Love	1915	US
The Hope of His Side	1935	GB--UA
In Folly's Trail	1920	Univ.
Larceny Street	1941	GB
Lights of Victory	1919	Univ.
Limelight	1936	GB
The Mints of Hell	1919	US
Mother of His Children	1920	Fox
The Outcast	1915	US
Raffles, the Amateur Cracksman	1917	US
The Right to Happiness *	1919	Univ.
Rose of Nome	1920	Fox
The Secret of Stamboul	1936	GB
Shooting Stars *	1928	GB
A Sister to Salome	1920	Fox
The Sky's the Limit	1937	GB
The Soul of Magdalene	1917	Metro.
Street Singer	1937	GB
West of the Water Tower	1924	Par.
White Lies	1920	Fox
Whitewashed Walls	1919	US

255. WALTER HARVEY

Account Rendered	1957	GB
Bad Blonde	1953	Lip.
Broth of a Boy	1958	GB
Bulldog Drummond at Bay	1937	GB--Rep.
Castle of Crimes	1940	GB
The Creeping Unknown	1956	GB--Ham./UA
Kill Her Gently	1958	GB
Man Bait	1952	GB--Lip.
Murder in Eden	1962	GB
North Sea Patrol	1940	GB
Ourselves Alone	1936	GB
The Saint's Girl Friday	1954	GB--Ham./ RKO
Sensation	1936	GB
Shadow of Fear	1963	GB
Spring Meeting	1940	GB
Stolen Face	1952	GB--Ham./Lip.
The Tenth Man	1936	GB
The Terror	1938	GB
The Tower of Terror	1941	GB--Mon.
Whispering Smith Hits London	1951	GB--Ham./RKO
Yellow Sands	1938	GB
Yes, Madam	1938	GB

256. BYRON HASKIN (1899-1984)

Across the Pacific	1926	WB
As the Earth Turns	1934	WB
Broken Chains	1922	Gold.
Colleen *	1936	WB
The Deadline	1932	Col.
Don Juan	1926	WB
Glad Rag Doll	1929	WB
The Green Light	1937	WB
The Guilty Generation	1931	Col.
His Majesty Bunker Bean	1925	WB
Hurricane's Gal *	1922	FN
I Married a Doctor	1936	WB
Madonna From Avenue 'A'	1929	WB
A Midsummer Night's Dream *	1935	WB
Millionaires *	1926	WB
On Thin Ice	1925	WB
On Trial	1928	WB
Personal Maid's Secret	1935	WB
The Sea Beast *	1926	WB
The Singing Fool	1928	WB
Slander the Woman	1923	FN
Stage Struck	1936	WB
Tough To Be Famous *	1932	FN
When a Man Loves *	1927	WB
Where the Worst Begins	1925	US
Wolf's Clothing *	1927	WB
World's a Stage	1922	US

257. PHILIP HATKIN

The Bluffer	1919	US
Bolshevism On Trial	1919	US
The Brand of Satan	1919	US
Carnival	1921	US
The Cost	1920	Par.
The Cross Bearer	1918	US
The Divine Sacrifice	1918	US
Guilty of Love	1920	Par.
Half an Hour	1920	Par.
Heart of Gold	1919	US
Home Wanted	1919	US
The Iron Ring	1917	US
Just Sylvia	1918	US
Love and the Woman	1919	US
The Maid of Belgium	1917	US
The Man Who Forgot *	1917	US
Moral Courage	1917	US
The Moral Deadline	1919	US

Old Nest *	1921	Gold.
Perils of Divorce	1916	US
A Romantic Adventuress	1920	Par.
The Social Highwayman	1916	US
The Social Pirate	1917	US
The Trap	1918	US
What Love Forgives *	1919	US
Yankee Pluck	1917	US
The Zero Hour	1918	US

258. ROBERT HAUSER

Final Chapter-Walking Tall	1977	AIP
The Frisco Kid	1979	WB
Hail Hero!	1969	NG
How To Steal the World	1968	US
Le Mans *	1971	NG
Lost in the Stars	1974	AFT
A Man Called Horse	1970	NG
Mean Dog Blues	1978	AIP
Norwood	1969	Par.
The Odd Couple	1968	Par.
Riot	1968	Par.
Soldier Blue	1970	AE
The Sweet Ride	1968	TCF
Twilight's Last Gleaming	1977	AA
Willard	1971	US

259. GEORGE HEATH

Ants in His Pants	1940	Aus.
Bitter Springs	1950	Aus.
Broken Melody	1937	Aus.
Bush Christmas	1947	Aus.--Univ.
Dad and Dave Come to Town	1938	Aus.
Dad Rudd, M.P.	1940	Aus.
40,000 Horsemen	1941	Aus.
Gone To the Dogs	1939	Aus.
It Isn't Done	1937	Aus.
Lovers and Luggers	1938	Aus.
Massacre Hill	1949	GB--Eal.
Mr. Chedworth Steps Out	1939	Aus.
Orphan of the Wilderness	1937	Aus.
Pacific Adventure	1947	Aus.--Col.
Rats of Tobruk	1945	Aus.
Tall Timbers	1937	Aus.
Thoroughbred	1936	Aus.
Vengeance of the Deep	1940	Aus.
Wherever She Goes	1953	Aus.--Eal.
Wild Innocence	1937	Aus.

260. OTTO HELLER (1896-1970)

Alfie	1966	GB--Par.
Alibi	1943	GB
The Amazing Quest of Ernest Bliss	1936	GB
Before Matriculation *	1932	Ger.
The Big Show	1961	TCF
Bila Nemoc	1937	GB
Bloomfield	1969	GB
Bond Street *	1948	GB
Can Hieronymous Merkin Ever Forget	xxx	
Mercy Humppe and Find True		
Happiness?	1969	GB--Univ.
Candlelight in Algeria *	1943	GB
Child in the House	1956	GB
The Crimson Pirate	1952	GB--WB
The Cruel Girl Friend	1932	Ger.
Curse of the Mummy's Tomb	1964	GB--Col.
The Dark Tower	1943	GB--WB
The Divided Heart	1954	GB--Eal.
A Dog of Flanders	1959	TCF
Don't Raise the Bridge, Lower the Water	1967	GB--Col.
Dreams Come True	1936	GB
Duffy	1968	GB--Col.
The Duke Wore Jeans	1958	GB
Ferry to Hong Kong	1959	GB--Rank
La Fille du Regiment	1933	Fr.
Die Fledermaus	1932	Fr.
Flesh and Blood	1951	GB
Flight From Folly	1944	GB--WB
Forty Years	1938	Holl.
Funeral in Berlin	1967	GB--Par.
Gaiety George	1946	GB
A Girl Friend as Sweet as You	1931	Ger.
Golden Arrow	1949	GB
Her Paneled Door	1950	GB
The High Command *	1936	GB
His Majesty O'Keefe	1954	GB--WB
The Hundred Pound Window	1943	GB--WB
I Live in Grosvenor Square *	1945	GB
I Married a Spy	1938	GB--GN
I'll Get You for This	1950	GB
I'll Never Forget What's His Name	1967	GB--Univ.
In Search of Gregory *	1969	GB--Univ.
The Ipcress File	1965	GB--Rank
The Ladykillers	1955	GB--Eal.
The Last Days of Dolwyn *	1949	GB
Life for Ruth	1962	GB--Rank
Light in the Piazza	1962	GB--MGM
Mademoiselle Docteur *	1937	GB
The Man Who Watched the Trains		
Go By	1952	GB

Manuela	1957	GB
Masquerade	1965	GB--UA
Mr. Emmanuel *	1944	GB
The Naked Runner	1967	GB--WB
Never Take No for an Answer	1951	GB
Night Boat to Dublin	1945	GB
A Night in Paradise	1933	Ger.
The Night Invader	1942	GB--WB
Now Barabbas Was a Robber	1949	GB--WB
The Passionate Stranger	1956	GB
Peeping Tom	1959	GB
Port Arthur	1941	Czech.
The Private Secretary	1935	GB
The Queen of Spades	1948	GB
The Rainbow Jacket	1954	GB--Eal.
Richard III	1955	GB
Sacred Waters	1961	Switz.
The Sheriff of Fractured Jaw	1958	GB--TCF
The Silent Enemy *	1958	GB
The Singer Not the Song	1960	GB--Rank
Sorcerer	1932	Ger.
The Square Ring	1953	GB--Eal.
Temptation Harbour	1946	GB
That Riviera Touch	1966	GB--Rank
They Made Me a Fugitive	1947	GB--WB
They Met in the Dark	1943	GB--Rank
They Met on Skis *	1940	Fr.
Those of the Side Show *	1932	Ger.
Tiara Tahiti	1962	GB--Rank
To Squeal	1931	Ger.
Tomorrow It Will Be Better *	1939	Holl.
Too Hot to Handle	1960	GB
The Truth About Women	1957	GB
Two Women	1940	Fr.
Under Secret Orders	1943	GB
The Vicious Circle	1957	GB
Victim	1961	GB--Rank
We Joined the Navy	1962	GB
West Eleven	1963	GB
What a Crazy World	1963	GB
Who Done It?	1956	GB--Eal.
Woman of Straw	1964	GB--UA
The Woman With No Name	1950	GB

261. PETER HENNESSY

Carry On Sergeant	1958	GB
Cat Girl	1957	GB
The Eyes of Annie Jones	1963	GB
Life in Danger	1964	GB

The Quare Fellow	1962	GB
Rock Around the World	1957	GB
The Savage Innocents *	1960	Fr./GB/It.
The Solitary Child	1958	GB
Time Lock	1957	GB

262. SID HICKOX (1895-   )

All Through the Night	1942	WB
Along the Great Divide	1950	WB
Always in My Heart	1942	WB
The Avenger	1933	Mon.
Battle Cry	1955	WB
Bedside	1934	WB
The Big Shakedown	1934	WB
The Big Shot	1942	WB
The Big Sleep	1946	WB
A Bill of Divorcement	1932	RKO
Blackwell's Island	1939	WB
Blonde Crazy	1931	WB
Blowing Wild	1953	WB
Brides Are Like That	1936	WB
Bright Lights	1935	WB
British Intelligence	1940	WB
Broadminded	1931	FN
The Case of the Velvet Claws	1936	WB
Central Airport	1933	WB
Central Park	1932	WB
Cheyenne	1947	WB
Colorado Territory	1949	WB
Confession	1937	WB
Convicted	1931	US
The Crowd Roars *	1932	WB
Dames *	1935	WB
Dance Goes On	1930	WB
Dark Passage	1947	WB
Democracy *	1920	US
Distant Drums	1951	US
The Doctor Takes a Wife	1940	Col.
East of the River	1940	WB
Edge of Darkness	1943	WB
Everybody's Hobby	1939	WB
Female	1933	WB
Fighter Squadron	1948	WB
First Lady	1937	WB
Flirting Widow	1930	FN
Flowing Gold	1940	WB
Footlights and Fools *	1929	WB
Fort Worth	1951	WB
Freshman Love	1936	WB

Frisco Jenny	1933	WB
Gentleman Jim	1942	WB
Give Me Your Heart	1936	WB
God Is My Co-Pilot	1945	WB
Goose and the Gander	1935	WB
The Gorilla	1930	WB
Grand Slam	1933	WB
The Great Jewel Robber	1940	WB
Happiness Ahead	1928	FN
The Hatchet Man	1932	WB
Heat Lightning	1934	WB
The Horn Blows at Midnight	1945	WB
Hot Stuff	1929	WB
I Am a Thief	1935	WB
I Found Stella Parish	1935	WB
I Sell Anything	1935	WB
The Kid From Kokomo	1939	WB
King of the Lumberjacks	1940	WB
King of the Underworld	1939	WB
The Last Flight	1931	WB
The Law in Her Hands	1936	WB
Law of the Tropics	1941	WB
Lightning Strikes Twice	1951	WB
Lilac Time *	1928	FN
The Little Giant	1926	Univ.
The Little Giant	1933	WB
Living On Velvet	1935	WB
A Lost Lady	1934	WB
Love Is a Racket	1932	WB
The Love Racket	1929	WB
The Man I Love	1946	WB
The Man Who Talked Too Much	1940	WB
Marriage Morals *	1923	US
Mary Stevens MD	1933	WB
Men Are Such Fools	1938	WB
Missing Witness	1937	WB
My Bill	1938	FN/WB
The Naughty Flirt	1931	WB
Northern Pursuit	1943	WB
Oh, Kay!	1928	FN
One Sunday Afternoon *	1943	WB
Party Husband	1931	WB
Private Life of Helen of Troy *	1927	FN
The Purchase Price	1932	WB
Registered Nurse	1934	WB
The Return of Doctor X	1939	WB
The Right to Live	1935	WB
Safe in Hell	1931	WB
Sailors' Wives	1928	FN
The St. Louis Kid	1934	WB
San Quentin	1937	WB

School Days	1921	WB
Secrets of an Actress	1938	WB
Sensation Hunter	1934	Mon.
Silver River	1948	WB
A Slight Case of Murder	1938	WB
Slim	1937	WB
Smiling Irish Eyes *	1929	WB
So Big	1932	WB
Special Agent	1935	WB
Stolen Holiday	1937	WB
A Stolen Life *	1946	WB
Stranded	1935	WB
Strictly Modern	1930	WB
Sweet Mama	1930	WB
Synthetic Sin	1929	WB
Tear Gas Squad	1940	WB
Them!	1954	WB
Thieves Fall Out	1941	FN/WB
Those Who Dance	1930	WB
Three Secrets	1949	WB
To Have and Have Not	1944	WB
Too Young to Marry	1931	WB
Top Speed	1930	WB
Trailin' West *	1936	WB
Twenty Thousand Sweethearts	1934	WB
Two Against the World	1936	WB
Two Weeks Off	1929	WB
Uncertain Glory	1944	WB
Under 18	1931	WB
Underground	1941	WB
The Wagons Roll at Night	1941	WB
West Point Story	1950	WB
White Heat	1949	WB
Why Be Good?	1929	FN
The Winning Team	1952	WB
Women Are Like That	1938	WB
Women in the Wind	1939	WB
Your Best Friend *	1922	WB

263. ARTHUR HIGGINS

The Adorable Outcast *	1928	Aus.
The Blue Mountains Mystery	1922	Aus.
The Bushwhackers	1925	Aus.
Circumstance	1922	Aus.
Diggers in Blighty	1933	Aus.
Fisher's Ghost	1924	Aus.
Ginger Mick	1920	Aus.
Harmony Row	1933	Aus.
Hills of Hate	1926	Aus.

His Royal Highness	1932	Aus.
The Kid Stakes	1927	Aus.
Odds On	1928	Aus.
On Our Selection	1920	Aus.
Peter Vernon's Silence	1926	Aus.
Rudd's New Selection	1921	Aus.
The Sentimental Bloke	1919	Aus.
Son Is Born	1946	Aus.
Sunshine Sally	1922	Aus.
Townies and Hayseeds	1923	Aus.
Trooper O'Brien	1928	Aus.
White Death *	1936	Aus.
The Woman Suffers	1918	Aus.

264. ERNEST HIGGINS

The Church and the Woman	1917	Aus.
East Lynne	1922	Aus.
Struck Oil	1919	Aus.
Sweet Nell of Old Drury	1911	Aus.
The Waybacks	1918	Aus.

265. KEN HIGGINS

Cop-Out	1967	GB
Darling	1965	GB
French Dressing	1963	GB
Games That Lovers Play	1971	GB
Georgy Girl	1966	GB--Col.
Golden Rendezvous	1977	US
Hot Millions	1968	MGM
I'm Not Feeling Myself Tonight	1976	GB
The Idol	1966	GB
Julius Caesar	1969	GB
The Midas Run	1969	US
Salt and Pepper	1968	GB--UA
Spy With a Cold Nose	1966	GB--Par.
Stranger in the House	1967	GB
Swingers' Paradise	1965	GB--AIP
Up Jumped a Swagman	1965	GB
The Virgin Soldiers	1969	GB--Col.
You Can't Win 'Em All	1970	GB--Col.

266. TASMAN HIGGINS

A Coo-ee From Home	1918	Aus.
A Daughter of the East	1924	Aus.
Heritage	1935	Aus.

The Hordern Mystery	1920	Aus.
In the Wake of the Bounty	1933	Aus.
Jeweled Nights *	1925	Aus.
The Life Story of John Lee	1921	Aus.
The Rushing Tide	1927	Aus.
Uncivilized	1936	Aus.

267. PERCY HILBURN

After Midnight	1927	MGM
Ben-Hur *	1925	MGM
Beverly of Graustark	1926	MGM
Black Bird	1926	MGM
Body and Soul	1927	MGM
The Branding Iron	1920	Gold.
Broken Barriers	1924	MGM
Bunty Pulls the Strings	1921	Gold.
Clear All Wires	1933	MGM
Confessions of a Queen	1925	MGM
The Cossacks	1928	MGM
Dangerous Days	1920	Gold.
The Demi-Bride	1927	MGM
The Dixie Handicap	1925	MGM
The Eternal Struggle	1923	Metro.
Flame of the Desert *	1919	US
The Flaming Forest	1926	MGM
The Girl From the Outside *	1919	Gold.
Godless Men	1921	Gold.
Good News	1930	MGM
The Goose Girl	1915	Par.
The Great Divide	1925	MGM
Hearts Aflame	1923	Metro.
The Hell Cat	1918	US
His Glorious Night	1929	MGM
The Iron Man	1931	Univ.
A Japanese Nightingale *	1918	Pathe
Man With Two Mothers	1922	Gold.
Man, Woman and Sin	1927	MGM
Mary Ellen Comes to Town	1920	Par.
Memory Lane	1926	FN
Mysterious Island	1929	MGM
The Narrow Path *	1918	Pathe
The Old West *	1921	Gold.
The Pest	1919	Gold.
The Poverty of Riches	1921	Gold.
The Puppet Crown	1915	Par.
Redemption	1930	MGM
The Rogue Song *	1930	MGM
Shadows	1919	Gold.
Sis Hopkins	1919	Gold.

Snowblind	1921	Gold.
The Storm	1922	Univ.
The Stronger Vow	1919	Gold.
The Sunset Trail	1917	US
Tower of Lies	1925	MGM
The Turn of the Wheel	1918	Gold.
The Unholy Three	1930	MGM
Valencia	1926	MGM
Way for a Sailor	1930	MGM
West of Zanzibar	1928	MGM
The White Desert	1925	MGM
Woman and the Puppet *	1920	US
The World and Its Women	1919	Gold.

268. JACK HILDYARD (1915-   )

Anastasia	1956	TCF
Another Time, Another Place	1958	GB--Par.
Battle of the Bulge	1965	WB
The Beast Must Die	1974	GB
Blue Movie Blackmail	1973	GB
The Bridge On the River Kwai	1957	GB--Col.
Caesar and Cleopatra *	1945	GB--Rank
Cardboard Cavalier *	1949	GB--Rank
Casino Royale	1967	GB--Col.
Cat and Mouse	1974	GB
Charley Moon	1956	GB
The Chiltern Hundreds *	1949	GB--Rank
Circus World	1964	US
The Deep Blue Sea	1955	GB--TCF
The Devil's Disciple	1959	GB--UA
Emily	1976	GB
55 Days at Peking	1962	US
The First Gentleman	1948	GB--Col.
The First of the Few	1942	GB
Folly To Be Wise	1952	GB
French Without Tears *	1939	GB--Par.
The Green Scarf	1954	GB
The Gypsy and the Gentleman	1957	GB--Rank
Hard Contract	1969	TCF
The Heart of the Matter	1953	GB
Hobson's Choice	1953	GB
Home at Seven *	1952	GB
Jet Storm	1959	GB
The Journey	1959	MGM
The Lamp Still Burns *	1943	GB
The Last Chapter	1974	GB--Rank/TCF
Lion of the Desert	1980	US
Live Now, Pay Later	1962	GB
The Living Idol	1956	Mex.--MGM

The March Hare	1956	GB
The Millionairess	1960	GB--TCF
Mrs. Brown, You've Got a Lovely Daughter	1968	GB--MGM
Modesty Blaise	1966	GB--TCF
Mohammed, Messenger of God	1976	Leb.
Not Now Comrade	1977	GB
Perfect Woman *	1949	GB
Puppet On a Chain *	1970	GB
The Reluctant Widow	1950	GB--Rank
Road to Hong Kong	1962	GB--UA
School for Secrets	1946	GB--Rank
Sixth and Main *	1977	US
Sleeping Car to Trieste *	1948	GB
The Sound Barrier	1952	GB
Suddenly Last Summer	1959	GB--Col.
Summertime	1955	GB
The Sundowners	1960	Aus./GB--WB
The Teckman Mystery	1954	GB
Topaz	1969	Univ.
The VIPs	1963	GB--MGM
Vice Versa	1947	GB--Rank
Villa Rides!	1968	Par.
While the Sun Shines	1946	GB
Wild Geese	1978	GB--Rank
You Can't Beat the Irish	1951	GB

269. GEORGE W. HILL

Buckshot John	1915	Par.
Burning Daylight in Alaska	1914	Par.
Burning Daylight in Civilization	1914	Par.
The Flying Torpedo	1916	US
The Hypocrites *	1915	Par.
Less Than the Dust	1916	US
Martin Eden	1914	US
Polly of the Circus	1917	Gold.
Pretty Mrs. Smith	1915	Par.
The Pursuit of the Phantom	1914	Par.
Remodeling Her Husband *	1920	Par.
The Sea Wolf	1913	US
Turning the Tables	1919	Par.
The Waiting Soul	1917	Metro.

270. ERWIN HILLIER (1911-   )

Boy Ten Feet Tall	1963	GB
The Butler's Dilemma	1943	GB
A Canterbury Tale	1944	GB--Rank

Castle in the Air	1952	GB
Chase a Crooked Shadow	1957	GB
The Dam Busters	1954	GB
Duel in the Jungle	1954	GB
Eye of the Devil	1967	GB--MGM
Father's Doing Fine	1952	GB
Girls At Sea	1958	GB
Go To Blazes	1961	GB
Happy Go Lovely	1950	GB
I Know Where I'm Going	1945	GB
The Interrupted Journey *	1949	GB
Isn't Life Wonderful?	1952	GB
Let's Be Happy	1957	GB
London Town	1946	GB
The Long and the Short and the Tall	1960	GB
The Mark of Cain	1947	GB
The Mark of the Hawk *	1958	Univ.
A Matter of Who	1961	GB--MGM
Mr. Perrin and Mr. Traill *	1948	GB
Naked Earth	1958	GB--TCF
The Naked Edge	1961	GB
Now and Forever	1955	GB
The October Man *	1947	GB
Operation Crossbow	1965	GB--MGM
The Pot Carriers	1962	GB
Private Angelo *	1949	GB
The Quiller Memorandum	1966	GB--Rank
Sands of the Kalahari	1965	GB
School For Scoundrels	1960	GB
Shadow of the Eagle *	1950	GB
Shake Hands With the Devil	1959	Ire.--UA
The Shoes of the Fisherman	1968	MGM
The Silver Fleet	1943	GB
They Knew Mr. Knight	1945	GB
The Valley of Gwangi	1968	WB
The Weaker Sex *	1948	GB
Where's Charley?	1952	GB--WB
Will Any Gentleman?	1953	GB
The Woman's Angle	1952	GB

271. PAUL HIPP

Blood and Lace	1971	AIP
The Boogens	1982	US
Fandango	1970	US
Grave of the Vampire	1972	US
Hangar 18	1980	US
The Incredible Two-Headed Transplant *	1970	AIP
The Politicians *	1970	US

President Must Die	1981	US
Psycho From Texas	1982	US
The Ribald Tales of Robin Hood	1969	US
Starlet	1969	US
Sweet Jesus, Preacher Man	1973	MGM
Sweet Trash	1970	US
Thar She Blows	1969	US
Trader Hornee	1970	US

272. GERALD HIRSCHFELD

Americathon	1979	UA
The Bell Jar	1979	Avco
C Man	1949	US
The Car	1977	Univ.
Child's Play	1972	Par.
Coma *	1978	MGM
Cotton Comes to Harlem	1970	UA
Days in My Father's House	1968	Den.--US
Diary of a Mad Housewife	1970	Univ.
Doc	1971	UA
Fail Safe	1964	Col.
Goodbye Columbus	1969	Par.
The Gravy Train	1974	Col.
Guilty Bystander	1950	US
Head Office	1986	Tri-S.
The House of God	1984	UA
The Incident	1967	TCF
Last Summer	1969	US
Malone	1987	Orion
Mr. Universe	1951	EL
My Favorite Year	1982	MGM-UA
Neighbors	1981	Col.
One Summer Love	1976	AIP
Some Kind of a Nut *	1969	UA
Summer Wishes, Winter Dreams	1973	Col.
T. R. Baskin	1971	Par.
To Be or Not To Be	1983	TCF
Two Gals and a Guy	1951	UA
Two Minute Warning	1976	Univ.
Two People	1973	Univ.
The Ultimate Warrior	1973	WB
W	1973	US
Why Would I Lie?	1980	UA
With These Hands	1950	US
World's Greatest Lover	1977	TCF
Young Frankenstein	1974	TCF

273. WINTON HOCH (1910-   )

The Big Circus	1959	AA
Bird of Paradise	1951	TCF
Darby O'Gill and the Little People	1959	Dis.
Dive Bomber *	1941	WB
Dr. Cyclops *	1940	Par.
Five Weeks in a Balloon	1962	TCF
The Green Berets	1968	WB
Halls of Montezuma *	1950	TCF
Jet Pilot	1957	US
The Lost World	1960	TCF
Melody Time	1948	Dis.
The Missouri Traveler	1958	Dis.
Mr. Roberts	1955	WB
Necromancy	1973	US
The Quiet Man *	1952	Rep.
The Redhead From Wyoming	1953	Univ.
The Reluctant Dragon *	1941	Dis.
Robinson Crusoe on Mars	1964	Par.
The Searchers	1956	WB
Sergeants Three *	1961	UA
She Wore a Yellow Ribbon	1949	RKO
So Dear to My Heart	1948	Dis.
The Sundowners	1950	EL
Tap Roots *	1948	Univ.
This Earth Is Mine *	1959	Univ.
Three Godfathers	1948	MGM
Tulsa	1949	EL
Voyage to the Bottom of the Sea *	1961	TCF
The Young Land *	1959	Col.

274. KEN HODGES

Assault	1970	GB--Rank
Assignment K	1968	GB--Col.
Baffled!	1972	GB
Behemoth the Sea Monster	1959	GB
The Comedy Man	1964	GB
Confessions From a Holiday Camp	1977	GB
Confessions of a Driving Instructor	1976	GB
David Copperfield	1969	GB
Day in the Life of Joe Egg	1971	GB--Col.
Dead Man's Evidence	1962	GB
Desert Mice	1959	GB
The Dream Maker	1964	GB--Univ.
Every Home Should Have One	1970	GB
Faces in the Dark	1960	GB--Rank
Feelings	1976	GB
The File of the Golden Goose	1969	GB--UA

Great St. Trinian's Train Robbery	1966	GB
Inadmissable Evidence	1968	GB--Par.
It's All Happening	1963	GB
The Jokers	1967	GB--Univ.
Lost Paradise	1978	Belg.
Negatives	1968	GB
Never Mind the Quality, Feel the Width	1973	GB--EMI/MGM
No Sex Please, We're British	1973	GB--Col.
The Odd Job	1978	GB--Col./EMI/ WB
Penny Gold	1973	GB
Professor Popper's Problems	1975	GB
Revenge	1971	GB--Rank
The Ruling Class	1971	GB
The Shuttered Room	1967	GB--WB
The Spiral Staircase	1975	GB--WB
Stand Up Virgin Soldiers	1977	GB--WB
Sword of Sherwood Forest	1960	GB--Col.
A Weekend With Lulu	1961	GB--Col./Ham.

275. CARL HOFFMAN

Battle of the Waltzes	1934	Ger.--UFA
The Challenge Accepted	1918	Pathe
Congress Dances	1931	Ger.--UFA
Dawn	1933	Ger.
Dr. Mabeuse	1922	Ger.
False Husband	1932	Ger.
Faust *	1926	Ger.
Flute Concert of Sansoucci	1931	Ger.--UFA
Halbblut	1919	Ger.
Harikari *	1919	Ger.
Hokuspocus	1930	Ger.
Homunculus	1916	Ger.
The Immoral Vagabond	1931	Ger.--UFA
In Secret Service	1931	Ger.--UFA
Man Without a Name	1932	Ger.--UFA
Morgenrot	1933	Ger.--UFA
Die Niebelungen *	1923	Ger.
A Student Song	1930	Ger.--UFA
The Tiger Murder Case	1930	Ger.--UFA
Der Tunnel	1933	Ger.
2 Hearts in One Beat	1932	Ger.--UFA
The White Demon	1932	Ger.--UFA
Wonderful Lives of Nina Petrova	1930	Ger.
The Wrong Husband	1931	Ger.--UFA
York	1932	Ger.--UFA

276. ADAM HOLENDER

The Boy Who Could Fly *	1986	Lor.
Dream Team	1989	Univ.
The Effect of Gamma Rays on Man-in-the-Moon Marigolds	1972	TCF
The Idolmaker	1980	UA
If Ever I See You Again *	1978	Col.
Man On a Swing	1974	Par.
Midnight Cowboy	1969	UA
Panic in Needle Park	1971	TCF
Promises in the Dark	1979	Orion
Puzzle of a Downfall Child	1970	Univ.
Seduction of Joe Tynan	1979	Univ.
Simon	1980	Orion
Street Smart	1987	Cannon
To Kill a Priest	1988	Fr.

277. GEORGE K. HOLLISTER

Bad Men's Money	1929	US
The Belgian *	1917	US
Divorcee	1919	Metro.
Don Caesar de Bazar	1915	US
From the Manger to the Cross	1912	US
Kerby Gow	1912	US
The Silent Woman	1918	Metro.
Someone in the House	1920	Metro.
Why Germany Must Pay	1919	Metro.

278. JOHN HORA

Explorers	1985	Par.
Further Adventures of the Wilderness Family-Part 2	1978	US
Gremlins	1984	WB
Gremlins 2: The New Batch	1990	WB
The Howling	1981	AE
Liar's Moon	1982	US
Loverboy	1989	Tri-S.
Maurie	1973	NG
Moonwalker	1988	WB
Twilight Zone-The Movie *	1983	WB

279. EDWARD HORN

As in a Looking Glass	1916	US
Dust of Desire	1919	US

Forest Rivals	1919	US
Manon Lescaut	1914	US
Officer 666	1914	US
Stop Thief!	1915	US
Through the Toils	1919	US

280. PLINY HORNE

The Circus Cyclone	1925	Univ.
Fighting Back	1917	US
Fire Flingers *	1919	Univ.
The Flames of Chance	1918	US
Flying Colors	1917	US
The Gun Woman *	1918	US
The Hard Rock Breed	1918	US
The Hero of the Hour	1917	US
An Honest Man	1918	US
Innocent's Progress	1918	US
Man Above the Law	1918	US
Prudence Off Broadway	1919	US
The Secret Code	1918	US
Shifting Sands	1918	US
The Shoes That Danced	1918	US
Society for Sale	1918	US
The Spindle of Life	1917	US
Wee Lady Betty	1917	US
Who Is To Blame?	1918	US

281. JAMES WONG HOWE (1899-1976)

Abe Lincoln in Illinois	1940	RKO
The Adventures of Tom Sawyer *	1938	Selz.
After Tomorrow	1932	Fox
Air Force *	1943	WB
The Alaskan	1924	Par.
Algiers	1938	US
Amateur Daddy	1932	Fox
The Baron of Arizona	1950	Lip.
Beauty for Sale	1933	MGM
Behave Yourself	1951	RKO
Bell, Book and Candle	1958	Col.
The Best People	1925	Par.
Biography of a Bachelor Girl	1935	MGM
Body and Soul	1947	US
The Brave Bulls *	1951	Col.
The Breaking Point	1924	Par.
The Call of the Canyon	1923	Par.
Chandu the Magician	1932	Fox
The Charmer	1925	Par.

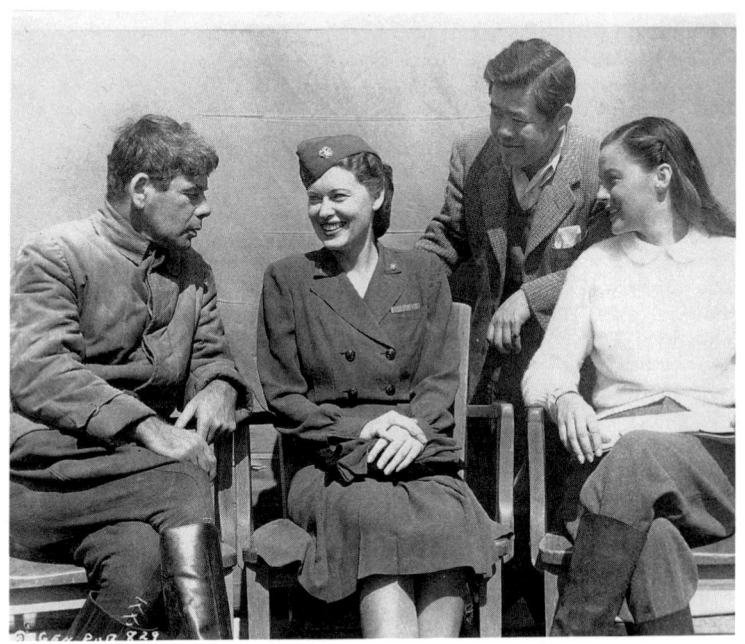

James Wong Howe (standing) visits the set of The Commandos Strike at Dawn (1942) with Paul Muni (left).

City for Conquest *	1940	WB
Come Back Little Sheba	1952	Par.
Comet Over Broadway	1938	WB
Confidential Agent	1945	WB
Counterattack	1945	Col.
The Criminal Code *	1931	Col.
Dance Team	1932	Fox
Danger Signal	1945	WB
Daughters Courageous	1939	WB
Death of a Scoundrel	1956	RKO
Desert Nights	1928	MGM
A Dispatch From Reuters	1940	WB
Dr. Ehrlich's Magic Bullet	1940	WB
Drango	1957	UA
Drums of Fate	1923	Par.
Dust Be My Destiny	1939	WB
The Eagle and the Hawk	1949	Par.
Farewell Again *	1937	GB
The Fighter	1952	US
Fire Over England *	1936	GB
The Flame Within	1935	MGM
Four Walls	1928	MGM
Funny Lady	1975	Col.
The Glory Guys	1965	UA
Hangmen Also Die	1943	US
The Hard Way	1942	WB
Have a Heart	1934	MGM
He Ran All the Way	1951	UA
The Heart Is a Lonely Hunter	1968	WB
Hello Sister	1933	Fox
Hollywood Party	1934	MGM
Hombre	1967	TCF
Hud	1963	Par.
Jennifer	1953	AA
The King on Main Street	1925	Par.
Kings Row	1941	WB
The Lady Says No	1951	UA
The Last Angry Man	1959	Col.
The Last of the Mobile Hot Shots	1969	WB
Laugh, Clown, Laugh	1928	MGM
Main Street to Broadway	1953	US
Man About Town	1932	Fox
Manhattan Melodrama	1934	MGM
Mantrap	1926	Par.
Mark of the Vampire	1935	MGM
Mr. Blandings Builds His Dream House	1948	RKO
The Molly Maguires	1970	Par.
My Reputation	1946	WB
The Night Is Young	1934	MGM
Nora Prentiss	1946	WB

North Star	1943	Gold.
Not So Long Ago	1925	Par.
O'Shaughnessy's Boy	1935	MGM
Objective Burma!	1944	WB
The Oklahoma Kid	1939	WB
The Old Man and the Sea *	1958	WB
On Your Toes *	1939	WB
Out of the Fog	1941	WB
The Outrage	1964	MGM
Padlocked	1926	Par.
Passage to Marseilles	1944	WB
Perfect Crime	1928	US
Peter Pan	1924	Par.
Picnic	1956	Col.
The Power and the Glory	1933	Fox
The Prisoner of Zenda	1937	Selz.
Pursued	1947	WB
The Rose Tattoo	1955	Par.
The Rough Riders	1927	Par.
Saturday's Children	1940	WB
Sea Horses	1926	Par.
Seconds	1966	Par.
Shining Victory	1941	WB
The Show Off	1934	MGM
The Side Show of Life	1924	Par.
The Song and Dance Man	1926	Par.
Song Without End	1960	Col.
Sorrell and Son	1927	UA
The Spanish Dancer	1923	Par.
The Spider	1931	Fox
Stamboul Quest	1934	MGM
The Story on Page One	1960	TCF
The Strawberry Blonde	1941	WB
Surrender	1931	Fox
Sweet Smell of Success	1957	UA
Tess of the Storm Country	1960	TCF
They Made Me a Criminal	1939	WB
The Thin Man	1934	MGM
This Property Is Condemned	1966	Par.
The Time of Your Life	1948	US
To the Last Man *	1923	Par.
Today	1930	US
Torrid Zone	1940	WB
Trail of the Lonesome Pine	1923	Par.
Transatlantic	1931	Fox
Tripoli	1950	Par.
Under the Red Robe *	1937	GB
Viva Villa! *	1934	MGM
Whipsaw	1934	MGM
Woman With Four Faces	1923	Par.
Yankee Doodle Dandy	1942	WB
The Yellow Ticket	1931	Fox

282. GILBERT HUBBS

Enter the Dragon	1973	WB
Flowers in the Attic *	1983	US
Force Five	1981	US
Golden Needles	1974	AIP
The Hellcats	1968	US
Master Piece	1970	US
Sword of Heaven	1985	US
This Is Elvis	1981	WB
The Wrestler	1974	US

283. ROGER HUBERT (1903-   )

L'Air de Paris	1954	Fr.
Angel On Earth	1961	Fr.
Le Baron Fantome	1943	Fr.
The Battle	1934	Fr.
The Big Chief	1959	Fr.
Blind Desire	1948	Fr.
Bonaparte and the Revolution	1971	Fr.
La Bonne Soupe	1963	Fr.
Chevalier de La Nuit	1953	Fr.
Cooking With Butter	1964	Fr.
The Cow and I	1960	Fr./Ger./It.
Cresus	1960	Fr.
The Devil's Envoys	1947	Fr.
Dynamic Jack	1961	Fr.
Elisa	1957	Fr.
The End of the World	1930	Fr.
Les Enfants du Paradis	1945	Fr.
L'Eternel Retour	1943	Fr.
Fanny	1948	Fr.
Female	1960	Fr.
La Fete a Henriette	1952	Fr.
The Good Shoup	1964	Fr.
Iceland Fisherman	1935	Fr.
J'Accuse	1938	Fr.
The Knight of the Night	1954	Fr.
Lafayette *	1961	Fr.
The Last Days of Pompeii	1950	Fr.
Leathernoose	1952	Fr.
Love Eternal	1943	Fr.
The Lovers of Brassmort	1951	Fr.
Lovers of Lisbon	1954	Fr.
The Lovers of Tage	1955	Fr.
The Mad Girl	1952	Fr.
The Man in the Raincoat	1957	Fr.
Man of the Hour	1940	Fr.
My Wife's Husband	1965	Fr./It.

Napoleon Bonaparte *	1955	Fr.
Oasis	1956	Fr.
Paris Holiday	1957	Fr.
Paris to New York	1940	Fr.
Pension Mimosas	1934	Fr.
Portrait of an Assassin	1950	Fr.
Queen Margot *	1955	Fr.
Room Upstairs	1948	Fr.
The Seven Deadly Sins *	1953	It.
Tempest in the Flesh	1954	Fr.
Therese Raquin	1953	Fr.
The Trip to Biaritz	1963	Fr.
White Cargo	1958	Fr.
Woman Thief	1938	Fr.

284. MICHAEL HUGO

The April Fools	1969	US
Bless the Beasts and Children	1973	Col.
Bug *	1975	Par.
Cover Me Babe	1970	TCF
Fools	1970	US
Head	1968	Col.
Live a Little, Steal a Lot	1974	AIP
Manitou	1978	US
Model Shop	1969	US
The Mountain Men	1980	Col.
Murph the Surf	1974	AIP
Number One	1969	UA
Ode to Billy Joe	1976	WB
One Is a Lonely Number	1972	MGM
Pandemonium	1982	MGM-UA
The Phynx	1970	WB
RPM	1970	Col.
The Spook Who Sat by the Door	1973	UA
They Only Kill Their Masters	1972	MGM
Trouble Man	1972	TCF

285. BOB HUKE

Conduct Unbecoming	1975	GB
The Lovers	1972	GB
Porridge	1979	GB
Powerforce *	1983	US
Reach for Glory	1962	GB--Col.
Under Milk Wood	1971	GB
Vengeance	1962	Ger./GB
The Very Edge	1962	GB
The Virgin and the Gypsy	1970	GB
The War Lover	1962	Col.

286. ALAN HUME

The Amsterdam Kill	1977	HgKg.
Arabian Adventure	1979	GB
At the Earth's Core	1976	GB
Bear Island	1979	Can./GB--Col.
Beware of Children	1960	GB
The Big Job	1965	GB
Birth of the Beatles	1979	GB
Bless This House	1973	GB
The Bofors Gun	1968	GB--Rank
Captain Nemo and the Underwater City *	1969	GB--MGM
Carry On Abroad	1972	GB--Rank/TCF
Carry On Cabby	1967	GB
Carry On Cleo	1964	GB
Carry On Cowboy	1965	GB
Carry On Cruising	1962	GB
Carry On Doctor	1968	GB
Carry On Emanuelle	1978	GB
Carry On Girls	1973	GB--Rank/TCF
Carry On Jack	1964	GB
Carry On Regardless	1961	GB
Carry On Screaming	1966	GB
Carry On Spying	1964	GB
Caveman	1981	UA
Cleopatra Jones and the Casino of Gold	1975	WB
Confessions of a Pop Performer	1975	GB
Dr. Terror's House of Horrors	1965	GB
Don't Lose Your Head	1967	GB
Eye of the Needle	1981	GB--UA
Father Dear Father	1973	GB--Rank/TCF
Finders Keepers	1966	GB--UA
A Fish Called Wanda	1988	MGM-UA
Follow That Camel	1967	GB--Rank
For the Love of Ada	1972	GB
For Your Eyes Only	1981	GB--UA
From Beyond the Grave	1973	GB--WB
Gulliver's Travels	1976	GB--EMI
Hearts of Fire	1987	Lor.
In the Doghouse	1961	GB--Rank
Iron Maiden	1962	GB
Kiss of the Vampire	1962	GB--Ham./Univ.
The Land That Time Forgot	1974	GB
The Last Grenade	1969	GB
The Legacy *	1978	GB--Col.
The Legend of Hell House	1973	GB--TCF
Lifeforce	1985	Tri-S.
Not Now Darling	1973	GB
Nurse On Wheels *	1963	GB
Octopussy	1983	GB
People That Time Forgot	1977	GB--AIP

Perfect Friday	1970	GB
Roommates	1962	GB
Runaway Train	1985	Cannon
The Second Victory	1986	GB
Sex Play	1974	GB
Shirley Valentine	1989	Par.
Supergirl	1984	GB--Col./EMI/ WB
This Is My Street	1963	GB
Three Hats for Lisa	1965	GB
Trial By Combat	1976	GB--WB
Twice Around the Daffodils	1962	GB
A View to a Kill	1985	GB--UA
The Violent Enemy	1968	GB
Warlords of Atlantis	1978	GB--EMI
The Watcher in the Woods	1980	Dis.
Without a Clue	1988	Orion
Wombling Free	1977	GB--Rank

287. J. ROY HUNT

Ace of Cads	1926	Par.
Action in Arabia	1944	RKO
The Age of Consent	1932	RKO
Alias French Gertie	1930	RKO
Almost a Gentleman	1939	RKO
The American Venus	1926	Par.
Annie Oakley	1935	RKO
Argentine Love	1924	Par.
The Arizona Ranger	1948	RKO
The Avenging Rider	1943	RKO
Beau Geste	1926	Par.
Beau Ideal	1931	RKO
Black Beauty	1946	TCF
Border Treasure	1950	RKO
Boy Slaves	1939	RKO
The Branded Woman	1920	US
Breakfast for Two	1937	RKO
Bride Walks Out	1936	RKO
The Brighton Strangler	1945	RKO
Brothers in the Saddle	1949	RKO
Call Out the Marines *	1942	RKO
The Case of Sergeant Grischa	1930	RKO
Close Harmony	1929	Par.
Consolation Marriage	1931	RKO
Cross Country Romance	1940	RKO
Crossfire	1947	RKO
The Crowded Hour	1925	Par.
The Dance of Life	1929	Par.
Dancing Mothers	1926	Par.

Dangerous Corner	1934	RKO
Dangerous Money	1924	Par.
A Daughter of the Gods	1916	Fox
The Devil Thumbs a Ride	1947	RKO
Dixiana	1930	RKO
Doctor's Secret	1929	Par.
Double Harness	1933	RKO
The Dummy	1929	Par.
Eight Iron Men	1952	Col.
Emergency Call	1933	RKO
The Eternal Sin	1917	US
Ex-Mrs. Bradford	1936	RKO
The Falcon and the Coeds	1943	RKO
Feel My Pulse	1928	Par.
The Fifty-Fifty Girl	1928	Par.
Finishing School	1934	RKO
Fixer Dugan	1939	RKO
Flying Down to Rio	1933	RKO
The Flying Irishman *	1939	RKO
Forgotten Faces	1928	Par.
Friends and Lovers	1931	RKO
Full Confession	1939	RKO
A Game of Death	1945	RKO
Girl Crazy	1932	RKO
Gun Smugglers	1948	RKO
Gunplay	1951	RKO
Hat, Coat and Glove	1934	RKO
Heavenly Days	1944	RKO
Help Yourself	1920	Gold.
Her Own Free Will	1924	US
Hitting a New High	1937	RKO
I Walked With a Zombie	1943	RKO
I'm Still Alive	1940	RKO
In Name Only	1939	RKO
Indian Agent	1948	RKO
The Juggler	1953	Col.
Kill or Be Killed	1950	EL
A Kiss for Cinderella	1926	Par.
The Lady Consents	1936	RKO
The Last Days of Pompeii *	1935	RKO
The Law West of Tombstone	1938	RKO
Lawful Larceny	1930	RKO
The Lawless	1949	Par.
Leathernecking	1930	RKO
Let's Try Again	1934	RKO
The Life of the Party	1937	RKO
A Likely Story	1947	RKO
Little Orvie	1940	RKO
The Lone Wolf	1917	Selz.
Love Comes Along	1930	RKO
Love's Redemption	1921	FN

Lucky Devils	1933	RKO
A Man to Remember	1938	RKO
The Man Who Found Himself	1937	RKO
The Manicure Girl	1925	Par.
Married and In Love	1940	RKO
The Meanest Gal in Town	1934	RKO
The Mighty	1929	Par.
Mighty Joe Young	1949	RKO
Miss Bluebeard	1925	Par.
Mother Carey's Chickens	1938	RKO
Muss 'Em Up *	1936	RKO
New Faces of 1937	1937	RKO
New York	1927	Par.
Oliver Twist	1933	Mon.
One Crowded Night	1940	RKO
Overland Telegraph	1951	RKO
Pagan Love *	1920	US
Panama Lady	1939	RKO
Parachute Battalion	1941	RKO
The Passing of the Third Floor Back	1918	FN
The Passion Flower	1921	FN
The Pay-Off	1930	RKO
Pistol Harvest	1951	RKO
Polly of the Follies	1922	FN
Prairie Law	1940	RKO
Race Street	1948	RKO
Radio City Revels *	1938	RKO
The Rejected Woman	1924	Gold.
Reno	1939	RKO
Return of the Bad Men	1948	RKO
Riders of the Range	1949	RKO
Rio Grande Patrol	1950	RKO
Road Agent	1952	RKO
The Roadhouse Murder	1930	RKO
Rubber Heels	1927	Par.
Saddle Legion	1951	RKO
Second Youth	1924	Gold.
She	1935	RKO
She's a Sheik	1927	Par.
Sherlock Holmes	1922	Gold.
The Sign on the Door	1921	FN
The Silver Streak *	1935	RKO
Smartest Girl in Town	1936	RKO
Smilin' Through *	1922	FN
Something Always Happens	1928	Par.
Spider Webs *	1927	US
The Sport Parade	1932	RKO
Stage to Chino	1940	RKO
Star of Midnight	1935	RKO
Storm Over Wyoming	1950	RKO
Swim, Girl, Swim	1927	Par.

Syncopation	1942	RKO
Take Me Home	1928	Par.
Target	1952	RKO
That Girl from Paris	1936	RKO
They Met in Argentina	1941	RKO
Thundering Hoofs	1942	RKO
Trail Street	1947	RKO
Triple Justice	1940	RKO
Trouping With Ellen	1924	US
The Truth	1920	Gold.
Under the Tonto Rim	1947	RKO
The Virginian *	1929	Par.
Walking On Air	1936	RKO
War Brides	1916	Selz.
Way Back Home	1932	RKO
We're Only Human	1936	RKO
What a Blonde	1945	RKO
What Women Will Do	1921	Pathe
Why Bring That Up?	1929	Par.
Wild, Wild Susan	1925	Par.
Wildfire	1925	Vita.
Without Orders	1936	RKO
The Woman Between	1931	RKO
Woman's Place 8	1921	FN
The Wonderful Thing	1921	FN
You Can't Buy Luck	1937	RKO
You Can't Fool Your Wife	1940	RKO

288. WILLIAM HYER

Amateur Crook	1938	US
Bars of Hate	1936	US
Brothers of the West	1938	US
Caryl of the Mountains	1936	US
Cheyenne Rides Again	1937	US
Code of the Range	1927	US
The Feud of the Trail	1938	US
The Flying Fists	1938	US
Gun Play	1935	US
Harlem on the Prairie	1937	US
The Kid From Santa Fe	1940	Mon.
The Laffin' Fool	1927	US
Land of the Six Guns *	1940	Mon.
Lost Ranch	1937	US
Orphan of the Pecos	1938	US
The Phantom of the Range	1936	US
Phantom Ranger	1938	Mon.
Pinto Rustlers	1937	US
Prison Shadows	1936	US
Put on the Spot	1936	US

Racing Blood *	1938	US
The Ranger's Roundup	1938	US
Reform School	1939	US
Riders From Nowhere *	1940	Mon.
Rio Grande Romance	1936	US
The Rogues' Tavern	1936	US
Santa Fe Bound	1936	US
Six-Shootin' Sheriff	1938	GN
Speed Limited	1940	US
Speed Reporter	1938	US
Taming the Wild	1937	US
Thunderbolt's Tracks	1927	US
Trigger Fingers	1939	US
Two Minutes to Play	1937	US

289. ARTHUR IBBETSON (1921-   )

All Coppers Are	1972	GB
The Angry Silence	1960	GB
Anne of a Thousand Days	1969	GB--Univ.
The Blue Lagoon *	1949	GB
The Bounty	1984	DeL.
The Bridal Path	1959	GB
The Canadians	1961	GB--TCF
The Chalk Garden	1964	GB--Univ.
A Doll's House	1973	GB
Eleven Harrowhouse	1974	GB--TCF
Fanatic	1965	GB--Ham.
The Fighting Prince of Donegal	1966	GB--Dis.
Frankenstein: The True Story	1973	GB--Univ.
Hopscotch	1980	Avco
I Could Go On Singing	1963	GB--UA
The Inspector	1961	GB--TCF
Inspector Clousseau	1968	GB--UA
It Shouldn't Happen to a Vet	1976	GB--EMI
The League of Gentlemen	1960	GB--Rank
Little Lord Fauntleroy	1980	GB
A Little Night Music	1977	Aust./Ger.
The Medusa Touch	1978	Fr./GB
Melba *	1953	GB
Mistress Pamela	1973	GB--EMI/MGM
Murder at the Gallop	1963	GB--MGM
Nothing Personal	1980	AIP
Out of Season	1975	GB--EMI
Poet's Pub *	1949	GB
Pretty Polly	1967	GB--Univ.
Prisoner of Zenda	1979	Univ.
The Railway Children	1970	GB--EMI
Santa Claus	1985	GB
The Sellout	1975	GB/It.--WB

Sky West and Crooked	1965	GB--Rank
The Spider and the Fly *	1949	GB
Stop Press Girl *	1949	GB--Rank
There Was a Crooked Man	1960	GB--UA
Tunes of Glory	1960	GB--UA
The Walking Stick	1970	GB--MGM
When Eight Bells Toll	1971	GB
Where Eagles Dare *	1969	GB--MGM
Whistle Down the Wind	1961	GB--Rank
The Wild Affair	1965	GB
Willy Wonka and the Chocolate		
Factory	1971	US

290. TONY IMI

American Roulette	1988	GB
Brass Target	1976	MGM
Buster	1988	GB
Christmas Carol	1984	GB
Dulcima	1971	GB--EMI
Fire Birds	1990	BV/Touch.
Firefighters	1975	GB
International Velvet	1978	GB--MGM
It's Not the Siege That Counts	1979	GB
It's 2'6" Above the Ground World	1972	GB
Junket 89	1970	GB
The Likely Lads	1976	GB--EMI
Nate and Hayes	1983	Par.
Night Crossing	1982	Dis.
North Sea Hijack	1979	GB--Univ.
Not Quite Jerusalem	1985	GB--Rank
Options *	1989	US
Percy's Progress	1974	GB--EMI
The Raging Moon	1970	GB--EMI
Robin Hood Junior	1975	GB
Sakharov	1984	HBO
The Sea Wolves	1980	GB/Switz.--US
Sergeant Steiner	1979	Ger.
The Slipper and the Rose	1976	GB
That's Carry On	1978	GB
Universal Soldier	1971	GB
Wired	1989	US
The Zoo Robbery	1973	GB

291. SILVANO IPPOLITI

Act of Aggression	1975	Fr.
Action	1980	It.
Aladdin	1986	It.

Alone Against Rome	1963	It.
Attention	1985	It.
The Bandit	1969	Bulg./It.
Caligula *	1979	It.--US
Capriccio	1987	It.--DeL.
The Cry	1970	It.
Deadly Sweet	1969	It.
Le Gang	1977	It.
God With Us	1970	It.
Hercules, Samson and Ulysses	1965	It.--MGM
The Humanoid	1979	It.--Col.
I Hate Blondes *	1981	It.
In the Year of Our Lord	1969	It.
The Iron Prefect	1977	It.
The Key	1983	It.
Madam Kitty	1977	Fr./Ger./It.
Miranda	1985	It.
Morel's Invention	1974	It.
Navajo Joe	1966	It./Sp.--UA
No Way Out	1973	Fr./It.
The Outside Man *	1973	Fr.--UA
Repenter	1985	It.
Sacco and Vanzetti	1971	Fr./It.
Seven Magnificent Gladiators *	1985	It.
Sodom and Gomorrah *	1962	Fr./It.--TCF
Specters	1987	It.
Super Fuzz	1981	US
Supersnooper	1981	It.
2 + 5: Mission Hydra	1966	It.
The Vacation	1971	It.
White Slave	1986	It.

292. MARK IRWIN

Bat 21	1988	Tri-S.
The Blob	1988	Tri-S.
Blood and Guts	1978	Can.
The Brood	1979	US
Buckeye and Blue	1988	US
Burnin' Love	1987	DeL.
Class of 1999	1990	US
The Dead Zone	1983	Par.
Fast Company	1979	US
The Fly	1986	TCF
Fright Night: Part 2	1988	Aus.
Funeral Home	1982	US
The Hanoi Hilton	1987	Cannon
I Come in Peace	1990	US
Night School	1981	Lor./Par.
Paint It Black	1990	US

Pass the Ammo	1988	US
The Protector	1985	US
Robocop 2	1990	Orion
Scanners	1981	AE
Spasms	1984	US
Starship Invasions	1977	Can.--WB
Tanya's Island	1980	US
Videodrome	1983	Univ.
Youngblood	1986	MGM-UA

293. PAUL IVANO (1900-1984)

About Face	1942	UA
All by Myself	1943	Univ.
The Bashful Bachelor	1942	RKO
Battle of Greed	1934	US
The Black Angel	1946	Univ.
Blazing Barriers	1937	Mon.
Breakdown	1952	Lip.
Captive Women	1952	RKO
Cavalcade of the West	1936	US
Champagne for Caesar	1950	UA
Chubasco *	1967	WB
Concert Magic	1948	US
The Dark Horse	1946	Univ.
Dead Man's Eyes	1944	Univ.
Destiny *	1944	Univ.
Fangs of the Wild	1954	Lip
Flesh and Fantasy *	1943	Univ.
For Men Only	1952	Lip.
The Frozen Ghost	1945	Univ.
Fun On a Weekend	1946	UA
Fury Below	1938	US
The Gangster	1947	AA
The Girl From Rio	1939	Mon.
The Girl on the Bridge	1951	TCF
Gold Raiders	1952	UA
Hello God *	1951	It.--US
Hi, Beautiful	1944	Univ.
Hitler-Dead or Alive	1942	US
Hold Back Tomorrow	1955	Univ.
Honeymoon Lodge	1943	Univ.
Hoosier Schoolboy	1937	Mon.
I Am a Criminal	1939	Mon.
The Imposter	1944	Univ.
Larceny With Music	1943	Univ.
Little Miss Big	1946	Univ.
Lizzie	1957	MGM
The Lovable Cheat	1949	US
Men in Her Diary	1945	Univ.

Million Dollar Weekend	1948	EL
The Naked Flame	1970	Can.
No Other Woman *	1928	Fox
The Nun and the Sergeant	1962	UA
One Girl's Confession	1953	Col.
Pardon My Rhythm	1946	Univ.
Pickup	1951	Col.
Pursuit to Algiers	1945	Univ.
Red Snow	1952	Col.
The Riding Avenger	1936	US
Search for Danger	1949	US
The Second Face	1950	EL
Senorita From the West	1945	Univ.
The Shanghai Gesture	1941	UA
She's for Me	1943	Univ.
Should a Girl Marry?	1939	Mon.
Slightly Terrific	1944	Univ.
The Spider Woman Strikes Back	1946	Univ.
The Strange Affair of Uncle Harry	1945	Univ.
Strange Fascination	1952	Col.
Street Angel *	1928	Fox
The Suspect	1944	Univ.
The 13th Man	1937	Mon.
Thy Neighbor's Wife	1953	TCF
Vengeance of the Deep	1923	US
You're a Lucky Fellow, Mr. Smith	1943	Univ.

294. FRED JACKMAN (1881-1959)

The Battling Orioles *	1924	Pathe
Black Cyclone *	1925	Pathe
The California Mail *	1936	WB
Charge of the Light Brigade *	1936	WB
The Crossroads of New York *	1922	FN
Down On the Farm *	1920	US
Home Talent *	1921	US
Married Life *	1920	US
A Midsummer Night's Dream *	1935	WB
Molly O	1921	FN
Moonlight Over the Prairie	1935	WB
She Loved a Sailor	1916	US
Small Town Idol *	1921	US
Suzanna *	1922	US
The White Sheep *	1924	Pathe

295. FRED JACKMAN, JR.

The Adventures of Don Coyote	1947	UA

Aerial Gunner	1943	Par.
Alaska Highway	1943	Par.
Albuquerque	1948	Par.
Apache Ambush	1955	Col.
Big Town	1947	Par.
Blackjack Ketchum	1956	Col.
Canadian Pacific	1949	TCF
The Cariboo Trail	1949	TCF
The Case Against Brooklyn	1958	Col.
Cell 2455 Death Row	1955	Col.
Coroner Creek	1948	Col.
Creature With the Atomic Brain	1955	Col.
Danger Flight	1939	Mon.
Dark Mountain	1944	Par.
Double Exposure	1944	Par.
Drums of the Desert	1940	Mon.
Earth vs. The Flying Saucers	1956	Col.
Flying Blind	1941	Par.
The Flying Fontaines	1959	Col.
Follow That Woman	1945	Par.
Forced Landing *	1941	Par.
Gambler's Choice	1944	Par.
The Gunfighters	1947	Col.
Harum Scarum	1965	MGM
High Explosive	1943	Par.
High Powered	1945	Par.
Hot Cargo	1946	Par.
I Live On Danger	1942	Par.
Juke Box Rhythm	1959	Col.
Julie	1956	MGM
Laughing At Danger	1940	Mon.
Life Begins at 17	1958	Col.
The Man With My Face	1951	UA
Minesweeper	1943	Par.
The Navy Way	1945	Par.
The Night Holds Terror	1955	Col.
No Hands on the Clock	1941	Par.
One Body Too Many	1944	Par.
One Exciting Night	1944	Par.
People Are Funny	1945	Par.
Phantom of Chinatown	1941	Mon.
The Prince of Thieves	1948	Col.
Scared Stiff	1945	Par.
Senior Prom	1958	Col.
Sign of the Wolf	1941	Mon.
Sky Patrol	1939	Mon.
Slaughter on Tenth Avenue	1957	Univ.
The Strawberry Roan	1948	Col.
Stunt Pilot	1939	Mon.
Submarine Alert	1943	Par.
Swamp Fire	1946	Par.

Take It Big	1944	Par.
They Made Me a Killer	1946	Par.
Timber Queen	1944	Par.
Tokyo Rose	1945	Par.
Tornado	1943	Par.
Torpedo Boat	1942	Par.
Unknown Island	1948	US
Up in the Air	1940	Mon.
Uranium Boom	1956	Col.
Wild West	1946	PRC
Wildcat	1942	Par.
Wolf Call	1939	Mon.
Wrecking Crew	1942	Par.
You're Out of Luck	1941	Mon.

296. ANDREW JACKSON

The Castaway Cowboy	1974	Dis.
Death of a Gunfighter	1969	Univ.
The Shakiest Gun in the West	1967	Univ.
The Strongest Man in the World	1975	Dis.
Superdad	1974	Dis.
3 Guns for Texas *	1968	Univ.

297. HARRY JACKSON (1896-1953)

An American Guerrila in the Philippines	1950	TCF
Anne of the Indies	1951	TCF
Apartment for Peggy	1948	TCF
The Band Wagon	1953	MGM
The Beautiful Blonde From Bashful Bend	1949	TCF
Broadway Scandals	1929	Col.
Carnival in Costa Rica	1947	TCF
Charlie Chan at the Race Track	1936	TCF
Charlie Chan on Broadway	1937	TCF
Chicken Every Sunday	1949	TCF
Circumstantial Evidence	1945	TCF
City Girl	1937	TCF
Clancy in Wall Street	1930	US
The Costello Case	1930	US
Dancing in the Dark	1949	TCF
Floating College	1928	US
45 Fathers	1937	TCF
Fury at Furnace Creek	1948	TCF
George Washington Cohen	1928	US
Give My Regards to Broadway	1948	TCF
The Great Hospital Mystery	1937	TCF
Greenwich Village *	1944	TCF

The Gun Runner	1928	US
Halls of Montezuma *	1950	TCF
Here Comes Trouble	1936	TCF
In His Steps	1936	GN
Johnny Comes Flying Home	1946	TCF
Jungle Bride	1933	Mon.
Kathleen Mavoureen	1930	US
The Kid From Left Field	1953	TCF
Ladies of the Night Club	1928	US
Life Begins at 40	1935	Fox
Lucky Boy	1929	US
Lydia Bailey	1952	TCF
The Man in Hobbles	1928	US
Mother Wore Tights	1947	TCF
My Lady's Past	1929	US
New Orleans	1929	US
Oh You Beautiful Doll	1949	TCF
Partners	1932	Pathe/RKO
Pony Soldier	1952	TCF
Reno	1930	US
She Learned About Sailors	1934	Fox
Strange Triangle	1946	TCF
Take Care of My Little Girl	1951	TCF
$10 Raise	1935	Fox
Think Fast, Mr. Moto	1937	TCF
Three Hours	1927	FN
365 Nights in Hollywood	1934	Fox
Three Little Words	1950	MGM
A Ticket to Tomahawk	1950	TCF
Two Men and a Maid	1929	US
Wake Up and Dream	1946	TCF
Way of a Gaucho	1952	TCF
We Go Fast	1941	TCF
When My Baby Smiles at Me	1948	TCF
Whispering Winds *	1929	US
The White Legion	1936	GN
Wild and Woolly	1937	TCF
Your Uncle Dudley	1935	Fox

298. JULIUS JAENZON

Atonement of Gosta Berling	1923	Swed.
For Her Sake	1930	Swed.
Gosta Berling's Saga	1923	Swed.
Gunnar Hede's Saga	1922	Swed.
Ingmar Arvet: Till Osterland	1924	Swed.
Johan	1920	Swed.
Karin Ingmarsdotter *	1919	Swed.
Korkarlen	1920	Swed.
Outlaw and His Wife	1917	Swed.

Les Proscrits	1917	Swed.
Sir Arne's Treasure	1919	Swed.
Terje Vigen	1916	Swed.
Vem Domer	1921	Swed.

298a. PETER JAMES

Caddie	1976	Aus.
Driving Miss Daisy	1989	WB
Echoes in Paradise	1989	US
The Irishman	1978	Aus.
The Killing of Angel Street	1983	Aus.
Mr. Johnson	1990	US
Rebel	1986	Aus.
The Right Hand Man	1987	US
Shadows of the Peacock	1987	Aus.
The Wild Duck	1983	Aus.

299. HAROLD JANES

Beautifully Trimmed	1920	Univ.
The Conflict	1921	Univ.
The Path She Chose	1920	Univ.
Reputation	1921	Univ.
The Road to Divorce	1920	Univ.
The Secret Gift	1920	Univ.
Wanted at Headquarters	1920	Univ.
When a Man's a Man *	1924	FN

300. GORDON JENNINGS (1897-1953)

Dixie *	1943	Par.
Frenchman's Creek *	1944	Par.
Give Us This Night *	1936	Par.
Here Come the Waves *	1944	Par.
Hold That Blonde *	1945	Par.
Lady in the Dark *	1944	Par.
Our Hearts Were Young and Gay *	1944	Par.

301. J. DEVEREUX JENNINGS (1885-1952)

Battling Butler	1926	MGM
Bells of San Juan	1922	Fox
Born to the West	1937	Par.
Boss of Camp Four *	1922	Fox
Brass Commandments	1923	Fox
Bride of the Regiment *	1930	FN

Cheating the Public	1918	Fox
Children of Jazz	1923	Par.
Civilization *	1916	US
Cobra *	1925	Par.
College *	1927	UA
The Coming of the Law	1919	Fox
Cowardice Court *	1919	Fox
Daredevil	1920	Fox
Divorce Among Friends	1930	WB
Dumbbells in Ermine	1930	WB
The Eagle *	1925	UA
The Edge of the Abyss	1915	US
Evangeline	1919	Fox
Fame and Fortune	1918	Fox
The Famous Ferguson Case	1932	FN/WB
The Feud *	1919	Fox
Flying Romeos	1928	FN
Footlight Ranger	1923	Fox
The Forbidden Room	1919	Fox
The General *	1927	UA
Glory of Clementina	1922	US
Golden Dawn	1930	WB
The Great Lover	1920	Gold.
The Gunfighter	1923	Fox
Heart Trouble *	1928	FN
Hold Everything	1930	WB
Life of the Party	1930	WB
The Lure of Jade	1921	US
Madame X	1920	Gold.
Manhattan Parade	1931	WB
The Matrimonial Bed	1930	FN/WB
Matrimony	1915	US
The Million Dollar Handicap *	1923	US
Miss Adventure	1919	Fox
The Missing Link	1927	WB
Mr. Logan U.S.A.	1918	Fox
Mistress of Shenstone	1921	US
North of 53	1917	Fox
Oh! Sailor, Behave!	1930	WB
Public Enemy	1931	WB
Roads of Destiny	1921	Gold.
Sally *	1930	FN/WB
Salvage	1921	US
The Sap	1929	WB
Scarlet Pimpernel	1917	Fox
Should a Husband Forgive?	1919	Fox
Side Show	1931	WB
Song of the West	1930	WB
The Spy	1917	Fox
Steamboat Bill, Jr. *	1928	UA
Steel Preferred	1926	US

The Sting of the Lash	1921	US
Stranger in Town	1932	WB
Those Who Dare	1924	US
Treat 'Em Rough	1919	Fox
Two Kinds of Women	1922	US
Vamping Venus	1928	FN
What No Man Knows	1921	US
The Winged Idol	1915	US
Without Compromise	1922	Fox
The Woman in Room 13	1920	Gold.

302. ROBERT C. JESSUP

The Big Brawl	1980	WB
Deadly Blessing	1981	US
Drive In	1976	Col.
In the Year 2889	1966	AIP
Mars Needs Women	1966	US
Race With the Devil	1975	TCF
The 7th Commandment	1961	US
Silent Rage *	1982	Col.
A Small Town in Texas	1976	AIP
Split Image	1982	Orion
Strange Compulsion	1964	US
Sugar Hill	1973	AIP

303. AL JONES

Blazing Days	1927	Univ.
The Border Cavalier	1927	Univ.
The Bronco Buster	1927	Univ.
The Gate Crasher	1928	Univ.
Hands Off	1927	Univ.
The Kid's Clever	1929	Univ.
A Made-to-Order Hero	1928	Univ.
A One Man Game *	1927	Univ.
Painting the Town	1927	Univ.
Quick Triggers	1928	Univ.
Range Courage	1927	Univ.
Skinner Steps Out	1929	Univ.
The Stolen Ranch	1926	Univ.
The Yellow Back	1926	Univ.

304. MICHAEL JOYCE

Do Your Duty	1928	FN
Head Man	1928	FN
My Old Kentucky Home *	1922	US

Queen of the Moulin Rouge	1922	US
When the Desert Calls	1922	US

305. ROBERT JUILLARD

Behind the Facade *	1939	Fr.
The Boss	1960	Fr.
The Children of Love	1953	Fr.
Count of Monte Cristo	1955	Fr./It.
Emile's Boat	1962	Fr.
The Enclosure	1961	Fr.
The Father of the Girl	1953	Fr.
Future Stars	1955	Fr.
Germany Year Zero	1947	Ger.
Gervaise	1956	Fr.
Les Grandes Manoeuvers *	1955	Fr.
Happy Road	1956	Fr.
Huis Clos	1954	Fr.
It Happened On the 36 Candles	1957	Fr.
Les Jeux Interdits	1952	Fr.
Look Out Girls	1957	Fr.
Nobody's Boy	1958	Fr.
Le Rendezvous	1961	Fr.
Road to Shame	1962	Fr.
Secret Game	1953	Fr.
Service Entrance	1954	Fr.
The She Wolves	1957	Fr.
You Are the Venom	1958	Fr.

306. RAY JUNE

Above and Beyond	1952	MGM
Alias a Gentleman	1947	MGM
Alibi	1929	US
And One Was Beautiful	1940	MGM
Another Language	1932	MGM
Arrowsmith	1932	Gold.
Babes in Arms	1939	MGM
Barbary Coast	1935	Gold.
The Bat Whispers *	1930	US
The Beginning or the End	1947	MGM
The Block Signal	1926	US
Blondes by Choice	1927	US
Born to Dance	1936	MGM
Bought	1931	WB
Boy of Mine *	1922	FN
The Bride Goes Wild	1948	MGM
A Broadway Butterfly	1925	WB
By Divine Right	1924	US

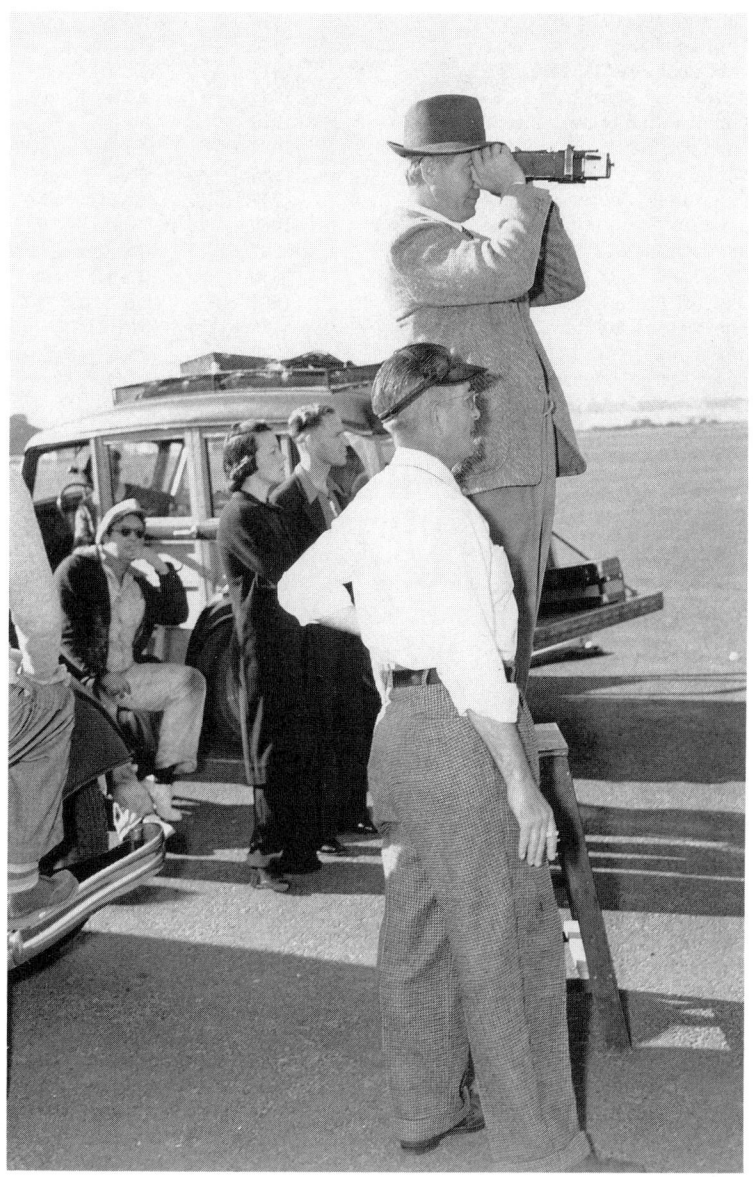

Ray June (front) with director Victor Fleming (at the viewfinder) on the set of <u>Test Pilot</u> (1938).

Cairo	1941	MGM
Callaway Went Thataway	1951	MGM
Calling Dr. Gillespie	1942	MGM
China Seas	1935	MGM
The Cockeyed Miracle	1946	MGM
Code 2	1953	MGM
The Companionate Marriage	1928	FN
Cornered	1924	WB
Corsair *	1931	US
The Court Jester	1955	Par.
Crisis	1950	MGM
Cross Breed	1927	US
Cynara	1930	Gold.
Day of Tiumph	1954	US
The Desert Bride	1928	Col.
Disorderly Conduct	1932	Fox
The Earl of Chicago	1940	MGM
Easy to Love	1953	MGM
Espionage	1937	MGM
Eyes of the World *	1930	UA
Fast and Furious	1939	MGM
The Feminine Touch	1941	MGM
The Final Extra	1927	US
Funny Face	1956	Par.
The Gay Bride	1934	MGM
The Girl From Missouri	1934	MGM
The Girl From Rio	1927	US
The Golden Web	1926	US
The Great Ziegfeld *	1936	MGM
H. M. Pulham, Esquire	1940	MGM
Hellship Bronson	1928	US
Heroes of the Night	1927	US
Hideout	1934	MGM
Honolulu	1938	MGM
The Hoodlum Saint	1946	MGM
Horse Feathers	1932	Par.
Hot Blood	1955	Col.
Houseboat	1958	Par.
I Cover the Waterfront	1933	TC/UA
I Dood It!	1943	MGM
I Married an Angel	1942	MGM
Indiscreet *	1931	UA
Inside Straight	1951	MGM
Invitation	1952	MGM
It's a Big Country *	1952	MGM
Journey for Margaret	1942	MGM
Just This Once	1952	MGM
Keep Your Powder Dry	1945	MGM
King of the Pack	1926	US
Little Nellie Kelly	1940	MGM
Live, Love and Learn	1937	MGM

The Lottery Bride	1930	UA
Love Crazy	1941	MGM
Lucky Night	1939	MGM
Man From Dakota	1940	MGM
Marriage Is a Private Affair	1943	MGM
Midnight Life	1928	US
Missing Daughters	1924	Selz.
Mrs. O'Malley and Mr. Malone	1950	MGM
Money To Burn	1926	US
Mountains of Manhattan	1927	US
Nancy Goes to Rio	1950	MGM
The Narrow Street	1924	WB
New York Nights	1929	UA
Night Must Fall	1937	MGM
One of the Bravest	1925	US
The Opening Night	1927	Col.
Penrod *	1922	FN
Penrod and Sam *	1923	FN
Phantom of the Forest	1926	US
Puttin' On the Ritz	1930	UA
Quarantined Rivals	1927	US
Racing Blood	1926	US
Racing Luck	1924	US
Reaching for the Moon *	1931	UA
The Reformer and the Redhead	1950	MGM
Rich Man, Poor Girl	1938	MGM
Riff Raff	1935	MGM
Riptide	1934	MGM
The River Woman	1928	US
Roman Scandals *	1933	Gold.
Saratoga	1937	MGM
The Satin Woman	1927	US
Scrambled Wives *	1921	FN
The Secret Garden	1949	MGM
Secrets	1933	UA
A Self-Made Failure *	1924	FN
The Seventh Sin	1957	MGM
The Shadow of the Law	1926	US
The Shadow on the Wall	1925	US
Shadow on the Wall	1949	MGM
The Sign of the Claw	1926	US
The Silent Avenger	1927	US
The Silent Power	1926	US
Sinews of Steel	1927	US
The Siren	1927	Col.
Sky Full of Moon	1952	MGM
A Slight Case of Larceny	1953	MGM
So This Is Love	1928	Col.
Sombrero	1953	MGM
A Southern Yankee	1948	MGM
The Sporting Age	1928	Col.

Strictly Dishonorable	1951	MGM
Strike Up the Band	1940	MGM
The Sun Comes Up	1949	MGM
Suzy	1936	MGM
Test Pilot	1938	MGM
This Is My Love	1954	RKO
Three Daring Daughters	1948	MGM
Three Men in White	1944	MGM
Through the Breakers	1928	US
Through Thick and Thin	1927	US
Times Square	1929	US
Tracked in the Snow Country	1925	WB
Twice Blessed	1945	MGM
United States Smith	1928	US
The Unknown Soldier	1926	US
Vacation From Love	1938	MGM
Vanessa, Her Love Story	1935	MGM
Wandering Husbands	1924	US
The Warning	1927	Col.
When Ladies Meet	1933	MGM
Wife vs. Secretary	1936	MGM
The Wife's Relations	1928	Col.
Woman Against Woman	1938	MGM
Woman Who Did Not Care	1927	US
A Woman's Way	1928	Col.
Women in His Life	1933	MGM
Ziegfeld Girl	1941	MGM

307. OTTO KANTUREK

Abdul the Damned	1935	GB
Adventures of Tunis *	1931	Ger.
April Blossoms	1934	MGM
A Clown Must Laugh	1936	GB--UA
Freedom of the Seas	1934	GB
Girl in the Case	1940	GB
Girl in the News	1940	GB--MGM/TCF
Gretel und Leisel	1931	Ger.
Her Majesty Love	1931	Ger.
Hold My Hand	1938	GB
Housemaster	1938	GB
The Inn at the Rhine	1931	Ger.
Kohlhisel's Daughters	1930	Ger.
Let's Make a Night Of It	1937	GB--Univ.
Longing 202	1932	Ger.
Love In Exile	1936	GB
Missing Ten Days	1941	GB
Mister Cinders	1934	GB
A Night at the Grand Hotel	1931	Ger.
Night Train	1940	GB--TCF
One Night in Paris	1940	GB

The Opera Ball	1931	Ger.
Over She Goes	1937	GB
Pirate of the Seven Seas	1941	GB
Please Teacher	1937	GB
Prisoner of Corbal	1939	GB
Queer Cargo	1938	GB
Shipyard Sally	1939	GB--TCF
So This Is London	1939	GB--TCF
A Song for You *	1933	Ger.
The Student's Romance	1936	GB
Those Were the Days	1934	GB
Three Days Love	1931	Ger.
24 Hours Out of the Life of a Woman *	1931	Ger.
Under False Flag	1932	Ger.--Univ.

308. STEVEN M. KATZ

And God Created Woman	1988	US
Backstreet Dreams	1990	US
Best Friends	1974	US
Bittersweet Love	1976	AE
Blues Brothers	1980	Univ.
Dead People	1974	US
18 Again	1988	US
Joyride	1977	AIP
The Kentucky Fried Movie	1977	US
Las Vegas Lady	1976	US
The Little Dragons	1980	US
Our Winning Season	1978	AIP
Pom Pom Girls	1976	US
The Silent Partner *	1978	Can.
Sister, Sister	1987	US
The Student Teachers	1973	US
Who's Harry Crumb?	1989	TRI-S.
Your Three Minutes Are Up	1973	US

309. BORIS KAUFMAN (1906-1980)

A Propos de Nice	1930	Fr.
All the Way Home	1963	Par.
L'Atalante	1934	Fr.
Baby Doll	1956	WB
The Brotherhood	1968	Par.
Bye Bye Braverman	1968	WB
Cinderella	1937	Fr.
Crowded Paradise	1946	US
The Fugitive Kind	1960	UA
Garden of Eden	1954	US

Gone Are the Days!	1963	US
The Group	1966	UA
Long Day's Journey Into Night	1961	US
On the Waterfront	1954	Col.
Patterns	1956	UA
The Pawnbroker	1965	US
Serenade	1940	Fr.
Singing in the Dark	1956	US
Splendor in the Grass	1961	WB
Tell Me That You Love Me Junie Moon	1969	Par.
That Kind of Woman	1959	Par.
Twelve Angry Men	1957	UA
Up Tight	1968	Par.
The World of Henry Orient *	1964	UA
You Can't Fool Antonette *	1936	Fr.--Par.
Zero de Conduite	1933	Fr.

310. CHARLES KAUFMAN

The Bearcat	1922	Univ.
The Bells	1918	Pathe
A Branded Soul	1917	Fox
Dead Game	1923	Univ.
The Deadlier Sex	1920	Pathe
Don Quickshot of the Rio Grande	1923	Univ.
The False Code	1919	Pathe
Fighting Cressy	1919	Pathe
The Flirt	1922	Univ.
Gates of Brass	1919	Pathe
The Girl in the Web	1920	Pathe
The Girl on the Stairs *	1924	PDC
The Gray Wolf's Ghost	1919	US
The Joyous Liar	1919	US
The Law Forbids *	1924	Univ.
The Master Man	1919	Pathe
The Midnight Stage	1919	Pathe
The Silver Girl	1919	Pathe
Step On It!	1922	Univ.
To Honor and Obey	1917	Fox
Todd of the Times	1919	Pathe
Trimmed in Scarlet	1923	Univ.
What Wives Want	1923	Univ.
A White Man's Chance	1919	US
The World Aflame	1919	Pathe

311. HARRY KEEPERS

The Eyes of Mystery	1918	Metro.
His Greatest Sacrifice	1921	Fox

Johnny Ring and the Captain's Sword *	1921	US
Just a Song at Twilight	1922	US
The Legion of Death	1918	Metro.
Lost Paradise *	1914	Par.
Marrying Money	1915	US
Outcast	1917	US
The Rip-Tide	1923	US
Something Different	1920	US
Who's Your Brother?	1919	US

312. MICHEL KELBER (1908-   )

The Affair Nina	1961	Fr./Ger.
After Goya	1944	Fr.
The Ambassador's Daughter	1956	US
Bal Tabarin	1952	Rep.
Beauty and the Devil	1950	Fr.
La Belle Otero	1954	Fr./It.
The Big Game	1954	Fr./It.
Bitter Victory	1957	Fr.--Col.
Boiling Pot	1957	Fr.
Bonsoir Paris, Bonsoir L'Amour	1957	Fr.
Un Carnet de Bal *	1936	Fr.
College Boarding House	1959	Sp.
Courier of Lyons	1938	Fr.
Dance Program *	1937	Fr.
The Devil and the Pulpit	1954	Fr./It.
Le Diable au Corps	1947	Fr.
Diary of a Woman in White	1965	Fr.
Do That to Me	1961	Fr.
The Empire of Night	1963	Fr.
The Fanatics	1960	Fr.
40 Little Mothers	1939	Fr.
La Franciscan de Bourges	1968	Fr.
French Can-Can	1955	Fr.
Girls in Distress	1940	Fr.
Good Luck, Charlie!	1962	Fr.
Grand Rue	1956	Fr.
Heart of Paris *	1939	Fr.
Heels Go to Hell	1956	Fr.
Hercule *	1938	Fr.
How To Rob a Department Store	1965	Fr.
Hunchback of Notre Dame	1956	Fr.
I Am a Dancer	1972	Fr.
I Was An Adventuress	1939	Fr.
In the French Style	1962	Fr.--Col.
Incognito	1958	Fr.
Is There a Frenchman in the House?	1982	Fr.
It's Your Birthday	1961	Fr.

Jack of Spades	1961	Fr.
John Paul Jones	1959	WB
Johnny Banco	1969	Fr./Ger./It.
Katia	1960	Fr.
Love and Desire	1952	Fr.
The Lovers of Midnight	1953	Fr.
The Lovers of Toledo	1952	Fr.
Lulu	1962	Aust.
Magnificent Sinner	1963	Fr.
Main Street	1956	Fr./Sp.
Mata Hari	1964	Fr./It.
Me Faire ca a Moi	1961	Fr.
The Naked Woman	1950	Fr.
Nights of Farewell	1966	Fr./USSR
100 Million and Trouble	1965	Fr.
Les Parents Terribles	1948	Fr.
The Pass	1967	Fr.
Petition for Pardon	1960	Fr.
Phedra	1968	Fr.
The Plotters	1954	Fr.
The Potatoes	1969	Fr.
Rasputin	1939	Fr.
Le Rouge et Le Noir	1954	Fr./It.
Ruy Blas *	1948	Fr.
The Story of a Three Day Pass	1968	Fr.
The Stream	1938	Fr.
A Swelled Head	1962	Fr.
The Tempest	1940	Fr.
Under Western Eyes	1936	Fr.
A View From the Bridge	1961	Fr./It.
The Wench	1949	Fr.
White Slave	1939	Fr.

313. ALFRED KELLER

Along the Oregon Trail	1947	Rep.
GI War Brides	1946	Rep.
The Last Crooked Mile *	1946	Rep.
Oregon Trail Scouts	1947	Rep.
Spoilers of the North	1947	Rep.
Under Colorado Skies	1947	Rep.
Vigilantes of Boomtown	1947	Rep.
Western Heritage	1948	RKO
The Wild Frontier	1947	Rep.

314. GEORGE F. KELLEY

Buckaroo From Powder River	1948	Col.
Carolina Blues	1944	Col.

Last Days of Boot Hill	1947	Col.
The Lone Hand Texan	1947	Col.
Outlaws of the Rockies	1945	Col.
Phantom Valley	1948	Col.
Six-Gun Law	1948	Col.

315. W. WALLACE KELLEY

Apache Uprising	1965	Par.
The Big Mouth *	1967	Col.
Buckskin	1968	Par.
The Comic	1969	Col.
The Disorderly Orderly	1964	Par.
The Errand Boy	1961	Par.
The Family Jewels	1965	Par.
The Fastest Guitar Alive	1966	MGM
The Greatest Show On Earth *	1952	Par.
Hook, Line and Sinker	1968	Col.
It's Only Money	1962	Par.
The Ladies Man	1961	Par.
Look In Any Window	1961	AA
The Nutty Professor	1963	Par.
Paradise Hawaiian Style	1965	Par.
The Patsy	1964	Par.
Red Tomahawk	1967	Par.
Sangaree *	1953	Par.
Stage to Thunder Rock	1964	Par.
Three On a Couch	1966	Col.
Town Tamer	1965	Par.
Watermelon Man	1970	Col.
Who's Minding the Store?	1963	Par.
The Young Captives	1959	Par.

316. ROY KELLINO (1912-1956)

Aren't Men Beasts?	1937	GB
The Big Blockade *	1941	GB--Eal.
Convoy *	1941	GB--Eal.
Foreign Affairs	1935	GB
I Met a Murderer *	1939	GB
Johnny Frenchman	1945	GB--Eal.
Kate Plus Ten	1938	GB
The Last Adventurers	1937	GB
Nine Men	1943	GB--Eal.
O.H.M.S.	1936	GB
The Phantom Light	1934	GB
Pot Luck *	1936	GB
The Proud Valley *	1939	GB--Eal.
San Demetrio London *	1943	GB--Eal.
Ships With Wings *	1941	GB--Eal.

317. VICTOR J. KEMPER

And Justice For All	1979	Col.
Audrey Rose	1977	UA
Author, Author!	1982	TCF
The Candidate	1972	WB
Chu Chu and the Philly Flash	1981	TCF
Clue	1985	Par.
Cohen and Tate	1988	Tri-S.
Coma *	1978	MGM
Crazy People	1990	Par.
Dog Day Afternoon	1975	WB
Eyes of Laura Mars	1978	Col.
The Final Countdown	1980	UA
The Four Seasons	1981	Univ.
The Friends of Eddie Coyle	1973	Par.
From the Mixed-Up Files of Mrs. Basil Frankweiler	1973	US
The Gambler	1975	Par.
Gordon's War	1973	TCF
The Hospital	1971	UA
Hot To Trot	1988	WB
Husbands	1970	Col.
The Jerk	1987	Univ.
Last of the Red Hot Lovers	1972	Par.
The Last Tycoon	1976	Par.
The Lonely Guy	1981	Univ.
Magic	1978	TCF
The Magic Garden of Stanley Sweetheart	1970	MGM
Mikey and Nicky	1976	Par.
Mr. Mom	1984	US
National Lampoon's Vacation	1983	WB
Night of the Juggler	1980	Col.
Oh God!	1977	WB
The One and Only	1978	Par.
Partners	1982	US
Pee Wee's Big Adventure	1985	WB
The Reincarnation of Peter Proud	1975	AE
Secret Admirer	1985	Orion
See No Evil, Hear No Evil	1989	Tri-S.
Shamus	1972	Col.
Slap Shot *	1977	Univ.
Stay Hungry	1976	UA
They Might Be Giants	1972	Univ.
Walk Like a Man	1987	MGM-UA
Who Is Harry Kellerman and Why Is He Saying These Things About Me?	1971	US
Xanadu	1980	Univ.

318. DAVID KESSON

Bits of Life	1921	FN
Bob Hampton of Placer	1921	FN
Diplomacy *	1926	Par.
Dinty	1920	FN
The Eternal Three	1923	Gold.
Everybody's Acting *	1926	Par.
The Flame of the Yukon	1926	PDC
Fools First *	1922	FN
Go and Get It	1920	FN
Hill Billy	1924	US
The Lotus Eater	1921	FN
Lovers of Robert Burns	1930	GB
Mike	1926	MGM
Minnie *	1922	FN
The Poor Nut	1927	FN
The Rendezvous	1923	Gold.
Rookery Nook	1930	GB
Silk Husbands and Calico Wives	1920	FN
The Skyrocket	1926	US
Splinters	1929	GB
The Sporting Venus	1925	Metro.-Gold.
The Stranger's Banquet *	1922	Gold.
Tess of the D'Urbervilles	1924	Metro.-Gold.
Three-Ring Marriage	1928	FN
The Unholy Three	1925	MGM
Wanted Men	1930	GB
Wild Oats Lane *	1926	PDC

319. FRANK KESSON

Bobbed Hair	1925	WB
The Climbers	1927	WB
Hills of Kentucky	1927	WB
His Majesty Bunker Bean	1925	WB
Land of the Silver Fox	1928	WB
Matinee Ladies	1927	WB
The Midnight Taxi	1928	WB
Millionaires *	1926	WB
My Man	1928	WB
No Defense	1929	WB
One Stolen Night	1929	WB
Powder My Back	1928	WB
Rinty of the Desert	1928	WB
Sailor Izzy Murphy	1927	WB
A Sailor's Sweetheart	1927	WB
The Sea Beast *	1926	WB
The Silver Slave	1926	WB
Simple Sis	1927	WB

When a Man Loves *	1927	WB
While London Sleeps	1926	WB
Why Girls Go Home *	1926	WB
Women They Talk About	1928	WB

320. HERBERT KIRKPATRICK

Boss Rider of Gun Creek *	1936	Univ.
Burning Up Broadway	1929	US
The Cancelled Debt	1927	US
The Cattle Thief	1936	Col.
Closed Gates	1927	US
The Cowboy and the Kid *	1936	Univ.
The Cruel Truth	1927	US
Empty Saddles *	1937	Univ.
Face Value	1927	US
For the Service *	1936	Univ.
The Fourth Alarm	1930	US
Heir to Trouble	1936	Col.
Hunted Men	1930	US
In the First Degree	1927	US
Ivory-Handled Gun *	1935	Univ.
Lawless Riders	1936	Col.
Marry the Girl	1928	US
Million for Love	1928	US
Motive for Revenge	1935	US
Oh, What a Night!	1926	US
The Oklahoma Sheriff	1930	US
Outcast Souls	1928	US
The Perfect Clue	1935	US
Phantom in the House	1929	US
Pretty Clothes	1927	US
The Rampant Age	1930	US
Red Signals	1927	US
Ride 'Em Cowboy *	1936	Univ.
Sandflow *	1937	Univ.
Second Honeymoon	1930	US
She's My Baby	1927	US
Silver Spurs *	1936	Univ.
Sunset of Power *	1936	Univ.
Throwback *	1935	Univ.
Thumbs Down	1927	US
Undressed	1928	US
Western Courage	1935	Col.
Western Frontier *	1935	Col.
Wolves of the Air	1927	US
Worldly Goods	1930	US

321. ROY KLAFFKI

The Adorable Deceiver	1926	US
Borrowed Clothes	1918	US
Flame of the Argentine	1926	US
Forbidden *	1919	Univ.
Her Five Foot Highness	1920	Univ.
His Divorced Wife	1919	Univ.
Home	1919	Univ.
Human Stuff	1920	Univ.
The Imposter	1926	US
The Infamous Miss Revel	1921	Metro.
The Jade Cup	1926	US
Married in Haste	1919	Fox
Queen o' Diamonds	1926	US
Secret Orders	1926	US
Three Wise Crooks	1925	US
The Tired Business Man *	1927	US
The Unattainable	1916	US
The Wedding March *	1928	Par.
Words and Music By ...	1919	Fox

322. BENJAMIN KLINE (1895-1974)

After Your Own Heart	1921	Fox
All-American Sweetheart	1937	Col.
Apache Chief	1949	Lip.
Arson Squad	1945	PRC
Arthur Takes Over	1948	TCF
Awakening of Jim Burke	1935	Col.
Babies for Sale	1940	Col.
Backlash	1947	TCF
Bad Men of the Hills	1942	Col.
Badman's Country	1958	TCF
Before I Hang	1940	Col.
The Big Boss *	1942	Col.
Big Town Round-Up	1921	Fox
Black Gold	1924	US
Blades of Musketeers	1953	US
The Bolted Door	1934	Univ.
Branded *	1931	Col.
Cafe Hostess	1940	Col.
The California Trail	1933	Col.
Call of the Rockies	1938	Col.
Calypso Heat Wave	1957	Col.
Cha-Cha-Cha Boom	1956	Col.
A Chapter in Her Life	1923	Univ.
Chasing the Moon	1922	Fox
Chinese Parrot	1927	Univ.
Club Havana	1946	PRC

The Colorado Trail	1938	Col.
Convicted Woman	1940	Col.
The Count of Ten *	1928	Univ.
Crash Landing	1958	Col.
Crimson Key	1947	TCF
Crossed Wires	1923	Univ.
Danger Street	1947	Par.
A Dangerous Adventure	1937	Col.
Dangerous Millions	1946	TCF
Dangerous Years	1948	TCF
Daring Danger	1932	Col.
Daring Days	1925	Univ.
Deadline For Murder	1946	TCF
Detour	1945	PRC
Don't Knock the Rock	1956	Col.
End of the Trail	1932	Col.
Escape from San Quentin	1957	Col.
Ever Since Venus	1944	Col.
Everybody's Dancin'	1950	Lip.
Extortion	1938	Col.
The Face on the Bar Room Floor	1932	US
Fighting Back	1948	TCF
Fighting Buckaroo	1943	Col.
The Fighting Fool	1932	Col.
Final Edition	1932	Col.
The First Degree	1923	Univ.
Five Little Peppers in Trouble	1940	Col.
The Flaming Hour	1922	Univ.
Fog	1934	Col.
The Frameup	1937	Col.
Frontier Fury	1943	Col.
Gallant Defender	1935	Col.
The Game That Kills	1937	Col.
The Giant Claw	1957	Col.
Girl in Danger	1934	Col.
Going Steady	1958	Col.
Guard That Girl	1935	Col.
Hail to the Rangers	1943	Col.
Half Past Midnight	1948	TCF
Hands Off	1921	Fox
Hell Bent for Love	1934	Col.
The Hell Cat	1934	Col.
Hello Trouble	1932	Col.
Hitchin' Posts	1920	Univ.
Holiday Rhythm	1950	Lip.
Homicide Bureau	1939	Col.
Honor Bound	1920	Univ.
How Do You Do?	1945	PRC
I Ring Doorbells	1946	PRC
I'll Fix It	1934	Col.
In Spite of Danger	1935	Col.

The Invisible Wall	1947	TCF
Island of Doomed Men	1940	Col.
Jewels of Brandenberg	1947	TCF
Joe Palooka, Champ	1946	Mon.
Journey's End	1930	US
The Judge	1949	US
Juvenile Court	1938	Col.
The King of Dodge City	1941	Col.
Konga, the Wild Stallion	1939	Col.
The Lady From Longacre	1921	Fox
The Last Man	1932	Col.
Last of the Lone Wolf	1930	Col.
Last of the Wild Horses	1948	Lip.
Law of the Northwest	1943	Col.
Law of the Plains	1938	Col.
Lawless Plainsman	1943	Col.
Let's Fall in Love	1934	Col.
Let's Go Steady	1945	Col.
Little Miss Roughneck	1938	Col.
Lone Star Vigilantes	1941	Col.
The Man From Sundown	1939	Col.
Man They Could Not Hang	1939	Col.
The Man Trailer	1934	Col.
The Man Who Turned to Stone	1957	Col.
The Man With Nine Lives	1940	Col.
McGuire of the Mounted	1923	Univ.
McKenna of the Mounted	1932	Col.
The Medico of Painted Springs	1941	Col.
Men of the Hour	1935	Col.
Men Without Souls	1940	Col.
Miami Expose	1956	Col.
Miss Mink of 1949	1949	TCF
Munster Go Home!	1966	Univ.
My Son Is Guilty	1939	Col.
My Woman	1933	Col.
The Night Horseman	1921	Fox
The Night the World Exploded	1957	Col.
Night Wind	1948	TCF
No Escape	1953	UA
Nobody's Children	1940	Col.
Omoo-Omoo	1949	US
Operation Haylift	1949	Lip.
Out West With the Peppers	1940	Col.
The Outlaw's Daughter	1925	Univ.
Panic On the Air	1936	Col.
Parole Girl	1933	Col.
The Party's Over	1934	Col.
Peacock Alley *	1930	US
The Phantom Submarine	1940	Col.
Police Car 17	1933	Col.
Prairie Stranger	1941	Col.

The Prescott Kid	1936	Col.
Pride of the Marines	1936	Col.
Pure Grit	1923	Univ.
The Range Feud	1931	Col.
The Red Lane	1920	Univ.
Rendezvous 24	1946	TCF
Riders of the Badlands	1942	Col.
Riders of the Northland	1942	Col.
Ridin' for Justice	1932	Col.
A Ridin' Romeo	1921	Fox
The Riding Tornado	1932	Col.
Riding West	1944	Col.
The Road Demon *	1921	Fox
Robin Hood of the Range	1943	Col.
Rock Around the Clock	1956	Col.
Roses Are Red	1947	TCF
The Rough Diamond	1921	Fox
Rumble on the Docks	1956	Col.
Scandal Sheet	1939	Col.
The Scarlet West *	1925	FN
Secret of Treasure Mountain	1956	Col.
Sensation Seekers	1927	Univ.
Shadows of Sing Sing	1934	Col.
She's a Sweetheart	1945	Col.
Shoot To Kill	1947	US
Silver City Raiders	1943	Col.
The Six-Fifty	1923	Univ.
Sky High	1922	Fox
The Son of Davy Crockett	1941	Col.
South of Arizona	1938	Col.
South of the Rio Grande	1932	Col.
Speed To Spare	1937	Col.
State Trooper	1933	Col.
Strange Journey	1946	TCF
Superspeed	1935	Col.
Tahiti Nights	1945	Col.
Ten Cents a Dance	1945	Col.
The Texas Cyclone	1932	Col.
Thunder Over the Prairie	1941	Col.
The Tijuana Story	1957	Col.
Tough Assignment	1949	Lip.
Trail of the Mounties	1947	US
Trailin'	1921	Fox
Treasure of Monte Cristo	1949	Lip.
Troopers Three *	1930	US
Trouble Preferred	1948	TCF
Tucson	1949	TCF
Two-Fisted Law	1932	Col.
Untameable *	1924	Univ.
Up and Going *	1922	Fox
Utah Blaine	1957	Col.

War Correspondent	1932	Col.
West of Cheyenne	1938	Col.
Westbound Mail	1936	Col.
Western Caravans	1939	Col.
The Western Code	1933	Col.
When Strangers Marry	1933	Col.
Whirlpool	1934	Col.
White Lies	1935	Col.
Whom the Gods Destroy	1934	Col.
Wolf Law	1922	Univ.
Woman I Stole	1933	Col.
A Woman Is the Judge	1939	Col.
Women in Prison	1938	Col.
The World Was His Jury	1958	Col.
Zombies of Mora Tau	1957	Col.

323. RICHARD H. KLINE (1926-   )

The Andromeda Strain	1970	Univ.
Backtrack *	1969	Univ.
Battle for the Planet of the Apes	1973	TCF
Black Gunn	1972	Col.
Body Heat	1981	WB
The Boston Strangler	1968	TCF
Breathless	1982	US
Camelot	1967	WB
Chamber of Horrors	1966	WB
The Competition	1980	Col.
Deal of the Century	1983	WB
Death Wish II *	1982	US
The Don Is Dead	1973	Univ.
Downtown	1990	TCF
A Dream of Kings	1969	NG
The Fury	1978	TCF
Gaily Gaily	1969	UA
Hammersmith Is Out	1972	US
Hang 'Em High *	1967	UA
Hard To Hold	1984	Univ.
The Harrad Experiment	1973	US
The Harrad Summer	1974	US
Howard the Duck	1986	Univ.
King Kong	1976	DeL.
Kotch	1971	ABC
Man, Woman and Child	1983	US
Mandingo	1975	DeL.
The Mechanic *	1972	UA
Mr. Majestyk	1974	UA
The Moonshine War	1970	MGM
My Stepmother Is An Alien	1988	Col.
Soylent Green	1973	MGM

Star Trek: The Motion Picture *	1979	Par.
The Terminal Man	1974	WB
Tilt	1979	WB
Touch and Go	1986	Tri-S.
Touched By Love	1980	Col.
Tristan und Isolt	1981	US
When the Legends Die	1972	US
Who'll Stop the Rain?	1978	UA
Won Ton Ton, the Dog That Saved Hollywood	1976	Par.

324. NICK KNOWLAND

Alf Garnett Saga	1972	US
The Children	1990	Ger./GB
Derek and Clive Get the Horn	1981	GB
Double Pisces, Scorpio Rising	1970	GB
Imagine	1973	US
Ping Pong	1986	GB
Playing Away	1986	GB
Secrets *	1971	US
Take It or Leave It	1983	GB
Testimony	1987	GB

325. BERNARD KNOWLES (1900-   )

Brown On Resolution	1935	GB
Canaries Sometimes Sing	1930	GB
Day Will Dawn *	1942	GB
The Demi-Paradise	1943	GB
East Meets West	1936	GB
English Without Tears *	1944	GB
Falling for You	1933	GB
Freedom Radio	1941	GB--Col.
French Leave	1930	GB
French Without Tears *	1939	GB--Par.
Gaslight	1939	GB
The Good Companions	1932	GB
Hound of the Baskervilles	1931	GB
Jack Ahoy	1934	GB
Jamaica Inn *	1939	GB
Jeannie *	1941	GB
Jew Suss	1934	GB
King of the Damned	1935	GB
Love Story	1944	GB
The Mikado *	1939	GB
Quiet Wedding	1940	GB--Par.
Rhodes of Africa *	1936	GB
Sabotage	1936	GB

Saint's Vacation	1941	RKO
Secret Mission *	1942	GB
Soldiers of the King	1933	GB
Take My Tip	1937	GB
Talk About Jacqueline *	1942	GB
The Thirty Nine Steps	1935	GB
Unpublished Story *	1942	GB--Col.
Young and Innocent	1937	GB

326. FRED J. KOENEKAMP

The Amityville Horror	1979	AIP
The Bad News Bears in Breaking Training	1977	Par.
Beyond the Valley of the Dolls	1970	TCF
Billy Jack	1971	WB
Carbon Copy	1981	Hem./RKO
The Champ	1979	MGM
Doc Savage, Man of Bronze	1975	WB
Doctor, You've Got To Be Kidding	1967	MGM
The Domino Principle *	1977	US
Embryo	1976	US
First Family	1980	WB
First Monday in October	1981	Par.
Flap!	1970	WB
Fun With Dick and Jane	1976	Col.
The Great Bank Robbery	1969	WB
Happy Birthday Wanda June	1971	Col.
Harry In Your Pocket	1973	UA
Heaven With a Gun	1969	MGM
The Helicopter Spies	1967	MGM
The Hunter	1980	Par.
Islands in the Stream	1976	Par.
Kansas City Bomber	1972	MGM
The Karate Killers	1967	MGM
Listen to Me	1989	Col.
Live a Little, Love a Little	1968	MGM
Love and Bullets *	1978	US
The Magnificent Seven Ride	1972	UA
One of Our Spies Is Missing	1966	MGM
One Spy Too Many	1966	MGM
The Other Side of Midnight	1972	TCF
Papillon	1973	US
Patton	1969	TCF
Posse	1975	Par.
Rage	1972	WB
The Skin Game	1971	WB
Sol Madrid	1968	MGM
Spencer's Mountain *	1963	WB
The Spy in the Green Hat	1966	MGM

The Spy With My Face	1966	MGM
Stay Away Joe	1968	MGM
Stewardess School	1987	US
Stand Up and Be Counted	1971	Col.
The Swarm	1978	WB
The Towering Inferno *	1974	TCF
Two of a Kind *	1983	TCF
Uptown Saturday Night	1974	WB
Welcome Home	1989	Col.
When Time Ran Out	1980	WB
White Line Fever	1974	Can.
Wrong Is Right	1982	Col.
Yes, Giorgio	1982	MGM-UA

327. HENRY KOTANI

Believe Me, Xantippe	1918	Par.
The Goat	1918	US
The House of Silence	1918	Par.
Johnny Get Your Gun	1919	Par.
Mrs. Temple's Telegram	1920	Par.
Puppy Love	1919	Par.
Rustling Bride	1919	Par.
The Sable Lorcha *	1915	US
The Secret Garden	1919	Par.
Under the Top	1919	US
Young Mrs. Winthrop	1920	Par.

328. LASZLO KOVACS

Alex in Wonderland	1970	MGM
At Long Last Love	1975	TCF
Baby Blue Marine	1976	Col.
Blood of Dracula's Castle	1969	US
Butch and Sundance: The Early Years	1979	TCF
Crackers	1984	Univ.
Day With the Boys	1969	US
Easy Rider	1969	Col.
F.I.S.T.	1978	UA
Five Easy Pieces	1970	Col.
For Pete's Sake!	1974	Col.
Frances	1982	EMI
Freebie and the Bean	1974	WB
Getting Straight	1970	Col.
Ghostbusters *	1984	Col.
Harry and Walter Go to New York	1976	Col.
Heart Beat	1979	WB
Hell's Angels On Wheels	1967	US

Hell's Blood Devils	1970	US
Huckleberry Finn	1974	UA
Inside Moves	1980	US
The King of Marvin Gardens	1972	Col.
Kiss Me Quick!	1964	US
The Last Movie	1971	Univ.
Legal Eagles	1986	Univ.
The Legend of the Lone Ranger	1981	US
Little Nikita	1988	Col.
A Man Called Dagger	1968	MGM
Marriage of a Young Stockbroker	1971	TCF
New York, New York	1977	UA
Nickelodeon	1976	Col.
Paper Moon	1973	Par.
Paradise Alley	1978	Univ.
Pocket Money	1972	US
Psych-Out	1968	AIP
Rebel Rousers *	1970	US
Reflection of Fear	1971	Col.
The Runner Stumbles	1979	US
Say Anything	1989	TCF
The Savage Seven	1968	AIP
Shampoo	1975	Col.
Single Room Unfurnished	1968	US
Slither	1972	MGM
Steelyard Blues *	1972	WB
Targets	1967	Par.
That Cold Day in the Park	1969	Can.
The Toy	1982	Col.
What's Up Doc?	1972	WB

329. GUNTHER KRAMPF (1899-   )

Alraune	1930	Ger.--UFA
The Amateur Gentleman	1936	GB
The Bells	1931	GB
Black Eyes	1939	GB
Black Sheep of Whitehall	1941	GB--Eal.
Brave Sinner	1933	GB
Convoy *	1940	GB--Eal.
Daughter of Evil	1930	Ger.--UFA
Dead Men's Shoes	1939	GB
Death at Broadcast House	1934	GB
Everything Is Thunder	1936	GB
False Rapture	1941	US
Fame Is the Spur *	1947	GB
The Franchise Affair	1950	GB
The Fugitive	1940	GB--Univ.
The Ghoul	1933	GB
Good Sinner	1931	Ger.

His Lordship	1936	GB
Kuhle Wampe	1933	Ger.
Latin Quarter *	1945	GB
Little Friend	1934	GB
Little Stranger	1934	GB--MGM
The Lucky Number	1933	GB
Marigold	1938	GB
Meet Me at Dawn	1946	GB--TCF
The Night Has Eyes	1942	GB
Nosferatu *	1922	Ger.
On the Night of the Fire	1939	GB
The Outsider	1931	GB--MGM
The Outsider	1939	GB
Pandora's Box	1929	Ger.
Paradise for Two	1937	GB--Korda
Portrait of Claire	1950	GB
Power	1934	GB
Queen of a Night	1931	Ger.
Rome Express	1932	GB
Sabotage at Sea	1942	GB
Sailors Three	1940	GB--Eal.
Student of Prague *	1926	Ger.
Suspected Person	1943	GB
13 Men and a Girl	1931	Ger.
This Was a Woman *	1948	GB
Tinker	1949	GB
The Tunnel	1935	GB
Warn That Man	1943	GB
Women Aren't Angels	1942	GB

330. ROBERT KRASKER (1913-1981)

Alexander the Great	1956	UA
Another Man's Poison	1951	GB
The Angel With the Trumpet	1949	GB
Behind the Mask	1958	GB
Billy Budd	1962	GB
Bonnie Prince Charlie *	1948	GB
Brief Encounter	1945	GB
Caesar and Cleopatra *	1945	GB--Rank
The Collector *	1965	Col.
The Criminal	1960	GB
Cry the Beloved Country	1951	GB
Cry Wolf	1980	GB--Par.
The Doctor's Dilemma	1958	GB--MGM
El Cid	1961	US
Fall of the Roman Empire *	1964	US
Guns of Darkness	1962	GB
Henry V	1944	GB--Rank
The Heroes of Telemark	1965	GB--Rank

Lamp Still Burns *	1943	GB
Libel	1959	GB--MGM
The Malta Story	1953	GB
Men Are Not Gods *	1936	GB--Korda
Never Let Me Go	1953	GB--MGM
Odd Man Out	1946	GB
The Quiet American	1957	UA
The Rising of the Moon	1957	WB
Romanoff and Juliet	1961	Univ.
Romeo and Juliet	1954	GB--Rank
The Running Man	1963	GB--Col.
Saint Meets the Tiger	1943	Rep.
Senso *	1953	It.
State Secret	1950	GB
Story of Esther Costello	1957	GB--Col.
That Lady	1955	GB--TCF
The Third Man	1949	GB--Korda/Selz.
The Trap	1966	Can./GB
Trapeze	1956	UA
Uncle Silas	1947	GB
Wonder Child *	1951	GB

331. MILTON KRASNER (1904-1987)

The Accused	1948	Par.
Advance to the Rear	1964	MGM
An Affair to Remember	1957	TCF
All About Eve	1950	TCF
Along Came Jones	1945	UA
Arabian Nights *	1942	Univ.
Bachelor Daddy	1941	Univ.
Ballad of Josie	1967	Univ.
The Bank Dick	1940	Univ.
Bells Are Ringing	1960	MGM
Beneath the Planet of the Apes	1969	TCF
Boy on a Dolphin	1957	TCF
Buck Privates	1941	Univ.
Bus Stop	1956	TCF
A Certain Smile	1958	TCF
Cheers of the Crowd	1936	Mon.
Count Your Blessings *	1959	MGM
The Courtship of Eddie's Father	1962	MGM
Crash Donovan	1936	Univ.
Crime of Dr. Hallett	1938	Univ.
The Dark Mirror	1946	Univ.
Deadline USA	1952	TCF
Death on the Diamond	1934	US
Delightfully Dangerous	1945	UA
Demetrius and the Gladiators	1954	TCF
Desiree	1954	TCF

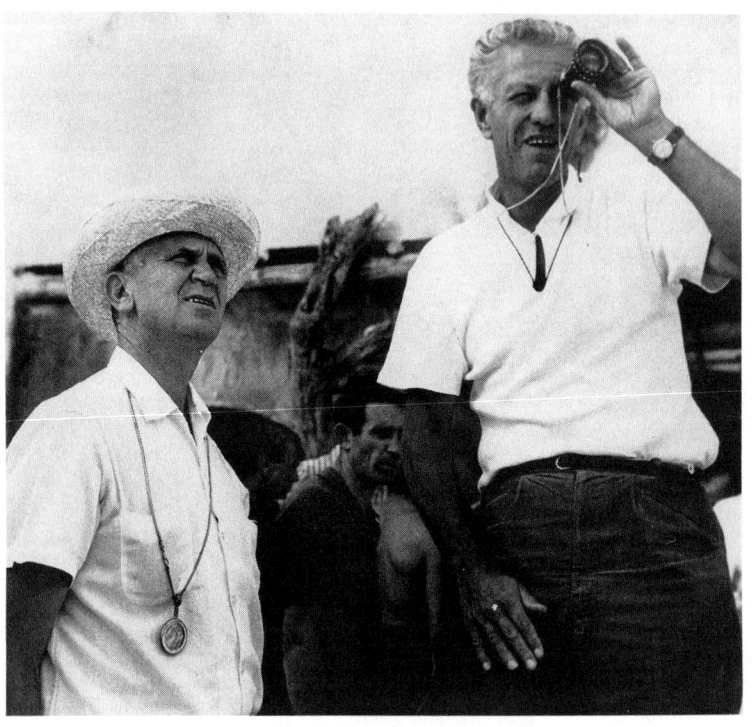

Milton Krasner (left) with director Nicholas Ray.

The Devil's Party	1938	Univ.
Diamond Frontier	1940	Univ.
Don't Just Stand There	1967	Univ.
A Double Life	1947	Univ.
Dream Wife	1953	MGM
Dreamboat	1952	TCF
The Egg and I	1947	Univ.
The Farmer's Daughter	1947	Selz.
Fate Is the Hunter	1964	TCF
Forbidden Heaven	1936	Rep.
The Four Horsemen of the Apocalypse	1961	MGM
Garden of Evil	1954	TCF
A Gentleman After Dark	1943	US
The Ghost of Frankenstein *	1942	Univ.
The Gift of Love	1958	TCF
The Girl in the Red Velvet Swing	1955	TCF
The Girl on the Front Page	1936	Univ.
Girl With Ideas	1937	Univ.
Go Naked in the World	1961	MGM
Golden Harvest	1933	Par.
Goodbye Charlie	1964	TCF
The Great Flirtation	1934	Par.
The Great God Gold	1935	Mon.
The Great Impersonation	1935	Univ.
Gung Ho!	1943	Univ.
Half Angel	1951	TCF
Hat Check Honey	1944	Univ.
Hired Wife	1940	Univ.
Hold 'Em Yale	1935	Par.
Holiday Affair	1949	RKO
Home From the Hill	1959	MGM
Honeymoon Limited	1936	Mon.
The House of Fear	1939	Univ.
The House of Seven Gables	1940	Univ.
House of Strangers	1949	TCF
How the West Was Won *	1962	MGM
How to Be Very Very Popular	1955	TCF
Hurry Sundown *	1967	Par.
I Can Get It for You Wholesale	1951	TCF
I Love That Man	1933	Par.
I Stole a Million	1939	Univ.
The Invisible Man Returns	1940	Univ.
The Invisible Man's Revenge	1944	Univ.
The Jury's Secret	1938	Univ.
Kiss Them for Me	1957	TCF
The Lady Fights Back	1937	Univ.
The Lady From Cheyenne	1941	Univ.
Laughing Irish Eyes *	1936	Rep.
The Little Accident	1939	Univ.
Looking for Love	1964	MGM
Love With the Proper Stranger	1964	Par.

The Mad Ghoul	1943	Univ.
Made in Paris	1966	MGM
Make a Million	1935	Mon./Rep.
The Man From Montreal	1940	Univ.
The Man Who Understood Women	1959	TCF
Men of Texas	1942	Univ.
Midnight Intruder	1938	Univ.
The Missing Guest	1938	Univ.
Mister Cinderella	1936	MGM
The Model and the Marriage Broker	1952	TCF
Monkey Business	1952	TCF
Murder in the Fleet	1935	MGM
Mysterious Crossing	1937	Univ.
Newsboys' Home	1939	Univ.
No Way Out	1950	TCF
Nurse From Brooklyn	1938	Univ.
O. Henry's Full House *	1952	TCF
Pardon My Sarong	1942	Univ.
Paris Calling	1941	Univ.
Paris Interlude	1934	MGM
People Will Talk	1951	TCF
Phone Call From a Stranger	1952	TCF
Prescription for Romance	1937	Univ.
Private Affairs	1940	Univ.
Private Scandal	1934	Par.
The Rains of Ranchipur	1955	TCF
Rawhide	1950	TCF
Red Line 7000 *	1965	Par.
The Remarkable Mr. Pennypacker	1958	TCF
The St. Valentine's Day Massacre	1967	TCF
The Sandpiper	1965	MGM
Sandy Is a Lady	1940	Univ.
The Saxon Charm	1948	Univ.
Scarlet Street	1946	Univ.
The Set Up	1949	RKO
The Seven Year Itch	1955	TCF
She Made Her Bed	1934	Par.
She's Dangerous	1937	Univ.
The Singing Nun	1966	MGM
Sitting Pretty	1933	Par.
Ski Patrol	1940	Univ.
So's Your Uncle *	1943	Univ.
Something in the Wind	1948	Univ.
The Spoilers	1942	Univ.
The Sterile Cuckoo	1969	Par.
The Storm	1938	Univ.
Sweet Bird of Youth	1962	MGM
Taxi	1952	TCF
There Goes the Groom	1937	RKO
This Woman Is Mine	1941	Univ.
Three Came Home	1950	TCF

Three Coins in the Fountain	1954	TCF
A Ticklish Affair	1963	MGM
Too Many Blondes	1941	Univ.
Trail of the Vigilantes *	1940	Univ.
Twenty-Three Paces to Baker Street	1956	TCF
Two Tickets to London	1943	Univ.
Two Weeks in Another Town	1962	MGM
Up in Central Park	1948	Univ.
The Venetian Affair *	1966	MGM
Vicki	1953	TCF
The Virginia Judge	1935	Par.
We Have Our Moments	1937	Univ.
We've Never Been Licked	1943	Univ.
Without Reservations	1946	RKO
The Woman in the Window	1944	US
Women Must Dress	1935	Mon.
Yellowstone	1936	Univ.
You Can't Cheat an Honest Man	1939	Univ.
Zanzibar	1940	Univ.

332. RICHARD KRATINA

Aaron Loves Angel	1975	Col.
The Angel Levine	1970	UA
Believe in Me *	1971	MGM
Born to Win *	1971	UA
Chapter Two *	1979	Col.
Come Back Charleston BLue	1972	WB
Firepower *	1979	US
Hair *	1979	UA
The Happy Hooker	1975	Cannon
Love Story	1970	Par.
The Pursuit of Happiness	1970	Col.
A Safe Place	1971	Col.
The Sentinel	1976	Univ.
The Super Cops	1974	MGM-UA

333. GEORG KRAUSE

At Night When the Devil Comes	1957	Ger.
Berliner Ballad	1949	Ger.
Court Martial	1962	Ger.--UA
The Doctor of Stalingrad	1958	Ger.
Encounter in Salzburg	1964	Ger.
Escape From East Berlin	1962	MGM
The Fair	1960	Ger.
Isle of Sin	1963	Ger.
It's Hot in Paradise	1962	Ger.
Der Katzensteg	1938	Ger.

Man on a Tightrope	1953	TCF
08/15-Part II	1955	Ger.
Paths of Glory	1957	UA
Seven Daring Girls	1962	Ger.
The Stars Are Shining	1938	Ger.
Taiga	1958	Ger.
The Truth About Rosemarie	1960	Ger.
Time of the Innocent	1964	Ger.--Col.
The Ways of Love Are Strange	1937	Ger.

334. EDWARD KULL

The Apache Raider	1928	Pathe
Arctic Fury *	1949	RKO
Arizona Whirlwind	1944	Mon.
The Black Ace	1928	Pathe
Black Market Rustlers	1943	Mon.
Border Blackbirds	1927	Pathe
Boss of Rustlers' Roost	1928	Pathe
A Boy, a Girl and a Dog	1946	US
The Bronc Stomper	1928	Pathe
Carnival Lady	1933	US
The Cheyenne Kid	1940	Mon.
Covered Wagon Trails	1940	Mon.
Cowboy Commandos	1943	Mon.
Creaking Stairs	1919	Univ.
Cyclone Kid	1931	US
Death Valley Rangers	1943	Mon.
The Devil's Twin	1927	Pathe
Ferocious Pal	1934	US
The Fighting Gentleman	1932	US
45 Caliber War	1929	Pathe
Forty-Niners	1932	US
Gambling Sex	1932	US
Headin' for Trouble	1931	US
High Gear	1933	US
The Lonely Woman	1918	US
The Lure of Luxury	1918	US
Making the Varsity	1928	US
The Man From New Mexico	1932	Mon.
The Man Trackers	1921	Univ.
Manhattan Knights *	1928	US
Mesquite Buckaroo	1939	US
The Millionaire Pirate	1919	US
Murder at Dawn	1932	US
New Adventures of Tarzan *	1935	Rep.
The Penal Code	1933	US
Pioneer Days	1940	Mon.
Rodeo Rhythm	1941	PRC
The Savage Girl	1933	US

Scarlet Brand	1932	US
Smoky Trails	1939	US
The Sundown Trail	1919	Univ.
Teen Age	1944	US
Tundra *	1936	US
War of the Range	1933	US
When a Man Rides Alone	1933	US
Who Killed Walton?	1918	US
Yellow Contraband	1928	Pathe

335. ROBERT C. KURRLE (1890-1932)

Abraham Lincoln *	1924	UA
All the Brothers Were Valiant	1923	Metro.
Blackie's Redemption	1919	Metro.
Blind Man's Eyes	1919	Metro.
Breakfast at Sunrise	1927	FN
Breakers Ahead *	1918	Metro.
Crooked Circle	1932	US
Crooner	1932	FN
Dancing Sweeties	1930	WB
Demon Des Meeres	1931	US
Easy To Make Money	1919	Metro.
Evangeline	1929	UA
The Expert	1932	WB
Faith	1919	Metro.
The Four Feathers *	1929	Par.
Furies	1930	FN
Her Mad Bargain	1921	FN
Her Majesty Love	1931	WB
High Pressure	1932	WB
High Steppers	1926	FN
Hit the Deck	1930	RKO
Hitting the High Spots	1918	Metro.
I Am the Law	1922	US
Illicit	1931	WB
The Invisible Fear	1921	FN
Isobel	1920	US
Jewel Robbery	1932	WB
Joanna *	1925	FN
Lady Who Lied	1925	FN
Lawyer Man	1932	WB
The Lion's Den	1919	Metro.
Lombardi, Ltd.	1919	Metro.
The Lure of Youth	1921	Metro.
Madonna of the Streets	1924	FN
The Match King	1932	FN/WB
Maybe It's Love	1930	WB
Moby Dick	1930	WB
One Way Passage	1932	WB

One-Thing-at-a-Time O'Day	1919	Metro.
Pals First	1926	FN
Playthings of Destiny	1921	FN
A Question of Honor	1922	FN
Ramona *	1928	UA
The Red Rider *	1925	Univ.
Resurrection *	1927	UA
Resurrection *	1931	Univ.
Revenge *	1928	UA
The Right of Way	1920	Metro.
Rio Grande	1920	Pathe
Rio Rita *	1929	RKO
River's End	1930	WB
Road to Singapore	1931	WB
Sackcloth and Scarlet *	1925	Par.
Sadie Thompson *	1928	UA
Silver Wings *	1922	Fox
Smart Money	1931	WB
A Son of the Sahara	1924	FN
The Spender	1919	Metro.
The Stolen Bride	1927	FN
The Strange Love of Molly Louvain	1932	FN/WB
The Tender Hour	1927	FN
The Trail to Yesterday	1918	Metro.
Unexpected Places	1918	Metro.
Why Women Love	1925	FN
Wings of the Storm	1926	Fox

336. LUIGI KUVEILLER

Age of Discretion	1990	IT.
Avanti!	1972	UA
Banana Joe	1982	Ger./It.
Blood for Dracula	1974	Fr./It.--US
The Boss and the Worker	1974	It.--UA
Carne per Frankenstein	1973	Fr./It.--US
Come Home and Meet My Wife	1974	It.
Count Tacchia	1983	It.
Deep Red	1976	It.
Double Murder	1978	It.
Escalation	1968	It.
Flirt	1983	It.
Fraulein Doctor	1968	It./Yugo.--Par.
Harem	1968	Fr./Ger./It.
I'm Getting a Yacht	1981	It.
Investigation of a Citizen Above Suspicion	1970	It.--Col.
Italian Fast Food	1986	It.
The Lady of Monza	1970	It.
Life Is Wonderful	1982	It./USSR

A Lizard in Woman's Skin	1971	Fr./It./Sp.--AIP
Malamore	1982	It.
A Man Called Sledge	1970	It.--Col.
Monte Napoleone	1987	It.--Col.
My Dearest Son	1985	It.
My First Forty Years	1987	It.
My Friends	1975	It.
New York Ripper	1982	It.
The Payoff	1978	It.--UA
Property Is No Longer a Theft	1973	Fr./It.
A Quiet Place in the Country	1970	Fr./It.--UA
Quite By Chance	1988	It.
Secret Access	1988	It.
Secret Scandal	1990	It.
Slap the Monster on Page One *	1972	It.
Somewhere Beyond Love	1974	It.
Strogoff	1970	Ger./It.
To Each His Own	1967	It.--UA
Todo Modo	1980	It.
We Still Kill the Old Way	1968	It.
The Working Class Goes to Heaven	1972	It.
Yuppies, Youngsters Who Succeed	1986	It.

337. LELAND LANCASTER

Across the Dead-Line	1922	Univ.
Doctor Jim	1921	Univ.
The Fighting Lover	1921	Univ.
Go Straight	1921	Univ.
The Shark Master	1921	Univ.
The Smart Sex	1921	Univ.
Tracked to Earth	1922	Univ.

338. SAM LANDERS

Bonnie May	1920	US
The Devil's Riddle	1920	Fox
The Fate of a Flirt	1925	Col.
Fighting Through	1919	US
Heartsease	1919	Gold.
Her Temporary Husband	1923	FN
The House of Intrigue	1919	US
It's a Bear	1919	US
The Mayor of Filbert	1919	US
A Regular Fellow	1919	US
Sealed Lips	1925	Col.
Sign of the Rose	1922	US
What No Man Knows	1921	US
When Husbands Flirt	1925	Col.

339. GEORGE W. LANE

Blind Wives	1920	Fox
The Broadway Peacock	1922	Fox
Buchanan's Wife	1918	Fox
Driven	1923	Univ.
Eastward Ho!	1919	Fox
Envy	1917	US
Footfalls	1921	Fox
It Is the Law	1924	Fox
Kathleen Mavoureen	1919	Fox
La Belle Russe	1919	Fox
The Lights of New York	1922	Fox
Sacred Silence	1919	Fox
The Silent Command	1923	Fox
Thou Shalt Not	1920	Fox
Thunderclap	1921	Fox
While New York Sleeps	1920	Fox

340. CHARLES B. LANG, Jr. (1902-   )

Aaron Slick From Pumpkin Creek	1952	Par.
Ace in the Hole	1951	Par.
Adventure in Diamonds	1940	Par.
Angel	1937	Par.
Anybody's Woman	1930	Par.
Are Husbands Necessary?	1942	Par.
Arise My Love	1940	Par.
The Atomic City	1952	Par.
Autumn Leaves	1956	Col.
A Bedtime Story	1933	Par.
Behind the Make-Up	1930	Par.
The Big Heat	1953	Col.
Blue Hawaii	1962	US
Blue Skies *	1946	Par.
Bob and Carol and Ted and Alice	1969	Col.
Branded	1950	Par.
Buck Benny Rides Again	1940	Par.
Butterflies Are Free	1972	Col.
Cactus Flower	1969	Col.
The Cat and the Canary	1939	Par.
Caught!	1931	Par.
Charade	1964	Univ.
Copper Canyon	1949	Par.
Cradle Song	1933	Par.
Critic's Choice	1963	WB
Cross My Heart	1945	Par.
Dancing on a Dime	1940	Par.
Death Takes a Holiday	1934	Par.
Desert Fury *	1947	Par.

Desire *	1936	Par.
Devil and the Deep	1932	Par.
Dr. Rhythm	1938	Par.
Doctors' Wives	1970	Col.
The Facts of Life	1960	UA
Fancy Pants	1950	Par.
A Farewell to Arms	1932	Par.
Father Goose	1964	Univ.
The Female on the Beach	1955	Univ.
A Flea in Her Ear	1968	TCF
The Flim Flam Man	1967	TCF
For the Defense	1930	Par.
A Foreign Affair	1948	Par.
The Forest Rangers *	1942	Par.
Forty Carats	1973	Col.
Gambling Ship	1933	Par.
The Ghost and Mrs. Muir	1947	TCF
The Ghost Breakers	1940	Par.
A Girl Named Tamiko	1962	Par.
The Gracie Allen Murder Case	1939	Par.
The Great Lover	1949	Par.
Gunfight at the O.K. Corral	1947	Par.
Here Come the Waves *	1944	Par.
Hotel	1967	WB
How the West Was Won *	1962	MGM
How To Commit Marriage	1969	US
How To Steal a Million	1966	TCF
I Love a Soldier	1944	Par.
Innocents of Paris	1929	Par.
Inside Daisy Clover	1965	WB
It Should Happen to You	1954	Col.
The Lady Has Plans	1942	Par.
Last Train From Gun Hill	1959	Par.
The Light of Western Stars	1930	Par.
Lives of a Bengal Lancer	1935	Par.
The Love Machine	1971	Col.
Loving You	1957	Par.
The Magnificent Lie	1931	Par.
The Magnificent Seven	1960	UA
The Man From Laramie	1955	Col.
The Matchmaker	1958	Par.
The Mating Season	1950	Par.
Midnight	1939	Par.
Miss Susie Slagle's	1946	Par.
Miss Tatlock's Millions	1948	Par.
Mississippi	1935	Par.
Mrs. Wiggs of the Cabbage Patch	1934	Par.
My Own True Love	1948	Par.
No One Man	1932	Par.
No Time for Love	1943	Par.
Not With My Wife You Don't! *	1966	WB

Nothing But the Truth	1941	Par.
Once a Lady	1931	Par.
One-Eyed Jacks	1961	Par.
Paris When It Sizzles	1963	Par.
Peking Express	1951	Par.
Peter Ibbetson	1935	Par.
Phfft	1954	Col.
Practically Yours	1944	Par.
Queen Bee	1955	Col.
The Rainmaker	1946	Par.
Red Mountain	1951	Par.
The Right to Love	1930	Par.
Rope of Sand	1949	Par.
Sabrina	1954	Par.
Salome	1953	Col.
Sarah and Son	1930	Par.
Separate Tables	1958	UA
September Affair	1950	Par.
Seven Days Leave	1920	Par.
Sex and the Single Girl	1964	WB
Shadow of the Law	1930	Par.
She Done Him Wrong	1933	Par.
Shepherd of the Hills *	1941	Par.
Shopworn Angel	1928	Par.
Skylark	1941	Par.
So Proudly We Hail!	1943	Par.
The Solid Gold Cadillac	1956	Col.
Some Like It Hot	1959	Par.
Souls at Sea	1937	Par.
Spawn of the North	1938	Par.
The Stalking Moon	1968	NG
Standing Room Only	1944	Par.
The Stork Club	1945	Par.
Strangers When We Meet	1960	Col.
Street of Chance	1930	Par.
Sudden Fear	1952	RKO
Summer and Smoke	1961	Par.
Sundown	1941	US
Thunder Below	1932	Par.
Tom Sawyer	1930	Par.
Tomorrow and Tomorrow	1932	Par.
Tovarich	1937	WB
True to Life	1943	Par.
Unfaithful	1931	Par.
The Uninvited	1944	Par.
Vice Squad	1931	Par.
Wait Until Dark	1967	WB
A Walk in the Spring Rain	1969	Col.
The Way to Love	1933	Par.
We're Not Dressing	1934	Par.
The Wheeler Dealers	1963	MGM

Where There's Life	1947	Par.
Wiengenlied	1930	Par.
Wild Is the Wind	1957	Par.
Women Without Names	1940	Par.
You and Me	1938	Par.
Zaza	1939	Par.

341. BRYAN LANGLEY

April Blossoms	1937	GB--MGM
Bond Street *	1948	GB
Daddy Long Legs	1938	Holl.
Dance Band	1935	GB
Dark Eyes of London	1939	GB
Dead Men Tell No Tales	1938	GB
Honours Easy	1935	GB
I Killed the Count	1939	GB
Kathleen	1937	GB
The Lilac Domino *	1937	GB
The Limping Man	1936	GB
Living Dangerously	1936	GB
Meet Mr. Penny	1938	GB
Mrs. Pym of Scotland Yard	1939	GB
The Mutiny of the Elsinore	1937	GB
No Escape	1936	GB
Ourselves Alone *	1935	GB
Piccadilly Incident *	1946	GB
Someone at the Door	1936	GB
Spare a Copper	1940	GB--Eal.
Spies of the Air	1939	GB
The Student's Romance	1935	GB
Wanted by Scotland Yard	1939	GB
When the Bough Breaks *	1947	GB

342. REGGIE LANNING

Abbott and Costello Meet the Keystone Cops	1955	Univ.
Angel in Exile	1948	Rep.
Angel on the Amazon	1948	Rep.
Bal Tabarin *	1952	Rep.
Belle Le Grand	1951	Rep.
Bells of Capistrano	1942	Rep.
The Big Bonanza	1944	Rep.
Blackmail	1947	Rep.
Calendar Girl	1947	Rep.
California Firebrand	1948	Rep.
Call of the Canyon	1942	Rep.
The Cameraman *	1928	MGM

Carolina Cannonball	1954	Rep.
Casanova in Burlesque	1944	Rep.
The Catman of Paris	1946	Rep.
The Cheaters	1945	Rep.
The Cherokee Flash	1945	Rep.
China Bound	1929	MGM
City of Shadows	1955	Rep.
Code of the Outlaw	1942	Rep.
The Cowboy and the Senorita	1944	Rep.
Crime of the Century	1946	Rep.
Cuban Fireball	1951	Rep.
Days of Jesse James	1939	Rep.
Days of Old Cheyenne	1943	Rep.
Dead Man's Gulch *	1943	Rep.
Down Dakota Way	1949	Rep.
The Fabulous Texan	1947	Rep.
Faces in the Fog	1944	Rep.
Fighting Coast Guard	1951	Rep.
The Flame	1947	Rep.
Flight Nurse	1953	Rep.
Frontier Vengeance	1940	Rep.
Gaucho of El Dorado	1941	Rep.
Gaucho Serenade	1940	Rep.
Grand Canyon Trail	1948	Rep.
Grandpa Goes Home	1940	Rep.
The Great Train Robbery	1941	Rep.
Hands Across the Border	1944	Rep.
Heart of the Rockies	1951	Rep.
Heroes of the Hills	1938	Rep.
Hit Parade of 1951	1950	Rep.
Hoodlum Empire	1952	Rep.
Hoosier Holiday	1943	Rep.
I Cover the Underworld	1955	Rep.
I Dream of Jeannie	1952	Rep.
I, Jane Doe	1948	Rep.
Idaho	1943	Rep.
The Inner Circle	1946	Rep.
The Inside Story	1948	Rep.
King of the Cowboys	1943	Rep.
King of the Texas Rangers	1941	Rep.
The Lady Wants Mink	1953	Rep.
Laughing Irish Eyes *	1936	Rep.
Lights of Old Santa Fe	1944	Rep.
Man From Cheyenne	1942	Rep.
Mercy Island	1941	Rep.
Mr. District Attorney	1941	Rep.
New Frontier	1939	Rep.
Northwest Outpost	1947	Rep.
One Man's Law	1940	Rep.
The Outcast	1954	Rep.
Pals of the Pecos	1941	Rep.

Pals of the Saddle	1938	Rep.
The Phantom Cowboy	1941	Rep.
The Pilgrim Lady	1947	Rep.
Pistol Packing Mama	1943	Rep.
The Pittsburgh Kid	1941	Rep.
The Plainsman and the Lady	1946	Rep.
Rainbow Over Texas	1946	Rep.
The Ranger and the Lady	1940	Rep.
The Road to Denver	1955	Rep.
Rosie the Riveter	1944	Rep.
Sabotage	1939	Rep.
Sands of Iwo Jima	1949	Rep.
Santa Fe Scouts	1943	Rep.
Santa Fe Stampede	1938	Rep.
Savage Horde	1950	Rep.
A Scream in the Dark	1943	Rep.
Sea of Lost Ships	1953	Rep.
The Showdown	1950	Rep.
Silver Spurs	1943	Rep.
Sing, Neighbor, Sing	1944	Rep.
Singing Guns	1950	Rep.
Sioux City	1946	Rep.
Song of Arizona	1946	Rep.
Song of Texas	1943	Rep.
Spite Marriage	1929	MGM
Steppin' in Society	1945	Rep.
Sunset in Wyoming	1941	Rep.
Sunset on the Desert	1942	Rep.
Surrender	1950	Rep.
Susanna Pass	1949	Rep.
Sweethearts on Parade	1953	Rep.
Three Little Sisters	1944	Rep.
Thunderbirds	1952	Rep.
The Timber Trail	1948	Rep.
Toughest Man in Arizona	1942	Rep.
Train to Alcatraz	1948	Rep.
Untamed Heiress	1954	Rep.
Valley of the Zombies	1946	Rep.
Wagon Tracks West	1943	Rep.
Wake of the Red Witch	1948	Rep.
Westward Ho!	1942	Rep.
Who Killed Aunt Maggie?	1940	Rep.
The Wild Blue Yonder	1952	Rep.
Wolf of New York	1940	Rep.
Woman They Almost Lynched	1952	Rep.
Wyoming Outlaw	1939	Rep.

343. VILIS LAPENIEKS (1931-1987)

Capone	1975	TCF

Capture That Capsule!	1961	US
Cisco Pike	1971	Col.
Deathwatch	1966	US
Eegah!	1962	US
Fallguy	1962	US
The Hideous Sun Demon *	1959	US
I Love My Wife	1970	Univ.
If It's Tuesday This Must Be Belgium	1969	UA
Magic Spectacles	1961	US
Mother Goose A-Go-Go	1966	US
Newman's Law	1974	Univ.
Night Tide *	1963	AIP
Queen of Blood	1966	AIP
Rainbow Bridge	1972	US
Shell Shock	1963	US
Third of a Man	1962	UA
Two	1974	US
V.D.	1961	US
Voyage to the Prehistoric Planet	1965	AIP
Walk the Angry Beach	1961	US

344. STEVEN LARNER

Almost Summer	1978	Univ.
Badlands *	1974	WB
Buddy Holly Story	1978	Col.
Burnt Offerings *	1976	UA
Caddyshack	1980	Orion
Goldengirl	1979	AE
Gray Lady Down	1978	Univ.
Lions Love	1969	US
Pipe Dreams	1976	AE
Steelyard Blues *	1972	WB
The Student Nurses	1970	US
Twilight Zone-The Movie *	1983	WB

345. JOSEPH LA SHELLE (1905-   )

The Abductors	1957	TCF
All in a Night's Work	1961	Par.
The Apartment	1960	UA
The Bachelor Party	1957	UA
Barefoot in the Park	1967	Par.
A Bell for Adano	1945	TCF
The Bermuda Mystery	1944	TCF
Career	1959	Par.
The Chase	1966	Col.
A Child Is Waiting	1963	UA
Claudia and David	1946	TCF

Cluny Brown	1946	TCF
Come to the Stable	1949	TCF
The Conqueror *	1955	US
Crime of Passion	1956	UA
Dangerous Crossing	1953	TCF
Deep Waters	1948	TCF
Doll Face	1945	TCF
Eighty Steps to Jonah	1969	WB
Elopement	1952	TCF
The Eve of St. Mark	1944	TCF
Everybody Does It	1949	TCF
Fallen Angel	1945	TCF
The Fan	1949	TCF
The Fortune Cookie	1966	UA
The Foxes of Harrow	1947	TCF
Fury at Sundown	1957	UA
The Fuzzy Pink Nightgown	1957	UA
The Guy Who Came Back	1951	TCF
Hangover Square	1944	TCF
Happy Land	1943	TCF
The Honeymoon Machine	1961	MGM
How the West Was Won *	1962	MGM
I Was a Teenage Werewolf	1957	AIP
Irma La Douce	1963	UA
The Jackpot	1950	TCF
Kiss Me Stupid	1964	UA
Kona Coast	1968	WB
The Late George Apley	1946	TCF
Laura	1944	TCF
The Long Hot Summer	1958	TCF
The Luck of the Irish	1947	TCF
Marty	1955	UA
Les Miserables	1952	TCF
Mr. Belvedere Rings the Bell	1951	TCF
Mr. 880	1950	TCF
Mr. Scoutmaster	1953	TCF
Mother Didn't Tell Me	1950	TCF
My Cousin Rachel	1952	TCF
The Naked and the Dead	1958	RKO
No Down Payment	1957	TCF
Our Miss Brooks	1956	WB
The Outcasts of Poker Flat	1952	TCF
The Outsider	1961	Univ.
River of No Return	1954	TCF
Road House	1948	TCF
Rocking Moon *	1926	US
Run for the Sun	1956	UA
Seven Women	1966	MGM
Something for the Birds	1952	TCF
Storm Fear	1955	UA
Take It or Leave It	1944	TCF

The Thirteenth Letter	1951	TCF
Under My Skin	1949	TCF
Where the Sidewalk Ends	1950	TCF
Whispering Smith *	1926	US
Wild and Wonderful	1963	Univ.

346. WALTER LASSALLY (1926-   )

The Adding Machine	1968	GB--Univ.
Angels of Iron	1981	Ger.--US
Autobiography of a Princess	1975	GB
'Beat' Girl	1960	GB
The Blood of Hussain	1980	GB
The Bostonians	1984	GB
The Clown	1976	Ger.
Day Shall Dawn *	1958	Pakistan
Day the Fish Came Out	1967	GB/Greece--TCF
Electra	1962	Greece
Girl in Black	1955	Greece
Happy Mother's Day-Love George	1973	US
Heat and Dust	1983	GB
Hullabaloo	1980	GB
Indian Summer	1987	GB
Joanna	1968	GB--TCF
The Loneliness of the Long Distance Runner	1962	GB
Madalena	1961	Greece
Malachi's Cove	1973	GB
A Matter of Dignity	1957	Greece
Memoirs of a Survivor	1981	GB--EMI
No More Credit	1958	Greece
Oedipus the King	1967	GB
Open Letter	1968	Greece
Our Last Spring	1960	Greece
The Perfect Murder	1988	GB/US
Pleasantville	1976	US
Price for Survival	1980	Ger.
Private School	1983	Univ.
Psyche 59	1964	GB
Savages	1972	US
Shenanigans	1977	US
Something for Everyone	1970	NG
Something Short of Paradise	1979	AIP
A Taste of Honey	1961	GB
Three Into Two Won't Go	1969	GB--Univ.
To Kill a Clown	1971	GB
Together	1956	GB
Tom Jones *	1963	GB--UA
Too Far to Go	1982	US

Twinky	1969	GB--Rank
Wild for Kicks	1960	GB
The Wild Party	1974	AIP
The Woman Across the Way	1978	Ger.
Zorba the Greek	1964	GB--TCF

347. ANDREW LASZLO (1926-)

Class of '44	1973	WB
Comeback	1983	TCF
Countdown at Kusini	1976	Col.
First Blood	1982	Orion
The Funhouse	1981	Univ.
Ghost Dad	1990	Univ.
I, the Jury	1982	TCF
Innerspace	1987	WB
Jennifer on My Mind	1971	UA
Lovers and Other Strangers	1969	ABC
The Night They Raided Minsky's	1968	UA
One Potato, Two Potato	1964	US
The Out-of-Towners	1970	Par.
The Owl and the Pussycat *	1970	Col.
Poltergeist II	1986	MGM
Remo Williams: The Adventure Begins	1985	Orion
Shogun	1981	Par.
Somebody Killed Her Husband *	1978	Col.
Southern Comfort	1981	TCF
Star Trek V: The Final Frontier	1989	Par.
Streets of Fire	1984	Univ.
Thieves *	1977	Par.
To Find a Man	1971	Col.
The Warriors	1979	Par.
You're a Big Boy Now	1967	US

348. ERNEST LASZLO (1906-1984)

About Mrs. Leslie	1954	Par.
Airport	1969	Univ.
Apache	1954	UA
Attack of the Puppet People	1958	US
Baby, the Rain Must Fall	1964	Col.
Bandido!	1956	UA
The Big Knife	1955	UA
The Big Mouth *	1967	Col.
The Big Wheel	1949	UA
Cover Up	1948	UA
DOA	1949	US
Daddy's Gone A-Hunting	1969	WB
Dear Ruth	1947	Par.

The Domino Principle *	1977	US
Fantastic Voyage	1966	TCF
The First Time	1968	UA
Four for Texas	1963	WB
The Girl From Manhattan	1948	UA
Gunsight Ridge	1957	UA
The Hitler Gang	1944	Par.
Houdini	1953	Par.
Impact	1949	UA
Inherit the Wind	1960	UA
It's a Mad, Mad, Mad, Mad World	1963	UA
The Jackie Robinson Story	1950	EL
Judgment at Nuremberg	1961	UA
The Kentuckian	1955	UA
Kiss Me Deadly	1955	UA
Lady in the Iron Mask	1952	TCF
The Last Sunset	1961	Univ.
Let's Live a Little	1948	EL
Linda *	1930	US
Logan's Run	1976	MGM
The Lucky Stiff	1948	UA
Lulu Belle	1948	Col.
Luv	1967	Col.
Luxury Liner *	1948	MGM
M	1951	Col.
Manhandled	1949	Par.
The Moon Is Blue	1953	US
Mutiny	1952	UA
The Naked Jungle	1954	Par.
Omar Khayam	1957	Par.
One Man's Way	1964	UA
The Pace That Kills	1928	US
The Restless Years	1958	Univ.
Riding High *	1950	Par.
Road to Rio	1947	Par.
Scared Stiff	1953	Par.
Ship of Fools	1965	Col.
Showdown	1972	Univ.
The Space Children	1958	Par.
Stalag 17	1953	Par.
The Star	1952	TCF
Star!	1968	TCF
The Steel Trap	1952	TCF
Ten Seconds to Hell	1959	GB--Ham.
Three for Bedroom C	1952	US
Two Years Before the Mast	1946	Par.
Valerie	1957	UA
Vera Cruz	1954	UA
The Well	1951	US
When I Grow Up	1951	US
While the City Sleeps	1956	RKO

| The White Outlaw | 1929 | US |
| Wings * | 1929 | Par. |

349. PHILIP LATHROP (1916-   )

Airport 1975	1974	Univ.
Airport '77	1977	Univ.
The All-American Boy	1973	WB
All Night Long	1981	Univ.
The Americanization of Emily	1964	MGM
The Black BIrd	1975	Col.
A Change of Seasons	1980	TCF
The Cincinnati Kid	1965	MGM
Concorde: Airport '79	1979	Univ.
Cry Tough	1959	UA
Days of Wine and Roses	1962	WB
Deadly Friend	1986	WB
A Different Story	1978	AE
Dime With a Halo	1963	MGM
Don't Make Waves	1967	MGM
The Driver	1978	EMI/TCF
Earthquake	1974	Univ.
Every Little Crook and Nanny	1972	MGM
Experiment in Terror	1962	Col.
Finian's Rainbow	1968	WB
Foolin' Around	1979	Col.
Girl Happy	1965	MGM
Girls on the Loose	1958	Univ.
Gunn	1967	Par.
The Gypsy Moths *	1969	MGM
Hammett *	1982	Orion
The Happening	1967	Col.
Hard Times	1975	Col.
The Hawaiians	1970	UA
I Love You, Alice B. Toklas	1968	WB
The Illustrated Man	1969	WB
Jekyll and Hyde Together Again	1982	Par.
The Killer Elite	1975	UA
Little Miss Marker	1980	Univ.
Live Fast, Die Young	1958	Univ.
Lolly Madonna XXX	1973	MGM
Lonely Are the Brave	1962	Univ.
Loving Couples	1980	US
Mame	1974	WB
Moment by Moment	1979	Univ.
Money, Women and Guns	1958	Univ.
National Lampoon's Class Reunion	1982	US
Never Too Late	1965	WB
The Perfect Furlough	1958	Univ.
The Pink Panther	1963	UA

Point Blank	1967	MGM
Portnoy's Complaint	1972	WB
The Prisoner of Second Avenue	1975	WB
Private Lives of Adam and Eve	1961	Univ.
Rabbit Run	1970	WB
The Saga of Hemp Brown	1958	Univ.
Soldier in the Rain	1963	AA
Swashbuckler	1976	Univ.
They Shoot Horses, Don't They?	1969	US
The Thief Who Came to Dinner	1973	WB
Thirty Six Hours	1964	MGM
Together Brothers *	1974	TCF
The Traveling Executioner	1970	MGM
Twilight of Honor	1963	MGM
What Did You Do in the War, Daddy?	1966	UA
Wild Heritage	1958	Univ.
Wild Rovers	1971	MGM

350. CHARLES LAWTON (1904-1965)

Abroad With Two Yanks	1944	US
Affairs of Martha	1942	MGM
All Ashore	1952	Col.
Andy Hardy Meets a Debutante	1940	MGM
The Big Store	1941	MGM
The Black Arrow	1948	Col.
Boots Malone	1952	Col.
Brewster's Millions	1945	US
Bring Your Smile Along	1955	Col.
Captain Pirate	1952	Col.
Cargo to Capetown	1950	Col.
The Chaser	1938	MGM
Commanche Station	1960	Col.
Congo Maisie	1940	MGM
Cowboy	1958	Col.
Cruisin' Down the River	1953	Col.
The Doolins of Oklahoma	1949	Col.
Drive a Crooked Road	1954	Col.
Dulcy	1940	MGM
Ensign Pulver	1964	WB
Eyes in the Night *	1942	MGM
Fingers at the Window *	1942	MGM
Forty Little Mothers	1940	MGM
Free and Easy *	1941	MGM
Full of Life	1956	Col.
Fuller Brush Girl	1950	Col.
The Gallant Blade *	1948	Col.
The Gene Krupa Story	1959	Col.
Getting Gertie's Garter	1945	UA
Gold Rush Maisie	1940	MGM

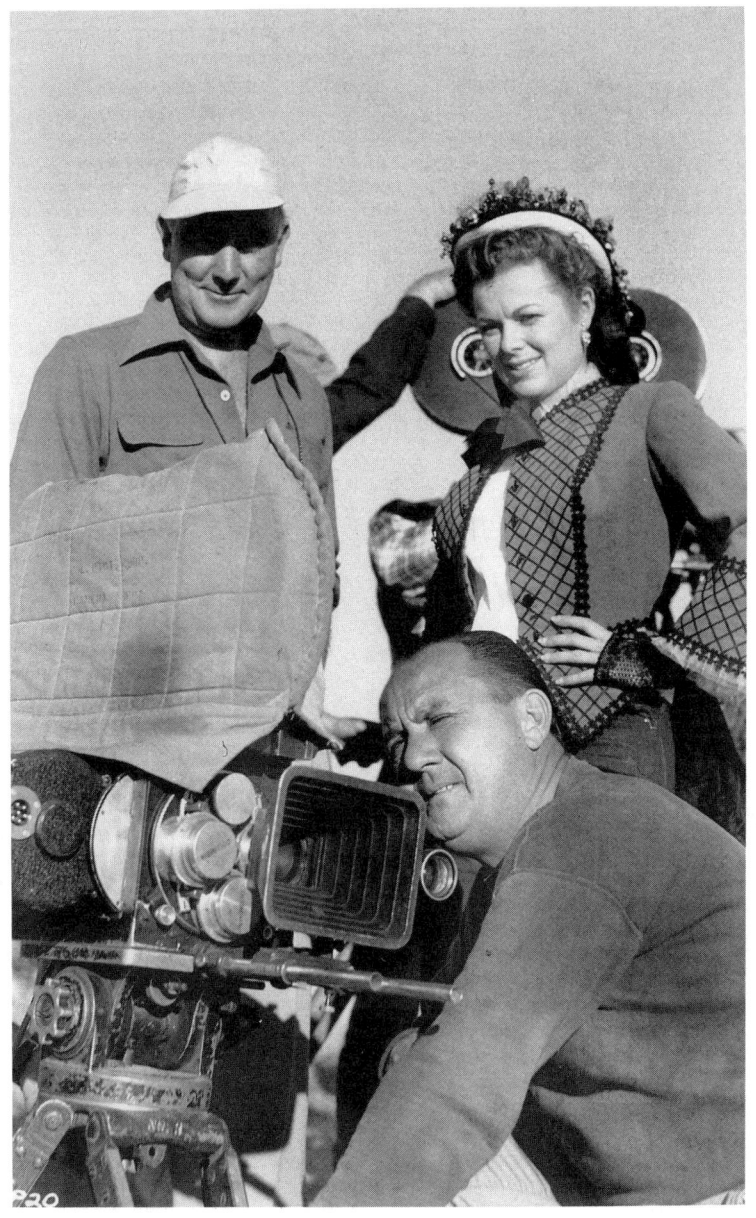

Charles Lawton (standing) with Barbara Hale on location for The
Last of the Commanches (1953).

Gunman's Walk	1958	Col.
Hangman's Knot	1952	Col.
The Happy Time	1952	Col.
Her First Romance	1951	Col.
Her Husband's Affairs	1947	Col.
I Love Trouble	1947	Col.
It Happened to Jane	1959	Col.
Joe Smith American	1942	MGM
Jubal	1956	Col.
Kill the Umpire	1950	Col.
Kiss and Tell	1945	Col.
The Lady From Shanghai	1948	Col.
The Last Hurrah	1958	Col.
The Last of the Commanches	1953	Col.
Let's Do It Again	1953	Col.
Listen, Darling	1938	MGM
The Long Gray Line	1955	Col.
Maisie Was a Lady	1941	MGM
Man in the Saddle	1951	Col.
Man on a String	1960	Col.
Mask of the Avenger	1951	Col.
Miracles for Sale	1939	MGM
Miss Grant Takes Richmond	1949	Col.
Miss Sadie Thompson	1953	Col.
Mr. Soft Touch *	1949	Col.
My Dear Miss Aldrich	1937	MGM
My Sister Eileen	1955	Col.
The Nevadan	1950	Col.
Nick Carter Master Detective	1939	MGM
One Way to Love	1942	Col.
Operation Mad Ball	1957	Col.
Paul	1952	Col.
Perilous Holiday	1945	Col.
A Rage to Live	1965	UA
A Raisin in the Sun	1961	Col.
The Return of Monte Cristo	1946	Col.
Ride Lonesome	1959	Col.
Ringside Maisie	1941	MGM
Rogues of Sherwood Forest	1950	Col.
Rome Adventure	1962	WB
Santa Fe	1951	Col.
See Here Private Hargrove	1944	MGM
Shockproof	1949	Col.
Sky Murder	1940	MGM
Slightly French	1948	Col.
Spencer's Mountain *	1963	WB
Stage to Tucson	1951	Col.
The Tall T	1957	Col.
They Rode West	1954	Col.
13 West Street	1962	Col.
This Time for Keeps	1942	MGM

Three Hours to Kill	1954	Col.
3 Is a Family	1944	UA
3:10 to Yuma	1957	Col.
The Thrill of Brazil	1946	Col.
Tokyo Joe	1949	Col.
Two Rode Together	1961	Col.
The Untamed Breed	1948	Col.
Up in Mabel's Room	1944	US
The Vanishing Virginian	1941	MGM
The Wackiest Ship in the Army	1960	Col.
The Walking Hills	1949	Col.
The Walls Come Tumbling Down	1946	Col.
Within the Law	1939	MGM
A Yank at Eton *	1942	MGM
You Can't Run Away From It	1956	Col.
Young Ideas	1943	MGM
Youngblood Hawke	1964	WB
Youngest Profession	1943	MGM

351. H. ALDERSON LEACH

Bonnie Annie Laurie	1918	Fox
The Love Auction	1919	Fox
Lure of Ambition	1919	Fox
Miss USA	1917	Fox
Putting One Over	1919	Fox
Swat the Spy	1918	Fox
Tell It to the Marines	1918	Fox
The Winning Stroke	1919	Fox

352. SAM LEAVITT (1904-1984)

Advise and Consent	1962	Col.
An American Dream	1966	WB
Anatomy of a Murder	1959	Col.
An Annapolis Story	1955	AA
The Bold and the Brave	1956	RKO
Brainstorm	1965	WB
Cape Fear	1962	Univ.
The Careless Years	1957	UA
Carmen Jones	1954	TCF
China Venture	1953	Col.
The Court Martial of Billy Mitchell	1955	US
Crime in the Streets	1956	AA
The Crimson Kimono	1959	Col.
The Defiant Ones	1958	UA
The Desperados	1968	Col.
Diamond Head	1962	Col.
Dr. Goldfoot and the Bikini Machine	1965	AIP

Eighteen and Anxious	1957	Rep.
Exodus	1960	UA
The Fearmakers	1958	US
Five Gates to Hell	1959	TCF
The Grasshopper	1969	US
Guess Who's Coming to Dinner?	1967	Col.
Hot Rod Girl	1956	AIP
I Deal in Danger	1966	TCF
Johnny Cool	1963	UA
Major Dundee	1965	Col.
The Man in the Glass Booth	1975	AFT
The Man With the Golden Arm	1955	UA
Murderer's Row	1966	Col.
My Blood Runs Cold	1965	WB
Pork Chop Hill	1959	UA
The Right Approach	1961	TCF
Seven Thieves	1960	TCF
Shock Treatment	1964	WB
Sierra Stranger	1957	Col.
Southwest Passage	1954	UA
Spanish Affair	1958	Par.
A Star Is Born	1954	WB
The Star Spangled Girl	1971	Par.
The Thief	1952	US
Time Limit	1957	UA
Two on a Guillotine	1965	WB
Where Angels Go ... Trouble Follows	1968	Co.
The Wild Party	1956	UA
The Wrecking Crew	1968	Col.

353. JOHN LEEZER

Acquitted	1916	US
The Arizona Streak	1926	US
Boots	1919	Par.
Cheerful Givers	1917	US
The Cowboy Cop	1926	US
The Cowboy Musketeer	1925	US
The Feud *	1919	Fox
The Heart of Twenty	1920	US
"Hell to Pay" Austen	1916	US
The Hope Chest *	1918	Par.
I'll Get Him Yet *	1919	Par.
Just Like a Woman *	1922	US
The Kid Is Clever	1918	Fox
Let's Go Gallagher *	1925	US
The Lily and the Rose *	1915	US
The Love Master *	1924	FN
The Masquerade Bandit	1926	US
The Mystery of the Leaping Fish *	1916	US

Nuggett Nell	1919	Par.
Out of Luck	1919	Par.
Out of the West	1926	US
Peppy Polly	1919	Par.
Red Hot Hoofs	1926	US
Tom and His Pals *	1926	US
The Triflers	1920	Univ.
White Fang *	1925	US
Wild to Go	1926	US
The Wyoming Wildcat	1925	US

354. RICHARD LEITERMAN

And Then You Die	1987	Can.
Cadence	1990	US
The Climb	1987	Can.
The Far Shore	1976	Can.
The First Season	1989	Can.
Get Back	1973	Can.
Goin' Down the Road	1970	Can.
A Married Couple	1970	Can.
Mother Lode	1982	US
My American Cousin	1985	Can.
Rad	1986	Tri-S.
Recommendation for Mercy	1975	Can.
Rip-Off	1971	Can.
Silence of the North	1981	Can.--Univ.
The Squeamish Five	1989	US
Surfacing	1981	Can.
Ticket to Heaven	1981	UA
Utilities	1983	Can.
Wedding in White	1973	Can.--AE
Who Has Seen the Wind?	1977	Can.
Wild Horse Hank	1979	Can.

355. CLAUDE LELOUCH (1937-   )

Adventure Is Adventure	1972	Fr.
The Good Guys and the Bad Guys	1976	Fr.
Good Year *	1973	Fr./It.
Happy New Year	1973	Fr.
Life, Love, Death *	1969	Fr.--UA
Live for Life	1967	Fr./It.--UA
Love Is a Funny Thing	1970	Fr./It.--UA
A Man and a Woman	1966	Fr.--UA
Marriage	1975	Fr.
Smic, Smac, Smoc	1971	Fr.

356. MATTHEW F. LEONETTI

Action Jackson	1988	Lor.
Another 48 Hours	1990	Par.
Breaking Away	1979	TCF
Budding System	1984	TCF
The Chicken Chronicles	1977	AE
Commando	1985	TCF
Dragnet	1987	Univ.
Extreme Prejudice	1987	Tri-S.
Eyewitness	1981	TCF
Fast Times at Ridgemont High	1982	Univ.
Hard to Kill	1990	WB
The Ice Pirates	1984	MGM-UA
Jagged Edge	1985	Col.
Johnny Handsome	1989	Tri-S.
Jumpin' Jack Flash	1986	TCF
Mr. Billion	1977	TCF
Poltergeist	1982	MGM-UA
Raise the Titanic!	1980	US
Red Heat	1988	Tri-S.
Weird Science	1985	Univ.

357. MARCEL LE PICARD

Alaska Patrol	1949	US
Almost a Husband	1919	Gold.
America *	1924	UA
Angels' Alley	1948	Mon.
Angels in Disguise	1949	Mon.
Ashes of Love	1918	US
Back to Liberty	1927	US
Bad Company *	1925	US
Behind Prison Walls	1943	PRC
Blazing Guns	1943	Mon.
Blonde Dynamite	1950	Mon.
Blues Busters	1950	Mon.
Borrowed Hero	1941	Mon.
Boss of Big Town	1943	PRC
Bowery Battalion	1951	Mon.
Bowery Buckaroos	1947	Mon.
Boys Will Be Boys	1921	Gold.
The Broadway Boob	1926	US
The Broadway Drifter	1927	US
Caravan Trail	1946	PRC
College Sweethearts	1942	Mon.
Combat	1927	US
Conquered Hearts	1918	US
Cowboy From Sundown	1940	Mon.
Crazy Knights	1944	Mon.

Crazy Over Horses	1951	Mon.
Cupid the Cowpuncher	1920	Gold.
Cyclone Jones	1923	US
Daughter of Mine	1919	Gold.
A Daughter of the Gods *	1916	Fox
Day Dreams	1919	Gold.
Doubling for Romeo	1922	Gold.
Down the Wyoming Trail	1939	Mon.
The Enchanted Forest	1945	PRC
Enlighten Thy Daughter	1917	US
Feudin' Fools	1952	Mon.
For Woman's Favor	1924	US
Forgotten Women	1949	Mon.
Gang War	1940	US
Gangs of the Waterfront	1945	Rep.
Ghost Chasers	1951	Mon.
The Girl From Monterey	1944	PRC
Golden Trail	1940	Mon.
Guile of a Woman	1921	Gold.
Headlines *	1925	US
Her Surrender	1916	US
Here Come the Marines	1952	Mon.
Here's Flash Casey	1937	GN
Hillbilly Blitzkrieg	1942	Mon.
His Rise to Fame	1927	US
Hold That Line	1952	Mon.
Home on the Range	1946	Rep.
Honest Hutch	1920	Gold.
Hotel Variety *	1933	US
I Am the Man	1924	US
Incident	1948	Mon.
Inspiration	1928	US
International Crime	1938	GN
The Invisible Ghost	1941	Mon.
Jes' Call Me Jim	1920	Gold.
Jet Job	1952	Mon.
Jinx Money	1948	Mon.
Joe Palooka in the Squared Circle	1950	Mon.
Jubilo	1919	Gold.
Lady From Chungking	1943	PRC
The Law Rides Again	1943	Mon.
Leave It to Susan	1919	Gold.
The Legion of Missing Men	1937	Mon.
Let's Go Navy!	1951	Mon.
Life or Honor?	1918	US
The Lost Trail	1945	Mon.
The Lost Volcano	1950	Mon.
Lucky Losers	1950	Mon.
Mad Youth *	1940	US
Man From Texas	1938	Mon.
Man of Courage	1943	PRC

Master Minds	1949	Mon.
Minstrel Man	1944	PRC
Miss V From Moscow	1943	PRC
Murder By Invitation	1941	Mon.
News Hounds	1947	Mon.
A Night for Crime	1943	PRC
Oh, Baby! *	1926	Univ.
One Law for Both	1917	US
One Thrilling Night	1942	Mon.
The Outer Gate	1937	Mon.
Outlaw's Paradise	1939	US
The Outlaw's Revenge	1915	US
Pals of the Silver Sage	1940	Mon.
The Panther's Claw	1942	PRC
A Perfect Lady	1918	Gold.
The Phantom Killer	1942	Mon.
The Pioneers	1941	Mon.
A Poor Relation	1921	Gold.
Prison Girl	1942	PRC
Prison Train	1938	US
Private Snuffy Smith	1942	Mon.
Rainbow Over the Range	1940	Mon.
Return of the Ape Man	1944	Mon.
Rhythm of the Rio Grande	1940	Mon.
Riders of the Frontier	1939	Mon.
Ridin' the Cherokee Trail	1941	Mon.
Riding the Sunset Trail	1941	Mon.
Riot Squad	1942	Mon.
Roll, Wagons, Roll	1939	Mon.
Rollin' Home to Texas	1941	Mon.
Rollin' Westward	1939	Mon.
Romance of the West	1946	PRC
Scared to Death	1947	US
Shadows of Suspicion	1944	Mon.
The Silent Enemy	1930	Par.
Silver Stallion	1941	Mon.
Smugglers Cove	1948	Mon.
Song of Old Wyoming	1945	PRC
Spooks Run Wild	1941	Mon.
Strictly Confidential	1919	Gold.
The Strange Boarder	1920	Gold.
Submarine Base	1943	PRC
Swingin' On a Rainbow	1945	Rep.
Texas Wildcats	1939	US
Through the Wrong Door	1919	Gold.
Triple Trouble	1950	Mon.
Trouble Makers	1948	Mon.
Two Men and a Woman	1917	US
An Unwilling Hero	1921	Gold.
Voodoo Man	1944	Mon.
Water, Water, Everywhere	1920	Gold.

Westbound Stage	1940	Mon.
Western Mail	1942	Mon.
Westward Bound	1944	Mon.
What a Man!	1944	Mon.
When Men Betray	1918	US
White Mice	1926	US
Wild Horse Stampede	1943	Mon.
Wildfire	1945	US
Wildness of Youth	1922	US
The Window Opposite	1919	US
The Winning Oar	1927	US
The Yanks Are Coming	1942	PRC

358. ELGIN LESSLEY

Alias Mary Brown	1918	US
The Atom	1918	US
The Cameraman *	1928	MGM
The Chaser *	1928	FN
Daughter Angele	1918	US
Go West *	1925	Metro.-Gold.
Her Decision	1918	US
High Stakes	1918	US
Irish Eyes	1918	US
Long Pants *	1927	FN
Marked Cards	1918	US
The Navigator	1924	MGM
Our Hospitality *	1923	Metro.
The Servant in the House	1920	FBO
Seven Chances *	1925	Metro.-Gold.
Sherlock, Jr. *	1924	Metro.
Station Content	1918	US
Three Ages *	1923	Metro.
Three's a Crowd *	1927	FN
Tramp, Tramp, Tramp	1926	FN
You Can't Believe Everything	1918	US

359. AL LIGOURI

The Belgian *	1917	US
Boomerang Bill	1922	Par.
A Daughter of MacGregor	1916	US
The Embarrassment of Riches	1918	US
The Firing Line	1919	Par.
The Innocent Lie	1916	US
Marie Ltd.	1919	US
The Passionate Pilgrim	1921	Par.
Redhead	1919	US
Romance of the Air *	1919	US

The Scar of Shame	1927	US
The Silver King	1919	Par.
The Smugglers	1916	US
Straight Is the Way	1921	Par.
Timothy's Quest *	1922	US
The Woman God Changed	1921	Par.
The World and His Wife	1920	Par.
The World to Live In	1919	US

360. EDDIE LINDEN (1896-1956)

Action Craver	1927	US
Arizona Cyclone *	1928	Univ.
California Frontier	1938	Col.
City of Missing Girls	1941	US
Crashin' Thru	1939	Mon.
Crusade Against the Rackets	1937	US
Dawn Express	1942	PRC
Hard Fists	1927	Univ.
Hard Guy	1941	PRC
Isle of Destiny	1940	RKO
Kazan *	1921	US
King Kong *	1933	RKO
Last Days of Pompeii *	1935	RKO
Last of the Desperadoes	1956	US
Law of the Texan	1938	Col.
Lazy Lightning	1926	Univ.
Loco Luck	1927	Univ.
Lost City	1935	US
The Man from the West	1926	Univ.
The Man in the Saddle	1926	Univ.
The Mask	1921	US
Mine to Keep *	1923	US
Mysterious Pilot	1937	Col.
One Glorious Scrap	1927	Univ.
Other Men's Duaghters	1923	US
Paroled From the Big House	1938	US
The Range Busters	1940	Mon.
The Range Riders	1927	US
Riders of the West	1927	US
Ridin' Comet	1925	US
The Ridin' Rascal	1926	Univ.
The Rosary	1922	FN
Rustlers Ranch	1926	Univ.
Saddle Jumpers	1927	US
Scar Hanan	1925	US
Set Free	1927	Univ.
The Set-Up	1926	Univ.
Sky Bandits	1940	Mon.
Sky High Corral	1926	Univ.

Son of Kong *	1933	RKO
Speeding Hoofs	1927	US
Spurs and Saddles	1927	Univ.
Stranger from Arizona	1938	Col.
Swamp Woman	1941	PRC
The Terror	1926	Univ.
Today I Hang	1942	PRC
Trailin' Double Trouble	1940	Mon.
The Werewolf	1956	Col.
West of Pinto Basin	1940	Mon.
Western Courage	1927	US
Western Pluck *	1926	Univ.
The Western Rover	1927	Univ.
Without Honors	1932	US
Wolves of the Sea	1938	US
A Yank in Libya	1942	PRC

360a. JOHN LINDLEY

Field of Dreams	1989	Col.
The Goodbye People	1984	US
Home of the Brave	1986	US
Immediate Family	1989	Col.
In the Mood	1987	Lor.
Killer Party	1986	MGM/UA
Lily in Love	1985	US
The Serpent and the Rainbow	1988	Univ.
Shakedown	1988	Univ.
Stepfather	1987	US
True Believer	1989	Col.
Vital Signs	1990	TCF

361. LIONEL LINDON (1905-1971)

Alias Jesse James	1958	US
Alias Nick Beal	1949	Par.
All Fall Down	1962	MGM
Around the World in Eighty Days	1956	UA
Bailout at 43,000	1957	UA
The Big Caper	1957	UA
The Black Scorpion	1957	WB
The Blazing Forest	1952	Par.
The Blue Dahlia	1946	Par.
Boy Did I Get a Wrong Number	1966	UA
Caribbean	1952	Par.
Casanova's Big Night	1954	Par.
Conquest of Space	1955	Par.
Dead Heat on a Merry Go Round	1968	Col.
Destination Moon	1950	Univ.

Drums in the Deep South	1951	RKO
Duffy's Tavern	1945	Par.
The Extraordinary Seaman	1968	MGM
Generation	1969	AE
Going My Way	1944	Par.
Grand Prix	1966	MGM
The Great Rupert	1950	EL
Hell's Island	1955	Par.
Here Come the Girls	1953	Par.
Hong Kong	1951	Par.
I Want to Live	1958	UA
Isn't It Romantic?	1948	Par.
Jamaica Run	1953	Par.
Japanese War Bride	1952	TCF
Jivaro	1953	Par.
Let's Face It	1943	Par.
The Lonely Man	1957	Par.
Lucy Gallant	1955	Par.
A Man Alone	1955	Rep.
The Manchurian Candidate	1962	UA
Masquerade in Mexico	1945	Par.
McHale's Navy Joins the Air Force	1965	Univ.
A Medal for Benny	1945	Par.
Monsieur Beaucaire	1946	Par.
My Favorite Brunette	1947	Par.
O.S.S.	1946	Par.
Only the Valiant	1951	WB
Pendulum	1969	Col.
Prehistoric Women	1951	EL
Quicksand	1950	UA
Rhubarb	1951	Par.
Road to Utopia	1945	Par.
The Sainted Sisters	1948	Par.
Sangaree *	1953	Par.
The Scarlet Hour	1955	Par.
The Secret of the Incas	1954	Par.
The Stars Are Singing	1952	Par.
Submarine Command	1951	Par.
The Sun Sets at Dawn	1950	EL
Tap Roots *	1948	Univ.
Those Redheads From Seattle	1953	Par.
3 Guns for Texas	1968	Univ.
Too Late Blues	1961	Par.
Top 'O the Morning	1949	Par.
Tropic Zone	1953	Par.
The Trouble With Angels	1966	Col.
The Trouble With Women	1947	Par.
The Turning Point	1952	Par.
The Vanquished	1953	Par.
Variety Girl *	1947	Par.
Welcome Stranger	1947	Par.

Without Honor	1949	UA
The Young Savages	1961	UA

362. IRVING LIPPMAN

Angel Unchained	1970	US
Apache Territory	1958	Col.
Domino Kid	1957	Col.
The Great Sioux Massacre	1965	Col.
Gunmen of Laredo	1959	Col.
Hellcats of the Navy	1957	Col.
The Loners	1972	US
The Outlaws Is Coming!	1965	Col.
Safe at Home!	1962	Col.
Tarzan and the Great River	1967	Par.
Tarzan and the Valley of Gold	1966	NG
Three Stooges Go Round the World in a Daze	1963	Col.
Twenty Million Miles to Earth	1957	Col.

363. HAROLD LIPSTEIN

The Adventures of Hajji Baba	1954	AA
Ambush	1949	MGM
Any Wednesday	1966	WB
Assignment To Kill *	1967	WB
Bannerline	1951	MGM
The Chapman Report	1962	WB
Chief Crazy Horse	1954	Univ.
Confidentially Connie	1953	MGM
Cry of the Hunted	1953	MGM
Damn Yankees	1958	WB
Desperate Search	1952	MGM
Drums Across the River	1954	Univ.
Fast Company	1953	MGM
Fearless Fagin	1952	MGM
Forever Darling	1956	MGM
The Great Man	1956	Univ.
Gypsy Colt	1954	MGM
Hell Is for Heroes	1962	Par.
Heller in Pink Tights	1960	Par.
Honeymoon Hotel	1964	MGM
Let's Kill Uncle	1966	Univ.
A Man Called Peter	1955	TCF
Never Steal Anything Small	1958	Univ.
The Night of the Grizzly	1966	Par.
No Name on the Bullet	1958	Univ.
No Questions Asked	1951	MGM
None But the Brave	1965	WB

The Painted Hills *	1951	MGM
Pal Joey	1957	Col.
Palm Springs Weekend	1963	WB
Pillars of the Sky	1956	Univ.
The Private War of Major Benson	1955	Univ.
Rampage	1963	WB
Ride a Crooked Trail	1958	Univ.
The River's Edge	1956	TCF
The Skipper Surprised His Wife	1950	MGM
Spring Reunion	1957	UA
Three Young Texans	1954	TCF
Von Ryan's Express *	1965	TCF
Walk the Proud Land	1956	Univ.
Wichita	1955	AA
Wild and the Innocent	1959	Univ.

364. ART LLOYD (1897-1954)

Babes in Toyland *	1934	US
Blockheads	1938	US
The Bohemian Girl *	1936	US
Bonnie Scotland *	1935	MGM/US
A Chump at Oxford	1939	US
The Flying Deuces *	1939	US
Fra Diavolo *	1933	MGM/US
General Spanky *	1936	MGM/US
Kelly the Second	1936	MGM
Pack Up Your Troubles	1931	US
Saps at Sea	1940	US
Way Out West *	1937	US

365. BRUCE LOGAN

Big Bad Mama	1974	US
Cat Murkil and the Silks	1976	US
Crazy Mama *	1975	US
Dracula's Dog	1978	US
Howzer	1972	US
I Never Promised You a Rose Garden	1977	US
Idaho Transfer	1975	US
The Incredible Shrinking Woman	1981	Univ.
Jackson County Jail	1976	US
Stunts *	1977	US
This Is a Hijack	1973	US
Tron	1982	Dis.

366. DIETRICH LOHMANN

The American Soldier	1970	Ger.

As Far As the Eye Can Sees	1980	Ger.
Bach B Minor Mass	1979	Ger.
The Baker's Bread	1977	Ger.
Bomber and Paganini	1977	Ger.
Bums	1984	Ger.
Cadillac	1969	Ger.
The Cat Has Nine Lives	1968	Ger.
Colder Than Death	1969	Ger.
Effi Briest *	1974	Ger.
The Fall	1979	Ger.
Final Call	1984	Ger.
Forester's Sons	1985	Ger.
Games Pass	1976	Ger.
Grmany in Autumn	1978	Ger.
Gods of Pestilence	1970	Ger.
Good-For-Nothings	1978	Ger.
Ein Grosser Grau-Blauer Vogel *	1970	Ger.
Harlis	1973	Ger.
Hitler: A Film From Germany	1977	Fr./Ger./GB
Karl May	1976	Ger.
Kassbach	1979	Aust.
Katzenmacher	1969	Ger.
The Last Cry	1977	Ger.
Lethal Obsession *	1988	Ger.
Love Is Not an Argument	1984	Ger.
The Maidens' War	1977	Ger.
Our Hitler	1980	Ger.
The Outsider	1976	Ger.
Peddlar of Four Seasons	1971	Ger.
Purity of Heart	1980	Ger.
Put On Ice	1980	Ger.
Recruits in Ingolstadt	197	Ger.
Requiem for a Virginal King	1972	Ger.
Silence Like Glass	1989	Ger.
The Tailor From Ulm	1979	Ger.
Vera Romeyke Is Not Acceptable	1976	Ger.
Why Does Mr. R Run Amok?	1970	Ger.

367. PAUL LOHMANN

Buffalo Bill and the Indians	1976	UA
California Split	1974	Col.
Charlie Chan and the Curse of the Dragon Queen	1981	US
Coffy	1973	AIP
Delta Pi	1985	US
Endangered Species	1982	MGM-UA
An Enemy of the People	1977	WB
Extreme Close-Up	1973	NG
Free Ride	1986	US

Hell's Angels	1969	AIP
Hide in Plain Sight	1980	MGM-UA
High Anxiety	1977	TCF
Looker	1981	WB
Meteor	1979	AIP
Mommie Dearest	1981	Par.
Nashville	1975	Par.
North Dalls Forty	1979	Par.
Silent Movie	1976	TCF
Time After Time	1979	WB
White Buffalo	1977	UA

368. RAUL LOMAS

Children of the Corn	1984	US
Prowler	1981	US
Rosebud Beach Hotel	1985	US
Stacy's Knights	1983	US
Young Giants	1983	US

369. BERT LONGNECKER

Across the Plains	1939	Mon.
The Air Hawk	1924	US
Behind Two Guns	1924	US
Better Days *	1927	US
Between Men	1935	US
Boothill Brigade	1937	Rep.
Buffalo Bill on the U.P. Trail	1926	US
The Crime Patrol	1936	US
Danger Valley	1938	Mon.
Desert Phantom	1936	US
Desert Rider	1923	US
Doomed at Sundown	1937	Rep.
Drifting Westward	1939	Mon.
Dynamite Dan	1924	US
$50,000 Reward	1924	US
Flying Fool *	1925	US
The Gambling Terror	1937	Rep.
God's Country and the Man	1937	Mon.
Gun Lords of Stirrup Basin	1937	Rep.
Gun Packer	1938	Mon.
The Gun Ranger	1937	Rep.
In High Gear	1924	US
Kit Carson Over the Great Divide	1925	US
Last of the Warrens	1936	US
Lawman Is Born	1937	Rep.
Lightnin' Crandall	1937	Rep.
Man's Country	1938	Mon.

Mexicali Kid	1938	Mon.
Oklahoma Terror	1939	Mon.
Overland Mail	1939	Mon.
The Painted Trail	1938	Mon.
Reckless Ranger	1937	Col.
Red Rope	1937	Rep.
Riders of Mystery	1925	US
Riders of the Dawn	1937	Mon.
Romance of the Rockies	1937	Mon.
Scream in the Night	1943	US
Slow as Lightning	1923	US
Stars Over Arizona	1937	Mon.
Sundown on the Prairie	1939	Mon.
Sundown Saunders	1936	US
Trail of Vengeance	1937	Rep.
Trigger Smith	1939	Mon.
The Trusted Outlaw	1937	Rep.
Wanted by the Police	1939	Mon.
Wild Horse Canyon	1939	Mon.

370. WILLIAM LUBTCHANSKY

After Darkness	1985	Fr.
The Butcher, the Star and the Orphan *	1975	Fr.
Cap Canaille	1983	Belg./Fr.
Class Relations	1984	Fr./Ger.
Comedy!	1987	Fr.
Every Man for Himself	1980	Fr.
Every Other Weekend	1990	Fr.
FM-Frequency Murder	1988	Fr.
First Voyage	1980	Fr.
Forbidden to Know	1973	Fr.--TCF
Frankenstein 90	1984	Fr.
The Games of the Countess Dolinger of Gratz *	1981	Fr.
Handsome Face	1972	Fr.
House of Jade	1988	Fr.
I Love You	1986	Fr.
The Indiscretion	1982	Fr.
It Only Happens to Others	1971	Fr./It.
Klann/Grand Guignol	1970	Fr.
Last Exit Before Roissy	1977	Fr.
Love on the Ground	1984	Fr.
The Mahabharata	1989	Fr./GB/US
Neige	1981	Fr.
New Wave	1990	Fr./Switz.
Next Summer	1985	Fr.
North Bridge	1981	Fr.
Northwest Wind	1977	Fr.
Prude	1986	Fr.

The Red Shadow	1982	Fr.
A Savage Summer	1970	Fr.
The Savior	1971	Fr.
Seasons of Pleasure	1988	Fr.
Short Memory	1979	Fr.
Speak to Me of Love	1975	Fr.
Stray Bullets	1983	Fr.
Temptation of Isabelle	1985	Fr.
Thomas	1975	Fr.
Time to Live	1969	Fr.
Trouble Agent	1987	Fr.
Violins at the Ball	1974	Fr.
Well-Filled Day	1973	Fr.
Why Israel?	1973	Fr.
The Woman Next Door	1981	Fr.--UA
Women Duelling	1976	Fr.

371. WALTER LUNDIN

Air Raid Wardens	1943	MGM
Doctor Jack	1922	US
Feet First *	1930	Par.
For Heaven's Sake	1926	Par.
The Freshman *	1925	Pathe
Girl Shy *	1924	Pathe
Grandma's Boy	1922	US
Hot Water	1924	Pathe
The Kid Brother	1927	Par.
Movie Crazy	1932	Par.
Safety Last	1923	Pathe/US
A Sailor-Made Man	1921	US
Speedy	1928	Par.
Way Out West *	1937	US
Welcome Danger *	1929	Par.
Why Worry?	1923	Pathe/US

372. IGOR LUTHER

The Age of Christ	1967	Czech.
Beiss Mich Liebling	1970	Ger.
Beyond Control	1970	Ger.
Birds, Orphans and Madmen	1970	Czech./Fr.
Bite Me Darling	1970	Ger.
Circle of Deceit	1981	Fr./Ger.--UA
Conquest of the Citadel	1977	Ger.
Coup de Grace	1976	Fr./Ger.
Danton	1983	Fr.
The Dream House	1981	Ger.

Eden and After	1970	Czech./Fr.
Fear Not, Jacob!	1981	Ger.
Freckles	1968	Ger./It.
The Handmaid's Tale	1990	US
He Who Lives in a Glass House	1971	Ger.
Killing Me Softly	1976	Ger.
Lethal Obsession *	1988	Ger.
A Love in Germany	1983	Fr./Ger.
The Man Who Lies	1970	Czech./Fr.
O.K.	1970	Ger.
One	1971	Ger.
Parsifal	1983	Fr.
Slavers	1977	Ger.
The Tin Drum	1979	Fr./Ger./Pol./ Yugo
Top Hat	1977	Ger.
War and Peace *	1983	Ger.
Yesterday's Tomorrow	1978	Ger.

373. WARREN LYNCH

Blondes at Work	1938	WB
Fly-Away Baby	1937	WB
Midnight Court	1937	WB
Murder in the Clouds	1935	FN/WB
Over the Goal	1937	FN/WB
Red Hot Tires	1935	WB
Six Day Bike Rider	1934	FN
Smart Blonde	1936	WB
Torchy Blaine in Chinatown	1938	WB
Torchy Runs for Mayor	1939	WB
The Widow From Monte Carlo	1936	WB

374. CHESTER LYONS

The Age of Desire	1923	FN
Alarm Clock Andy	1920	Par.
As Young as You Feel	1931	Fox
Bachelor's Paradise	1928	US
Back Pay	1922	FN
Bad Girl	1931	Fox
Bill Henry	1919	Par.
Bombshell *	1933	MGM
The Bootlegger's Daughter	1922	US
The Busher	1920	Par.
Children of Dust	1923	FN
The Circle	1925	MGM
Clothes Make the Woman	1928	US
Crooked Straight	1919	Par.

Daddy's Gone A-Hunting	1925	MGM
Deception	1933	Col.
The Egg Crate Wallop	1919	Par.
The Family Skeleton	1918	Par.
The First Year	1926	Fox
45 Minutes From Broadway	1920	FN
Frivolous Sal *	1925	FN
Fugitives	1929	Fox
The Gateway of the Moon	1928	Fox
The Gentle Cyclone	1926	Fox
Get-Rich-Quick Wallingford	1921	Par.
The Girl Dodger	1919	Par.
The Good Provider	1922	Par.
Greased Lightning	1919	Par.
Happiness	1924	Metro.
Hay Foot, Straw Foot	1919	Par.
The Hired Man	1918	Par.
Homer Comes Home	1920	Par.
Just Like a Woman *	1923	US
The Law of the North *	1918	Par.
Lightnin'	1930	Fox
Liliom	1930	Fox
Love Makes' Em Wild	1927	FOx
Love or Justice	1917	US
Lucky Star *	1929	Fox
Mad Love *	1935	MGM
Man and Maid	1925	Metro.-Gold.
The Man Life Passed By	1923	Metro.
Mother Machree	1928	Fox
Nameless Men	1928	US
The Naughty Duchess *	1928	US
Night Life	1927	US
Nineteen and Phyllis	1920	FN
Not Damaged	1930	Fox
The Nth Commandment	1923	Par.
An Old Fashioned Boy	1920	Par.
The Only Thing	1925	MGM
Paris Green	1920	Par.
Peaceful Valley	1920	FN
Playing the Game	1918	Par.
The Power of the Press *	1928	Col.
The Pride of the Palomar	1922	Par.
Ramona *	1936	TCF
Red Hot Dollars	1920	Par.
Robin Hood of Eldorado	1936	MGM
Sequoia	1934	MGM
The Sheriff's Son	1919	Par.
Sisters	1922	US
Song o' My Heart *	1930	Fox
String Beans	1918	Par.
They Had to See Paris *	1929	Fox

Under the Pampas Moon	1935	Fox
The Valley of Silent Men	1922	Par.
A Village Sleuth	1920	Par.
White Hunter	1936	TCF
A Woman Against the World	1928	US
Women's Wares	1927	US

375. EDGAR LYONS

Death Valley Outlaws	1941	Rep.
Do It Now *	1924	US
The Fighting Trooper	1935	US
The Firebrand	1922	US
Montana Bill	1921	US
Northern Frontier	1935	US
The Old Corral	1937	Rep.
The Reckless Sex	1925	US
Shadows on the Sage	1942	Rep.
Smiling Jim	1922	US
Stagecoach to Denver	1947	Rep.
The Torrent *	1924	US
A Western Demon	1922	US

376. REGGIE LYONS

Angel Citizens	1922	US
Black Beauty	1921	Vita.
Black Jack	1927	Fox
Blood Will Tell	1927	Fox
The Branded Sombrero	1928	Fox
The Cave Man	1915	Vita.
Chain Lightning	1927	Fox
The Cowboy and the Countess	1926	Fox
Danger Ahead	1923	US
Desert Valley	1926	Fox
The Desert's Price	1925	Fox
The Family Upstairs	1926	Fox
The Fighting Buckaroo	1926	Fox
The Gold Grabbers	1922	US
Good As Gold	1927	Fox
Hills of Peril	1927	Fox
Just Like a Woman *	1923	US
A Man Four Square	1926	Fox
Mortmain	1915	Vita.
Mother's Roses	1915	Vita.
So This Is Arizona	1922	US
30 Below Zero	1926	Fox
The Trail Rider	1925	Fox
The Unfortunate Sex	1920	US

The War Horse	1927	Fox
The Wheels of Justice	1915	Vita.
Whispering Sage	1927	Fox
The White Masks	1921	US

377. JOHN MacBURNIE

Alias the Champ	1949	Rep.
Arizona Manhunt	1951	Rep.
Bandit King of Texas	1949	Rep.
Bandits of Dark Canyon	1947	Rep.
Bells of Coronado	1950	Rep.
Border Saddlemates	1952	Rep.
Buckaroo Sheriff of Texas	1951	Rep.
The Bushwhackers	1952	US
California Passage	1950	Rep.
Campus Honeymoon	1948	Rep.
Canyon City	1943	Rep.
Captive of Billy the Kid	1952	Rep.
Code of the Silver Sage	1950	Rep.
Colorado Sundown	1952	Rep.
The Dakota Kid	1951	Rep.
Daredevils of the Clouds	1948	Rep.
Daughter of the Jungle	1949	Rep.
Desert of Lost Men	1951	Rep.
Desperadoes of Dodge City	1948	Rep.
Desperadoes' Outpost	1952	Rep.
Destination Big House	1951	Rep.
Down Laredo Way	1953	Rep.
Duke of Chicago	1949	Rep.
El Paso Stampede	1953	Rep.
Federal Agent at Large	1950	Rep.
Flame of Youth	1949	Rep.
Flaming Fury	1949	Rep.
Fort Dodge Stampede	1951	Rep.
Frisco Tornado	1950	Rep.
Ghost of Zorro	1949	Rep.
Gobs and Gals	1952	Rep.
Harbor of Missing Men	1950	Rep.
Heart of Virginia	1948	Rep.
Hideout	1949	Rep.
Homicide for Three	1948	Rep.
Insurance Investigator	1951	Rep.
Jesse James, Jr.	1942	Rep.
The Last Musketeer	1952	Rep.
Lightnin' in the Forest	1948	Rep.
Madonna of the Desert	1948	Rep.
The Main Street Kid	1947	Rep.
The Man From Rio Grande	1943	Rep.
Marshal of Amarillo	1948	Rep.

Marshal of Cedar Rock	1953	Rep.
Missing Women	1951	Rep.
The Missourians	1950	Rep.
Navajo Trail Raiders	1949	Rep.
Night Riders of Montana	1951	Rep.
Oklahoma Badlands	1948	Rep.
Old Oklahoma Plains	1952	Rep.
Old Overland Trail	1953	Rep.
Out of the Storm	1948	Rep.
Outlaws of Santa Fe	1944	Rep.
Overland Mail Robbery	1943	Rep.
Pioneer Marshal	1949	Rep.
Post Office Inspector	1949	Rep.
Powder River Rustlers	1949	Rep.
Pride of Maryland	1951	Rep.
Pride of the Plains	1944	Rep.
The Red Menace	1949	Rep.
Redwood Forest Trail	1950	Rep.
Rose of the Yukon	1949	Rep.
Rough Riders of Durango	1951	Rep.
Rustlers on Horseback	1950	Rep.
Salt Lake Raiders	1950	Rep.
San Antone Ambush	1949	Rep.
Secret Service Investigator	1948	Rep.
Sheriff of Wichita	1949	Rep.
Silver City Bonanza	1951	Rep.
Slippy McGee	1948	Rep.
Son of God's Country	1948	Rep.
Sons of Adventure	1948	Rep.
South of Rio	1949	Rep.
South Pacific Trail	1952	Rep.
Stagecoach Express	1942	Rep.
Street Bandits	1951	Rep.
Streets of San Francisco	1949	Rep.
Tarnished	1950	Rep.
Texas Terrors	1940	Rep.
Thunder in God's Country	1951	Rep.
Thundering Caravans	1952	Rep.
Trail of Robin Hood	1950	Rep.
Trial Without Jury	1950	Rep.
Tropical Heat Wave	1952	Rep.
The Tulsa Kid	1940	Rep.
Twilight in the Sierras	1950	Rep.
Under Mexicali Stars	1950	Rep.
Utah Wagon Train	1951	Rep.
Vigilante Hideout	1950	Rep.
Wells Fargo Gunmaster	1951	Rep.
Wild Horse Ambush	1952	Rep.
Woman in the Dark	1952	Rep.
Women of Headquarters	1950	Rep.
The Wyoming Bandit	1949	Rep.

378. JOSEPH MacDONALD (1906-1968)

Alvarez Kelly	1966	Col.
As Young As You Feel	1951	TCF
Behind Green Lights	1946	TCF
The Big Noise	1944	TCF
Bigger Than Life	1956	TCF
Blindfold	1965	Univ.
Broken Lance	1954	TCF
Call Northside 777	1948	TCF
Captain Eddie	1945	TCF
The Carpetbaggers	1964	Par.
Charlie Chan in Rio	1941	TCF
The Dark Corner	1946	TCF
Down to the Sea in Ships	1949	TCF
The Fiend Who Walked the West	1958	TCF
Flight From Ashiya *	1963	UA
Forty Pounds of Trouble	1963	Univ.
Fourteen Hours	1951	TCF
The Gallant Hours	1959	UA
A Guide For the Married Man	1967	TCF
A Hatful of Rain	1957	TCF
Hell and High Water	1954	TCF
Hilda Crane	1956	TCF
House of Bamboo	1955	TCF
How To Marry a Millionaire	1953	TCF
In the Meantime, Darling	1944	TCF
Invitation to a Gunfighter	1964	UA
It Happens Every Spring	1949	TCF
Kings of the Sun	1963	UA
The Last Time I Saw Archie	1961	UA
The List of Adrian Messenger	1963	Univ.
Little Tokyo USA	1942	TCF
The Man Who Wouldn't Die	1942	TCF
McKenna's Gold *	1969	Col.
Mirage	1965	Univ.
Moss Rose	1947	TCF
My Darling Clementine	1946	TCF
Niagara	1952	TCF
O. Henry's Full House *	1952	TCF
On the Threshold of Space	1956	TCF
Panic in the Streets	1950	TCF
Pepe	1960	Col.
Pickup on South Street	1953	TCF
Pinky	1949	TCF
The Postman Didn't Ring	1942	TCF
Quiet Please, Murder	1943	TCF
The Racers	1955	TCF
The Reward	1965	TCF
Rio Conchos	1964	TCF
Rose of France	1936	TCF

The Sand Pebbles	1966	TCF
Shock *	1946	TCF
Stella	1950	TCF
The Street With No Name	1948	TCF
Sunday Dinner for a Soldier	1944	TCF
Taras Bulba	1962	UA
Teenage Rebel	1956	TCF
Ten North Frederick	1958	TCF
That Other Woman	1942	TCF
Titanic	1953	TCF
The True Story of Jesse James	1956	TCF
The View From Pompey's Head	1955	TCF
Viva Zapata!	1952	TCF
Walk on the Wild Side	1962	Col.
Warlock	1959	TCF
What Price Glory?	1952	TCF
Where Love Has Gone	1964	Par.
Will Success Spoil Rock Hunter?	1947	TCF
Woman's World	1954	TCF
Yellow Sky	1948	TCF
The Young Lions	1958	TCF
You're in the Navy Now	1951	TCF

379. JACK MacKENZIE

Adventures of a Rookie	1943	RKO
Another Face	1935	RKO
Beau Bandit	1930	RKO
Belle of Alaska	1922	US
Black Lightning	1924	US
Boy From Indiana	1950	EL
Breaking the Ice	1938	RKO
Bring Him In	1921	Vita.
Caught Plastered	1931	RKO
Child of Divorce	1946	RKO
Code of the West	1947	RKO
Colleen of the Pines	1922	US
Crime Ring	1938	RKO
Dance Hall	1929	RKO
Diamonds Adrift	1921	Vita.
Divorce	1923	US
Dixie Jamboree	1945	PRC
Don't Turn 'Em Loose	1936	RKO
Duke of Chimney Butte	1921	US
Escape	1930	RKO
Eternal Love	1917	Univ.
Falcon Strikes Back	1943	RKO
False Ambition	1918	US
The Flame Barrier	1958	UA
Gambling	1934	Fox

The Ghost Flower	1918	US
The Gift Supreme	1920	US
Gildersleeve On Broadway	1943	RKO
Gildersleeve's Bad Day	1943	RKO
Gildersleeve's Ghost	1943	RKO
Girl From Mexico *	1939	RKO
Go Chase Yourself	1938	RKO
Great Guy	1936	GN
Hawaii Calls	1938	RKO
Hi Gaucho!	1936	RKO
Hi Ya, Sailor *	1943	Univ.
Hideaway	1937	RKO
High Flyers *	1937	RKO
His Master's Voice	1925	US
Hold That Lion	1926	Par.
Hot Tip	1935	RKO
Introduce Me *	1925	US
Isle of the Dead	1945	RKO
It Can Be Done	1921	Vita.
Jazz Heaven	1929	RKO
The Jolt	1921	Fox
Jungle Woman	1944	Univ.
Ladies' Day	1943	RKO
Ladies' Night in a Turkish Bath	1928	FN
Ladies of the Jury	1932	RKO
Last Outlaw	1936	RKO
The Last Rebel	1918	US
Let It Rain	1927	Par.
Let's Make Music	1940	RKO
Little Orphan Annie	1932	RKO
The Lodge in the Wilderness	1926	US
The Lullaby	1924	US
Make Mine Laughs *	1949	RKO
Mama Loves Papa	1945	RKO
The Marshal's Daughter	1953	UA
Massacre River	1949	AA/Mon.
Meet the Missus	1937	RKO
Mexican Spitfire	1939	RKO
Mexican Spitfire at Sea	1942	RKO
Mexican Spitfire Out West	1940	RKO
Mexican Spitfire's Baby	1941	RKO
Mexican Spitfire's Elephant	1942	RKO
Michael O'Halloran	1948	Mon.
Mug Town	1943	Univ.
Mummy's Boys *	1936	RKO
My Pal Wolf	1944	RKO
Never Say Die	1924	US
The Night Ship	1925	US
The Nut-Cracker	1926	US
On Again-Off Again	1937	RKO
On the Threshold	1925	US

The Overland Limited	1925	US
Part Time Wife	1925	US
Partners in Time	1946	RKO
Passport to Destiny	1944	RKO
Peach O' Reno	1931	RKO
Peck's Bad Boy WIth the Circus	1938	RKO
Pop Always Pays	1940	RKO
Private Affairs	1925	US
The Purple Cipher	1920	Vitz.
Radio City Revels *	1938	RKO
Rainbow Man	1929	Par.
The Return of Dracula	1958	UA
The Romance Promoters	1920	Vita.
Scattergood Baines	1941	RKO
Scattergood Meets Broadway	1941	RKO
Scattergood Pulls the Strings	1941	RKO
Scattergood Rides High	1942	RKO
Scattergood Survives a Murder	1942	RKO
Secret of the Hills	1921	Vita.
Seven Keys to Baldpate	1925	Par.
Seven Keys to Baldpate	1947	RKO
Shattered Lives	1925	FN
She's Got Everything	1937	RKO
Should a Doctor Tell? *	1931	GB
Silent Pal	1925	US
The Silver Car	1921	Vita.
The Snowshoe Trail	1922	US
Soft Cushions	1927	Par.
Sued for Libel	1939	RKO
A Texas Steer	1927	FN
That's My Baby	1926	Par.
Thelma	1922	US
Three Sevens	1921	Vita.
Thunder Mountain	1947	RKO
Timber	1942	RKO
Toton	1919	US
23½ Hours Leave	1937	GN
Two In Revolt	1936	RKO
Two O'Clock Courage	1945	RKO
Two Weeks To Live	1943	RKO
Unmarried Wives	1924	US
Vagabond Lady	1935	MGM
The Vampire	1957	UA
Whispering Winds *	1929	US
Whom the Gods Would Destroy	1919	FN
Wildcat Bus	1940	RKO
Zombies On Broadway	1945	RKO

380. GLENN MacWILLIAMS

A-Haunting We Will Go	1942	TCF

Ankles Preferred	1927	Fox
Arizona *	1918	US
The Arizona Kid	1930	Fox
Blue, White and Perfect	1941	TCF
The Camels Are Coming *	1934	GB
Captain January	1924	US
Chetniks	1943	TCF
The Clairvoyant *	1934	GB--Fox
Comon Clay	1930	Fox
The Dangerous Maid	1923	FN
Deserted at the Altar *	1922	US
Dressed to Kill	1941	TCF
Ever Since Eve	1921	Fox
Evergreen	1934	GB
First a Girl	1935	GB
The Front Page	1931	UA
Gangway	1937	GB
The Golden Strain	1925	Fox
Great Guns	1941	TCF
Hat Check Girl	1932	FOx
He Hired the Boss	1943	TCF
Head Over Heels in Love	1937	GB
The Heart of Salome	1927	Fox
Hearts in Dixie	1929	Fox
Heat Wave	1935	GB
Helen's Babies *	1924	US
His Majesty the American *	1919	UA
If I'm Lucky	1945	TCF
It Shouldn't Happen to a Dog	1946	TCF
It's Love Again	1936	GB
King Solomon's Mines *	1937	GB
Kismet *	1920	US
The Knickerbocker Buckaroo *	1919	US
Ladies Must Dress	1927	Fox
Lady in Distress	1942	GB
The Lamplighter	1921	Fox
Lazybones *	1925	Fox
Lifeboat	1944	TCF
Lily	1926	Fox
Love Hungry	1928	Fox
Lovetime	1921	Fox
The Luck of the Irish *	1920	US
Man in the Trunk	1942	TCF
The Mine With the Iron Door	1924	US
The Mother Heart	1921	Fox
My Boy *	1921	FN
My Heart Is Calling	1935	GB
Oliver Twist *	1922	FN
Orders Is Orders	1935	GB
Pajamas	1927	Fox
Partners of Fate *	1921	Fox

Pleasure Crazed *	1929	Fox
The Poor Simp *	1920	Selz.
The Proud Valley *	1939	GB--Eal.
Quicksands *	1923	Par.
The Re-Creation of Brian Kent	1925	US
Rebecca of Sunnybrook Farm	1932	Fox
The Return of Peter Grimm	1926	Fox
Roger Touhy Gangster	1944	TCF
Rupert of Hentzau *	1923	Selz.
Sailing Along	1938	GB
Say! Young Fellow *	1918	US
The Sea Wolf *	1930	Fox
The Secret Studio	1927	Fox
Shock *	1946	TCF
Siberia *	1926	Fox
Silent Barriers	1937	GB
The Spider	1945	TCF
The Spider and the Rose *	1923	US
A Splendid Hazard	1920	FN
Stage Madness	1927	Fox
Sundown Jim	1942	TCF
Things Are Looking Up	1935	GB
Thunder Mountain	1925	Fox
Trouble *	1922	FN
Valiant *	1929	Fox
Waltzes From Vienna	1934	GB
The Wheel	1925	Fox
While Paris Sleeps	1932	Fox
Win That Girl	1928	Fox
Wing and a Prayer	1944	TCF
Wing Toy	1921	Fox
Winged Victory	1944	TCF
Wintertime	1943	TCF
Within These Walls	1945	TCF

381. DON MALKAMES (1904-1987)

Beware	1946	US
Big Town	1932	US
The Burglar	1957	Col.
Citizen Saint	1947	US
Cry Murder	1950	US
Hi-De-Ho	1947	US
Jigsaw	1949	UA
Miracle in Harlem	1948	US
Pie in the Sky	1964	AA
Project X	1949	US
St. Benny the Dip	1951	UA
Sarumba	1950	UA
So Young, So Bad	1950	UA
That Man From Tangier	1953	UA

382. THOMAS MALLOY

The Adventure Shop	1918	Vita.
Any Wife	1922	Fox
The Blue Envelope Mystery	1916	Vita.
The Custard Cup	1923	Fox
The Fortune Hunter	1920	Vita.
A Girl at Bay	1919	Vita.
The Girl Problem	1919	Vita.
The Heart of Maryland	1921	Vita.
Her Unborn Child *	1930	US
Indiscretion	1917	Vita.
The Island of Retribution	1915	Vita.
The Judgment House	1917	Par.
Moonshine Valley	1922	Fox
No Mother to Guide Her	1923	Fox
Oil	1920	US
Over the Top	1918	Vita.
Shackles of Gold	1922	Fox
Sisters of the Golden Circle	918	US
A Stage Romance	1922	Fox
Thin Ice	1919	Vita.
The Tower of Jewels	1920	Vita.
The Unknown Quality	1919	Vita.
Unmasked *	1929	US
Without Fear	1922	Fox

383. JOSEPH MANGINE

Alone in the Dark	1982	US
Alligator	1980	US
Black Panther	1977	GB
Captain Lust	1977	US
Dreamland *	1983	US
Erika/One	1969	US
Hot Skin and Cold Cash	1965	US
The Lords of Flatbush *	1974	Col.
Mother's Day	1980	US
New Maniacs *	1986	US
Pleasure Plantation *	1970	US
Squirm	1976	AIP
The Sword and the Sorcerer	1982	US
Van Nuys Blvd.	1979	US
Whispers of Fear	1976	US

384. ISIDORE MANKOFSKY

Better Off Dead	1985	WB
Blood Money (Clinton and Nadine)	1988	US

Homebodies	1974	AE
The Jazz Singer	1980	US
Jud	1971	US
Muppet Movie	1979	US
One Crazy Summer	1986	WB
Say Yes	1986	US
Scream Blacula Scream	1973	AIP
Second Coming of Suzanna	1974	US
Skin Deep	1989	TCF
Somewhere in Time	1980	Univ.
Trick Baby	1973	Univ.
Werewolves on Wheels	1971	US

385. WILLIAM MARGULIES (1906-1987)

Angel in My Pocket	1969	Univ.
Arson for Hire	1959	AA
The Broken Star	1956	UA
Clambake	1967	UA
Crime Against Joe	1956	UA
Easy Come, Easy Go	1966	Par.
Emergency Hospital	1956	UA
Ghost and Mr. Chicken	1965	Univ.
The Girl in Black Stockings	1957	UA
Gunpoint	1966	Univ.
Hot Cars	1956	UA
How to Frame a Figg	1970	Univ.
Incident at Phantom Hill	1966	Univ.
Johnny Rocco	1958	AA
Jungle Heat	1957	UA
The Love God?	1969	Univ.
The Magic of Lassie	1978	US
A Man Called Gannon	1969	Univ.
McHale's Navy	1964	Univ.
Outlaw's Son	1957	UA
Pharaoh's Curse	1957	UA
Revolt at Fort Laramie	1957	UA
Revolt in the Big House	1958	AA
Sword of Ali Baba	1965	Univ.
Taggart	1965	Univ.
Tomahawk Trail	1957	UA
War Drums	1957	UA

386. J. PEVERELL MARLEY (1901-1964)

Adam Had Four SOns	1941	Col.
Alexander's Ragtime Band	1938	TCF
Bulldog Drummond Strikes Back	1934	UA
Cardinal Richelieu	1935	Fox

Celebrity	1928	Pathe
The Charge at Feather River	1953	WB
Charley's Aunt	1941	TCF
Chicago	1927	Pathe
Clive of India	1935	Fox
The Count of Monte Cristo	1934	US
The Country Doctor	1927	Pathe
Daytime Wife	1939	TCF
Dixie Dugan	1943	TCF
Dress Parade	1927	Pathe
Drumbeat	1954	US
Dynamite	1929	MGM
Fast Workers	1933	MGM
Feet of Clay *	1924	Par.
A Fever in the Blood	1960	WB
Folies Bergere *	1935	Fox
Forty Winks	1925	Par.
Four Jills in a Jeep	1944	TCF
Gallant Lady	1933	Fox/UA
The Godless Girl	1929	Pathe
The Golden Bed	1925	FP
The Great American Broadcast *	1941	TCF
The Greatest Show on Earth *	1952	Par.
The Groom Wore Spurs	1951	Univ.
Hell's Highroad	1925	US
Her Man O' War	1926	US
Homicide	1949	WB
Hotel for Women	1939	TCF
The Hound of the Baskervilles	1939	TCF
The House of Rothschild	1934	Fox
Hudson's Bay *	1940	TCF
Illegal	1955	WB
In Old Chicago	1937	TCF
It Had to Happen	1936	TCF
It's a Great Life	1929	MGM
John Loves Mary	1948	WB
Johnny Trouble	1957	US
Judgment of Lake Balatov *	1933	Hung.
Jump Into Hell	1955	WB
King of Burlesque	1936	TCF
King of Kings *	1927	Pathe
King Richard and the Crusaders	1954	WB
Kiss Tomorrow oodbye	1950	WB
A Lady of Chance *	1928	MGM
The Left-Handed Gun	1958	WB
Life With Father *	1947	WB
Look for the Silver Lining	1949	WB
The Magnificent Dope	1942	TCF
The Man I Married	1940	TCF
Marie	1933	Ger.
The Meanest Man in the World	1943	TCF

The Mighty Barnum	1934	Fox
Moon Over Miami *	1941	TCF
Night and Day *	1946	WB
Night Before the Divorce	1942	TCF
Night Club	1925	Par.
Night Unto Night	1949	WB
Of Human Bondage	1946	WB
Off Limits	1953	Par.
One Rainy Afternoon	1935	US
Perfect Strangers	1950	WB
Phantom of the Rue Morgue	1954	WB
Power	1928	Pathe
Pretty Baby	1950	WB
Pride of the Marines *	1945	WB
Private Number	1936	TCF
Return of the Frontiersman	1950	WB
The Road to yesterday	1925	US
Sally, Irene and Mary	1938	TCF
Sensations of 1945 *	1944	US
Serenade	1956	WB
Show Folks *	1928	Pahte
Silence	1926	US
Sing, Baby, Sing	1936	TCF
Sleepers West	1941	TCF
The Spirit of St. Louis *	1957	WB
Spring Shower	1932	Hung.
Star Dust	1940	TCF
The Steel Jungle	1956	WB
Suez	1938	TCF
Sunny Side Up	1926	US
Swamp Water	1941	TCF
The Ten Commandments *	1923	Par.
Thanks a Million	1935	TCF
This Day and Age	1933	Par.
This Mad World *	1930	MGM
Three Musketeers	1935	RKO
The Toast of New York	1937	RKO
The Two Mrs. Carrolls	1945	WB
Up the River	1938	TCF
The Volga Boatman *	1926	US
Westbound	1959	WB
Whiplash	1948	WB
Winterset	1936	RKO
Wise Girl	1937	RKO
The Woman Racket	1930	MGM
Women of Glamour *	1937	Col.
Young April	1926	US

387. CARL F. (BRICK) MARQUARD

Act of Vengeance	1974	AIP

All the Loving Couples	1969	US
Castle of Evil	1966	US
Dayton's Devils	1968	US
Destination Inner Space	1966	US
Don't Worry, We'll Think of a Title	1966	UA
Foxy Brown	1974	AIP
Where Does It Hurt?	1971	US

388. JACQUES MARQUETTE

Arizona Raiders	1965	Col.
Attack of the Fifty Foot Woman	1958	AA
Battle of Blood Island	1960	US
The Brain From Planet Arous	1958	US
A Bucket of Blood	1959	AIP
Burnt Offerings *	1976	UA
The Christine Jorgenson Story	1970	UA
Creature From the Haunted Sea	1961	US
Flight of the Lost Balloon	1961	AIP
Forty Guns to Apache Pass	1967	Col.
Frankie and Johnny	1966	UA
Fuzz	1972	UA
The Gatling Gun	1972	UA
The Last Woman on Earth	1960	US
More Dead Than Alive	1968	UA
Once You Kiss a Stranger	1969	WB
Return to Macon County	1975	AIP
The Strangler	1963	AA
Teenage Thunder	1957	US
Trauma	1962	US
Trouble With Girls	1969	MGM
War Is Hell	1964	AA
Wild on the Beach	1965	TCF
Winter A-Go-Go	1965	Col.

389. OLIVER MARSH (1892-1941)

After the Thin Man	1936	MGM
All Woman	1918	Gold.
Annie Laurie	1927	MGM
Another Thin Man *	1939	MGM
Arsene Lupin	1932	MGM
Baby Face Harrington	1935	MGM
Bachelor Father	1931	MGM
Bitter Sweet *	1940	MGM
Blonde Inspiration *	1941	MGM
The Bondage of Barbara	1919	Gold.
The Brand	1919	Gold.
Broadway Melody of 1940 *	1939	MGM

Broadway Rose	1922	Metro.
Broadway Serenade	1939	MGM
But the Flesh Is Weak	1932	MGM
Camille	1927	FN
Circe the Enchantress	1924	Metro.
The Crimson Gardenia	1919	Gold.
Dancing Lady	1933	MGM
Dangerous Business	1920	FN
Daring Love *	1924	US
David Copperfield	1935	MGM
The Divine Woman	1928	MGM
Divorce in the Family	1932	MGM
Dodging a Million	1918	Gold.
The Dove	1927	UA
Dream of Love *	1928	MGM
DuBarry, Woman of Passion	1930	UA
The Duchess of Buffalo	1926	FN
Emma	1932	MGM
The Enemy	1927	MGM
Eternal Love	1929	UA
Faithless	1932	MGM
Fascination	1922	Metro.
Fashion Row	1923	Metro.
The Firefly	1937	MGM
The Floor Below	1918	Gold.
The Floradora Girl	1930	MGM
The French Doll	1923	Metro.
The Girl from the Outside *	1919	Gold.
The Girl of the Golden West	1938	MGM
Good References	1920	FN
The Great Ziegfeld *	1936	MGM
Hidden Fires	1918	Gold.
His Brother's Wife	1936	MGM
I Love You Again	1940	MGM
Ice Follies of 1939 *	1939	MGM
In Gay Madrid	1930	MGM
In Search of a Sinner	1920	FN
It's a Wonderful WOrld	1939	MGM
Jazzmania	1923	Metro.
Joan of Plattsburg	1918	Gold.
Just a Gigolo	1931	MGM
Kiki	1926	FN
Lady Be Good *	1941	MGM
Lady of Scandal *	1930	MGM
Lessons in Love	1921	FN
Letty Lyndon	1932	MGM
Looking Forward	1933	MGM
The Love Expert	1920	FN
Love On the Run	1936	MGM
Love's Blindness *	1926	MGM
Love's Wilderness	1924	FN

Mademoiselle Midnight	1924	Metro.
Mama's Affair	1921	FN
Man in Possession	1931	MGM
Marianne	1929	MGM
Married Flirts	1924	MGM
The Masked Bride	1925	MGM
The Masks of the Devil	1928	MGM
The Merry Widow *	1925	MGM
Merry Widow	1934	MGM
The Midshipman	1925	MGM
The Mohican's Daughter *	1922	MGM
Mystery of Mr. X	1934	MGM
New Moon	1930	MGM
New Adventures of Get-Rich-Quick		
Wallingford	1931	MGM
Night Flight *	1933	MGM
No More Ladies	1935	MGM
Not So Dumb	1930	MGM
One New York Night	1935	MGM
Our Modern Maidens	1929	MGM
Peacock Alley	1922	MGM
The Perfect Woman	1920	FN
Phantom of Paris	1931	MGM
Possessed	1931	MGM
The Racing Strain	1919	Gold.
Rage in Heaven	1941	MGM
Rain	1932	UA
Red Hot Romance *	1922	FN
The Road to Romance	1927	MGM
Rosalie	1937	MGM
Sadie McKee	1934	MGM
Sadie Thompson *	1928	UA
The Sin of Madelon Claudet	1931	MGM
The Single Standard	1929	MGM
Small Town Girl *	1936	MGM
The Smart Set	1928	MGM
The Son-Daughter	1932	MGM
Soul Mates	1925	MGM
Strictly Unconventional	1930	MGM
Sweethearts	1938	MGM
A Tale of Two Cities	1936	MGM
Today We Live	1933	MGM
The Toy Wife	1938	MGM
Two Weeks	1920	FN
The Unknown Purple	1923	US
Untamed	1929	MGM
Wedding Bells	1921	FN
The Wild Man of Borneo	1941	MGM
The Woman Disputed	1928	UA
Woman's Place *	1921	FN
The Women *	1939	MGM
Women Are Trouble	1936	MGM

390. WILLIAM C. MARSHALL

The Amazons	1917	Par.
All of a Sudden Peggy	1920	Par.
American Manners *	1924	US
Amos and Andy	1930	RKO
The Bachelor Daddy *	1922	Par.
Crooked Streets	1920	Par.
A Daughter of the Gods *	1916	Fox
Eyes of the Heart	1920	US
The Fighting Demon *	1925	US
Flaming Waters	1925	US
Fools for Luck	1928	Par.
The Ghost Breaker	1922	Par.
A Girl Named Mary	1920	Par.
Great Expectations	1917	Par.
The Great Impersonation	1921	Par.
Hot News	1928	Par.
Hula	1927	Par.
In Fast Company	1924	US
In Mizzoura	1919	Par.
The Isle of Hope *	1925	US
Itching Palsm	1923	US
The Jilt	1922	Univ.
Jimmie's Millions	1925	US
The Ladder of Lies	1920	Par.
A Lady in Love	1920	Par.
The Land of Promise	1917	Par.
Laughing at Danger	1924	US
Let's Get a Divorce	1918	Par.
Lights Out	1923	US
Little Miss Hoover	1918	Par.
The Make-Believe Wife	1918	Par.
Moran of the Lady Letty	1922	Par.
Night Parade	1929	GB--RKO
On Time	1924	US
Our Leading Citizen *	1922	Par.
Partners in Crime	1928	Par.
The Prince of Pep *	1925	US
Rose of the River	1919	Par.
Second Wife	1930	RKO
Secret Service	1919	Par.
The Sheik	1921	Par.
Step Lively *	1924	US
Sweet Lavender	1920	US
Tearin' Loose	1925	US
Tearing Through	1925	US
Tea--With a Kick *	1923	US
Terror Island	1920	Par.
Time to Love	1927	Par.
The Wall Street Whiz *	1925	US

Wedding Bill$	1927	Par.
Wet Paint	1926	Par.
A Wise Fool	1921	Par.
The Woman Thou Gavest Me	1919	Par.
You'd Be Surprised	1926	Par.
Youth and Adventure	1925	US

391. JACK MARTA

Affair in Reno	1957	Rep.
The Ambushers *	1967	Col.
An Angel Comes to Brooklyn	1945	Rep.
Angel Baby *	1960	US
Any Man's Wife	1937	Rep.
Apache Rose	1947	Rep.
Beginning of the End	1957	Rep.
Behind the News	1940	Rep.
Belle of Old New York	1950	Rep.
Bells of San Angelo	1947	Rep.
Bill and Coo	1947	Rep.
Billy Jack Goes to Washington	1977	US
Blue Montana Skies	1939	Rep.
Bold Caballero *	1937	Rep.
The Bonnie Parker Story	1958	AIP
The Border Legion	1940	Rep.
Bordertown Gun Fighters	1943	Rep.
Born to Be Wild	1938	Rep.
Brazil	1944	Rep.
Brimstone	1949	Rep.
Bulldog Edition	1936	Rep.
Cat Ballou	1965	Col.
Circus Girl	1937	Rep.
The City	1971	Univ.
Colorado	1940	Rep.
Come Next Spring	1956	Rep.
Company of Killers	1970	Univ.
Confidential *	1935	Rep.
Cowboy Serenade	1942	Rep.
Dakota	1945	Rep.
The Dark Command	1940	Rep.
Dancing Feet *	1936	Rep.
A Desperate Adventure	1938	Rep.
Down Mexico Way	1941	Rep.
Duel at Apache Wells	1957	Rep.
Eat Carroll's Sketchbook	1946	Rep.
Earl Carroll's Vanities	1945	Rep.
Earl of Puddlestone	1940	Rep.
Earth vs. The Spider	1958	US
Eyes of Texas	1948	Rep.
The Fabulous Senorita	1952	Rep.

Fair Wind to Java	1952	Rep.
The Far Frontier	1949	Rep.
Fighting Thoroughbreds	1939	Rep.
Flying Tigers	1942	Rep.
Forged Passport	1939	Rep.
Framed	1975	Rep.
The Gallant Legion	1948	Rep.
The Gay Ranchero	1948	Rep.
Gentleman From Louisiana *	1936	Rep.
Ghost Town Gold	1937	Rep.
Girl From Alaska *	1942	Rep.
Girl From God's Country	1940	Rep.
Girl from Mandalay *	1936	Rep.
Girl in the Woods	1958	Rep.
The Golden Stallion	1949	Rep.
Grand Ole Opry	1940	Rep.
Harmony Lane *	1935	Rep.
Heart of the Golden West	1942	Rep.
Heart of the Rockies	1937	Rep.
Hearts in Bondage *	1936	Rep.
Hellfire	1949	Rep.
Hell's Outpost	1955	Rep.
The Higgins Family	1938	Rep.
Hit Parade of 1941	1940	Rep.
Hit Parade of 1943	1943	Rep.
Hit the Saddle	1937	Rep.
Hitch Hike Lady *	1936	Rep.
Hitchhike to Happiness	1945	Rep.
Honeychile	1951	Rep.
The House of a Thousand Candles *	1936	Rep.
I Stand Accused	1938	Rep.
Ice Capades	1941	Rep.
In Old Amarillo	1951	Rep.
In Old California	1942	Rep.
In Old Oklahoma	1943	Rep.
In Old Sacramento	1946	Rep.
Invisible Enemy	1938	Rep.
It Could Happen to You	1937	Rep.
Jim Hanvey Detective	1937	Rep.
Jubilee Trail	1954	Rep.
The Kid From Cleveland	1949	Rep.
King of the Newsboys	1938	Rep.
King of the Pecos	1936	Rep.
Ladies in Distress	1938	Rep.
Lady From Louisiana	1941	Rep.
Larceny on the Air	1937	Rep.
The Last Bandit	1949	Rep.
The Last Command	1955	Rep.
The Leathernecks Have Landed *	1936	Rep.
The Leavenworth Case *	1936	Rep.
Lisbon	1956	Rep.

London Blackout Murders	1942	Rep.
Loves of Carmen *	1927	Fox
Main Street Lawyer	1939	Rep.
A Man Betrayed	1941	Rep.
Man From Frisco	1944	Rep.
Man From Music Mountain	1938	Rep.
The Mandarin Mystery	1936	Rep.
Manhattan Merry-Go	1937	Rep.
Master Gunfighter	1975	US
The Maverick Queen	1955	Rep.
Mexicana	1945	Rep.
Mickey, the Kid	1939	Rep.
A Missouri Outlaw	1942	Rep.
Montana Belle	1952	RKO
Murder in the Music Hall *	1946	Rep.
My Best Gal	1944	Rep.
My Buddy	1944	Rep.
My Wife's Relatives	1939	Rep.
Navy Blues	1937	Rep.
Navy Born *	1936	Rep.
The Night Hawk	1938	Rep.
The Night Riders	1939	Rep.
Night Time in Nevada	1948	Rep.
North of the Great Divide	1950	Rep.
Oh! Susanna	1951	Rep.
Oklahoma Annie	1952	Rep.
On the Old Spanish Trail	1947	Rep.
Outside of Paradise	1938	Rep.
Pals of the Golden West	1951	Rep.
Panama Sal	1957	Rep.
Paradise Express	1937	Rep.
A Parilous Journey	1953	Rep.
Perils of Pauline	1967	Univ.
Petticoat Politics	1941	Rep.
Pioneers of the West	1940	Rep.
Plaza Suite	1971	Par.
The Plunderers	1947	Rep.
Port of 40 Thieves	1944	Rep.
Pride of the Navy	1939	Rep.
Public Cowboy No. 1	1937	Rep.
Puddin'Head	1941	Rep.
Range Defenders	1937	Rep.
Red Dance *	1928	Fox
Red River Range	1938	Rep.
Red River Valley	1941	Rep.
Rhythm of the Saddle	1938	Rep.
Ride, Tenderfoot, Ride	1940	Rep.
Ride the Man Down	1952	Rep.
Riders of the Whistling Skull	1937	Rep.
Ridin' Down the Canyon	1942	Rep.
Robin Hood of the Pecos	1941	Rep.

Rock Island Trail	1950	Rep.
Rocky Mountain Rangers	1940	Rep.
Rough Riders' Roundup	1939	Rep.
SOS Tidal Wave	1939	Rep.
Saga of Death Valley	1940	Rep.
The Shanghai Story	1954	Rep.
The Sheik Steps Out	1937	Rep.
Should Husbands Work?	1939	Rep.
Sierra Sue	1941	Rep.
Sis Hopkins	1941	Rep.
Smuggled Cargo	1939	Rep.
Someone to Remember	1943	Rep.
Song of Nevada	1944	Rep.
South of Caliente	1951	Rep.
Southward Ho!	1939	Rep.
The Spider	1958	AIP
Spoilers of the Forest	1957	Rep.
Spoilers of the Plains	1951	Rep.
Springtime in the Sierras	1947	Rep.
Sunset in the West	1950	Rep.
Tahiti Honey	1943	Rep.
Taming Sutton's Gal	1957	Rep.
That Brennan Girl	1946	Rep.
Thou Shalt Not Kill	1939	Rep.
$1,000 a Minute *	1935	Rep.
Timberjack	1954	Rep.
Trial of Billy Jack	1974	US
Trigger, Jr.	1950	Rep.
Under California Stars	1948	Rep.
Under Western Stars	1938	Rep.
The WAC From Walla Walla	1952	Rep.
Walking Tall	1973	US
Wall Street Cowboy	1939	Rep.
War of the Colossal Beast	1958	AIP
The Wayward Girl	1957	Rep.
West Side Kid	1943	Rep.
What Price Glory? *	1926	Fox
Woman of the North Country	1952	Rep.
Women in War	1940	Rep.
X Marks the Spot	1942	Rep.
Yellow Rose of Texas	1944	Rep.
You'll Like My Mother	1972	Univ.

392. OTELLO MARTELLI (1903-   )

Anna	1952	It.--DeL.
Il Bidone	1955	Fr./It.
Bitter Rice	1949	It.--DeL.
Boccacio '70	1962	Fr./It.--TCF
Cyrano and D'Artagnan	1964	Fr./It./Sp.

Days of Love	1954	It.
La Dolce Vita	1960	Fr./It.--AIP
The Duchess of Parma	1937	It.
Francis, God's Jester	1950	It.
Giacomo Casanova	1938	It.
Girl in the Window	1961	Fr./It.
The Glass Mountain	1949	GB
Gold of Naples	1955	It.
The Golden Madonna *	1949	GB--/Mon.
Guedalina	1957	Fr./It.
A Husband for Anna Zaccheo	1953	It.
I'll Give a Million *	1935	It.
It Happened in Rome	1952	Fr./It.
The Law	1959	Fr./It.
Lights of Variety	1950	It.
Loves of Don Juan	1948	It.
Lucky to Be a Woman	1955	It.
Menage, Italian Style	1966	It.
My Wife *	1964	It.
Nights of Cabiria *	1956	It.
Paisan	1946	It.
The Redhead	1962	Ger.
Rome Eleven O'Clock	1952	It.
La Strada	1954	It.
Stromboli	1949	It.--RKO
The Teacher From Vigevano	1964	It.
This Angry Age	1958	Fr./It.--Col.
Three Faces of a Woman *	1965	It.--DeL.
I Vitelloni *	1953	Fr./It.
Where the Hot Wind Blows	1958	Fr./It.--MGM
Who Is Happier Than I?	1938	It.
Woman Is a Wonderful Thing *	1964	It.
Woman of the River	1955	Fr./It.--Col.

393. H. KINLEY MARTIN

An Amateur Devil	1920	Par.
Brewster's Millions	1921	Par.
The Campus Flirt	1926	Par.
Ducks and Drakes	1921	US
The Escape	1928	Fox
Eve's Secret	1925	Par.
Fashions for Women	1927	Par.
Fireman, Save My Child	1927	Par.
First Love	1921	Par.
Food for Scandal	1920	US
A Full House	1920	Par.
The Golden Princess	1925	Par.
Hands Up!	1926	Par.
It	1927	Par.

A Kiss in a Taxi	1927	Par.
March Hare	1921	US
Midnight	1922	Par.
Oh, Lady, Lady	1920	US
One Wild Week	1921	US
Paths to Paradise	1925	Par.
The Rainmaker	1926	Par.
Senorita	1927	Par.
The Sleepwalker	1922	Par.
The Speed Girl	1921	Par.
Tell It to Sweeney	1927	Par.
Two Flaming Youths	1927	Par.
Two Weeks With Pay	1921	US
What Happened to Jones?	1920	Par.
Wife Savers *	1928	Par.

394. JOHN MARTIN

Betrayed Woman	1955	AA
The Big Tip Off	1955	AA
Bullwhip	1958	AA
Highway Dragnet	1954	AA
Las Vegas Shakedown	1955	AA
Port of Hell	1955	AA
Racing Blood	1954	TCF
Sea Tiger	1952	Mon.
Security Risk	1954	AA
Toughest Man Alive	1955	AA

395. ROBERT MARTIN

Autumn Crocus	1934	GB
Black Feather	1928	US
Crooks Can't Win	1928	FBO
Danger Street	1928	FBO
Girls Don't Gamble	1920	US
Hardboiled	1929	FBO
Hit of the Show	1928	FBO
Hey Rube!	1928	FBO
Java Head	1935	FB
Look On the Bright Side	1931	GB
Look Up and Laugh	1935	GB
Lorna Doone	1935	GB
Love of Sunya	1927	UA
Loyalties	1933	GB
Making the Grade *	1921	US
Sing As We Go	1934	GB
Smiling All the Way	1920	US
Strange Evidence	1932	GB--Par.
Voice of the Storm	1929	FBO

396. ARTHUR MARTINELLI (1882-1967)

Alias Ladyfingers	1921	Metro.
The Amateur Adventuress	1919	Metro.
Because of Eve *	1948	US
Charlie Chan in Black Magic	1944	Mon.
Cinderella Swings It	1943	RKO
Cipher Bureau	1938	GN
Convict's Code	1939	Mon.
County Fair	1937	Mon.
The Covered Trailer	1939	Rep.
Crime Afloat	1937	US
Criminals WIthin	1941	PRC
Deerslayer	1943	Rep.
The Devil Bat	1942	PRC
Double Cross	1941	PRC
Drums of Destiny	1937	US
East Side, West Side	1923	US
Ella Cinders	1926	FN
The Face Between	1922	Metro.
Fair and Warmer	1919	Metro.
A Favor to a Friend	1919	Metro.
Federal Fugitives	1941	PRC
Female Fugitive	1938	Mon.
Fools and Their Money	1919	Metro.
Gang Bullets	1938	Mon.
The Glory Trail	1936	US
The Greater Glory *	1926	FN
Her Fighting Chance	1917	US
Here Comes Kelly	1943	Mon.
I Believe in You	1940	RKO
I Conquer the Sea	1936	US
The Idle Rich	1921	Metro.
In Old New Mexico	1945	Mon.
Inside Information	1939	Univ.
Johnny-On-the-Spot	1919	Metro.
Kildare of Storm	1919	Metro.
The Law Commands	1938	US
The Long Shot	1939	GN
Love, Honor and Obey	1920	Metro.
Mad Empress *	1940	WB
The Man Who	1921	Metro.
Meanest Man in the World	1923	FN
A Message From Mars	1921	Metro.
Miracle Kid	1942	PRC
The Misleading Lady *	1920	Metro.
Mr. Celebrity	1942	PRC
Nation Aflame	1937	US
Old Louisiana	1937	US
Panama Patrol	1939	GN
Paper Bullets	1941	PRC

Polly With a Past	1920	Metro.
Raw Timber	1938	US
Rebellion	1938	US
Revolt of the Zombies *	1936	US
The Right That Failed	1922	Metro.
Secret Evidence	1941	PRC
Shadows Over Shanghai	1938	GN
Sherlock Brown	1922	Metro.
Star Reporter	1939	Mon.
A Successful Adventure	1918	Metro.
Supernatural	1933	Par.
Swing Out the Blues	1944	Col.
Sylvia on a Spree	1918	Metro.
10 Laps to Go	1938	US
That's Good	1919	Metro.
The Trail of the Shadow	1917	Metro.
A Trip to Paradise	1921	Metro.
Under Strange Flags	1937	US
Undercover Agent	1939	Mon.
The Walk-Offs	1920	Metro.
White Zombie	1932	UA
The Winning of Beatrice	1918	Metro.
The Witness Vanishes	1939	Univ.
Youth to Youth	1922	Metro.

397. HAROLD MARZORATI (1893-1964)

Gun Glory	1957	MGM
Handle With Care	1958	MGM
High School Confidential	1958	MGM
The Hired Gun	1958	MGM
Hot Summer Night	1957	MGM
Marauders	1955	MGM
Slander	1956	MGM
World, the Flesh and the Devil	1949	MGM

398. RUDOLF MATE (1898-1964)

Address Unknown	1944	Col.
The Adventures of Marco Polo	1938	Gold.
Aren't We All?	1932	GB--Par.
Blockade	1938	US
Charlie Chan's Secret	1936	TCF
Come and Get It *	1936	Gold.
Cover Girl *	1944	Col.
Dante's Inferno	1935	Fox
Le Dernier Milliardaire *	1936	Fr.
Dodsworth	1936	Gold.
Down To Earth	1947	Col.

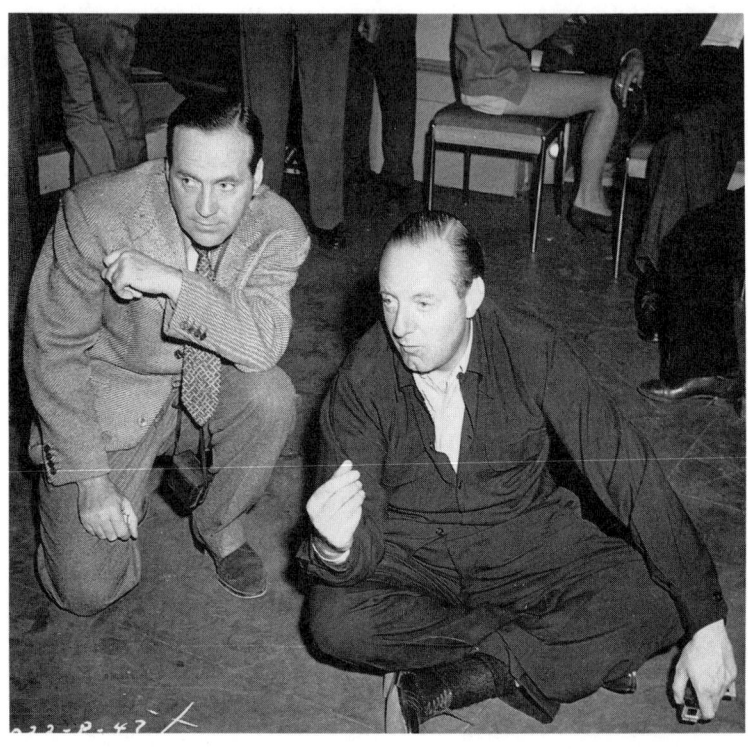

Rudolph Mate (left) with director Victor Saville at work on Tonight and Every Night (1945).

Dressed To Thrill	1935	Fox
Flame of New Orleans	1941	Univ.
Foreign Correspondent	1940	US
Gilda	1946	Col.
It Had To Be You *	1947	Col.
It Started With Eve	1941	Univ.
Liliom *	1934	Fr.--Fox
Love Affair	1939	RKO
A Message to Garcia	1936	TCF
Metropolitan	1935	Fox
My Favorite Wife	1940	RKO
Our Relations	1936	US
Outcast	1937	Par.
Passion of Joan of Arc *	1928	Fr.
The Pride of the Yankees	1942	Gold.
Professional Soldier	1936	TCF
The Real Glory	1939	Gold.
Sahara	1943	Col.
Seven Sinners	1940	Univ.
Song of the Streets	1939	Fr.
Stella Dallas	1937	Gold.
That Hamilton Woman!	1941	GB--Korda
They Got Me Covered	1943	Gold.
To Be or Not To Be	1942	Korda/UA
Tonight and Every Night	1945	Col.
Trade Winds	1939	US
Vampyr *	1931	Fr./Ger.
Youth Takes a Fling	1938	Univ.

399. CHRISTIAN MATRAS (1903-   )

Adorable Creatures	1952	Fr.
All Roads Lead to Rome	1949	Fr.
Angel and Sinner	1947	Fr.
Artists' Entrance *	1938	Fr.
Les Avenues de Till L'Espiegle	1957	Fr./Ger.
The Ball of Count Orgel	1970	Fr.
Beast at Bay	1959	Fr.
Beauty up His Sleeve	1958	Fr.
Birds in Peru	1968	Fr.--Univ.
Bluebeard	1951	Fr.
Boule de Suif	1945	Fr.
Cafe de Paris *	1938	Fr.
Cartouche	1961	Fr./It.
Christine	1959	Fr.
Crime Does Not Pay	1962	Fr.
Daughters of Destiny	1954	Fr./It.
The Desperate Ones	1968	Sp.--AIP
Diary of a Madman	1963	Fr.
Double Deception	1960	Fr.

Eagle With Two Heads	1948	Fr.
Earrings of Madame De	1954	Fr.
Eye for an Eye	1956	Fr./It.
Fanfan La Tulipe	1951	Fr.
The Game of Truth	1961	Fr.
La Fin de Jour	1939	Fr.
The French Game	1963	Fr.
The French They are a Funny Race	1956	Fr.
Le Grande Illusion *	1937	Fr.
Gypsy Fury	1950	Fr.--Mon.
L'Idiot	1946	Fr.
The Lace Wars	1966	Fr./Rom.
Legions of Honor *	1938	Fr.
Les Jeux sont Faits	1947	Fr.
The Lions are Loose	1961	Fr.
Lola Montes	1955	Fr./Ger.
Lost Souvenirs	1951	Fr.
Lucretia Borgia	1952	Fr./It.
Madame Du Barry	1954	Fr./It.
The Majordomo	1965	Fr.
Maldone *	1927	Fr.
The Man to Men	1948	Fr.
Maxime	1962	Fr.
Meeting in Paris	1956	Fr.
The Milky Way	1969	Fr./It.
The Mirror Has Two Faces	1958	Fr.
Modigliani of Montparnasse	1961	Fr./It.
Mother Love	1937	Fr.
Nana	1955	Fr.
Not Dumb, the Bird	1972	Fr.
Olivia	1951	Fr.
L'Or des Mers	1931	Fr.
Paradise Lost	1939	Fr.
Paris Blues	1961	UA
Paris Waltz	1950	Fr.
Particular Friendships	1964	Fr.
Le Plaisir *	1952	Fr.
Pontcarrel	1942	Fr.
Prison without Bars *	1938	Fr.
Risks of the Profession	1968	Fr.
La Ronde	1950	Fr.
Scheherazade	1965	Fr./It./Sp.
Secrets d'Alcove	1954	Fr./It.
The Spies	1958	Fr.
Students' Road	1960	Fr.
Therese Desqueroux	1962	Fr.
This Special Friendship	1967	Fr.
Towards Ecstasy	1960	Fr.
Varieties	1971	Fr.
Virginie	1962	Fr.
Why Do You Come So Late?	1959	Fr.

Woman from Beirut	1965	Fr./It./Sp.
Woman Times Seven	1967	Fr./It.--TCF

400. THOMAS MAUCH

Abschied von Gestern *	1966	Ger.
Aguirre, Wrath of God	1972	Ger.
The Artists Under the Big Top: Perplexed	1968	Ger.
Assault of the Present Upon the Rest of Time	1985	Ger.
Bread and Butter	1990	Ger.
Deadline *	1987	Ger.
Desperado City	1981	Ger.
Erika's Passions	1978	Ger.
Fitzcarraldo	1982	Ger.--US
Der Gross Verhau	1971	Ger.
Heinrich	1977	Ger.
Hell's Kitchen	1983	Ger.
Kingdom of Naples	1978	Ger.
Mary of the Stars	1989	Ger.
Mealtimes	1967	Ger.
Midgets Also Begin Small	1970	Ger.
No Mercy, No Future	1981	Ger.
Not Nothing Without You	1985	Ger.
Occasional Work of a Slave	1974	Ger.
Odds and Ends *	1987	Ger.
Palermo-Wolfsburg	1980	Ger.
Passionate People	1983	Aust./Ger./ Switz.
The Patriot *	1979	Ger.
Signs of Life	1968	Ger.
Slave Coast *	1988	Ger.
Strong Ferdinand	1976	Ger.
Stroszek	1977	Ger.
Under the Pavement Lies the Strand	1975	Ger.
Unknown Country	1987	Aust./Fr.
An Unusual Girl	1976	Fr.
Walter's Last Trip	1989	Ger.
War and Peace *	1983	Ger.

401. DONALD McALPINE

Adventures of Barry Mackenzie	1972	Aus.
Barry Mackenzie Holds His Own	1975	Aus.
Blue Skies Again	1983	WB
Breaker Morant	1980	Aus.
The Club	1980	Aus.
Don's Party	1976	Aus.

Don't Cry, It's Only Thunder	1982	US
Down and Out in Beverly Hills	1986	Touch.
The Earthling	1981	US
The Getting of Wisdom	1977	Aus.
Harry & Son	1984	Orion
Money Movers	1978	Aus.
Moon Over Parador	1988	Univ.
Moving	1988	WB
My Brilliant Career	1979	Aus.
My Man Adam	1986	Tri-S.
Now and Forever	1983	Aus.
Odd Angry Shot	1979	Aus.
Orphans	1987	Lor.
Parenthood	1989	Univ.
Patrick	1978	Aus.
Predator *	1987	TCF
Puberty Blues	1982	Aus.
See You in the Morning	1989	WB
Stanley and Iris	1990	MGM/UA
Tempest	1982	Col.

402. HUGH McCLUNG

Arizona *	1918	US
A Child of God	1915	US
Fickle Woman	1920	US
He Comes Up Smiling	1918	US
The Lily and the Rose *	1915	US
A Man and His Mate	1915	US
Mr. Fix It	1918	US
Overland Red	1920	Univ.
The Sable Lorcha	1915	US
Say! Young Fellow *	1918	US

403. TED McCORD (1898-1976)

Action in the North Atlantic	1943	WB
Adventures of Huckleberry Finn	1960	MGM
Beyond the Rockies	1932	Selz.
The Big Stampede	1932	WB
Blazing Sixes	1937	WB
The Breaking Point	1950	WB
Bullet Scars	1942	WB
Bullets for O'Hara	1941	WB
The Burning Hills	1956	WB
The California Mail *	1936	WB
Calling All Husbands	1940	WB
The Canyon of Adventure	1928	FN
Carnival Boat	1932	RKO

The Case of the Black Parrot	1941	WB
Cattle Town	1952	WB
Cherokee Strip *	1937	WB
The Code of the Scarlet	1928	FN
Code of the Secret Service	1939	WB
Cowboy Quarterback	1939	WB
The Crash	1928	FN
The Damned Don't Cry	1950	WB
Daredevil Drivers	1938	FN/WB
The Dawn Trail	1930	Col.
Deep Valley	1947	WB
The Desert Flower	1925	FN
Desert Vengeance	1931	Col.
The Devil's Saddle Legion	1937	WB
East of Eden	1954	WB
Empty Holsters	1937	WB
Fargo Express	1933	US
Father Is a Prince	1940	FN/WB
Feud of the West	1936	US
The Fiddlin' Buckaroo	1933	Univ.
The Fighting Legion	1930	Univ.
A Fine Madness	1966	WB
Flamingo Road	1949	WB
Flirting With Love	1924	FN
For Sale	1924	FN
Force of Arms	1951	WB
Freighters of Destiny	1932	RKO
Fugitive in the Sky	1937	WB
Ghost Valley	1932	RKO
Girl He Left Behind	1956	WB
Goodbye My Fancy	1951	WB
Gun Justice	1934	Univ.
Guns of the Pecos	1937	FN/WB
The Hanging Tree	1958	WB
The Helen Morgan Story	1957	WB
Hell Fire Austin *	1932	US
Hero's Island	1962	UA
Highway West	1941	WB
Honor of the Range	1934	Univ.
I Died a Thousand Times	1955	WB
I Was Framed	1942	WB
Irene	1926	FN
Johnny Belinda	1948	WB
June Bride	1948	WB
Knockout	1941	FN/WB
Ladies Must Live	1940	WB
The Lady Takes a Sailor	1949	WB
Land Beyond the Law	1937	WB
The Lone Rider	1930	Col.
Lucky Larkin	1930	Univ.
The Man from Monterey	1933	WB

The Marriage Whirl	1925	FN
The McConnell Story *	1955	WB
Men without Law	1930	Col.
Mountain Justice	1930	Univ.
Murder in the Air	1940	FN/WB
Murder in the Big House	1942	WB
Nine Lives Are Not Enough	1941	WB
Operation Secret	1952	WB
The Pace That Thrills	1925	FN
Parade of the West	1930	Univ.
The Phantom City	1928	FN
Prairie Thunder *	1937	FN/WB
Pride of the Bluegrass	1939	WB
Private Detective	1939	FN/WB
Private Property	1960	US
The Proud Rebel	1958	MGM
The Rainmakers	1935	US
Ride Him Cowboy	1932	Vita./WB
Rocky Mountain	1950	WB
Rocky Rhodes	1934	Univ.
The Royal Rider	1929	FN
Sacred and Profane Love	1921	Par.
Saddle Buster	1932	Pathe/RKO
Sally	1925	FN
Secret Service of the Air	1939	WB
Senor Americano	1929	Univ.
Sergeant Murphy	1938	WB
Shadow Ranch	1930	Col.
She Couldn't Say No	1941	WB
Singapore Woman	1941	FN/WB
Smart Girls Don't Talk	1948	WB
Smog	1962	It.
Smoling Guns	1934	Univ.
So Big	1924	FN
Somewhere in Sonora	1933	WB
Song of the Caballero	1930	Univ.
Sons of the Saddle	1930	Univ.
The Sound of Music	1965	TCF
South Seas Woman	1953	WB
Starlift	1951	WB
Stone of Silver Creek	1935	Univ.
Stop, You're Killing Me	1953	WB
Strawberry Roan	1933	Univ.
Sundown Trail	1931	Pathe/RKO
The Telegraph Trail	1933	FN/WB
That Way With Women	1947	WB
This Woman Is Dangerous	1952	WB
Tombstone Canyon	1932	US
The Trail Drive	1933	Univ.
Trailin' West *	1936	FN/WB
The Treasure of the Sierra Madre	1948	WB

Two for the Seesaw	1962	UA
The Upland Rider	1928	FN
Valley of the Giants	1927	FN
The Wagon Master	1929	Univ.
War Hunt	1961	US
We Moderns	1925	FN
Wheels of Destiny	1934	Univ.
When a Man Sees Red	1935	Univ.
Wild Bill Hickok Rides	1941	WB
Young At Heart	1954	WB
Young Man With a Horn	1950	WB

404. WILLIAM H. McCOY

Bab's Candidate	1920	Vita.
If Women Only Knew	1921	US
The Man Who Couldn't Beat God	1915	Vita.
The Midnight Bride	1920	Vita.
The Sea Rider	1920	Vita.

405. BARNEY McGILL (1892-1942)

Across the Atlantic	1928	WB
Alias the Doctor	1932	FN/WB
Battle of Broadway	1938	TCF
The Beast of the City *	1932	MGM
Beauty and the Boss	1932	WB
Born To Be Bad	1934	TC
The Bowery	1933	TC
Breezy Jim	1919	US
Brewster's Millions *	1935	GB
Broadway Thru a Keyhole	1933	UA
Bureau of Missing Persons	1933	WB
Cabin in the Cotton	1932	WB
Casey at the Bat	1927	Par.
Charlie Chan in Shanghai	1935	Fox
The Cisco Kid	1931	Fox
The College Widow	1927	WB
The Country Beyond	1936	TCF
Crack Up	1936	TCF
The Crimson City	1928	WB
Critical Age	1922	US
Desert Song	1929	WB
Devil McCare	1919	US
Doorway To Hell	1930	WB
Employees' Entrance	1933	WB
Everybody's Old Man	1936	TCF
Evidence	1929	WB
First Baby	1935	Fox

Folies Bergere *	1935	TC
Girls Under 21	1940	Col.
Gold Diggers of Broadway *	1929	WB
Good Time Charley	1927	WB
Hard To Handle	1933	WB
High Tension	1936	TCF
The Home Towners	1928	WB
The House of Scandal	1928	US
Husbands For Rent	1927	WB
I Believed in You	1934	Fox
Jaws of Steel	1927	WB
Keep Smiling *	1925	US
The Keyhole	1933	WB
Lancer Spy	1937	TCF
The Last Gentleman	1934	Fox
Laughing at Trouble	1937	TCF
Lone Wolf Keeps a Date	1941	Col.
The Mad Genius	1931	WB
Mammy	1930	WB
The Mayor of Hell	1933	WB
Midnight Taxi	1937	TCF
Miss Pinkerton	1932	WB
The Mouthpiece	1932	WB
Murder in Trinidad	1934	Fox
My Lady Friends	1921	FN
My Marriage	1936	TCF
My Past	1931	WB
Nancy Steele Is Missing *	1937	TCF
Noah's Ark *	1929	WB
Off to the Races	1937	TCF
Other Men's Women	1931	WB
The Phantom Submarine	1941	Col.
The President Vanishes	1934	Par.
Redheads on Parade *	1935	Fox
The Rejuvenation of Aunt Mary	1927	US
A Self-Made Failure *	1924	FN
She Had to Eat	1937	TCF
Sharpshooters	1938	TCF
Show of Shows	1929	WB
Skin Deep	1929	WB
The Song and Dance Man	1936	TCF
Stark Mad	1929	WB
State Street Sadie	1928	WB
Svengali	1931	WB
The Terror	1928	WB
Thank You, Jeeves	1936	TCF
Three Faces West	1930	WB
Twenty Thousand Years in Sing Sing	1932	WB
A Trip to Chinatown	1926	Fox
What Price Glory *	1926	Fox

406. NICK McLEAN

Cannonball Run II	1984	WB
Cobra *	1986	WB
The Goonies	1985	WB
Mac and Me	1988	Orion
Spaceballs	1987	MGM-UA
Staying Alive	1983	Par.
Stick	1985	Univ.
Stoker Ace	1983	Univ./WB
Twice in a Lifetime	1985	US

407. GEORGE MEEHAN

Across the Sierras		
Alibi For Murder	1936	Col.
The Bandit of Sherwood Forest *	1946	Col.
Battling Buddy	1924	US
Ben-Hur *	1925	MGM
Beyond the Sacramento	1940	Col.
The Black Parachute	1944	Col.
Blazing Six Shooters	1940	Col.
Boston Blackie and the Law	1946	Col.
Boston Blackie Booked on Suspicion	1945	Col.
Boston Blackie's Rendezvous	1945	Col.
Bullets for Rustlers	1940	Col.
Code of the Range	1936	Col.
Convicted	1938	Col.
Cowboy in the Clouds	1943	Col.
Cowboy Canteen	1944	Col.
Criminals in the Air	1937	Col.
The Desperadoes *	1943	Col.
Down Rio Grande Way	1942	Col.
Escape in the Fog	1945	Col.
A Fight to the Finish	1925	Col.
A Fight to the Finish	1937	Col.
Fighting Youth	1925	Col.
Gallant Journey *	1946	Col.
The Ghost Talks	1929	Fox
Girl I Loved	1923	UA
Girls of the Road	1940	Col.
The Great Sensation	1925	Col.
The Handsome Brute	1925	Col.
Heart Punch	1932	US
Her First Beau	1941	Col.
Inside Information	1935	US
Justice of the Range	1935	Col.
Landrush	1946	Col.
The Last Horseman	1944	Col.
The Last Warning	1938	Univ.

Lawless Empire	1946	Col.
Legion of Terror	1936	Col.
Lure of the Wild	1925	Col.
The Man From Tumbleweeds	1940	Col.
A Man's World	1942	Col.
Manhattan Shakedown	1939	Col.
The Mark of the Whistler	1944	Col.
Mary of the Movies *	1923	US
Meet Miss Bobby Socks	1944	Col.
Murder Is News	1939	Col.
The Mysterious Avenger	1936	Col.
New Champion	1925	Col.
North of the Yukon	1939	Col.
The Officer and the Lady	1941	Col.
Out of the Storm *	1926	US
Outlaws of the Panhandle	1941	Col.
Outpost of the Mounties	1939	Col.
Paid to Dance	1937	Col.
Pardon My Gun	1943	Col.
Parole Racket	1937	Col.
Paying the Price	1927	Col.
The Phantom Thief	1946	Col.
The Pinto Kid	1941	Col.
Pioneers of the Frontier	1940	Col.
Prairie Schooners	1940	Col.
The Return of Wild Bill	1940	Col.
Riders of Black River	1939	Col.
Rough, Tough and Ready	1945	Col.
The Royal Mounted Patrol	1941	Col.
S.O.S. Perils of the Sea	1925	Col.
Secret Patrol *	1936	Col.
Singin' in the Corn	1946	Col.
Special Inspector	1939	US
Speed Mad	1925	Col.
Stampede *	1936	Col.
The Stranger From Texas	1940	Col.
Sundown Valley	1944	Col.
A Tailor Made Man *	1922	UA
Taming of the West	1939	Col.
Tarzan's Revenge	1938	TCF
Texas	1941	Col.
Texas Stagecoach	1940	Col.
Thanks For Everything *	1938	TCF
The Thundering Frontier	1940	Col.
There's Something About a Soldier *	1944	Col.
Too Tough To Kill	1935	Col.
Two in a Taxi	1941	Col.
Two-Fisted Rangers	1940	Col.
Voice of the Whistler	1945	Col.
West of Abilene	1940	Col.
West of Tombstone	1942	Col.

The Westerner	1936	Col.
The Wildcat of Tucson	1940	Col.
Youth On Trial	1945	Col.

408. WILLIAM MELLOR (1904-1963)

Abie's Irish Rose	1946	UA
Across the Wide Missouri	1951	MGM
Affairs of Dobie Gillis	1953	MGM
Alaska Seas	1953	Par.
Ambush	1939	Par.
Back From Eternity	1956	RKO
Bad Day at Black Rock	1954	MGM
The Best of Everything	1959	TCF
Beyond the Blue Horizon *	1942	Par.
The Big Gamble *	1960	TCF
Big Leaguer	1953	MGM
The Birth of the BLues	1941	Par.
Blaze of Noon	1947	Par.
Bulldog Drummond in Africa	1938	Par.
Car 99	1935	Par.
Carbine Williams	1952	MGM
Champagne Waltz	1937	Par.
College Holiday *	1936	Par.
Collegiate	1936	Par.
Comin' Round the Mountain	1940	Par.
The Commandos Strike at Dawn	1942	Col.
Compulsion	1959	TCF
Crack in the Mirror	1960	TCF
The Diary of Anne Frank	1959	TCF
Disputed Passage	1939	Par.
Dixie *	1943	Par.
Elmer and Elsie	1934	Par.
Enter Madame *	1935	Par.
Exclusive	1937	Par.
The Fleet's In	1942	Par.
Giant *	1956	WB
Give a Girl a Break	1953	MGM
The Great Man's Lady	1942	Par.
The Great McGinty	1940	Par.
The Greatest Story Ever Told *	1965	UA
Home on the Range	1935	Par.
Hotel Imperial	1939	Par.
It's a Big Country *	1952	MGM
Johnny Concho	1956	UA
Las Vegas Nights	1941	Par.
The Last Frontier	1955	Col.
Love Happy	1949	US
Love in the Afternoon	1957	AA
The Magnificent Fraud	1939	Par.

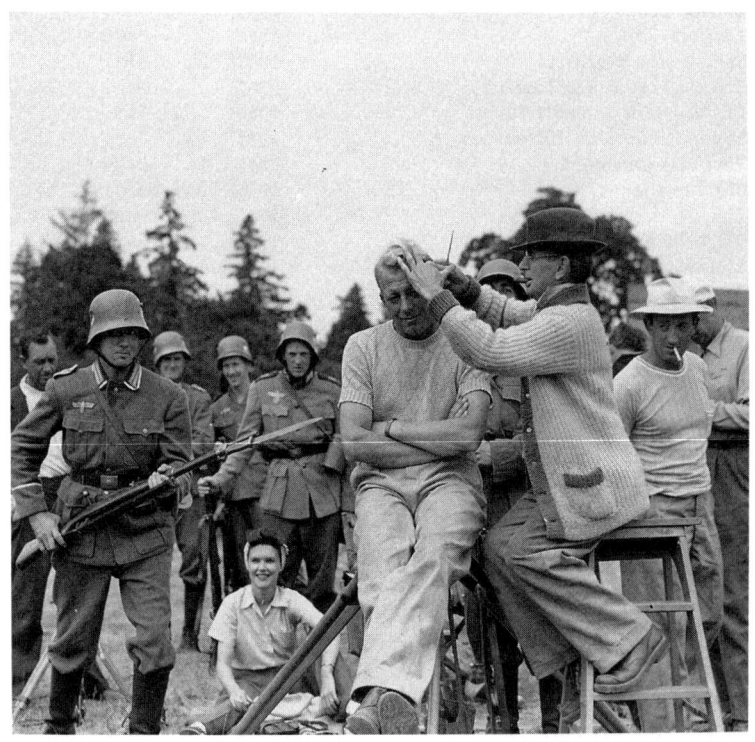

William Mellor gets his hair cut in this gag shot on the set of The Commandos Strike at Dawn (1942).

Make Way for Tomorrow	1937	Par.
Man-Eater of Kumaon	1948	Univ.
Mr. Hobbs Takes a Vacation	1962	TCF
Moon Over Burma	1940	Par.
My Favorite Blonde	1942	Par.
My Man and I	1952	MGM
The Naked Spur	1953	MGM
The Next Voice You Hear	1950	MGM
One Foot in Hell	1960	TCF
One Third of a Nation	1939	US
Peyton Place	1957	TCF
A Place in the Sun	1951	Par.
Poppy	1936	Par.
Reaching for the Sun	1941	Par.
Ride a Crooked Mile	1938	Par.
Road to Morocco	1942	Par.
Road to Singapore	1940	Par.
Romance in the Dark	1938	Par.
The Senator Was Indiscreet	1947	Univ.
Sing, Boy, SIng	1958	TCF
Skirts Ahoy!	1952	MGM
Sky Parade	1936	Par.
Soldiers Three	1951	MGM
A Son Comes Home	1936	Par.
State Fair	1962	TCF
Stolen Heaven	1938	Par.
Texas, Brooklyn and Heaven	1948	UA
$1000 a Touchdown	1939	Par.
Thrill of a Lifetime	1937	Par.
Tokyo After Dark	1959	Par.
Too Late for Tears	1949	UA
Typhoon *	1940	Par.
Undercover Doctor	1939	Par.
The Unknown Man	1951	MGM
Wagon Wheels	1934	Par.
Wake Island *	1942	Par.
Westward the Women	1951	MGM
Wild in the Country	1961	TCF
Wings in the Dark *	1935	Par.
Woman Obsessed	1959	TCF
Woman Trap	1936	Par.

409. CHRIS MENGES

Angel	1982	GB
Babylon	1980	GB
Black Beauty	1971	GB
Black Jack	1980	GB
Bloody Kids	1979	GB
Comfort and Joy	1984	Univ.

Fatherland	1986	Ger./GB
Gumshoe	1971	GB--Col.
High Season!	1987	GB
Kes	1969	GB--UA
The Killing Fields	1984	WB
Local Hero	1983	WB
Looks and Smiles	1981	GB
Loving Walter	1986	GB
Marie	1985	MGM-UA
The Mission	1986	WB
Shy People	1987	Cannon
Winter Flight	1984	GB

410. JOHN MESCALL (1899-   )

Affairs of a Gentleman	1934	Univ.
All's Fair in Love	1921	Gold.
Almost Married	1932	Fox
Andy Hardy's Double Life *	1942	MGM
Below the Line *	1925	WB
The Black Cat	1934	Univ.
Born To Love	1931	RKO
The Bride of Frankenstein	1935	Univ.
The Bridge of Sighs	1925	WB
Brothers under the Skin	1922	Gold.
By Candlelight	1934	Univ.
Dangerous Curve Ahead	1921	Gold.
Dark Waters *	1944	UA
Davy Crockett, Indian Scout *	1950	UA
The Desperadoes Are in Town	1956	TCF
The Easiest Way	1931	MGM
Follow Your Heart *	1936	Rep.
From the Ground Up	1921	Gold.
Gimme	1923	Gold.
The Glorious Fool	1922	Gold.
Happy Landing	1938	TCF
Henry Aldrich for President	1941	Par.
High Voltage	1929	Pathe
His First Command *	1929	Pathe
His Hour	1924	Metro.-Gold.
Hold Your Horses	1921	Gold.
I've Been Around	1935	Univ.
It's a Great Life	1920	Gold.
Josette	1938	TCF
Kit Carson *	1940	UA
The Leatherneck	1929	Pathe
The Leopard Lady	1928	Pathe
Love Over Night	1928	Pathe
The Love Toy	1926	WB
Magnificent Obsession	1935	Univ.

Make a Wish	1937	RKO
Man-Made Woman	1928	Pathe
My Lucky Star	1938	TCF
New Morals for Old	1932	MGM
New Wine	1941	UA
A Night in New Orleans	1942	Par.
Night Life of the Gods	1935	Univ.
Night of January 16th	1941	Par.
Night Work	1930	Pathe
Not of This Earth	1947	AA
Oh, What a Nurse!	1926	WB
One More River	1934	Univ.
The Poor Rich	1934	Univ.
The Quiet Gun	1957	TCF
Red Hot Rhythm	1929	Pathe
Reno	1923	Gold.
Return of Casey Jones	1933	Mon.
The Road Back *	1937	Univ.
Sal of Singapore	1929	Pathe
Sensations of 1945	1944	UA
Shady Lady	1929	Pathe
Showboat	1936	Univ.
Silken Shackles *	1926	WB
Sin Takes a Holiday	1930	Pathe/RKO
Six Days	1923	Gold.
Skyline	1931	Fox
Smart Girl	1935	Par.
So This Is Paris	1926	WB
The Social Highwayman	1926	WB
The Sophomore	1929	Pathe
Souls For Sale	1923	Gold.
South of Pago Pago	1940	UA
The Student Prince in Old Heidelberg	1927	MGM
Sweater Girl	1942	Par.
Take a Letter, Darling	1942	Par.
The Tenth Woman	1924	WB
Three Russian Girls	1944	UA
Three Weeks	1924	Gold.
True As Steel	1924	Gold.
Walking Back	1928	Pathe
The Wall Flower	1922	Gold.
Watch Your Step	1922	Gold.
When Tomorrow Comes	1939	Univ.
Wife Who Wasn't Wanted *	1925	WB
Wine of Youth	1924	Metro.-Gold.
The Woman Hater	1925	WB
The Wreck of the Hesperus	1927	Pathe
Youth Runs Wild	1944	RKO

411. RUSSELL METTY (1906-1978)

The Affairs of Annabel	1938	RKO
Against All Flags	1952	Univ.
All My Sons	1948	Univ.
All That Heaven Allows	1955	Univ.
Annabel Takes a Tour	1938	RKO
Annapolis Salute	1937	RKO
The Appaloosa	1966	Univ.
Arch of Triumph	1948	US
Around the World	1943	RKO
Army Surgeon	1942	RKO
The Art of Love	1965	Univ.
Bagdad	1949	Univ.
Battle Hymn	1957	Univ.
Because of You	1952	Univ.
Behind the Headlines	1937	RKO
Behind the Rising Sun	1943	RKO
Ben	1972	US
Betrayal From the East	1945	RKO
The Big Street	1942	RKO
Breakfast in Hollywood	1946	UA
Bringing Up Baby	1938	RKO
Buccanneer's Girl	1949	Univ.
Bus Riley's Back in Town	1965	Univ.
By Love Possessed	1961	UA
Cancel My Reservation	1972	WB
Captain Newman MD	1963	Univ.
Change of Habit	1969	Univ.
Congo Crossing	1956	Univ.
Counterpoint	1967	Univ.
Crashout	1955	US
Cult of the Cobra	1955	Univ.
Curtain Call	1940	RKO
Curtain Call at Cactus Creek	1949	Univ.
Dance, Girl, Dance	1940	RKO
The Desert Hawk	1950	Univ.
Everything's On Ice	1939	RKO
Eye of the Cat *	1969	Univ.
The Falcon's Brother	1942	RKO
The Female Animal	1957	Univ.
Flame of Araby	1952	Univ.
Flower Drum Song	1961	Univ.
Forever and a Day *	1943	RKO
40 Naughty Girls	1937	RKO
Four Guns to the Border	1954	Univ.
Four Jacks and a Jill	1941	RKO
A Girl, a Guy and a Gob	1941	RKO
The Girl and the Gambler	1939	RKO
The Golden Horde	1951	Univ.
The Great Man Votes	1939	RKO

Hitler's Children	1943	RKO
How Do I Love Thee?	1970	ABC
I'd Rather Be Rich	1964	Univ.
If a Man Answers	1962	Univ.
Imitation of Life	1959	Univ.
The Interns	1962	Col.
Irene	1940	RKO
It Happens Every Thursday	1953	Univ.
It's in the Bag	1945	UA
Ivy	1947	Univ.
Joan of Paris	1942	RKO
Katie Did It	1951	Univ.
Kiss the Blood Off My Hands	1948	Univ.
The Lady Gambles	1949	Univ.
Little Egypt	1951	Univ.
Madame X	1965	Univ.
Madigan	1968	Univ.
Magnificent Obsession	1954	Univ.
Man Afraid	1957	Univ.
The Man From Bitter Ridge	1955	Univ.
The Man From the Alamao	1953	Univ.
The Man of a Thousand Faces	1957	Univ.
Man without a Star	1955	Univ.
The Master Race	1944	RKO
Mexican Spitfire Sees a Ghost	1942	RKO
Midnight Lace	1960	Univ.
The Midnight Story	1957	Univ.
Miracle in the Rain	1956	WB
The Misfits	1961	UA
Mister Cory	1957	Univ.
Mr. Doodle Kicks Off	1938	RKO
Mr. Peabody and the Mermaid	1948	Univ.
Monster on the Campus	1958	Univ.
Music In Manhattan	1944	RKO
Naked Alibi	1954	Univ.
Next Time I Marry	1938	RKO
Night Waitress	1936	RKO
No, No, Nanette	1940	RKO
The Omega Man	1971	WB
Pardon My Past	1945	Col.
Peggy	1950	Univ.
The Perfect Marriage	1946	Par.
The Pink Jungle	1968	Univ.
Platinum High School	1960	MGM
Portrait in Black	1960	Univ.
Private Affairs of Bel Ami	1947	UA
The Raging Tide	1951	Univ.
Ride the Pink Horse	1947	Univ.
Room Service	1938	RKO
Rough Night in Jericho	1967	Univ.
The Scarlet Angel	1952	Univ.

The Secret War of Harry Frigg	1967	Univ.
Seminole	1953	Univ.
Seven Days Ashore	1944	RKO
Sierra	1950	Univ.
Sign of the Pagan	1954	Univ.
The Sky's the Limit *	1943	RKO
Spartacus	1960	Univ.
The Spellbinder	1939	RKO
Step Down to Terror	1958	Univ.
The Story of GI Joe	1945	UA
The Stranger	1946	RKO
Sunny	1941	RKO
Take Me to Town	1953	Univ.
Tammy and the Doctor	1963	Univ.
Taza, Son of Cochise	1954	Univ.
Tender Comrade	1943	RKO
Texas across the River	1966	Univ.
That Touch of Mink	1962	Univ.
That's Right, You're Wrong	1939	RKO
There's Always Tomorrow	1956	Univ.
They Wanted to Marry	1937	RKO
The Thing That Couldn't Die	1958	Univ.
This Earth Is Mine *	1959	Univ.
Thoroughly Modern Millie	1967	Univ.
Three Sons	1939	RKO
The Thrill of It All	1963	Univ.
A Time to Love and a Time to Die *	1958	Univ.
Touch of Evil	1958	Univ.
Treasure of Lost Canyon	1952	Univ.
Tribes	1970	TCF
Tumbleweed	1953	Univ.
Up Front	1951	Univ.
Veils of Bagdad	1953	Univ.
The War Lord	1965	Univ.
We Were Strangers	1949	Col.
Weekend For Three	1941	RKO
West of the Pecos *	1934	RKO
Whistle Stop	1946	UA
A Woman's Vengeance	1948	Univ.
The World in His Arms	1952	Univ.
Written on the Wind	1956	Univ.
Wyoming Mail	1950	Univ.
Yankee Buccaneer	1952	Univ.
You Can't Beat Love	1937	RKO
You Gotta Stay Happy	1948	Univ.

412. REXFORD METZ

Every Which Way But Loose	1978	WB
Forced Vengeance	1982	MGM-UA

The Gauntlet	1977	WB
Jim, the World's Greatest *	1976	Univ.
Serial	1980	Par.

413. RUSS MEYER (1923-   )

Beneath the Valley of the Ultravixens	1979	US
Cherry, Harry and Raquel	1969	US
Desperate Women	1954	US
Eve and the Handyman	1961	US
Finders Keepers, Lovers Weepers	1968	US
Good Morning and Goodbye!	1968	US
Heavenly Bodies	1963	US
The Immoral West and How It Was Lost	1962	US
The Immortal Mr. Teas	1960	US
Lorna	1964	US
Motor Psycho	1965	US
Supervixens	1975	US
Up	1976	US
Vixen	1968	US

414. PIERRE MIGNOT

L'Affaire Coffin	1980	Can.
Anne Trister	1986	Can.
Beyond Therapy	1987	US
Blizzard	1990	Can.
The Boy in BLue	1986	TCF
Come Back to the Five & Dime...		
Jimmie Dean, Jimmie Dean	1982	US
Cordelia	1980	Can./Fr.
Day in a Taxi	1982	Can.
Fool For Love	1985	Cannon
J. A. Martin: Photographe	1977	Can.
Lucien Brouillard	1983	Can.
Maria Chapdelaine	1983	Can.
Mario	1984	Can.
Meet Market	1989	Can.
O. C. and Stiggs	1987	MGM-UA
Secret Honor	1984	US
Straight to the Heart	1988	Can./Switz.
Streamers	1983	UA

415. ARTHUR MILLER (1895-1970)

The Angel of Broadway	1927	Pathe
Anna and the King of Siam	1946	TCF
Annapolis	1928	Pathe

Arms and the Woman	1916	US
The Avalanche	1919	Par.
Bad Company	1931	RKO
The Baroness and the Butler	1938	TCF
Bella Donna	1923	Par.
Big Jim Garrity	1916	US
The Big Shot	1931	RKO
Black Sheep	1935	Fox
The Blue Bird *	1940	TCF
The Blue Danube	1928	Pathe
Bottoms Up	1934	Fox
Breach of Promise	1941	MGM
Brigham Young Frontiersman	1940	TCF
Bright Eyes	1934	Fox
The Cheat	1923	Par.
The Clinging Vine	1926	Pathe
Common Clay	1919	Pathe
The Coming of Amos	1925	PDC
Convict 993	1918	Pathe
The Cop	1928	Pathe
Counterfeit	1919	Par.
The Cry of the Weak	1919	Pathe
Cytherea	1924	FN
Dragonwyck	1946	TCF
The Eternal City	1923	FN
Eve's Leaves	1926	PDC
Experience	1921	Par.
Father's Son	1931	FN/WB
The Fighting Eagle	1927	Pathe
Flying Fool	1929	Pathe
For Alimony Only	1926	PDC
Forever	1921	Par.
Gentleman's Agreement	1947	TCF
The Gunfighter	1950	TCF
Handy Andy	1934	Fox
Heidi	1937	TCF
Her I Am a Stranger	1939	TCF
The Hillcrest Mystery	1918	Pathe
His First Command *	1929	Pathe
His House in Order	1920	Par.
His Supreme Moment	1925	FN/Gold.
Hold 'Em Yale!	1928	Pathe
How Green Was My Valley	1941	TCF
The Hunting of the Hawk	1917	Pathe
Iceland	1942	TCF
Idols of Clay	1920	Par.
In Hollywood With Potash and Perlemutter *	1924	FN/Gold.
Immortal Sergeant	1943	TCF
It's a Small World	1935	Fox
A Japanese Nightingale *	1918	Pathe

Johnny Apollo	1940	TCF
The Keys of the Kingdom	1944	TCF
Kick In	1922	Par.
Lady of Scandal *	1930	MGM
Lady Rose's Daughter	1920	Par.
The Last Trail	1934	Fox
A Letter to Three Wives	1949	TCF
The Little Colonel	1935	Fox
Little Miss Broadway	1938	TCF
The Little Princess *	1939	TCF
Love Time	1934	Fox
The Mad Game	1933	Fox
Made for Love	1926	PDC
Man Hunt	1941	TCF
The Man Who Dared	1933	Fox
The Mark of Cain	1917	Pathe
The Mark of Zorro	1940	TCF
Me and My Gal	1932	Fox
The Men in Her Life *	1941	Col.
The Moon Is Down	1943	TCF
The Narrow Path *	1918	Pathe
The Naulakha	1918	Pathe
New York	1916	US
Nobody's Widow	1927	PDC
Officer O'Brien	1930	Pathe
Oh, Yeah!	1929	Pathe
Okay America	1932	Univ.
On Their Own	1940	TCF
On with the Dance	1920	Par.
Our Better Selves	1919	Pathe
The Ox-Bow Incident	1943	TCF
Paddy O'Day	1935	Fox
Panama Flo	1932	RKO
Paying the Piper	1921	Par.
Pigskin Parade	1936	TCF
The Profiteers	1919	Pathe
The Prowler	1951	UA
The Purple Heart	1944	TCF
The Rains Came	1939	TCF
The Razor's Edge	1946	TCF
Rebecca of Sunnybrook Farm	1938	TCF
The Recoil	1917	Pathe
The Right To Love	1920	Par.
The Romantic Journey	1916	US
A Royal Scandal	1945	TCF
Sailor's Holiday	1929	Pathe
Sailor's Luck	1933	Fox
See America Thirst	1933	Fox
A Society Exile	1919	Par.
Son of Fury	1942	TCF
The Song of Bernadette	1943	TCF

The Spieler	1928	Pathe
Stranded in Arcady	1917	US
Strange Cargo	1929	Pathe
Stowaway	1936	TCF
Submarine Patrol	1938	TCF
Sylvia of the Secret Service	1917	Pathe
Tarnish *	1924	FN/Gold.
The Thief in Paradise	1925	FN
36 Hours to Kill	1936	TCF
This Above All	1942	TCF
Three Live Ghosts	1922	Par.
To Have and To Hold	1922	Par.
Tobacco Road	1941	TCF
The Truth About Youth	1930	FN
Vanity	1927	PDC
Vengeance Is Mine	1918	US
The Volga Boatman *	1926	PDC
The Walls of Jericho	1948	TCF
Wee Willie Winkie	1937	TCF
Welcome Home	1935	Fox
Whirlpool	1950	TCF
White Fang	1936	TCF
The White Parade	1934	Fox
The Witness for the Defense *	1919	Par.
Young Bride	1932	RKO

416. ERNEST MILLER

Affairs of Cappy Ricks	1937	Rep.
The Albany Night Boat	1928	US
Alias the Night Wind	1923	Fox
Alimony Madness	1933	US
All over Town	1937	Rep.
Angels With Broken Wings	1941	Rep.
Arizona Terrors	1942	Rep.
Arkansas Judge	1941	Rep.
Army Girl	1938	Rep.
Arson Gang Busters	1938	Rep.
Back in the Saddle	1941	Rep.
Bandit Queen	1950	Lip.
Barnyard Follies	1940	Rep.
Battle Zone	1952	AA
Beating the Game	1921	Gold.
Behind Green Lights	1935	US
Behind Jury Doors	1933	GB
Bells of Rosarita	1945	Rep.
Beneath Western Skies	1944	Rep.
Billy the Kid Returns	1938	Rep.
Bitter Creek	1954	AA
Black Hills	1948	EL

Black Hills Express	1943	Rep.
Black Lash	1952	US
The Bold Frontiersman	1948	Rep.
Border Rangers	1950	Lip.
The Border Whirlwind	1926	US
The Boss of Camp Four *	1922	Fox
Bowery Boy	1941	Rep.
Bulldog Pluck	1927	US
Cactus Trails	1927	US
California Joe	1944	Rep.
Call of the Yukon	1938	Rep.
Calling All Marines	1939	Rep.
Calling Wild Bill Elliott	1943	Rep.
Chance of a Lifetime	1943	Col.
Chastity *	1923	FN
Chatterbox	1943	Rep.
Check Your Guns	1947	EL
Cheyenne Takes Over	1947	EL
Citadel of Crime	1941	Rep.
Clearing the Range	1931	US
Colorado Ranger	1940	Lip.
Come On Cowboys	1937	Rep.
Come On Leathernecks	1938	Rep.
Confidential *	1935	Rep.
Country Fair	1941	Rep.
Country Fair	1941	Rep.
Country Gentleman	1937	Rep.
Cowboys from Texas	1939	Rep.
Crimson Romance	1934	US
Crooked River	1950	Lip.
The Crooked Road	1940	Rep.
Dancing Feet *	1936	Rep.
Dead Man's Gulch *	1943	Rep.
Death Valley Gunfighter	1949	Rep.
Death Valley Manhunt	1943	Rep.
The Devil's Apple Tree	1929	US
The Devil's Skipper	1928	US
Domestic Meddlers	1928	US
Down in Arkansaw	1938	Rep.
Driven from Home	1927	US
The Dude Cowboy	1926	US
Eager Lips *	1927	US
The Enchanted Valley	1948	EL
Ex-Flame	1930	US
Exiled to Shanghai	1937	Rep.
Fair Play	1925	US
Fast on the Draw	1950	Lip.
The Fighting Hombre	1927	US
The Fighting Vigilantes	1947	EL
Flight at Midnight	1939	Rep.
Forgotten Girls	1940	Rep.

The Fortyniners	1954	AA
Friendly Neighbors	1940	Rep.
Frontier Investigator	1949	Rep.
Galloping Thunder	1927	US
Gangs of New York	1938	Rep.
The Gay Amigo	1949	UA
Gentleman from Louisiana *	1936	Rep.
Ghost Town Renegades	1947	PRC
Ghost Valley Raiders	1940	Rep.
Girl from Havana	1940	Rep.
Girl from Mandalay *	1936	Rep.
The Grain of Dust	1928	US
Grand Canyon	1949	Lip.
Gunfire	1940	Lip.
Guns and Guitars	1937	Rep.
Hair Trigger Baxter *	1926	US
Happy Go Lucky	1937	Rep.
Harmony Lane *	1935	Rep.
The Hawk of Powder River	1948	EL/PRC
The Headline Woman	1935	US
Hearts in Bondage *	1936	Rep.
Hellgate	1952	Lip.
Her Adventurous Night	1946	Univ.
Her Resale Value	1933	US
Hitch Hike Lady *	1936	Rep.
Hollywood Mystery	1934	US
Hollywood Stadium Mystery	1938	Rep.
Home in Wyomin'	1942	Rep.
The Homesteaders	1953	AA
Honor of the Press	1932	US
Hostile Country	1950	Lip.
The House of a Thousand Candles *	1936	Rep.
Hurricane Smith	1942	Rep.
Hutch of the U.S.A.	1924	US
I Shot Billy the Kid	1950	Lip.
I Shot Jesse James	1949	Lip.
Identity Unknown	1945	Rep.
In Old Missouri	1940	Rep.
In Old Monterrey	1939	Rep.
In Old Santa Fe *	1934	US
The Jazz Girl	1926	US
Jeepers Creepers	1939	Rep.
Joan of Ozark	1942	Rep.
Join the Marines	1937	Rep.
Joy Street	1929	Fox
Kansas Territory	1952	Mon.
Kansas Terrors	1939	Rep.
King of the Bullwhip	1951	US
Ladies at Ease	1927	US
Ladies Crave Excitement *	1935	US
The Ladybird *	1927	US

Laughing at Life *	1933	US
Law of the Golden West	1949	Rep.
Lawless Cowboys	1952	Mon.
The Leathernecks Have Landed *	1936	Rep.
The Leavenworth Case *	1936	Rep.
Life of an Actress	1927	US
The Lightning Warrior *	1931	US
Little Big Horn	1951	Lip.
Little Men *	1935	US
The Longhorn	1951	Mon.
Love Trader *	1930	US
Made in Heaven	1921	Gold.
Mama Runs Wild	1938	Rep.
The Man from the Black Hills	1952	Mon.
Man's Size *	1923	Fox
The Marines Are Coming *	1935	US
Marriage by Contract	1928	US
Marshal of Heldorado	1950	Lip.
The Maverick	1952	AA
Meet the Boy Friend	1937	Rep.
Meet the Missus	1940	Rep.
Melody and Moonlight	1940	Rep.
Melody Trail	1935	Rep.
Mister Antonio	1929	US
Molly and Me *	1929	US
Money to Burn	1940	Rep.
Motor Patrol	1950	Lip.
Mountain Rhythm	1939	Rep.
The Mysterious Miss X	1939	Rep.
Naughty	1927	US
The Naughty Duchess *	1928	US
Navy Born *	1936	Rep.
The Night Flyer	1928	Pathe
Night Raiders	1952	Mon.
No Holds Barred	1952	Mon.
The Old Barn Dance	1938	Rep.
The Old Homestead	1943	Rep.
On Probation	1924	US
On to Reno	1928	Pathe
One Frightened Night	1935	US
Orphans of the Street	1939	Rep.
Outlaw Country	1949	US
Pioneer Justice	1947	PRC
Poison	1924	US
Prairie Pioneers	1941	Rep.
The President's Mystery	1936	Rep.
Prison Nurse	1938	Rep.
Prowlers of the Sea	1928	US
Public Enemies	1942	Rep.
The Purple V	1943	Rep.
The Purple Vigilantes	1938	Rep.

Radar Secret Service	1950	Lip.
Ragtime *	1927	US
Raiders of the Range	1942	Rep.
The Rebel City	1953	AA
Red Desert	1949	Lip.
Refuge *	1923	FN
Remember Pearl Harbor	1942	Rep.
Return of the Lash	1947	EL/PRC
The Return of Wildfire	1948	Lip.
Revenge at Monte Carlo	1933	US
Riders of the Rio Grande	1944	Rep.
Rimfire	1949	Lip.
Ringside	1949	Lip.
Road to Alcatraz	1945	Rep.
Romance on the Run	1938	Rep.
Rookies on Parade	1941	Rep.
Sagebrush Troubadour	1936	Rep.
Sailors on Leave	1941	Rep.
Saved by Radio	1922	US
Say It with Diamonds	1927	US
The Scarlet Dove	1928	US
Scatterbrain	1940	Rep.
Scotland Yard Investigator *	1945	Rep.
Sea Racketeers	1937	Rep.
Secrets of the Underground	1942	Rep.
Shadow Valley	1947	EL/PRC
The Shamrock and the Rose	1927	US
Shantytown	1943	Rep.
She Married a Cop	1939	Rep.
She-Wolf	1931	Univ.
Shep Comes Home	1949	Lip.
Shepherd of the Ozarks	1942	Rep.
Sing, Dance, Plenty Hot	1940	Rep.
Skipalong Rosenbloom	1951	US
Son of a Badman	1949	US
Son of Billy the Kid	1949	US
Springtime in the Rockies	1937	Rep.
Stage to Blue River	1952	Mon.
Square Dance Jubilee	1949	Lip.
Star of Texas	1953	AA
Stars over Texas	1946	PRC
The Steel Helmet	1951	Lip.
Storm over Bengal	1938	Rep.
Stormy Waters	1928	US
Street of Missing Men	1939	Rep.
The Sundown Kid	1943	Rep.
Sunshine of Paradise Alley *	1926	US
Surging Seas	1924	US
Tell It to a Star	1945	Rep.
Tenth Avenue Kid	1938	Rep.
Terror of Bar X	1927	US

Texas City	1952	Mon.
Texas Lawmen	1951	Mon.
$1000 a Minute *	1935	Rep.
Three Texas Steers	1939	Rep.
Thumbs Up	1943	Rep.
The Thundering Trail	1951	US
Ticket To Paradise	1936	Rep.
The Tiger Woman	1945	Rep.
The Tioga Kid	1948	EL/PRC
The Toilers	1928	US
Topeka	1953	AA
A Tragedy at Midnight	1942	Rep.
Train to Tombstone	1950	Lip.
Trigger Trio	1937	Rep.
Troopers Three *	1930	US
Tropical Nights *	1928	US
Tumbleweed Trail	1946	PRC
Tumbling Tumbleweeds	1935	Rep.
Turned Up	1924	US
Tuxedo Junction	1941	Rep.
Two Wise Maids	1937	Rep.
Untamed Fury	1947	PRC
Valiant Hombre	1948	UA
The Valley of Bravery	1926	US
The Valley of Hate	1924	US
Village Barn Dance	1940	Rep.
Virtue's Revolt	1924	US
Waco	1952	Mon.
Wagons Westward	1940	Rep.
Was It Bigamy?	1925	US
Waterfront Lady	1935	Rep.
West of the Brazos	1950	Lip.
Western Pacific Agent	1950	Lip.
The Westward Trail	1948	EL/PRC
Whistling Hills	1951	Mon.
Wild Horse	1931	US
Woman Doctor	1939	Rep.
The Wrong Road	1937	Rep.
Yokel Boy	1942	Rep.
Youth on Parade	1943	Rep.
The Zero Hour	1939	Rep.

417. VIRGIL MILLER (1887-1974)

Alex the Great	1928	FBO
Amazing Vagabond	1929	RKO
Berlin Correspondent	1942	TCF
The Big Adventure	1921	Univ.
The Black Bag *	1922	Univ.
Blinky	1923	Univ.

Broadway or Bust	1924	Univ.
Broken Hearts of Hollywood *	1926	WB
Calling Dr. Death	1943	Univ.
Careless	1928	US
Charlie Chan at the Wax Museum	1940	TCF
Charlie Chan at Treasure Island	1939	TCF
Charlie Chan in City of Darkness	1939	TCF
Charlie Chan in Panama	1940	TCF
Charlie Chan in Reno	1939	TCF
Charlie Chan's Murder Cruise	1940	TCF
Chasing Danger	1939	TCF
Cheated Hearts	1921	Univ.
Colorado	1921	Univ.
Come and Get It	1929	FBO
Courage of the West	1937	Univ.
The Count of Ten *	1928	Univ.
Crazylegs All-American	1953	Rep.
Danger, Love at Work	1937	TCF
Dr. Renault's Secret	1942	TCF
Don't Shoot	1922	Univ.
Drift Fence	1937	Par.
Find the Witness	1937	Col.
The Falcon in San Francisco	1945	RKO
Finders Keepers	1928	Univ.
Finger Prints	1927	WB
The Flame of Life	1923	Univ.
The Flaming Frontier	1926	Univ.
40 Horse Hawkins	1924	Univ.
Gang War	1928	US
The Gay Old Bird	1927	WB
The Gentleman From America	1923	Univ.
Guardians of the Wild	1928	Univ.
Headin' For Danger	1928	RKO
Hit and Run	1924	Univ.
The Honeymoon's Over	1939	TCF
Hook and Ladder	1924	Univ.
The House of Fear	1945	Univ.
The Hurricane Kid	1925	Univ.
I Killed Wild Bill Hickok	1956	US
The Inside Story	1939	TCF
Irish Hearts	1927	WB
Kindled Courage	1923	Univ.
Laughing At Death	1929	FBO
Let 'Er Buck	1925	Univ.
The Little Savage	1929	RKO
The Lone Hand	1922	Univ.
Lorraine of the Lions	1925	Univ.
Luring Lips	1921	Univ.
Man At Large	1941	TCF
The Man Under Cover	1922	Univ.
Manhattan Heartbeat	1940	TCF

The Michigan Kid	1947	Univ.
Miss Robin Crusoe	1954	TCF
Mr. Moto Takes a Chance	1938	TCF
Mr. Moto's Last Warning	1939	TCF
Murder over New York	1940	TCF
Murder without Tears	1953	AA
Mysterious Mr. Moto	1938	TCF
Navajo	1952	Lip.
Nobody's Bride	1923	Univ.
Out of Luck	1923	Univ.
Pals of the Prarie	1929	FBO
The Pearl of Death	1944	Univ.
Phantom of the Opera *	1925	Univ.
Pier 13	1940	TCF
Pink Tights	1920	Univ.
Private Izzy Murphy	1926	WB
Private Nurse	1941	TCF
The Ramblin' Kid	1923	Univ.
Red Courage	1921	Univ.
The Red Stallion	1947	EL
Ride for Your Life	1924	Univ.
Ride, Kelly, Ride	1941	TCF
The Ridin' Kid from Powder River	1924	Univ.
Ridin' Wild	1922	Univ.
Ridin' Wild	1925	US
Right to the Heart	1942	TCF
The Runaway Express	1926	Univ.
The Saddle Hawk	1925	Univ.
The Sawdust Trail	1924	Univ.
The Scarlet Car	1923	Univ.
Scotland Yard	1941	TCF
The Scrapper	1922	Univ.
Shootin' For Love	1923	Univ.
The Silent Barrier *	1920	US
Singing Outlaw	1938	Univ.
Single Handed	1923	Univ.
Small Town Deb	1941	TCF
Stocks and Blondes	1928	FBO
Street Corner	1948	US
Sure Fire	1921	Univ.
Thank You, Mr. Moto	1937	TCF
The Thrill Chaser	1923	Univ.
Time Out for Murder	1938	TCF
The Trap	1922	Univ.
Two Kinds of Love	1920	Univ.
The Two Outlaws	1928	Univ.
Unchained	1955	WB
Under Western Skies	1926	Univ.
The Vagabond Cub	1929	FBO/RKO
The Vigilantes Return	1947	Univ.
Walking Down Broadway	1938	TCF

Weird Woman	1944	Univ.
Who Is Hope Schuyler?	1942	TCF
Woman I Love	1929	FBO
The Woman in Green	1945	Univ.
Young Whirlwind	1928	FBO

418. WILLIAM MILLER

Broken Barriers *	1928	US
Carnegie Hall	1947	UA
Chinatown Charlie *	1928	FN
The Clean-Up *	1929	US
Close-Up	1948	EL
Code of the Air	1928	US
The Dream Melody *	1929	US
Dynamite Delaney	1938	US
Green Fields *	1937	US
Home Made *	1927	FN
Lew Tyler's Wives	1926	US
Lost Boundaries	1949	US
Montmarte Rose *	1929	US
Moonlight and Pretzels	1933	Univ.
The Moral Sinner	1924	Par.
One Splendid Hour *	1929	US
The Romance of a Million Dollars *	1926	US
The Shock Punch	1925	Par.
Singing Blacksmith	1938	US
The Sleeping City	1940	Univ.
Sweet Surrender	1935	Univ.
Tango Bar	1935	Par.
Teresa	1951	MGM
The Wright Idea *	1928	FN

418a. ALEC MILLS

Biddy	1983	GB
Hot Target	1985	NZ
King Kong Lives	1986	US
License to Kill	1989	GB--MGM/UA
Lionheart	1987	Orion
Living Daylights	1987	MGM/UA

419. VICTOR MILNER (1893-   )

All of Me	1934	Par.
Artists and Models	1937	Par.
Blonde Or Brunette	1927	Par.
Broken Lullaby	1932	Par.

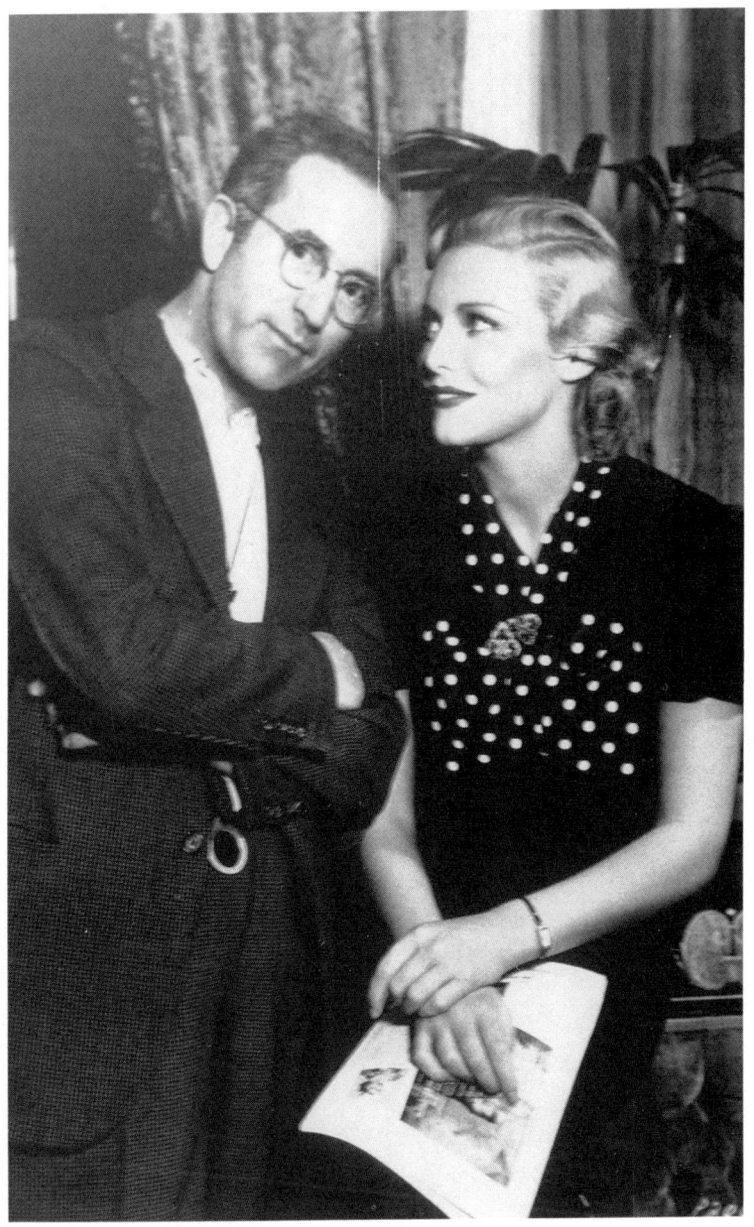

Victor Milner with Madeleine Carroll (ca. 1936).

The Buccaneer	1938	Par.
Bulldog Drummond Escapes	1937	Par.
The Cabaret Girl	1919	Univ.
Carrie	1952	Par.
The Cat's Pajamas	1926	Par.
Cause for Divorce	1923	Selz.
The Cave GIrl	1921	FN
Children of Divorce	1927	Par.
Christmas in July	1940	Par.
Cleopatra	1934	Par.
College Swing	1938	Par.
The Crusades	1935	Par.
A Dangerous Game	1922	Univ.
Dark City	1950	Par.
Daughter of the Dragon	1931	Par.
Design for Living	1933	Par.
Desire *	1936	Par.
Dice of Destiny	1920	Pathe
East of Suez	1925	Par.
Felix O'Day	1920	Pathe
Fugitive from Matrimony	1919	US
The Furies	1950	Par.
The General Died at Dawn	1936	Par.
The Gilded Lily	1935	Par.
Give Me a Sailor	1938	Par.
Give Us This Night *	1937	Par.
Gossip	1923	Univ.
The Great Moment	1944	Par.
The Great Victor Herbert	1939	Par.
Half a Bride	1928	Par.
Haunting Shadows	1920	US
Her Night of Nights	1922	Univ.
Her Unwilling Husband	1920	Pathe
High, Wide and Handsome	1937	Par.
Hostages	1943	Par.
Human Hearts	1922	Univ.
Hunted Men	1938	Par.
I Take This Woman	1931	Par.
It's a Wonderful Life *	1946	RKO
Jeopardy	1952	MGM
The Kentucky Derby	1922	Univ.
Kick-In	1931	Par.
Kid Boots	1926	Par.
Ladies' Man	1931	Par.
Lady of the Harem	1926	Par.
The Lavendar Bath Lady	1922	Univ.
Learning To Love	1925	FN
Let's Go Native	1930	Par.
Live Wires	1921	Fox
The Love Letter	1923	Univ.
Love Me Tonight	1932	Par.

The Love Parade	1929	Par.
Loves of an Actress	1928	Par.
Lucky Lady	1926	Par.
Luxury Liner	1933	Par.
The Man I Killed	1932	Par.
Man Who Lost Himself	1941	Univ.
The Marriage Playground	1929	Par.
Monte Carlo	1930	Par.
My Favorite Spy	1951	Par.
My Life with Caroline	1941	RKO
No Limit	1931	Par.
Northwest Mounted Police *	1940	Par.
On the Stroke of Three *	1924	US
One Hour before Dawn	1920	Pathe
One Hour with You	1932	Par.
One Sunday Afternoon	1933	Par.
The Other Love	1947	US
Our Leading Citizen	1939	Par.
Out of the Dust	1920	US
The Palm Beach Story	1942	Par.
Paramount on Parade *	1930	Par.
The Plainsman *	1936	Par.
Play Square	1921	Fox
The Princess and the Pirate *	1944	Gold.
Reap the Wild Wind *	1942	Par.
The Red Lily	1924	Metro.-Gold.
The River of Romance	1929	Par.
Rolled Stockings	1927	Par.
Say It in French	1938	Par.
The Sealed Envelope	1919	Univ.
Seventeen	1940	Par.
Shadows of Conscience	1921	US
The Showdown	1928	Par.
Sins of the Fathers	1928	Par.
So Red the Rose	1935	Par.
Song of Songs	1933	Par.
The Spaniard	1925	Par.
The Spotlight	1927	Par.
The Story of Dr. Wassell *	1944	Par.
The Strange Love of Martha Ivers	1946	Par.
The Street of Sin *	1928	Par.
The Studio Murder Mystery	1929	Par.
The Texan	1930	Par.
Those Were the Days	1940	Par.
Three Sinners	1928	Par.
Thy Name Is Woman	1924	Metro.
Till We Meet Again	1936	Par.
Touchdown, Army!	1938	Par.
The Town Scandal	1923	Univ.
Trouble in Paradise	1932	Par.
True to the Navy	1930	Par.

Unchartered Channels	1920	US
Undercover Man	1933	Par.
Unfaithfully Yours	1948	TCF
Union Pacific *	1939	Par.
The Velvet Hand	1918	US
The Wanderer	1926	Par.
The Way of All Flesh	1927	Par.
Wharf Angel	1934	Par.
What a Life!	1939	Par.
What Love Will Do	1921	Fox
When We Were Twenty-One	1921	Pathe
The White Dove	1920	US
The Wild Party	1929	Par.
The Wolf of Wall Street	1929	Par.
The Woman from Moscow	1928	Par.
Wonder Man *	1945	Gold.
You Never Know Women	1926	Par.
You Were Meant for Me	1948	TCF

420. HAL MOHR (1894-1974)

An Act of Murder	1948	Univ.
Another Part of the Forest	1948	Univ.
As Husbands Go	1934	Fox
Baby Face Nelson	1957	UA
Back Door to Heaven *	1938	Par.
Bag and Baggage	1923	Selz.
The Bamboo Saucer	1968	US
Because of Him	1945	Univ.
The Big Gamble	1931	RKO
The Big Night	1951	UA
Bitter Apples	1927	WB
The Boss	1956	UA
Broadway	1929	Univ.
Bullets or Ballots	1936	WB
Captain Blood	1935	WB
Carolina	1934	Fox
Cat Creeps *	1930	Univ.
Change of Heart	1934	Fox
Cheers for Miss Bishop	1941	Par.
Charlie Chan's Courage	1934	Fox
The Climax *	1944	Univ.
Cohens and Kellys in Africa	1930	Univ.
The Common Law	1931	RKO
The County Chairman	1935	Fox
Creation of the Humanoids	1962	US
David Harum	1934	Fox
Destry Rides Again	1939	Univ.
The Devil's in Love	1933	Fox
Devotion	1931	RKO

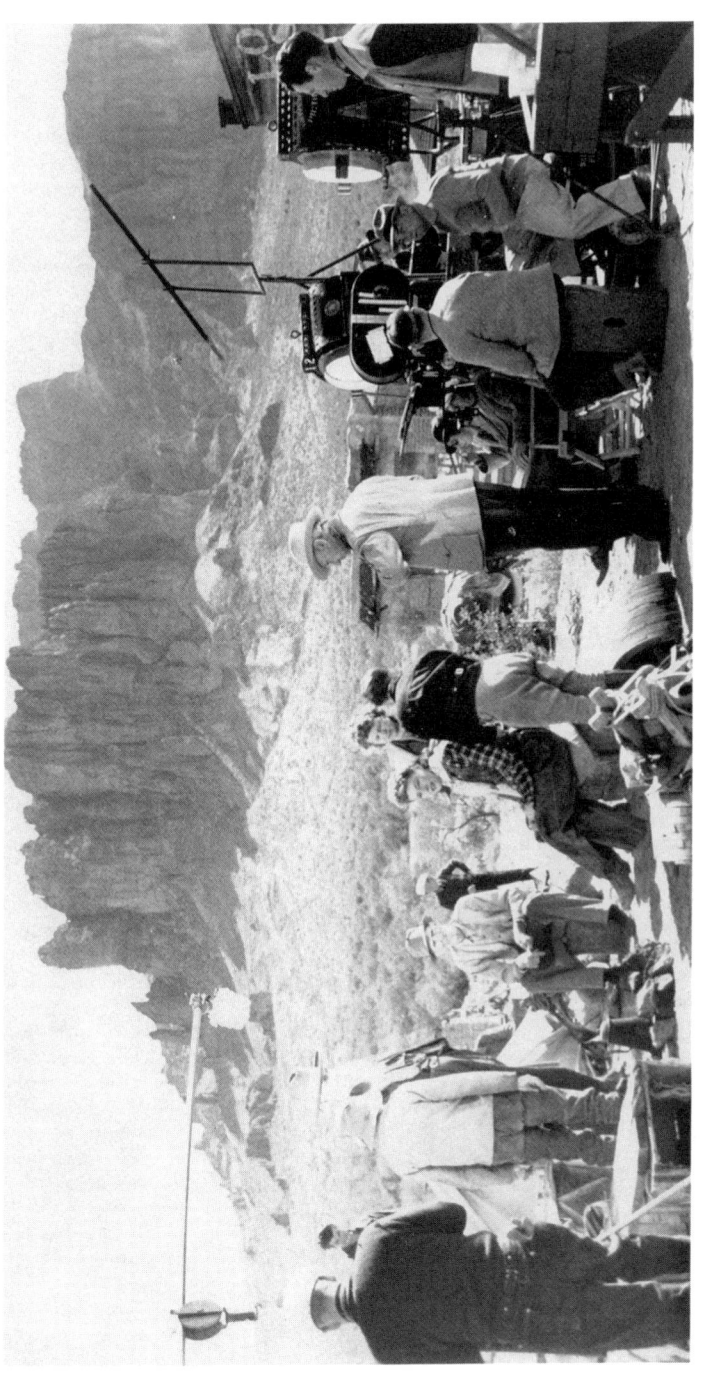

Hal Mohr (center, in white hat) on location with Irene Dunne and crew.

The First Year	1932	Fox
The Four-Poster	1952	Col.
Free Love	1930	Univ.
The Girl from Chicago	1927	WB
Glorious Betsy	1928	WB
The Green Pastures	1936	WB
The Gun Runners	1958	UA
He Who Laughs Last	1925	US
The Heart of Maryland	1927	WB
The High Hand	1926	Pathe
I Loved You Wednesday	1933	Fox
I Met My Love Again	1937	US
I'll Be Yours	1947	Univ.
The Impatient Years *	1944	Col.
International Lady	1941	US
The Jazz Singer	1927	WB
Johnny Holiday	1949	UA
King of Jazz *	1930	Univ.
Ladies Courageous	1944	Univ.
Ladies in Love	1936	TCF
Lady in a Jam	1942	Univ.
Lady with a Past	1932	RKO
The Last Performance	1929	Univ.
The Last Voyage	1960	MGM
The Last Warning	1929	Univ.
The Lineup	1958	Col.
Little Annie Rooney *	1925	UA
The Lost Moment	1947	Univ.
The Man from the Diner's CLub	1963	Col.
The Marriage Clause	1926	Univ.
The Member of the Wedding	1953	Col.
A Midsummer Night's Dream *	1935	WB
A Million Bid	1927	WB
The Monster	1925	Metro.-Gold.
My Gal Loves Music	1944	Univ.
A Night in Paradise	1946	Univ.
Noah's Ark *	1929	WB
Old San Francisco	1927	WB
Outward Bound	1930	WB
The Phantom of the Opera *	1943	Univ.
Pirates of Monterey *	1947	Univ.
Playing with Souls	1925	FN
Pot O Gold	1941	UA
Rancho Notorious	1952	RKO
Rio	1939	Univ.
Salome Where She Danced *	1945	Univ.
San Diego I Love You *	1944	Univ.
The Second Woman	1950	UA
The Servant's Entrance	1934	Fox
Shady Lady	1945	Univ.
Shanghai Lady	1929	Univ.

Slightly Used	1927	WB
Song of Scheherezade *	1947	Univ.
Sparrows *	1926	UA
State Fair	1933	Fox
Tenderloin	1928	WB
Tess of the Storm Country	1932	Fox
The Third Degree	1926	WB
This Is the Life	1943	Univ.
Top Man	1943	Univ.
Twin Beds	1942	US
Under Pressure *	1935	Fox
The Underpup	1939	Univ.
Underworld USA	1960	Col.
The Unfoldment *	1922	US
Vanity's Price	1924	US
The Walking Dead	1936	WB
The Warrior's Husband	1933	Fox
Watch Him Step	1922	US
Watch on the Rhine *	1943	WB
The Wedding March *	1928	Par.
Week-Ends Only	1932	Fox
When the Daltons Rode	1940	Univ.
The WIld One	1954	Col.
A Woman Commands	1932	RKO
A Woman of Experience	1931	RKO
Woman on the Run	1950	Univ.
A Woman Who Sinned *	1924	US
Worst Woman in Paris	1933	Fox

421. JACQUES MONTERAN

America *	1914	US
Come On In	1918	Par.
The Fairy and the Waif	1915	US
The Fortune Teller	1920	US
Good-Bye Bill	1919	Par.
The Money Maniac	1921	Pathe
Neighbors	1918	US
Oh, You Women!	1919	Par.
The Oldest Law	1918	US
The Test of Honor	1919	Par.
T'Other Dear Charmer	1918	US
The Way Out	1918	US

422. VINCENT MONTON

Blue Fire Lady	1978	Aus.
Crosstalk	1982	Aus.
The Day After Halloween	1980	Aus.

Fantasm Comes Again	1977	Aus.
Heatwave	1982	Aus.
Hostage-The Christian Maresch Story	1983	Aus.
Innocent Prey	1984	Aus.
Long Weekend	1978	Aus.
Molly	1983	Aus.
Moving Out	1982	Aus.
Norman Loves Rose	1982	Aus.
Race to the Yankee Zephyr	1981	Aus./NZ
Road Games	1981	Aus.
Street Hero	1984	Aus.
Thirst	1979	Aus.
The Trespassers	1976	Aus.

423. CARLO MONTUORI (1885-   )

Bambole *	1965	It.--Col.
The Bicycle Thief	1948	It.
Bullet for Stefano	1950	It.
Children of Chance	1950	It.
La Citta Si Defende	1951	It.
Crooked Love	1936	It.
Difficult Years	1950	It.
Enemy	1953	It.
For Men Only	1939	It.
Frisky	1955	It.
Gold of Naples	1955	It.
Henry IV	1948	It.
His Last 12 Hours	1953	It.
I Love You Only	1936	It.
I'll Give a Million	1938	It.
In Olden Days *	1952	It.
It's Easier for a Camel	1950	Fr./It.
The Last Five Minutes	1955	Fr./It.--Col.
Leave All Hope	1937	It.
Love and Poisons	1950	It.
Lovers without Love	1948	It.
Motherland	1931	It.
Pact with the Devil	1949	It.
Prelude to Madness	1949	It.
Professor, My Son	1949	It.
Rome-Paris-Rome	1951	Fr./It.
The Roof	1956	Fr./It.
The Sign of Venus	1955	It.
30 Seconds of Love	1937	It.
Time Gone By	1953	It.
The Voice of Love	1950	It.
The White Line	1952	It.

424. MARIO MONTUORI (1920-   )

Age of Love	1954	Fr.--US
Age of the Medici	1979	It.
Battle of the Mods	1968	It.
Bigamist	1956	It.
A Breath of Scandal	1960	Par.
Chen-Bibi	1955	Fr./It.
Goliath and the Dragon	1961	Fr./It.--AIP
Heart and Soul	1950	It.
How, When, WIth Whom?	1969	It.--Col.
Kiss the Other Sheik	1968	Fr./It.--MGM
Love Is Twenty Years Old *	1962	Fr./It./Jap.
The Messiah	1978	It.
O.K. Nero	1952	It.
The Overcoat	1952	It.
Queen of Sheba	1953	It.
Paolo and Francesca	1953	It.
Paranoia *	1966	Fr./It.
Prisoner of the Volga	1960	Fr./It.--Par.
Roman Tales	1956	It.
Sodom and Gomorrah *	1962	Fr./It.--TCF
Squaricio	1958	Fr./It.
3 Nights of Love *	1969	It.
Women and Bandits	1951	It.
Year One	1974	It.

425. MILTON MOORE

College Days *	1926	US
Daughters of Today	1924	Selz.
Don't Get Personal	1922	Univ.
The Earth Woman	1926	US
The Girl He Didn't Buy	1928	US
Golden Shackles	1928	US
The Goose Woman	1925	Univ.
The Guttersnipe	1922	Univ.
He Who Gets Slapped	1924	MGM
One Hour of Love *	1927	US
Out of the Past	1927	US
Passionate Youth	1925	US
Playing with Fire	1921	Univ.
The Rose of Kildare	1927	US
Skyfire	1920	US
Stella Maris	1925	Univ.
The Tomboy	1924	US
Web of Fate	1927	US
Wilful Youth	1927	US
Woman's Law	1927	US

426. RICHARD MOORE

Annie	1982	Col.
Changes	1969	US
Devil's Angels	1967	AIP
The Life and Times of Judge Roy Bean	1972	NG
Maryjane	1968	AIP
Myra Breckinridge	1970	TCF
Operation CIA	1965	AA
The Reivers	1970	US
The Scalphunters *	1968	UA
Sometimes a Great Notion	1971	Univ.
The Stone Killer	1973	Col.
WUSA	1970	Par.
The Wild Angels	1966	AIP
Wild in the Streets	1968	AIP
Winning	1969	Univ.

427. TED MOORE (1914-   )

The Amorous Adventures of Moll Flanders	1965	GB--Par.
The Bandit of Zhobe	1959	GB
Call Me Bwana	1962	GB--Rank
Clash of the Titans	1981	GB--MGM
Cockleshell Heroes *	1955	GB--Col.
Country Dance	1969	GB--MGM
Day of the Triffids	1962	GB
Diamonds Are Forever	1971	GB--UA
Dr. No	1972	GB--UA
Dominque	1978	GB
From Russia with Love	1963	GB--UA
The Gamma People	1956	GB--Col.
The Golden Voyage of Sinbad	1973	GB--Col.
The Hellions	1961	GB--Col.
High Flight	1958	GB--Col.
How To Murder a Rich Uncle	1957	GB--Col.
Idle On Parade	1959	GB
In the Nick	1960	GB--Col.
Interpol	1957	GB--Col.
Jazzboat	1960	GB--Col.
Johnny Nobody	1960	GB--Col.
The Killers of Kilimanjaro	1959	GB--Col.
THe Last Safari	1967	GB--Par.
Let's Get Married	1960	GB
Live and Let Die	1973	GB--UA
A Man for All Seasons	1966	GB--Col.
The Man Inside	1958	GB--Col.
Man With the Golden Gun *	1974	GB--UA
Mix Me a Person	1961	GB

Most Dangerous Man in the World	1969	GB--TCF
Odongo	1956	GB--Col.
Orca-Killer Whale	1977	DeL.
Priest of Love	1981	GB
The Prime of Miss Jean Brodie	1969	GB--TCF
A Prize of Gold	1955	GB--Col.
Prudence and the Pill	1968	GB--TCF
Psychomania	1972	GB
Safari *	1956	GB
Shalako	1968	GB
She'll Follow You Anywhere	1971	GB
Sinbad and the Eye of the Tiger	1977	GB--Col.
Tank Force!	1958	GB--Col.
Thunderball	1965	GB--UA
The Trials of Oscar Wilde	1960	GB
Zarak *	1956	GB--Col.

428. DONALD MORGAN

Ace Eli and Rodger of the Skies *	1973	TCF
Christine	1983	Col.
Hysterical	1983	US
I Wanna Hold Your Hand	1978	Univ.
Let's Do It Again	1975	WB
Off the Wall	1983	US
One on One	1972	US
A Piece of the Action	1977	WB
Santee	1972	US
Sheila Levine Is Dead and Living in New York	1975	Par.
Skatetown USA	1979	Col.

429. IRA MORGAN (1889-1959)

Along Came Love	1937	Par.
Barbary Pirate	1949	Col.
The Barrier	1926	MGM
Beauty's Worth	1922	Par.
The Black Doll	1983	Univ.
The Blazing Trail	1949	Col.
Border Buckaroos	1943	PRC
The Bride's Play	1921	Par.
Brown of Harvard	1926	MGM
Buttons	1927	MGM
The Callahans and the Murphys	1927	MGM
Captain Applejack	1931	WB
Captive Girl	1950	Col.
Chain Gang	1950	Col.
Charlie Chan in Secret Service	1944	Mon.

Chasing Rainbows	1929	MGM
The Chinese Cat	1944	Mon.
Corregidor	1943	PRC
Cyclops	1956	AA
Delinquent Daughters	1944	PRC
Detective Kitty O'Day	1944	Mon.
Devil Goddess	1955	Col.
The Duke Steps Out	1929	MGM
Enchantment	1921	Par.
The Enemies of Women	1923	Gold.
Excess Baggage	1928	MGM
Face in the Fog *	1922	Par.
The Family Honor	1920	FN
Fighting Valley	1943	PRC
Find the Woman	1922	Par.
Flying Fleet	1929	MGM
Fog Island	1945	PRC
Fury of the Congo	1951	Col.
Girl o' My Dreams	1935	Mon.
Girl of the Limberlost	1934	Mon.
Girl Overboard	1937	Univ.
The Girl Said No	1930	MGM
Girls in Chains *	1943	PRC
Glamour Girl	1947	Col.
The Great Gabbo	1929	MGM
Gunsmoke Mesa	1944	PRC
High School Hero	1946	Mon.
Hollywod and Vine	1945	PRC
Hot Rhythm	1944	Mon.
I Escaped from the Gestapo	1943	Mon.
I'd Give My Life	1936	Par.
Isle of Forgotten Sins	1943	PRC
The Jack Knife Man	1920	FN
Janice Meredith *	1924	Metro.-Gold.
Jimmy the Gent	1934	WB
Jive Junction	1943	PRC
Johnny Doesn't Live Here Anymore	1944	Mon.
Junior Prom	1946	Mon.
Last of the Redmen *	1947	Col.
Leave It to the Irish	1944	Mon.
Lena Rivers	1932	US
Lights of Old Broadway	1925	Metro.-Gold.
A Little Journey	1927	MGM
Little Old New York *	1923	Gold.
Lost in the Stratosphere	1935	Mon.
The Lost Tribe	1949	Col.
Lovey Mary	1926	MGM
Man to Man	1930	WB
Manhattan Angel	1948	Col.
Mark of the Gorilla	1950	Col.
Mary Lou	1948	Col.

Modern Times *	1936	UA
The Mutineers	1949	Col.
The Mystic	1925	MGM
Never the Twain Shall Meet	1925	Metro.-Gold.
On the Great White Trail	1938	GN
The Other Half	1919	US
The Payoff	1943	PRC
Poor Relations	1919	US
Pygmy Island	1950	Col.
Racing Luck	1948	Col.
Red Head	1934	Mon.
The Red Mark	1928	Pathe
Revenue Agent	1950	Col.
Rogues' Gallery	1945	PRC
Rookies	1927	MGM
The Sea Bat	1930	MGM
The Sea Master	1917	US
Seeing It Through	1920	US
Sensation Hunters	1945	Mon.
The Ship from Shanghai	1930	MGM
Sin of Nora Moran	1933	US
Sing, Sinner, Sing	1933	US
Sinner's Holiday	1930	MGM
Social Briars	1918	US
Spring Fever	1927	MGM
State Penitentiary	1950	Col.
The Strange Mr. Gregory	1945	Mon.
Sweethearts of the U.S.A.	1944	Mon.
The Taxi Dancer	1927	MGM
The Three Legionaires	1937	US
Tiger Fangs	1943	PRC
Trail of Terror	1944	PRC
Twelve Miles Out	1927	MGM
Two Blondes and a Redhead	1947	Col.
Tyrant of the Sea	1950	Col.
The Unholy Night	1929	MGM
Unknown Blonde	1934	US
The Unwritten Law	1933	US
The Vampire Bat	1933	US
A Very Honorable Guy	1934	FN/WB
Washington Merry-Go-Round	1932	Col.
West of Sonora	1948	Col.
West of Texas	1943	EL/PRC
West Point	1927	MGM
The Westland Case	1937	Univ.
When the Lights Go On Again	1944	PRC
When Knighthood Was in Flower *	1922	Par.
When Strangers Marry	1944	Mon.
Where Are Your Children? *	1943	Mon.
The World Gone Mad	1933	US
Yolanda *	1924	Metro.-Gold.

430. JOHN ARTHUR MORRILL

A Boy and His Dog	1975	US
The Brotherhood of Satan	1970	Col.
Brothers	1977	WB
The Dark	1979	US
The Day Time Ended	1980	US
The Grass Eater	1961	US
The Hideous Sun Demon *	1959	US
Hollywood Horor House	1975	US
Kingdom of the Spiders *	1977	US
Mr. Sycamore	1975	US
Odd Birds	1985	US
One Way Wahini	1965	US
The Quick and the Dead	1963	US
Saturday Morning *	1971	Col.
Steel Arena	1973	US
Truck Stop WOmen	1974	US
The Witchmaker	1969	US

431. OSWALD MORRIS

The Adventurers	1950	GB--Rank
Battle of the Villa Fiorita	1964	GB--WB
Beat the Devil	1953	GB
Beau Brummel	1954	GB--MGM
Cairo Road	1950	GB
The Card	1952	GB
The Ceremony	1963	UA
Circle of Danger	1951	GB
Come Fly with Me	1962	MGM
The Dark Crystal	1982	GB--Univ.
Dracula	1974	GB
The Entertainer	1960	GB
Equus	1977	GB--UA
A Farewell to Arms *	1957	Selz./TCF
Fiddler on the Roof	1971	UA
Fragment of Fear	1970	GB--Col.
The Golden Salamander *	1949	GB
Goodbye Mr. Chips	1969	GB--MGM
Great Catherine	1968	GB--WB
The Great Muppet Caper	1981	GB
The Guns of Navarone	1961	GB--Col.
Heaven Knows Mr. Allison	1957	TCF
The Hill	1965	GB--MGM
Just Tell Me What You Want	1980	WB
The Key	1958	GB--Col.
Knave of Hearts	1954	GB
Lady Caroline Lamb	1972	GB--EMI
Life at the Top	1965	GB--Col.

Lolita	1962	GB--MGM
Look Back in Anger	1959	GB
The Mackintosh Man	1973	WB
The Man Who Never Was	1955	GB--TCF
The Man Who Would Be King	1975	Col.
Man with the Golden Gun *	1974	GB--UA
Mr. Moses	1965	GB--UA
Moby Dick	1956	GB--WB
Moulin Rouge	1952	GB
The Odessa File	1974	GB--Col.
Of Human Bondage	1964	GB--MGM
Oliver!	1968	GB--Col.
Our Man in Havana	1959	GB--Col.
The Passionate Friends *	1948	GB
The Pumpkin Eater	1964	GB--Col.
The Roots of Heaven	1958	TCF
Satan Never Sleeps	1962	TCF
Saturday Island	1951	GB
Scrooge	1970	GB
The Seven Per Cent Solution	1976	Univ.
Sleuth	1972	GB
So Little Time	1952	GB
South of Algiers	1952	GB
Spy Who Came in From the Cold	1966	GB--Par.
Stop the World--I Want to Get Off	1966	GB--WB
The Taming of the Shrew *	1967	Col.
Term of Trial	1962	GB
The Wiz	1978	Univ.

432. REG MORRIS

Bells	1981	Can.
Black Christmas	1974	Can.
A Christmas Story	1983	MGM--UA
Drylanders	1965	Can.--Col.
Empire of the Ants	1977	AIP
The Food of the Gods	1976	AIP
King of the Grizzlies	1976	Dis.
Loose Cannons	1990	Tri-S.
Love *	1982	Can.
Marie-Ann	1978	Can.
Middle Age Crazy	1980	Can.
Murder By Decree	1978	Can./GB
Phobia	1980	Can.
Porky's	1982	Can.
Porky's II: The Next Day	1983	TCF
Second Wind	1976	Can.
Shadow of the Hawk *	1973	Can.--Col.
The Shape of Things To Come	1979	Can.
Tribute	1980	Can.--TCF
Welcome to Bloody City	1977	Can.

433. ROBBY MULLER

Alice in the Cities *	1974	Ger.
The American Friend	1977	Fr./Ger.--US
Barfly	1987	Cannon
The Believers	1987	Orion
Body Rock	1984	US
The Cheaters	1984	Fr./Ger.
Class Enemy	1983	Ger.
A Cop's Sunday	1983	Fr.
The Country Is Calm	1976	Ger.
Down By Law	1986	US
The Glass Cell	1978	Ger.
The Goalie's Anxiety at the Penalty Kick	1972	Ger.
Honeysuckle Rose	1980	WB
In for Treatment	1980	Ger.
In the Course of TIme	1976	Ger.
Jonathan *	1973	Ger.
Korczak	1990	Pol.
The Left-Handed Woman	1980	Ger.
The Little Devil	1988	It.
The Longshot	1986	Orion
Mysteries	1979	Holl.
Mystery Train	1989	Jap./US
Paris, Texas	1984	Fr./Ger.
Repo Man	1984	Univ.
St. Jack	1979	US
The Scarlet Letter	1973	Ger.
They All Laughed	1981	TCF/UA
To Live and Die in L.A.	1985	MGM-UA
The Wild Duck	1976	Ger.
Wrong Moment	1975	Ger.

434. FRED MURPHY

Best Seller	1987	Orion
The Dead	1987	US
Death of an Angel	1985	TCF
Eddie and the Cruisers	1983	US
Enemies: A Love Story	1989	TCF
Five Corners	1987	GB--US
Fresh Horses	1988	Col.
Full Moon in Blue Water	1988	US
Funny about Love	1990	Par.
Girlfriends	1978	US
Heartland	1979	US
Hoosiers	1986	Orion
Imposters	1979	US
Key Exchange	1985	TCF

Local Color	1978	US
Night Game	1989	US
Q-The Winged Serpent	1983	US
The Scenic Route	1978	US
The State of Things *	1983	Ger./Port.--US
Tell Me a Riddle	1980	US
Touched	1983	US
The Trip to Bountiful	1985	US
Winners Take All	1987	US

435. NICHOLAS MUSURACA (1890-   )

Allegheny Uprising	1939	RKO
The Avenging Rider	1928	FBO
The Bachelor and the Bobby Soxer *	1947	RKO
Back to Bataan	1945	RKO
The Bandit's Son	1927	FBO
Bedlam	1946	RKO
The Big Shot	1937	RKO
Bill of Divorcement	1940	RKO
Blind Alibi	1938	RKO
Blood on the Moon	1948	RKO
The Blue Gardenia	1953	WB
Bombardier	1943	RKO
Border Cafe	1937	RKO
Born To Be Bad	1950	RKO
Bride by Mistake	1944	RKO
Bride of the Storm	1926	WB
By Your Leave	1935	RKO
Call Out the Marines *	1942	RKO
Cat People	1942	RKO
Chance at Heaven	1933	RKO
The Charge of the Gauchos *	1928	FBO
The Cherokee Kid	1927	FBO
China Sky	1945	RKO
Clash by Night	1952	RKO
Come On Danger	1932	RKO
The Company She Keeps	1940	RKO
Condemned Women	1938	RKO
Crashing Hollywood *	1937	RKO
Crossfire	1933	RKO
Curse of the Cat People	1944	RKO
Cyclone of the Range	1927	RKO
Danger Patrol	1937	RKO
Deadline at Dawn	1946	RKO
Devil's Canyon	1953	RKO
Dog Justice	1928	FBO
Dynamite Pass	1950	RKO
Everybody's Doing It *	1938	RKO
Everything's Rosie	1931	RKO

The Falcon in Hollywood	1944	RKO
The Fallen Sparrow	1943	RKO
The Farmer in the Dell	1936	RKO
Five Came Back	1939	RKO
Flight from Glory *	1937	RKO
Flying Devils	1933	RKO
Forever and a Day *	1943	RKO
The Freckled Rascal	1929	FBO/RKO
Gangway for Tomorrow	1943	RKO
The Gay Falcon	1941	RKO
The Ghost Ship	1943	RKO
The Gilded Highway	1926	WB
A Girl in Every Port	1951	RKO
Girl Rush	1944	RKO
Glorious Adventure *	1922	US
Golden Boy *	1939	Col.
Gun Law	1929	FBO/RKO
Half Shot at Sunrise	1930	RKO
Haunted Gold	1932	WB
Headline Shooter	1933	RKO
Hell Bent for Heaven	1926	WB
His New York Wife	1926	US
The Hitch-Hiker	1953	RKO
Hook, Line and Sinker	1930	RKO
Hot Lead	1951	RKO
Hunt the Man Down	1950	RKO
Hurry, Charlie, Hurry	1941	RKO
I Remember Mama	1948	RKO
Idaho Red	1929	FBO
Inside the Lines	1930	RKO
Lady Scarface	1941	RKO
Last Lap	1928	US
Law of the Underworld	1938	RKO
Lightning Lariats	1927	US
Little Men	1940	RKO
Living On Love	1937	RKO
The Locket	1946	RKO
Long Lost Father	1934	RKO
The Mad Miss Manton	1938	RKO
Man on the Prowl	1947	UA
Marine Raiders	1944	RKO
Men of Chance	1931	RKO
Murder on a Bridle Path	1936	RKO
Murder on a Honeymoon	1935	RKO
Murder on the Blackboard	1934	RKO
The Mysterious Desperado	1949	RKO
The Navy Comes Through	1942	RKO
Night Spot	1938	RKO
Obliging Lady	1941	RKO
Old Man Rhythm	1935	RKO
On the Banks of the Wabash	1923	Vita.

Orphan of the Sage	1928	FBO
Out of the Past	1947	RKO
Pacific Liner	1938	RKO
The Passionate Quest	1926	WB
Phantom of the Range	1928	FBO
Play Girl	1940	RKO
The Plot Thickens	1936	RKO
The Pride of Pawnee	1929	FBO
Red Riders of Canada	1928	FBO
The Red Sword	1929	FBO/RKO
Repent at Leisure	1941	RKO
The Richest Girl in the World	1934	RKO
Rider from Tucson	1950	RKO
Roadblock	1951	RKO
Romance in Manhattan	1934	RKO
Rough Ridin' Red	1928	FBO
Saturday's Heroes	1937	RKO
Scarlet River	1933	RKO
Second Wife	1936	RKO
The Seventh Victim	1943	RKO
Shameful Behavior?	1926	US
Side Street *	1929	RKO
Silly Billies	1936	RKO
The Sin Ship	1931	RKO
Sky Giant	1938	RKO
Smart Women	1931	RKO
Smashing the Rackets	1938	RKO
The Sonora Kid	1927	US
Sorority House	1939	RKO
The Spiral Staircase	1945	RKO
Spliting the Breeze	1927	US
Stagecoach Kid	1949	RKO
The Story of Mankind	1957	WB
Stranger on the Third Floor	1940	RKO
Susan Slept Here	1954	RKO
Swiss Family Robinson	1940	RKO
Tarnished Angel	1938	RKO
Terror	1928	FBO
They Made Her a Spy	1939	RKO
Three Who Loved	1931	RKO
To Beat the Band	1935	RKO
Tom Brown's Schooldays	1940	RKO
Tom's Gang	1927	US
Too Many Cooks	1931	RKO
Too Many Wives	1937	RKO
Too Much Too Soon *	1958	WB
Trail Guide	1952	RKO
The Trail of the Horse Thieves	1929	FBO/RKO
Tropic Madness	1928	FBO
The Tuttles of Tahiti	1942	RKO
12 Crowded Hours	1939	RKO

Two in the Dark	1936	RKO
Tyrant of Red Gulch	1928	FBO
Village Tale	1935	RKO
We're on the Jury	1937	RKO
We're Rich Again	1934	RKO
When the Law Rides	1928	FBO
Where Danger Lives	1950	RKO
Where Sinners Meet	1934	RKO
The Whip Hand	1951	RKO
The Woman on Pier 13	1949	RKO

436. DAVID MYERS

Die Laughing	1980	Orion/WB
FM	1978	Univ.
Hard Traveling	1985	US
Human Highway	1983	US
Mysterious Monster *	1976	US
Renaldo and Clara *	1978	US
Roadie	1980	UA
Sammy Stops the World	1978	US
Uforia	1984	Univ.
Welcome to LA	1976	UA
Zoot Suit	1982	Univ.

437. ARMANDO NANNUZZI

Appassionata	1974	It.
Bailiff of Griefensee	1979	It.
Il Bell Antonio	1960	It.--Emb.
Beyond Good and Evil	1977	Fr./Ger./It.--UA
La Boheme	1988	Fr./It.
The Boom	1963	It.
The Brigand	1961	It.
La Cage aux Folles	1978	Fr./It.--UA
La Cage aux Folles II	1980	Fr./It.--UA
Careless	1982	It.
Caller	1987	US
Chino	1973	Fr./It./Sp.
The Cross-Eyed Saint	1971	It.
The Damned	1969	Ger./It.--WB
Diary of a Cloistered Nun	1973	Fr./Ger./It.
Doll That Took the Town	1965	It.
Don Camillo in Moscow	1965	It.
Frankenstein Unbound *	1990	TCF
La Fuga	1966	It.--TCF
The Girl from Parma	1963	It.
The Girl of the Day	1957	It.

Gold Rimmed Glasses	1987	Fr./It./Yugo.
Good King Dagobert	1984	Fr./It.
Grand Piano	1984	It.
Head of the Family	1967	Fr./It.--Par.
The Hypochondriac	1980	It.
I Knew Her Well	1966	It.
I Love N.Y.	1987	US
Italian Secret Service	1968	It.
Liberty, Equality, Sauerkraut	1985	It.
Lissy	1957	It.
Love a La Carte	1965	It.
Ludwig	1972	Fr./Ger./It.--
Mafioso	1962	It. MGM
The Magnificent Cuckold	1965	Fr./It.
Maximum Overdrive	1986	It.
Merry Christmas! Happy New Year	1990	Fr./It.
Milarepa	1974	It.
The Miser	1990	Fr./It./Sp.
Misunderstood	1967	Fr./It.
Mussolini and I	1985	It.
My Name Is Nobody *	1973	Fr./Ger./It.--
Nana	1983	It. Cannon
Nest of Vipers	1979	It.--Par.
La Notte Brava	1962	Fr./It.
La Nuit de Varennes	1983	Fr./It.--Col.
Okay Okay	1983	It.
Pigsty *	1969	Fr./It.
The Queens *	1968	Fr./It.--Col.
Sahara *	1984	MGM-UA
Sandra	1966	It.
Silent Night	1988	Ger.
Silver Bullet	1985	It.
Six Days a Week	1966	Fr./It./Sp.
The Skin	1981	Fr./It.
State Reasons	1978	Fr./It.
Strange Events *	1977	It.
Tigers in Lipstick *	1985	It.
Tonight's the Night	1960	It.
Too Soon To Die	1966	Fr./It.
The Visit	1964	Fr./Ger./It.-- TCF
Wake Up and Die	1967	Fr./It.
Waterloo	1970	It./USSR--Par.
Weekend, Italian Style	1967	Fr./It./Sp.
When a Man Grows Old	1962	It.--Col.
The Window to Luna Park	1957	It.
Young Husbands	1958	Fr./It.

438. RONALD NEAME (1911-   )

Blithe Spirit	1945	GB

Cheer Boys Cheer	1939	GB
Come On George *	1939	GB
Crimes of Stephen Hawke	1936	GB--MGM
Dangerous Moonlight *	1941	GB--RKO
Dangerous Secrets	1938	GB
Feather Your Nest	1937	GB
The Four Just Men	1939	GB--Eal.
The Gaunt Stranger	1938	GB
Give Her a Ring *	1934	GB
I See Ice *	1938	GB
In Which We Serve	1942	GB--Rank
The Improper Duchess	1936	GB
Invitation to the Waltz	1935	GB
It's in the Air *	1938	GB
Keep Fit *	1937	GB
Let George Do It *	1940	GB--Eal.
Let's Be Famous *	1939	GB--Eal.
Major Barbara	1941	GB
Music Hath Charms *	1936	GB
Once in a Million	1936	GB
One of Our Aircraft Is Missing	1941	GB
Penny Paradise *	1938	GB
Return to Yesterday	1940	GB--Eal.
Saloon Bar	1940	GB--Eal.
This Happy Breed	1944	GB
Trouble Brewing	1939	GB
The Ware Case	1938	GB--Eal.
Young Man's Fancy	1940	GB--Eal.

439. HARRY NEUMANN

According to Mrs. Hoyle	1951	Mon.
Across the Rio Grande	1949	Mon.
African Treasure	1952	Mon.
Air Devils	1938	Univ.
Allotment Wives	1945	Mon.
The Apache Kid	1941	Rep.
The Ape *	1940	Mon.
Are These Our Parents?	1944	Mon.
Arizona Bound	1941	Mon.
The Arizona Sweepstakes	1926	Univ.
Arizona Territory	1950	Mon.
Army Bound	1952	Mon.
The Back Trail	1924	Univ.
Beauty and the Bandit	1946	Mon.
Below the Border	1942	Mon.
Below the Deadline	1946	Mon.
Black Gold	1947	Mon.
Black Market Babies	1946	Mon.
The Boiling Point *	1932	US

Bomba and the Jungle Girl	1952	Mon.
Border Wolves	1938	Univ.
The Bowery Boys Meet the Monster	1954	AA
Bowery to Bagdad	1955	AA
Boys' Reformatory	1939	Mon.
The Buckaroo Ki	1926	Univ.
Bulldog Courage	1922	US
A Bullet for Joey	1955	UA
Burning the Wind	1929	Univ.
The Calgary Stampede	1925	Univ.
California Straight Ahead	1937	Univ.
The Californian	1937	TCF
Calling Homicide	1956	AA
Cappy Ricks Returns	1935	Rep.
Captain Tugboat Annie	1945	Rep.
Cavalry Scout	1951	Mon.
Chain of Evidence	1957	AA
Chasing Trouble	1940	Mon.
Cheers of the Crowd *	1936	Mon.
Chip of the Flying U	1926	Univ.
Cisco Kid Returns	1945	Mon.
Clearing the Trail	1928	Univ.
Clipped Wings	1953	AA
Cole Younger, Gunfighter	1958	AA
The Concentratin' Kid	1930	Univ.
Courtin' Trouble	1949	Mon.
Courtin' Wildcats	1929	Univ.
Cow Country	1953	
Cowboy Counsellor *	1932	US
Crashing Las Vegas	1956	AA
Crossed Trails	1948	Mon.
The Danger Rider	1928	Univ.
Daring Chances	1924	Univ.
Dawn on the Great Divide	1942	Mon.
Deep in the Heart of Texas	1942	Univ.
The Denver Dude	1927	Univ.
Disc Jockey	1950	AA
The Disembodied	1957	AA
Divorce	1945	Mon.
Dizzy Dames	1936	US
Don Dare Devil	1925	Univ.
Doomed to Die	1940	Mon.
Down Texas Way	1942	Mon.
Down to the Sea	1936	Rep.
Dragonfly Squadron	1954	AA
Drifting Along	1946	Mon.
The Dude Bandit *	1933	US
The Duke Comes Back	1937	Rep.
The Face of Marble	1946	Mon.
False Feathers	1929	US
Fashion Model	1945	Mon.
The Fatal Hour	1940	Mon.

Fence Riders	1950	Mon.
Fighter Attack	1953	AA
Fighting Fury	1924	Univ.
The Fighting Parson	1933	US
Fighting Trouble	1956	AA
Flame of the West	1945	Mon.
Flashing Guns	1947	Mon.
Flat Top	1952	AA/Mon.
Flight to Mars	1951	Mon.
The Flyin' Cowboy	1928	Univ.
Flying Hoofs	1925	Univ.
Footsteps in the Night	1957	AA
Forbidden Trails	1941	Mon.
Forced Landing	1936	Rep.
Forever Yours	1945	Mon.
Fort Osage	1952	Mon.
Fort Vengeance	1953	AA
Frontier Feud	1945	Mon.
GI Honeymoon	1945	Mon.
Galloping Fury	1927	Univ.
Gangster's Boy	1938	Mon.
The Gay Buckaroo	1932	US
A Gentle Gangster	1943	Rep.
Ghost Town Law	1942	Mon.
The Girl from Calgary	1932	Mon.
The Golden Idol	1954	AA
Gun Battle at Monterey	1957	AA
Gun Runner	1949	Mon.
Gun Talk	1948	Mon.
The Gunman from Bodie	1941	Mon.
Gunslingers	1950	Mon.
Hard Hombre	1931	US
Hats Off	1937	GN
Haunted House	1940	Mon.
Heart of the Rio Grande	1942	Rep.
A Hero on Horseback	1927	Univ.
Heroes in Blue	1939	Mon.
Hey! Hey! Cowboy	1927	Univ.
Hiawatha	1952	Mon.
Hidden Danger	1949	Mon.
Hidden Enemy	1940	Mon.
High Society	1955	AA
The Highwayman	1951	Mon.
Hold That Hypnotist	1947	AA
Honor of the West	1939	Univ.
The Hoosier Schoolmaster	1935	Mon.
Hot Shots	1596	AA
The Hunted	1948	AA
I Cover the War	1937	Univ.
I Killed That Man	1941	Mon.
I Was an American Spy	1951	AA/Mon.

Idol of the Crowds	1937	Univ.
In the Money	1958	AA
Intruder	1933	US
Irish Luck	1939	Mon.
The Iron Master *	1933	US
It Happened Out West	1937	TCF
The Jade Mask	1945	Mon.
Jalopy	1953	AA
Jungle Gents	1954	AA
Kansas Pacific	1953	AA
Keeper of the Bees	1935	Mon.
Killer Leopard	1954	AA
King of the Rodeo	1929	Univ.
King of the Royal Mounted	1936	TCF
The Land of Missing Men	1930	US
The Lariat Kid	1929	Univ.
The Last Stand	1938	Univ.
Law Men	1944	Mon.
Law of the Panhandle	1950	Mon.
Law of the West	1949	Mon.
Let's Sing Again	1936	RKO
Local Bad Man *	1932	US
The Long Long Trail	1929	Univ.
Looking for Danger	1957	AA
Loose in London	1953	AA/Mon.
Lord of the Jungle	1955	AA
Man from God's Country	1958	AA
Man with Two Lives	1942	Mon.
Marked Trails	1944	Mon.
The Maze	1953	AA
The Mesa of Lost Women	1956	US
Midnight Limited	1940	Mon.
Million Dollar Baby	1935	Mon.
Mr. Wong, Detective	1938	Mon.
Mr. Wong in Chinatown	1939	Mon.
The Mounted Stranger	1930	Univ.
Murder on the Waterfront	1943	WB
Mutiny in the Big House	1939	Mon.
My Gun Is Quick	1957	UA
Mysterious Mr. Wong	1935	Mon.
The Mystery Man	1935	Mon.
The Mystery of Mr. Wong	1939	Mon.
Navy Bound	1951	Mon.
Navy Secrets	1939	Mon.
No Greater Sin	1941	US
No Ransom	1935	US
The Nut Farm	1935	Mon.
Officer 13 *	1933	US
The Old Homestead	1935	US
Old Swimmin' Hole	1941	Mon.
On the Spot	1940	Mon.

Once to Every Bachelor	1934	US
Outlaw Express	1938	Univ.
Over the Border	1950	Mon.
Painted Ponies	1927	Univ.
Panhandle	1948	AA
Paris Playboys	1954	AA
Partners of the Trail	1944	Mon.
The Phantom Bullet	1926	Univ.
The Phantom Stage	1939	Univ.
The Phenix City Story	1955	AA
Picture Brides *	1934	US
Points West	1929	Univ.
Port of Missing Men	1930	US
The Prarie King	1927	Univ.
Pride of the Blue Grass	1954	AA
Prison Break	1938	Univ.
Queen of the Yukon	1940	Mon.
Raiders of the Border	1944	Mon.
Range Justice	1949	Mon.
Range Land	1949	Mon.
Range Law	1944	Mon.
The Rawhide Kid	1928	Univ.
The Red Rider *	1925	Univ.
Return from the Sea	1954	AA
Riders of the Dusk	1950	Mon.
Riders of the West	1942	Mon.
Ridgeway of Montana	1924	Univ.
Ridin' Thunder	1925	Univ.
Riding For Fame	1928	Univ.
Roar of the Crowd	1953	AA
Roar of the Press	1941	Mon.
A Roaring Adventure	1925	Univ.
Roaring Ranch	1930	Univ.
Rodeo	1952	Mon.
Roll Along Cowboy	1937	TCF
The Rose Bowl Story	1952	Mon.
Sabu and the Magic Ring	1957	AA
Safari Drums	1953	AA
School for Girls	1935	US
Screaming Eagles	1956	AA
Shadows of the West	1949	Mon.
She's in the Army	1942	Mon.
Short Grass	1950	AA /Mon.
A Shriek in the Night *	1933	US
The Sign of the Cactus	1925	Univ.
The Silent Rider	1927	Univ.
Silver Raiders	1950	Mon.
Silver Trails	1948	Mon.
Smiling Guns	1929	Univ.
Son of Belle Starr	1953	AA
Son of the Navy	1940	Mon.

South of Santa Fe	1942	Rep.
Spirit of the West	1932	US
Spook Busters	1946	Mon.
Spook Chasers	1955	AA
Spook Ranch	1925	Univ.
Spurs	1930	Univ.
Spy Chasers	1955	AA
Spy Ship	1942	WB
Stage Struck	1948	Mon.
Stampede	1949	AA/Mon.
Stoker *	1932	US
The Stranger from Pecos	1943	Mon.
Streets of New York	1939	Mon.
Sunbonnet Sue	1945	Mon.
Sweepstake Annie	1935	US
Take the Stand *	1934	US
The Taming of the West	1925	Univ.
Tarzan the Fearless *	1933	US
The Texas Kid	1944	Mon.
The Thirteenth Guest	1932	Mon.
Tomboy	1940	Mon.
Tough Kid	1939	Mon.
Trail's End	1949	Mon.
Trailin' Trouble	1930	Univ.
A Trick of Hearts	1928	Univ.
Trigger Tricks	1930	Univ.
Truck Busters	1943	WB
Two Heads on a Pillow	1934	US
Two Sinners	1935	Rep.
Two-Fisted Jones	1925	Univ.
Unholy Love *	1932	US
Up in Smoke	1956	AA
Vanity Fair *	1932	US
Wagons West	1952	Mon.
The Wasp Woman	1960	AA
West of Eldorado	1949	Mon.
West of Singapore *	1933	Mon.
West of the Alamo	1946	Mon.
West of the Law	1942	Mon.
West of Wyoming	1950	Mon.
Western Gold	1937	TCF
Western Pluck *	1926	Univ.
Western Renegades	1949	Mon.
Western Trails	1938	Univ.
The Western Wallop	1924	Univ.
Wife Wanted	1946	Mon.
Wild Brian Kent	1936	TCF
Wild Stallion	1952	Mon.
The Wild West Show	1928	Univ.
The Winged Horseman	1929	Univ.
The Women of Pitcairn Island	1957	TCF

440. PETER NEWBROOK

The Black Torment	1964	GB
Corruption	1967	GB--Col.
Crucible of Terror	1972	GB
Gonks Go Beat	1965	GB
Gutter Girls	1964	GB
In the Cool of the Day	1962	MGM
Press for Time	1966	GB--Rank
The Sandwich Man	1966	GB--Rank
Saturday Night Out	1963	GB
School for Unclaimed Girls	1969	GB
That Kind of Girl	1963	GB
Third Time Lucky *	1949	GB

441. ROBERT NEWHARD

Big Happiness	1920	US
The Coward	1915	US
Crimson Gold *	1923	US
Diane of the Green Van	1919	US
Dollar for Dollar	1920	Pathe
Everybody's Sweetheart	1920	Selz.
Fuss and Feathers	1918	Par.
Happy Though Married	1919	Par.
His Birthright	1918	US
The Hunchback of Notre Dame *	1923	Univ.
Hungry Hearts	1922	Gold.
The Iron Strain	1915	US
The Lure of the Night Club	1927	US
Making the Grade *	1921	US
A Man in the Open	1919	US
A Man's Fight	1919	US
Nobody's Kid	1921	US
On the Night Stage	1915	US
Rubber Tires	1927	Pathe
Smouldering Embers	1920	Pathe
Social Ambition	1918	Gold.
The Street Called Straight	1920	Gold.
The Trail of the Axe	1922	US
When Do We Eat?	1918	Par.
With Hoops of Steel	1918	US

442. JOHN M. NICHOLAS, Jr.

Air Patrol	1962	TCF
Ambush at Cimarron Pass	1958	TCF
Apache Warrior	1957	TCF
Attack of the Giant Leeches	1959	AIP

The Day Mars Invaded the Earth	1962	US
Demons of the Swamp	1959	US
Desert Hell	1958	TCF
Four Fast Guns	1959	Univ.
Gang War	1958	TCF
Ghost Diver	1957	TCF
Guns of Diablo	1964	MGM
Harbor Lights	1964	TCF
Hot Rod Girl	1958	AIP
House of the Damned	1963	TCF
Night of the Blood Beast	1958	AIP
Police Nurse	1963	TCF
Showdown at Boot Hill	1958	TCF
Tank Commandos	1959	AIP
Terror	1963	AIP
Thunder Island	1963	TCF
Thundering Jets	1958	TCF
Under Fire	1957	TCF
Young and Dangerous	1957	TCF
Young Guns of Texas	1962	TCF

443. WILLIAM NOBLES

The Adventures of Red Ryder	1940	Rep.
Air Police	1931	US
The Arizona Kid	1939	Rep.
Bad Man of Deadwood	1941	Rep.
Bar L Ranch	1930	US
Barb Wire	1922	US
Beware of Ladies	1937	Rep.
Beyond the Rio Grande	1930	US
The Big Show *	1936	Rep.
Bill Cracks Down	1937	Rep.
Boots and Saddles	1937	Rep.
The Border Sheriff	1927	Univ.
Branded a Coward	1935	US
Bustin' Through	1925	Univ.
Call the Mesketeers	1938	Rep.
Carolina Moon	1940	Rep.
Carson City Kid	1940	Rep.
Child of M'Sieur	1919	US
Colorado Sunset	1939	Rep.
Comin' Round the Mountain	1936	Rep.
Covered Wagon Days	1940	Rep.
Crow's Nest	1922	US
Cyclone Bliss	1921	US
Dangerous Holiday	1937	Rep.
The Demon	1926	Univ.
Desert Bandit	1941	Rep.
Doughnuts and Society	1936	Rep.

The Drifter	1932	US
Drums of Fu Manchu	1943	Rep.
The Fighting Peacemaker	1926	Univ.
The Fighting Three	1927	Univ.
Firebrand Jordan	1930	US
Frontier Pony Express	1939	Rep.
Gold Mine in the Sky	1938	Rep.
Grinning Guns	1927	Univ.
Heroes of the Saddle	1940	Rep.
Hi-Yo Silver	1940	Rep.
Hidden Loot	1925	Univ.
Hurricane Horseman	1931	US
In Old Caliente	1939	Rep.
In Old Cheyenne	1941	Rep.
In Old Santa Fe *	1934	US
Jesse James at Bay	1941	Rep.
Jimmy Valentine	1936	Rep.
Kansas Cyclone	1941	Rep.
Ladies Crave Excitement	1935	US
The Lawless Nineties	1936	Rep.
The Lightning Warrior *	1931	US
Little Men *	1935	US
Lone Star Raiders	1940	Rep.
The Lonely Trail	1936	Rep.
Looking for Trouble *	1926	Univ.
The Man from Hell	1934	US
A Man from Nowhere	1920	US
The Marines Are Coming *	1935	US
Men of Daring	1927	Univ.
Mexicali Rose	1939	Rep.
Nevada City	1941	Rep.
Oh Susanna	1937	Rep.
Outlaw Justice	1932	US
Outlaws of Sonora	1938	Rep.
Overland Bound	1929	US
Overland Stage Raiders	1938	Rep.
Phantom of the Desert	1930	US
Prarie Moon	1938	Rep.
Rags to Riches	1941	Rep.
The Rambling Ranger	1927	Univ.
Rancho Grande	1940	Rep.
Red Fork Range	1931	US
Red Hot Leather	1926	Univ.
Red River Valley	1936	Rep.
The Red Warning	1923	Univ.
Ride, Ranger, Ride	1937	Rep.
Riders of the Black Hills	1938	Rep.
Ridin' Law	1930	US
Ridin' on a Rainbow	1941	Rep.
Roarin' Lead	1936	Rep.
Romance on the Range	1942	Rep.

Rootin' Tootin' Rhythm	1937	Rep.
Rough and Ready	1927	Univ.
Roundup Time in Texas	1937	Rep.
Rovin' Tumbleweeds	1939	Rep.
SOS Coast Guard	1941	Rep.
Saddlemates	1941	Rep.
A Scarlet Weekend	1932	US
The Scrappin' Kid	1926	Univ.
Sheriff of Tombstone	1941	Rep.
Shine On Harvest Moon	1939	Rep.
The Singing Cowboy *	1936	Rep.
The Singing Vagabond	1935	Rep.
A Six-Shootin' Romance	1926	Univ.
The Slingshot Kid *	1927	FBO
South of the Border	1939	Rep.
Swanee River	1931	US
The Three Mesquiteers	1937	Rep.
The Trail Blazers	1940	Rep.
Trails of Danger	1931	US
Two Gun Sheriff	1941	Rep.
Under Texas Skies	1940	Rep.
West of Cheyenne	1931	US
Western Jamboree	1938	Rep.
The Western Whirlwind	1927	Univ.
Westward Bound	1930	US
The White Outlaw	1925	Univ.
Wild Horse Rodeo	1937	Rep.
The Wild Horse Stampede	1926	Univ.
Winds of the Wasteland	1936	Rep.
Wolves of the Border	1923	US
Yodelin' Kid from Pine Ridge	1937	Rep.
Young Bill Hickok	1940	Rep.
Young Buffalo Bill	1940	Rep.

444. STEVE NORTON

Another Man's Wife	1924	US
Beauty Shoppers *	1927	US
Beyond the Shadows	1918	US
Black Butterflies *	1928	US
Bluebeard, Jr.	1922	US
The Broken Gate *	1927	US
Bubbles	1920	US
Closin' In	1918	US
The Enchanted Island *	1927	US
The Follies Girl	1919	US
Ghost City	1921	US
Gloriana	1916	US
Heiress for a Day	1918	US
Hell's End	1918	US

Husband Hunters *	1927	US
Love's Whirlpool	1924	US
The Man Who Woke Up	1918	US
Nancy Comes Home	1918	US
The Peddler of Lies	1920	Univ.
Restless Souls	1919	US
Shore Acres *	1920	Metro.
The Silent Command	1915	Univ.
Too Much Married	1921	US
The Wolverines	1921	US

445. BRUNO NUYTTEN

At Night All Cats Are Gray	1977	Fr.
Barocco	1976	Fr.
The Best Way to Get Along	1976	Fr.
The Bronte Sisters	1979	Fr.
Brubaker	1980	TCF
Detective	1985	Fr.
Fort Saganne	1984	Fr.
French Postcards	1979	Fr./Ger.--Par.
Going Places	1974	Fr.
The Grilling	1981	Fr.
Hotel of the Americas	1982	Fr.
India Song	1975	Fr.
The Inquisitor	1982	Fr.
Insider Memories of France	1975	Fr.
Invitation au Voyage	1983	Fr.
Jean de Florette	1986	Fr.
Life Is a Bed of Roses	1984	Fr.
Life Is a Novel	1983	Fr.
Like a Turtle on Its Back	1981	Fr.
Manon of the Springs	1986	Fr.
Musician Killer	1975	Fr.
My Heart Is Red	1977	Fr.
A Passing Killer	1981	Fr.
La Pirate	1984	Fr.
Possession	1981	Fr./Ger.
So Long, Stooge	1984	Fr.
The Truck	1977	Fr.
The Waltzers	1974	Fr.

446. SVEN NYKVIST (1922-   )

Agnes of God	1985	Col.
Another Woman	1988	Orion
Autumn Sonata	1978	Ger./Swed.
Black Moon	1975	Fr.
Cannery Row	1982	MGM

Cries and Whispers	1972	Swed.
Crimes and Misdemeanors	1989	Orion
The Dove	1974	US
Dream Lover	1986	MGM-UA
The Dress	1965	Swed.
Fanny and Alexander	1982	Fr./Ger./Swed.
First Love	1970	Ger./Switz.
From the Life of the Marionettes	1980	Ger.
Gay Old Time	1947	Swed.
Girl In Tails	1957	Swed.
Girl of Solbakken	1958	Swed.
The Gorilla *	1956	Swed.
The Hour of the Wolf	1967	Swed.
Hurricane	1979	DeL.
The Judge	1961	Swed.
Katinka	1988	Den./Swed.
King of the Gypsies	1978	Par.
Lady Lena and Blue-Eyed Per	1947	Swed.
The Last Run	1971	MGM
Laughing in the Sunshine	1953	GB/Swed.--UA
Lend Me Your Wife	1959	Swed.
Loving Couples	1964	Swed.
Maj la Male	1948	Swed.
Make Way for Lila	1962	Ger./Swed.
The Marriage of Mr. Mississippi	1961	Ger.--UFA
Masks	1966	Swed.
A Matter of Morals	1960	Swed.--UA
Monismanien 1995	1975	Swed.
Murder Game	1962	Ger.
The Naked Night *	1953	Swed.
New York Stories *	1989	BV/Touch.
Now About these Women...	1964	Swed.
One Day in the Life of Ivan Denisovich	1971	GB
One Plus One	1978	Swed.
The Passion of Anna	1970	Swed.
Persona	1966	Swed.
The Postman Always Rings Twice	1981	Lor.
Pretty Baby	1978	Par.
Ransom	1975	GB
The Ritual	1970	Swed.
The Sacrifice	1986	Fr./Swed.
Scenes From a Marriage	1973	Swed.
The Serpent's Egg	1977	Ger.
Shame	1968	Swed.
Siddhartha	1973	Col.
The Silence	1963	Swed.
Snow White and the Seven Jugglers	1963	Swed.
Star 80	1983	WB
Starting Over	1979	Par.
Summer Lightning	1972	Ger.
Swann in Love	1983	Fr.

The Tenant	1976	Fr.--Par.
Through a Glass Darkly	1961	Swed.
To Love	1964	Swed.
The Touch	1970	Swed.--US
The Tragedy of Carmen	1983	Fr.
The True and the False	1955	Swed.
The Unbearable Lightness of Being	1988	Orion
The Virgin Spring	1959	Swed.
Willie and Phil	1980	TCF
Winter Light	1963	Swed.

447. L. WILLIAM O'CONNELL

Accidents Will Happen	1938	WB
Adventures of Jane Arden	1939	WB
Adventures of Rusty	1945	Col.
After Midnight With Boston Blackie	1943	Col.
Alcatraz Island	1938	WB
April Fool	1926	US
Baby Take a Bow	1934	Fox
Bachelor of Arts	1935	Fox
Beautiful but Broke	1944	Col.
Behold This Woman *	1924	Vita.
The Bells	1926	US
The Beloved Brute	1924	Vita.
Bengal Tiger	1936	WB
Best of Enemies	1936	TCF
The Big Noise	1936	GB--TCF
Big Time	1929	Fox
The Blonde from Singapore	1941	Col.
Blondie's Lucky Day	1946	Col.
Border Law	1931	Col.
Bringing Up Father	1946	Mon.
A Broken Doll	1921	US
Calling Philo Vance	1939	WB
Charlie Chan in London	1934	Fox
Cherokee Strip *	1937	FN/WB
Come On Over	1922	Gold.
The Cradle Snatchers	1927	Fox
The Crime Doctor's Courage	1945	Col.
The Crime Doctor's Warning	1945	Col.
Criminal Code *	1931	Col.
Cry of the Werewolf	1944	Col.
Dancing in Manhattan	1945	Col.
Dangerously They Live	1941	WB
Decoy	1947	Mon.
Doughboys in Ireland	1943	Col.
Enter Madame	1922	Metro.
Fashionable Fakers	1923	US
Fazil	1928	Fox

Flight Angels	1940	FN/WB
Forbidden Trail	1936	Col.
Four Devils *	1929	Fox
The Fourth Musketeer	1923	US
Fox Movietone Follies of 1930	1930	Fox
Gambling On the High Seas *	1940	WB
General Custer at Little Big Horn	1926	US
Get Hep to Love	1942	Univ.
A Girl in Every Port *	1928	Fox
Girl in the Case	1944	Col.
Granny Get Your Gun	1939	FN/WB
The Hands of Nara	1922	Metro.
Heart of the North	1938	WB
Here's to Romance	1935	Fox
Hey, Rookie	1944	Col.
Humanity	1933	Fox
In Old Kentucky	1935	Fox
The Invisible Menace	1938	WB
Is Everybody Happy?	1943	Col.
It's a Great Life	1943	Col.
Jam Session	1944	Col.
Jiggs and Maggie in Society	1948	Mon.
Jiggs and Maggie Out West	1950	Mon.
King of Hockey	1935	WB
Klondike Fury	1942	Mon.
Life With Blondie	1945	Col.
The Little Grey Mouse	1920	Fox
Little Miss Thoroughbred	1938	WB
Lost Honeymoon	1947	EL
Louisiana Hayride	1944	Col.
The Lunatic at Large	1927	FN
Maker of Men	1931	Col.
Making the Grade	1929	Fox
Man of Iron	1935	FN/WB
The Menace	1932	Col.
The Missing Juror	1944	Col.
Money and the Woman	1940	FN/WB
The Monkey Talks	1927	Fox
Murder in Times Square	1943	Col.
Music Is Magic	1935	Fox
My Son	1925	FN
Mystery House	1938	FN/WB
Mystery Ship	1941	Col.
Nancy Drew and the Hidden Staircase	1939	WB
Nancy Drew-Detective	1938	WB
Nancy Drew-Troubleshooter	1939	WB
No Babies Wanted	1928	US
An Old Sweetheart of Mine	1923	Metro.
Olsen's Night Out	1934	Fox
On the Level *	1930	Fox
On Trial	1939	WB

Once a Doctor	1937	FN/WB
One Dangerous Night	1943	Col.
One Mysterious Night	1944	Col.
One Woman Idea	1929	Fox
Paid To Love	1927	Fox
Passport to Suez	1943	Col.
Penrod and Sam	1937	FN/WB
Polo Joe	1936	WB
The Power of the Whistler	1945	Col.
Prarie Thunder *	1937	FN/WB
The Princess and the Plumber *	1930	Fox
Public Wedding	1937	WB
Pursued	1934	Fox
Rackety Rax	1932	Fox
The Redeeming Sin	1925	WB
Renegades	1930	Fox
Repeat Performance	1947	EL
Return of the Vampire *	1943	Col.
Rubber Racketeers	1942	Mon.
Scarface *	1932	UA
Sergeant Mike	1945	Col.
She Loved a Fireman	1938	FN/WB
Sir Lumberjack	1926	US
The Skywayman *	1920	Fox
Slaves of Beauty	1927	Fox
Stand Up and Cheer *	1934	Fox
Stars On Parade	1944	Col.
The Stork Pays Off	1941	Col.
Such Men Are Dangerous	1930	Fox
Sweetheart of Sigma Chi	1946	Mon.
They Shall Play	1921	US
Three Girls Lost	1931	Fox
The Three Sisters	1930	Fox
Through the Dark *	1924	Gold.
Times Square Playboy	1936	WB
Treachery Rides the Range	1936	WB
Trick for Trick	1933	Fox
2 Senoritas from Chicago	1943	Col.
The Unchastened Woman	1925	US
Under Pressure *	1935	Fox
Underground Agent	1942	Col.
West of Shanghai	1937	FN/WB
When Were You Born?	1938	FN/WB
White Bondage	1937	WB
White Eagle	1932	Col.
Wild Company	1930	Fox
Wolf Fangs	1927	Fox
The Woman of Bronze	1923	Metro.

448. MIROSLAV ONDRICEK

Amadeus	1984	Orion
Audition	1968	Czech.
Awakenings	1990	Col.
Big Shots	1987	Lor./TCF
Cerne Slunce	1979	Czech.
Competition	1968	Czech.
Dark Sun	1980	Czech.
Diane's Body	1969	Czech./Fr.
The Divine Emma	1980	Czech.
F/X	1986	Orion
The Fireman's Ball	1967	Czech.
Funny Farm	1988	WB
Game of the Apple	1977	Czech.
Hair *	1979	UA
Hotel Pacific	1975	Czech.
If	1968	GB--Par.
Intimate Lighting	1969	Czech.
Jakub	1977	Czech.
Loves of a Blonde	1965	Czech.
Martyrs of Love	1968	Czech.
O Lucky Man!	1973	GB--WB
Ragtime	1981	DeL.
Silkwood	1983	ABC
Slaughterhouse Five	1972	Univ.
Taking Off	1971	Univ.
Valmont	1989	Orion
World According to Garp	1982	WB

449. S. D. ONIONS

The Amorous Sex	1963	GB
Black Memory	1947	GB
Bless 'Em All	1949	GB
The Curse of the Wraydons	1946	GB
Don Giovanni	1954	GB
Give a Dog a Bone	1966	GB
The Golden Rabbit	1962	GB
The Greed of William Hart	1948	GB
King of the Underworld	1952	GB
A Matter of Murder	1949	GB
Murder at 3AM	1953	GB
The Mysterious Mr. Nicholson	1947	GB
The Night We Got the Bird	1960	GB
Romeo and Juliet	1966	GB--Emb.
Der Rosenkavalier	1962	GB
Six Men	1951	GB
Skid Kids	1953	GB
Stars in Your Eyes	1956	GB

The Temptress	1949	GB
Tim Driscoll's Donkey	1955	GB

450. ARTHUR ORNITZ (1917-1985)

Act One	1963	WB
The Anderson Tapes	1971	Col.
Badge 373	1973	Par.
The Boys in the Band	1970	US
Change of Mind	1969	US
Charly	1968	US
The Chosen	1981	US
The Connection	1961	US
Death Wish	1974	Par.
Forever Young, Forever Free	1976	Univ.
The Goddess	1958	Col.
Hanky Panky	1982	Col.
Heart of the Garden *	1985	US
House of Dark Shadows	1970	MGM
Jacktown	1962	US
Law and Disorder	1975	US
Me, Nathalie	1969	US
A Midsummer Night's Dream	1967	US
Minnie and Moskowitz	1971	Univ.
Next Stop Greenwich Village	1975	TCF
Oliver's Story	1978	Par.
The Possession of Joel Delaney	1971	US
The Pusher	1960	UA
Requiem for a Heavyweight	1962	Col.
Serpico	1973	Par.
Sweet Suzy	1973	US
Tattoo	1980	US
Thieves *	1977	Par.
A Thousand Clowns	1965	UA
The Tiger Makes Out	1967	Col.
An Unmarried Woman	1977	TCF
Without Each Other	1962	US
The World of Henry Orient *	1964	UA
The Young Doctors	1961	UA

451. ALFRED ORTLIEB

The ABC of Love	1919	Pathe
The Bait	1921	Par.
The Black Panther's Club *	1921	US
The Fair Cheat	1923	US
Greater Love Hath No Man *	1915	Metro.
The Heart of a Painted Woman	1915	Metro.
Lafayette We Come!	1918	US

Lifting Shadows	1920	Pathe
The Light in the Dark *	1922	FN
Love's Penalty	1921	FN
Lover's Island	1925	US
A Modern Salome *	1920	Metro.
None So Blind	1923	US
The Shooting of Dan McGrew	1915	Metro.
Stardust	1921	FN
Stars of Glory	1919	US
The Streets of New York	1922	US
Tarnished Reputations *	1920	Pathe
The Thirteenth Chair *	1919	Pathe
The Unfair Sex	1926	US
The Unknown Love	1919	Pathe
When Love Grows Cold *	1925	US
The White Circle	1920	Par.

452. LOUIS OSTLAND

By Hook or Crook	1918	US
The Purple Lily *	1918	US
Road to France	1918	US
Susan's Gentleman	1917	US
The Wasp	1918	US

453. ROY OVERBAUGH

American-That's All	1917	US
Away Goes Prejudice	1920	Par.
The Beautiful City *	1925	FN
The Bishop Murder Case	1930	MGM
A Case At Law	1917	US
Classmates *	1924	FN
A Dark Lantern	1920	US
Dr. Jekyll and Mr. Hyde	1920	Par.
Erstwhile Susan	1919	US
Footlights	1921	Par.
Fury	1923	FN
Grafters	1917	US
Little Accident	1931	Univ.
Love's Boomerang	1922	Par.
The Magic Cup	1921	US
The Man from Home	1922	Par.
The Man Who Made Good	1917	US
Nell Gwyn	1926	GB--FN
New Toys	1925	FN
On the Jump	1918	Fox
Outside the Law	1930	Univ.
Panthea *	1917	Selz.

Penrod and Sam	1931	FN
Sadie Love	1920	Par.
Sentimental Tommy	1921	Par.
Shore Leave *	1925	FN
Soul-Fire	1925	FN
The Spanish Jade	1922	Par.
A Successful Failure	1917	US
39 East	1920	US
Together We Live	1935	Col.
Wanted-A Husband	1919	Par.
What Men Want	1930	Univ.
The White Sister	1923	Metro.
Women Men Marry	1922	US
Young Desire	1930	Univ.

454. TED PAHLE

Affair Lafort	1939	Fr.
Augustina of Aragon	1950	Fr.
The Big Noise	1928	FN
Conflict	1939	Fr.
Entente Cordiale *	1939	Fr.
It Happened in Gibraltar	1943	Fr.
The Jazz Age	1929	FBO
Loyola, the Soldier Saitn	1952	US
Marius	1931	Fr.
My Heart Hesitates	1932	Fr.--Par.
Rebel	1931	Fr.--Par.
Stolen Love	1928	FBO
Storm over Asia	1938	Fr.
Ultimatum *	1938	Fr.

455. ERNEST PALMER (1885-1978)

Ali Baba Goes to Town	1937	TCF
Always the Woman	1922	Gold.
Banjo on My Knee	1936	TCF
Belle Starr *	1941	TCF
The Bells Go Down	1943	GB--UA
Berkeley Square	1933	Fox
Birds of a Feather	1935	GB--Univ.
Blood and Sand *	1941	TCF
Broken Arrow	1950	TCF
Business and Pleasure	1932	Fox
Can This Be Dixie?	1936	TCF
Caravan *	1934	Fox
Cavalcade	1933	Fox
Centennial Summer	1946	TCF
Chad Hanna	1940	TCF

Chamber of Horrors	1940	GB--Mon.
Champion of Lost Causes	1925	Fox
Charlie Chan in Paris	1935	Fox
Charlie Chan's Greatest Case	1933	Fox
Cheaters at Play	1932	Fox
Child Thou Gavest Me	1921	FN
City Girl	1930	Fox
Coney Island	1943	TCF
A Connecticut Yankee	1931	Fox
Courageous Mr. Penn	1941	GB
The Crime of Dr. Forbes	1936	TCF
The Dancers	1925	Fox
Delicious	1931	Fox
Devil's Lottery	1932	Fox
Diamond Horsehoe	1945	TCF
The Dolly Sisters	1945	TCF
Down to Earth	1932	Fox
Early To Wed	1926	Fox
East Lynne	1925	Fox
Edge of the World	1937	GB
Even As Eve	1920	FN
Everything Is Rhythm	1940	GB
Facts of Love *	1949	GB
Farmer Takes a Wife *	1935	Fox
Fine Clothes	1925	FN
Flames of Desire	1924	Fox
For You Alone	1944	GB
Four Devils *	1929	Fox
Four Men and a Prayer	1938	TCF
The Gables Mystery	1931	GB--MGM
Gentle Julia	1936	TCF
Ghosts of Berkeley Square	1947	GB
Goldie	1931	Fox
The Goose Steps Out	1942	GB--UA
Great Hotel Murder	1934	Fox
The Great Profile	1940	TCF
Green Fingers	1946	GB
He Found a Star	1941	GB
He Married His Wife	1940	TCF
High School Hero	1927	Fox
Hollywood Cavalcade *	1939	TCF
Honesty-The Best Policy	1926	Fox
Hoopla	1933	Fox
I Wonder Who's Kissing Her Now?	1947	TCF
Ivanhoe	1913	GB
It Could Happen to You	1939	TCF
Just Imagine	1930	Fox
Kentucky *	1938	TCF
The Lisbon Story *	1946	GB
Little Miss Molly	1940	GB
Love Is News	1937	TCF

Love under Fire	1937	TCF
Man Who Broke the Bank at Monte Carlo	1935	Fox
"Marriage License"?	1926	Fox
Married Alive	1927	Fox
Meet the Navy *	1946	GB
Million Dollar Manhunt	1962	GB
The Miracle Man	1919	Par.
Murder in Reverse	1945	GB
Music in the Air	1934	Fox
My Gal Sal	1942	TCF
Mystery Woman	1935	Fox
The New Commandment *	1925	FN
News Is Made at Night	1939	TCF
Next of Kin	1942	GB--Eal./UA
No Other Woman *	1928	Fox
Now I'll Tell	1934	Fox
One Clear Call	1922	FN
Out of the Blue *	1931	GB
Painted Woman	1932	Fox
The Palace of Pleasure	1926	Fox
Pin Up Girl	1944	TCF
Pleasure Crazed *	1928	Fox
Pleasure Cruise	1933	Fox
Prisoners of Love	1921	Gold.
Public Deb Number One	1940	TCF
Red Hot Romance *	1922	FN
The River	1928	Fox
Sailor's Lady	1940	TCF
San Demetrio London *	1943	GB--Eal.
Scudda Hoo! Scudda Hay!	1948	TCF
Second Honeymoon	1937	TCF
7th Heaven *	1927	Fox
Shooting High	1940	TCF
Six Cylinder Love	1931	Fox
Slave Ship	1937	TCF
Sleepers East	1934	Fox
Something for the Boys	1944	TCF
The Song of Life	1922	FN
Song of the Islands	1942	TCF
The Spider	1940	TCF
Springtime *	1948	GB
Springtime in the Rockies	1942	TCF
Stand Up and Cheer *	1934	Fox
Star for a Night	1936	TCF
The Stars Look Down *	1939	GB
Straight, Place and Show	1938	TCF
Street Angel *	1928	Fox
Sunny Side Up	1929	Fox
Sweet Rosie O'Grady	1943	TCF
Tall, Dark and Handsome	1941	TCF

Three Blind Mice	1938	TCF
Three Little Girls in Blue	1946	TCF
The Three Weird Sisters *	1948	GB
Thru Different Eyes *	1929	Fox
Thunderbirds	1942	TCF
The Trial of Vivenne Ware	1932	Fox
The Trojan Brothers *	1946	GB
The Twenty Questions Murder Mystery	1949	GB
20,000 Men a Year	1939	TCF
Under Two Flags	1936	TCF
Uneasy Terms	1948	GB
Wages for Wives	1925	Fox
Waltz Time	1945	GB
The Wanters	1923	FN
Way Down East	1935	Fox
Weekend In Havana	1941	TCF
When the Door Opened	1925	Fox
Wings of Youth	1925	Fox
The Woman Eater	1959	GB--Col.
Women Everywhere	1930	Fox
Yellow Fingers *	1926	Fox

456. CECILIO PANIAGUA

Commando	1962	Belg./Ger./It./ Sp.--AIP
Companys, Catalonia on Trial	1979	Sp.
Custer of the West	1968	Sp.--US
Dr. Coppelius	1968	Sp.--US
The Great Day	1957	It./Sp.
Hunting Party	1977	GB--UA
Island of the Doomed	1967	Ger./Sp.--AA
Mathias Sandorf	1963	Fr.
The Mistress	1976	Sp.
My Daughter Hildegart	1977	Sp.
The Mysterious House of Dr. C	1976	US
100 Rifles	1969	TCF
Remains of the Shipwreck	1978	Sp.
The Revolt of the Slaves	1961	Ger./It./Sp.-- UA
Sonatas *	1959	Sp.
Treasure Island	1971	Fr./Ger./GB/Sp.
Whom God Forgives	1957	Sp.

457. JACK PARKER

Boadicea	1926	GB
Dance Pretty Lady	1932	GB
Dandy Dick	1935	GB

The Return of Bulldog Drummond	1934	GB
Spy 77 *	1933	GB
Tell England *	1931	GB
Wanted	1937	GB

458. RAY PARSLOW

England Made Me	1972	GB
Madhouse	1974	AIP
The Strange Vengeance of Rosalie	1972	TCF
Under the Doctor	1976	GB
The World Is Full of Married Man	1979	GB

459. EDWARD PAUL

Back to Life	1925	US
The Chief	1933	MGM
Children of the Whirlwind	1925	US
The Darling of the Rich	1922	US
Daughters Who Pay *	1925	US
Greater Than Marriage *	1924	Vita.
The Hoosier Schoolmaster	1924	US
The Iron Man	1925	US
The Leavenworth Case	1923	Vita.
Lilies of the Streets *	1925	US
Love of Women	1924	Selz.
Loyal Lives	1923	Vita.
The Man without a Heart	1924	US
Modern Marriage	1923	US
Scandal Sheet	1925	US
Sinner or Saint	1923	Selz.
Solomon in Society	1922	US
The Truth about Wives	1923	US
Two Shall Be Born	1924	Vita.
Virrtuous Liars	1924	Vita.

460. STAN PAVEY

The Belles of St. Trinian's	1954	GB
Curtain Up	1952	GB
Daughter of Darkness *	1947	GB--Par.
Dead of Night *	1945	GB--Rank/Univ.
Dreaming	1944	GB--Eal.
Fame Is the Spur *	1947	GB
The Galloping Major	1951	GB
Guilty?	1956	GB
Happiest Days of Your Life	1950	GB
The Happiness of Three Women	1954	GB

Happiness Ever After	1954	GB
Here Comes the Sun	1945	GB
Hideout	1948	GB
Home Is the Hero	1961	Ire.
Hour of Decision	1957	GB
Mr. Potts Goes to Moscow	1953	GB
The Model Murder Case	1964	GB
My Son the Vampire	1952	GB
Mystery Submarine	1962	GB--Univ.
Pink String and Sealing Wax *	1945	GB--Eal.
The Poacher's Daughter	1958	GB
The Projected Man	1966	GB--Univ.
The Runaway Bus	1954	GB
Shoot First	1953	GB--UA
They Came to a City	1944	GB--Eal.
Tonight's the Night	1954	GB
Too Many Crooks	1958	GB--Rank
Your Past Is Showing	1958	GB--Rank

461. ROBERT PAYNTER

An American Werewolf in London	1981	GB
The Big Sleep	1977	US
Chato's Land	1971	UA
Curtains *	1983	Can.
The Final Conflict *	1981	TCF
Firepower *	1979	US
The Games	1970	TCF
Hannibal Brooks	1968	UA
Lawman	1970	UA
Little Shop of Horrors	1986	WB
The Mechanic *	1972	UA
National Lampoon's European Vacation	1985	WB
The Nightcomers	1971	GB
Scorpio	1972	UA
Scream For Help	1984	Lor.
Spies Like Us	1985	WB
Strike It Rich	1990	GB/US
Superman II *	1980	WB
Superman III	1983	GB
Terminus *	1961	GB
Trading Places	1983	Par.
When the Whales Came	1989	GB--TCF

462. KENNETH PEACH (1903-1987)

Battle at Bloody Beach	1961	TCF
Blood on the Arrow	1964	AA
Born Wild	1968	AIP

Chicago Confidential	1957	UA
City Beneath the Sea	1970	TCF
Curse of the Faceless Man	1958	UA
A Dog's Best Friend	1960	UA
Five Steps to Danger	1956	UA
The Girl from San Lorenzo	1950	UA
Gun Brothers	1956	UA
Guns, Girls and Gangsters	1958	UA
Hell's Belles	1969	AIP
The Incredible Journey *	1963	Dis.
The Iron Sheriff	1957	UA
It! The Terror From Beyond Space	1958	UA
Jesse James' Women	1954	UA
Lone Ranger and the City of Gold	1958	UA
The Lost Missile	1958	UA
Pufnstuf	1970	Univ.
Sniper's Ridge	1961	TCF
Sons of the Desert	1934	MGM
A Time for Killing	1967	Col.
Toughest Gun in Tombstone	1958	UA
When the Clock Strikes	1961	UA

463. C. M. PENNINGTON-RICHARDS

Always a Bride	1953	GB
All Over the Town	1949	GB
Aunt Clara	1954	GB
A Christmas Carol	1951	GB--UA
Desperate Moment	1953	GB
Esther Waters *	1947	GB
Forbidden Cargo	1934	GB
The Frightened Bride	1952	GB
The Hidden Room	1949	GB--EL/Rank
It's Never Too Late	1956	GB
The Magic Garden	1952	S.Afr.
1984	1956	GB--Col.
The Reluctant Saint	1962	It.--US
Salt to the Devil	1949	GB--EL/Rank
Something Money Can't Buy	1952	GB--Univ.
Star of India	1956	GB--UA
Tarzan and the Lost Safari	1957	GB--MGM
Tom Brown's School Days *	1951	GB--UA
Treasure Hunt	1952	GB
White Corridors	1951	GB
Woman in the Hall *	1947	GB--Rank
The Wooden Horse	1950	GB

464. JEAN PENZER

The African	1983	Fr.

Aloise	1975	Fr.
Bernadette	1988	Fr.
The Blockhead Fair	1963	Fr.
The Body of My Enemy	1976	Fr.
Le Bon Plaisir	1984	Fr.
Buffet Froid	1979	Fr.
Les Caprices de Marie	1970	Fr.--UA
Chariots Go to Spain	1972	Fr.
Chimney No. 4	1966	Ger.
Destroy, She Said	1970	Fr.
The Devil by the Tail	1969	Fr./It.--UA
Fear in the City	1975	Fr.
Five Day Lover	1961	Fr.
5% Risk	1980	Belg./Fr.--Orion
Games of Love	1960	Fr.
Get Your Handkerchiefs Ready	1978	Fr.
Give Her the Moon	1970	Fr./It.--UA
Go See Mother...Father Is Working	1978	Fr.
Hail the Artist	1973	Fr.
Happiness Is for Tomorrow	1962	Fr.
The Heir	1973	Fr.
Hell Train	1984	Fr.
L'Incorrigible	1975	Fr.
Inheritor	1973	Fr.
The Joker	1961	Fr.
Lady Oscar	1979	Fr./Jap.
A Man to Kill	1967	Fr./Sp.
The Meetings of Anna	1978	Belg./Fr./Ger.
My Buddy's Girl	1983	Fr.
Our Story	1984	Fr.
Papa's Cinema	1970	Fr.--Col.
The Passerby of the Sans Souci Caf	1982	Fr./Ger
Playtime	1963	Fr.
The Predator	1976	Fr.
La Recreation	1961	Fr.
Red Pants	1963	Fr.--Col.
A Room in Town	1982	Fr.
Rumba	1987	Fr.
Seven Capital Sins *	1963	Fr./It.--Emb.
The Thousandth Window	1960	Fr.
Three Seats for the 26th	1988	Fr.
20,000 Leagues across the Earth *	1961	Fr./USSR
The Two of Us	1968	Fr.
Without Apparent Motive	1972	Fr.--TCF
You Only Die Twice	1985	Fr.

465. LACEY PERCIVAL

The Adventures of Algy *	1925	Aus.

Around the Boree Log	1925	Aus.
The Betrayer	1921	Aus.
The Birth of White Australia	1928	Aus.
The Digger Earl	1921	Aus.
The Dingo	1923	Aus.
The Dinkin Bloke	1923	Aus.
Dope	1924	Aus.
Down Under *	1927	Aus.
The Face at the Window	1919	Aus.
£ 500 Reward	1918	Aus.
His Convict Bride	1918	Aus.
Joe	1924	Aus.
The Kingdom of Twilight *	1929	Aus.
The Mystery of the Hansom Cab	1925	Aus.
Painted Daughters	1925	Aus.
Possum Padlock	1921	Aus.
Prehistoric Hayseeds	1923	Aus.
Robbery under Arms	1920	Aus.
The Sealed Room	1926	Aus.
Tall Timber	1926	Aus.

466. JAMES PERGOLA

Hardly Working	1981	TCF
Hot Stuff	1979	Col.
Love Child	1982	WB
Nobody's Perfekt	1981	Col.
Police Academy 5: Assignment Miami Beach	1988	WB
Smokey and the Bandit III	1983	Univ.
Thunder and Lightning	1977	TCF
What Comes Around	1986	US

467. GEORGES PERINAL (1897-1965)

A Nous la Liberte	1932	Fr.
Affairs of Adelaide	1948	GB--TCF
Blood of a Poet	1930	Fr.
Bonjour Tristesse	1957	Col.
Catherine the Great	1934	GB--UA
The Challenge	1938	GB
Dangerous Moonlight *	1941	GB
Dark Journey *	1937	GB--Korda/UA
David Golder *	1932	Fr.
The Day They Robbed the Bank of of England	1960	GB--MGM
Drums *	1938	GB--Korda/UA
Escape Me Never *	1935	GB--UA
The Fallen Idol	1948	GB

First of the Few *	1942	GB--RKO
The Four Feathers *	1939	GB--Korda/UA
The Girl from Maxim's	1936	GB
Honeymoon *	1959	GB
I'll Never Forget You	1951	GB--TCF
An Ideal Husband *	1947	GB
If This Be Sin	1950	GB
Immoral Charge	1962	GB
A King in New York	1957	GB
Lady Chatterley's Lover	1955	Fr.--Col.
The Life and Death of Colonel Blimp *	1943	GB
Loser Takes All	1956	GB
Maldone *	1927	Fr.
A Man about the House *	1947	GB
The Man Who Loved Redheads	1954	GB--UA
Le Million *	1931	Fr.
The Mudlark	1950	GB--TCF
Murder on Diamond Row	1937	GB--UA
No Highway	1951	GB--TCF
Les Nouveaux Messieurs *	1928	Fr.
Old Bill and Son	1940	GB
Once More With Feeling	1960	Col.
Operation X	1951	GB--Col.
Oscar Wilde	1959	GB
Prison without Bars	1938	GB--UA
Private Life of Don Juan	1934	GB--UA
Private Life of Henry VIII	1933	GB--UA
Quartorze Juillet	1933	Fr.
Rembrandt *	1937	GB--UA
St. Joan	1957	UA
Sanders of the River	1936	GB--UA
Satellite in the Sky *	1956	WB
Serious Charge	1959	GB
Sous Les Toits de Paris	1930	Fr.
The Thief of Baghdad *	1940	GB--UA
Things To Come	1936	GB--UA
Three Cases of Murder	1954	GB
Tom Thumb	1958	GB--MGM
Under the Red Robe *	1937	GB--TCF
Vacation from Marriage *	1945	GB--MGM
The Woman for Joe	1955	GB--Rank

468. HARRY PERRY

April Showers	1923	US
Are You a Failure?	1923	US
Borderland	1922	Par.
The Breath of Scandal	1924	US
The Broken Wing	1923	US
Cappy Ricks	1921	Par.

City of Silent Men	1921	Par.
The Conquest of Canaan	1921	Par.
The Crimson Challenge	1922	Par.
The Easy Road	1921	Par.
The Faith Healer	1921	Par.
The Fighting American	1924	Univ.
Flattery *	1925	US
The Girl Who Came Back	1923	US
Go Straight	1925	US
Hell's Angels *	1930	UA
If You Believe It, It's So	1922	Par.
The Mansion of Aching Hearts	1925	US
The Midnight Flyer	1925	US
Now We're in the Air	1927	Par.
The Ordeal	1922	Par.
A Prince There Was	1921	Par.
Shadows	1922	US
Sins of Roxanne *	1920	Par.
The Vanishing American *	1925	Par.
The Virginian	1923	US
White and Unmarried	1921	Par.
Wings *	1927	Par.

469. PAUL PERRY (?-1963)

The Air Legion	1929	FBO/RKO
At the End of the World	1921	Par.
Behold My Wife!	1920	Par.
The City of Dim Faces	1918	Par.
The Cruise of the Make-Believes	1918	Par.
David Golder *	1932	Fr.
Everywoman	1919	Par.
Forbidden Paths	1917	Par.
The Ghost House	1917	Par.
Good Gracious Annabelle	1919	Par.
Hidden Pearls	1918	Par.
The House That Jazz Built	1921	US
Introduce Me *	1925	US
Jane Goes a'Wooing	1919	Par.
The Jucklins	1920	Par.
The Lash	1916	FP
The Little Minister	1921	Par.
Love in the Desert	1929	FBO
Men, Women and Money	1919	Par.
Nan of Music Mountain	1917	Par.
On the Stroke of Three	1924	US
The Outside Woman	1921	US
Over the Border	1922	Par.
Pettigrew's Girl	1919	Par.
Pink Gods	1922	Par.

Ponjola	1923	FN
The Round Up	1920	Par.
The Sea Wolf	1920	Par.
Singed Wings	1922	Par.
Sinners in Love	1928	FBO
Souls for Sables	1925	US
A Sporting Chance	1919	Par.
Such a Little Pirate	1918	Par.
Sweet Kitty Bellairs	1916	FP
The Thousand Dollar Husband	1916	FP
Told in the Hills *	1919	Par.
Waking Up the Town *	1925	UA
What Money Can't Buy	1917	Par.
Wild Youth	1918	Par.

470. HENRI PERSIN

Angelique	1964	Fr.
Angelique and the King	1966	Fr./It.
Angelique et Le Sultan	1968	Fr.
Angelique Marquise des Anges	1965	Fr./It.
Big Gamble	1960	Fr.
Brigade Anti-Gangs	1966	Fr.
Catherine, One Love Is Enough	1969	Fr.
Coplan FX Casse Tout	1965	Fr.
Une Corde, Un Colt	1969	Fr./It.
El Condor	1970	NG
The Exterminators	1965	Fr.
I Killed Rasputin	1965	Fr.
The Knight from Pardaillan	1962	Fr.
Laissez Tirer Les Tireurs	1964	Fr.
The Legend of Frenchie King	1971	Fr./GB/It./Sp.
The Longest Day *	1962	TCF
Marvelous Angelique	1965	Fr.
Oil Girls	1971	Fr.
The Sergeant	1968	WB
Seven Guys and a Girl	1967	Fr./It./Rom.
Three Disordered Children	1966	Fr.
A Toi de Faire, Mignonne	1963	Fr.
Unite Congo	1962	Congo/Fr.
Untameable Angelique	1967	Fr./Ger./It.
You Do It, Cutie	1963	Fr.

471. DON PETERMAN

American Flyers	1985	WB
Cocoon	1985	TCF
Flashdance	1983	Par.
Gung Ho!	1986	Par.

King of the Mountain	1981	Univ.
Kiss Me Goodbye	1982	TCF
Planes, Trains and Automobiles	1987	Par.
Rich and Famous	1981	MGM-UA
She's Having a Baby	1988	Par.
She's Out of Control	1989	Col.
Splash	1984	Dis.
Star Trek IV: The Voyage Home	1986	Par.
When a Stranger Calls	1979	Col.
Young Doctors in Love	1982	TCF

472. GEORGE PETERS

The Adventurous Sex	1925	US
All Aboard	1927	FN
The Bandolero	1924	Metro.-Gold.
The Broken Violin	1923	US
The Brown Derby *	1926	FN
The Girl with the Jazz Heart	1920	Gold.
The Highest Bidder	1921	Gold.
Jacqueline *	1923	US
Piccadilly Jim	1920	Selz.
The Power Within	1921	Pathe
Serenade	1921	FN
Sooner or Later	1920	Selz.
Stepping Along *	1926	FN
Taxi	1919	US
Upside Down	1919	US
Wanted For Murder	1919	US

473. C. GUS PETERSON

Adventure's End	1937	Univ.
Arizona Days	1937	GN
Ashes of Hope	1917	US
The Beachcomber	1915	US
Black Bandit	1938	Univ.
Career Girl	1944	PRC
Charley's Aunt	1925	US
The Chechako	1914	Par.
Divorce Made Easy *	1929	Par.
Get Along, Little Dogies	1937	Rep.
Golden Dreams	1922	Gold.
The Gray Dawn	1922	US
Guilty Trails	1938	Univ.
Gunsmoke Ranch	1937	Rep.
The Hand at the Window	1918	US
Heart's Haven	1922	US
Her Purchase Price	1919	US

His Enemy the Law	1918	US
Hold Your Breath *	1924	US
I Love You	1918	US
Lady in the Death House	1944	PRC
Machine Gun Mama	1944	PRC
Madame Behave *	1925	US
Mademoiselle Paulette	1918	US
The Mysterious Rider	1921	Par.
The Mystery of the Hooded Horseman	1937	GN
The New Frontier	1935	Rep.
An Odyssey of the North	1914	Par.
Old Loves for New	1918	US
The Oregon Trail	1936	Rep.
Pagan Lady *	1931	Col.
Prarie Justice	1938	Univ.
Reckless Romance *	1924	US
Riders of the Rockies	1937	GN
Rogue and Riches	1920	Univ.
Sing Cowboy Sing	1937	GN
The Sky Pilot	1921	FN
Sweethearts On Parade	1930	Col.
Tex Rides with the Boy Scouts	1937	GN
Trouble in Texas	1937	GN
When Romance Rides *	1924	Gold.

474. ALEX PHILLIPS (1901-1977)

The Absentee	1952	Mex.
Adam and Eve	1956	Mex.
Adventures of Joselito and Tom Thumb	1960	Mex.
The Adventures of Robinson Crusoe	1953	UA
Arde	1971	Mex.
Cafe Concordia	1943	Mex.
Castle of Purity	1974	Mex.
Come On Now, Ponciano	1937	Mex.
Divorce Made Easy *	1929	Par.
El Baul Macabro	1936	Mex.
The Female Soldier	1966	Mex.
For the Love of Mike	1960	TCF
Geronimo	1962	UA
Glorious Nights	1938	Mex.
Green Shadow	1955	Mex.
Hold Your Breath *	1924	US
Jalisco Don't Backslide	1941	Mex.
The Last of the Fast Guns	1958	Univ.
Little Red Riding Hood	1963	Mex.
Little Village	1962	Mex.
The Littlest Outlaw *	1955	Dis.
The Mad Empress *	1940	Mex.--WB
Mad Woman	1952	Mex.

Madame Behave *	1925	PDC
Man Friday	1975	GB
The Nervous Wreck	1926	PDC
The Net	1953	Mex.
Night of a Thousand Cats	1972	Mex.
Of Love and Desire	1963	TCF
One Life for Another	1934	Mex.--Col.
The Other One	1947	Mex.
Pancho Villa Returns	1950	Mex.
Papa's Intrigues	1939	Mex.
The Proud Ones	1953	Fr./Mex.
The Queen's Swordsman	1963	Mex.
Santa	1932	Mex.
See My Lawyer *	1921	US
Seven Days *	1925	PDC
The Shame of the Sabine Women	1962	Mex.
Sierra Baron	1958	TCF
The Sinner of Magdala	1950	Mex.
Ten Days to Tulara	1958	Mex.
Time to Die	1966	Mex.
Tizoc	1957	Mex.
Up and Down	1959	Mex.--Col.
Up in Mabel's Room *	1926	PDC
Vertigo	1946	Mex.
Villa!	1958	TCF
We Two	1957	Mex.
The Wonderful Country *	1959	UA
Yolanda	1943	Mex.

475. ALEX PHILLIPS, JR.

Allan Quatermain and the Lost City of Gold *	1987	Cannon
Born in East LA	1987	Univ.
The Bricklayers	1977	Mex.
Bring Me the Head of Alfredo Garcia	1974	UA
Buck and the Preacher	1971	Col.
Caboblanco	1981	AE
Canoa	1976	Mex.
Chac *	1975	Mex.
Un Chileno en Espana *	1963	Chile
The Cubs	1975	Mex.
Demonoid	1981	US
The Devil's Rain	1975	Mex.--US
The Distant Wind *	1965	Mex.
Fade To Black	1980	US
Firewalker	1986	Cannon
The Fool Killer	1965	AA
Foxtrot	1976	Mex./Switz.
The Goat	1982	Fr.

Good Luck, Miss Wyckoff	1979	US
The Great Scout and Cathouse Thursday	1976	AIP
The Heist	1976	Mex.
High Risk	1981	US
King Solomon's Mines	1985	Cannon
Little Treasure	1985	Tri-S.
Monday's Child	1967	Arg.--US
Murphy's Law	1986	Cannon
National Mechanics	1975	Mex.
Number One with a Bullet	1987	Cannon
Las Poquianchis	1977	Mex.
The Savage Is Loose	1974	US
The Seduction	1981	Mex.
Sorceress	1983	US
Sunburn	1979	Par.
Surf II	1984	US
Survival Run	1980	US
Swap	1980	Mex.
To Kill a Stranger	1985	US
Torchlight	1984	US
Traitors of San Angel	1967	Mex.
Trouble in Spies	1987	DeL./HBO
Wolf Lake	1984	US
The Wrath of God	1972	MGM
Yanco	1961	Mex.

476. FRANK PHILLIPS

The Apple Dumpling Gang	1974	Dis.
The Apple Dumpling Gang Rides Again	1979	Dis.
Bedknobs and Broomsticks	1971	Dis.
The Black Hole	1979	Dis.
The Computer Wore Tennis Shoes	1970	Dis.
Darker Than Amber	1970	NG
Escape to Witch Mountain	1975	Dis.
Goin' Coconuts	1978	US
Going Ape!	1981	Par.
Gus	1976	Dis.
Herbie Goes Bananas	1980	Dis.
Herbie Rides Again	1974	Dis.
Hot Lead and Cold Feet	1978	Dis.
The Island at the Top of the World	1974	Dis.
Midnight Madness	1980	Dis.
No Deposit, No Return	1976	Dis.
Now You See Him, Now You Don't	1972	Dis.
One and Only Genuine Original Family Band	1968	Dis.
Pete's Dragon	1977	Dis.
Return from Witch Mountain	1978	Dis.
Rider on a Dead Horse	1962	AA

Scandalous John	1971	Dis.
The Shaggy DA	1976	Dis.
Snowball Express	1972	Dis.
Treasure of Matecumbe	1976	Dis.
The Wild Country	1970	Dis.
Wild Wild Winter	1966	Univ.
The World's Greatest Athlete	1973	Dis.

477. LOUIS PHYSIOC

Bab's Diary	1917	Par.
Call of the Circus	1930	US
A Girl Like That	1917	Par.
The Glorious Lady	1919	Selz.
God of Mankind	1928	US
The Knife	1918	US
The Millionaire Cowboy	1924	US
The No-Gun Man	1924	US
Peck's Bad Girl	1918	Gold.
A Perfect 36	1918	Gold.
The Reason Why	1918	US
Rolling Stones	1916	FP
The Spite Bride	1919	Selz.
Thundering Dawn *	1923	Univ.
Upstairs and Down	1919	Selz.
Western Limited	1932	Mon.

478. TONY PIERCE-ROBERTS

Cold Room	1984	GB
Kipperbang	1984	GB--MGM-UA
Mr. & Mrs. Bridge	1990	US
Moonlighting	1982	GB--Univ.
Out Cold	1989	GB
A Private Function	1985	GB
Slaves of New York	1989	Tri-S.
Tiger's Tale	1987	GB

479. KEVIN PIKE

Apprentice to Murder	1988	US
Bad Medicine	1985	TCF
Betsy's Wedding	1990	Touch.
The Dresser	1983	Col.
A Dry White Season *	1989	MGM/UA
Gulag	1985	HBO
A New Life	1988	Par.

480. TOMISLAV PINTER

Artificial Paradise	1990	Yugo
Battle of the Neretva	1970	Ger./It./Yugo--AIP
Birch Tree	1967	Yugo.
Crusoe	1988	US
Cyclops	1982	Yugo.
Dancing On Water	1986	US
Dare Devil's Time	1977	Yugo.
The Eleventh Commandment	1970	Yugo.
Fear	1975	Yugo.
The Fourth Companion	1967	Yugo.
Gamblers	1970	US
Gazija	1981	Yugo.
Girl	1987	GB
Happy Gypsies	1967	Yugo.
Heritage	1985	US
The House	1975	Yugo.
Jaws of Life	1984	Yugo.
Journalist	1979	Yugo.
Knockout	1971	Yugo.
Manifesto	1988	Cannon
Meeting Place	1989	Yugo.
Monday or Tuesday	1966	Yugo.
Montenegro	1981	GB/Swed.
Nothing but Words of Praise for the Deceased	1984	Yugo.
Pavle Pavlovoc	1975	Yugo.
Petria's Wrath	1983	Yugo.
Pigs and Pearls	1981	GB/Swed.
Point 995	1960	Yugo.
Private Vices, Public Virtue	1976	It./Yugo.
Return	1979	Yugo.
Rondo	1967	Yugo.
Round Trip	1978	Yugo.
Search	1979	Yugo.
Sleep Well, My Love	1987	GB
Snowstorm	1977	Yugo.
Steppenwolf	1974	US
Sutjeska	1973	Yugo.
That Summer of White Roses	1989	GB/Yugo.
Three	1966	Yugo.
Transylvania 6-5000	1985	US
Twilight Time	1983	Yugo.--MGM-UA
The Way to Paradise	1971	Yugo.
The Widowhood of Karolina Zasler	1976	Yugo.

481. ROBERT PITTACK

All-American Co-Ed	1941	UA

Bells of San Fernando	1947	US
Brooklyn Orchid	1942	UA
Calaboose	1943	UA
The Devil with Hitler	1942	UA
Dudes Are Pretty People	1942	UA
Fall In	1943	UA
Fiesta *	1941	UA
The Girl from Scotland Yard	1937	Par.
Goin' to Town	1944	RKO
Kit Carson *	1940	UA
Little Iodine	1946	UA
Mad Wednesday	1947	RKO
Meet Dr. Christian	1939	RKO
Midnight Madonna	1937	Par.
Mind Your Business	1937	Par.
Miss Polly	1941	UA
Niagara Falls	1941	UA
Pennies from Heaven	1936	Col.
Prarie Chickens	1943	UA
Susie Steps Out	1946	UA
Tanks a Million	1941	UA
Taxi, Mister	1943	UA
That Nazty Nuisance	1943	UA
That's My Baby	1944	Rep.
The Vampire's Ghost *	1945	Rep.
Waco	1966	Par.
Yankee Fakir	1947	Rep.
Yanks Ahoy	1943	UA

482. LARRY PIZER

All Neat in Black Stockings	1969	GB--NG/WB
Cattle Annie and Little Britches	1980	Univ.
The Europeans	1979	GB
Four in the Morning	1965	GB
Isadora	1968	GB--Univ.
Killing Hour	1985	US
Morgan! *	1966	GB
Night-Flowers	1979	US
The Optimists	1973	GB--Par.
Our Mother's House	1967	GB--MGM
The Party's Over	1963	GB--AA
Phantom of the Paradise	1974	TCF
Pussy Galore	1965	US
Pussycat Alley	1965	GB
Timerider	1983	US
Where Are the Children?	1986	Col.

483. ROBERT PLANCK (1894-   )

Above Suspicion	1943	MGM
Always Goodbye	1938	TCF
Anchors Aweigh *	1945	MGM
Athena	1954	MGM
The Bat Whispers *	1930	UA
The Belle of New York	1952	MGM
Broken Dreams	1933	Mon.
The Canterville Ghost	1943	MGM
Career Woman *	1936	TCF
Cass Timberlane	1947	MGM
Corsair *	1931	US
Diane	1956	MGM
The Doctor and the Girl	1949	MGM
The Duke of West Point	1938	US
Escape	1940	MGM
Eyes in the Night *	1942	MGM
Frontier Marshal	1934	Fox
Gaby	1956	MGM
Girl Crazy *	1943	MGM
The Girl Most Likely	1956	RKO
The Heavenly Body	1943	MGM
Her Cardboard Lover *	1942	MGM
Hold That Co-Ed	1938	TCF
It Happened in Brooklyn	1947	MGM
It's Great To Be Alive	1933	Fox
Jane Eyre	1935	Mon.
Jane Eyre *	1943	TCF
Jeanne Eagels	1957	Col.
Kentucky Moonshine	1938	TCF
King Kelly of the U.S.A.	1934	Mon.
King of the Turf	1939	US
The King's Thief	1955	MGM
Last of the Mohicans	1936	US
Life Begins in College	1937	TCF
Life in the Raw	1933	Fox
Life Returns	1939	Univ.
Lili	1952	MGM
Little Women *	1949	MGM
Love and Hisses	1937	TCF
Luxury Liner *	1948	MGM
Madame Bovary	1949	MGM
Maisie Goes to Reno	1944	MGM
Man in the Iron Mask	1939	US
Manhattan Love Song	1934	Mon.
The Melody Lingers On	1935	US
Money Means Nothing	1934	Mon.
Moonfleet	1955	MGM
The Moonstone	1934	Mon.
Our Daily Bread	1934	UA

Please Believe Me	1950	MGM
Prisoner of War	1954	MGM
Reaching for the Moon *	1930	UA
Red Salute	1935	US
Remains To Be Seen	1953	MGM
Rendezvous At Midnight	1935	Univ.
Reunion In France	1943	MGM
Rhapsody	1954	MGM
Rich, Young and Pretty	1951	MGM
Royal Wedding	1951	MGM
Scandal at Scourie	1953	MGM
Secret of the Chateau	1935	Univ.
The Secret Witness	1931	Col.
Ship Ahoy *	1942	MGM
The Show-Off	1946	MGM
Silver Lining *	1932	UA
Strange Cargo	1940	MGM
Summer Stock	1950	MGM
Susan and God	1940	MGM
Texas Carnival	1951	MGM
That I May Live	1937	TCF
Thin Ice *	1937	TCF
This Is My Affair	1937	TCF
Three Live Ghosts	1929	UA
The Three Musketeers	1948	MGM
Time Out for Romance	1937	TCF
Torch Song	1953	MGM
Up Goes Maisie	1946	MGM
We Were Dancing	1942	MGM
We Who Are About to Die	1937	RKO
Weekend at the Waldorf	1945	MGM
When Ladies Meet	1941	MGM
Woman Wise	1937	TCF
A Woman's Face	1941	MGM
The Young Stranger	1957	RKO

484.   FRANZ PLANER (1894-1963)

Adventure in Sahara	1938	Col.
Adventures of Martin Eden	1942	Col.
Appointment in Berlin	1943	Col.
Bad for Each Other	1954	Col.
The Beloved Vagabond	1936	Col.
The Big Country	1958	UA
The Blue Veil	1951	RKO
Breakfast at Tiffany's	1961	Par.
A Bullet Is Waiting	1954	Col.
The Caine Mutiny	1954	Col.
Canal Zone	1942	Col.

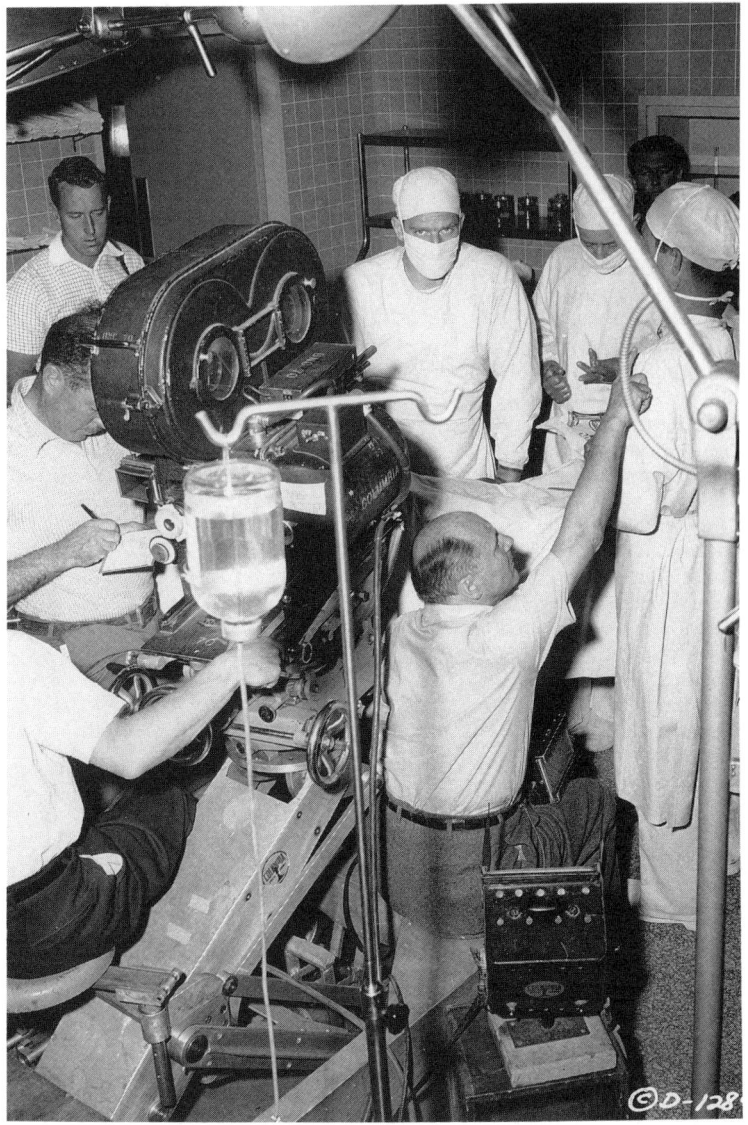

Franz Planer (center, pointing) sets up a shot with Charlton Heston in Bad for Each Other (1954).

Champion	1949	US
Charm of La Boheme	1938	Aust.
The Chase	1947	Col.
Countess of Monte Cristo	1933	Univ.
Criss Cross	1948	Univ.
Cyrano de Bergerac	1950	US
Death of a Salesman	1951	Col.
Decision before Dawn	1951	TCF
Destroyer	1943	Col.
The Dictator	1936	GB
Escape to Glory	1940	Col.
The Exile	1948	Univ.
The Face behind the Mask	1941	Col.
The Five Thousand Fingers of Doctor T	1953	Col.
Flight Lieutenant	1942	Col.
Gasoline Station	1930	Ger.--UFA
Harvard Here I Come	1942	ol.
The Heat's On	1943	Col.
Her Sister's Secret	1946	PRC
His Divorce Reason *	1931	Ger.--UFA
Holiday	1938	Col.
Honolulu Lu	1941	Col.
I Love a Bandleader	1945	Col.
King of Kings *	1961	MGM
Leave It to Blondie	1945	Col.
The Left Hand of God	1955	TCF
Letter from an Unknown Woman	1948	Univ.
Liebelei	1932	Ger.
The Long Wait	1954	UA
Maskerade	1934	Aust.
Meet Boston Blackie	1941	Col.
The Mountain	1956	Par.
My Kingdom for a Cook	1943	Col.
99 River Street	1953	UA
North of Shanghai	1939	Col.
Not As a Stranger	1955	UA
The Nun's Story	1959	WB
Office Manager	1932	Ger.
Once More My Darling	1949	Univ.
Once Upon a Time	1944	Col.
One Touch of Venus	1948	Univ.
Our Wife	1941	Col.
Party Doesn't Answer	1932	Ger.
The Pride and the Passion	1957	UA
The Rebel Son *	1939	GB
Retreat on the Rhine *	1933	Ger.
Roman Holiday *	1953	Par.
Sabotage Squad	1942	Col.
The Scarf	1951	UA
Secret Command	1944	Col.

711 Ocean Drive	1950	Col.
Sing for Your Supper	1941	Col.
Snafu	1945	Col.
Something To Shout About	1943	Col.
The Spirit of Stanford *	1942	Col.
Stage Struck	1957	RKO
The Stork Arrives	1931	Ger.
Strange Affair	1944	Col.
Submarine Raider	1942	Col.
Sweetheart of the Campus	1941	Col.
Take One False Step	1949	Univ.
They Dare Not Love	1941	Col.
Three Girls about Town	1942	Col.
Three Husbands	1950	UA
Time Out for Rhythm	1941	Col.
A Town Is All Upset	1933	Ger.
Twenty Thousand Leagues under the Sea *	1954	Dis.
Unfinished Symphony	1934	Ger.
The Unforgiven	1960	UA
Vendetta *	1950	RKO
The Wife Takes a Flyer	1942	Col.
Zapfenstreich am Rhein *	1930	Ger.

485. H. G. PLIMPTON

Checkers	1919	Fox
For Another Woman	1924	US
The Jungle Trail	1919	Fox
Nero	1922	It.--Fox
Why I Would Not Marry	1918	Fox

486. GABOR POGANY

Antonio Gramsci--The Days of Prison	1977	It.
Assunta Spina	1948	It.
Bluebeard	1972	US
Buona Sera, Mrs. Campbell	1968	It.--UA
Carmela	1949	It.
Cavern	1965	Ger./It./Yugo-- TCF
Dark Purpose	1964	Univ.
Don't Trifle with Women	1957	It.
Double Face	1969	Ger./It.
Duel without Honor	1950	It.
El Amor Brujo *	1967	Sp.
Europe by Night	1959	It.
La Fille de Mata Hari	1954	Fr.
For One Who Dies	1973	It.

Friends for Life	1964	It.
Il Giudizio Universale	1961	It.
The Golden Arrow	1964	It.--MGM
Hornet's Nest	1969	UA
The House of Intrigue	1959	It.--AA
Imperial Venus	1963	Fr./It.
In Olden Days *	1952	It.
Jeanne au Bucher	1954	Fr.
Joan at the Stake	1954	Fr./It.
Judgment in Berlin	1988	US
Kiss of a Dead Woman	1949	It.
The Lady Doctor *	1963	Fr./It./Sp.
The Last Judgment	1961	Fr./It.
Love and Chatter	1958	Fr./It./Sp.
Maddalena	1971	It.
The Magistrate	1959	It./Sp.
A Man Could Get Killed	1966	Univ.
The Man with the Grey Glove	1949	It.
A Nun at the Crossroads	1970	It./Sp.--Univ.
One of Those	1953	It.
Our Times	1953	It.
Pezzo, Capopezzo, e Capitano	1958	Ger./It.
The Player Pianos	1965	Fr./Sp.
The Queen of Babylon	1956	It.--TCF
Romeo and Juliet	1968	It./Sp.
Sins of Rome	1954	It.
Snow Job	1972	WB
Spartacus the Gladiator	1953	It.
Storm	1954	Fr./It.
Stormbound	1952	It.--Rep.
Strange Deception	1953	It.
10:30 PM Summer	1966	It./Sp.
Those Daring Young Men in Their Jaunty Jalopies	1969	Fr./GB/It.-- Par.
Three Bites of the Apple	1966	MGM
Times Gone By	1953	It.
Torpedo Bay	1964	It.
Toto, Vittorio and the Doctor	1958	Fr./It./Sp.
Trapped In Tangiers	1960	It./Sp.--TCF
Turn the Other Cheek	1975	Fr./It.
Two Women	1960	Fr./It.--Emb.
The Uninhibited	1968	Fr./It./Sp.
Valdez Is Coming	1970	UA
The Voice of Silence	1953	It.
War of the Zombies	1965	It.--AIP
Wives and Obscurities	1957	IT.
Women without Names	1950	Fr.

487. GENE POLITO

The Bad News Bears Go to Japan	1978	Par.
Colossus: The Forbin Project	1969	Univ.
Five on the Black Hand Side	1973	UA
Futureworld *	1976	AIP
My Sweet Charlie	1970	Univ.
The Plunderers	1960	AA
Portrait of a Mobster	1961	WB
Prime Cut	1972	NG
The Ride to Hangman's Tree	1967	Univ.
Trackdown	1976	UA
Twist All Night *	1961	AIP
Up in Smoke	1978	Par.
Westworld	1973	MGM

488. SOL POLITO (1892-1960)

The Adventures of Mark Twain	1944	WB
The Adventures of Robin Hood *	1938	WB
Alias Jimmy Valentine	1920	Metro.
Angels with Dirty Faces	1938	WB
Anna Lucasta	1949	Col.
Are You Legally Married?	1919	US
Arsenic and Old Lace	1944	WB
The Bad Lands *	1925	US
The Bad Man	1923	FN
Beyond the Border	1925	US
Big Business Girl	1931	WB
Bill Apperson's Boy	1919	FN
The Bishop of the Ozarks	1923	US
Blessed Event	1932	WB
The Border Patrol	1928	Pathe
Boy Meets Girl	1938	WB
Burning Bridges	1928	Pathe
Burning Daylight	1928	FN
Burglar by Proxy	1919	FN
The Butterfly	1915	US
A Butterfly on the Wheel *	1915	US
A Cafe in Cairo	1924	US
Captains of the Clouds *	1942	WB
Charge of the Light Brigade *	1936	WB
Cinderella Jones	1946	WB
City for Conquest *	1940	WB
Cloak and Dagger	1946	WB
Colleen *	1936	WB
Confessions of a Nazi Spy	1939	WB
The Corn Is Green	1945	WB
The Cotton King	1915	US
The Crimson Runner	1925	US

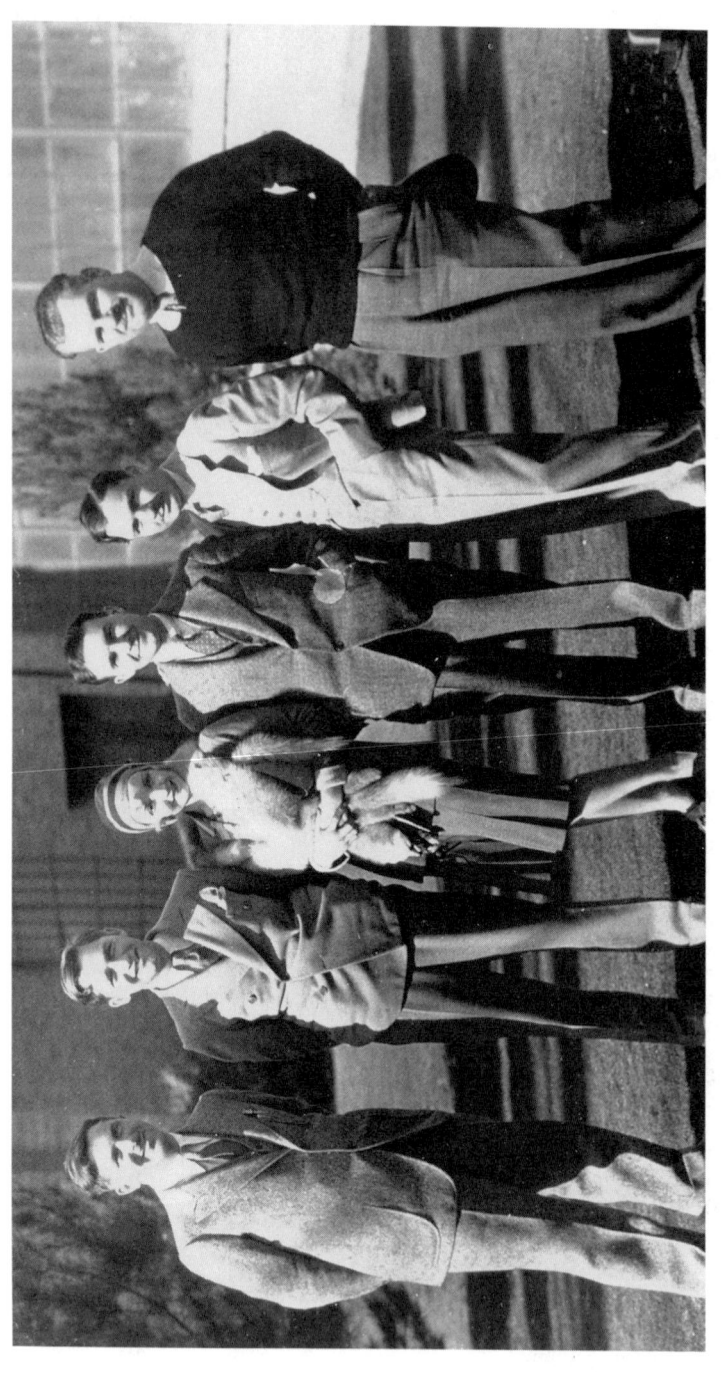

Sol Polito (left) with director Mervyn LeRoy (second from left) and others involved with Show Girl in Hollywood (1930)

Dark Hazard	1934	WB
The Dark House	1932	WB
Dr. Monica	1934	WB
Dodge City *	1939	WB
Driftin' Thru	1926	Pathe
Escape Me Never	1947	WB
Fireman Save My Child	1932	WB
Five Star Final	1931	WB
The Flaming Forties	1924	US
Flirtation Walk *	1934	WB
Forty-Second Street	1933	WB
Four Wives	1939	WB
The Frontier Trail	1926	Pathe
G-Men	1935	WB
The Gay Sisters	1942	WB
The Girl of the Golden West *	1923	FN
The Girl of the Golden West	1930	WB
Go into Your Dance *	1935	WB
Going Wild	1930	WB
Gold Is Where You Find It	1938	WB
Golddiggers of 1933	1933	WB
Golddiggers of Paris *	1938	WB
Gun Gospel	1927	FN
Hard-Boiled Haggerty	1927	FN
The Haunted House	1928	FN
The Hawk's Nest	1928	FN
Heart to Heart	1928	FN
Her Husband's Honor	1918	US
Hi Nellie	1934	WB
The House of Horror *	1929	WB
I Am a Fugitive from a Chain Gang	1932	WB
In Caliente *	1935	WB
Isle of Lost Ships	1929	FN
The Land beyond the Law	1927	FN
The Lightning Rider	1924	US
Local Boy Makes Good	1931	WB
Lonesome Ladies *	1927	FN
The Long Night	1947	RKO
The Love Defender	1919	US
Madame DuBarry	1934	WB
Madonna of the Streets	1930	Col.
Man and the Moment	1929	WB
Mighty Lak' a Rose	1923	FN
The Misleading Lady *	1920	Metro.
M'Liss *	1915	US
No, No, Nanette	1930	WB
Now, Voyager	1942	WB
Numbered Men	1930	WB
On Your Toes *	1939	WB
The Overland Stage	1927	FN
Paint and Powder	1925	US

Paris	1929	WB
The People vs. Nancy Preston	1925	US
The Petrified Forest	1936	WB
Picture Snatcher	1933	WB
Playing Around	1930	WB
The Price of Redemption	1920	Metro.
The Prince and the Pauper	1937	WB
The Private Lives of Elizabeth and		
Essex	1939	WB
Queen X	1917	US
Ready, Willing and Able	1937	WB
The Reckoning Day	1918	US
Rhapsody in Blue *	1945	WB
Rip Van Winkle	1914	US
Roaring Rails	1924	US
The Roof Tree	1921	Fox
Ruling Passions	1918	US
The Ruling Voice	1931	WB
The Santa Fe Trail	1940	WB
Satan Town	1926	Pathe
Scarley Seas	1929	FN
The Sea Hawk	1940	WB
The Sea Wolf	1941	WB
Senor Daredevil	1926	FN
Seven Footsteps to Satan	1929	WB
The Seventh Bandit	1926	Pathe
The Shepherd of the Hills	1928	FN
Shipmates Forever	1935	WB
Should a Woman Tell?	1920	Metro.
Show Girl	1928	FN/WB
Showgirl in Hollywood	1930	WB
Silent Sanderson	1925	US
The Sins of Society	1915	US
The Siren of Seville	1924	US
Soft Shoes	1923	US
Soldiers of Fortune *	1919	US
Somewhere in Sonora	1927	FN
Sons O Guns	1936	WB
Sorry Wrong Number	1948	Par.
A Stolen Life *	1946	WB
Strength of the Pines *	1922	Fox
Suicide Fleet	1931	Pathe/RKO
Sweet Adeline	1935	WB
This Is the Army *	1943	WB
Three Men on a Horse	1936	WB
Three on a Match	1932	WB
Tough To Be Famous *	1932	FN
Treason	1918	US
Trimmed	1922	Univ.
Twin Beds	1929	WB
Union Depot	1932	WB

The Unknown Cavalier	1926	FN
The Variety Show *	1937	WB
Virginia City	1940	WB
The Voice of the Turtle	1948	WB
What Love Forgives *	1919	US
Who Loved Him Best	1918	US
Why Men Leave Home	1924	FN
The Widow from Chicago	1930	WB
Wildfire	1915	US
The Woman in Red	1935	WB
Wonder Bar	1934	WB
The Working Man	1933	WB
You Can't Get Away with Murder	1939	WB

489. PIERO PORTALUPI

Aida	1954	It.
And a Man Came	1965	It.--Par.
Bellissima	1952	It.
The Biggest Bundle of Them All	1968	MGM
Carthage in Flames	1961	Fr./It.--Col.
A Farewell to Arms *	1957	Selz./TCF
Francis of Assisi	1961	TCF
House of Cards	1968	Univ.
Incantesimo Tragico	1950	It.
The Invincible Six	1970	Iran--US
Jessica	1962	Fr./It.--UA
The Loves of Salammbo	1963	Fr./It.--TCF
Love Prelude	1948	It.
Luxury Girls	1953	It.--UA
Monte Cassino	1948	It.
Neapolitan Fantasy	1953	It.
No Peace among the Olives	1950	It.
Romance of a Horsethief	1971	AA
The Statue	1970	GB
Story of a Woman	1969	It.--Univ.
Tombolo	1949	It.
Tragic Spell	1952	It.
Vacation with a Gangster	1952	It.
The Wastrel	1963	It.

490. EDWIN S. PORTER (1869-1941)

Count of Monte Cristo	1913	FP
The Eternal City	1915	FP
A Good Little Devil	1914	FP
Tess of the Storm Country	1914	FP

491. STEPHEN POSEY

American Drive-In	1985	US
Bloody Birthday	1986	US
Emma Mae	1976	US
House Where Death Lives	1982	US
Modern Day Houdini	1983	US
Penitentiary II	1982	MGM-UA
The Slumberparty Massacre	1982	US
Three for the Road	1987	US
Welcome to 18	1986	US

492. G. O. POST

Gentle Julia	1923	Fox
Havoc	1925	Fox
Just Off Broadway	1924	Fox
The Man without a Country	1925	Fox
A Man's Mate	1924	Fox
Marriage in Transit	1925	Fox
The Outsider	1926	Fox
Shirley of the Circus	1922	Fox
The Silver Treasure	1926	Fox
That French Lady	1924	Fox
The Whirlwind of Youth	1927	Par.
You Can't Get Away with It	1923	Fox

493. STEVEN POSTER

Aloha Summer	1988	US
Big Top Pee Wee	1988	Par.
Blood Beach	1981	US
The Boy Who Could Fly *	1986	Lor.
Dead and Buried	1981	AE
The Heavenly Kid	1985	Orion
Next of Kin	1989	WB
Opportunity Knocks	1990	Univ.
Rocky V *	1990	MGM/UA
Someone to Watch Over Me	1987	Col.
Spring Break	1983	Col.
Strange Brew	1983	MGM-UA
Testament	1983	Par.

493a. ROGER PRATT

Batman	1989	WB
Brazil	1985	Univ.
Consuming Passions	1988	GB/US

High Hopes	1988	GB
Meantime	1986	GB
Mona Lisa	1986	GB
Paris by Night	1989	GB
The Sender	1982	Par.

494. ROLAND PRICE

Blood and Steel	1925	US
Call of the Mate	1924	US
The Cowboy and the Flapper	1924	US
A Desperate Moment	1926	US
Do It Now *	1924	US
Down by the Rio Grande	1924	US
Man from God's Country	1924	US
The Martyr Sex	1924	US
Morals for Men	1925	US
The Other Kind of Love	1924	US
The Sword of Valor	1924	US
That Wild West	1924	US
The Thoroughbred	1925	US

495. JACK PRIESTLEY

Across 110th Street	1972	UA
Born To Win *	1971	UA
The First Deadly Sin	1980	US
A Man Called Adam	1966	Emb.
The Midnight Man	1974	Univ.
No Way To Treat a Lady	1968	Par.
Stiletto	1969	AE
The Subject Was Roses	1968	MGM
Where's Poppa?	1970	UA

496. BRIAN PROBYN

Call Him Mr. Shatter *	1976	GB
Count Dracula and His Vampire Bride	1978	GB--Ham.
Downhill Racer	1969	Par.
Far East	1982	GB
Frankenstein and the Monster from Hell	1973	GB--HAm.
Holiday on the Buses	1973	GB
Inn of the Damned	1974	Aus.
Innocent Bystanders	1972	GB--Par.
The Jerusalem File *	1971	Isr.--MGM
The Long Day's Dying	1968	GB--Par.

Man at the Top	1973	GB
The Mango Tree	1977	Aus.
Poor Cow	1967	GB
The Revolutionary	1970	GB--UA
Straight On Till Morning	1972	GB--Ham.

497. ARTHUR QUINN

Blackbirds	1920	US
The Girl Philippa	1917	Vita.
His Brother's Keeper *	1921	US
Kennedy Square	1916	Vita.
Mortmain	1915	Vita.
Philip Holden-Water	1916	US
The Suspect	1916	Vita.

498. JEAN RABIER (1927-   )

Alice or The Last Escapade	1977	Fr.
Banana Skin	1963	Fr.
Bay of Angels	1964	Fr.
The Beautiful Swindlers *	1967	Fr./Holl./It./
Blood Relations	1978	Can./Fr.
Le Bonheur	1966	Fr.
Le Boucher	1970	Fr./It.
The Breakup	1970	Fr.
The Champagne Murders	1968	Fr.--Univ.
Cleo from Five to Seven	1961	Fr.
Cold Sweat	1971	Fr./It.
Cry of the Owl	1987	Fr./It.
Dirty Hands	1976	Fr./Ger./It.
The Evil Eye	1962	Fr.
The Enchanted Isles	1965	Fr./Port.
La Femme Infidele	1968	Fr./It.--AA
From the Boys	1971	Fr./It.
The Hatter's Ghost	1982	Fr.
Heartbreak Ridge	1955	Fr.
High Heels	1972	Fr.
House of Pride	1980	Fr.
An Idiot in Paris	1967	Fr.
Innocents with Dirty Hands	1975	Fr./Ger./It.
Just Before Nightfall	1971	Fr./It.--Col.
Landru	1962	Fr./It.
Let the Beast Die	1969	Fr.
Line of Demarcation	1966	Fr.
The Little Virtuous	1968	Fr.
Marie Chantal against Dr. Kha	1965	Fr./It./Mor./S
Masks	1987	Fr.
The Nada Gang	1974	Fr./It.

No Harm Intended	1987	Fr./It.
The One Man Band	1970	Fr.
Ophelia	1964	Fr.
Les Parapluies de Cherbourg	1964	Fr./Ger.
Paris Seen By ... *	1965	Fr.
Une Partie de Plaisir	1975	Fr.
Poulet au Voyage	1984	Fr.
Quiet Days in Clichy	1990	Fr./Ger./It.
Reckonings Against the Grain	1971	Fr.
Red Wedding Night	1973	Fr.
The Road to Corinth	1967	Fr.
Rogopag *	1963	It.--US
The Scandal	1967	Fr.--Univ.
Seven Capital Sins *	1963	Fr./It.--Emb.
Six in Paris *	1968	Fr.
Ten Days' Wonder	1971	Fr.
The Third Lover	1963	Fr./It.
This Man Must Die	1970	Fr./It.--AA
Le Tigre Aime La Chair Fraiche	1964	Fr.
Le Tigre Se Parfume a La Dynamite	1965	Fr./It./Sp.
To Our Late Unlamented Husband	1988	Fr.
The Twist	1976	Fr.
Violent Noziere	1978	Fr.
Violette	1978	Fr.
Who's Got the Black Box?	1970	Fr./Ger./It.
The Wise Guys	1961	Fr.
Women's Affair	1988	Fr.

499. THOMAS RAE

The Adorable Savage	1920	Univ.
The Fire Cat	1921	Univ.
Lasca	1919	Univ.
Thunder Island	1921	Univ.
A Tokio Siren	1920	Univ.
White Youth	1920	Univ.
Wolves of the North	1921	Univ.

500. OUSAMA RAWI

Alfie Darling	1975	GB--EMI
The Black Windmill	1974	GB--Univ.
The 14	1973	GB--EMI
Little Girl in Blue Velvet	1978	Fr.
Pulp	1972	GB--UA
Skyriders	1976	Greece--TCF
Zulu Dawn	1979	GB--WB

501. DON REDDY

Benji	1974	US
Benji the Hunted	1987	Dis.
The Double McGuffin	1979	US
For the Love of Benji	1977	US
Oh Heavenly Dog	1980	TCF

502. FRANK REDMAN

Along the Rio Grande	1941	RKO
Anne of the Windy Poplars	1940	RKO
Bad Lands	1939	RKO
Bamboo Blonde	1946	RKO
Beauty for the Asking	1939	RKO
Beat the Band	1947	RKO
Career	1939	RKO
Conspiracy	1939	RKO
Crashing Hollywood	1937	RKO
Criminal Court	1946	RKO
Dick Tracy	1945	RKO
Dick Tracy Meets Gruesome	1947	RKO
Dick Tracy's Dilemma	1947	RKO
Ding Dong Williams	1946	RKO
Double Danger	1938	RKO
Double Deal	1950	RKO
Eyes of the Underworld	1929	Univ.
The Falcon in Danger	1943	RKO
The Falcon in Mexico	1944	RKO
The Falcon's Adventure	1946	RKO
The Falcon's Alibi	1946	RKO
Footlight Varieties	1951	RKO
Fugitives for a Night	1938	RKO
Government Girl	1943	RKO
The Great Gildersleeve	1942	RKO
Hawk of the Hills *	1929	Pathe
Having Wonderful Crime	1945	RKO
Here We Go Again	1942	RKO
I'm from the City	1938	RKO
If You Knew Susie	1948	RKO
A Lady Takes a Chance	1943	RKO
Little Orphan Annie	1938	Par.
Look Who's Laughing *	1941	RKO
Maid's Night Out	1938	RKO
Man Alive	1945	RKO
The Marines Fly High	1940	RKO
Men against the Sky	1940	RKO
A Night of Aeventure	1944	RKO
The Pace That Thrills	1952	RKO
Pan-Americana	1945	RKO

Patrick the Great	1945	Univ.
Petticoat Larceny	1943	RKO
Playmates	1941	RKO
Powder Town	1942	RKO
The Saint in New York *	1938	RKO
The Saint Strikes Back	1939	RKO
The Saint Takes Over	1940	RKO
San Quentin	1946	RKO
Shed No Tears	1948	EL
Sing Your Way Home	1945	RKO
Sing Your Worries Away	1942	RKO
Step by Step	1946	RKO
Sunset Pass	1946	RKO
This Land Is Mine	1943	RKO
Too Many Girls	1940	RKO
The Truth About Murder	1945	RKO
Wild Horse Mesa	1947	RKO
You'll Find Out	1940	RKO

503. ART REED

All at Sea	1929	MGM
Baby Face Morgan	1942	PRC
Beyond the Sierras	1928	MGM
Black Dragons	1942	Mon.
Born To Fight	1938	US
The Bushranger	1928	MGM
The Corpse Vanishes	1942	Mon.
Dark Manhattan	1937	US
Death in the Sky *	1937	US
The Desert Rider	1929	MGM
Drums of Jeopardy	1931	US
East Side Kids	1940	Mon.
Fighting Renegade	1939	US
Fighting Thru	1930	US
Flaming Lead	1939	US
Frontier Justice	1936	US
The Girl in the Show	1929	MGM
Girl's Town	1942	PRC
Gold *	1932	US
Hold for Ransom *	1938	US
I Cover Chinatown	1938	US
Lucky Terror	1936	US
Madame X	1929	MGM
Misbehaving Husbands	1941	PRC
Morgan's Last Raid	1929	MGM
The Overland Telegraph	1929	MGM
Phantom Patrol	1936	US
Ranger Courage	1937	Col.
Red Blood of Courage	1935	US

Sioux Blood	1929	MGM
Six Gun Rhythm	1939	GN
Song of the Trail	1936	US
Straight Shooter	1940	US
Swifty	1936	US
A Tenderfoot Goes West	1937	US
The Utah Kid	1930	US
Wild Horse Round Up	1937	US
Wildcat Trooper	1936	US
With Love and Kisses	1937	US

504. MICHAEL REED

Bang, Bang, You're Dead *	1966	AIP
The Devil Ship Pirates	1963	GB--Col./Ham.
Dracula Prince of Darkness	1965	GB--Ham./TCF
Galileo	1976	AFT
Ghost in the Noonday Sun	1984	GB
The Gorgon	1964	GB--Col./Ham.
The Groundstar Conspiracy	1972	Can.--Univ.
Guns in the Heather	1968	GB--Dis.
The Hireling	1973	GB--Col./WB
Leopard in the Snow	1978	GB
Loophole	1980	GB
The McKenzie Break	1970	UA
No Longer Alone	1978	US
October Moth	1959	GB--Rank
On Her Majesty's Secret Service	1969	GB--UA
The Passage	1979	GB--UA
Pleasure Girls	1966	GB
Prehistoric Women	1967	GB--TCF
Rasputin-The Mad Monk	1966	GB--TCF
Shout at the Devil	1976	GB--AIP
The Stick Up	1977	GB
The Traitors	1962	GB--Univ.
Two a Penny	1967	GB
Von Richtofen and Brown	1971	UA
Wild Geese II	1985	GB--Univ.
Zero Population Growth	1971	Par.

505. WILLIAM REESE

Atta Boy *	1926	Pathe
Case of the Howling Dog	1934	WB
Convention City	1933	WB
Don't Bet On Blondes	1935	WB
Fancy Baggage	1929	WB
Fashions of 1934	1934	FN
From Headquarters	1933	WB

The Gamblers	1929	WB
Going Highbrow	1935	WB
Hardboiled Rose	1929	WB
Hearts in Exile	1929	WB
Housewife	1934	WB
The Kennel Murder Case	1933	WB
The Maltese Falcon	1931	WB
A Modern Hero	1934	WB
Meet the Mayor	1938	US
Midnight Alibi	1934	FN/WB
The Office Wife	1930	WB
On the Border	1930	WB
Rough Waters	1930	WB
Scarlet Pages	1930	FN
Under a Texas Moon	1930	WB
When Danger Calls	1927	US

506. ART REEVES

Afraid to Fight	1922	Univ.
The Alster Case *	1915	US
Any Night	1922	US
Arizona Whirlwind	1927	Pathe
Ashes	1922	US
The Bloodhound	1925	US
Body and Soul	1920	Metro.
A Bowery Cinderella	1927	US
Broadway Madness	1927	US
The Dead Line	1926	US
The Fighting Boob	1926	US
The Galloping Kid	1922	Univ.
Galloping Vengeance	1925	US
The Greater Claim	1921	Metro.
Man Rustlin'	1926	US
Man Who Married His Own Wife	1922	Univ.
The Medicine Man *	1930	US
Mile-a-Minute Man	1926	US
The Misfit Ways	1920	Metro.
Out of the Silent North	1922	Univ.
The Phantom of the North	1929	US
The Power of the Weak	1926	US
Pride of Sunshine Alley	1924	US
The Range Terror	1925	US
Satan and the Woman	1928	US
The Stronger Will	1928	US
Sunny Skies *	1930	US
The Swellhead *	1930	US
The Test of Donald Norton	1926	US
That Man Jack! *	1926	US
Untamed Justice	1929	US

Wild Bill Hickok *	1923	Par.
Wings of Adventure	1930	US
Women Who Dare	1928	US

507. WILLIAM REINHART

Ace High	1918	Fox
The Gown of Destiny	1918	US
The Hopper	1918	US
The Isle of Love	1916	US
The Sea Panther	1918	US
Sins of the Children *	1918	US
The Witching Hour	1916	US

508. RAY REIS

Ace of Action	1926	US
The Ballyhoo Booster	1928	Pathe
Between Dangers	1927	Pathe
The Bonanza Buckaroo	1926	US
Code of the Cow Country	1927	Pathe
The Cowboy Cavalier	1928	Pathe
The Cyclone Cowboy	1927	Pathe
Dark Skies *	1929	US
The Desert Demon	1925	US
The Desert of the Lost	1927	Pathe
Desperate Courage	1928	Pathe
Double Action Daniels	1925	US
Fast Fightin'	1925	US
The Fightin' Comeback	1927	Pathe
The Flying Buckaroo	1928	Pathe
The Galloping Gobs	1927	Pathe
Interferin' Gent	1927	Pathe
The Meddlin' Stranger	1927	Pathe
The Obligin' Buckaroo	1927	Pathe
On the Go	1925	US
Pals in Peril	1927	Pathe
The Ramblin' Galoot	1926	uS
Reckless Courage	1925	US
Ride 'Em High	1927	Pathe
The Ridin' Rowdy	1927	Pathe
Roarin' Broncs	1927	Pathe
Saddle Cyclone	1925	US
Saddle Mates	1928	Pathe
Skedaddle Gold	1923	Pathe
Soda Water Cowboy	1927	Pathe
Tearin' into Trouble	1927	Pathe
Thundering Romance	1924	US
Twisted Triggers	1926	US

The Valley of Hunted Men	1928	Pathe
White Pebbles	1927	Pathe

509. RAY RENNAHAN (1896-1980)

Arrowhead	1953	Par.
At Sword's Point	1951	RKO
Becky Sharp	1935	RKO
Belle of the Yukon	1945	Univ.
Belle Starr *	1941	TCF
Blood and Sand *	1941	TCF
Blood Test	1923	US
Blue Bird *	1940	TCF
California	1946	Par.
A Connecticut Yankee at King Arthur's Court	1949	Par.
Denver and the Rio Grande	1952	Par.
Doctor X *	1932	WB
Down Argentine Way *	1940	TCF
Drums along the Mohawk *	1939	TCF
Duel in the Sun *	1946	Selz.
Fanny Foley Herself	1931	RKO
Flaming Feather	1951	Par.
Flight to Tangier	1953	Par.
For Whom the Bell Tolls	1943	Par.
Gold Diggers of Broadway *	1929	WB
Gone with the Wind *	1939	MGM/Selz.
Great Missouri Raid	1950	Par.
Guns of Fort Petticoat	1957	Col.
The Halliday Brand	1956	UA
Her Jungle Love	1938	Par.
Hurricane Smith	1952	Par.
Incendiary Blonde	1945	Par.
Kentucky *	1938	TCF
Kid Millions	1934	UA
King of Jazz *	1930	Univ.
Lady in the Dark *	1944	Par.
A Lawless Street	1955	Col.
Louisiana Purchase *	1941	Par.
Maryland *	1940	TCF
The Merry Widow *	1925	MGM
Mystery of the Wax Museum	1933	WB
Paleface	1948	Par.
Perils of Pauline	1947	Par.
Pony Express	1953	Par.
Rage at Dawn	1955	RKO
Redskin *	1929	Par.
The Runaround	1931	RKO
Seventh Cavalry	1956	Col.
Silver City	1951	Par.

Stranger on Horseback	1955	UA
Streets of Laredo	1949	Par.
Terror in a Texas Town	1958	UA
Texas Lady	1955	RKO
A Thousand and One Nights	1945	Col.
The Ten Commandments *	1923	Par.
Unconquered	1947	Par.
Up in Arms	1944	Gold.
The Vagabond King	1930	Par.
Vogues of 1938	1937	US
Warpath	1951	Par.
Whispering Smith	1948	Par.
The White Tower	1950	RKO
Whoopee! *	1930	Gold.
Wings of the Morning *	1937	GB--TCF

510. CLAUDE RENOIR (1914-   )

The Adventurers	1970	Par.
Alice in Wonderland *	1949	GB
Amazing Monsieur Fabre	1952	Fr.--US
And Die of Pleasure	1960	Fr./It.--Par.
L'Animal	1977	Fr.
Appointment with Life	1949	Fr.
Attention: The Kids Are Watching	1978	Fr.--UA
Barbarella	1967	Fr./It.--Par.
Big Runaround	1966	Fr.
Blood and Roses	1960	Fr./It.--Par.
Born of an Unknown Father	1951	Fr.
The Burglars	1971	Fr./It.--Col.
The Cheaters	1961	Fr.
Circus World	1964	Par.
Clara De Montargis	1951	Fr.
Cool, Calm and Collected	1976	Fr.
Crime and Punishment	1958	Fr.
The Crucible	1958	Fr.
Doctor Laennee	1949	Fr.
Don't Look Now	1969	Fr./GB
End of Desire	1962	Fr./It.
A Faithful Woman	1976	Fr.
French Connection II	1975	TCF
The Game Is Over	1967	Fr.
The Golden Coach	1952	Fr./It.
Gorilla's Waltz	1959	Fr.
Le Grande Illusion *	1937	Fr.
The Green Glove	1950	UA
Helle	1972	Fr.
Hit and Run	1959	Fr.
The Horsemen	1970	Col.
Ideal Couple	1946	Fr.

Impossible Object	1973	Fr.
In the Kingdom of Heaven	1949	Fr.
The Kill	1966	Fr.
The Killer	1972	Fr.
Knock	1951	Fr.
The Lady in the Car with Glasses and a Gun	1969	Fr.--Col.
Lafayette *	1961	Fr.
Legions of Honor *	1938	Fr.
A Life	1958	Fr.
Life Is Ours *	1936	Fr.
Lights of Paris *	1938	Fr.
The Lovers of Tereul	1962	Fr.
Madame Butterfly	1955	It./Jap.
Maddalena	1955	It.
The Madwoman of Chaillot *	1969	WB
The Married Couple of Year Two	1971	Fr.
The Medic	1979	Fr.
A Missionary	1956	Fr.
Monsieur Vincent	1947	Fr.
No Time for Breakfast	1975	Fr.
Paris Does Strange Things	1956	Fr./It.--WB
Paris in the Month of August	1968	Fr.
Une Partie de Campagne *	1936	Fr.
Paul and Michelle	1974	Fr./GB--Par.
Prelude to Glory	1950	Fr.
Prison without Bars *	1938	Fr.
Puccini	1979	Fr.
The Queer Assignment	1945	Fr.
Rendezvous de Juillet	1949	Fr.
The River *	1951	UA
Sergeant X	1960	Fr.
The Serpent	1974	Fr./Ger./It.--AE
Soluna	1968	Fr.
The Spat	1978	Fr.
Spirits of the Dead *	1969	Fr./It.
The Spy Who Loved Me	1977	GB--UA
Symphony for a Massacre	1965	Fr./It.
Tales of Mystery and Imagination	1968	Fr./It.
Toni *	1934	Fr.
The Track	1975	Fr.
Les Tricheurs	1958	Fr.
The Unvanquished	1964	Fr.--MGM
The Waste-Land	1960	Fr.
Ways of Love	1950	Fr./It.
The Wing and the Thigh	1976	Fr.

511. GAYNE RESCHER

Book of Numbers	1973	AE

Claudine	1974	TCF
The Doctor and the Playgirl	1965	US
A Face in the Crowd *	1957	WB
Fiend of Dope Island	1961	US
John and Mary	1969	TCF
Mad Dog Coll	1961	Col.
Murder Incorporated	1960	TCF
A New Leaf	1970	Par.
Norman, Is That You?	1976	MGM
Olly Olly Oxen Free		
Open the Door and See All the People	1964	US
Rachel Rachel	1968	WB
Star Trek: The Wrath of Khan	1982	Par.
Such Good Friends	1971	Par.
The Troublemaker	1964	US

512. LARRY REVENE

Bad Blood	1989	US
Bedroom Eyes II	1990	US
C.O.D.	1983	Ger.--US
Cleo/Leo	1989	US
Delivery Boys	1986	US
Deranged!	1987	US
Doom Asylum	1988	US
Enrapture	1990	US
Hollywood Hot Tubs	1984	US
Hot T Shirts	1980	US
If Looks Could Kill	1987	US
In Love	1983	US
The Marilyn Diaries	1990	US
Party Incorporated	1989	US
Preppies	1984	US
R.S.V.P.	1984	US
Sensations	1988	US
Sex Appeal	1986	US
Sexpot	1988	US
Slammer Girls	1987	US
Student Affairs	1988	US
Vampires *	1988	US
Wildest Dreams	1990	US
Wimps	1987	US
Young Nurses in Love	1989	US

513. BEN REYNOLDS

Alias Mary Dodd	1920	Univ.
Another Man's Shoes	1922	Univ.
Beans	1918	US

Blarney	1926	MGM
Blind Husbands	1919	Univ.
Butterfly	1924	Univ.
Cheyenne's Pal	1917	Univ.
Come On Marines	1934	Par.
Common Property	1919	Univ.
The Denial	1925	MGM
The Devil's Circus	1926	MGM
The Devil's Passkey	1920	Univ.
Exchange of Wives	1925	MGM
False Kisses	1921	Univ.
The Fast Worker	1924	Univ.
A Fight for Love *	1919	Univ.
Foolish Wives *	1922	Univ.
The Fourflusher	1928	Univ.
Freedom of the Press	1928	Univ.
The Ghost Patrol	1923	Univ.
The Golden Gallows	1922	Univ.
Greed *	1925	MGM
The Greyhound Limited	1929	WB
Hell Bent	1918	Univ.
His Secretary	1925	MGM
Honky Tonk	1929	WB
The House without Children	1919	US
It's a Great Life	1936	Par.
Kid Gloves	1929	WB
The Little Wildcat	1928	WB
The Long Chance	1922	Univ.
Man of the Forest	1933	Par.
Man, Woman and Wife	1929	Univ.
McFadden's Flats	1935	Par.
Menace	1934	Par.
The Merry Widow *	1925	MGM
Name The Woman	1928	Col.
The Old Fashioned Way	1934	Par.
One Hour Late	1935	Par.
The Prisoner	1923	Univ.
Queen Kelly *	1928	UA
Riders Up	1924	Univ.
The Scarlet Drop	1918	Univ.
The Secret Man	1917	Univ.
Shattered Dreams	1922	Univ.
She Hired a Husband	1919	US
The Signal Tower	1924	Univ.
The Silk-Lined Burglar	1919	Univ.
Silk Stockings	1927	Univ.
A Slave of Fashion	1925	MGM
Sonny Boy	1929	WB
Stolen Kisses	1929	WB
Stormswept	1923	US
Straight Shooting *	1917	Univ.

The Supreme Passion *	1917	Univ.
A Taste of Life	1919	US
There You Are!	1926	MGM
The Thirteenth Juror	1927	Univ.
The Thundering Herd	1933	Par.
Tillie and Gus	1933	Par.
Tin Hats	1926	MGM
To the Last Man	1933	Par.
Under Suspicion	1919	Univ.
Vengeance	1930	Col.
Wanderer of the Wasteland	1935	Par.
The Waning Sex	1926	MGM
The Way of the Strong	1928	Col.
The Wedding March *	1928	Par.
When a Woman Strikes	1919	US
The Witching Hour	1934	Par.
A Woman's Fool	1918	Univ.
A Wonderful Wife	1922	Univ.

514. EDMOND RICHARD

And Hope To Die	1972	Fr.--TCF
Ankle Bone	1969	Fr.
The Bad Starters	1976	Fr.
Boodle	1988	Fr.
Chimes at Midnight	1966	Sp./Switz.
De L'Amour	1965	Fr./It.
The Discreet Charm of the Bourgeosie	1972	Fr.--TCF
Free Escape	1964	Fr.
How Short Is the Time for Love?	1970	Ger.
July in September	1988	Fr.
Kill	1971	Fr.
Kill the Referee	1984	Fr.
Les Miserables	1982	Fr.
Litan	1982	Fr.
Manon 70	1967	Fr.
The Marvelous Visit	1974	Fr.--Orion
The Miser	1980	Fr.
Night of Lust	1965	Fr.
The Phantom of Liberty	1974	Fr.--TCF
Red Caviar	1985	Fr.
Sex Power	1970	Fr.
That Obscure Object of Desire	1978	Fr./Sp.
The Trial	1962	Fr./Ger./It.
Unsewing Machine	1986	Fr.
Young Rebels	1968	Fr.

514a. ROBERT RICHARDSON

Born on the Fourth of July	1989	Univ.

Dudes	1987	US
Eight Men Out	1988	Orion
Platoon	1986	Orion
Repo Man *	1984	Univ.
Salvador	1986	Hemdale
Talk Radio	1988	Univ.
Wall Street	1987	TCF

515. ANTHONY RICHMOND

The American Success Company	1979	Col.
Bad Timing	1980	GB--Rank
Cat Chaser	1989	US
Don't Look Now	1973	GB
The Eagle Has Landed	1976	GB--Col.
The Greek Tycoon	1978	Univ.
Head On	1980	Can.
Improper Channels	1979	Can.
The In Crowd	1988	Orion
Love and Bullets *	1978	GB
Madame Sin	1972	US
The Man Who Fell to Earth	1976	GB
Old Dracula	1974	GB--AIP
Only When I Larf	1968	GB--Par.
Silver Bears	1977	Col.
Slapstick of Another Kind	1984	US
Stardust	1974	GB--Col.
Sunset	1988	Tri-S.
That's Life	1986	Col.

516. TOM RICHMOND

The Bikini Shop	1987	US
The Chocolate War	1988	US
Chopping Mall	1986	US
Hard Rock Zombies	1987	US
Hardbodies	1984	Col.
Hardbodies 2	1986	US
I'm Gonna Get You Sucka	1988	MGM-UA
Running Hot	1984	US
Stand Alone *	1986	US
Stand and Deliver	1988	WB
Straight to Hell	1987	US

517. IRVING RIES

Biff Bang Buddy	1924	US
Breaking into Society	1923	US

The Business of Love	1925	US
Gold and Grit	1925	US
The Ladder Jinx	1922	Vita.
Too Much Business	1922	Vita.

518. GUNTER RITTAU (1893-1971)

Asphalt	1929	Ger.
A Blonde Dream *	1932	Ger.--UFA
Blue Angel *	1930	Ger.--Par./UFA
Bombs over Monte Carlo	1931	Ger.--UFA
Darling of the Gods *	1930	Ger.--UFA
Einbrecher	1931	Ger.--UFA
F.P.I. Doesn't Answer	1933	Ger.--UFA
Gold *	1934	Ger.--UFA
The Great Tenor *	1931	Ger.--UFA
Happy after Ever	1932	Ger.--UFA
Heimkehr	1928	Ger.
Kriemhild's Revenge	1924	Ger.--UFA
Lady Killer	1937	Fr.
Love Is Love *	1932	Ger.--UFA
Metropolis *	1927	Ger.--UFA
Monte Carlo Madness	1932	Ger.--UFA
Die Niebelungen *	1924	Ger.
Nightclub Hostess	1941	Fr.
L'Or *	1934	Ger.
SOS Sahara	1938	Ger.--UFA
Siegfried *	1924	Ger.--UFA
Storms Of Passion	1932	Ger.--UFA
Tempest	1932	Ger.--UFA
The Winner	1932	Ger.--UFA

519. GEORGE RIZARD

Alias Julius Caesar	1922	FN
The Barnstormer	1922	FN
The Blue Moon	1920	Pathe
Courtship of Miles Standish	1923	US
The Dangerous Talent	1920	Pathe
The Deuce of Spades *	1922	FN
The Gamesters	1920	Pathe
Gas, Oil and Water *	1922	FN
The Girl I Loved *	1923	UA
The Girl Woman *	1919	Vita.
Held to Answer	1923	Metro.
The Hoosier Schoolmaster	1914	US
Jack Chanty	1915	US
A Midnight Bell *	1921	FN
Old Swimmin' Hole	1921	FN

Payment Guaranteed	1921	Pathe
R.S.V.P. *	1921	FN
Scrap Iron	1921	FN
Six Feet Four	1919	Pathe
Smudge	1922	FN
A Sporting Chance	1919	Pathe
Their Mutual Child	1920	Pathe
This Hero Stuff	1919	Pathe
The Truth Wagon	1914	US
Two Minutes to Go *	1921	FN
The Valley of Tomorrow	1920	Pathe

520. GEORGE ROBINSON

Abbott and Costello in the Foreign Legion	1950	Univ.
Abbott and Costello Meet Dr. Jekyll and Mr. Hyde	1953	Univ.
Abbot and Costello Meet the Invisible Man	1951	Univ.
Abbott and Costello Mee the Mummy	1955	Univ.
Ali Baba and the Forty Thieves *	1944	Univ.
The All-American	1932	Univ.
Allergic to Love	1944	Univ.
Back to God's Country	1927	Univ.
Behind the Eight Ball	1942	Univ.
The Big Cage	1933	Univ.
Black Horse Canyon	1954	Univ.
Blondes Are Dangerous	1937	Univ.
Captive Wild Women	1943	Univ.
Carnival Queen	1937	Univ.
The Cat Creeps	1946	Univ.
The Challenge	1948	TCF
Charlie McCarthy Detective	1939	Univ.
Cheating Cheaters	1934	Univ.
Chinatown Squad	1935	Univ.
Cobra Woman *	1944	Univ.
Comin' Round the Mountain	1951	Univ.
The Creeper	1948	TCF
Cross Country Cruise	1934	Univ.
Dance with Me, Henry	1956	UA
Destiny *	1944	Univ.
Destry	1954	Univ.
Diamond Jim	1935	Univ.
Dracula's Daughter	1936	Univ.
Drums of the Congo	1942	Univ.
East of Borneo	1931	Univ.
East Side of Heaven	1939	Univ.
Easy To Take	1936	Par.

Eyes of the Underworld	1943	Univ.
The Falcon Takes Over	1942	RKO
The Fighting Guide	1922	Vita.
Francis in the Haunted House	1956	Univ.
Frankenstein Meets the Wolf Man	1943	Univ.
Free For All	1949	Univ.
Frontier Gal *	1945	Univ.
Get Going	1943	Univ.
Gift of Gab *	1934	Univ.
Give Out Sisters	1942	Univ.
Glamour	1934	Univ.
Goodbye Broadway	1938	Univ.
Great Expectations	1934	Univ.
The Great Impersonation	1942	Univ.
Guardians of the Wild *	1928	Univ.
A Guilty Conscience	1921	Vita.
Gun for a Coward	1956	Univ.
Gypsy Wildcat *	1944	Univ.
Half a Sinner	1934	Univ.
Heading for Heaven	1947	EL
The Harvest of Hate	1929	Univ.
Hell's Heroes	1930	Univ.
Her First Mate	1933	Univ.
Here Come the Coeds	1945	Univ.
A Hero for a Night	1927	Univ.
Homicide Squad	1931	Univ.
Hoofbeats of Vengeance	1929	Univ.
Horseplay	1934	Univ.
House of Dracula	1945	Univ.
House of Frankenstein	1944	Univ.
Idea Girl	1946	Univ.
If I Had My Way	1940	Univ.
The Invisible Ray *	1936	Univ.
The Irresistible Lover *	1927	Univ.
It Happened in New York	1935	Univ.
Jack and the Beanstalk	1952	WB
Joe Dakota	1957	Univ.
The Kettles in the Ozarks	1956	Univ.
King Solomon of Broadway	1935	Univ.
Linda Be Good	1947	PRC
Little Tough Guys in Society	1938	Univ.
Lost in Alaska	1952	Univ.
Love, Honor, Oh Baby!	1933	Univ.
Ma and Pa Kettle on Vacation	1953	Univ.
Madame Spy	1942	Univ.
The Man in Blue	1937	Univ.
The Man Who Cried Wolf	1937	Univ.
Million Dollar Ransom	1934	Univ.
Mr. Big	1943	Univ.
Mr. Dynamite	1935	Univ.
The Mummy's Tomb	1942	Univ.

Murder in the Blue Room	1944	Univ.
The Mystery of Edwin Drood	1935	Univ.
Nagana	1933	Univ.
The Naughty Nineties	1945	Univ.
Night Key	1937	Univ.
The Night Runner	1957	Univ.
No Defense	1921	Vita.
Once in a Lifetime	1933	Univ.
One Hour to Live	1939	Univ.
Open Secret	1948	EL
Phyllis of the Follies	1928	Univ.
The Plainsman *	1936	Par.
Playing It Wild	1923	Vita.
Plunging Hoofs	1929	Univ.
Postal Inspector	1936	Univ.
Racing Youth	1932	Univ.
Reported Missing	1937	Univ.
Restless Souls	1922	Vita.
Rhythm of the Islands	1943	Univ.
Ricochet Romance	1954	Univ.
The Road Back *	1937	Univ.
The Road to Reno	1938	Univ.
Rock Pretty Baby	1956	Univ.
The Runaround	1946	Univ.
The Scarlet Claw	1944	Univ.
Service De Luxe	1938	Univ.
She Wrote the Book	1946	Univ.
The Silent Vow	1922	Vita.
Sin Town	1942	Univ.
Sinners in Paradise	1938	Univ.
Slave Girl *	1947	Univ.
Slightly Scandalous	1946	Univ.
Son of Dracula	1943	Univ.
Son of Frankenstein	1939	Univ.
Son of Monte Cristo	1940	UA
The Spirit of Notre Dame	1931	Univ.
The Square Jungle	1955	Univ.
Steelheart	1921	Vita.
Stop That Man	1928	Univ.
Strange Wives	1935	Univ.
Sudan	1945	Univ.
The Sun Never Sets	1939	Univ.
Sutter's Gold *	1936	Univ.
Tales of Robin Hood	1952	Lip.
Tarantula	1955	Univ.
13 Lead Soldiers	1948	TCF
3 Kids and a Queen	1935	Univ.
The Tie That Binds	1923	WB
Top Sergeant	1942	Univ.
Tower of London	1939	Univ.
The Toy Tiger	1956	Univ.

Treat 'Em Rough	1942	Univ.
Unexpected Father	1939	Univ.
The Vicious Circle	1948	UA
Walk a Crooked Mile *	1948	Col.
When Danger Smiles	1922	Vita.
When Johnny Comes Marching Home	1942	Univ.
When's Your Birthday?	1937	RKO
Where Men Are Men	1921	Vita.
Wild Blood	1929	Univ.
Wives under Suspicion	1938	Univ.
The Yellow Mountain	1954	Univ.
The Wrong Mr. Wright	1927	Univ.
You're a Sweetheart	1937	Univ.

521. GUY ROE

Amazon Quest	1949	US
Armored Car Robbery	1950	RKO
Behind Locked Doors	1948	EL
The Cobra Strikes	1948	EL
The Fortress	1947	Can.
Godzilla *	1956	Jap.
In This Corner	1948	EL
My Six Convicts	1952	Col.
Queen for a Day	1951	UA
Railroaded	1947	EL
A Scandal in Paris	1946	UA
The Silver Star		
The Sound of Fury	1950	UA
Target Earth	1954	AA
Trapped	1949	EL
Two-Gun Lady	1956	US
Whispering City *	1947	Can.--EL

522. NICHOLAS ROEG (1928-)

Code 7, Victim 5!	1965	GB--Col.
Dr. Crippen	1962	GB--WB
Fahrenheit 451	1966	GB--Univ.
Far from the Madding Crowd	1967	GB--MGM
A Funny Thing Happened on the Way to the Forum	1966	UA
The Girl Getters	1966	GB--AIP
Glastonbury Fayre	1973	GB
The Great Van Robbery	1963	GB--UA
The Guest	1964	GB
Information Received	1962	GB--Univ.
Just for Fun	1963	GB--Col.
Masque of the Red Death	1964	GB--AIP

Nothing but the Best	1964	GB
Performance	1970	GB
Petulia	1968	GB--WB
Seaside Swingers	1965	GB
Walkabout	1970	Aus.--TCF

523. OWEN ROIZMAN

Absence of Malice	1981	Col.
The Black Marble	1980	Avco.
The Electric Horseman	1979	Col./Univ.
The Exorcist	1973	WB
The French Connection	1971	TCF
The Gang That Couldn't Shoot Straight	1971	MGM
Havana	1990	Univ.
The Heartbreak Kid	1972	TCF
I Love You to Death	1990	Tri-S.
Network	1976	MGM-UA
Play It Again Sam	1972	Par.
Return of a Man Called Horse	1976	UA
Sergeant Pepper's Lonelyhearts Club Band	1978	Univ.
The Stepford Wives	1975	US
Stop	1970	WB
Straight Time	1978	WB
The Taking of Pelham 123	1974	UA
Taps	1981	TCF
Three Days of the Condor	1975	DeL./Par.
Tootsie	1982	Col.
True Confessions	1981	UA

524. JACKSON ROSE

Alias the Deacon *	1928	Univ.
The Alster Case *	1915	US
The Beautiful Cheat	1926	Univ.
Behind the Curtain	1924	Univ.
Big Game	1921	Metro.
Big Timber	1924	Univ.
Born To Speed	1947	PRC
Bungalow 13	1948	TCF
Burning Daylight	1920	Metro.
Cheating Cheaters	1927	Univ.
The Checkered Coat	1948	TCF
The Dangerous Age *	1922	FN
The Dangerous Blonde	1924	Univ.
Destination Murder	1950	RKO
Dillinger	1945	Mon.

Excitement	1924	Univ.
Experiment Alcatraz	1950	RKO
Fear	1946	Mon.
The Foreign Legion	1928	Univ.
The Girl from Woolworth's	1929	FN/WB
The Girl on the Barge	1929	Univ.
Graustark	1915	US
Great Plane Robbery	1950	UA
Green Grass Widows	1928	US
The Grip of the Yukon	1928	Univ.
Held by the Law	1927	Univ.
His Last Race	1923	US
I Cheated the Law	1949	TCF
A Lady Surrenders	1930	Univ.
Law and Order	1932	Univ.
The Last Card	1921	Metro.
Lingerie	1928	US
Lost Zeppline	1929	US
Love Me and the World Is Mine	1928	Univ.
Main Street after Dark	1944	MGM
Mama Steps Out	1937	MGM
The Man from Texas	1948	EL
The Marriage of William Ashe	1921	Metro.
The Married Flapper	1922	Univ.
The Measure of a Man	1924	Univ.
The Midnight Sun *	1926	Univ.
Midstream	1929	US
The Mutiny on the Elsinore	1920	Metro.
My Dear Secretary	1948	UA
The Mystery Club	1926	Univ.
The Night Message	1924	Univ.
Northwest Rangers	1942	MGM
The Old Soak	1926	Univ.
Once a Gentleman	1930	US
One Wonderful Night	1914	US
Out of the Blue	1947	EL
Paid Back *	1922	Univ.
Painted Fences	1929	US
The Phantom Thunderbolt	1933	Fox
Philo Vance Returns	1947	PRC
Philo Vance's Gamble	1947	PRC
Philo Vance's Secret Mission	1947	PRC
Prejudice	1949	US
Radio Patrol	1932	Univ.
Ridin' Pretty	1925	Univ.
Seed	1931	Univ.
Skinner's Dress Suit	1917	US
The Slim Princess	1915	US
Smoldering Fires	1925	Univ.
The Star Rover	1920	Metro.
Stepchild	1947	PRC

Straight Through	1925	Univ.
Strictly Dishonorable	1931	Univ.
The Sunset Trail	1924	Univ.
The Swellhead *	1930	US
The Three Wise Guys	1936	MGM
Trocadero	1944	Rep.
Troopers Three *	1930	US
The Unknown Guest	1943	Mon.
Up the Ladder	1925	Univ.
We Americans	1928	Univ.
The Whispered Name	1924	Univ.

525. PHIL ROSEN

The Blindness of Devotion *	1915	Fox
The Clemenceau Case	1915	Fox
The Darling of Paris	1917	Fox
The Eternal Magdalene	1919	Gold.
The Green-Eyed Monster	1916	Fox
The Heart of Maryland	1915	Metro.
Her Greatest Love	1917	Fox
Hypocrisy	1916	Fox
Kreutzer Sonata	1915	Fox
A Little Brother of the Rich	1915	Univ.
The Littlest Rebel	1914	US
Love Hunger	1919	US
Romeo and Juliet	1916	Fox
Sin		
The Soul of Broadway	1915	Fox
The Spider and the Fly	1916	Fox
The Spreading Dawn	1917	Gold.
The Tiger Woman	1917	Fox
Under Crimson Skies	1920	Univ.
The Unfaithful Wife	1915	Fox
A Wife's Sacrifice	1916	Fox

526. CHARLES ROSHER (1885-1974)

The Affairs of Cellini	1934	TC
After Office Hours	1935	MGM
After Tonight	1933	RKO
Annie Get Your Gun	1950	MGM
Anton the Terrible	1916	Par.
Assignment in Brittany	1943	MGM
At First Sight	1917	Par.
Atlantic	1929	GB
The Beloved Bachelor	1931	Par.
Blackbirds	1915	Par.
Blacklist	1916	FP

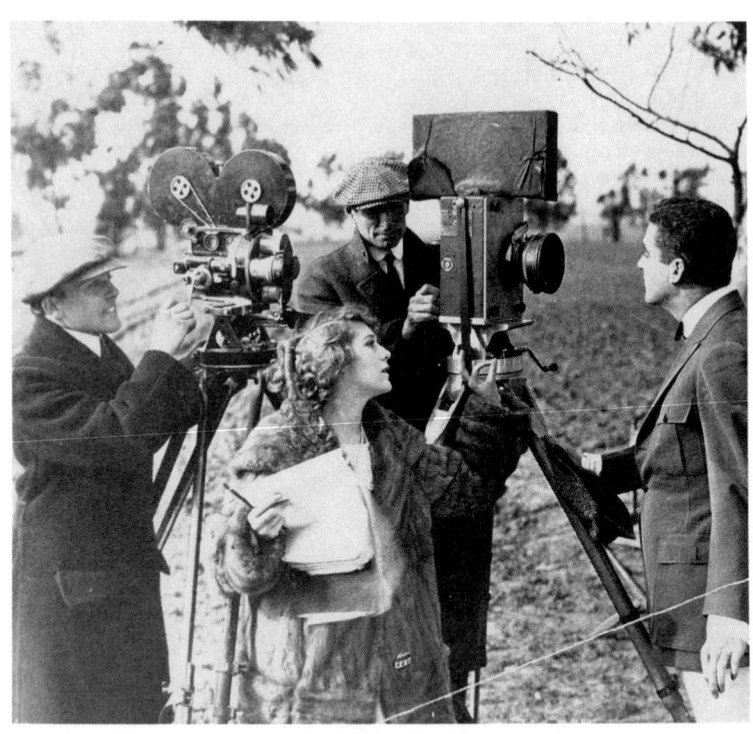

Charles Rosher (left) with Mary Pickford.

Broadway Melody of 1936	1935	MGM
Brother Rat and a Baby	1939	WB
Call of the Wild	1935	TC
Captain Kidd, Jr.	1919	Par.
A Child Is Born	1939	WB
The Clown *	1916	FP
Common Ground	1916	FP
Daddy Long Legs *	1919	FN
Dance Fools Dance	1930	MGM
Dark Delusion	1947	MGM
Dorothy Vernon of Haddon Hall	1924	UA
The Dub	1919	Par.
East Side West Side	1949	MGM
Espionage Agent	1939	WB
Fiesta *	1947	MGM
Four Mothers	1940	WB
Hard To Get	1938	WB
Hashimure Togo	1917	FP/Par.
Heart o' the Hills *	1919	FN
Hell's Kitchen	1937	WB
Hollywood Hotel *	1937	WB
The Hoodlum	1919	FN
How Could You, Jean?	1918	US
Husband's Holiday	1931	Par.
Johanna Enlists	1918	US
Jupiter's Darling *	1954	MGM
Kismet	1944	MGM
Knowing Men	1930	GB--UA
Laughing Sinners	1931	MGM
Little Annie Rooney *	1925	UA
Little Lord Fauntleroy	1921	UA
Little Lord Fauntleroy	1936	Selz.
The Little Princess *	1917	US
The Love Hunger	1919	US
The Love Light *	1921	UA
Men Are Not Gods	1937	GB--Korda
Million Dollar Baby	1941	WB
A Mormon Maid	1917	US
Moulin Rouge	1934	TC
My Best Girl	1927	UA
My Lover Came Back	1940	WB
Mystery of the Poison Pool	1914	US
Neptune's Daughter	1949	MGM
Off the Record	1939	WB
On an Island with You	1948	MGM
On Record	1917	Par.
One Foot in Heaven	1941	WB
One More American	1918	Par.
Our Betters	1933	RKO
Outcast Lady	1934	MGM
Pagan Love Song	1950	MGM

Paid	1930	MGM
The Perfect Specimen	1937	WB
Pierre of the Plains	1942	MGM
The Plow Girl	1916	FP
Pretty Maids All in a Row	1971	MGM
The Price of Things	1930	GB--UA
The Primrose Ring	1917	FP/Par.
Pudd'nhead Wilson	1916	FP
The Red Danube	1950	MGM
Romeo and Juliet	1916	Fox
Rosita	1923	UA
Scaramouche	1952	MGM
The Secret Game	1917	Par.
Showboat	1951	MGM
Silence	1931	Par.
Silver Cord	1933	RKO
Sin	1915	Fox
Small Town Girl *	1936	MGM
Smilin' Through *	1922	FN
Song of the Thin Man	1947	MGM
The Soul of Broadway	1915	Fox
The Sowers	1916	FP
Sparrows *	1926	UA
The Spider and the Fly	1916	Fox
The Spreading Dawn	1917	Gold.
Stand By for Action	1943	MGM
The Story of Three Loves *	1953	MGM
Suds	1920	UA
Sunrise--A Song of Two Humans *	1927	Fox
Swing Fever	1943	MGM
Tempest	1928	UA
Tess of the Storm Country *	1922	UA
This Modern Age	1931	MGM
Three Cheers for the Irish	1940	WB
Through the Back Door	1921	UA
Tiger Rose	1923	WB
The Tiger Woman	1917	Fox
Till I Come Back to You *	1918	Par.
Too Many Millions	1918	Par.
Two World	1930	GB
Under Crimson Skies	1920	Univ.
The Unfaithful Wife	1915	Fox
Vagabond Queen	1931	GB
The Voice in the Fog	1915	Par.
War Nurse	1930	MGM
White Banners	1938	WB
The White Man's Law	1918	Par.
A Wife's Sacrifice	1916	Fox
The Woman I Love	1937	RKO
The Yearling *	1946	MGM
Yes My Darling Daughter	1939	WB

Yolanda and the Thief	1945	MGM
Young Bess	1953	MGM
Ziegfeld Follies *	1944	MGM

527. ART ROSS

Closed Doors	1921	Vita.
Daring Hearts *	1919	Vita.
The Darkest Hour	1920	Vita.
Deadline at Eleven	1920	Vita.
The Fire Brigade	1922	US
Human Collateral	1920	Vita.
Island Wives	1922	Vita.
It Isn't Being Done This Season	1921	Vita.
Miss Ambition	1918	Vita.
Received Payment	1922	Vita.
A Virgin's Sacrifice	1922	Vita.
What's Your Reputation Worth?	1921	Vita.

528. HAROLD ROSSON (1895-1987)

Abie's Irish Rose	1928	Par.
The Actress	1953	MGM
Almost a Lady	1926	US
An American Romance	1944	MGM
Any Number Can Play	1949	MGM
Are You Listening?	1932	MGM
As You Like It *	1936	GB--TCF
The Asphalt Jungle	1950	MGM
The Bad Seed	1956	WB
The Barbarian	1933	MGM
Between Two Women	1945	MGM
Bombshell *	1933	MGM
Boom Town	1940	MGM
Buried Treasure	1921	Par.
Captains Courageous	1937	MGM
Case of Lena Smith	1929	Par.
Cat and the Fiddle *	1933	MGM
The Cinema Murder	1920	Par.
Classified	1925	FN
Command Decision	1949	MGM
The Cradle	1922	Par.
Cuban Love Song	1931	MGM
Dangerous When Wet	1953	MGM
Dark Secrets	1923	Par.
David Harum	1915	FP
The Devil Is a Sissy	1936	MGM
The Docks of New York	1928	Par.
Dr. Kildare Goes Home	1940	MGM

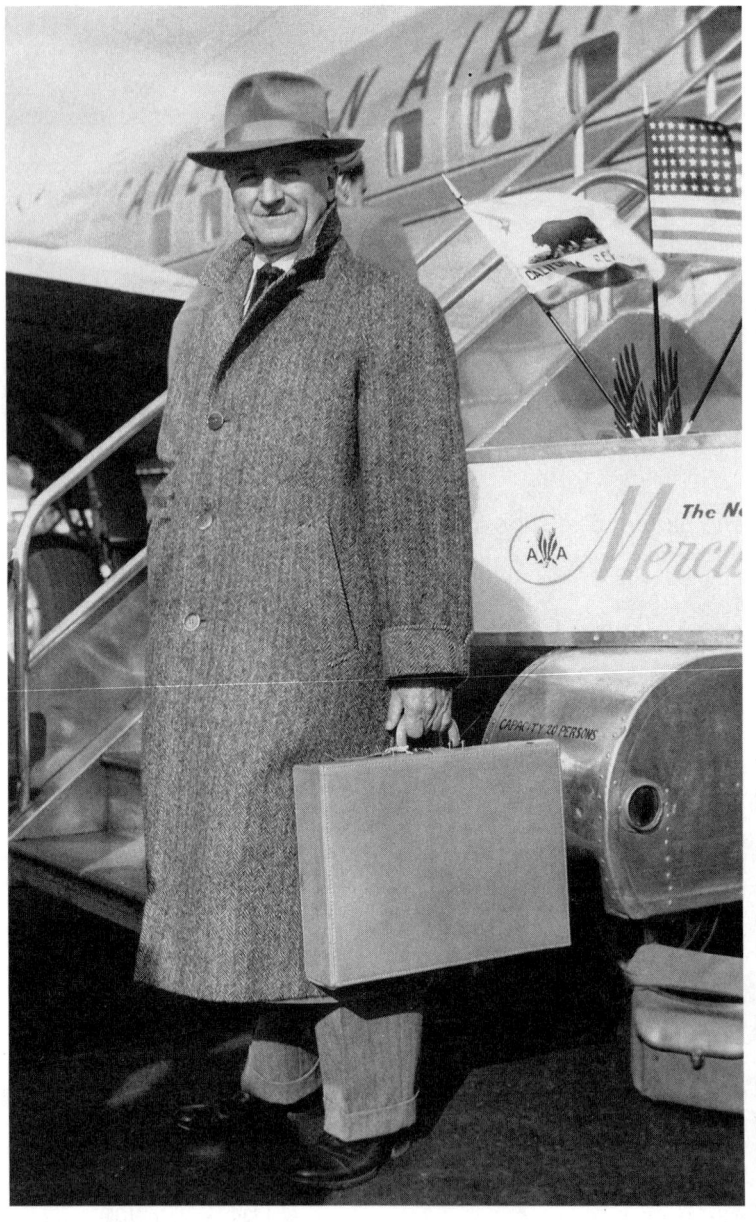

Harold Rosson in New York airport (ca. 1953).

Downstairs	1932	MGM
The Dragnet	1928	Par.
Duel in the Sun *	1946	Selz.
Edison the Man	1940	MGM
El Dorado	1966	Par.
The Emperor's Candlesticks	1937	MGM
The Enemy Below	1957	TCF
Evening Clothes	1927	Par.
Everything for Sale	1921	Par.
The Far Call	1929	Fox
Feller Needs a Friend	1932	US
Flight Command	1940	MGM
For the Defense	1922	Par.
For Wives Only	1926	US
Frozen Justice	1929	Fox
The Garden of Allah *	1936	Selz.
Garrison's Finish	1923	US
A Gentlemen Prefer Blondes	1928	Par.
Getting Gertie's Garter	1927	US
The Ghost Goes West	1936	GB--Korda
Glimpses of the Moon	1923	Par.
Heliotrope	1920	Par.
Hello Sister	1930	US
Hold Your Man	1933	MGM
Homecoming	1948	MGM
A Homespun Vamp	1922	Par.
Honky Tonk	1941	MGM
The Hucksters	1947	MGM
I Love Melvin	1953	MGM
I Take This Woman	1939	MGM
Infatuation	1925	FN
Jim the Conqueror	1927	US
Johnny Eager	1941	MGM
Key To the City	1950	MGM
Kongo	1932	MGM
Lawful Larceny	1923	Par.
The Little French Girl	1925	Par.
Living in a Big Way	1947	MGM
Love Is Better Than Ever	1951	MGM
Madame Satan	1930	MGM
Mambo	1954	It.
Man Bait	1926	US
A Man Must Live	1925	Par.
Man Who Could Work Miracles	1936	GB--Korda
Manhandled	1924	Par.
Manhattan	1924	Par.
Men Call It Love	1931	MGM
Men of Boy's Town	1941	MGM
My Brother Talks to Horses *	1946	MGM
No Leave, No Love *	1946	MGM
No Time for Sergeants	1958	WB

Oliver Twist	1916	FP
On the Town	1949	MGM
Onionhead	1958	WB
Open Range	1927	Par.
Panthea *	1917	Selz.
Passion Flower	1930	MGM
The Penalty	1941	MGM
Penthouse *	1933	MGM
Pete Kelly's Blues	1955	WB
Polly of the Storm Country	1920	FN
The Prodigal	1931	MGM
Quicksands *	1923	Par.
The Red Badge of Courage	1951	MGM
Red Dust	1932	MGM
Red Headed Woman	1932	MGM
Rough House Rosie *	1927	Par.
The Sawdust Paradise	1928	Par.
The Scarlet Pimpernel	1934	GB--Korda
Service for Ladies	1927	Par.
Singin' in the Rain	1952	MGM
Slightly Dangerous	1943	MGM
A Society Scandal	1924	Par.
Somewhere I'll Find YOu	1942	MGM
South Sea Rose	1929	Fox
Sporting Blood	1931	MGM
The Squaw Man	1931	MGM
The Story of Three Loves *	1953	MGM
The Story without a Name	1924	Par.
Strange Lady in Town	1955	WB
The Stratton Story	1949	MGM
The Street of Forgotten Men	1925	Par.
Tarzan the Ape Man *	1932	MGM
Tennessee Johnson	1943	MGM
They Gave Him a Gun	1937	MGM
Thirty Seconds over Tokyo *	1944	MGM
This Mad World *	1930	MGM
This Side of Heaven	1934	MGM
Three Week-Ends	1928	Par.
Three Wise Fools	1946	MGM
Through a Glass Window	1922	Par.
To Please a Lady	1950	MGM
Too Hot To Handle	1938	MGM
Too Many Kisses	1925	Par.
Toward the Unknown	1956	WB
Treasure Island	1934	MGM
Trent's Last Case	1929	Fox
Turn Back the Clock	1933	MGM
Ulysses	1954	It.
Up in Mabel's Room *	1926	US
A Virginia Courtship	1921	Par.
Washington Melodrama	1942	MGM

The Wizard of Oz	1939	MGM
A Yank at Oxford	1938	MGM
Zaza	1923	Par.

529. GIUSEPPE ROTUNNO (1923-   )

The Adventures of Baron Munchausen	1989	GB--Col.
All Screwed Up	1974	It.
All That Jazz	1979	Col./TCF
Amarcord	1973	It.--WB
American Dreamer	1984	WB
And the Ship Sails On	1983	Fr./It.
The Angel Wore Red	1960	MGM
Anna of Brooklyn	1958	It.--RKO
The Assisi Underground	1985	US
The Beast	1974	Fr./It.--WB
The Best of Enemies	1961	Col.
The Bible	1966	TCF
Boccacio '70	1962	Fr./It.--TCF
Candy	1968	Fr./It.
Carnal Knowledge	1971	AE
Casanova	1976	It.--Univ.
City of Women	1980	Fr./It.
Desire	1984	It.
Divine Creature	1976	It.
End of the World in Our Usual Bed in a Night Full of Rain	1978	It.--WB
Everything Ready, Nothing Works	1974	It.
Family Diary	1963	It.--MGM
Fast and Sexy	1960	Fr./It.--Col.
Fellini Satyricon	1969	It.--UA
Five Branded Women	1960	Par.
Five Days One Summer	1982	Ladd/WB
Ghosts in Rome	1960	It.
The Girl and the Palio	1958	It.
The Great War *	1959	It.
Haunted Summer	1988	Cannon
Hotel Colonial	1987	It.--US
Julia and Julia	1987	It.
The Leopard	1963	It.--TCF
The Love Specialist	1959	It.
Man of La Mancha	1972	UA
The Monte Carlo Story	1956	It.--UA
The Naked Maja	1959	It.--UA
On the Beach *	1959	UA
Orchestra Rehearsal	1979	Fr./Ger./It.
The Organizer	1964	Fr./It./Yugo.
Orpheus	1985	It.
Policarpo	1959	Fr./It./Sp.
Popeye	1980	Par.

Red Sonja	1985	DeL./MGM-UA
Rent-a-Cop	1987	US
Rocco and His Brothers	1960	Fr./It.
Rollover *	1981	Orion/WB
Roma	1972	Fr./It.--UA
Scandal in Sorrento	1955	Fr./It.
The Secret of Santa Vittoria	1969	UA
Senso	1968	It.
Spirits of the Dead *	1969	Fr./It.--AIP
Stormtroopers	1977	It.
Story of Love and Anarchy	1973	It.
The Stranger	1967	Alg./Fr./It.--Par.
Strikers	1963	It.--Par.
Sunflower	1969	Fr./It.--AE
Tales of Mystery and Imagination *	1968	Fr./It.
Tosca	1960	It.
White Nights	1957	Fr./It.
The Witches	1968	Fr./It.
Yesterday, Today and Tomorrow	1963	Fr./It.--Emb.

530. STEVE ROUNDS

The Boss of the Lazy Y	1918	US
Business Is Business	1915	Univ.
By Proxy	1918	US
Cactus Crandall	1918	US
The Day She Paid	1919	Univ.
Faith and Endurin'	1918	US
The Frame-Up	1915	Univ.
Paying His Debt	1918	US
The Pretender	1918	US
A Red-Haired Cupid	1918	US
So Long Letty	1920	US
Wolves of the Border	1918	US

531. PHILIPPE ROUSSELOT

The Bear	1988	Fr.
Cocktail Molotov	1980	Fr.
Dangerous Liaisons	1988	WB
Diablo Mewnthe	1977	Fr.
Diva	1981	Fr.
La Doloresse	1981	Fr.
Dream One	1984	Fr.
Emerald Forest	1985	Emb.
For Clemence	1977	Fr.
A Girl from Lorraine	1983	Fr./Switz.
The Guinea Pig Couple	1977	Fr.

Guy De Maupassant	1982	Fr.
Henry and June	1990	Univ.
Hope and Glory	1987	GB--Col.
The Hussy	1979	Fr.
It Always Rains When It's Wet	1974	Fr.
The Jaws of the Wolf	1982	Fr.
Marie for Memory *	1968	Fr.
The Moon in the Gutter	1983	Fr./It.--Col.
Nemo	1984	Fr./GB
Night Magic	1985	Fr.
Paradise	1977	Fr.
Peppermint Soda	1979	Fr.
Repeated Absences	1972	Fr.
The Right of the Maddest *	1973	Fr.
The Roads of Exile	1978	Fr.
Therese	1986	Fr.
Thieves after Dark	1984	Fr.
Too Beautiful for You	1989	Fr.
We're No Angels	1989	Par.

532. JOHN L. RUSSELL

Arctic Flight	1952	Mon.
The Atomic Kid	1954	Rep.
Backtrack *	1969	Univ.
The Beast from Twenty Thousand Fathoms	1953	WB
Billie	1965	UA
The Cabinet of Caligari	1962	TCF
Champ for a Day	1953	Rep.
City That Never Sleeps	1953	Rep.
The Eternal Sea	1955	Rep.
Geraldine	1953	Rep.
Girls Town	1959	MGM
The Golden Gloves Story	1950	EL
The Green Promise	1949	RKO
Guilty of Treason	1950	EL
Hell's Crossroads	1957	Rep.
Hell's Half Acre	1954	Rep.
The Indestructible Man	1956	AA
Invasion USA	1952	Col.
Jigsaw	1968	Univ.
Lay That Rifle Down	1955	Rep.
Macbeth	1948	Rep.
Make Haste To Live	1954	Rep.
The Man from Planet X	1951	UA
Moonrise	1948	Rep.
Out of Sight	1966	Univ.
Park Row	1952	UA
Problem Girls	1953	Col.

Psycho	1960	Par.
So This Is New York	1948	UA
Star in the Dust	1956	Univ.
Sword of Venus	1953	RKO
Tobor the Great	1954	Rep.
The Vanishing American	1955	Rep.

533. JOSEPH RUTTENBERG (1889-1983)

Ada	1961	MGM
Adventure	1945	MGM
B.F.'s Daughter	1948	MGM
Bachelor in Paradise	1961	MGM
Balalaika *	1939	MGM
Because You're Mine	1952	MGM
Beyond Price	1921	Fox
Big City	1937	MGM
The Blue Streak	1917	Fox
The Bribe	1949	MGM
Brigadoon	1954	MGM
Broadway Melody of 1940 *	1939	MGM
Butterfield Eight *	1960	MGM
Cause for Alarm	1951	MGM
Comrade X	1940	MGM
Crossroads	1942	MGM
A Day at the Races	1937	MGM
The Debt of Honor	1918	Fox
Desire Me	1947	MGM
Dr. Jekyll and Mr. Hyde	1941	MGM
Does It Pay?	1923	Fox
Doing Their Bit	1918	Fox
Everybody Sing	1937	MGM
A Fallen Idol	1919	Fox
First 100 Years	1938	MGM
The Fool	1925	Fox
Frankie and Johnnie	1936	Rep.
From Now On	1920	Fox
Fury	1936	MGM
Gaslight	1944	MGM
Gigi	1958	MGM
Gigolette	1935	RKO/Selz.
A Global Affair	1963	MGM
The Great Caruso	1950	MGM
The Great Diamond Robbery	1954	MGM
Green Mansions	1959	MGM
Harlow	1965	Emb./Par.
A Heart's Revenge	1918	Fox
Her Twelve Men	1954	MGM
The Hook	1962	MGM
Ice Follies of 1939 *	1939	MGM

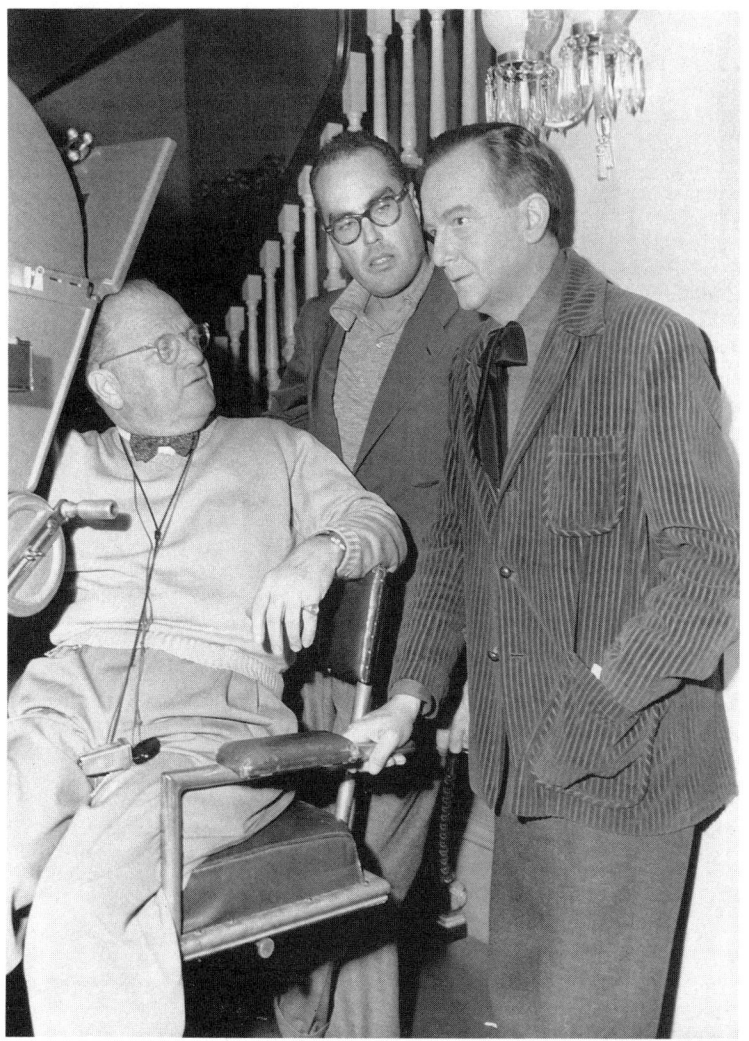

Joseph Ruttenberg (left) with director John Sturges (center) and actor Maurice Evans on the set of <u>Kind Lady</u> (1951).

If Winter Comes	1923	Fox
Interrupted Melody *	1955	MGM
Invitation to the Dance *	1954	MGM
It Happened at the World's Fair	1962	MGM
It's a Big Country *	1952	MGM
Julia Misbehaves	1948	MGM
Julius Caesar	1953	MGM
Killer McCoy	1947	MGM
Kind Lady	1951	MGM
Kismet	1955	MGM
Know Your Men	1921	Fox
The Last Time I Saw Paris	1954	MGM
Latin Lovers	1953	MGM
Love Has Many Faces	1964	Col.
Mad Holiday	1936	MGM
Madame Curie	1944	MGM
The Magnificent Yankee	1951	MGM
Man Hunt	1936	WB
Man on Fire	1957	MGM
The Miniver Story	1950	MGM
Mrs. Miniver	1942	MGM
Mrs. Parkington	1944	MGM
The Mountain Woman	1921	Fox
My Brother Talks to Horses *	1946	MGM
My Friend, the Devil	1922	Fox
My Little Sister	1919	Fox
On Borrowed Time	1939	MGM
The Oscar	1966	Par.
The Painted Madonna	1917	Fox
Peg of the Pirates	1918	Fox
The People's Enemy	1935	RKO/Selz.
The Philadelphia Story	1940	MGM
Piccadilly Jim	1936	MGM
Presenting Lily Mars	1943	MGM
The Prisoner of Zenda	1952	MGM
The Prodigal	1955	MGM
Random Harvest	1942	MGM
The Reluctant Debutante	1958	MGM
School for Wives *	1925	Vita.
The Shark	1920	Fox
Side Street	1950	MGM
Silver Wings *	1922	Fox
The Slave	1917	Fox
Small Town Girl	1953	MGM
Somebody Up There Likes Me	1956	MGM
Speedway	1968	MGM
Spring Madness	1938	MGM
The Struggle	1931	UA
The Subterraneans	1960	MGM
Summer Bachelors	1926	Fox
The Swan *	1956	MGM

Sylvia	1964	Par.
Tell No Tales	1938	MGM
That Forsythe Woman	1949	MGM
The Thief	1920	Fox
Thou Shalt Not Steal	1917	Fox
Three Comrades	1938	MGM
The Three Godfathers	1936	MGM
Tiger's Cub	1920	Fox
Too Young To Kiss	1951	MGM
Town That Forgot God *	1922	Fox
Two Loves	1961	MGM
Two-Faced Woman	1941	MGM
Until They Sail	1957	MGM
The Valley of Decision	1947	MGM
The Vintage	1947	MGM
A Virgin Paradise *	1921	Fox
Waterloo Bridge	1940	MGM
Who's Been Sleeping in My Bed?	1963	Par.
Who's Got the Action?	1962	Par.
Wife Number Two	1917	Fox
Woman in the Dark	1935	RKO
Woman of the Year	1942	MGM
The Woman Who Gave	1918	Fox
Woman! Woman!	1919	Fox
The Women *	1939	MGM
The Wreck of the Mary Deare	1959	MGM
The Yellow Dog	1916	Univ.
Young Man with Ideas	1952	MGM

534. ERIC SAARINEN

Boxoffice	1982	US
Eat My Dust	1976	US
Golden Seal	1983	US
The Hills Have Eyes	1977	US
Juan Perez Jolote *	1975	Mex.
Modern Romance	1981	Col.
Real Life	1979	Par.
Star Hops	1978	US
You Light Up My Life	1977	Col.

535. CHARLES SALERNO

The Arnelo Affair	1946	MGM
Barbary Coast Gent	1944	MGM
Bewitched	1945	MGM
Boys' Ranch	1946	MGM
Faithful in My Fashion	1946	MGM
Gentle Annie	1944	MGM
Nothing But Trouble	1945	MGM

She Went to the Races	1945	MGM
Undercover Maisie	1947	MGM

535a. MIKAEL SALOMON

The Abyss	1989	TCF
Always	1989	Univ.
Arachnophobia	1990	Dis.
Peter Von Scholten	1987	Den.
Stealing Heaven	1988	WB
Street of My Childhood	1986	Den.
Torch Song Trilogy	1988	US
Wolf at My Door	1986	Den./Fr.
Zelly and Me	1988	Col.

536. HENDRIK SARTOV

America	1924	UA
La Boheme	1926	MGM
Broken Blossoms *	1919	UA
Dream Street	1921	UA
Hearts of the World *	1918	US
Isn't Life Wonderful? *	1924	UA
One Exciting Night *	1922	UA
Orphans of the Storm *	1921	UA
Quality Street	1927	MGM
The Red Mill	1927	MGM
The Scarlet Letter	1926	MGM
Under the Black Eagle	1928	MGM
Way Down East *	1920	UA
The White Rose *	1923	UA

537. TED SCAIFE (1912-   )

All Night Long	1961	GB
Beautiful Stranger *	1954	GB
The Birthday Present	1957	GB
The Boy and the Bridge	1959	GB--Col.
The Captain's Paradise	1953	GB
Carry On Constable	1960	GB
Catlow	1970	SP.--MGM
The Constant Husband	1954	GB
Cry of the Penguins	1971	GB
Curse of the Demon	1958	Col.
Dark of the Sun	1968	GB--MGM
The Dirty Dozen	1967	GB--MGM
Follow the Boys	1963	MGM
Hannie Calder	1971	GB--Par.

Happy Is the Bride	1957	GB
His and Hers	1960	GB
The Holly and the Ivy	1952	GB
House of the Seven Hawks	1959	MGM
An Inspector Calls	1959	GB
The Intruder	1953	GB
Khartoum *	1966	GB--UA
A Kid for Two Farthings	1955	GB
The Kremlin Letter	1970	TCF
The Last Blitzkrieg	1958	Col.
Law and Disorder	1958	GB
The Lion	1962	GB--TCF
The Liquidator	1965	GB--MGM
Melba *	1953	GB--UA
Murder on Monday	1952	GB
Operation Snafu	1965	GB--AIP
The Passionate Sentry	1953	GB
Play Dirty	1969	GB--UA
Please Turn Over	1960	GB--Col.
The Ringer	1952	GB
Sea Wife	1957	GB--TCF
Sinful Davey *	1968	GB--UA
Sitting Target	1972	GB--MGM
633 Squadron *	1964	UA
Smiley *	1956	GB--TCF
Smiley Gets a Gun	1958	GB--TCF
Storm over the Nile *	1955	GB--Col.
Tarzan the Magnificent	1960	GB--Par.
Tarzan's Greatest Adventure	1959	GB--Par.
Tarzan's Three Challenges	1963	MGM
Trial and Error	1962	GB--MGM
The Truth about Spring	1964	GB--Univ.
The Two-Headed Spy	1958	GB--Col.
A Walk with Love and Death	1969	TCF
Watch Your Stern	1960	GB
The Water Babies	1978	GB
Young Cassidy	1964	GB--MGM

538. RIAL B. SCHELLINGER

Cynthia-of-the-Minute	1920	US
The Kaiser's Finish	1918	WB
The Master-Mind *	1920	FN
The Mischief Maker	1916	Fox
A Modern Cinderella	1917	Fox
My Four Years in Germany	1918	US
Never Say Quit	1919	Fox
The Rose of Blood	1917	Fox

539. MAX SCHNEIDER

An Amateur Widow	1919	US
Appearance of Evil	1918	US
Battler	1919	US
The Black Circle	1919	US
The Blue Pearl	1920	US
Journey's End	1918	US
Phil-For-Short	1919	US
The Power and the Glory	1918	US
The Praise Agent	1919	US
The Riddle: Woman	1920	Pathe
Spurs of Sybil	1918	US
Stolen Hours	1918	US
The Unveiling Hand	1919	US
The Whims of Society	1918	US
The Witch Woman	1918	US
Woman the Germans Shot	1918	US

540. GEORGE SCHNEIDERMAN

The Auctioneer	1927	Fox
Bare Knuckles	1921	Fox
Black Paradise	1926	Fox
The Blue Eagle	1926	Fox
Born Reckless	1930	Fox
Boston Blackie	1923	Fox
Cameo Kirby	1923	Fox
Carmen *	1915	Fox
Charlie Chan Carries On	1931	Fox
Children of the Night	1921	Fox
Colleen	1927	Fox
Colorado Pluck	1921	Fox
The Devil Is a Sissy	1936	MGM
Dr. Bull	1933	Fox
Elinor Norton	1935	Fox
The Face on the Barroom Floor	1923	Fox
The Fast Mail *	1922	Fox
52nd Street	1937	US
Flirting with Fate	1938	MGM
A Fool There Was	1915	Fox
Four Sons *	1928	Fox
The Gay Caballero	1932	Fox
George White's Scandals *	1934	Fox
George White's 35 Scandals	1935	Fox
Gladiator	1937	Col.
Good Intentions	1930	Fox
Hangman's House	1928	Fox
Hearts of Oak	1924	Fox
The Hell Ship	1920	Fox

Hold That Girl	1934	Fox
Hoodman Blind	1923	Fox
Infernal Machine	1933	Fox
The Iron Horse *	1924	Fox
Is Zat So?	1927	Fox
Jackie	1921	Fox
The Johnstown Flood	1926	Fox
Judge Priest	1934	Fox
Just Pals	1920	Fox
Kentucky Pride	1925	Fox
Lazybones *	1925	Fox
The Little Wanderer	1920	Fox
The Lost Princess	1919	Fox
Love Is Love	1919	Fox
Love's Harvest	1920	Fox
Man's Size *	1923	Fox
Michael Shayne Private Detective	1940	TCF
Molly and I	1920	Fox
Orient Express	1934	Fox
Pardon My Nerve!	1922	Fox
Part Time Wife	1930	Fox
Pawn Ticket 210	1922	Fox
Pilgrimage	1933	Fox
Queenie	1921	Fox
Riders of the Purple Sage	1931	Fox
Road House	1928	Fox
Robbers' Roost	1933	Fox
The Roughneck	1924	Fox
Scotland Yard	1930	Fox
The Shamrock Handicap	1926	Fox
Singing River	1921	Fox
Snowdrift	1923	Fox
Steamboat Round the Bend	1935	Fox
Sunset Sprague	1920	Fox
Thank You	1925	Fox
Three Bad Men	1926	Fox
2 Girls Wanted	1927	Fox
Vagabond Luck	1919	Fox
The Village Blacksmith	1922	Fox
Walls of Gold	1933	Fox
Western Speed	1922	Fox
Whispering Wires	1926	Fox
The World Moves On	1934	Fox
Young America	1932	Fox
Youth Must Have Love	1922	Fox

541. ERNEST SCHOEDSACK (1893-   )

Chang	1927	Par.
The Four Feathers *	1929	Par.

Greed *	1925	MGM
Lost Empire	1924	US

542. CHARLES EDGAR SCHOENBAUM

Abbott and Costello in Hollywood	1945	MGM
Across the Continent	1922	Par.
Adventure	1925	Par.
Always a Bride	1940	FN/WB
Always Audacious	1920	Par.
Arizona Bound	1927	Par.
Bad Bascomb	1946	MGM
Beau Sabreur	1928	Par.
The Best Man	1919	US
Born to the West	1926	Par.
Bride of the Regiment *	1930	FN
Burglar Proof	1920	Par.
Challenge to Lassie	1949	MGM
The Charm School	1921	Par.
Code of the Sea	1924	Par.
Command Performance	1931	FN
Cynthia	1947	MGM
Daughter of Shanghai	1937	Par.
Desert Gold	1926	Par.
The Devil's Cargo	1925	Par.
Drums of the Desert	1927	Par.
Duchess of Idaho	1950	MGM
Empty Hands	1924	Par.
Escape to Paradise	1939	RKO
Exit the Vamp	1921	Par.
Fires of Faith *	1919	Par.
Fisherman's Wharf	1939	RKO
Forlorn River	1926	Par.
The Girl Who Came Back	1918	Par.
Good News	1947	MGM
Goodbye Love	1934	RKO
The Heart Raider	1923	Par.
Held by the Enemy	1920	Par.
THe Hell Diggers	1921	Par.
Here Comes the Band	1935	MGM
Heritage of the Desert	1924	Par.
Hi Diddle Diddle	1943	UA
The Hills of Home	1948	MGM
In the Name of Love	1925	Par.
It's in the Air	1935	MGM
It Pays To Advertise	1919	Par.
Junior Army	1943	Col.
The Last Frontier	1926	US
Little Women *	1949	MGM
Love Insurance	1920	Par.

Love on Toast	1937	Par.
Man of the Forest	1926	Par.
Men Are Such Fools	1933	RKO
The Mighty McGurk	1946	MGM
Miss Hobbs	1920	US
Mr. Billings Spends His Dime	1923	Par.
The Mysterious Rider	1927	Par.
The Mystery Girl	1918	Par.
Nevada	1927	Par.
New York Town	1941	Par.
Nobody's Money	1923	Par.
On Such a Night	1937	Par.
On the High Seas	1922	Par.
The Outriders	1950	MGM
Rainbow on the River	1936	RKO
Rent Free	1922	Par.
The Rogue Song *	1930	MGM
Sailor Be Good	1933	RKO
Sally *	1930	FN/WB
Salute to the Marines *	1943	MGM
Secret Valley	1937	TCF
She Got What She Wanted	1930	US
The Siren Call	1922	Par.
The Six Best Cellars	1920	Par.
Something To Do *	1919	Par.
A Son of His Father	1925	Par.
Son of Lassie	1945	MGM
Songs of the Legion	1938	Par.
Stars in My Crown	1950	MGM
Summer Holiday	1948	MGM
Tomorrow at Seven	1933	RKO
Too Much Johnson	1920	Par.
Too Much Speed	1921	Par.
Under the Tonto Rim	1928	Par.
The Vanishing American *	1925	Par.
The Vanishing Pioneer	1925	Par.
Venus in the East	1919	Par.
The Very Good Young Man	1919	Par.
Vicky Van	1919	Par.
The Water Hole	1928	Par.
Way Down South	1939	RKO
Why Smith Left Home	1919	Par.
The Winning Girl	1919	Par.
Woman's Weapons	1918	Par.
Women Go On Forever	1931	US
The World's Champion	1922	Par.

543. ABE SCHOLTZ

Damaged Hearts	1924	US
Eyes of the Totem	1925	Pathe

The Heart of the Yukon *	1927	Pathe
Hearts and Fists	1926	US
The Light in the Clearing	1921	US

544. EUGENE SCHUFFTAN (1880-1971)

L'Atlantide	1932	Ger.
The Big Scare	1964	Fr.
Bizarre, Bizarre	1937	Fr.
Bloody Brood	1959	Can.--AA
Bluebeard *	1944	PRC
Captain Sinbad *	1963	MGM
Chappaqua	1967	US
A Couple	1960	Fr.
Crimson Curtain	1952	Fr.
The Doctor's Diagnosis	1966	Ger./Switz.
The Drama of Shanghai *	1938	Fr.
Farewell	1930	Ger.
Foggy Quay *	1938	Fr.
The Grouch *	1931	Ger.--UFA
Hatred	1941	Fr.
Hitler's Madmen *	1943	MGM/PRC
The Horror Chamber of Dr. Faustus	1962	Fr./It.
The Hustler	1961	TCF
It Happened Tomorrow *	1944	UA
Lilith *	1964	Col.
Menscham am Sontag	1929	Ger.
My Wife the Swindler *	1931	Ger.--UFA
Norah O'Neale *	1934	GB
An Old Spanish Custom	1936	GB--MGM
Quai des Brumes	1938	Fr.
The Respectable Prostitute	1952	Fr.
The Robber Symphony	1937	GB
A Scandal in Paris	1946	UA
The Smuggler's Ball	1952	Belg./Fr.
Something Wild	1961	UA
The Stolen Face *	1930	Ger.
The Tender Enemy *	1938	Fr.
La Tete Contre Les Murs	1958	Fr.
Three Rooms in Manhattan	1965	Fr.
Three Waltzes	1939	Fr.
Trap	1958	Fr.
Two Love Crimes	1953	Fr.
Ulysses *	1955	It.--Par.
Under Secret Orders	1943	Fr.
The Virgins	1963	Fr.
Without Tomorrow	1940	Fr.
Yoshiwara	1937	Fr.

545. FRED SCHULER

Amityville 3-D	1983	Orion
Armed and Dangerous	1986	Col.
Arthur	1981	Orion/WB
Easy Money	1983	Orion
Fletch	1985	Univ.
Gloria	1980	Col.
Haunted Honeymoon	1986	Orion
King of Comedy	1983	TCF
Love and Money	1980	Lor.
Maxie	1985	Orion
Nothing Lasts Forever	1984	MGM-UA
Soup for One	1982	WB
Stir Crazy	1980	Col.
Wise Guys	1986	MGM-UA

546. HOWARD SCHWARTZ

Batman	1966	TCF
The Big Bounce	1969	WB
The Case of Patty Smith	1962	US
The Devil and Max Devlin	1981	Dis.
Futureworld *	1976	AIP
Incredible Hulk *	1978	US
A Public Affair	1962	US

547. XAVIER SCHWARZENBERGER

Ace of Aces	1982	Fr./Ger.
Berlin Alexanderplatz	1980	Ger./It.
The Condemned	1975	Aust./Ger.
Fear of Falling	1984	Ger.
Kamikaze 89	1982	Ger.
Lili Marleen	1980	Ger.--UA
Lola	1982	Ger.--UA
Misfire	1977	Ger.
Momo	1987	Ger./It.
Odipussi	1988	Ger.
Otto-The New Movie	1987	Ger.
The Outsider	1983	Fr.
Querelle	1982	Fr./Ger.
The Silent Ocean	1983	Aust./Ger.
Student Gerber	1982	Aust./Ger.
Veronika Voss	1982	Ger.--UA
Waltzes of the Danube	1984	Ger.

548. HOMER SCOTT

The American Beauty	1916	US
The Clue	1915	Par.
The Extra Girl *	1923	US
The Happiness of Three Women	1917	Par.
Her Father's Son	1916	US
The House of Lies	1916	US
Huck and Tom	1918	Par.
The Key to Yesterday	1914	US
The Light of Western Stars	1918	US
The Man Who Could Not Lose	1914	US
Pasquale	1916	US
The Shepherd of the Hills	1920	US
The Shriek of Araby	1923	US
Vengeance of the Deep *	1923	US

549. JOHN SEALE

Alvin Purple	1974	Aus.
BMX Bandits	1983	Aus.
Children of a Lesser God	1986	Par.
Dead Poets Society	1989	BV/Touch.
Deathcheaters	1976	Aus.
Doctor and Nurses	1982	Aus.
The Empty Beach	1985	Aus.
Fatty Finn	1980	Aus.
Fighting Back	1982	GB
Ginger Meggs	1982	Aus.
Goodbye Paradise	1982	Aus.
The Hitcher	1986	Tri-S.
The Mosquito Coast	1986	WB
Rain Man	1988	MGM-UA
Silver City	1984	Aus.
Stakeout	1987	Dis.
Survivor	1981	Aus.

550. EDMOND SECHAN

Adventures of Arsene Lupin	1956	It.
All Mad about Him	1967	Fr.
Backfire *	1965	Fr.
The Bear	1963	Fr.
The Blue Country	1977	Fr.
Le Boum	1983	Fr.
Chinese Adventures in China	1965	Fr.
Crin Blanc	1953	Fr.
Fraudulent Death	1957	Fr.
Free Escape	1964	Fr.

Funny Money	1966	Fr.
The Girl Hunters	1959	Fr.
La Gendarme a New York	1965	Fr.
La Grand Maffia	1971	Fr.
Happy Easter	1984	Fr.
Heaven on One's Head	1965	Fr.
The Little Wheedlers	1978	Fr.
Love and Cool Water	1976	Fr.
Love Is a Ball	1962	UA
Le Metaf	1973	Fr.--MGM
Monsieur Papa	1977	Fr.
Out of It	1978	Fr.
The Party	1981	Fr.
Le Peau de Toledo	1970	Fr.
Perched on a Tree	1971	Fr.
Piaf	1974	Fr.
Piaf-The Early Years	1982	Fr.--TCF
The Possessed	1956	Fr.
The Red Balloon	1956	Fr.
Seventh Target	1985	Fr.
Sky above Heaven *	1964	Fr./It.
Tamango	1958	Fr.
Tender Scoundrel	1967	Fr./It.--Emb.
That Man from Rio	1964	Fr./It.
Torpedo Skin	1970	Fr./Ger./It.-- Par.
The Triumph of Michael Strogoff	1962	Fr.
Two Weeks in September	1967	Fr./GB--Par.
Up to His Ears	1966	Fr./It.
The Vultures	1984	Fr.
With Joyous Heart	1967	Fr./GB
Women	1983	Fr.
Your Shadow Is Mine	1963	Fr./It.

551. GUIDO SEEBER (1879-1940)

Arbored Colony	1933	Ger.
Die Freudlose Gasse	1925	Ger.
Golem	1914	Ger.
Golem *	1920	Ger.--UFA
King Fredericus *	1921	Ger.
New Year's Eve *	1923	Ger.
Secrets in a Soul *	1926	Ger.
Storm in a Water Glass	1931	Aust.
Student of Prague	1913	Ger.
Sylvester	1923	Ger.
Tragedie der Strasse	1927	Ger.
The Woman They Talk About	9133	Ger.

552. JOHN F. SEITZ (1893-1979)

Across to Singapore	1928	MGM
Adorable	1933	Fox
Adoration	1928	FN
Adventures of Huckleberry Finn	1939	MGM
All Men Are Enemies	1934	Fox
Appointment with Danger	1951	Par.
The Arab	1924	MGM
Bad Little Angel	1939	MGM
The Bad Man	1930	FN
The Badlanders	1958	MGM
Beauty and the Rogue	1918	US
Between Two Women	1937	MGM
Beyond Glory	1948	Par.
The Big Land	1957	WB
Botany Bay	1952	Par.
The Bride's Silence	1917	US
Calcutta	1946	Par.
Captain Carey USA	1951	Par.
Captain January	1936	TCF
Careless Lady	1932	Fox
Casanova Brown	1944	Univ.
Chicago Deadline	1949	Par.
Classmates *	1924	FN
Coming Out Party	1934	Fox
The Conquering Pwoer	1921	Metro.
The Country Doctor *	1936	TCF
The Crowd Roars	1938	MGM
A Cry in the Night	1956	WB
Curly Top	1935	Fox
Dangerously Yours	1933	Fox
Dear Brat	1951	Par.
The Deep Six	1958	US
Desert Legion	1953	Univ.
The Divine Lady	1929	WB
Dr. Kildare's Crisis	1940	MGM
Dr. Kildare's Strange Case	1940	MGM
Double Indemnity	1944	Par.
East Lynne	1931	Fox
The Fair Co-Ed	1927	MGM
The Farmer Takes a Wife	1935	Fox
Fifteen Maiden Lane	1936	TCF
Five Graves to Cairo	1943	Par.
Fly By Night	1942	Par.
Fort Algiers	1953	UA
The Four Horsemen of the Apocalypse	1921	Metro.
A Game of Wits	1917	US
The Goldbergs	1950	Par.
The Great Gatsby	1949	Par.
Guns of the Timberland	1960	US

Hail the Conquering Hero	1944	Par.
Hard to Get	1929	FN/WB
Hardys Ride High	1939	MGM
Hearts Are Trumps	1920	Metro.
Hell on Frisco Bay	1955	US
Helldorado	1935	Fox
Her Private Life	1929	FN/WB
Home Sweet Homicide	1946	TCF
The Hour before the Dawn	1944	Par.
Hush Money	1931	Fox
The Imperfect Lady	1946	Par.
In the Next Room	1930	WB
Invaders from Mars	1953	US
The Iron Mistress	1952	WB
Kismet	1930	WB
Ladies They Talk About	1933	WB
A Little Bit of Heaven	1940	Univ.
The Littlest Rebel	1935	Fox
Lord Jeff	1938	MGM
The Lost Weekend	1945	Par.
Love Is a Headache	1938	MGM
Lucky Jordan	1942	Par.
Madame X	1937	MGM
The Magician	1926	MGM
The Man in the Net	1959	UA
Many Rivers to Cross	1955	MGM
Marie Galante	1934	Fox
The Mate of the Sally Ann	1917	US
The McConnell Story *	1955	WB
Merely Mary Ann	1931	Fox
The Miracle of Morgan's Creek	1943	Par.
Mr. Skitch	1933	Fox
The Moon and Sixpence	1943	US
A Most Immoral Lady	1929	FN/WB
Murder Will Out	1930	FN/WB
Navy Blue and Gold	1937	MGM
Navy Wife	1935	Fox
Night Has a Thousand Eyes	1948	Par.
On Our Merry Way *	1948	US
One More Spring	1935	Fox
Our Little Girl	1935	Fox
Outcast	1928	FN
Over the Hill	1931	Fox
Paddy the Next Best Thing	1933	Fox
The Painted Angel	1929	FN/WB
Passport to Hell	1932	Fox
The Patsy	1928	MGM
Poor Little Rich Girl	1936	TCF
Powers That Prey	1918	US
The Price of a Party	1924	US
Prisoner of Zenda	1922	Metro.

Redheads on Parade *	1935	Fox
Road to Paradise	1930	FN
The Rocket Man	1954	TCF
Rogue Cop	1954	MGM
The Sagebrusher	1920	US
Saigon	1947	Par.
The San Francisco Story	1952	WB
Santiago	1956	WB
Saskatchewan	1954	Univ.
Saturday's Children	1929	FN/WB
The Savage	1952	Par.
Scaramouche	1923	Metro.
Sergeant Madden	1939	MGM
She Wanted a Millionaire	1932	Fox
Shore Acres *	1920	Metro.
Six Hours To Live	1932	Fox
Souls in Pawn	1917	US
Springtime for Henry	1934	Fox
The Squall	1929	WB
Stablemates	1938	MGM
Sullivan's Travels	1941	Par.
Sunset Boulevard	1950	Par.
Sweethearts and Wives	1930	FN
This Gun for Hire	1942	Par.
Thunder Afloat	1939	MGM
The Trail of '98	1929	MGM
Trifling Women	1922	Metro.
Turn to the Right	1922	Metro.
Unchartered Seas	1921	Metro.
The Unseen	1945	Par.
Up Romance Road	1918	US
The Well Groomed Bride	1946	Par.
The Westerners	1919	US
When Worlds Collide *	1951	Par.
Where the Pavement Ends	1923	Metro.
Whose Wife?	1917	US
Wild Harvest	1947	Par.
Young Doctor Kildare	1938	MGM
Young Sinners	1931	Fox

553. DEAN SEMLER

Bullseye	1987	Aus.
Cocktail	1988	Dis./Touch.
The Coca-Cola Kid	1985	Aus.
Dances with Wolves	1990	Orion
Dead Calm	1989	Aus.--WB
Farewell to the King	1989	Orion
Going Sane!	1986	Aus.
Hoodwink	1981	Aus.

Impulse	1990	WB
K-9	1989	Univ.
Kitty and the Bagman	1983	Aus.
Let the Balloon Go	1976	Aus.
Mad Max Beyond Thunderdome	1985	Aus.--WB
Razorback	1984	Aus.--WB
Road Warrior	1982	Aus.--WB
Stepping Out	1981	Aus.
Undercover	1984	Aus.
Young Guns	1988	TCF
Young Guns II	1990	TCF

554. MICHAEL SERESIN

Angel Heart	1987	Tri-S.
Come See the Paradise	1990	TCF
Fame	1980	MGM-UA
Midnight Express	1978	GB--Col.
The Undertaker Parlor Computer	1976	Fr.
The Ragman's Daughter	1972	GB
Shoot the Moon	1982	MGM
Sleeping Dogs	1977	NZ
Watch Out for the Eyes	1976	Fr.

555. LEON SHAMROY (1901-1974)

Accent on Youth	1935	Par.
The Adventures of Sherlock Holmes	1939	TCF
The Agony and the Ecstasy	1965	TCF
Alma De Gaucho	1930	US
Behold My Wife!	1934	Par.
Beloved Infidel	1959	TCF
The Best Things in Life Are Free	1956	TCF
Bitter Sweets	1928	US
The Black Swan	1942	TCF
Blossoms on Broadway	1937	Par.
The Blue Angel	1959	TCF
The Bravados	1958	TCF
Buffalo Bill	1944	TCF
Call Me Madam	1953	TCF
Caprice	1967	TCF
The Cardinal	1963	Col.
Cheaper by the Dozen	1950	TCF
Claudia	1943	TCF
Cleopatra	1963	TCF
Confirm or Deny	1941	TCF
Crash Dive	1943	TCF
Daddy Longlegs	1955	TCF
Daisy Kenyon	1947	TCF

David and Bathsheba	1951	TCF
Desk Set	1957	TCF
Do Not Disturb	1965	TCF
Down among the Sheltering Pines	1952	TCF
Down Argentine Way *	1940	TCF
The Egyptian	1954	TCF
Fatal Lady	1936	Par.
Forever Amber	1947	TCF
Four Sons	1940	TCF
The Girl Can't Help It	1956	TCF
The Girl Next Door	1953	TCF
The Glass Bottom Boat	1966	MGM
Good Dame	1934	Par.
Good Morning Miss Dove	1955	TCF
The Great American Broadcast *	1941	TCF
The Great Gambini	1937	Par.
Greenwich Village *	1944	TCF
Her Bodyguard *	1938	Par.
Her Husband Lies	1937	Par.
Hidden Aces	1927	Pathe
I Was an Adventuress	1940	TCF
Jennie Gerhardt	1933	Par.
John Goldfarb, Please Come Home!	1965	TCF
Justine	1969	TCF
The King and I	1956	TCF
King of the Khyber Rifles	1954	TCF
Kiss and Make Up	1934	Par.
Land of the Lawless	1927	Pathe
The Last Moment	1928	US
Leave Her to Heaven	1945	TCF
Lilliam Russell	1940	TCF
Little Old New York	1940	TCF
Love Is a Many Splendored Thing	1955	TCF
Made for Each Other	1938	UA
Mary Burns, Fugitive	1935	Par.
Moon over Miami *	1941	TCF
North to Alaska	1960	TCF
On the Riviera	1951	TCF
Out with the Tide	1928	US
Pirates of the Sky	1927	Pathe
Planet of the Apes	1968	TCF
Porgy and Bess	1959	Col.
Prince of Foxes	1949	TCF
Private Worlds	1935	Par.
Rally Round the Flag, Boys	1958	TCF
Ready for Love	1934	Par.
The Robe	1953	TCF
Roxie Hart	1942	TCF
Second Fiddle	1939	TCF
The Secret Life of an American Wife	1968	TCF
She Asked for It	1937	Par.

She Couldn't Take It	1935	Col.
She Married Her Boss	1935	Col.
The Shocking Miss Pilgrim	1946	TCF
Skidoo	1968	Par.
Snow White and the 3 Stooges	1961	TCF
The Snows of Kilimanjaro	1952	TCF
Soak the Rich	1935	Par.
South Pacific	1958	TCF
Spendthrift	1936	Par.
State Fair	1945	TCF
Stormy Weather	1943	TCF
The Story of Alexander Graham Bell	1939	TCF
Strange Adventure	1933	Mon.
Ten Gentlemen from West Point	1942	TCF
Tender Is the Night	1961	TCF
That Lady in Ermine	1948	TCF
That Night in Rio	1941	TCF
There's No Business Like Show Business	1954	TCF
Thirty Day Princess	1934	Par.
Three Cornered Moon	1933	Par.
Tin Pan Alley	1940	TCF
Tongues of Scandal	1927	US
Tonight We Sing	1953	TCF
A Tree Grows in Brooklyn	1945	TCF
The Trunk Mystery	1927	Pathe
Twelve O'Clock High	1949	TCF
Two Flags West	1950	TCF
Wait Til the Sun Shines, Nellie	1952	TCF
Wake Me When It's Over	1960	TCF
Wedding Present	1936	Par.
What a Way to Go!	1963	TCF
Where Do We Go from Here?	1945	TCF
White Witch Doctor	1953	TCF
Wilson	1944	TCF
With a Song in My Heart	1952	TCF
A Yank in the RAF	1941	TCF
You Only Live Once	1937	UA
The Young in Heart	1938	UA

556. HARRY SHARP (1892-1966)

The Accusing Finger	1936	Par.
Adventure in Washington	1941	Col.
All the King's Horses	1935	Par.
Anna Christie	1923	FN
Around the World in 80 Minutes With Douglas Fairbanks *	1931	UA
Barbara Fritchie	1924	PDC
Beau Revel	1921	Par.

The Big City	1928	MGM
The Black Pirate	1926	UA
Blonde Trouble	1937	Par.
Booloo	1938	Par.
The Boy Friend	1926	MGM
Broadway Limited	1941	UA
Broken Wing	1932	Par.
Campus Confessions	1938	Par.
The Case of Clara Deane	1932	Par.
Christine of the Hungry Heart	1924	FN
Crime by Night	1944	WB
The Crowd	1928	MGM
Daughter of the West	1949	US
Diamond Handcuffs	1928	MGM
Dr. Cyclops *	1940	Par.
Don Q, Son of Zorro *	1925	UA
Duck Soup	1933	Par.
Dynamite Smith	1924	Pathe
Early to Bed	1936	Par.
Enticement	1925	FN
The Fabulous Suzanne	1946	Rep.,
The False Madonna	1932	Par.
From Hell to Heaven	1937	Par.
Geronimo!	1939	Par.
Girl of the Limberlost	1924	US
The Glass Alibi	1946	Rep.
The Glass Key	1935	Par.
Golden Gloves	1940	Par.
The Guilty	1947	Mon.
Hail the Woman	1921	US
Henry Aldrich, Editor	1942	Par.
Here Comes the Groom	1934	Par.
The Hidden Hand	1942	WB
High Tide	1947	Mon.
His Exciting Night	1938	Univ.
Hold 'Em Navy!	1937	Par.
Homespun Folk	1920	US
Hotel Haywire	1937	Par.
The Hottentot	1922	FN
Human Wreckage	1923	FBO
Illegal Traffic	1938	Par.
The Iron Mask	1929	UA
It Happened on Fifth Avenue	1947	Mon.
It's a Gift	1934	Par.
Jealousy	1945	Rep.
Judgment of the Storm *	1924	US
Just around the Corner	1938	Par.
Ladies Should Listen	1934	Par.
Lady Be Careful	1936	Par.
The Lawton Story	1949	US
The Lemon Drop Kid	1934	Par.

Lion and the Lamb	1931	Col.
Lord Byron of Broadway	1930	MGM
Lorna Doone	1922	FN
Love in the Rough	1930	MGM
The Lovelorn	1927	MGM
Lying Lips *	1921	US
Madame Racketeer	1932	Par.
Madison Square Garden	1932	Par.
Man in Half Moon Street	1944	Par.
Many Happy Returns	1934	Par.
The Marriage Cheat	1924	FN
Melody in Spring	1934	Par.
Ministry of Fear	1944	Par.
The Mirage	1924	US
Mother O'Mine	1921	US
Murder Goes to College	1937	Par.
The Mysterious Doctor	1942	WB
The National Barn Dance	1944	Par.
Partners in Crime	1937	Par.
Perilous Waters	1948	Mon.
Rose Bowl	1936	Par.
Scandal Sheet	1937	Par.
70,000 Witnesses	1932	Par.
Sins of the Children	1930	MGM
Six of a Kind	1934	Par.
Slide, Kelly, Slide	1927	MGM
Song of the Eagle	1933	Par.
Soul of the Beast	1923	Metro.
Speedway	1929	MGM
Strangers In Love	1932	Par.
Sudden Money	1939	Par.
The Sunshine Trail	1923	FN
The Third Alarm	1922	US
This Reckless Age	1932	Par.
Thunder	1929	MGM
Tiger Thompson	1924	US
Tomorrow the World	1944	UA
Trial of Mary Dugan	1931	MGM
Violence	1947	Mon.
Way Out West	1930	MGM
What a Wife Learned	1923	FN
What Next Corporal Hargrove?	1945	MGM
Where East Is West	1929	MGM
While the City Sleeps	1928	MGM
Wild Money	1937	Par.
Woman Who Came Back	1945	Rep.
The Young Land *	1957	Col.

557. JOSEPH SHELDERFER

The Cambric Mask	1919	Vita.

The Captain's Captain	1919	Vita.
Cousin Kate	1920	Vita.
Divorce Coupons	1922	Vita.
Dollars and the Woman	1920	Vita.
The Dust of Egypt	1915	Vita.
Her Lord and Master	1921	Vita.
The Lion and the Mouse	1919	Vita.
The Prey	1920	Vita.
A Price for Folly *	1915	Vita.
The Prodigal Judge *	1922	Vita.
The Scarab Ring	1921	Vita.
The Spark Divine	1919	Vita.
Sowers and Reapers	1917	Metro.
Splendid Duchess *	1920	Vita.
The Two-Edged Sword	1916	Vita.
The Vengeance of Durand	1919	Vita.
The Vice of Fools	1920	Vita.
The Winchester Woman	1919	Vita.

558. LESTER SHORR

Arizona Bushwhackers	1968	Par.
Hot Rod Rumble	1957	AA
Law of the Lawless	1963	Par.
The McMasters	1969	US
The Peacemaker	1956	UA
The Quick Gun	1964	Col.
Ride beyond Vengeance	1966	Col.
Take the Money and Run	1968	US
Three Bad Sisters	1956	UA

559. DON SHORT

Ace of Hearts	1921	Gold.
Calvert's Valley	1922	Fox
The Devil Within	1921	Fox
Don't Neglect Your Wife	1921	Gold.
The Eleventh Hour	1923	Fox
The Fast Mail *	1922	Fox
Gleam O'Dawn	1922	Fox
Iron to Gold	1922	Fox
The Little Shepherd of Kingdom Come	1920	Gold.
Oath-Bound	1922	Fox
The Penalty	1920	Gold.
Second Hand Love	1923	Fox
Skid Proof	1923	Fox
Strange Idols	1922	Fox
Strength of the Pines *	1922	Fox

Three Who Paid	1923	Fox
While Justice Waits	1922	Fox
The Wolf Man *	1924	Fox
The Yellow Stain	1922	Fox
The Yosemite Trail	1922	Fox

560. WILLIAM SICKNER

Arizona Trail	1943	Univ.
Bad Man from Red Butte	1940	Univ.
Behind the Mask	1946	Mon.
Belle Starr's Daughter	1948	TCF
Big Timber	1950	Mon.
Black Diamonds	1940	Univ.
Black Midnight	1949	Mon.
Blonde Savage	1947	EL
Bomba and the Elephant Stampede	1951	Mon.
Bomba and the Hidden City	1950	Mon.
Bomba on Panther Island	1950	Mon.
Bomba the Jungle Boy	1949	Mon.
Border Bandits	1946	Mon.
Border Brigands	1935	Univ.
Bowery Bombshell	1946	Mon.
Call of the Klondike	1950	Mon.
Casa Manana	1951	Mon.
Cheyenne Roundup	1943	Univ.
The Chinese Ring	1947	Mon.
Chip of the Flying U	1939	Univ.
Cry Vengeance	1954	AA
Danger in the Pacific	1942	Univ.
Dangerous Money	1946	Mon.
Dark Alibi	1946	Mon.
Desert Pursuit	1952	Mon.
Docks of New Orleans	1948	Mon.
Don't Gamble With Strangers	1946	Mon.
Father Takes the Air	1951	Mon.
The Feathered Serpent	1948	Mon.
Fighting Fools	1949	Mon.
Finger Man	1955	AA
French Leave	1948	Mon.
Frontier Bad Men	1943	Univ.
Gas House Kids Go West	1947	PRC
Henry the Rainmaker	1949	Mon.
Hold That Baby!	1949	Mon.
Hot Steel	1940	Univ.
Humphrey Takes a Chance	1950	Mon.
In Fast Company	1946	Mon.
Jack Slade	1953	AA
Joe Palooka in Fighting Mad	1948	Mon.
Joe Palooka in Winner Takes All	1948	Mon.

Joe Palooka Meets Humphrey	1950	Mon.
Keep 'Em Slugging	1943	Univ.
Kidnapped	1948	Mon.
Killer Dill	1947	US
Killer Shark	1950	Mon.
Kilroy Was Here	1947	Mon.
King of the Bandits	1947	Mon.
Leave It to Henry	1949	Mon.
Left Handed Law *	1937	Univ.
The Lion Hunters	1951	Mon.
Little Joe the Wrangler	1942	Univ.
Live Wires	1946	Mon.
The Lone Star Trail	1943	Univ.
Lonesome Trail	1945	Mon.
Loophole	1954	AA
Louisiana	1947	Mon.
Mississippi Rhythm	1949	Mon.
A Modern Marriage	1950	Mon.
The Mummy's Ghost	1944	Univ.
The Mystery of the Golden Eye	1948	Mon.
Night Freight	1955	AA
Northern Patrol	1953	AA
Northwest Territory	1952	Mon.
Oklahoma Raiders	1944	Univ.
Old Chisholm Trail	1942	Univ.
Outlawed Guns *	1935	Univ.
Penthouse Rhythm	1945	Univ.
Pony Post	1940	Univ.
Prarie Express	1947	Mon.
Raiders of San Joaquin	1943	Univ.
Return of Jack Slade	1955	AA
Rhythm Inn	1951	Mon.
Riders of Pasco Basin	1940	Univ.
Riders of the Dawn	1946	Mon.
The Scarlet Clue	1945	Mon.
The Shadow Returns	1946	Mon.
Shadows over Chinatown	1946	Mon.
The Shanghai Chest	1948	Mon.
Sideshow	1950	Mon.
Sierra Passage	1950	Mon.
Sky Dragon	1949	Mon.
Son of Roaring Dan	1940	Univ.
South of the Rio Grande	1945	Mon.
The Steel Fist	1952	Mon.
Stormy *	1935	Univ.
Tangier Incident	1953	AA
Tenting Tonight on the Old Camp Ground	1943	Univ.
There Goes Kelly	1945	Mon.
Torpedo Alley	1952	AA
Trail of the Yukon	1949	Mon.

Tuna Clipper	1949	Mon.
The Undead	1957	AIP
Weekend Pass	1944	Univ.
The Wolf Hunters	1950	Mon.
Yellow Fin	1951	Mon.

561. ALLEN SIEGLER

Against the Law	1934	Col.
Ain't Love Funny?	1927	US
Air Hostess	1949	Col.
Anybody's War	1930	Par.
April Folly	1920	Par.
Behind Prison Gates	1939	Col.
Beware Spooks!	1939	Col.
Beyond the Law	1934	Col.
The Big Little Person	1919	Univ.
Black Room	1935	Col.
The Blackmailer	1936	Col.
Blind Date	1934	Col.
Blondie's Big Moment	1947	Col.
The Body Disappears	1941	WB
Breed of the Sea	1926	US
Burning Up	1930	Par.
Carnival	1935	Col.
The Case of Missing Man	1935	Col.
Case of the Black Cat	1936	WB
City Streets	1938	Col.
Contraband	1925	Par.
Counterfeit Lady	1937	Col.
Cowboy Star	1936	Col.
Crime of Helen Stanley	1934	Col.
Damaged Lives	1937	US
Dan Matthews	1936	Col.
Danger, Go Slow	1918	Univ.
The Dangerous Age *	1922	FN
Death Flies East	1935	Col.
The Delicious Little Devil	1919	Univ.
The Devil Commands	1941	Col.
The Devil Is Driving	1937	Col.
Devil Ship	1947	Col.
The Devil's Trademark	1928	FBO
Driftin' Sands	1928	FBO
L'Enigmatique Monsieur Parkes	1930	Par.
Faint Perfume	1925	US
Father's Son	1941	WB
The Fighting Code	1934	Col.
The Fighting Sheriff	1925	US
Five Little Peppers at Home	1940	Col.
A Fool's Awakening	1924	Metro.

Fugitive Lady	1934	Col.
The Girl Who Wouldn't Work	1925	US
Girls Men Forget	1924	US
The Harvester	1927	US
Hate	1922	Metro.
Hell's House	1932	US
The Hole in the Wall	1921	Metro.
Human Tornado *	1925	US
Inner Sanctum	1948	US
The Inside of the Cup	1921	Par.
It Can't Last Forever	1937	Col.
Jesse James	1927	Par.
Judgment of the Hills	1927	US
June Moon	1931	Par.
Killer at Large	1935	Col.
Kisses	1922	Metro.
Kosher Kitty Kelly	1926	US
Laddie	1926	US
The Lady Objects	1938	Col.
Little Mickey Grogan	1927	FBO
The Little Yellow House	1928	FBO
The Lone Wolf in Mexico	1947	Col.
The Lone Wolf Spy Hunt	1939	Col.
Love among the Millionaires	1930	Par.
Loves of Ricardo	1926	US
The Magic Garden	1927	US
The Main Event	1938	Col.
Make Me a Star	1932	Par.
A Man's Game	1934	Col.
Meet the Baron	1933	MGM
Military Academy	1940	Col.
Mills of the Gods	1935	Col.
The Miracle of Love	1920	Par.
Modern Love	1918	Univ.
Mother	1927	US
Motor Madness	1937	Col.
Moulders of Men	1927	US
My Lady's Lips	1925	US
My Son Is a Criminal	1939	Col.
Naughty Nanette	1927	US
Never Trust a Gambler	1951	Col.
No Time to Marry	1938	Col.
Not for Publication	1927	US
The Old Wyoming Trail	1937	Col.
One Man Justice *	1937	Col.
The Other Woman's Story *	1925	US
Over the Wire	1921	Metro.
Parisian Love	1925	US
Party Wire	1935	Col.
Plastic Age *	1925	US
Port Said	1948	Col.

The Price of a Good Time	1918	US
The Restless Sex	1920	Par.
Roaming Lady	1936	Col.
Romance of the Redwoods	1939	Col.
Rough Going	1925	US
Saving the Family Name	1916	US
The Scarlet Trail	1919	US
Sea Legs	1930	Par.
Shadows on the Stairs	1941	WB
Slightly Scarlet	1930	Par.
Smashing the Spy Ring	1939	Col.
Smuggler's Gold	1951	Col.
So You Won't Talk?	1940	Col.
The Social Lion	1930	Par.
Someone To Love	1928	Par.
Speed Wings	1934	Col.
Spoilers of the Range	1939	Col.
Strange Alibi	1941	FN/WB
Take the Heir	1930	US
Through the Dark *	1924	Gold.
The Timid Terror	1926	US
Trapped	1937	Col.
Trapped by Television	1936	Col.
The Truant Husband	1920	US
Trucker's Top Hand	1924	US
Two Fisted Sheriff	1937	Col.
Unknown World *	1951	Lip.
The Unpainted Woman	1919	Univ.
Unseeing Eyes *	1923	Gold.
Wallflowers *	1928	FBO
The Weaker Vessel *	1919	Univ.
West of Santa Fe	1938	Col.
What Am I Bid?	1919	Univ.
When a Girl Loves	1919	US
White Thunder	1925	US
Wolf Song	1929	Par.
Woman In Distress	1937	Col.
You May Be Next	1936	Col.

562. HAL SINTZENICH

America *	1924	UA
The Challenge	1922	US
Free Air *	1922	US
Girl of the Sea *	1920	US
Has the World GOne Mad!	1923	US
Isn't Life Wonderful? *	1924	UA
Out Yonder *	1920	Selz.
Over the Hill to the Poorhouse	1920	Fox
Sally of the Sawdust *	1925	UA

"That Royle Girl" *	1925	Par.
The White Heather *	1919	US
White Rose *	1923	UA
The Woman God Sent *	1920	Selz.

563. WILLIAM SKALL (1898-1976)

All Mine to Give	1957	RKO
Arabian Nights *	1942	Univ.
Billy the Kid *	1941	MGM
Brave Warrior	1952	Col.
Cripple Creek	1952	Col.
Dancing Pirate	1936	RKO
Everything I Have Is Yours	1952	MGM
The Forest Rangers *	1942	Par.
The Golden Hawk	1952	Col.
The Half-Breed	1952	RKO
Kim	1950	MGM
Life with Father *	1947	WB
The Little Princess *	1939	TCF
The Mikado *	1939	GB--Univ.
My Wild Irish ROse *	1947	WB
Night and Day *	1946	WB
Northwest Passage *	1940	MGM
Quo Vadis *	1951	MGM
Ramona *	1936	TCF
Reap the Wild Wind *	1942	Par.
Return of Frank James *	1940	TCF
Rope *	1948	WB
The Silver Chalice	1955	WB
Song of Scheherezade *	1947	Univ.
The Time, the Place and the Girl	1946	WB
Two Guys from Texas *	1948	WB
Victoria the Great *	1937	GB
Virginia *	1941	Par.

564. DOUGLAS SLOCOMBE (1913-   )

All at Sea	1958	GB--MGM
Another Shore	1948	GB--Eal.
The Bawdy Adventures of Tom Jones	1976	GB--Univ.
The Blue Max	1966	TCF
Boom!	1968	Univ.
The Boy Who Stole a Million	1960	GB
The Buttercup Chain	1970	Col.
Cage of Gold	1950	GB--Eal.
The Captive Heart *	1946	GB--EL/Eal.
Caravans	1978	Iran--Univ.
Circus of Horrors	1960	GB--AIP

Crash of Silence	1952	GB
Dance Hall	1950	GB--Eal.
Davy	1957	GB--Eal./MGM
Dead of Night *	1945	GB--Eal./Rank/ Univ.
Decision Against Time	1956	GB--MGM
The Destructors	1974	GB--AIP
Fathom *	1967	TCF
Fearless Vampire Killers	1967	MGM
Freud	1963	Univ.
Girl on the Canal	1947	GB--Eal.
The Great Gatsby	1974	Par.
Guns at Batasi	1964	GB--TCF
Hedda	1975	GB
A High Wind in Jamaica	1965	TCF
His Excellency	1951	GB--Eal.
Hue and Cry *	1946	GB--Eal.
Indiana Jones and the Temple of Doom *	1984	Par.
Indiana Jones and the Last Crusade *	1989	Par.
It Always Rains on Saturday	1947	GB--EL/Rank
The Italian Job *	1968	GB--Par.
Jesus Christ Superstar	1973	Univ.
Julia	1977	TCF
Kind Hearts and Coronets *	1949	GB--Eal.
The L-Shaped Room	1962	GB--Col.
Lady Jane	1986	Par.
The Lady Vanishes	1979	GB--Rank
The Lavender Hill Mob	1951	GB--Eal./Univ.
Lease of Life	1954	GB
The Light Touch	1955	GB--Eal./Univ.
The Lion in Winter	1968	GB--AE
Lost and Found	1979	Col.
The Love Lottery	1953	GB--Eal.
The Loves of Joanna Gooden	1947	GB--Eal.
Ludwig II	1955	Ger.
The Maids	1974	GB--AFT
Man in the White Suit	1951	GB--Eal./Rank/ Univ.
The Mark	1961	GB--TCF
Murphy's War	1971	GB--Par.
The Music Lovers	1970	GB--UA
Nasty Habits	1976	GB
Never Say Never Again	1983	GB--WB
Nijinsky	1980	GB--Par.
Panic in the Parlour	1956	GB
The Pirates of Penzance	1983	Univ.
Promise Her Anything	1966	GB--Par.
Raiders of the Lost Ark	1981	Par.
The Return	1973	GB
Robbery	1967	GB

Rollerball	1975	UA
A Run for Your Money	1949	GB--Eal./Univ.
Sailor Who Fell from Grace with the Sea	1975	GB--AE
Saraband for Dead Lovers	1948	GB--EL/Eal.
Scream of Fear	1961	GB--Col./Ham.
The Servant	1963	GB
The Smallest Show on Earth	1957	GB
That Lucky Touch	1975	GB--AA/Rank
The Third Secret	1964	GB--TCF
The Titfield Thunderbolt	1952	GB--Eal./Univ.
Travels with My Aunt	1972	GB--MGM
Tread Softly Stranger	1958	GB
Water	1985	GB--Rank
Wonderful to Be Young!	1962	GB--Par.

565. LEONARD SMITH (1894-1947)

At the Circus	1939	MGM
Best Foot Forward	1943	MGM
Billy the Kid *	1941	MGM
Blue Sierra	1946	MGM
Broadway Rhythm	1943	MGM
The Captain Is a Lady	1940	MGM
Caught Short	1930	MGM
Courage of Lassie	1946	MGM
Design for Scandal *	1941	MGM
The Devil Doll	1936	MGM
Doughboys	1930	MGM
Four Girls in White	1938	MGM
Free and Easy	1930	MGM
The Ghost Goes Home	1940	MGM
Go West	1940	MGM
The Golden Fleecing	1940	MGM
The Idle Rich	1929	MGM
Joe and Ethel Turp Call on the President	1939	MGM
Lassie Comes Home	1943	MGM
London by Night	1937	MGM
Maisie	1939	MGM
Married before Breakfast	1937	MGM
Murder in the Private Car *	1934	MGM
National Velvet	1944	MGM
Paradise for Three	1937	MGM
Parlor, Bedroom and Bath	1931	MGM
Prosperity	1932	MGM
Reducing	1931	MGM
Ship Ahoy *	1942	MGM
The Sidewalks of New York	1931	MGM
Sinner Take All	1936	MGM

Smilin' Through	1941	MGM
So This Is Africa	1933	Col.
So This Is College	1929	MGM
Song of the City	1937	MGM
Stand Up and Fight	1939	MGM
Tarzan Escapes	1936	MGM
Tarzan Finds a Son!	1939	MGM
They Learned About Women	1930	MGM
Thoroughbreds Don't Cry	1937	MGM
Tough Guy	1936	MGM
Wu Li Chang	1930	MGM
The Yearling *	1946	MGM

566. STEPHEN SMITH, JR.

The Angel of Crooked Street	1922	Vita.
Baree, Son of Kazan *	1925	Vita.
Between Friends	1924	Vita.
Borrowed Husbands	1924	Vita.
Captain Blood	1924	Vita.
The Clean Heart	1924	Vita.
The Count of Luxembourg	1926	US
Flower of the North	1921	Vita.
Fortune's Mask	1922	Vita.
A Girl's Desire	1922	Vita.
The Little Angel of Canyon Creek	1914	Vita.
The Little Minister	1922	Vita.
Little Wildcat	1922	Vita.
The Man Next Door	1923	Vita.
Masters of Men	1923	Vita.
The Midnight Alarm	1923	Vita.
My Man	1924	Vita.
My Wild Irish Rose	1922	Vita.
The Ninety and Nine	1922	Vita.
One Stolen Night	1923	Vita.
Pampered Youth *	1925	Vita.
Pioneer Trails	1923	Vita.
The Son of Wallingford	1921	Vita.
Steele of the Royal Mounted	1925	Vita.
Transcontinental Limited	1926	US

567. WILLIAM EDWARD SNYDER

Aloma of the South Seas *	1941	Par.
The Americano	1954	RKO
Appointment With a Shadow	1958	Univ.
The Bandit of Sherwood Forest *	1946	Col.
Beyond a Reasonable Doubt	1956	RKO
Big Business	1937	TCF

A Bit of Heaven *	1928	US
Blackbeard the Pirate	1952	RKO
Blue Skies *	1946	Par.
The Boatniks	1970	Dis.
Bon Voyage!	1962	Dis.
Borrowing Trouble	1937	TCF
Bundle of Joy	1956	RKO
Cattle King	1963	MGM
The Creature from the Black Lagoon	1954	Univ.
Dangerous Mission	1954	RKO
Destination Unknown	1933	Univ.
Down on the Farm	1938	TCF
Escapade in Japan	1957	RKO
Escape by Night	1937	Rep.
Everybody's Baby	1939	TCF
Fangs of Fate	1928	Pathe
The Fighting Marine	1926	Pathe
Fighting Youth	1935	Univ.
The First Traveling Saleslady	1956	RKO
Flying Leathernecks	1951	RKO
The Flying Missile	1950	Col.
Girl Loves Boy	1937	GN
Great Day in the Morning	1955	RKO
The Harvester	1936	Rep.
Hawk of the Hills *	1929	Pathe
Her Man	1930	Pathe
His Night Out	1935	Univ.
Hoof Marks *	1927	Pathe
Horse in the Gray Flannel Suit	1969	Dis.
Hot Water	1937	TCF
The House across the Street	1949	WB
Huk!	1956	UA
I Was a Convict	1939	Rep.
Jolson Sings Again	1949	Col.
The Jones Family in Hollywood	1939	TCF
Lonely Wives	1931	Pathe/RKO
Love on a Budget	1938	TCF
The Loves of Carmen	1948	Col.
The Man from Colorado	1949	Col.
Marked Money	1928	Pathe
Meet the Girls	1938	TCF
Million Dollar Duck	1971	Dis.
Monkeys Go Home!	1966	Dis.
Moon Pilot	1961	Dis.
Never a Dull Moment	1967	Dis.
New Mexico *	1951	UA
$1,000,000 Duck	1971	Dis.
One Minute to Zero	1952	RKO
Painted Desert	1931	Pathe
Pardon My Gun	1930	Pathe
Passport Husband	1938	TCF

The Petty Girl	1950	Col.
Princess and the Pirate *	1944	Gold.
Rascal	1969	Dis.
Red Sundown	1956	Univ.
Renegades	1946	Col.
The Return of October	1948	Col.
Road Demon	1938	TCF
Second Chance	1953	RKO
Small Town Boy	1937	GN
Son of Sinbad	1955	RKO
Speed To Burn	1938	TCF
The Story of Dr. Wassell *	1944	Par.
Summer Magic	1963	Dis.
Sweetheart of the Navy	1937	GN
The Swordsman	1947	Col.
Tarzan's Fight for Life	1958	MGM
Ten Tall Men	1951	Col.
They Just Had To Get Married	1933	Univ.
A Tiger Walks	1963	Dis.
The Tip-Off	1931	Pathe/RKO
The Toast of New Orleans	1950	MGM
Toby Tyler	1959	Dis.
The Treasure of Pancho Villa	1955	RKO
A Trip to Paris	1938	TCF
White Savage *	1943	Univ.
Wonder Man *	1945	Gold.
The Younger Brothers	1949	WB
Youth On Parole	1937	Rep.

567a. BARRY SONNENFELD

Big	1988	TCF
Blood Simple	1984	US
Compromising Positions	1985	Par.
Miller's Crossing	1990	TCF
Misery	1990	Col.
Raising Arizona	1987	TCF
Three O'Clock High	1987	Univ.
Throw Mama from the Train	1987	Orion
When Harry Met Sally ...	1989	Col.

568. LEONARD SOUTH

Amy	1981	Dis.
Family Plot	1976	Univ.
Hang 'Em High *	1967	UA
Herbie Goes to Monte Carlo	1977	Dis.
I Sailed to Tahiti With an All-Girl Crew *	1968	US
The North Avenue Irregulars	1978	Dis.

569. ALBERTO SPAGNOLI

La Baby Sitter	1975	Fr./Ger./It.
Black Pirate	1977	It.
Daisy Miller	1974	Par.
Fantozzi Takes It on the Chin Again	1984	It.
Fracchia, the Human Beast	1982	It.
Hercules	1983	It.--MGM-UA
Hercules II	1985	Cannon
Killer Fish	1979	Braz./It.
Policewoman	1975	It.--US
Really ... Incredible	1982	It.
We Want the Colonels	1973	It.

570. THEODOR SPARKUHL (1894-1945)

Alf's Carpet	1929	GB
All Women Have Secrets	1940	Par.
Among the Living	1941	Par.
The Bachelor's Daughters	1946	UA
Beau Geste *	1939	Par.
The Big Broadcast of 1937	1936	Par.
Blood on the Sun	1945	US
Buy Me That Town	1941	Par.
Caravan *	1934	Fox
Carmen	1918	Ger.
La Chienne *	1931	Fr.
College Holiday *	1936	Par.
College Scandal	1935	Par.
The Compulsory Husband	1930	GB
Dangerous To Know	1938	Par.
Dr. Broadway	1942	Par.
Enter Madame *	1935	Par.
Father Brown Detective	1935	Par.
The Flying Scotsman	1929	GB--WB
Forgotten Faces	1936	Par.
Four Hours To Kill	1935	Par.
The Glass Key	1942	Par.
The Good Fellows	1943	Par.
The Hardboiled Canary	1941	Par.
Harmony Heaven	1930	GB
High, Wide and Handsome *	1937	Par.
If I Were King	1938	Par.
The Informer	1929	GB
Internes Can't Take Money	1937	Par.
Johnny Come Lately	1943	US
Lady from the Sea	1929	GB
The Lady's From Kentucky	1939	Par.
The Last Outpost	1935	Par.
The Light That Failed	1939	Par.

Lone Cowboy	1934	Par.
Midnight Angel	1941	Par.
Midnight Club	1933	Par.
Murder He Says	1945	Par.
Night Plane from Chungking	1942	Par.
No More Women	1934	Par.
One Arabian Night	1921	Ger.--FN
Opened by Mistake	1940	Par.
Our Hearts Were Young and Gay *	1944	Par.
Pacific Blackout	1942	Par.
Passion	1919	Ger.--FN/UFA
Princess aux Huitres	1919	Ger.
Queen of the Mob	1940	Par.
Rangers of Fortune	1943	Par.
The Remarkable Andrew	1942	Par.
Rulers of the Sea *	1939	Par.
St. Louis Blues	1939	Par.
Salty O'Rourke	1945	Par.
Salute For Three	1943	Par.
Second Chorus	1941	Par.
Ship Cafe	1935	Par.
Star Spangled Rhythm *	1942	Par.
Street of Chance	1942	Par.
Sumurun	1920	Ger.
Suspense *	1930	GB
The Texans	1938	Par.
Thirteen Hours by Air	1936	Par.
Till We Meet Again	1944	Par.
Tip-Off Girls	1938	Par.
Wake Island *	1942	Par.
The Way of All Flesh	1940	Par.
Wells Fargo	1937	Par.
West Point Wide	1941	Par.
Yours for the Asking	1936	Par.

571. DANTE SPINOTTI

Aria *	1987	GB--US
The Basil Quartet	1982	It.
Beaches	1988	Touch.
Berlin Affair	1985	Ger./It.
Choke Canyon	1986	US
Cinderella '80	1984	Fr./It.
The Comfort of Strangers	1990	It./US
Crimes of the Heart	1986	US
Disobedience	1981	Fr./It.
From the Hip	1987	DeL.
Hearts in Armor	1983	It.
Illegally Yours	1988	MGM-UA
The Legend of the Holy Drinker	1988	It.

Mamba	1988	It.
Manhunter	1986	DeL.
A Midsummer Night's Dream	1983	It.
Minestrone	1981	It.
Photographing Patricia	1984	It.
Softly ... Softly	1985	It.
Thus Spake Bellavista	1984	It.
Torrents of Spring	1989	GB /It.
A Violent Life	1990	Fr. /Ger. /It.
Voyage of the Rock Aliens *	1988	US

572. FRANK STANLEY

The Big Fix	1978	Univ.
Breezy	1973	Univ.
Car Wash	1976	Univ.
The Carey Treatment	1972	MGM
Corvette Summer	1978	UA
The Eiger Sanction *	1975	Univ.
The Fish That Saved Pittsburgh	1979	UA
Grease 2	1982	Par.
A Hero Ain't Nothing But a Sandwich'	1977	US
Heroes	1977	Univ.
J. W. Coop	1971	Col.
Magnum Force	1973	WB
Mr. Ricco	1975	MGM-UA
A Separate Peace	1972	Par.
"10"	1979	Orion /WB
Thunderbolt and Lightfoot	1974	UA
Tom Sawyer	1973	UA
Under the Rainbow	1981	Orion /WB
Wholly Moses	1980	Col.
Willie Dynamite	1973	Univ.

572a. OLIVER STAPLETON

Absolute Beginners	1986	Orion
Aria *	1987	GB /US
Cookie	1989	WB
Earth Girls Are Easy	1988	US
The Grifters	1990	US
My Beautiful Laundrette	1986	GB
Prick Up Your Ears	1987	GB
Restless Natives	1986	Orion
Running Out of Luck	1985	US
Sammy and Rosie Get Laid	1987	GB
She-Devil	1989	Orion

573. ROBERT STEADMAN

Above the Law	1988	WB
Dogs	1976	US
Executive Action	1973	NG
Good Guys Wear Black	1978	US
Hammer	1972	UA

573a. PETER STEIN

Beach House	1982	US
C.H.U.D.	1984	US
Ernest Goes to Jail	1990	BV/Touch.
Ernest Saves Christmas	1988	BV
Friday the 13th, Part 2	1981	Par.
Good Dissonance Like a Man	1977	US
Graveyard Shift	1990	Par.
A Great Wall	1986	Orion
Just Crazy about Horses	1978	US
The Passage	1988	US
Pet Sematary	1989	Par.
Reuben, Reuben	1983	TCF
The Wild Pair	1987	US
Wildrose	1985	US

574. WILLIAM STEINER

The Battle of Paris	1929	Par.
Fast and Loose	1930	Par.
The Forbidden Range *	1923	US
Go Man Go	1954	UA
Heads Up	1930	Par.
His Woman	1931	Par.
Hotel Variety *	1933	US
The Lady Lies	1929	Par.
Love and Passion	1932	US
Middleton Family at the New York World's Fair	1939	US
Midnight	1934	Univ.
Queen High	1930	Par.
Roadhouse Nights	1930	Par.
Sins of the Fathers	1948	Can.
Take a Chance	1933	Par.
The Tattooed Stranger	1950	RKO
Two Tickets to Paris	1962	Col.
Wayward	1932	Par.
The Window	1949	RKO

575. MACK STENGLER (1895-1962)

Adventures of Kitty O'Day	1944	Mon.
The Ape Man	1943	Mon.
The Argyle Secrets	1948	US
Arizona Nights	1927	US
Army Wives	1944	Mon.
Bank Alarm	1937	GN
The Border Legion	1930	Par.
Borrowed Trouble	1948	UA
Bowery at Midnight	1942	Mon.
Breed of Courage	1927	US
Captain Calamity	1936	GN
Campus Rhythm	1943	Mon.
Campus Sleuth	1948	Mon.
Caught in the Act	1941	PRC
College Days *	1926	US
Danger Ahead	1940	Mon.
Dangerous Venture	1947	UA
The Dead Don't Dream	1948	UA
The Devil's Playground	1946	UA
Duke of the Navy	1942	PRC
Fall Guy	1947	Mon.
False Paradise	1948	UA
The First Night *	1927	US
Fool's Gold	1947	UA
Foreign Agent	1942	Mon.
Freckles Comes Home	1942	Mon.
Gambling Daughters	1941	PRC
The Gang's All Here	1941	Mon.
The Gay Intruders	1948	TCF
Ghosts on the Loose	1943	Mon.
Hell Harbor *	1930	UA
Hired Wife	1934	US
Hoppy's Holiday	1947	UA
I Wouldn't Be in Your Shoes	1948	Mon.
In a Moment of Temptation	1927	US
Jens Monson in America *	1947	Swed.
Joe Palooka in The Big Fight	1949	Mon.
Joselyn's Wife *	1926	US
Jungle Patrol	1948	TCF
Kit Carson	1928	Par.
Knight of the Plains	1938	US
Lady, Let's Dance	1944	Mon.
Let's Go Collegiate	1941	Mon.
Let's Live Again	1948	TCF
Lost at Sea *	1926	US
Love Takes Flight	1937	GN
The Marauders	1947	UA
Meet the Mob	1942	Mon.
Mystery of the 13th Guest	1943	Mon.

Navy Spy	1939	GN
Nearly Eighteen	1943	Mon.
Oh, What a Night	1944	Mon.
One Hour of Love	1927	US
One-Man Law	1932	Col.
The Pioneer Scout	1928	Par.
Regular Fellows	1941	PRC
Revenge of the Zombies	1943	Mon.
Rhythm Parade	1943	Mon.
Ride 'Em Cowgirl	1938	GN
Sarong Girl	1943	Mon.
Silent Conflict	1948	UA
Silver Comes Through	1927	US
Silver Skates	1943	Mon.
Sin Cargo *	1926	US
The Singing Cowgirl	1939	GN
Sinister Journey	1948	UA
Smart Guy	1943	Mon.
Smart Politics	1948	Mon.
A Song for Miss Julie	1945	Rep.
Songs and Bullets	1938	US
South of Panama	1941	PRC
Spotlight Scandals	1943	Mon.
Spy Train	1943	Mon.
Strange Gamble	1948	UA
The Sunset Legion *	1928	Par.
Sunset Murder Case	1941	US
Terror of Tiny Town	1938	Col.
That Model from Paris *	1926	US
Top Sergeant Mulligan	1941	Mon.
Unexpected Guest	1947	UA
Water Rustlers	1939	GN
We're in the Legion Now	1937	GN
Where Are Your Children? *	1943	Mon.
Why Girls Leave Home	1945	PRC
Wings Over the Pacific	1943	Mon.
Women in Bondage	1943	Mon.
Yellow Cargo	1936	GN
Yukon Flight	1940	Mon.

576. ALAN STENSVOLD

Affair in Havana	1957	AA
Air Strike	1955	Lip.
Chandler	1971	MGM
Clay Pigeon	1971	MGM
Country Boy	1966	US
The Destructors	1968	US
Dimension 5	1966	US
Eight on the Lamb	1966	UA

The Girl Who Knew Too Much	1969	US
The Hindu *	1953	GB--UA
It's a Bikini World	1967	US
The Money Jungle	1968	US
Panic in the City	1968	US
Please Murder Me	1956	US
The Private Navy of Sergeant O'Farrell	1968	UA
Saturday Night in Apple Valley	1965	US
Sundown Riders	1948	US
Thunder Road	1958	UA
Tiger by the Tail	1970	US
Track of Thunder	1967	UA

577. JOHN STEPHENS

Boxcar Bertha	1972	AIP
Bunny O'Hare *	1971	AIP
Crystalstone	1988	US
Foxtrap *	1986	It.--US
Heart Like a Wheel *	1983	TCF
Little Cigars	1973	AIP
Run, Angel, Run!	1969	US
Ski Patrol	1990	US
Sorcerer *	1977	Par./Univ.
Steele Justice	1987	US

578. GEORGE STEVENS (1904-1975)

The Battling Orioles *	1924	Pathe
Black Cyclone *	1925	Pathe
The Desert's Toll *	1925	MGM
The Devil Horse *	1926	Pathe
Girl from Gay Paree *	1927	US
Lightning *	1927	US
No Man's Law *	1927	Pathe
The Valley of Hell *	1927	MGM
The White Sheep *	1924	Pathe

579. JACK STEVENS

The Better Man	1926	US
The Blue Streak *	1926	US
The Broadway Gallant	1926	US
The Cuckoo Clock	1938	It.--MGM
The Merry Cavalier	1926	US
Mine To Keep *	1923	US
The Night Patrol *	1926	US

Pardon Us	1931	MGM
Wall Street Whiz *	1925	US

580. ERNEST STEWARD

Above Us the Waves	1955	GB--Rank/Rep.
Agent 8 3/4	1964	GB
The Assassins	1953	GB--UA
Bitter Harvest	1963	GB--Rank
The Brides of Fu Manchu	1966	US
Callan	1974	GB
Campbell's Kingdom	1957	GB--Rank
Carnaby M.D.	1967	GB--Rank
Carry On Again Doctor	1969	GB--Rank
Carry On at Your Convenience	1971	GB
Carry On Behind	1975	GB
Carry On Camping	1969	GB--Rank
Carry On Dick	1974	GB
Carry On England	1976	GB--Rank/TCF
Carry On Loving	1970	GB--Rank
Carry On Matron	1972	GB
Carry On Up the Khyber	1968	GB--Rank
Carry On Up the Jungle	1970	GB--Rank
Cash on Delivery	1956	GB--RKO
Checkpoint	1956	GB--Rank
A Coming-Out Party	1962	GB
Conspiracy of Hearts	1960	GB--Rank
Crooks Anonymous	1962	GB
Dark Places	1974	GB
A Day to Remember	1953	GB
Deadlier Than the Male	1967	GB--Univ.
Doctor at Large	1957	GB--Rank
Doctor at Sea	1955	GB--Rank
Doctor in Distress	1963	GB--Rank
Doctor in Love	1960	GB--Rank
Doctor in the House	1954	GB
Doctor in Trouble	1970	GB--Rank
Dulcimer Street	1948	GB
The Face of Fu Manchu	1965	GB
Get Charlie Tully	1972	GB
Hennessy	1975	GB--AIP
The High Commissioner	1968	GB--Rank
House of Mystery	1961	GB--AA
I've Gotta Horse	1965	GB
The Iron Petticoat	1956	GB--MGM
Island Rescue	1952	GB
McGuire, Go Home!	1966	GB--Rank
Mad about Men	1954	GB
The Magnificent Two	1967	GB--Rank
Make Mine a Double	1961	GB

No Love for Johnnie	1960	GB--Rank
No, My Darling Daughter	1961	GB--Rank
One More Time	1969	GB--UA
A Pair of Briefs	1961	GB--Rank
Passionate Summer	1958	GB--Rank
Payroll	1961	GB--AA
Percy	1971	GB--EMI/MGM
Piccadilly Third Stop	1960	GB--Rank
Psycho Circus	1967	GB--AIP
Quest for Love	1971	GB--Rank
The Secret Place	1957	GB--Rank
Simon and Laura	1955	GB--Univ.
Some Girls Do	1969	GB--Rank/UA
Steptoe and Son Ride Again	1973	GB--MGM
A Tale of Two Cities	1958	GB--Rank
Ten Little Indians	1966	GB
The Thirty Nine Steps	1960	GB--Rank/TCF
Trouble in Store	1953	GB--Rank/Rep.
24 Hours To Kill	1966	GB
Upstairs and Downstairs	1959	GB--Rank/TCF
The Wildcats of St. Trinian's	1980	GB
The Wind Cannot Read	1958	GB--Rank/TCF
The Wrong Arm of the Law	1962	GB
Young and Willing	1962	GB--Rank

581. CLIFFORD STINE (1906-1987)

Abbott and Costello Go to Mars	1953	Univ.
Air Cadet *	1951	Univ.
And Now Miguel	1966	Univ.
Away All Boats *	1956	Univ.
Back at the Front	1952	Univ.
Bedtime Story	1964	Univ.
The Brass Bottle	1964	Univ.
Bronco Buster	1952	Univ.
The Creature Walks among Us	1956	Univ.
East of Sumatra	1953	Univ.
Fireman Save My Child	1959	Univ.
Fluffy	1964	Univ.
Follow Me Boys!	1966	Dis.
For Love or Money	1963	Univ.
Gambit	1966	Univ.
Has Anybody Seen My Gal?	1952	Univ.
Hell Bent for Leather	1960	Univ.
It Came from Outer Space	1953	Univ.
The King's Pirate	1967	Univ.
Law and Order	1953	Univ.
Ma and Pa Kettle at Waikiki	1955	Univ.
The Milkman	1950	Univ.
Mystery Submarine	1950	Univ.

No Room for the Groom	1952	Univ.
Posse from Hell	1961	Univ.
Rosie!	1967	Univ.
Smoke Signal	1955	Univ.
Tammy Tell Me True	1961	Univ.
That Funny Feeling	1965	Univ.
This Island Earth	1955	Univ.
A Time to Love and a Time to Die *	1958	Univ.
The Ugly American	1962	Univ.
Weekend With Father	1951	Univ.
Wings of the Hawk	1953	Univ.

582. HAROLD STINE

Black Gold	1963	WB
The Busybody	1966	Par.
Caper of the Golden Bulls	1966	GB--Emb.
Chuka	1967	Par.
The Couch	1962	WB
For Those Who Think Young	1964	UA
Girl on the Run	1958	GB
A House Is Not a Home	1964	Emb.
House of Women	1962	WB
The Incredible Mr. Limpet	1964	WB
Johnny Reno	1966	Par.
The Last of the Secret Agents	1966	Par.
M.A.S.H.	1970	TCF
Man of Conflict	1953	US
The Night Walker	1964	Univ.
The Poseidon Adventure	1972	TCF
Project X	1968	Par.
The Spirit Is Willing	1966	Par.
The Todd Killings	1970	NG

583. VITTORIO STORARO

Agatha	1979	WB
Apocalypse Now	1979	UA
The Bird with the Crystal Plummage	1970	Ger./It.
Body of Love	1972	It.
The Conformist	1969	Fr./It.--Par.
Dick Tracy	1990	BV/Touch.
The Driver's Seat	1975	It.--AE
Giordano Bruno	1973	It.
Ishtar	1987	Col.
The Last Emperor	1987	Col.
Last Tango in Paris	1972	Fr./It.
Luna	1979	It.--TCF
Malizia	1973	It.--Par.

New York Stories *	1989	BV/Touch.
1900	1976	It.--Par./TCF/
		UA
One from the Heart	1982	Col.
Reds	1981	Par.
Spider's Strategem	1970	It.
Submission	1977	It.
Tis a Pity She's a Whore	1973	It.
Tucker: The Man and His Dreams	1988	Par.
Wagner	1983	Aust./GB/Hung
Youth March	1970	It.

584. ARCHIE STOUT (1886-   )

Abilene Town	1946	UA
Angel and the Badman	1947	Rep.
Bar 20 Rides Again	1935	Par.
Beau Geste *	1939	Par.
The Benson Murder Case	1930	Par.
Big Jim McLain	1952	US
Blue Steel	1934	Mon.
Borderland	1937	Par.
Call of the Prarie	1936	Par.
Captain Kidd	1945	UA
Conflict	1936	Univ.
The Conquering Horde	1931	Par.
Dangerous Paradise	1930	Par.
Dark Waters *	1944	UA
Darkened Rooms	1929	Par.
Dawn Rider	1935	US
Derelict	1930	Par.
Desert Trail	1935	Mon.
The Drivin' Fool	1923	US
The Eagle's Brood	1935	Par.
Fame Street	1932	Mon.
Feet of Clay *	1924	Par.
Fighting Champ	1933	Mon.
Flirting with Danger	1935	Mon.
Forgotten Women	1932	Mon.
Fort Apache	1948	RKO
The Fugitive	1933	Mon.
Galloping Romeo	1933	Mon.
Galloping Thru	1932	Mon.
Ghost City	1932	Mon.
God's Country and the Man	1931	US
Goodbye My Lady *	1956	WB
Gun Smoke	1931	Par.
Happy Landing	1934	Mon.
Hard, Fast and Beautiful	1951	RKO
Headin' North	1930	US

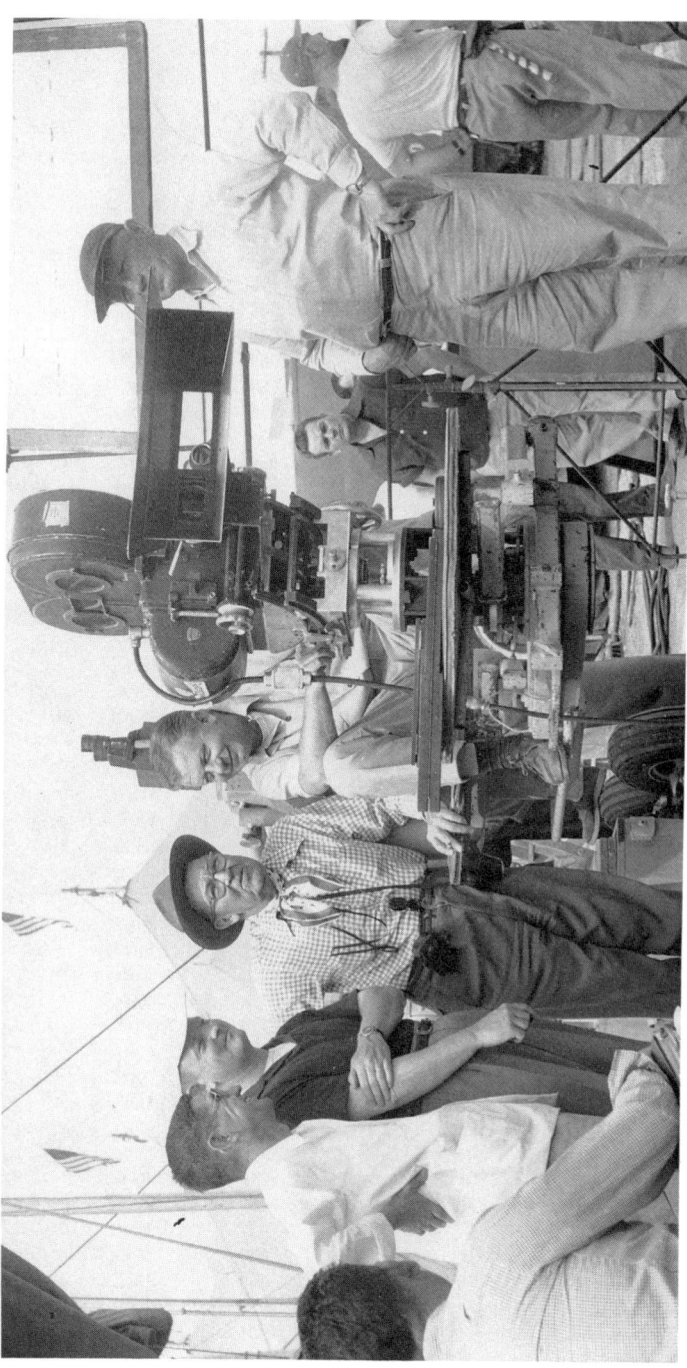

Archie Stout (in checkered shirt) on location for _Ring of Fear_ (1954).

Heart of the West	1936	Par.
Heritage of the Desert	1932	Par.
Hills of Old Wyoming	1937	Par.
His Nibs *	1921	US
Honor of the Mounted	1932	Mon.
Hop-a-Long Cassidy	1935	Par.
Hopalong Cassidy Returns	1936	Par.
Hondo *	1953	WB
Island in the Sky	1953	WB
It Happened Tomorrow *	1944	UA
It Pays To Advertise	1931	Par.
Land of Wanted Men	1932	Mon.
The Last Round-Up	1934	Par.
Law of the North *	1932	Mon.
Law of the Sea	1932	Mon.
Lawless Range	1935	Mon./Rep.
Lucky Larrigan	1933	Mon.
The Lucky Texan	1934	Mon.
Lust for Gold	1949	Col.
The Man from Utah	1934	Mon.
Manslaughter	1930	Par.
Mason of the Mounted	1932	Mon.
Men Are Like That	1930	Par.
The Montana Kid	1931	Mon.
Mother and Son	1931	Mon.
The Mysterious Rider	1933	Par.
Mystery Plane	1939	Mon.
Near the Trail's End	1931	US
'Neath the Arizona Skies	1934	Mon.
Nevada	1935	Par.
On the Loose	1951	RKO
Outrage	1950	RKO
Paradise Canyon	1935	Mon.
Partners of the Trail	1931	Mon.
Professor Beware	1938	Par.
The Quiet Man *	1952	Rep.
Rainbow Ranch	1933	Mon.
Randy Rides Alone	1934	Mon.
The Ranger's Code	1933	Mon.
The Return of Dr. Fu Manchu	1930	Par.
Rider of the Plains	1931	US
Riders of Destiny	1933	Mon.
Riders of the Desert	1932	US
Rio Grande *	1950	Rep.
Rocky Mountain Mystery	1935	Par.
Rulers of the Sea *	1939	Par.
Sagebrush Trail	1933	Mon.
The Sea God	1930	Par.
The Sea Spoilers	1936	Univ.
Ships of Hate	1931	Mon.
Singlehanded Sanders	1932	Mon.

16 Fathoms Deep	1934	Mon.
Son of the Plains	1931	US
The Star Packer	1934	Mon.
Summer Storm *	1944	UA
The Sun Shines Bright	1953	Rep.
Sunrise Trail	1931	US
Sunset Pass	1933	Par.
Tarzan and the Amazons	1945	RKO
Tarzan and the Huntress	1947	RKO
The Ten Commandments *	1923	Par.
Texas Rangers Ride Again	1940	Par.
Texas Terror	1935	Mon.
Three on the Trail	1936	Par.
The Trail Beyond	1934	Mon.
Trail Dust	1936	Par.
Trouble along the Way	1953	WB
Under the Tonto Rim	1932	Par.
Varsity	1928	Par.
Wagonmaster *	1950	RKO
West of the Divide	1934	Mon.
Young Eagles	1930	Par.

585. HARRY STRADLING (1902-1970)

Action for Slander	1937	GB
Androcles and the Lion	1952	RKO
Angel Face	1953	RKO
Auntie Mame	1958	WB
The Barkeleys of Broadway	1949	MGM
Bathing Beauty	1944	MGM
Burnt Fingers	1927	Pathe
The Citadel	1938	GB--MGM
The Corsican Brothers	1942	US
The Crowded Sky	1960	WB
Dark at the Top of the Stairs	1960	WB
Dark Journey *	1937	GB
The Devil and Miss Jones	1941	RKO
The Devil's Garden *	1920	FN
Dirty Dingus Magee	1970	MGM
Divorce of Lady X	1937	GB
Easter Parade	1948	MGM
Easty to Wed	1946	MGM
Edge of Doom	1950	Gold.
Episode	1937	Aus.
A Face in the Crowd *	1957	WB
Fair Lady *	1922	UA
Fingers at the Window *	1942	MGM
Five Finger Exercise	1962	Col.
Forever Female	1953	Par.
The Full Deck *	1934	Fr.

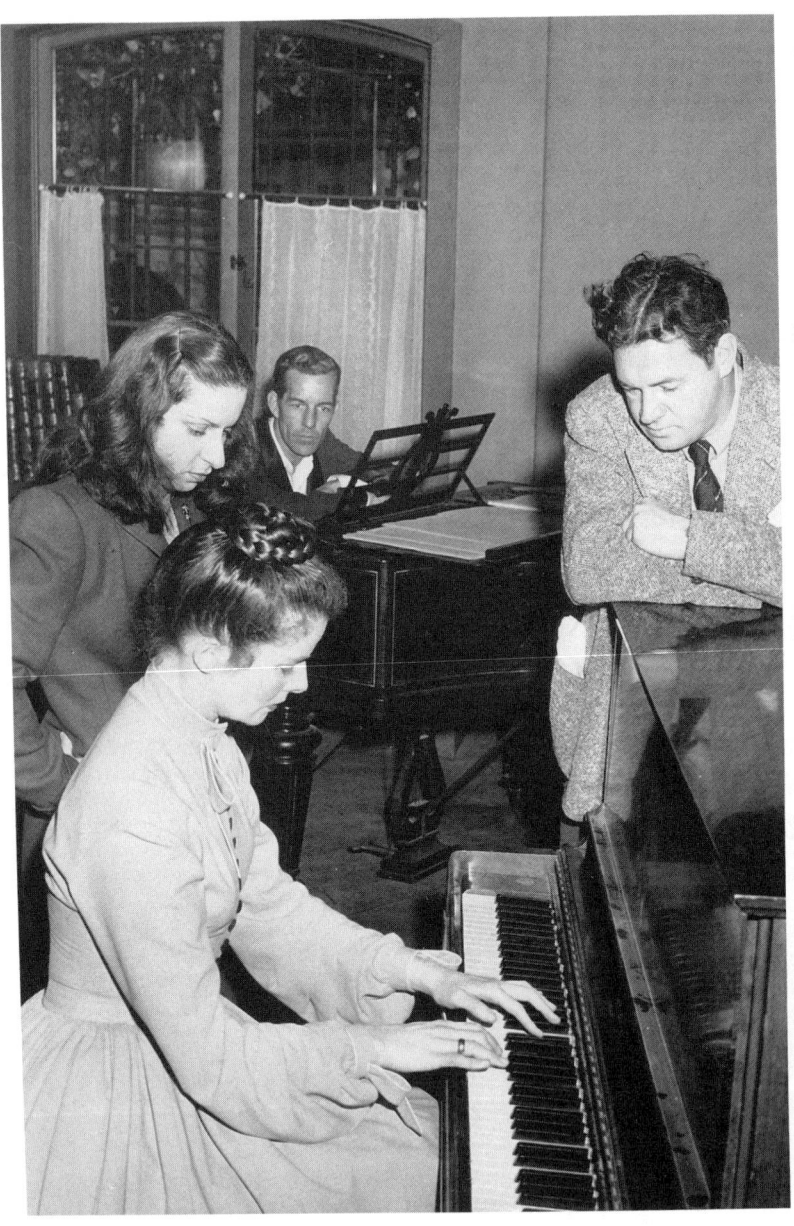

Harry Stradling (right) watches Katharine Hepburn rehearsing for
Song of Love (1947).

Funny Girl	1968	Col.
Le Grand Jeu *	1934	Fr.
The Great Adventure *	1921	FN
Guys and Dolls	1955	Gold.
Gypsy	1962	WB
Hans Christian Anderson	1952	Gold.
Helen of Troy	1955	WB
Hello, Dolly!	1969	TCF
Her Cardboard Lover *	1942	MGM
Her Highness and the Bellboy	1945	MGM
His Wife's Husband	1922	US
Holiday in Mexico	1946	MGM
How to Murder Your Wife	1964	UA
How Women Love	1922	US
The Human Comedy	1943	MGM
I Want You	1951	Gold.
In the Good Old Summertime	1949	MGM
Island Of Love	1963	WB
Jamaica Inn *	1939	GB
Jim the Penman *	1921	FN
Johnny Guitar	1954	Rep.
La Kermesse Herique	1935	Fr.
Knight without Armour	1937	GB
Lady of the Camelias *	1934	Fr.
The Lion Has Wings *	1939	GB--Korda
A Lion Is in the Streets	1953	WB
Little Big Man	1970	US
Lucky In Love *	1929	Pathe
Maisie Gets Her Man	1942	MGM
A Majority of One	1961	WB
Marjorie Morningstar	1958	WB
Mary Mary	1963	WB
Men in Her Life *	1941	Col.
A Millionaire for Christy	1951	TCF
Mr. and Mrs. North	1941	MGM
Mr. & Mrs. Smith	1941	RKO
Moment to Moment	1966	Univ.
Mother's Boy *	1929	Pathe
My Fair Lady	1964	CBS/WB
My Son John	1952	Par.
My Son My Son	1940	US
Nazi Agent	1942	MGM
The Nest	1927	US
On a Clear Day You Can See Forever	1970	Par.
On the Double *	1961	Par.
Over the Moon	1937	GB
The Owl and the Pussycat *	1970	Col.
The Pajama Game	1957	WB
Parrish	1961	WB
Penelope	1966	MGM
The Picture of Dorian Gray	1945	MGM

The Pirate	1948	MGM
Pygmalion	1938	GB
Q Planes	1939	GB
The Sea of Grass	1947	MGM
The Secrets of Paris *	1922	US
Song of Love	1947	MGM
Song of Russia	1944	MGM
South Riding	1937	GB
A Streetcar Named Desire	1951	WB
The Substitute Wife	1925	US
A Summer Place	1959	WB
Swing Shift Maisie	1943	MGM
Symphonie D'Amour	1946	Fr.
Synanon	1965	Col.
Tension	1950	MGM
They Knew What They Wanted	1940	RKO
Thrill of a Romance	1945	MGM
Till the Clouds Roll By *	1946	MGM
Valentino	1951	Col.
Walk, Don't Run	1966	Col.
Wandering Fires	1925	US
White Cargo	1942	MGM
Who Was That Lady?	1960	Col.
Words and Music *	1948	MGM
The Yellow Cab Man	1950	MGM
The Young Philadelphians	1959	WB

586. HARRY STRADLING, JR.

Bank Shot	1974	UA
Big Bus	1976	Par.
Bite the Bullet	1975	Col.
Blind Date	1987	Tri-S.
Born Again	1978	AE
Buddy Buddy	1981	MGM-UA
Caddyshack II	1988	WB
Carny	1980	UA
Convoy	1978	UA
Damnation Alley	1977	TCF
Fool's Parade	1971	Col.
Go Tell the Spartans	1978	AE
Good Guys and the Bad Guys	1969	WB
The Greatest	1977	GB--Col.
Late Liz	1971	US
McQ	1974	WB
The Mad Room	1969	Col.
The Man Who Loved Cat Dancing	1973	MGM
Midway	1976	Univ.
Mitchell	1975	AA
O'Hara's Wife	1982	US

Prophecy	1979	Par.
Pursuit of D. B. Cooper	1981	Univ.
Rooster Cogburn	1975	Univ.
S.O.B.	1981	Par.
1776	1972	Col.
Skyjacked	1972	MGM
Something Big	1971	NG
Special Delivery	1976	AIP
Support Your Local Gunfighter	1971	UA
Support Your Local Sheriff!	1968	UA
There Was a Crooked Man	1970	WB
Thumb Tripping	1972	AE
Up the Academy	1980	WB
The Way We Were	1973	Col.
Welcome To Hard Times	1967	MGM
With Six You Get Egg Roll *	1968	NG
Young Billy Young	1969	UA

587. WALTER STRADLING

Amarilly of Clothesline Alley	1918	Par.
Captain Alvarez	1914	Vita.
The Case of Becky	1915	Par.
A Chorus Lady	1915	Par.
A Gentleman of Leisure	1915	Par.
Hit-the-Trail Holiday	1918	US
Mr. Grex of Monte Carlo	1915	Par.
M'Liss	1918	US
Out of a Clear Sky	1918	Par.
Rebecca of Sunnybrook Farm	1917	US
The Secret Orchid *	1915	Par.
The Secret Sin	1915	Par.
Stella Maris	1918	US
Young Romance	1915	Par.

588. WALTER STRENGE (1899-1974)

Appointment with Murder	1948	US
Before Morning	1933	US
The Burning Cross	1947	US
Cry Terror	1958	MGM
The Devil's Cargo	1948	US
Down Memory Lane	1949	EL
Dragnet	1969	Univ.
Drums O'Voodoo	1934	US
Frontier Gun	1958	TCF
God Is My Partner	1957	TCF
Gun Fight	1961	UA
The Littlest Hobo *	1958	AA

Lone Texan	1959	TCF
The Love Kiss *	1930	US
Lure of the Swamp	1957	TCF
Messenger of Peace	1950	US
Million Dollar Pursuit	1951	Rep.
Mr. Walkie Talkie	1952	Lip.
Oklahoma Territory	1960	UA
Road to the Big House	1947	US
Rockabilly Baby	1957	TCF
Rodeo King and the Senorita	1951	Rep.
Secrets of Monte Carlo	1951	Rep.
Sergeant Ryker	1968	Univ.
Stagecoach to Fury	1956	TCF
The Talk of Hollywood	1929	US
13 Fighting Men	1960	TCF
Valley of Mystery	1967	Univ.

589. GEORGE STRETTON

Big Fella *	1937	US
Blackmailed	1950	GB
Blondes for Danger	1938	GB
Calling All Stars	1937	GB
It's You I Want	1936	GB
Jury's Evidence *	1936	GB
Live Wire	1937	GB
Maria Marten	1935	GB--MGM
The Missing People	1939	GB--GN/Mon.
The Mysterious Mr. Reeder	1940	GB--Mon.
Prelude to Fame	1950	GB--Univ.
Return of the Frog	1938	GB
A Royal Divorce	1938	GB
A Warning to Wantons	1948	GB

590. PERCY STRONG

After the Ball	1933	GB
Alf's Button	1930	GB
East Lynne on the Western Front	1931	GB
The Great Game	1930	GB
The Last Journey *	1935	GB
The Little People	1926	GB
Love, Life and Laughter *	1923	GB
No Lady	1931	GB
Reveille	1924	GB

591. KARL STRUSS (1886-1981)

Abraham Lincoln	1930	UA

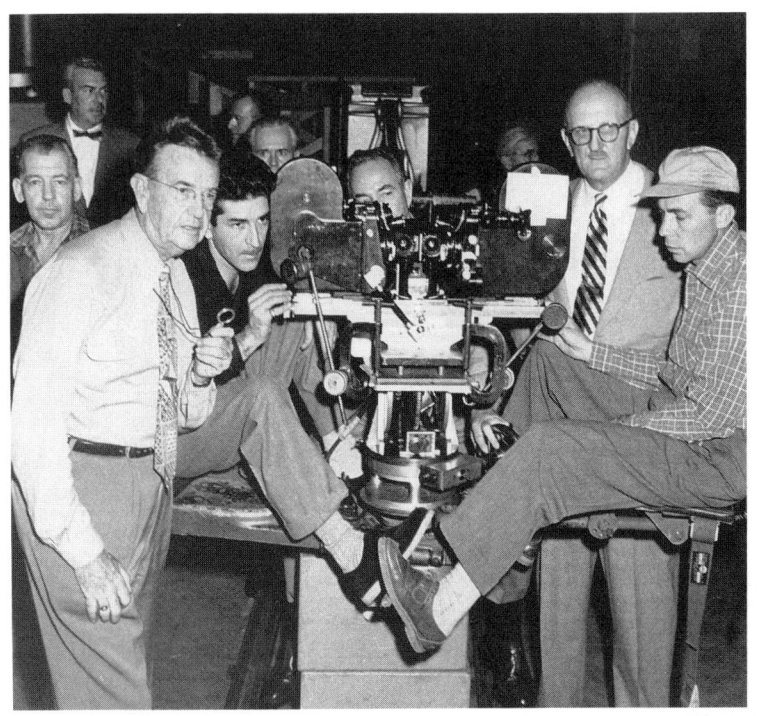

Karl Struss (right, standing).

The Affairs of Anatol *	1921	Par.
The Alligator People	1959	TCF
Aloma of the South Seas	1941	Par.
And the Angels Sing *	1941	Par.
Anything Goes	1936	Par.
Babe Comes Home	1927	FN
Bad Boy	1949	Mon.
The Bad One	1930	UA
Battle of the Sexes *	1928	UA
Belle of the Nineties	1934	Par.
Ben-Hur *	1925	MGM
Bring On the Girls	1945	Par.
Caught In the Draft	1941	Par.
Cavalleria Rusticana *	1953	It.
Dancers in the Dark	1932	Par.
Danger Lights *	1930	RKO
Daughters of the Rich	1923	US
The Deerslayer	1957	TCF
Disgraced	1933	Par.
Dr. Jekyll and Mr. Hyde	1931	Par.
Double or Nothing	1937	Par.
Drums of Love *	1928	UA
The Dude Goes West	1948	AA
Fatal Desire	1953	It.
The Fly	1958	TCF
Fool's Paradise *	1921	Par.
Fools First *	1922	FN
Forever After	1926	FN
Forgotten Commandments	1932	Par.
Four Frightened People	1934	Par.
The Funniest Show on Earth	1954	It.
The Girl in 419	1933	Par.
Go West Young Man	1936	Par.
Goin' to Town	1935	Par.
The Great Dictator *	1940	UA
Guilty As Hell	1932	Par.
Happy Go Lucky *	1943	Par.
Heaven Only Knows	1947	UA
Hell's 4000	1926	Fox
Here Come the Jets	1959	TCF
Here Is My Heart	1934	Par.
The Hero	1923	US
Hollywood Boulevard	1936	Par.
Hot Angel *	1958	Par.
Idle Tongues	1924	FN
Island of Lost Men	1939	Par.
Island of Lost Souls	1932	Par.
It's a Small World	1950	EL
Lady of the Pavements	1929	UA
The Law and the Woman	1922	Par.
The Legend of Hollywood	1924	US

Let's Make a Million	1937	Par.
Limelight	1952	US
Lummox	1930	UA
Machete	1958	UA
The Macomber Affair	1947	UA
Man from Yesterday	1932	Par.
Maytime	1923	US
Meet the Price	1926	US
Mesa of Lost Women *	1956	US
Minnie *	1922	FN
Mr. Ace	1946	US
Mohawk	1956	TCF
Mothers-In-Law	1923	US
Mountain Music	1937	Par.
Murder by the Clock	1931	Par.
The Neapolitan Turk *	1953	It.
The Night Watch	1928	FN
One Romantic Night	1930	UA
Paris Honeymoon	1938	Par.
Poisoned Paradise: The Forbidden Story of Monte Carlo	1924	US
Poor Men's Wives	1923	US
The Preview Murder Mystery	1936	Par.
The Pursuit of Happiness	1934	Par.
Rainbow Island	1944	Par.
The Rebel Set	1959	AA
Return of Jesse James	1950	Lip.
Rhythm on the Range	1936	Par.
Rich Men's Wives	1922	US
Riding High *	1943	Par.
The Road to Reno	1931	Par.
Rocketship XM	1950	Lip.
Rose of Cimarron	1952	TCF
The Sad Horse	1959	TCF
Saturday Night *	1922	Par.
She Devil	1957	TCF
The Sign of the Cross	1932	Par.
Sing You Sinners	1938	Par.
Siren of Atlantis	1949	UA
Skippy	1931	Par.
Some Like It Hot	1939	Par.
Something to Think About *	1920	Par.
Sparrows *	1926	UA
The Star Maker	1939	Par.
The Story of Temple Drake	1933	Par.
Sunrise-A Tale of Two Humans *	1927	Fox
Suspense	1946	Mon.
The Taming of the Shrew	1929	UA
Tarzan and the Leopard Woman	1946	RKO
Tarzan and the She Devil	1953	RKO
Tarzan's Magic Fountain	1949	RKO

Tarzan's Peril	1951	RKO
Tarzan's Savage Fury	1952	RKO
Texan Meets Calamity Jane	1950	Col.
Thanks for the Memory	1938	Par.
Thorns and Apple Blossoms	1922	US
Thunder Trail	1937	Par.
Tonight Is Ours	1933	Par.
Too Many Parents	1936	Par.
Torch Singer	1933	Par.
Two for Tonight	1935	Par.
Two Kinds of Women	1932	Par.
Two Nights with Cleopatra *	1953	It.
Up Pops the Devil	1931	Par.
Waikiki Wedding	1937	Par.
White Man	1924	US
The Winding Stair	1925	Fox
The Woman Accused	1933	Par.
The World and the Flesh	1932	Par.
Zenobia	1939	US

592. ROBERT A. STUART

Beating the Odds	1919	Vita.
Beauty Proof	1919	Vita.
Birth of a Soul	1920	Vita.
The Broadway Bubble *	1920	Vita.
The Enemy	1916	Vita.
Fighting Destiny	1919	Vita.
The Flaming Clue	1920	Vita.
A Florida Enchantment	1914	Vita.
French Heels *	1922	US
The Gamblers	1919	Vita.
The Gauntlet	1920	Vita.
The Green God	1918	Vita.
Her Right To Live	1917	Vita.
The Juggernaut	1915	Vita.
The King of Diamonds	1918	Vita.
A Million Bid	1914	Vita.
My Official Wife	1914	Vita.
No Trespassing	1922	US
Playing Dead	1915	Vita.
Rose of the South	1916	Vita.
The Sins of the Mothers	1915	Vita.
Soldiers of Chance	1917	Vita.

593. CHARLES STUMAR (1891-1955)

The Abysmal Brute	1923	Univ.
Anybody Here Seen Kelly?	1928	Univ.

The Badge of Marshal Brennan	1957	AA
The Biggest Show on Earth	1918	Par.
Billion Dollar Scandal	1932	Par.
Black Beauty	1933	US
Bombay Mail	1934	Univ.
Caught Bluffing	1922	Univ.
The Cohens and Kellys	1926	Univ.
The Cohens and Kellys in Paris	1928	Univ.
The Combat	1926	Univ.
Come Again Smith	1919	US
Command to Love	1931	Univ.
The Countess of Monte Cristo	1934	Univ.
Don't Doubt Your Wife	1922	US
The Drifters	1919	US
Embarrassing Moments	1934	Univ.
The End of the Game	1919	Pathe
Fifth Avenue Models	1925	Univ.
Forbidden Fire	1919	US
Forsaking All Others	1922	Univ.
The Freshie	1922	US
The Gaiety Girl	1924	Univ.
Greater Than Love	1921	US
The Heart of Humanity	1932	Univ.
A House Divided	1931	Univ.
I Am Guilty	1921	US
I Like It That Way	1934	Univ.
I'll Show You the Town	1925	Univ.
K-The Unknown	1924	Univ.
King for a Night	1933	Univ.
The Leopard Woman	1920	US
Let's Be Ritzy	1934	Univ.
Let's Talk It Over	1934	Univ.
The Lone Wolf's Daughter	1919	US
Love	1920	US
Love Madness	1920	US
Lying Lips *	1921	US
Manhattan Moon	1935	Univ.
The Michigan Kid	1928	Univ.
The Midnight Guest	1923	Univ.
The Mummy	1932	Univ.
Nice Women *	1932	Univ.
Peacock Feathers	1925	Univ.
Perch of the Devil	1927	Univ.
Poker Faces	1926	Univ.
Power of a Lie	1922	Univ.
The Price of Fear	1928	Univ.
Prisoner of the Pines	1918	US
Raffles the Amateur Cracksman	1925	Univ.
The Raven	1935	Univ.
Rhine Girl	1931	Ger.
Romance in the Rain	1934	Univ.

The Rose of Paris	1924	Univ.
Sahara	1919	Pathe
Saturday's Millions	1933	Univ.
Secret of the Blue Room	1933	Univ.
Sex	1920	US
The Shakedown *	1929	Univ.
Shams of Society *	1921	US
Siege	1925	Univ.
Skin Deep	1923	FN
Slim Fingers	1929	Univ.
Stolen Secrets	1924	Univ.
Storm over the Andes	1935	Univ.
Straight from the Heart	1935	Univ.
Those Who Pay	1918	US
The Tip-Off	1929	Univ.
Tom Brown of Culver	1932	Univ.
The Top O' the Morning	1922	Univ.
Trail of Hate	1922	US
Transient Lady	1935	Univ.
The Turmoil	1924	Univ.
Uncertain Lady	1934	Univ.
Uncle Tom's Cabin *	1927	Univ.
Wake Up and Dream	1934	Univ.
The Werewolf of London	1935	Univ.
What's Your Husband Doing?	1919	Par.
When Husbands Deceive	1922	US
When the Devil Drives	1922	US
Where Was I?	1925	Univ.
The Whole Town's Talking	1926	Univ.
Without Honor	1918	US
Wolves of the City	1929	Univ.

594. JOHN STUMAR

Above the Clouds	1934	Col.
Anne of Little Smoky	1921	US
Atlantic Adventure	1935	Col.
Before Midnight	1934	Col.
The Best Man WIns	1935	Col.
Black Is White	1920	Par.
Blaze Away	1922	US
Buck Privates	1928	Univ.
The Claw	1927	Univ.
Counterfeit *	1936	Col.
The Crowd Roars *	1932	WB
Daddies	1924	WB
The Dark Mirror	1920	Par.
The Darling of New York	1923	Univ.
Devil's Squadron	1936	Col.
Dollar Devils	1923	US

Down the Stretch	1927	Univ.
The Durango Kid	1940	Col.
End of the Trail	1936	Col.
Escape from Devil's Island	1935	Col.
Extravagance	1919	Par.
The Family Secret	1924	Univ.
The Flood	1931	Col.
The Forgotten Law	1922	Metro.
Fury of the Jungle	1934	Col.
Girl Overboard	1929	Univ.
Hard Boiled	1919	Par.
Harmon of Michigan	1941	Col.
He Loved an Actress	1938	GB
Head Winds	1925	Univ.
His Wife's Friend	1920	Par.
Home James	1928	Univ.
The Home Maker	1925	Univ.
The Homebreaker	1919	Par.
I Was a Prisoner on Devil's Island	1941	Col.
If You Could Only Cook	1935	Col.
The Irresistible Lover *	1927	Univ.
Jealousy	1934	Col.
The Kaiser's Shadow	1918	Par.
Kingdom Within	1922	US
Klondike Kate	1944	Col.
L'Apache	1919	Par.
The Lady and the Mob	1939	Col.
A Lady of Quality	1924	Univ.
The Lady of Red Butte	1919	Par.
Laughter in Hell	1933	Univ.
Leftover Ladies	1931	US
Listen Lester	1924	US
The Lone Wolf Takes a Chance	1941	Col.
Love Me	1918	Par.
The Love Thief	1926	Univ.
The Market of Souls	1919	Par.
The Marriage Ring	1918	Par.
The Mating of Marcella	1918	Par.
Mill on the Floss	1937	GB
A Million to Burn	1923	Univ.
Mr. Boggs Steps Out	1938	GN
Most Precious Thing in Life	1934	Col.
Mother Eternal	1921	US
Music in My Heart	1940	Col.
Name the Woman	1934	Col.
Naughty! Naughty!	1918	Par.
Naval Academy	1941	Col.
One Is Guilty	1934	Col.
One Man Justice *	1937	Col.
Other Men's Wifes	1919	Par.
Pardon My French	1921	Gold.

Parents on Trial	1939	Col.
Power of the Press	1943	Col.
The Price of Pleasure	1925	Univ.
Quicksands	1918	Par.
Recaptured Love	1930	WB
Red Lips	1928	Univ.
Return of the Vampire *	1943	Col.
Second Choice	1930	WB
The Secret Seven	1940	Col.
Shams of Society	1921	US
Something to Sing About	1937	GN
The Song of the Soul	1920	Gold.
The Spirit of Stanford *	1942	Col.
The Spoilers *	1923	Gold.
The Super-Sex	1922	US
Temporary Marriage	1923	US
13 Washington Square	1928	Univ.
Those High Grey Walls	1939	Col.
The Time, the Place and the Girl	1929	WB
The Tornado	1924	Univ.
Tramp, Tramp, Tramp	1942	Col.
2 Latins from Manhattan	1941	Col.
Two-Fisted Gentleman	1936	Col.
Tyrant Fear	1918	Par.
The Unwelcome Stranger	1935	Col.
Under Age	1941	Col.
Vive La France	1918	Par.
Wild Beauty	1927	Univ.
Wine	1924	Univ.
A Woman's Faith	1925	Univ.
Young and Beautiful	1934	US

595. TIMOTHY SUHRSTEDT

Android	1982	US
Bill and Ted's Excellent Adventure	1989	Orion
City Limits	1985	US
Critters	1986	US
Doin' Time on Planet Earth	1988	Cannon
Feds	1988	WB
Forbidden World	1982	US
The House on Sorority Row	1983	US
Mannequin	1987	TCF
Men at Work	1990	US
Mystic Pizza	1988	US
Remote Control	1988	US
Space Rage	1987	US
Split Decision	1988	US
Stand Alone *	1986	US
Teen Wolf	1985	US

596. BRUCE SURTEES

Back to the Beach	1987	Par.
Bad Boys *	1983	Univ.
The Beguiled	1971	Univ.
Big Wednesday *	1978	WB
Blume in Love	1973	US
Conquest of the Planet of the Apes	1972	TCF
Dirty Harry	1971	WB
Dreamer	1979	TCF
Escape from Alcatraz	1979	Par.
Firefox	1982	WB
The Great Northfield Minnesota Raid	1971	Univ.
High Plains Drifter	1972	Univ.
Honkytonk Man	1982	WB
Inchon	1981	MGM-UA
Joe Kidd	1972	Univ.
Ladies and Gentlemen: The Fabulous Stains	1982	Par.
Leadbelly	1976	Par.
Lenny	1974	UA
License to Drive	1988	TCF
Men Don't Leave	1990	WB
Movie Movie *	1978	WB
Night Moves	1975	WB
Out of Bounds	1986	Col.
The Outfit	1973	MGM
The Outlaw Josey Wales	1976	WB
Pale Rider	1985	WB
Play Misty for Me	1971	Univ.
Psycho III	1986	Univ.
Ratboy	1986	WB
Risky Business *	1983	WB
The Shootist	1976	Par.
Sparkle	1976	WB
Sudden Impact	1983	WB
Three Warriors	1977	US
White Dog	1982	Par.

597. ROBERT SURTEES (1906-1985)

Act of Violence	1949	MGM
The Arrangement	1969	WB
The Bad and the Beautiful	1952	MGM
Ben-Hur	1959	MGM
Big City	1948	MGM
Big Jack	1949	MGM
Bloodbrothers	1978	WB
Cimarron	1961	MGM
The Collector *	1965	Col.

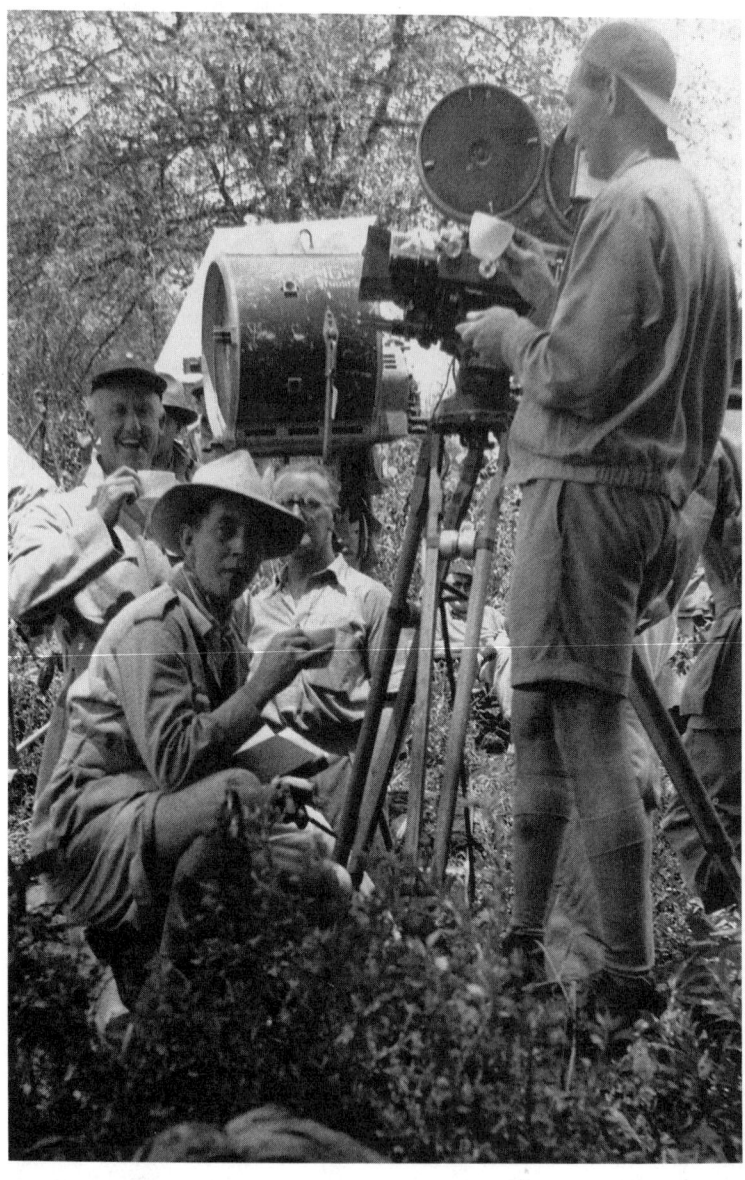

Robert Surtees (left, in dark cap) pauses for tea with his crew on Mogambo (1953).

The Cowboys	1972	WB
A Date with Judy	1948	MGM
Dr. Dolittle	1967	TCF
Escape from Fort Bravo	1953	MGM
The Graduate	1967	MGM
The Great Waldo Pepper	1975	Univ.
The Hallelujah Trail	1965	UA
The Hindenburg	1975	Univ.
Intruder in the Dust	1949	MGM
It Started in Naples	1960	Par.
King Solomon's Mines	1950	MGM
Kisses for My President	1964	WB
The Kissing Bandit	1948	MGM
The Last Picture Show	1971	MGM
The Law and Jake Wade	1958	MGM
Les Girls	1957	MGM
The Liberation of L. B. Jones	1970	Col.
The Light Touch	1951	MGM
The Long Long Trailer	1954	MGM
Lost Angel	1943	MGM
Lost Command	1966	Col.
Lost Horizon	1972	Col.
Meet the People	1944	MGM
Merry Andrew	1958	MGM
The Merry Widow	1952	MGM
Mogambo *	1953	MGM
Music for Millions	1944	MGM
Mutiny on the Bounty	1962	MGM
No Leave, No Love *	1946	MGM
Oklahoma!	1955	US
Oklahoma Crude	1973	Col.
The Other	1972	TCF
Our Vines Have Tender Grapes	1945	MGM
PT 109	1963	WB
Quo Vadis *	1951	MGM
Raintree County	1958	MGM
Ride, Vaquero!	1953	MGM
Same Time Next Year	1978	Univ.
The Satan Bug	1965	UA
A Star Is Born	1976	WB
The Sting	1973	Univ.
Strange Holiday	1945	US
The Strip	1951	MGM
Summer of '42	1971	WB
The Swan *	1956	MGM
Sweet Charity	1969	Univ.
Tenth Avenue Angel	1948	MGM
That Midnight Kiss	1949	MGM
The Third Day	1965	WB
Thirty Seconds over Tokyo *	1944	MGM
Trial	1955	MGM

Tribute to a Bad Man	1956	MGM
The Turning Point	1977	TCF
Two Girls and a Sailor	1944	MGM
Two Sisters from Boston	1946	MGM
The Unfinished Dance	1947	MGM
Valley of the Kings	1954	MGM
The Wild North	1951	MGM

598. PETER SUSCHITZKY

All Creatures Great and Small	1974	GB--EMI
The Charge of the Light Brigade *	1968	GB--UA
Charlie Bubbles	1968	GB--Univ.
Dead Ringers	1988	Can.
The Empire Strikes Back	1980	TCF
Falling in Love	1984	Par.
The Gladiators	1970	Swed.
Henry VIII and His Six Wives	1972	GB--EMI/MGM
It Happened Here	1963	GB--UA
Krull	1983	Col.
Leo the Last	1969	GB--UA
Lisztomania	1975	GB--WB
Lock Up Your Daughters	1969	GB--Col.
Melody	1971	GB
The Pied Piper	1971	Ger./Gb--Par.
Privilege	1967	GB--Univ.
The Rocky Horror Picture Show	1975	GB--TCF
Thank You All Very Much	1969	GB--Col.
That'll Be the Day	1973	GB--EMI
Valentino	1977	GB--UA
Where the Heart Is	1990	BV/Touch.

599. WOLFGANG SUSCHITZKY (1912-   )

The Bespoke Overcoat	1955	GB
Les Bicyclettes de Belsize	1969	GB
Cat and Mouse	1958	GB
The Chain	1985	GB--Rank
Entertaining Mr. Sloane	1969	GB--WB
Falling in Love Again *	1980	US
Get Carter	1971	GB--MGM
Good and Bad At Games	1983	GB
The Horse's Mouth	1953	GB--UA
Living Free	1972	GB--Col./WB
Moments	1974	GB
No Resting Place	1951	GB
The Oracle	1953	GB
Ring of Bright Water	1969	GB--Rank
Sands of Beersheba	1966	Isr.--AIP

The Small World of Sammy Lee	1962	GB
Some Kind of Hero	1972	GB
Something to Hide	1972	GB
Theatre of Blood	1973	GB--UA
Ulysses	1967	GB--US
The Vengeance of She	1967	GB--TCF
Young Visitors	1984	GB

600. LUCIEN TAINGUY

All Man	1916	US
Arizona	1913	US
The Beautiful Mrs. Reynolds	1918	US
Beauty and Bullets	1928	Univ.
The Beloved Adventuress	1917	US
The Boss	1915	US
Checkers	1913	US
Cleopatra	1912	US
Courage for Two	1919	US
A Damsel in Distress	1919	Pathe
Diane of Star Hollow	1921	US
The Echo of Youth	1919	US
The Family Honor	1917	US
The Girl from Porcupine	1921	US
God's Country and the Law	1921	US
His Royal Highness *	1918	US
Hit Or Miss	1919	US
In Walked Mary	1920	Pathe
Leap to Fame	1918	US
The Love Cheat	1919	Pathe
Love in a Hurry	1919	US
The Man Who Forgot *	1917	US
Mandarin's Gold	1919	US
The North Wind's Malice	1920	Gold.
The Purple Lily *	1918	US
The Scar	1919	US
The Shadow of Rosalie Byrnes	1920	Selz.
The Web of Desire	1917	US
What Women Want	1920	US

601. KENNETH TALBOT

Battle Beneath the Earth	1967	MGM
Born Free	1965	GB--Col.
Charley One-Eye	1972	GB--Par.
Countess Dracula	1972	GB--Ham./TCF
The Devil within Her	1976	GB--AIP/Ham.
Doomwatch	1972	GB
The Girl Hunters	1963	GB

Hammerhead *	1968	Col.
Hands of the Ripper	1971	GB--Univ.
Maroc 7	1967	GB--Par.
Nothing But the Night	1972	GB
Persecution	1974	GB
The Stranger from Venus	1954	GB
Underground	1970	GB--UA

602. PHILIP TANNURA

Alias Boston Blackie	1942	Col.
The Apple-Tree Girl	1917	US
The Babe Ruth Story *	1948	AA/Mon.
Blondie Knows Best	1946	Col.
Bodyhold *	1949	Col.
Break the News	1938	GB--Mon.
Bred in Old Kentucky	1926	US
The Camels Are Coming *	1934	GB
Channel Crossing	1933	GB
China Corsair	1951	Col.
The Confessions of Boston Blackie	1942	Col.
Counsel's Opinion	1933	GB--Par.
Counter-Espionage	1942	Col.
Counterspy Meets Scotland Yard	1950	Col.
The Crime Doctor's Gamble	1947	Col.
The Crime Doctor's Man Hunt	1946	Col.
Criminal Lawyer	1951	Col.
The Crimson Circle	1936	GB--Univ.
Customs Agent	1950	Col.
Cyclone Buddy *	1924	US
Dangerous Blondes	1943	Col.
Dangerous Cargo	1939	GB
Dinner at the Ritz	1937	GB--TCF
Dirty Work	1934	GB
Dishonour Bright	1936	GB
Dreaming Out Loud	1940	RKO
Fighting Stock	1935	GB
Flame of Stamboul	1951	Col.
The Flying Saucer	1950	US
Footlight Glamour	1943	Col.
For Valour	1937	GB
Good Luck, Mr. Yates	1943	Col.
Harlem Globetrotters	1951	Col.
Hello Annapolis	1942	Col.
Her Summer Hero	1928	FBO
Hi-Jacked	1950	Lip.
His Last Haul	1928	FBO
I Stand Condemned	1935	GB--UA
Inspector Hornleigh *	1938	GB--TCF
Jake the Plumber	1927	FBO

Just Before Dawn	1946	Col.
Key Witness	1947	Col.
Knickerbocker Holiday	1946	UA
Laugh Your Blues Away	1943	Col.
Legionaires in Paris	1927	US
Let's Have Fun	1943	Col.
The Little Chevalier	1917	US
The Lone Wolf and His Lady	1949	Col.
Love from a Stranger	1937	GB--UA
Lucky in Love *	1929	Pathe
Lucky Legs	1942	Col.
Man in the Rough	1928	FBO
The Man Who Returned to Life	1942	Col.
Matinee Idol	1928	Col.
The Millerson Case	1947	Col.
Mother's Boy *	1929	Pathe
Mysterious Intruder	1946	Col.
Night Editor *	1946	Col.
An Old-Fashioned Girl	1948	EL
Out of the Depths	1946	Col.
Parachute Nurse	1942	Col.
Poison Pen	1939	GB--Rep.
Prison Ship	1945	Col.
Redhead from Manhattan	1943	Col.
The Return of Daniel Boone	1941	Col.
The Return of the Whistler	1948	Col.
Reveille with Beverly	1943	Col.
The Richest Man in Town	1941	Col.
Sally of the Scandals	1928	FBO
School for Husbands	1937	GB
Shamrock Hill	1949	EL
She Has What It Takes	1943	Col.
Skinner's Big Idea	1928	FBO
Some Pun'kins *	1925	US
Stolen Life	1939	GB--Par.
Stormy Weather	1935	GB
Strange Illusion	1945	PRC
Sweet Adeline	1926	US
Sweetheart of the Fleet	1942	Col.
Taxi 13	1928	US
There's a Girl in My Heart	1949	AA
There's Something about a Soldier *	1942	Col.
The Tougher They Come	1950	Col.
The Town Went Wild	1945	PRC
Trapped by Boston Blackie	1948	Col.
2 Yanks in Trinidad	1942	Col.
The Unbeliever	1918	US
When a Dog Loves	1927	US
Yellowback	1929	FBO
You'll Never Get Rich	1941	Col.

603. JEAN-JACQUES TARBES

And Long Live Liberty	1978	Fr.
Association of Wrongdoing	1987	Fr.
Banzai	1983	Fr.
The Big Scare	1974	Fr.
Black Eye	1987	Fr.
Blackout	1978	Can./Fr.
Borsalino & Co.	1974	Fr.
Le Dimanche de La Vie	1966	Fr.
Easy Down There!	1971	Fr.
The Egg	1972	Fr.--Col.
Emergency Exit	1970	Fr.
Farewell, Friend	1968	Fr./It.
Fiancee Who Came in From the Cold	1983	Fr.
Gag Kings	1985	Fr.
The Gypsy	1975	Fr.--TCF
Hearth Fires	1972	Fr.
Jeff	1969	Fr.--WB
Joint Brothers	1986	Fr.
Justine De Sade	1972	Fr.
The Mad Dog	1966	Fr.
My New Partner	1984	Fr.
My New Partner 2	1990	Fr.
Popsy Pop	1971	Fr.
So Long, Friend	1968	Fr.
The Swimming Pool	1970	Fr.
Too Small, My Friend	1970	Fr.
Two	1989	Fr.
Two Men in Town	1973	Fr.
Ursulu et Grelu	1974	Fr.--TCF

604. GILBERT TAYLOR (1914-   )

Alive and Kicking	1959	GB
As Long as They're Happy	1955	GB--Rank
The Bedford Incident	1965	GB--Col.
Bedroom Window	1987	DeL.
Before Winter Comes	1968	GB--Col.
Blonde Sinner	1956	AA
Blood Fiend	1967	GB
Bottoms Up	1960	GB
Brighton Rock *	1947	GB
Call Me Genius	1961	GB
Crest of the Wave	1954	GB--MGM
Cul De Sac	1966	GB
A Day at the Beach	1970	Par.
Desert Attack	1958	GB--TCF
Dr. Strangelove	1963	Col.
Dracula	1979	Univ.

Escape to Athena	1979	GB
Ferry across the Mersey	1965	GB--UA
Flash Gordon	1980	Univ.
Frenzy	1972	GB--Univ.
Front Page Story	1953	GB
The Good Companions	1956	GB
Green Ice	1981	GB
A Hard Day's Night	1964	GB--UA
Hide and Seek	1963	GB--Univ.
High Treason	1951	GB
It's Great to Be Young	1956	GB
Josephine and Men	1955	GB
Lassiter	1984	WB
Losin' It	1983	Emb.
Macbeth	1971	GB--Col.
The Man Outside	1968	GB--AA
Meetings with Remarkable Men	1979	GB
A Nice Girl Like Me *	1969	GB--AE
No Time for Tears	1957	GB
No Tree in the Street	1958	GB
The Omen	1976	TCF
Operation Bullshine	1959	GB
The Outsider	1949	GB
Petticoat Pirates	1961	GB--WB
A Prize of Arms	1961	GB
Quackser Fortune Has a Cousin in the Bronx	1970	US
Repulsion	1965	GB
Ring-a-Ding Rhythm	1962	GB--Col.
Sailor of the King	1953	GB--TCF
Sands of the Desert	1960	GB
Seven Days to Noon	1950	GB
She Didn't Say No!	1958	GB--WB
The Silken Affair *	1956	GB--RKO
Star Wars	1977	TCF
Stop Me Before I Kill!	196	GB--Col./Ham.
Theatre of Death	1966	GB
Tommy the Toreador	1960	GB--WB
Undercovers Hero	1975	GB
Venom	1981	GB--Par.
Voyage of the Rock Aliens *	1988	US
The Weak and the Wicked	1953	GB--AA
Woman in a Dressing Gown	1957	GB--WB
Work Is a Four-Letter Word	1968	GB--Univ.
The Yellow Balloon	1952	GB--AA

605. J. O. TAYLOR

Afraid To Love	1927	Par.
Alias the Lone Wolf	1927	Col.

The Bachelor's Baby	1927	Col.
Behind the Door	1920	Par.
The Belle of Broadway	1926	Col.
Below the Surface	1920	Par.
The Better Way	1926	Col.
Bigger Than Barnum's	1926	US
Birds of Prey	1927	Col.
Blind Hearts	1921	US
The Blood Ship	1927	Col.
The Brute Master	1920	US
By Whose Hand?	1927	Col.
Chicago after Midnight	1928	FBO
Coney Island	1928	FBO
The Cup of Life	1921	US
A Daughter of the Wolf	1919	Par.
Fashion Madness	1928	Col.
For Ladies Only	1927	Col.
The Grim Game *	1919	Par.
Happy Days *	1929	Fox
The Haunted Ship *	1927	US
The House of Youth	1924	PDC
The Kid Sister	1927	Col.
King Kong *	1933	RKO
The Last Moment	1923	Gold.
The Lone Wolf Returns	1926	Col.
The Man Alone	1923	US
Obey the Law	1926	Col.
Pleasure before Business	1927	Col.
The Price of Honor	1927	Col.
A Private Scandal	1921	US
Remember	1926	Col.
Sally in Our Alley	1927	Col.
Scars of Jealousy	1923	FN
The Sea Lion	1921	US
The Sea Wolf	1926	PDC
Singapore Mutiny	1928	FBO
Smoke Bellew *	1929	US
A Soldier's Plaything	1930	WB
A Son of Erin	1916	US
Son of Kong *	1933	RKO
Song O' My Heart *	1930	Fox
Stolen Pleasures	1927	Col.
Sweet Rosie O'Grady	1926	Col.
A Thousand to One	1920	US
Uninvited Guest	1920	US
Wandering Girls	1927	Col.

606. RONNIE TAYLOR

Ballad in Blue	1964	GB--WB
Champions	1984	GB

A Chorus Line	1985	Col.
Circle of Iron	1979	GB
Cry Freedom	1987	GB--Univ.
The Experts	1989	Par.
Foreign Body	1986	GB--Orion
Gandhi *	1982	GB--Col.
High Road to China	1983	WB
Hound of the Baskervilles	1983	GB
Opera	1987	Col.
The Rainbow Thief	1990	GB
Savage Harvest	1981	TCF
Sea of Love	1989	Univ.
Splitz	1984	US
Suckalo	1976	US
Tommy *	1975	GB--Col.
Two and Two Make Six *	1961	GB

607. TED TETZLAFF (1903-   )

Acquitted *	1929	Col.
Ann Carver's Profession	1933	Col.
Annapolis Farewell	1935	Par.
Apache	1928	Col.
Arrest Bulldog Drummond	1939	Par.
Artists and Models Abroad	1938	Par.
Atta Boy *	1926	Pathe
Attorney for the Defense	1932	Col.
The Avenger *	1931	Col.
Behind Closed Doors	1929	Col.
Behind the Mask	1932	Col.
Brief Moment	1933	Col.
By Whose Hand? *	1932	Col.
Cafe Society	1939	Par.
Child of Manhattan	1933	Col.
College Rhythm *	1934	Par.
Comrades	1928	US
The Criminal Code *	1931	Col.
A Dangerous Affair	1931	Col.
Day of Reckoning	1933	MGM
The Devil's Cage	1928	US
The Donovan Affair	1929	Col.
Eager Lips *	1927	US
Easy Living	1937	Par.
The Enchanted Cottage	1945	RKO
The Faker	1929	Col.
The Fall of Eve	1929	Col.
Father and Son	1929	Col.
The Flying Machine	1929	Col.
Fools for Scandal	1938	WB
For the Love O' Lil	1930	Col.

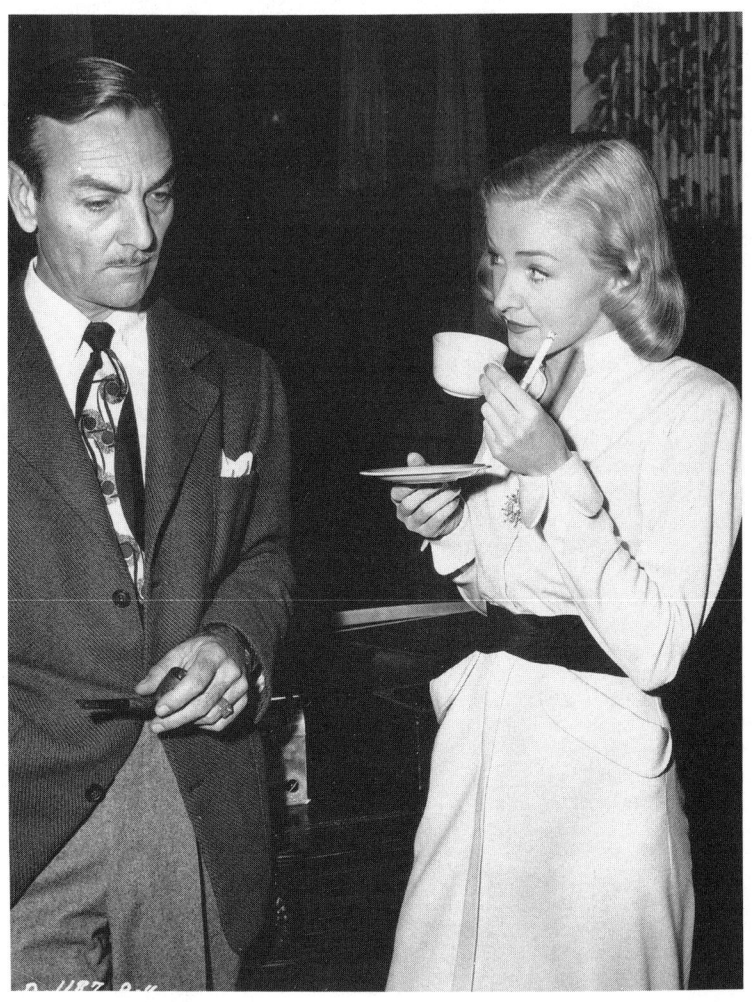

Ted Tetzlaff (functioning as the director on Johnny Allegro, 1949), with Nina Foch.

Fugitive Lovers	1934	Col.
The Good Bad Girl	1931	Col.
Guilty	1930	Col.
Hands across the Table	1935	Par.
Hell's Island	1930	Col.
His Greatest Gamble	1934	RKO
Hollywood Speaks	1932	Col.
Honeymoon in Bali	1939	Par.
Hurricane	1930	Col.
I Married a Witch	1942	UA
I Want a Divorce	1940	Par.
Into No Man's Land	1928	US
Kiss the Boys Goodbye	1941	Par.
Lady by Choice	1934	Col.
The Lady Is Willing	1942	Col.
Lady of Secrets	1936	Col.
The Ladybird *	1927	US
The Last Parade	1931	Col.
Life's Mockery	1928	US
Light Fingers	1929	Col.
The Lightning Flyer	1931	Col.
Love Affair	1932	Col.
Love before Breakfast	1936	Univ.
Love Thy Neighbor	1940	Par.
The Mad Doctor	1941	Par.
Man about Town	1939	Par.
Man against Woman	1932	Col.
Masked Angel	1928	US
The Melody Man	1930	Col.
Men Are Like That	1931	Par.
Men in Her LIfe	1931	Col.
Mexicali Rose	1929	Col.
The More the Merrier	1943	Col.
Murder with Pictures	1936	Par.
My Man Godfrey	1936	Univ.
Night Club Lady	1932	Col.
Night Mayor	1932	Col.
Notorious	1946	RKO
Paris in Spring	1935	Par.
Personality	1930	Col.
Polly of the Movies	1927	US
Prince of Diamonds	1930	Col.
The Princess Comes Across	1936	Par.
The Power of the Press *	1928	Col.
Ragtime *	1927	US
Remember the Night	1940	Par.
Rhythm on the River	1940	Par.
Road to Zanzibar	1941	Par.
A Royal Romance	1930	Col.
Rumba	1935	Par.
Safari	1940	Par.

Shanghaied Love	1931	Col.
Should Ladies Beware?	1933	MGM
Sisters	1930	Col.
Soldiers and Women	1930	Col.
Soldiers of the Storm	1933	Col.
Sophie Lang Goes West	1937	Par.
The Squealer	1930	Col.
Stool Pigeon	1928	Col.
Sunshine of Paradise Alley *	1926	US
Swing High, Swing Low	1937	Par.
Talk of the Town	1942	Col.
Temptations of a Shop Girl *	1927	US
The Texas Ranger	1931	Col.
This Sporting Age	1932	Col.
Those Endearing Young Charms	1945	RKO
Three Wise Girls	1932	Col.
The Thrill Hunter	1933	Col.
Tol'able David	1930	Col.
Tom Sawyer, Detective	1939	Par.
Transatlantic Merry Go Round	1934	UA
Tropic Holiday	1938	Par.
True Confession	1937	Par.
Turn Off the Moon	1937	Par.
Wall Street *	1929	Col.
You Were Never Lovelier	1942	Col.
You're the One	1941	Par.
Younger Generation	1929	Col.

608. BUD THACKERY

Accused of Murder	1956	Rep.
Asylum for a Spy	1967	Univ.
Bandits of the West	1953	Rep.
Beau Geste	1966	Univ.
Beyond the Last Frontier	1943	Rep.
Black Hills Ambush	1952	Rep.
Coogan's Bluff	1968	Univ.
The Cyclone Kid	1942	Rep.
Did You Hear the One about the Traveling Saleslady?	1967	Univ.
The Fatal Witness	1945	Rep.
Flame of the Islands	1955	Rep.
Gangs of Sonora	1941	Rep.
The Gay Vagabond	1941	Rep.
The Girl from Alaska *	1942	Rep.
The Girl Who Dared	1944	Rep.
Goodnight Sweetheart	1944	Rep.
Hanged Man	1964	Univ.
Headin' for God's Country	1943	Rep.
The Hell With Heroes	1968	Univ.

Here Comes Elmer	1943	Rep.
Iron Mountain Trail	1953	Rep.
Jaguar	1956	Rep.
Last Frontier Uprising	1947	Rep.
Leadville Gunslinger	1952	Rep.
The Man from Rainbow Valley	1946	Rep.
O, My Darling Clementine	1943	Rep.
Oregon Trail	1945	Rep.
Out California Way	1946	Rep.
Outcasts of the Trail	1949	Rep.
Outlaws of Pine Ridge	1942	Rep.
The Phantom Plainsman	1942	Rep.
The Plainsman	1966	Univ.
Prince of the Plains	1949	Rep.
The Raiders	1964	Univ.
Red River Shore	1953	Rep.
Saddle Pals	1947	Rep.
San Antone	1952	Rep.
Santa Fe Passage	1955	Rep.
Savage Frontier	1953	Rep.
Shadows of Tombstone	1953	Rep.
Son of Zorro	1947	Rep.
Sons of the Pioneers	1942	Rep.
Stardust on the Sage	1942	Rep.
Stranger at My Door	1956	Rep.
Strategy of Terror	1969	Univ.
Sunset Serenade	1942	Rep.
Swing Your Partner	1943	Rep.
Tammy and the Millionaire *	1967	Univ.
Terror at Midnight	1956	Rep.
That's My Gal	1947	Rep.
Thunder over Arizona	1956	Rep.
Traffic in Crime	1946	Rep.
The Traitor Within	1942	Rep.
The Twinkle in God's Eye	1955	Rep.
The Undercover Woman	1946	Rep.
Valley of Hunted Men	1942	Rep.
The Vampire's Ghost *	1945	Rep.

609. GARY THIELTGES

The Boss' Wife	1986	Tri-S.
Eating Raoul	1982	TCF
Retribution	1987	US
Sno-Line	1986	US
Sticky Fingers	1988	US
Under the Gun	1989	US
Vasectomy: A Delicate Matter	1986	US

610. ARMAND THIRARD (1899-   )

Act of Love	1953	UA
Altitude 3,200 *	1938	Fr.
And God Created Woman	1956	Fr.
Apres L'Amour	1948	Fr.
Babette s'en Va t-en-Guerre	1959	Fr.--Col.
Beauties of the Night	1952	Fr.
Black Sun	1969	Fr.
The Brain *	1969	Fr.--Par.
Castle in Sweden	1963	Fr.
The Citadel of Silence *	1939	Fr.
Dark Eyes	1938	Fr.
David Golder *	1932	Fr.
Deadlier Than the Male	1957	Fr.
The Devil's Daughter	1949	Fr.
The Devil's Hand	1946	Fr.
Les Diaboliques	1954	Fr.
Does One Ever Know?	1957	Fr.
Don't Tempt the Devil	1964	Fr./It.
Flight into Darkness	1938	Fr.
The Fortress of Silence	1937	Fr.
The Four Truths	1963	Fr.
Fric Frac	1939	Fr.
Gingerhead	1932	Fr.
Goldsmith's Embankment	1947	Fr.
The Good Causes	1963	Fr.
Goodbye Again	1961	UA
Le Grand Bluff	1957	Fr.
Guns for San Sebastian	1967	Fr./It./Mex.-- MGM
Heart of Paris *	1939	Fr.
Here Is the Beauty	1950	Fr.
If All the Guys in the World	1956	Fr.
Jenny Lamour	1948	Fr.
The Jewelers of Midnight	1958	Fr.--Col.
Lemmy pour Les Dames	1962	Fr.
The Liars	1964	Fr.
The Living Corpse	1940	Fr.
Look Lovely and Shut Up	1958	Fr.
Love on a Pillow	1963	Fr./It.
Mam'zelle Nitouche	1954	Fr.
Man about Town	1947	Fr.--RKO
Manon	1949	Fr.
Marco the Magnificent	1963	Afg./Egypt/Fr It./Yugo.-- MGM
Mayerling	1937	Fr.
Midnight Tradition *	1939	Fr.
Miquette and Her Mother	1950	Fr.
Moderato Cantabile	1964	Fr./It.

The Most Wanted Man	1962	Fr./It.
Murder of Father Christmas	1941	Fr.
The Murderer Lives at No. 21	1947	Fr.
The Naked Heart	1950	GB
The Night Heaven Fell	1958	Fr.
North Hotel *	1939	Fr.
Nutty Naughty Chateau	1964	Fr./It.
Open Door to the Sea *	1935	Fr.
Paris Still Sings	1952	Fr.
The Patriot *	1938	Fr.
Pique Dame *	1944	Fr.
Poil de Carotte	1932	Fr.
Port of Desire	1960	Fr.
Public Enemy No. 1	1954	Fr.
Queen of Spades *	1937	Fr.
Race For Life	1955	Fr.
The Regattas of San Francisco	1960	Fr.--Col.
Roger La Houte	1946	Fr.
Sheep Has Five Legs	1954	Fr.
Soft Singing	1960	Fr.
Spring, Autumn and Love	1955	Fr.
Storm *	1938	Fr.
Stormy Waters *	1946	Fr.--MGM
The Sultans	1966	Fr.
Symphonie Fantastique	1947	Fr.
Le Symphonie Pastorale *	1946	Fr.
Tales of Paris *	1962	Fr./It.
Terrible Lovers	1936	Fr.
Three Days To Live	1958	Fr.
3 Fables of Love *	1963	Fr./It./Sp.
The Three Musketeers	1961	Fr.
Time Bomb	1961	Fr./It.
Trap for Cinderella	1965	Fr.
Trouble with Widows	1964	Fr.
The Truth	1961	Fr./It.
Utopia	1950	Fr./It.
Voici Les Temps des Assassins	1956	Fr.
The Wages of Fear	1953	Fr.
Warrior's Rest	1962	Fr.
Wild Roots of Love	1962	Fr.
The Wind Rises	1959	Fr.
With a Smile *	1939	Fr.

611. ALLEN QUARRIER THOMPSON

Across the Divide	1921	US
Black Aces	1937	Univ.
Boss of Lonely Valley *	1937	Univ.
Boss Rider of Gun Creek *	1936	Univ.
The Cowboy and the Kid *	1936	Univ.

Dollar Down	1925	US
Empty Saddles *	1937	Univ.
The Fatal Mistake	1924	US
The Fearless Lover	1925	US
The Fighting Edge *	1926	WB
For the Service *	1936	Univ.
Hawaiian Buckaroo	1938	TCF
Headin' East	1937	Col.
Hollywood Round Up	1937	Col.
Ivory Handled GUn *	1935	Univ.
Law for Tombstone *	1937	Univ.
The Man Upstairs	1926	WB
The Overland Express	1938	Col.
Panamint's Bad Man	1938	TCF
Racing for Life	1924	Col.
Ranger of the Big Pines	1925	Vita.
Rawhide	1938	TCF
Ride 'Em Cowboy *	1936	Univ.
Sandflow *	1937	Univ.
Smoke Tree Range	1937	Univ.
Silverspurs *	1936	Univ.
Sudden Bill Dorn	1938	Univ.
Sunset of Power *	1936	Univ.
Tainted Money	1924	US
The Throwback *	1935	Univ.
Who Cares?	1925	Col.
Women First	1924	Col.

612. STUART THOMPSON

The Bride Wore Boots	1946	Par.
Calypso Joe	1957	AA
Dear Wife	1949	Par.
Death of a Champion	1939	Par.
Emergency Squad	1950	Par.
Ladies Man	1947	Par.
Our Hearts Were Growing Up	1946	Par.
Out of This World	1945	Par.
Variety Girl *	1947	Par.
You Can't Ration Love	1944	Par.

613. WILLIAM CREEVY THOMPSON

Absinthe	1914	Univ.
Arctic Fury *	1949	RKO
As the Sun Went Down	1918	Metro.
Bride of the Atom *	1955	US
The Claim	1918	Metro.
The Curse of Eve	1917	US

Dementia	1955	AIP
Destiny	1915	Metro.
The Fall of a Nation *	1916	US
The Garden of Lees	1915	Univ.
Glen or Glenda?	1953	Par.
The Golden Mistress	1954	UA
High School Girl	1935	US
In Judgment Of	1918	Metro.
Jail Bait	1954	US
The Lawless Rider	1954	UA
Lion's Paws	1931	US
Mother, I Need You	1918	US
No Greater Love	1932	Col.
Pals	1925	US
Plan 9 from Outer Space	1956	US
Revenge	1918	Metro.
Riders of the Golden Gulch	1932	US
Sealed Valley	1915	Metro.
Shore Acres	1914	US
Treasure of the Sea	1918	Metro.
Woman Untamed	1920	US
Wormwood	1915	Fox

614. ALEX THOMSON

Alfred the Great	1969	GB--MGM
Best House in London	1968	GB--MGM
Bullshot	1983	GB
The Cat and the Canary	1978	GB
The Class of Miss McMichael	1978	GB
Date with An Angel	1987	DeL.
Deathline	1972	GB--AIP
Dr. Phibes Rises Again	1972	GB--AIP
Duet for One	1986	Cannon
Electric Dreams	1984	MGM-UA
Eureka	1980	GB--UA
Erblinka	1967	Isr.
Excalibur	1981	Orion/WB
Fear Is the Key	1972	Par.
A Game for Vultures	1979	GB
Here We Go Round the Mulberry Bush	1967	GB--UA
High Spirits	1988	Tri-S.
I Start Counting	1970	GB--UA
The Keep	1983	Par.
The Krays	1990	GB
Labyrinth	1986	Tri-S.
Last of Linda Cleer	1982	GB
Legend	1985	TCF/Univ.
Leviathan	1989	MGM/UA
Mr. Destiny	1990	BV/Touch.

The Night Digger	1971	GB--MGM
The Rachel Papers	1989	GB--UA
The Rise and Fall of Michael Rimmer	1970	GB--WB
Rosie Dixon Night Nurse	1978	GB--Col.
The Sicilian	1987	TCF
Track 29	1988	GB
Wings of Fame	1990	Holl.
Year of the Dragon	1985	MGM-UA

615. DONALD THORIN

Against All Odds	1984	Col.
Bad Boys *	1983	Univ.
Collision Course	1990	US
Couch Trip	1987	Orion
The Golden Child	1986	Par.
Lock Up	1989	Tri-S.
Midnight Run	1988	Univ.
An Officer and a Gentleman	1982	Par.
Tango & Cash	1989	WB
Thief	1981	UA
Troop Beverly Hills	1989	Col.
Wildcats	1986	WB

616. WILLIAM THORNLEY

Better Times	1919	US
Border Vengeance	1925	US
The Breathless Moment	1924	Univ.
Burning Words	1923	Univ.
Crashin' Thru *	1923	US
The Dancing Cheat	1924	Univ.
Desert Driven *	1923	US
The Desperate Game	1926	Univ.
The Devil's Trail	1919	US
Dolly's Vacation	1918	Pathe
God's Crucible	1921	US
The Grey Devil	1926	US
His Mystery Girl	1923	Univ.
Jack O' Clubs	1924	Univ.
The Love Brand	1923	Univ.
Man to Man	1922	Univ.
The Miracle Baby	1923	US
The Near Lady	1923	Univ.
Silent Sheldon	1925	US
Triple Action	1925	Univ.
The Turn in the Road	1919	US
West of the Rainbow's End	1926	US

617. HARRY THORPE

Mark of Zorro *	1920	UA
A Modern Musketeer *	1918	US
The Mollycoddle *	1920	UA
The Nut *	1921	UA
Reaching for the Moon *	9117	US
The Wedding March *	1928	Par.
When the Clouds Roll By *	1919	UA
Wild Honey	1922	Univ.

618. FRANK TIDY

Code of Silence	1985	Orion
The Duellists	1977	GB--Par.
The Grey Fox	1983	Can.--UA
Hot Pursuit	1987	Par./RKO
John and the Missus	1987	Can.
The Lucky Star	1980	Can.
One Magic Christmas	1985	Dis.
The Package	1989	Orion
Raggedy Rawney	1988	GB
Slipstream	1989	GB
Spacehunter: Adventures in the Forbidden Zone	1983	Col.
Sweet Liberty	1986	Univ.

619. EDUARD TISSE (1897-1961)

Aerograd	1935	USSR
Alexander Nevsky	1938	USSR
Bezhin Meadow	1937	USSR
Hunger, Hunger, Hunger	1921	USSR
The Immortal Garrison	1957	USSR
Ivan The Terrible	1942-46	USSR
Man of Music	1953	USSR
October *	1927	USSR
Potemkin *	1925	USSR
Que Viva Mexico	1931	USSR
Seeds of Freedom	1943	USSR
Sierebristaya Pyl	1953	USSR
Silver Dust	1953	USSR
Statchka *	1924	USSR

620. ARTHUR TODD

According To Hoyle	1922	US
The Adventurous Blonde	1937	WB

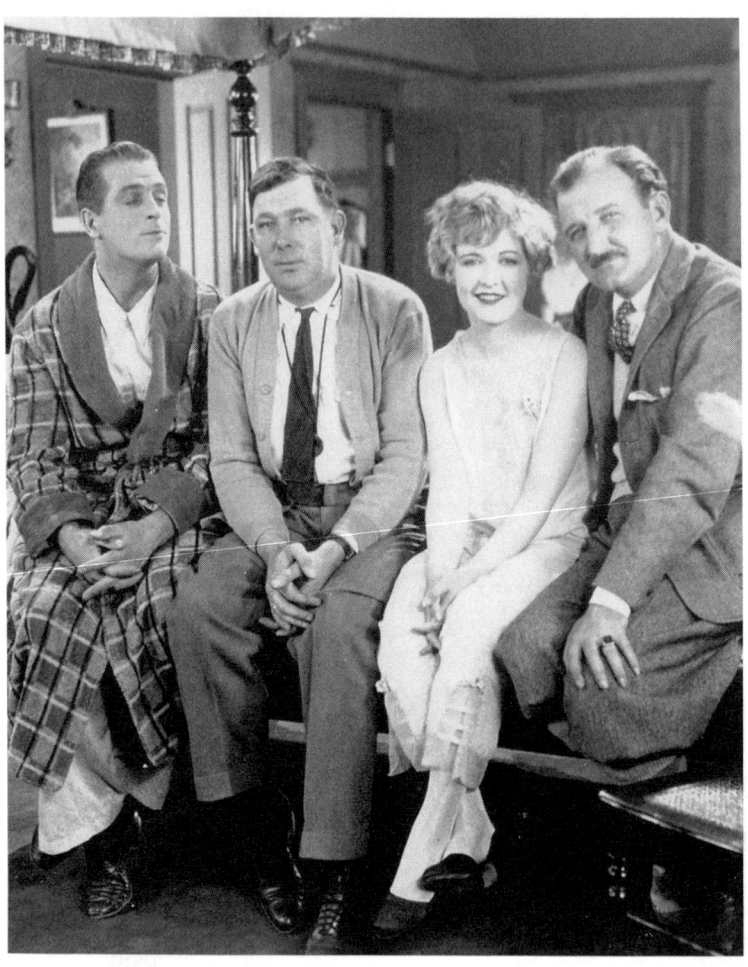

Arthur Todd (far right).

Alibi Ike	1935	WB
The Amazing Mr. Williams	1939	Col.
An Angel from Texas	1940	WB
Angels Wash Their Faces	1939	WB
Babbitt	1934	FN
Back in Circulation	1935	WB
Bad Men of Missouri	1941	WB
Betsy Ross	1917	US
Big-Hearted Herbert	1934	WB
Boulder Dam	1936	WB
The Brass Bottle	1923	FN
Broadway Hostess	1935	WB
The Challenge of Chance	1919	US
The Cheerful Fraud	1927	Univ.
Clear the Decks	1929	Univ.
The Coast of Opportunity	1920	US
College Coach	1933	WB
Crime School	1938	WB
The Dancers	1930	Fox
Dead End Kids on Dress Parade	1939	WB
Deliverance *	1919	US
Desert Gold *	1919	US
The Devil To Pay	1920	Pathe
A Devil With Women	1930	Fox
Down the Stretch	1936	WB
The Dream Cheater	1920	US
Earthworm Tractors	1936	WB
Elmer the Great	1933	WB
Embarrassing Moments	1930	Univ.
Ever in My Heart	1933	WB
Fast and Furious	1927	Univ.
The Florentine Dagger	1935	WB
Forget-Me-Not	1922	Metro.
The Forward Pass	1929	FN/WB
The Fourth Commandment	1927	Univ.
A Fugitive from Justice	1940	WB
Gambling on the High Seas	1940	WB
Girl Missing	1933	WB
Girls on Probation *	1938	WB
Going Places	1939	WB
Gold Heels	1924	Fox
Golf Widows	1928	Col.
Good Morning, Judge	1928	Univ.
The Great Mr. Nobody	1941	WB
The Green Flame	1920	US
Harold Teen	1934	WB
He Couldn't Say No	1933	WB
Her Big Night	1926	Univ.
Her Husband's Secretary	1937	WB
Here Comes Carter	1936	WB
His Lucky Day	1929	Univ.

Hot Heels	1928	Univ.
Hot Saturday	1932	Par.
The House of Whispers	1920	US
How to Handle Women	1928	Univ.
I Am Not Afraid	1939	WB
In Every Woman's Life	1924	US
The Isle of Lost Ships	1923	FN
I've Got Your Number	1934	WB
Jailbreak	1936	WB
Just a Woman	1925	FN
Lady Gangster	1942	WB
The Lawyer's Secret	1931	Par.
Live Sparks	1920	US
The Lone Eagle	1927	Univ.
Loose Ankles	1930	WB
The Lord Loves the Irish	1919	US
Marry the Girl	1937	WB
Melody for Two	1937	WB
Men in Exile	1937	WB
Million Dollar Legs	1932	Par.
Miss Pacific Fleet	1935	WB
Monkey Business	1931	Par.
Murder by an Aristocrat	1936	WB
The Murder of Dr. Harrington	1936	WB
Naughty But Nice	1939	WB
The Night Bird	1928	Univ.
No. 99	1920	US
One Hysterical Night	1929	Univ.
One Year To Live	1925	FN
Out All Night	1927	Univ.
The Payoff	1935	WB
Penrod and His Twin Brother	1938	WB
Penrod's Double Trouble	1938	WB
Red Hot Speed	1929	Univ.
The Return of the Terror	1934	WB
River's End	1940	WB
Rolling Home	1926	Univ.
Sh! The Octopus	1937	WB
She Couldn't Say No	1930	WB
Sing Me a Love Song	1936	WB
The Singing Marine	1937	WB
Skinner's Dress Suit	1926	Univ.
The Small Bachelor	1927	Univ.
The Smiling Ghost	1941	WB
Snowed Under	1936	FN/WB
Sooky	1931	Par.
South of Suez	1940	WB
Speed King	1923	US
Sporting Life	1925	Univ.
Take It from Me	1926	Univ.
Thanks for the Buggy Ride	1928	Univ.

That's My Daddy	1928	Univ.
$30,000	1920	US
Three Sons O Guns	1941	WB
Torchy Gets Her Man *	1938	WB
Torchy Plays with Dynamite	1939	WB
Torment	1924	FN
Watch Your Wife	1926	Univ.
We're in the Money	1935	WB
What a Man	1930	US
The White Moth	1924	FN
Wild Boys of the Road	1933	WB
Wild Horse Mesa	1932	Par.
You're in the Army Now *	1941	WB

621. GREGG TOLAND (1904-1948)

Ball of Fire	1942	Gold.
The Bat	1926	UA
Beloved Enemy	1936	Gold.
The Best Years of Our Lives	1946	Gold.
The Bishop's Wife	1947	Gold.
Bulldog Drummond *	1929	Gold.
Citizen Kane	1941	RKO
Come and Get It *	1936	Gold.
Condemned *	1930	Gold.
The Cowboy and the Lady	1938	Gold.
The Dark Angel	1935	Gold.
Dead End	1937	Gold.
The Devil To Pay *	1931	Gold.
Enchantment	1948	Gold.
Forsaking All Others *	1934	MGM
The Goldwyn Follies	1938	Gold.
The Grapes of Wrath	1940	TCF
History Is Made at Night	1937	US
Indiscreet *	1931	UA
Intermezzo	1939	Selz.
The Kid from Brooklyn	1946	Gold.
The Kid from Spain	1932	Gold.
Kid Millions	1935	Gold.
Kidnapped *	1938	TCF
The Little Foxes	1941	Gold.
The Long Voyage Home	1940	US
Mad Love *	1935	MGM
Man Wanted	1932	WB
The Masquerader	1935	Gold.
Les Miserables	1935	Fox
Nana	1934	Gold.
The Outlaw	1943	US
Palmy Days	1932	Gold.
Play Girl	1932	WB

Public Hero Number One	1935	MGM
Queen Kelly *	1928	UA
Raffles *	1930	UA
Raffles	1940	Gold.
The Road to Glory	1936	TCF
Roman Scandals *	1933	Gold.
A Song Is Born	1948	Gold.
Song of the South	1947	Dis.
Splendor	1935	Gold.
Strike Me Pink *	1936	Gold.
The Tenderfoot	1932	WB
These Three	1936	Gold.
They Shall Have Music	1939	Gold.
This Is Heaven *	1929	Gold./UA
Tonight or Never	1931	Gold.
The Trespasser *	1929	UA
Tugboat Annie	1933	MGM
The Unholy Garden *	1931	Gold.
Washington Masquerade	1932	MGM
We Live Again	1934	Gold.
The Wedding Night	1935	Gold.
The Westerner	1940	Gold.
Whoopee! *	1930	Gold.
Winning of Barbara Worth *	1926	Gold.
Woman Chases Man	1937	Gold.
Wuthering Heights	1939	Gold.

622. ALDO TONTI (1910-   )

Adam and Eve	1950	It.
Agostino	1963	It.--DeL.
L'Amore	1948	It.
The Ape Woman	1964	It.--Emb.
Ashanti	1979	Col.
Attila the Hun *	1954	Fr./It.
The Bandit	1946	It.
Barabbas	1962	It.--Col.
Big and the Bad	1971	Fr./It./Sp.
The Black Sheep	1968	It.
Botta e Riposta	1950	It.
Brancaleone alla Crociate	1971	Alg./It.
Cardinal Messias *	1940	It.
Casanova 70	1965	It.--Emb.
Cast a Giant Shadow	1966	UA
Castle of the Living Dead	1963	Fr./It.
Catch As Catch Can	1968	It.--Emb.
Cento Anni D'Amore	1954	It.
Count of Monte Cristo	1976	GB
Crazy Joe	1973	Col.
Damon and Pythias	1962	MGM

The Deserter	1970	It./Yugo.--Par.
The Devil	1963	It.
The Devil in Love	1968	It.--WB
Eager To Live	1953	It.
Easy Years	1953	It.
The Family	1970	Fr./It.
The Firemen of Viggin	1949	It.
Flesh Will Surrender	1950	It.
For the First Time	1959	Ger./It.--MGM
Forbidden	1955	It.
The Girl in Australia	1972	It.--Col.
The Greatest Love	1952	It.
Hell Raiders of the Deep	1954	It.
Hello Elephant	1954	It.
Hey Boy	1949	It.
How I Lost the War	1948	It.
The Hunchback of Rome *	1963	It.
I Love You, Love	1961	Fr./It.
I'll Find You Again	1949	It.
I'm in the Revue	1951	It.
It Happened in Rome	1959	It.
Kiss the Girls and Make Them Die	1966	It.--Col.
The Klansman *	1974	Par.
Lost Souls	1961	It.
Malia	1952	It.
The Man with the Balloons	1968	Fr./It.
Merchant of Slaves	1949	It.
The Mill on the Po	1948	It.
Miracle	1948	Fr./It.
Musilino the Bandit	1951	It.
Naples Millionaire	1951	It.
Nights of Cabiria	1957	It.
Obsession *	1942	It.
Outcry	1949	It.
Paranoia *	1966	Fr./It.
Peddlin' in Society	1949	It.
Reflections in a Golden Eye	1967	WB
Rene the Cane	1977	It.
The Savage Innocents *	1960	GB--Par.
Scorned Flesh	1948	It.
Sensulita	1952	It.--Par.
Serenade of a Big Love	1959	Ger.
Seven of the Big Bear	1953	It.
The She-Wolf	1953	It.
The Ship of Condemned Women	1953	It.
Slaves Still Exist	1964	It.
Souvenir d'Italie	1957	It.--Rank
Strange Events *	1977	It.
Street Has Many Dreams	1948	It.
Tempest	1958	Fr./It./Yugo.-- Par.

Three Tough Guys	1974	It.--Par.
To Bed or Not To Bed	1963	It.
Treasure of San Gennaro	1968	Fr./Ger./It.--Par.
Under Ten Flags	1960	It.--Par.
The Unfaithfuls	1960	It.--AA
Upon This Rock	1970	It.
The Valachi Papers	1972	Fr./It.--Col.
Violent City	1970	Fr./It.--Univ.
War and Peace *	1956	It.--Par.
Without Pity	1948	It.
The Wolf of the Sila	1950	It.
A Woman at Her Window	1976	Fr.
Woman Trouble	1949	It.
The Young Tigers	1968	It.

623. MARIO TOSI

The Betsy	1977	AA
Buster and Billie	1973	Col.
Carrie	1976	UA
Coast to Coast	1980	Par.
The Frogs	1972	GB--TCF
The Glory Stompers	1967	AIP
Hearts of the West	1975	MGM-UA
MacArthur	1977	Univ.
The Main Event	1979	WB
Outside In	1972	US
Report to the Commissioner	1974	UA
Resurrection	1981	Univ.
Six Pack	1982	TCF
Smoke in the Wind	1971	US
Some Call It Loving	1973	US
The Stunt Man	1978	TCF
Swamp Country	1966	US
Terror in the Jungle *	1968	US
Whose Life Is It Anyway?	1981	MGM-UA

624. ROLLIE TOTHEROH (1890-1967)

The Circus	1928	UA
City Lights *	1931	UA
The Gold Rush	1925	UA
Great Dictator *	1940	UA
The Kid	1921	FN
Modern Times *	1936	UA
Monsieur Verdoux *	1947	UA
The Pilgrim	1923	FN
Shoulder Arms	1918	FN

Song of My Heart	1947	AA
A Woman of Paris *	1923	UA

625. JEAN TOURNIER

Amelie	1961	Fr.
The Annuity	1972	Fr.--UA
Arms of Night	1961	Fr.
Black Thursday	1974	Fr.
The Cache	1983	Fr.
The Comeuppance	1970	Fr.
Counterfeit Constable	1966	Fr.
Day of the Jackal	1973	GB--Univ.
The Father's Trip	1966	Fr.
Feu a Volonte	1965	Fr.
The Fiendish Plot of Dr. Fu Manchu	1980	Orion
Fire at Will	1965	Fr.
For a Cop's Hide	1981	Fr.
Les Gaspards	1974	Fr.
Go France	1964	Fr.
Hello Anxiety	1988	Fr.
Un Homme de Trop	1967	Fr.
Ladies' Man	1960	Fr.
The Little Brother	1968	Fr.
Man, Woman and Child	1983	Par.
Moonraker	1979	GB--UA
Nobody's Women	1984	Fr.
On the Lam	1971	Fr.
One Man Too Many	1967	Fr.--UA
Shock Troops	1968	Fr./It.--UA
Shut Up, Gulls!	1974	Fr.--UA
The Sleeping Car Murders	1965	Fr.--TCF
Start he Revolution without Me	1969	WB
Target	1985	CBS/WB
The 1,001 Nights	1990	Fr./It.
Three Men To Destroy	1980	Fr.
Three Thousand Million Without an Elevator	1972	Fr.
The Train *	1964	Fr./It.--UA
We Don't Bury on Sundays	1959	Fr.

626. LEO TOVER (1902-1964)

All Hands on Deck	1961	TCF
Are These Our Children?	1931	RKO
The Arizona Raiders	1936	Par.
The Arkansas Traveller	1938	Par.
Bachelor Apartment	1931	RKO
Bahama Passage	1941	Par.

Between Heaven and Hell	1956	TCF
Big Broadcast of 1936	1935	Par.
The Biscuit Eater	1940	Par.
Blue Denim	1959	TCF
Bluebeard's Eight Wife	1938	Par.
A Blueprint for Murder	1953	TCF
Bolero	1934	Par.
The Bride Comes Home	1935	Par.
China	1943	Par.
Cocoanut Grove	1938	Par.
College Humor	1933	Par.
College Rhythm *	1934	Par.
The Conqueror *	1935	RKO/US
The Crystal Ball	1943	US
The Day the Earth Stood Still	1951	TCF
Dead Reckoning	1947	Col.
Ebb Tide	1937	Par.
The Fall Guy	1930	RKO
The Farmer's Daughter	1940	Par.
Fascinating Youth	1926	Par.
Florida Special	1936	Par.
Follow That Dream	1962	UA
Follow the Sun	1951	TCF
Framed	1930	RKO
Fraulein	1958	TCF
From the Terrace	1960	TCF
Gay Diplomat	1931	RKO
Girl of the Port	1930	RKO
Girl of the Rio	1932	RKO
Girl without a Room	1933	Par.
God Gave Me Twenty Cents	1926	Par.
The Great Gatsby	1926	Par.
The Great Jasper	1933	RKO
The Heiress	1949	Par.
Hold Back the Dawn	1941	Par.
I Met Him in Paris	1937	Par.
I Walk Alone	1948	Par.
I Wanted Wings	1941	Par.
I'm No Angel	1933	Par.
In Love and War	1958	TCF
Invitation to Happiness	1939	Par.
Is My Face Red?	1932	RKO
Island of the Blue Dolphins	1964	Univ.
Journey to the Center of the Earth	1959	TCF
King of Chinatown	1939	par.
The Lieutenant Wore Skirts	1955	TCF
Life with Henry	1941	Par.
Love in Bloom	1935	Par.
Love Me Tender	1956	TCF
Love's Greatest Mistake	1927	Par.
Maid of Salem	1936	Par.

The Major and the Minor	1942	Par.
Man in the Attic	1953	TCF
Marriage Go Round	1961	TCF
Mrs. Wiggs of the Cabbage Patch	1942	Par.
Misty *	1961	TCF
The Monkey's Paw	1933	RKO
Murder at the Vanities	1934	Par.
My Friend Irma	1949	Par.
My Pal Gus	1952	TCF
My Wife's Best Friend	1952	TCF
Never Say Die	1939	Par.
A Nice Little Bank That Should Be Robbed	1958	TCF
A Night at Earl Carroll's	1940	Par.
Night Club Scandal	1937	Par.
Night of Nights	1939	Par.
No Man of Her Own	1932	Par.
Paid in Full	1949	Par.
Payment on Demand	1951	RKO
The President's Lady	1953	TCF
Pride of St. Louis	1952	TCF
The Quarterback	1940	Par.
The Revolt of Mamie Stover	1956	TCF
Rose of the Rancho	1936	Par.
Royal Bed	1931	RKO
Runaway Bride	1930	RKO
Say One for Me	1959	TCF
Sealed Verdict	1948	Par.
The Secret Fury	1950	RKO
Secret of Convict Lake	1951	TCF
She's My Weakness	1930	RKO
Shoot the Works	1934	Par.
The Silver Horde	1930	RKO
The Snake Pit	1948	TCF
Soldier of Fortune	1955	TCF
Star Spangled Rhythm *	1942	Par.
State's Attorney	1932	RKO
Strange Bedfellows	1965	Univ.
Street Girl	1929	RKO
The Sun Also Rises	1957	TCF
Sunday in New York	1963	MGM
Symphony of Six Million	1932	RKO
The Tall Men	1955	TCF
Tanned Legs *	1929	RKO
The Telephone Girl	1927	FP
Thirteen Women	1932	RKO
Transgression	1931	RKO
Traveling Husbands	1931	RKO
Untamed *	1940	Par.
Untamed	1955	TCF
Vagabond Lover	1929	RKO

Valiant Is the Word for Carrie	1936	Par.
The Very Idea	1929	RKO
A Very Special Favor	1965	Univ.
Victory	1940	Par.
The Way to the Gold	1957	TCF
We're Not Married	1952	TCF
When Willie Comes Marching Home	1949	TCF
Woman on the Beach *	1947	RKO
You Belong to Me	1934	Par.
Young and Willing	1942	Par.

627. LUCIANO TOVOLI

The Adoption	1978	Fr.
Beyond the Door	1982	It.
Bianca	1984	It.
Bread and Chocolate	1973	It.
Bye Bye Monkey	1978	Fr./It.
La Cage aux Folles 3	1985	Fr./It.--Col./ WB
Captain Fracassa's Journey	1990	Fr./It.
The Desert of the Tartars	1976	Fr./Iran/It.
The Dirty Weekend	1973	It.--MGM
Fracchia vs. Dracula	1986	It.
Fugitives	1986	It.
General of the Dead Army *	1983	Fr./It.
Growing Up	1988	It.
In the Pope's Eye	1981	It.
Interior of a Convent	1978	It.
The Invited One	1969	Fr./It.
The Last Woman	1976	It.
Leonor	1975	Fr./It./Sp.
The Mystery of Oberwald	1980	It.
The Passenger	1975	It.--MGM-UA
The Peaceful Age	1975	It.
Police	1985	Fr.
Priceless Beauty	1989	It.
Reversal of Fortune	1990	WB
Roaring Forties	1982	Fr./Ger./SL
Rose Spot	1969	It.
Something Like Love	1968	It.
Sunday Woman	1976	Fr./It.--TCF
Suspira	1976	It.--TCF
Tulips of Haarlem	1970	Fr./It.--WB
Unsane	1987	It.
Vanilla Strawberry	1989	Fr./It.
We Will Not Grow Old Together	1972	Fr.
Weak Spot	1975	Fr./Ger./It.
What Time Is It?	1989	Fr./It.--WB
Where Are You Going on Holiday? *	1979	It.
White, Red and Vendome Green	1981	It.

628. WOLFGANG TREU

The Castle	1968	Ger.
Disorder and Early Torment	1977	Ger.
Every Year Again	1967	Ger.
Forbidden	1984	Ger.
Giselle	1978	Ger.
God Does Not Believe in Us Anymore	1988	Aust.
The Little Drummer Girl	1984	WB
Maschenka	1987	Ger.
Moritz, Dear Moritz	1978	Ger.
Night of the Askari	1978	Ger./S.Afr.
North Sea Is Dead Sea	1976	Ger.
Orpheus	1978	Ger./Switz.
The Pedestrian	1974	Ger.
St. Pauli Report	1972	Ger.
The Salzburg Conneaction	1972	TCF
Song for Europe	1985	Ger.
Trotta	1971	Ger.
Two Faces of January	1986	Ger.
The Wonderful Years	1980	Ger.

629. JAN TROELL (1931-)

The Baby Carriage	1963	Swed.
Bang	1977	Swed.
Eeny Meeny Miny Moe	1968	Swed.
The Emigrants	1970	Swed.--WB
Flight of the Eagle	1983	Swed.
4 X 4	1965	Den./Fin./Nor./ Swed.
Here's Your Life	1967	Swed.
The New Land	1973	Swed.--WB
Unto a Good Land	1972	Swed.

630. WILLIAM TROIANO

The Devil's Messenger	1961	US
Dracula (the Dirty Old Man)	1969	US
Handle with Care	1964	US
Horror of the Blood Monsters *	1970	US
Ride a Wild Stud	1966	US
The Ruined Bruin	1961	US
She Freak	1967	US
The Slime People	1963	US

631. WILLIAM TUERS

The Barricade *	1921	US

Beyond the Rainbow *	1922	US
Birthright	1920	US
Breed of the Border *	1924	US
The Dixie Flyer *	1926	US
Forest Havoc	1926	US
Frenzied Frames	1926	US
His Nibs *	1921	US
Moran of the Mounted	1926	US
The Night Owl	1926	US
One Million in Jewels	1923	US
Race Wild	1926	US
Racing Romance	1926	US
The Scorcher	1927	US
The Sixth Commandment *	1924	US
The Smoke Eaters	1926	US
Speed Wild	1925	US
Speeding Through	1926	US
Sunshine Harbor	1922	US
Tarnish *	1924	FN/Gold.
Till We Meet Again *	1922	US
The Triflers	1924	US
The Warning Signal	1926	US
Whispering Canyon *	1926	US

632. GERRY TURPIN

Battle Hell	1957	GB
The Bobo	1967	GB--WB
Deadfall	1968	GB--TCF
Diamonds for Breakfast	1968	GB--Par.
Doctor and the Devils *	1985	GB--TCF
Dutchman	1966	GB
Hoffman	1970	GB
Honeymoon *	1959	GB
I Want What I Want	1971	GB
The Last of Sheila	1973	WB
The Man Who Had Power over Women	1970	GB--AE
Morgan!	1966	GB
Oh What a Lovely War	1969	GB--Par.
The Queen's Guards	1960	GB--TCF
Seance on a Wet Afternoon	1964	GB
What Became of Jack and Jill?	1971	GB--TCF
The Whisperers	1966	GB--UA
The Wrong Box	1966	GB--Col.
Young Winston	1972	GB--Col.

633. EDWARD G. ULLMAN

The Blinding Trail	1919	Univ.

Father and the Boys	1915	Univ.
The Little White Savage	1919	Univ.
Out of the Night	1918	US
A Society Sensation	1918	US
The Wild Cat of Paris	1919	Univ.

634. GEOFFREY UNSWORTH (1914-1978)

The Abdication	1974	GB--WB
Alice's Adventures in Wonderland	1927	GB
The Assassination Bureau	1968	GB--Par.
Bachelor of Hearts	1958	GB--Rank
Baxter	1972	GB--NG
Becket	1964	GB--Par.
Blanche Fury *	1948	GB--Univ.
The Bliss of Mrs. Blossom	1968	GB--Par.
The Blue Lagoon *	1949	GB--Univ.
A Bridge Too Far *	1977	GB--UA
Cabaret	1972	AA
The Clouded Yellow	1950	GB
Cromwell	1970	GB--Col.
Dance of Death	1971	GB--Par.
Dangerous Exile	1957	GB--Rank
Don Quixote	1973	Aus.
Double Confession	1953	GB
First Great Train Robbery	1978	GB--UA
Flame over India	1959	GB--TCF
Fools Rush In	1949	GB--Rank
Genghis Khan	1964	Ger./GB/Yugo.-- Col.
Goodbye Gemini	1970	GB
Half a Sixpence	1967	GB--Par.
Hell Drivers	1957	GB--Rank
The Internecine Project	1974	GB--AA
Ivory Hunter	1951	GB--Eal./Univ.
Jacqueline	1956	GB--Rank
Jassy *	1947	GB--Univ.
Kisenga, Man of Africa *	1946	GB
Land of Fury	1954	GB--Univ.
The Laughing Lady	1946	GB
Love and Pain and the Whole Damn Thing	1972	Col.
Lucky Lady	1975	TCF
Made in Heaven	1953	GB
The Magic Christian	1970	GB
The Main Attraction	1962	GB--MGM
Man with a Million	1954	GB--UA
A Matter of Time	1976	AIP
Murder on the Orient Express	1974	GB--Par.
Oh Dad, Poor Dad, Mama's Hung You in the Closet and I'm Feelin' So Sad	1967	Par.

On the Double *	1961	Par.
Outpost in Malaya	1952	GB
Passage Home	1955	GB
Penny Princess	1952	GB--Univ.
The Purple Plain	1954	GB--Rank/UA
The Reckoning	1969	GB--Col.
The Return of the Pink Panther	1975	GB--UA
Royal Flash	1975	GB--TCF
Say Hello to Yesterday	1970	GB
Scott of the Antarctic *	1948	GB--Eal.
Simba	1955	GB--Lip.
The Smugglers	1948	GB--EL
The Spider and the Fly *	1949	GB
Superman	1978	WB
Superman II *	1980	WB
Sword and the Rose	1952	Dis./RKO
Tamahine	1964	GB--MGM
Tess *	1979	Fr./GB--MGM
The 300 Spartans	1962	TCF
Three Sisters	1970	GB--AFT
Tiger in the Smoke	1956	GB--Rank
A Town Like Alice	1956	GB--Rank
Trio *	1950	GB--Par.
Turn the Key Softly	1953	GB
2001: A Space Odyssey *	1968	GB--MGM
Unman, Wittering and Zigo	1971	GB--Par.
Value for Money	1955	GB--Rank
Voices	1973	GB
Whirlpool	1959	GB--Rank
Why Bother To Knock?	1964	GB
The World of Suzie Wong	1960	Par.

635. FRANK URSON (1887-1928)

Alias Mike Moran	1919	Par.
An Adventure in Hearts	1920	Par.
Hawthorne of the U.S.A.	1919	Par.
The Lottery Man	1919	Par.
The Love Burglar	1919	Par.
Nina the Flower Girl	1917	US
The Roaring Road	1919	Par.
Stranded	1916	US
You're Fired	1919	Par.

636. JOST VACANO

Das Boot	1981	Ger.
The Brothers	1976	Ger.
Dear Fatherland, Be At Peace	1976	Ger.

Death or Freedom	1978	Ger.
The Fifth Commandment	1979	Ger.
52 Pick-Up	1986	Cannon
Lost Honor of Katharina BLum	1975	Ger.--Orion/Par.
The Neverending Story	1984	Ger.--WB
No Shooting Time for Foxes	1966	Ger.
The Roarin' Fifties	1983	Ger.
Robocop	1987	Orion
Rocket Gibraltar	1988	Col.
Soldier of Orange *	1979	Holl.--Rank
Spetters	1983	Holl.
Supermarket	1974	Ger.
Total Recall	1990	TRI-S.

637. JOSEPH VALENTINE (1900-1949)

Alias Mary Dow	1935	Univ.
Appointment for Love	1943	Univ.
Are You There?	1930	Fox
Between Us Girls	1942	Univ.
The Boys from Syracuse	1940	Univ.
Bride for Sale	1949	RKO
Call It Luck	1934	Fox
Cheer Up and Smile	1930	Fox
Curlytop	1924	Fox
Doubting Thomas	1935	Fox
First Love	1939	Univ.
The Folly of Vanity *	1924	Fox
The Gay Deception	1935	Fox
The Girl from Havana	1929	Fox
Heartbeat	1946	RKO
Hold That Ghost *	1941	Univ.
In the Navy	1941	Univ.
It's a Date	1940	Univ.
Joan of Arc	1948	RKO/US
Keep 'Em Flying	1941	Univ.
Lover Come Back	1946	Univ.
Mad about Music	1938	Univ.
Magnificent Doll	1946	Univ.
The Man I Marry *	1936	Univ.
Merry Go Round of 1938	1937	Univ.
The Moon's Our Home	1936	Par.
My Husband's Wives	1924	Fox
My Little Chickadee	1939	Univ.
Myrt and Marge	1934	Univ.
The News Parade *	1928	Fox
Next Time We Love	1936	Univ.
Nice Girl?	1941	Univ.
Night of Terror	1933	Col.
One Hundred Men and a Girl	1937	Univ.

One Night in the Tropics	1940	Univ.
Possessed	1947	WB
Prep and Pep *	1928	Fox
Protection	1929	Fox
The Rage of Paris	1938	Univ.
Remember Last Night?	1936	Univ.
Rope *	1948	WB/US
Saboteur	1942	Univ.
The Scarlet Honeymoon	1925	Fox
7th Heaven *	1927	Fox
Shadow of a Doubt	1943	Univ.
Sleep My Love	1948	UA
So Goes My Love	1946	Univ.
Soup to Nuts	1930	Fox
Speakeasy	1929	Fox
Spring Parade	1940	Univ.
The Star Dust Trail	1924	Fox
Student Tour	1934	MGM
Swell-Head	1935	Col.
That Certain Age	1938	Univ.
3 On a Honeymoon	1934	Fox
Three Smart Girls	1936	Univ.
Three Smart Girls Grow Up	1939	Univ.
Tomorrow Is Forever	1945	RKO
Top of the Town	1937	Univ.
Trail of the Vigilantes *	1940	Univ.
Two in a Crowd	1936	Univ.
Unfinished Business	1941	Univ.
Wild Gold	1934	Fox
Wings over Honolulu	1937	Univ.
The Wolf Man	1940	Univ.

638. ENRIQUE (HARRY) JUAN VALLEJO

The Dwelling Place of a Light	1920	US
Her Sacrifice *	1926	US
The Killer	1921	Pathe
The Lure of Egypt	1921	Pathe
The Millionaire	1921	Univ.
The Money Changers	1920	Pathe
The Rage of Paris	1921	Univ.
Riders of the Dawn	1920	US
Romance of Tarzan	1918	FN
The Spanish Jade	1915	Par.
The Spenders	1920	US
Tarzan of the Apes *	1918	US
The Three Must-Get-Theres *	1922	US
The U.P. Trail	1920	US

639. A. H. VALLET

Cotton and Cattle	1921	US
A Cowboy Ace	1921	US
Flowing Gold	1921	FN
The Law of the Yukon *	1920	US
Out of the Clouds	1921	US
The Range Pirate	1921	US
Rustlers of the Night	1921	US
The Thrill Seekers *	1927	US

640. NED VAN BUREN

The Alien	1915	US
Ashes of Embers	1916	Par.
The Bandbox *	1919	US
A Broadway Saint	1919	US
Burn 'Em Up Barnes *	1921	US
Cardigan *	1922	US
Children of Eve	1915	US
Counsel for the Defense *	1925	US
Fedora	1918	Par.
Gladiola	1915	US
Has the World Gone Mad!	1923	US
The Headless Horseman	1922	US
The Kingdom of Youth	1918	Gold.
The Old Fool	1923	US
Sapho	1917	Par.
The Sin That Was His	1920	Selz.
The Slave Market	1917	Par.
La Tosca	1918	Par.
Twilight	1919	US
The Volcano	1919	US
When a Man's a Man *	1924	FN
Wild Honey	1919	US

641. JOHN VAN DEN BROEK

Barbary Sheep	1917	US
The Bluebird	1918	US
The Hand of Peril	1916	US
Mother	1914	US
The Pride of the Clan *	1917	US
Prunella	1918	Par.
The Velvet Paw	1916	US
The Whip	1917	US
The Wishing Ring	1914	US

642. EDDIE VAN DEN ENDEN

Because of the Cats	1973	Belg./Holl.
Black Rider	1983	Holl.
Butterfly	1981	US
Caught	1987	US
Daughters of Darkness	1971	Belg./Fr./Ger./ It.
Death of a Nun	1975	Belg./Holl.
Doctor in the Village	1958	Holl.
Fake-Out	1982	US
Flanagan	1976	Holl.
Frontier	1984	Holl.
Grunt: The Wrestling Movie	1985	US
If It Doesn't Come from Your Heart	1961	Holl.
In the Shadow of Victory	1986	Holl.
The Knife	1961	Holl.
Lifespan	1975	GB/Holl.--US
Louisa, A Word for Love	1972	Holl.
Mira	1971	Holl.
Monsieur Hawarden	1968	Belg./Holl.
Order and Security in the World	1978	Fr.
Red-Haired Revolver	1974	Belg./Fr.
Rififi in Amsterdam	1962	Holl.
Rigged	1985	Holl.
10:32 in the Morning	1966	Holl.
A Time to Die	1983	US
Traffic	1970	Holl.
Trompe L'Oeil	1975	Fr.
Village on the River	1959	Holl.

643. PAUL VAN DER LINDEN

Eliza's Horoscope	1975	Can.
High	1970	Can.
King Solomon's Treasure	1978	Can.
Kings and Desperate Men	1984	GB
The Last Chase	1981	US
Lies My Father Told Me	1975	Can--Col.
The Merry Wives of Tobias Rouke	1972	Can.

644. CHARLES VAN ENGER

Abbott and Costello Meet Frankenstein	1948	Univ.
Abbott and Costello Meet the Killer Boris Karloff	1949	Univ.
Africa Screams	1949	UA
Arizona Cyclone	1941	Univ.

Aunt Sally	1933	GB
Battles of Chief Pontiac	1953	US
Be My Wife	1921	Gold.
Bela Lugosi Meets a Brooklyn Gorilla	1952	US
Boss of Hangtown Mesa	1942	Univ.
Bowery to Broadway	1944	Univ.
The Brass Legend	1956	UA
Bride of the Gorilla	1951	US
Broadway after Dark	1924	WB
Buck Privates Come Home	1946	Univ.
Captain Bill	1935	GB
Chip Off the Old Block	1944	Univ.
The Chorus Kid	1928	US
The Christian	1923	Gold.
Combat Squad	1953	Col.
The Country Fair	1920	US
Cracked Nuts	1941	Univ.
Crazy House	1943	Univ.
The Daltons Ride Again	1945	Univ.
Daring Youth	1924	US
Daughters of Pleasure	1924	US
A Doll's House	1922	UA
Domestic Troubles	1928	WB
Easy Pickings	1927	FN
The Famous Mrs. Fair	1923	Metro.
Fighting Bill Fargo	1942	Univ.
The Foolish Matrons *	1921	US
Footloose Widows *	1926	WB
Forbidden Paradise	1924	Par.
Fox Movietone Follies	1929	Fox
Framed	1927	FN
Friday the Thirteenth	1933	GB
Frisco Lil	1942	Univ.
Frisco Sal	1945	Univ.
The Ghost Catchers	1944	Univ.
Give and Take	1928	Univ.
The Great Redeemer	1920	Metro.
Gun Fever	1958	UA
Half a Sinner	1940	Univ.
The Head of the Family	1928	US
Hello Sucker	1941	Univ.
Her Primitive Man	1944	Univ.
Hi Diddle Diddle *	1943	UA
Hi Ya Chum	1943	Univ.
High Society BLues	1930	Fox
Hit the Ice	1943	Univ.
Hogan's Alley *	1925	WB
Homesick	1928	Fox
Hot for Paris	1929	Fox
How To Educate a Wife	1924	WB
I Was a Spy	1933	GB

It Ain't Hay	1943	Univ.
Jack of All Trades	1936	GB
Jungle Captive *	1945	Univ.
Khyber Patrol	1954	UA
The Kid from Texas	1950	Univ.
Kid Monk Baroni	1952	US
Kindred of the Dust *	1922	FN
Kiss Me Again	1925	WB
Lady Windermere's Fan *	1925	WB
Law of the Range	1941	Univ.
The Last of the Mohicans *	1920	US
The Life of Riley	1927	FN
The Limited Mail *	1925	W
Little Giant	1946	Univ.
Lorna Doone	1951	Col.
Lover's Lane	1924	WB
Lucky Devils	1941	Univ.
Ma and Pa Kettle at the Fair *	1952	Univ.
Ma and Pa Kettle Back on the Farm	1951	Univ.
Ma and Pa Kettle Go to Town	1950	Univ.
The Magnetic Monster	1953	UA
Magnificent Roughnecks	1956	AA
Man from Montana	1941	Univ.
The Marriage Circle	1924	WB
Married in Hollywood *	1929	Fox
The Masked Rider	1941	Univ.
Meet the Wife *	1931	Col.
The Merry Monahans *	1944	Univ.
Mexican Hayride	1948	Univ.
Miracle on Main Street	1940	RKO
Moonlight in Havana	1942	Univ.
My Son for You	1935	GB
Name the Man	1924	Gold.
Never a Dull Moment	1943	Univ.
Never Give a Sucker an Even Break	1941	Univ.
Night Club Girl	1944	Univ.
The Night Monster	1942	Univ.
None But the Brave	1928	Fox
The Noose Hangs High	1948	EL
North to the Klondike	1942	Univ.
On Stage Everybody	1945	Univ.
One Mad Kiss *	1930	Fox
Other Women's Husbands	1926	FN
Paradise	1926	FN
The Phantom of the Opera *	1925	Univ.
The Port of Missing Girls	1928	US
Puppets	1926	FN
Rawhide Rangers	1941	Univ.
Red Hot Tires	1925	WB
Sabre Jet	1953	UA
Salome	1922	US

San Francisco Docks	1941	Univ.
The Sea Tiger	1927	FN
Seven Years Bad Luck	1921	US
Sherlock Holmes Faces Death	1943	Univ.
The Silver Bullet	1942	Univ.
The Singing Sheriff	1944	Univ.
Sitting Bull *	1954	UA
Slightly Tempted	1940	Univ.
Smile, Brother, Smile	1927	FN
Spider Woman	1944	Univ.
Strange Conquest	1946	Univ.
That Night with You *	1945	Univ.
That's The Spirit	1943	Univ.
Three Wise Fools	1923	Gold.
Three Women	1924	WB
The Time of Their Lives	1946	Univ.
Timetable	1955	UA
Turkey Time	1933	GB
Two Dollar Bettor	1951	US
Under Western Skies	1945	Univ.
Where There's a Will	1936	GB
White Tie and Tails	1946	Univ.
Who Done It?	1942	Univ.
Why Girls Go Back Home	1926	WB
The Wistful Widow of Wagon Gap	1947	Univ.
Words and Music *	1929	Fox

645. JAMES C. VAN TREES

Adventures in Iraq	1943	WB
Advice to the Lovelorn	1933	Fox
Age of Innocence	1934	RKO
Alexander Hamilton	1931	WB
Angel on My Shoulder	1946	UA
The Argyle Case	1929	WB
The Babe Ruth Story *	1948	AA
Baby Face	1933	WB
Bedside Manner	1945	UA
Big City Blues	1932	WB
Blood Money	1933	TC
The Bonded Woman	1922	Par.
Busses Roar	1942	WB
Captain Thunder	1931	WB
Career Woman *	1936	TCF
Chickie	1925	FN
The Crystal Cup	1927	FN
Don Juan's Three Nights	1926	FN
Escape from Crime	1942	WB
Every Night at Eight	1935	Par.
Expensive Husbands	1938	WB

The Fabulous Dorseys	1947	UA
Fifth Avenue	1926	PDC
The Final Closeup	1919	Par.
Find the Blackmailer	1943	WB
Flight from Destiny	1941	WB
Flying Hostess	1936	Univ.
The Furnace	1920	US
Gentlemen Are Born	1934	WB
The Girl from Tenth Avenue	1935	WB
Girls *	1919	Par.
Good Night Paul	1918	US
The Gorilla Man	1942	WB
The Great John L	1945	UA
The Green Goddess	1930	WB
The Green Temptation	1922	Par.
Happiness a La Mode	1919	US
The Heart of New York	1932	WB
Her Master's Voice	1936	Par.
Here Comes Happiness	1941	WB
Heroes for Sale	1933	WB
The Highway of Hope	1917	Par.
His Official Fiancee	1919	Par.
The Huntress	1923	FN
I Loved a Woman	1933	WB
I Want My Man	1925	FN
If I Marry Again	1925	FN
An International Marriage	1916	US
Intrigue	1916	Par.
It's Love I'm After	1937	WB
Jenny Be Good	1920	US
Judy of Rogues' Harbor	1920	US
The King's Vacation	1933	WB
A Lady's Name	1918	US
The Last Ride	1944	WB
Let Them Live	1937	Univ.
Life Begins	1932	WB
Lilies of the Field	1924	FN
Lily Turner	1933	WB
The Lone Wolf's Daughter	1929	Col.
Looking for Trouble	1933	UA
Lost at the Front	1927	FN
Love Is on the Air	1937	WB
The Making of Maddalena	1916	US
Man Crazy	1927	FN
The Man from Blankley's	1930	WB
The Man from Funeral Range	1918	Par.
The Man Hunter	1930	WB
Man Who Lived Twice	1936	Col.
The Man Who Played God	1932	WB
Midnight Lovers	1926	FN
Midnight Mary	1933	MGM

The Millionaire	1931	WB
Mrs. Leffingwell's Boots	1918	US
Morals	1921	Par.
More Deadly Than the Male	1919	Par.
Murder in the Private Car *	1934	MGM
A Night in Casablanca	1946	US
Nine Girls	944	Col.
Nurse Marjorie	1920	US
The Nurse's Secret	1941	WB
Old English	1930	WB
Over the Wall	1938	WB
A Pair of Silk Stockings	1918	US
Palm Springs	1936	Par.
The Parachute Jumper	1933	WB
The Patient in Room 18	1938	WB
The Perfect Flapper	1924	FN
The Prince of Headwaiters	1927	FN
The Prince of Pilsen	1926	PDC
The Reckless Hour	1931	WB
The Rescuing Angel	1919	Par.
The Road to Love	1916	US
Romance and Arabella	1919	US
The Rustle of Silk *	1923	Par.
Sacred and Profane Love	1921	Par.
The Sacred Flame	1929	WB
Sauce for the Goose	1918	US
The Scarlet Lady	1928	Col.
Secret Enemies	1942	WB
Shanghai	1935	Par.
She Couldn't Say No	1930	WB
The Shot in the Dark	1941	FN/WB
Silver Dollar	1932	WB
Single Wives *	1924	FN
Sinner's Parade	1928	Col.
Smashing the Money Ring	1939	WB
So Long Letty	1929	WB
The Soul of Youth	1920	US
Star Witness	1931	WB
Steel against the Sky	1941	WB
Stingaree	1934	RKO
The Stronger Love	1916	US
A Successful Calamity	1931	WB
Sweet Music	1934	WB
Taxi!	1932	WB
They Call It Sin	1932	WB
They Met in a Taxi	1936	Col.
The Thirteenth Commandment	1920	Par.
The Top of New York	1922	Par.
Twinkletoes	1926	FN
Unclaimed Goods	1918	Par.
The Unguarded Hour	1936	MGM

The Veiled Adventure	1919	Selz.
Viennese Nights	1930	WB
Waterfront	1939	WB
Wealth	1921	Par.
West of the Pecos *	1934	RKO
The Whip	1928	FN
The White Flower	1923	Par.
Who Cares?	1919	US
Widow by Proxy *	1919	Par.
The Wild Olive	1915	Par.
Wine, Women and Horses	1937	WB
The Witching Hour	1921	Par.
Woman on the Jury	1924	FN
You Can't Escape Forever *	1942	WB
You're in the Army Now *	1941	WB
The Young Rajah	1922	Par.

646. RENE VERZIER

The Awakening	1971	Can.
Breaking All the Rules	1985	Can.
Bullies	1986	Can.
City on Fire	1979	Can.--AE
Covergirl	1984	Can.
Cross Country	1983	Can.--MGM-UA
Deadly Eyes	1983	US
The Death of a Lumberjack	1973	Can.
Death Ship	1980	Can.--AE
Double Negative	1980	Can.
Eddie and the Cruisers II: Eddie Lives	1989	Can.
Fish Hawk	1979	Can.--AE
The Funny Farm	1983	Can.
Gas	1981	Can.--Par.
Heads or Tails	9171	Can.
High-Ballin	1978	AIP
Hog WIld	1980	Can.--AE
I Love You	1974	Can.
L'Initiation	1970	Can.
Jacques Brel Is Alive and Living in Paris	1975	AFT
Joy *	1983	Can./Fr.
Little Girl Who Lives Down the Lane	1976	Can.--AIP/Rank
Love Is a Four Letter Word	1970	Can.
The Men	1971	Can.
Morning Man	1987	Can.
Of Unknown Origin	1983	Can.--WB
One Night Only	1986	Can.
The Pyx	1973	Can.
Rabid	1977	Can.
Rats	1982	Can.

Rituals	1978	Can.
Search and Destroy	1981	US
Seven Times a Day	1971	Can./Isr.
Terror Train	1980	Can.--TCF
There's Always a Way To Find a Way	1973	Can.
Toby McTeague	1986	Can.
True Nature of Bernadette	1972	Can.
Two Solitudes	1978	Can.
Valerie	1969	Can.
Vindicator	1986	Can.
Visiting Hours	1981	Can.
Wild Thing	1987	US
With the Blood of Others	1974	Fr.

646a. ROBIN VIDGEON

The Fly II	1989	TCF
The Fool	1990	GB
Hellbound: Hellraiser II	1988	US
Hellraiser	1987	GB
Mr. North	1988	US
Nightbreed	1990	TCF
Parents *	1989	US
The Penitent	1988	US

647. SACHA VIERNY (1919-   )

Baxter, Vera Baxter	1977	Fr.
Beau Pere	1981	Fr.
Belle de Jour	1967	Fr.--AA
Belly of an Architect	1987	Fr.
The Bulgarian Night	1971	Fr.
The Burned Barns	1973	Fr.--TCF
Caroline Cherie	1968	Fr.
The Cook, the Thief, His Wife &		
Her Lover	1989	Fr./Holl.
Dance of the Herons	1966	Ger./Holl.
The Dead Season of Loves	1961	Fr.
The Devil in the Box	1977	Fr.
Drowning by Numbers	1988	GB
The Future of Emily	1984	Fr./Ger.
La Guerre Est Finie	1966	Fr./Swed.
The Hand	1969	Fr.--WB
Hiroshima, Mon Amour *	1959	Fr./Jap.
The Holy Family	1973	Fr./Switz.
Hypothesis of the Stolen Painting *	1979	Fr.
Last Year at Marienbad	196	Fr./It.
The Lost Way	1980	Belg./Fr./Switz.
Love Unto Death	1984	Fr.

Mon Oncle d'Amerique	1980	Fr.
The Monk	1973	Fr.
Muriel	1963	Fr./It.
La Musica	1967	Fr.--UA
The Public Woman	1984	Fr.
The Season for Love	1963	Fr.
Stavisky	1974	Fr.
Stepfather	1981	Fr.
A Taste for Women	1966	Fr./It.
The Tattooed One	1968	Fr.
The Three Crowns of a Sailor	1983	Fr.
Who Cares ... Anatomy of a Delivery Boy	1971	Fr.
Zed and Two Noughts	1985	Fr.

648. REYNALDO VILLALOBOS

The Ballad of Gregorio Cortez	1983	Emb.
Band of the Hand	1986	Tri-S.
Blame It on Rio	1984	TCF
Coupe de Ville	1990	Univ.
Desert Bloom	1986	Col.
Lucas	1986	TCF
Major League	1989	Par.
Mike's Murder	1984	WB
Nine to Five	1980	TCF
Punchline	1988	Col.
Risky Business *	1983	WB
Saving Grace	1986	Col./Emb.
Sibling Rivalry	1990	Col.
Urban Cowboy	1980	Par.
Windy City	1984	CBS/WB

649. ERNEST VINCZE

Biggles	1986	GB
Business As Usual	1987	GB--Cannon
Got It Made	1971	GB
Hitler's S.S.--Portrait in Evil	1985	GB--Cannon
Jane Austen in Manhattan	1981	US
Roseland	1977	US
Scrubbers	1982	GB
The Secret Policeman's Ball	1980	GB
Shanghai Surprise	1986	MGM
Sharma and Beyond	1986	GB
Winstanley	1975	GB

650. PAUL VOGEL (1899-1975)

Angels in the Outfield	1952	MGM
Arena	1953	MGM
The Bar Sinister	1955	MGM
Battleground	1949	MGM
Bernardine	1957	TCF
Black Hand	1949	MGM
The Clown	1952	MGM
Dial 1119	1950	MGM
Down in San Diego	1941	MGM
Drums of Africa	1963	MGM
Everybody's Doing It *	1938	RKO
Fit for a King	1937	RKO
The Gazebo	1959	MGM
The Girl in White	1952	MGM
The Girl Who Had Everything	1953	MGM
Go for Broke!	1951	MGM
Green Fire	1954	MGM
The Gun Hawk	1963	AA
Half a Hero	1953	MGM
The Happy Years	1950	MGM
High Society	1956	MGM
High Wall	1947	MGM
Hold On!	1966	MGM
Holiday for Sinners	1952	MGM
Interrupted Melody *	1955	MGM
It's a Dog's Life	1955	MGM
Jupiter's Darling *	1954	MGM
Kid Glove Killer	1942	MGM
Lady in the Lake	1946	MGM
A Lady without Passport	1950	MGM
The Magic Sword	1962	UA
Mail Order Bride	1963	MGM
Merton of the Movies	1947	MGM
The Money Trap	1966	MGM
Pacific Rendezvous	1942	MGM
Period of Adjustment	1962	MGM
Pilot Number Five	1943	MGM
The Potters	1927	Par.
Public Pigeon No. 1	1957	RKO/Univ.
The Rack	1956	MGM
The Return of the Seven	1966	UA
Riot On Sunset Strip	1967	AIP
Rogue's March	1953	MGM
Rose Marie	1954	MGM
The Rounders	1965	MGM
Running Wild	1927	Par.
The Scarlet Coat	1955	MGM
Scene of the Crime	1949	MGM
The Sellout	1951	MGM

Signpost to Murder	1967	MGM
The Student Prince	1954	MGM
Sunday Punch	1942	MGM
The Tall Target	1951	MGM
Tarzan the Ape Man	1959	MGM
The Tender Trap	1955	MGM
They All Came Out *	1939	MGM
Three Guys Named Mike	1951	MGM
The Time Machine	1960	MGM
Tish	1942	MGM
Village of the Giants	1965	US
Watch the Birdie	1950	MGM
When the Boys Meet the Girls	1965	MGM
Wide Open Faces *	1938	Col.
The Wings of Eagles	1957	MGM
The Wonderful World of the Brothers Grimm	1962	MGM
You for Me	1952	MGM

651. NICHOLAS VON STERNBERG

Appointment with Fear	1985	US
Beyond the Doors	1989	US
Dangerous Love	1988	US
Dr. Alien	1989	US
Dolemite	1975	US
Final Justice	1985	US
Gas Pump Girls	1979	US
Hospital Massacre	1982	Cannon
Joysticks	1983	US
Jungle Warriors	1984	Ger./Mex.
Petey Wheatstraw	1978	US
Pink Motel	1982	US
Slaughterhouse Rock	1988	US
Texasville	1990	Col.
Tourist Trap	1979	US
Uninvited	1988	US
Valet Girls	1987	US
Wacko	1983	US

652. BLAKE WAGNER

Arizona Express	1924	Fox
Atta Boy *	1926	Pathe
Finnegan's Ball	1927	US
Fools in the Dark *	1924	US
Play Safe	1927	Pathe

653.   FRITZ ARNO WAGNER (1889-1958)

Adrienne Lecouvreur	1938	Fr.
Amphytrion	1935	Ger.--UFA
April 1, 2000	1953	Aust.
Be Mine Tonight *	1933	GB
Beautiful Adventure *	1932	Ger.--UFA
Beggar's Opera	1931	Ger.--WB
Beloved Corinna	1957	Ger.
Blood Bonds	1983	Ger.
Brand in the Opera *	1930	Ger.
Der Brennende Acker *	1922	Ger.
The Broken Jug	1937	Ger.--UFA
Comrades of 1918 *	1931	Ger.
Destiny *	1921	Ger.
Dolly Gets Ahead *	1931	Ger.--UFA
Dolly's Career *	1930	Ger.--UFA
Eternal Love	1960	Ger.
Die Dreigroschenoper	1931	Ger.
Film without a Name	1950	Ger.
Fire in the Opera *	1932	Ger.
Four Infantry Men	1930	Ger.
Girls behind Bars	1950	Ger.
Glamourous Night	1937	Ger.--Rep.
Hotel Adlon	1955	Ger.
Kameradschaft	1931	Ger.
Die Liebe der Jeanne Ney *	1927	Ger.
M *	1931	Ger.--Par.
The Man Who Was Sherlock Holmes	1937	Ger.--UFA
Der Mude Tod *	1921	Ger.
Nosferatu *	1922	Ger.
Palace Scandal	1949	Ger.
Ronny	1932	Ger.--UFA
Rose of Stamboul	1953	Ger.
Schatten	1923	Ger.
The Song of Night	1932	Ger.--UFA
Spies	1928	Ger.--MGM/UFA
The Testament of Dr. Mabeuse	1933	Ger.
The Threepenny Opera	1931	Ger.--WB
Warning Shadows	1922	Ger.
Zu Chronik von Griesthuis *	1924	Ger.

654.   SIDNEY WAGNER

Andy Hardy Meets a Debutante *	1940	MGM
Apache Trail	1943	MGM
Bataan	1943	MGM
Blonde Inspiration	1941	MGM
Born To Sing	1941	MGM
Boys' Town	1938	MGM

Cabin in the Sky	1943	MGM
A Christmas Carol	1938	MGM
The Cross of Lorraine	1944	MGM
The Cyclone Rider	1924	Fox
Dragon Seed	1944	MGM
Fair Warning	1937	TCF
Fiesta *	1947	MGM
The Fighting Ranger	1934	Col.
Gallant Sons	1940	MGM
The Gay Retreat	1927	Fox
Getaway	1941	MGM
Henry Goes to Arizona *	1939	MGM
Hideout *	1934	MGM
High Barbaree	1947	MGM
I'll Wait For You	1941	MGM
Kathleen	1941	MGM
The Kid from Texas	1939	MGM
Let Freedom Ring	1939	MGM
The Man from Down Under	1943	MGM
Masked Emotions	1929	Fox
More Pay-Less Work	1926	Fox
The News Parade *	1928	Fox
Northwest Passage *	1940	MGM
The Omaha Trail	1942	MGM
One Mile From Heaven	1937	TCF
Prep and Pep *	1928	Fox
The Postman Always Rings Twice	1946	MGM
Rationing	1943	MGM
Rich But Honest	1927	Fox
The Romance of Rosy Ridge	1947	MGM
The Sailor Takes a Wife	1945	MGM
Why Sailors Go Wrong	1928	Fox
Sins of Man	1936	TCF
Sporting Blood	1940	MGM
A Stranger in Town	1943	MGM
Tarzan's New York Adventure	1942	MGM
This Man's Navy	1945	MGM
To Mary with Love	1936	TCF
Tortilla Flat	1942	MGM
Under Your Spell	1936	TCF
Whistling in the Dark	1941	MGM
Woman Wise	1928	Fox
Young Tom Edison	1940	MGM

655. WILLIAM WAGNER

The Country Cousin	1919	Selz.
The Dangerous Paradise	1920	Selz.
The Girl from Nowhere	1921	Selz.
The Imp	1920	Selz.

The Incorrigible Dukane	1915	Par.
Mary Moreland	1917	US
The Miracle of Manhattan	1921	Selz.
Poor Dear Margaret Kirby	1921	Selz.
The Pretenders	1916	Metro.
The Referee	1922	Selz.
Remorseless Love	1921	Selz.
The Way of a Maid	1921	Selz.
Whispers	1920	Selz.
Why Announce Your Marriage *	1922	Selz.
Wide Open Town	1922	Selz.
The Woman Game	1920	Selz.

656. KEITH WAGSTAFF

Backstage	1988	Aus.
The Coolangatta Gold	1984	Aus.
Man from Snowy River	1983	Aus.--TCF
Return to Snowy River: Part II	1988	Aus.
Running from the Guns	1987	Aus.

657. RIC WAITE

Adventures in Babysitting	1987	Dis.
Border *	1982	Univ.
Brewster's Millions	1985	Univ.
Class	1983	Orion
Cobra *	1986	Cannon/WB
Defiance	1980	US
Footloose	1984	Par.
Forty Eight Hours	1982	Par.
The Great Outdoors	1988	Univ.
The Long Riders	1980	UA
Marked for Death	1990	TCF
On the Nickel	1980	US
The Other Side of the Mountain Part 2	1977	Univ.
Summer Rental	1985	Par.
Tex	1982	Dis.
Volunteers	1985	Tri-S.

658. CLAUDE HENRY WALES

Deuce Duncan	1918	US
Madame Sphinx	1918	US
The Mask	1918	US
The Painted Lily	1918	US
The Price of Applause	1918	US

Tony America	1918	US
Until They Get Me	1917	US

659. JOSEPH WALKER (1892-1985)

Affair in Trinidad	1952	Col.
Aflame in the Sky	1927	US
After the Storm	1928	Col.
Air Hostess	1933	Col.
American Madness	1932	Col.
Arizona *	1941	Col.
Around the Corner	1930	Col.
The Awful Truth	1937	Col.
Back to God's Country	1919	FN
Baited Trap	1926	US
Bedtime Story	1941	Col.
Below the Sea	1933	Col.
Beware of Blondes	1928	Col.
The Bitter Tea of General Yen	1933	Col.
Born Yesterday	1950	Col.
Broadway Bill	1934	Col.
Broadway Hoofer	1929	Col.
By Whose Hand? *	1932	Col.
Chalk Marks *	1924	US
Clash of the Wolves	1925	WB
The College Hero	1927	Col.
Court-Martial	1928	Col.
Danger	1923	US
The Dark Past	1948	Col.
Death Valley	1927	US
The Deceiver	1931	Col.
Dirigible *	1931	Col.
The Dixie Flyer *	1926	US
Driftwood	1928	Col.
The Eternal Woman	1929	Col.
A Feather in Her Hat	1935	Col.
Fighting Courage	1925	US
Fire and Steel *	1927	US
First Comes Courage	1943	Col.
Flaming Fury	1926	US
Flight	1929	Col.
The Flying U Ranch	1927	US
Forbidden	1932	Col.
The Girl Friend	1935	Col.
Girl from God's Country	1921	US
The Great Mail Robbery	1927	US
The Grub Stake	1923	US
The Guilt of Janet Ames	1498	Col.
Harriet Craig	1950	Col.
He Stayed for Breakfast	1940	Col.

Here Comes Mr. Jordan	1941	Col.
His Girl Friday	1940	Col.
The Impatient Years *	1944	Col.
Isle of Forgotten Woman	1927	Col.
It Happened in Hollywood	1937	Col.
It Happened One Night	1934	Col.
It's a Wonderful Life *	1946	RKO
The Jolson Story	1946	Col.
Joy of Living	1938	RKO
Ladies Must Play	1930	Col.
Ladies of Leisure	1930	Col.
Lady for a Day	1933	Col.
Lady Raffles	1928	Col.
Let Women Alone	1925	PDC
Let's Live Tonight	1935	Col.
Lost Horizon	1937	Col.
Love Me Forever	1936	Col.
Lover Come Back	1931	Col.
The Marrying Kind	1952	Col.
Mating of Millie	1948	Col.
Midnight Mystery	1930	RKO
The Miracle Woman	1932	Col.
Mr. Deeds Goes to Town	1936	Col.
Mr. Smith Goes to Washington	1939	Col.
Mr. Soft Touch *	1949	Col.
Mr. Winkle Goes to War	1944	Col.
The Mob	1951	Col.
Modern Mothers	1928	Col.
Murder on the Roof	1930	Col.
The Music Goes Round	1936	Col.
My Sister Eileen	1941	Col.
Never a Dull Moment	1950	RKO
A Night To Remember	1942	Col.
North Star	1925	US
Nothing To Wear	1928	Col.
Object-Alimony	1928	Col.
One Night of Love	1934	Col.
Only Angels Have Wings *	1939	Col.
The Outlaw Dog	1927	US
Penny Serenade	1941	Col.
Platinum Blonde	1931	Col.
The Pleasure Buyers	1925	WB
The Quitter	1929	Col.
Rain or Shine	1930	Col.
Ransom	1928	Col.
Restless Youth	1928	Col.
Richard the Lion-Hearted	1923	US
Roughly Speaking	1945	WB
Say It with Sables	1928	Col.
Shanghaied	1927	US
She Wouldn't Say Yes	1945	Col.

Shopworn	1932	Col.
Shopworn Angel	1938	MGM
The Sideshow	1928	Col.
Song of Love	1929	Col.
Stage Kisses	1927	Col.
Start Cheering	1938	Col.
The Street of Illusion	1928	Col.
Submarine	1928	Col.
Subway Express	1931	Col.
Tales of Manhattan	1942	TCF
Tars and Spars	1946	Col.
Tarzan and the Golden Lion	1927	US
Tell It to the Judge	1949	Col.
Temporary Sheriff	1926	US
Tentacles of the North	1926	US
That Certain Thing	1928	Col.
Theodora Goes Wild	1936	Col.
There's That Woman Again	1938	Col.
They All Kissed the Bride	1942	Col.
This Thing Called Love	1941	Col.
The Tigress	1927	Col.
Together Again	1944	Col.
Too Many Husbands	1940	Col.
Trial Marriage	1929	Col.
The Velvet Touch	1948	RKO
Virgin Lips	1928	Col.
Virtue	1932	Col.
What a Woman!	1931	Col.
What Shall I Do?	1924	US
What's Buzzin' Cousin?	1943	Col.
When You're in Love	1937	Col.
The Wise Virgin	1924	PDC
A Woman of Distinction	1950	Col.
You Belong to Me	1941	Col.
You Can't Take It with You	1938	Col.

660. VERNON WALKER (1894-1948)

Crashing Hollywood *	1937	RKO
A Damsel in Distress *	1937	RKO
Don't Tell the Wife *	1937	RKO
End of the Rope	1923	US
Firebrand Trevision	1920	Fox
Flight from Glory *	1937	RKO
The Flying Irishman *	1939	RKO
Forbidden Trails	1920	Fox
The 40th Floor	1924	Pathe
A Front Page Story	1922	Vita.
Genius at Work *	1946	RKO
George White's Scandals *	1945	RKO

High Flyers *	1937	RKO
King Kong *	1933	RKO
THe Last Straw	1920	Fox
The Long Loop on the Pecos	1927	Pathe
Look Who's Laughing *	1941	RKO
The Man from Hardpan	1927	Pathe
Mary of the Movies *	1923	Col./US
Mummy's Boys *	1936	RKO
Music for Madame *	1937	RKO
None But the Lonely Heart *	1944	RKO
Nurse Edith Cavell *	1939	RKO
Purple Dawn *	1923	US
The Right of the Strongest	1924	Selz.
Robin Hood, Jr.	1923	US
Show Business *	1944	RKO
The Silver Streak *	1935	RKO
The Sky's the Limit *	1942	RKO
Son of Kong *	1933	RKO
Super Sleuth *	1937	RKO
Ten Nights in a Bar-Room	1931	US
Top Hat *	1935	RKO
Would You Forgive?	1920	Fox

661. FRED WALLER, JR

The Cradle Buster	1922	US
Grit	1924	US
Puritan Passions	1923	US
Second Fiddle	1923	US
Youthful Cheaters	1923	US

662. DAVID WALSH

Ace Eli and Rodger of the Skies *	1973	TCF
Cactus in the Snow	1972	US
California Suite	1978	Col.
Chapter Two *	1979	Col.
Cleopatra Jones	1973	WB
Corky	1971	MGM
The Crazy World of Julius Vrooder	1974	TCF
Evel Knievel	1971	US
Everything You Always Wanted to Know about Sex But Were Afraid to Ask	1972	UA
Fatal Beauty	1987	MGM-UA
Foul Play	1978	Par.
The Goodbye Birl	1977	MGM/WB
A Gunfight	1970	Par.
Hero at Large	1980	MGM
House Calls	1978	Univ.

I Ought to Be in Pictures	1982	TCF
I Walk the Line	1970	Col.
The In-Laws	1979	WB
Just You and Me, Kid	1979	Col.
The Laughing Policeman	1973	TCF
Making Love	1982	TCF
Max Dugan Returns	1983	TCF
Monte Walsh	1970	NG
Murder by Death	1976	Col.
My Science Project	1985	Dis.
Only When I Laugh	1981	Col.
Outrageous Fortune	1987	Dis.
The Other Side of the Mountain	1975	Univ.
Private Benjamin	1980	WB
Rollercoaster *	1977	Univ.
Romantic Comedy	1983	MGM-UA
Scott Joplin	1977	Univ.
Seems Like Old Times	1980	Col.
Silver Streak	1976	TCF
Sleeper	1973	UA
Summer School	1987	Par.
The Sunshine Boys	1975	UA
Taking Care of Business	1990	BV
Unfaithfully Yours	1984	TCF
W. C. Fields and Me	1975	Univ.
W.H.I.F.F.S.	1975	TCF

663. ANDY WARHOL (1927-   )

Blue Movie	1969	US
The Chelsea Girls	1966	US
I a Man	1967	US
The Life of Juanita Castro	1965	US
The Loves of Ondine	1968	US
More Milk Evette	1966	US
My Hustler	1965	US
Nude Restaurant		

664. DWIGHT WARREN

The Altar Stairs	1922	Univ.
Dangerous Traffic	1926	US
Double Dealing	1923	Univ.
In Slumberland	1917	US
The Midnight Patrol	1918	Selz.
Sand *	1920	Par.
The Shock	1923	Univ.
Singer Jim McKee	1927	Par.
The Spoilers *	1923	Gold.
Wild Bill Hickok *	1923	Par.

665. JOHN F. WARREN

Anything Goes	1956	Par.
Angel, Angel Down We Go	1969	AIP
Beau James	1957	Par.
The Colossus of New York	1958	Par.
The Cosmic Man	1959	AA
The Counterfeit Killer	1968	Univ.
The Country Girl	1954	Par.
Dark Intruder	1965	Univ.
Daughter of Dr. Jekyll	1957	AA
For Singles Only	1968	Univ.
The Love-Ins	1967	Col.
The Proud and the Profane	1956	Par.
The Search for Bridey Murphy	1956	Par.
The Seven Little Foys	1955	Par.
Tammy and the Millionaire *	1967	Univ.
A Time To Sing	1968	MGM
Torn Curtain	1966	MGM
The Young Runaways	1968	MGM
Zero Hour!	1957	Par.

666. GILBERT WARRENTON

Abilene Trail	1951	Mon.
Aladdin and His Lamp	1952	Mon.
Alias the Deacon	1928	Univ.
Alimony	1949	EL
Anna Ascends	1922	Par.
The Atomic Submarine	1960	AA
The Bachelor Daddy *	1922	Par.
The Barefoot Boy	1938	Mon.
Beauty and the Beast	1963	UA
Beggars in Ermine	1934	Mon.
Behind Masks	1921	Par.
Beware of Windows	1927	Univ.
Blue Blood	1951	Mon.
Blue Grass of Kentucky	1950	Mon.
Born to Gamble	1935	US
Boy of the Streets	1937	Mon.
Boy Who Caught a Crook	1961	UA
Breezing Home	1937	Univ.
A Bride for Henry	1937	Mon.
The Burning Trail	1925	Univ.
Butterflies in the Rain	1926	Univ.
California Straight Ahead	1925	Univ.
Captain of the Guard	1930	Univ.
The Cat and the Canary	1927	Univ.
Champagne for Breakfast	1935	Col.
Cherokee Uprising	1950	Mon.

City of Silent Men	1942	PRC
The Clown and the Kid	1961	UA
Colorado Ambush	1951	Mon.
Coronado	1935	Par.
County Fair	1950	Mon.
Cowboy and the Prizefighter	1950	EL
Dawn of the East	1921	Par.
Devil's Mate	1933	Mon.
Diary of a High School Bride	1959	AIP
Dragstrip Riot	1958	AIP
8 Girls in a Boat	1934	Par.
Federal Bullets	1937	Mon.
The Fighting Redhead	1949	EL
The Flight That Disappeared	1961	UA
Flowing Gold *	1924	FN
Forbidden Island	1959	Col.
Ghost of Dragstrip Hollow	1959	AIP
Ghost of the China Sea	1958	Col.
The Golden Fleece	1918	US
The Great Dan Patch	1949	UA
The Great Jesse James Raid	1953	Lip.
Gun Street	1961	UA
Headline Crasher	1937	US
Heart of the Hills	1919	FN
Hello Everybody	1933	Par.
Here Comes Cookie	1935	Par.
The Hide-Out	1931	Univ.
High School Hellcats	1958	AIP
High Tide	1918	US
Hold Your Man	1929	Univ.
Hot Rod	1950	Mon.
Humoresque	1920	Par.
Hush Money	1921	Par.
Incident in an Alley	1962	UA
Jazz Mad	1928	Univ.
A Lady's Profession	1933	Par.
The Land of Hope	1921	US
The Lane That Had No Turning	1922	Par.
The Last Edition	1925	US
The Law of the Great Northwest	1918	US
The Legend of Tom Dooley	1959	Col.
The Leopardess	1923	Par.
Little Italy	1921	US
Lonesome	1928	Univ.
The Loudspeaker	1934	Mon.
Love and Glory	1924	Univ.
The Love Thrill	1927	Univ.
The Love Trap	1929	Univ.
Mama Loves Papa	1933	Par.
The Man Who Laughs	1927	Univ.
A Man's Past	1927	Univ.

The Marines Are Here	1938	Mon.
Massacre	1956	TCF
Master of the World	1961	AIP
The Meddler	1925	Univ.
Mesa of Lost Women *	1956	US
Missing Millions	1922	Par.
Mississippi Gambler	1929	Univ.
Montana Desperado	1951	Mon.
More To Be Pitied Than Scorned	1922	US
Mother Knows Best	1928	Fox
Mother's Cry	1930	FN/WB
No Place to Hide	1956	AA
The Non-Stop Flight	1926	US
Oh, Doctor!	1925	Univ.
Operation Bikini	1963	AIP
The Other Woman's Story *	1925	US
Outlaw Gold	1951	Mon.
Outlaws of Texas	1950	Mon.
Panic in the Year Zero!	1962	AIP
Paradise Isle	1937	Mon.
Paratroop Command	1959	AIP
The Phantom Broadcast	1933	US
The Plastic Age *	1925	US
The Plaything of Broadway	1921	US
Rainbow's End	1935	US
Ride, Ryder, Ride!	1949	EL
Roll Thunder Roll	1949	EL
Romance of the Limberlost	1938	Mon.
Rose of the Rio Grande	1938	Mon.
Saintly Sinners	1962	UA
Saleslady	1937	Mon.
Scandal	1929	Univ.
Secret of Deep Harbor	1961	UA
Secrets of the Night	1925	Univ.
Seven Days *	1925	PDC
Show Boat	1929	Univ.
Sins of Jezebel	1953	Lip.
Smilin' at Trouble	1925	US
Spanish Cape Mystery	1935	US
The Sphinx	1933	Mon.
Submarine Seahawk	1959	AIP
Sunset Range	1935	US
Surrender	1927	Univ.
Taxi! Taxi!	1927	Univ.
Telephone Operator	1938	Mon.
Ten Cents a Dance *	1931	Col.
Texas Bad Man	1953	AA
They Raid by Night	1942	PRC
Ticket to Crime	1934	US
Tom and His Pals *	1926	US
The Traffic Cop	1926	US

Under the Big Top	1938	Mon.
Under the Red Robe *	1923	Gold.
The White Orchid	1954	UA
Woman Unafraid	1934	US
You Have To Run Fast	1961	UA
Young Daniel Boone	1950	Mon.

667. NORMAN WARWICK

The Abominable Dr. Phibes	1971	GB--AIP
Confessions of a Window Cleaner	1974	GB--Col.
The Creeping Flesh	1972	GB--Col.
Doctor and the Devils *	1985	GB--TCF
Dr. Jekyll and Sister Hyde	1971	GB--AIP/Ham.
During One Night	1961	GB
Follow That Horse!	1961	GB--WB
The Godsend	1980	Can.--Cannon
Italian Job *	1969	GB--Par.
Last Days of Man on Earth	1975	GB
The Last Valley *	1970	GB
One Night with You *	1948	GB--Univ.
Over the Odds	1961	GB--Rank
Private Angelo *	1949	GB
Spring and Port Wine	1970	GB--EMI
Stork Talk	1964	GB
Take Me High	1973	GB--EMI
Tales From the Crypt *	1972	GB
Tales That Witness Madness	1973	GB--Par.
They Came from Beyond Space	1967	GB
Torture Garden	1967	GB--Col.
The Trunk	1961	GB--Col.
The Young and the Guilty	1958	GB

668. DAVID WATKIN (1925-   )

The Bed Sitting Room	1969	GB--UA
The Boy Friend	1971	GB--MGM
Catch-22	1970	Par.
The Charge of the Light Brigade *	1968	GB--UA
Chariots of Fire	1981	GB--TCF
Cuba	1979	UA
A Delicate Balance	1973	AFT
Devils	1970	GB--WB
Endless Love	1981	Univ.
The Four Musketeers	1974	TCF
The Good Mother	1988	Dis./Touch.
Hamlet	1990	WB
Hanover Street	1979	GB--Col.

Help!	1965	GB--UA
The Homecoming	1973	AFT
How I Won the War	1967	GB--UA
Joseph Andrews	1977	GB--Par.
Journey to the Center of the Earth *	1989	Cannon
The Knack	1968	GB
Mademoiselle *	1966	Fr. GB--UA
Mahogany	1975	Par.
Marat/Sade	1966	GB--UA
Masquerade	1988	MGM-UA
Memphis Belle	1990	WB
Moonstruck	1987	MGM-UA
Out of Africa	1985	Univ.
Return to Oz	1985	Dis.
Robin and Marian	1976	GB--Col.
Sky Bandits	1986	GB
That Summer	1979	GB--Col.
The Three Musketeers	1973	TCF
To the Devil a Daughter	1975	GB--EMI
White Nights	1985	Col.
Yellow Dog		

669. FRANK WATTS

D.A.R.Y.L.	1985	Par.
Educating Rita	1983	GB--Col.
George and Mildred	1980	GB
Rising Damp	1980	GB
The Shillingbury Blowers	1980	GB

670. HARRY WAXMAN (1912-   )

Alf n' Family	1968	GB
The Anniversary	9168	GB--Ham./TCF
The Baby and the Battleship	1956	GB
The Bargee	1964	GB
The Beast in the Cellar	1970	GB--Cannon
Blue Blood	1973	GB
A Bridge Too Far *	1977	GB--UA
Brighton Rock *	1947	GB
Contraband Spain	1955	GB
The Cracksman	1963	GB--WB
Crooks in Cloisters	1964	GB
Cry of the Penguins	1971	GB
Dalia and the Sailors	1964	Isr.
Danger Route	1967	GB--UA
Day the Earth Caught Fire	1961	GB--Univ.
The Detective	1954	GB--Col.
Digby	1973	GB

Elephant Gun	1958	GB--Rank
Endless Night	1971	GB
Fame Is the Spur *	1947	GB
The Family Way	1966	GB--WB
Flight of the Doves	1971	Col.
Fury at Smugglers' Bay	1960	GB
The Gay Lady	1949	GB
Glory At Sea	1952	GB
The Golden Link	1954	GB
Green Grow the Rushes	1951	GB
I Thank a Fool	1962	GB--MGM
Innocent Sinners	1958	GB--Rank
Journey Together	1944	GB
Khartoum *	1966	GB--UA
Late Flowering Love	1981	GB
The Long Memory	1952	GB
Look Before You Love *	1948	GB
Man in the Moon	1960	GB
Meet Mr. Callaghan	1954	GB
My Sister and I	1948	GB
The Nanny	1965	GB--Ham./TC
Night Hair Child	1971	GB
Not Tonight Darling	1971	GB
The Pink Panther Strikes Again	1976	GB--UA
Robbery under Arms	1957	GB--Rank
The Roman Spring of Mrs. Stone	1961	GB--WB
Sapphire	1959	GB--Univ.
The Secret Partner	1961	GB--MGM
She	1965	GB--Ham./MC
The Sleeping Tiger	1954	GB
Some Will, Some Won't	1969	GB
Stolen Hours	1963	UA
Swiss Family Robinson	1960	Dis.
Sword of Lancelot	1962	GB--Univ.
Tears for Simon	1957	GB--Rank/Re
There's a Girl in My Soup	1970	GB--Col.
They Were Not Divided	1951	GB--Rank/UA
Third Man on the Mountain	1959	Dis.
Triple Deception	1956	GB--Rank
The Trygon Factor	1966	GB--WB
Twisted Nerve	1968	GB--NG
The Uncanny *	1977	Can./GB--Ra
Valley of Eagles *	1951	GB--Lip.
Vampyres, Daughters of Dracula	1974	GB
Waterfront	1950	GB
The Wicker Man	1973	GB--WB
Wonderwall	1969	GB

671. GEORGE WEBBER

An American Widow	1917	Metro.

Birth of a Boy	1938	US
The Blooming Angel	1920	Gold.
Boy! What a Girl	1947	US
Cinderella of the Hills	1921	Fox
The City of Comrades	1919	Gold.
The Coast of Folly	1925	Par.
The Concert	1921	Gold.
East Side, West Side	1927	Fox
The Eternal Mother	1917	Metro.
The Exciters	1923	FP
Extra! Extra!	1922	Fox
Fine Manners	1926	Par.
Follies Girl	1943	PRC
The Gay Lord Quex	1920	Gold.
Go West Young Man	1919	Gold.
Head over Heels	1922	Gold.
The House of Secrets	1929	US
Jinx	1919	Gold.
The Joy Girl *	1927	Fox
Just Out of College	1921	Gold.
The Little Red Schoolhouse	1923	US
Lord and Lady Algy	1919	Gold.
Love 'Em and Leave 'Em	1926	Par.
Madame Sans-Gene	1925	Par.
A Man and His Money	1919	Gold.
The Music Master *	1927	Fox
Night Life of New York	1925	Par.
One of the Finest	1919	Gold.
Pinto	1920	Gold.
Pots and Pans Peggie	1917	US
The Purple Highway *	1923	Par.
Sepia Cinderella	1947	US
The Slim Princess	1920	Gold.
The Snow Bride	1923	Par.
So's Your Old Man	1926	Par.
Stage Struck	1925	Par.
Syncopation *	1929	RKO
Thirty a Week	1918	Gold.
Tillie's Tomato Surprise	1915	US
The Untamed Lady	1926	Par.
Upstairs	1919	Gold.
Wages of Virtue	1924	Par.
What Happened to Rosa?	1921	Gold.

672. HAROLD WELLMAN

Andy Hardy Comes Home *	1958	MGM
Atlantis	1961	MGM
Darling Lili *	1970	Par.
First To Fight	1967	WB

The Great Race *	1965	WB
THe Invisible Boy	1957	MGM
Key Witness	1960	MGM
MacKenna's Gold *	1969	Col.
Muscle Beach Party	1964	AIP
Murder Is My Beat	1955	AA
The Virginian *	1929	Par.
Watusi	1959	MGM

673. CONRAD WELLS (1898-1930)

Behind That Curtain *	1929	Fox
Captain Lash	1929	Fox
Chicken a La King	1928	Fox
The Desired Woman	1927	WB
Dressed to Kill	1928	Fox
Dry Martini	1928	Fox
Ginsburg the Great	1927	WB
Let's Go Places	1930	Fox
New Year's Eve	1929	Fox
Romance of the Underworld	1928	Fox
The Sky Hawk	1929	Fox
The Swell-Head	1927	Col.
True Heaven	1929	Fox
The Woman from Hell	1929	Fox

674. HAROLD WENSTROM

Adam and Eva *	1923	Par.
The Arizonian	1935	RKO
The Beauty Shop	1922	Par.
The Big House	1930	MGM
Born to Battle	1926	US
The Face in the Fog *	1922	Par.
Fast Life	1932	MGM
Gift of Gab *	1934	Univ.
The Go-Getter	1923	Par.
Great White Way *	1924	Gold.
Hazardous Valley	1927	US
Hell Divers	1931	MGM
Huddle	1932	MGM
Into Her Kingdom	1926	FN
Laddie	1935	RKO
The Lady in Ermine	1927	FN
The Lost Patrol	1934	RKO
The Midnight Watch	1927	US
Min and Bill	1930	MGM
Powdersmoke Range	1935	RKO
Proxies *	1921	Par.

The Saphead	1921	Metro.
The Secret Six	1931	MGM
Speak Easily	1932	MGM
Syncopating Sue	1926	FN
Their Big Moment	1934	RKO
Under the Red Robe *	1923	Gold.
Wednesday's Child	1934	RKO
What! No Beer?	1933	MGM
When Knighthood Was in Flower *	1922	Par.
The Wild Goose	1921	Par.
The Young Diana	1922	Par.
Zander the Great *	1925	Metro.-Gold.

675. BRIAN WEST

Age of Innocence	1977	Can.
Billy Two Hats	1973	GB -UA
Bloodbath at the House of Death *	1984	GB--EMI
84 Charing Cross Road	1987	Co.
Finders Keepers	1984	CBS/WB
Jacknife	1989	US
The Lonely Lady	1983	Univ.
Marvin and Tige	1983	US
Outback	1970	Aus.--UA
Russian Roulette	1975	AE
The Spikes Gang	1974	UA
Squeeze a Flower	9170	Aus.
Stories from a Flying Trunk *	1979	GB--EMI
Sunstruck	1972	Aus.
Yesterday's Hero	1979	GB--EMI

676. FREDERICK E. WEST

The Bounty Killer	1965	Emb.
Dragstrip Girl	1957	AIP
Flesh and the Spur	1956	AIP
Girls in Prison	1956	AIP
Gunslinger	1956	US
Invasion of the Saucer Men	1957	AIP
It Conquered the World	1956	AIP
Jet Attack	1958	AIP
Motorcycle Gang	1957	AIP
My World Dies Screaming	1958	US
The Oklahoma Woman	1956	US
Requiem for a Gunfighter	1965	Emb.
Runaway Daughters	1957	AIP
Shake, Rattle and Rock!	1957	AIP
The She-Creature	1956	AIP
Swamp Women	1956	US

677. HASKELL WEXLER (1926-   )

America, America	1963	WB
Angel Baby *	1960	AA
The Best Man	1964	UA
Blaze	1989	BV/Touch.
Bound for Glory	1976	UA
Colors	1988	Orion
Coming Home	1978	UA
A Face in the Rain	1963	US
The Hoodlum Priest	1961	UA
In the Heat of the Night	1967	UA
Lookin' To Get Out	1982	Par.
Lonnie	1963	US
The Loved One	1965	MGM
Matewan	1987	US
Medium Cool	1969	Par.
One Flew Over the Cuckoo's Nest	1975	UA
Second-Hand Hearts	1981	Par.
Studs Lonigan *	1960	UA
The Thomas Crown Affair	1968	UA
Three Fugutives	1989	BV/Touch.
The Trial of the Catonsville Nine	1972	US
Who's Afraid of Virginia Woolf?	1966	WB

678. CHARLES F. WHEELER

The Barefoot Executive	1970	Dis.
The Best of Times	1986	Univ.
The Bubble	1966	US
C. C. & Company	1970	AE
C.H.O.M.P.s	1979	US
Cat from Outer Space	1978	Dis.
Charley and the Angel	1974	Dis.
Che!	1969	TCF
Cold Turkey	1970	UA
Condorman	1981	Dis.
Duel at Diablo	1965	UA
Freaky Friday	1976	Dis.
Last Flight of Noah's Ark	1980	Dis.
Limbo	1972	Univ.
Molly and Lawless John	1972	US
One Little Indian	1973	Dis.
Pieces of Dreams	1970	UA
Silent Running	1971	Univ.
Slaughter's Big Ripoff	1973	US
Tora! Tora! Tora! *	1970	Jap.--TCF
Truck Turner	1974	AIP
The War between Men and Women	1972	NG
Yours, Mine and Ours	1968	UA

679. LESTER WHITE (1907-1958)

Absolute Quiet	1936	MGM
Andy Hardy Gets Spring Fever	1939	MGM
Andy Hardy's Blonde Trouble	1944	MGM
Andy Hardy's Private Secretary	1941	MGM
Babes on Broadway	1941	MGM
Bad Guy	1937	MGM
Beyond Tomorrow	1940	RKO
Blonde Fever	1944	MGM
Burn 'Em Up O'Connor	1938	MGM
Calling Dr. Kildare *	1939	MGM
Calm Yourself	1935	MGM
The Courtship of Andy Hardy	1942	MGM
The Daring Caballero	1949	UA
Drums of Tahiti	1954	Col.
Exclusive Story	1934	MGM
A Family Affair	1937	MGM
The Fireball	1950	TCF
Five against the House	1955	Col.
Fort Ti *	1953	Col.
The 49th Man	1953	Col.
The Fuller Brush Man	1948	Col.
Gasoline Alley	1951	Col.
The Good Humor Man	1950	Col.
Gun Fury	1953	Col.
Harem Girl	1952	Col.
He's a Cockeyed Wonder	1950	Col.
Henry Goes to Arizona *	1939	MGM
The Hidden Eye	1945	MGM
Hurricane Island	1951	Col.
Invisible Agent	1942	Univ.
Jesse James vs. The Daltons	1954	Col.
Judge Hardy's Children	1938	MGM
Jungle Jim	1948	Col.
Life Begins for Andy Hardy	1941	MGM
Little Mister Jim	1946	MGM
The Lone Gun	1954	UA
The Longest Night	1936	MGM
Lost in a Harem	1944	MGM
Love Finds Andy Hardy	1938	MGM
Massacre Canyon	1954	Col.
Miss Annie Rooney	1942	US
Monster That Challenged the World *	1957	UA
The Murder Man	1935	MGM
Out West with the Hardys	1938	MGM
The Outlaw Stallion	1954	Col.
Overland Pacific	1954	UA
The Prizefighter and the Lady	1933	MGM
Pushover	1954	Col.
Sherlock Holmes and the Secret Weapon	1942	Univ.

Sherlock Holmes in Washington	1943	Univ.
Sky Commando	1953	Col.
Society Doctor	1935	MGM
Speed	1936	MGM
Spirit of West Point	1947	US
The Stranger Wore a Gun	1953	Col.
Sworn Enemy	1936	MGM
Times Square Lady	1935	MGM
Top Gun	1955	UA
We Went to College	1936	MGM
When the Redskins Rode	1951	Col.
Whistling in Brooklyn	1943	MGM
White Lightning	1953	AA/Mon.
White Savage *	1943	Univ.
A Wicked Woman	1934	MGM
The Women Men Marry	1937	MGM
Women's Prison	1955	Col.
Wyoming Renegades	1955	Col.
A Yank on the Burma Road	1942	MGM
Yellow Jack	1938	MGM
You're Only Young Once	1938	MGM

680. WILLIAM WHITLEY

Alaska Passage	1959	TCF
The Big Gusher	1951	Col.
Blonde Bait *	1956	GB
Cat Women of the Moon	1953	US
Gunsmoke in Tucson	1958	AA
Jungle Manhunt	1951	Col.
Juvenile Jungle	1958	Rep.
Killer Ape	1953	Col.
Purple Heart Diary	1951	Col.
Quantrill's Raiders	1958	AA
Queen of Outer Space	1958	AA
Savage Mutiny	1953	Col.
Tarzan's Hidden Jungle	1955	RKO
The 3 Stooges in Orbit	1962	Col.
Valley of the Headhunters	1953	Col.
Voodoo Tiger	1952	Col.
A Yank in Indo-China	1952	Col.
A Yank in Korea	1951	Col.

681. JOHN WILCOX

Au Pair Girls	1972	GB
The Belstone Fox	1973	GB--Rank/TCF
The Black Knight	1954	Col.
Call Him Mr. Shatter *	1975	AE/Ham.

Carve Her Name with Pride	1958	GB--Rank
The Chairman	1969	TCF
The Cockleshell Heroes *	1955	GB--Col.
Connecting Rooms	1969	GB
Craze	1973	GB--WB
Daleks-Invasion Earth	1966	GB
Dr. Who and the Daleks	1965	GB
Dracula and Seven Golden Vampires	1975	GB--Pam.
The Evil of Frankenstein	1964	GB--Ham./Univ.
Expresso Bongo	1959	GB
The Ghoul	1975	GB--Rank
Harry Black and the Tiger	1958	GB--TCF
Hell Below Zero	1954	GB--Col.
Hound of the Baskervilles *	1978	GB
Hysteria	1964	GB--MGM
I Like Money	1962	GB--TCF
Invitation to Monte Carlo	1959	GB
Judith	1965	Par.
The Last Valley *	1970	GB
Legend of the Werewolf	1975	GB
Light Up the Sky	1960	GB
The Limbo Line	1969	GB
Mr. Denning Drives North	1951	GB
The Mouse That Roared	1959	GB--Col.
Nightmare	1964	GB--Ham./Univ.
Only Two Can Play	1962	GB--Col.
Outcast of the Islands	1951	GB
Paratrooper	1954	GB--Col.
The Passionate Sentry	1952	GB
The Psychopath	1966	GB--Par.
Safari *	1956	Col.
633 Squadron *	1964	UA
The Skull	1965	GB--Par.
Some People	1962	GB--AIP
Steptoe and Son	1972	GB--EMI
Summer Holiday	1962	GB--AIP
A Touch of Larceny	1959	GB--Par.
Victor Frankenstein *	1977	Ire./Swed.
A Twist of Sand	1968	GB--UA
Waltz of the Toreadors	1962	GB
Where's Jack?	1968	GB--Par.
Zarak *	1956	GB--Col.

682. HARRY WILD

Affair with a Stranger	1953	RKO
Arizona Legion	1939	RKO
The Bandit Trail	1941	RKO
The Big Game	1936	RKO
The Big Steal	1949	RKO

Bullet Code	1940	RKO
Come On Danger	1942	RKO
The Conqueror *	1955	RKO
Cornered	1945	RKO
Cyclone on Horseback	1941	RKO
Don't Tell the Wife *	1937	RKO
Dude Cowboy	1941	RKO
Easy Living	1949	RKO
The Falcon Out West	1944	RKO
The Falcon's Adventure *	1946	RKO
Farewell My Lovely	1944	RKO
The Fargo Kid	1941	RKO
The Fighting Gringo	1939	RKO
First Yank into Tokyo	1945	RKO
The French LIne	1953	RKO
Gambling House	1950	RKO
Gentlemen Prefer Blondes	1953	TCF
His Kind of Woman	1951	RKO
Johnny Angel	1945	RKO
Laddie	1940	RKO
Lady Behave	1937	Rep.
Land of the Open Range	1942	RKO
Las Vegas Story	1952	RKO
Lawless Valley	1938	RKO
Legion of the Lawless	1940	RKO
Macao	1952	RKO
Mademoiselle Fifi	1944	RKO
The Marshal of Mesa City	1939	RKO
Millionaires In Prison	1940	RKO
My Forbidden Past	1951	RKO
Nevada	1944	RKO
The Painted Desert	1938	RKO
Pitfall	1948	US
Portia On Trial	1937	Rep.
Racing Lady	1937	RKO
Racketeers of the Range	1939	RKO
The Renegade Ranger	1938	RKO
Riding the Wind	1941	RKO
Robbers of the Range	1941	RKO
The Rookie Cop	1939	RKO
Rookies in Burma	1943	RKO
The Saint in Palm Springs	1941	RKO
She Couldn't Say No	1952	RKO
Six-Gun Gold	1941	RKO
So This Is Washington	1943	RKO
Son of Paleface	1952	**Par.**
Stage Door Canteen	1943	US
Station West	1498	RKO
Strange Bargain	1949	RKO
Tarzan Triumphs	1943	RKO
Tarzan's Desert Mystery *	1943	RKO

They Won't Believe Me	1947	RKO
The Threat	1949	RKO
Till the End of Time	1946	RKO
Top of the World *	1955	UA
Trouble in Sundown	1939	RKO
Two Tickets to Broadway *	1951	RKO
Tycoon	1947	RKO
Underwater!	1955	RKO
Valley of the Sun	1942	RKO
Wagon Train	1940	RKO
Walk Softly Stranger	1950	RKO
Wanderers of the Wasteland	1945	RKO
West of the Pecos	1945	RKO
The Woman on the Beach *	1947	RKO

683. L. GUY WILKY

Adam's Rib	1923	Par.
After the Show	1921	Par.
An Alien Enemy	1918	US
Alimony	1918	FN
All of a Sudden Norma	1919	US
Beautiful but Dumb	1928	US
The Bedroom Window	1924	Par.
Bought and Paid For	1922	Par.
Clarence	1922	Par.
Conrad in Quest of His Youth	1920	Par.
Don't Call It Love	1924	Par.
The Eagle's Nest	1915	US
The Fast Set	1924	Par.
Gimme	1923	Gold.
Goddess of Lost Lake	1918	US
Hearts Asleep	1919	US
Honor's Cross	1918	Gold.
Icebound	1924	Par.
Jack Straw	1920	Par.
Josselyn's Wife	1919	US
A Law unto Herself	1918	US
Locked Doors	1925	Par.
The Lost Romance	1921	Par.
Lost--A Wife	1925	Par.
The Man Who Fights Alone	1924	Par.
A Man's Man	1917	US
Manslaughter *	1922	Par.
The Marriage Maker	1923	Par.
Men and Women	1925	Par.
Midsummer Madness	1920	Par.
Miss Lulu Bett	1921	Par.
New Brooms	1925	Par.
New Lives for Old	1925	Par.

Nice People	1922	Par.
One Woman to Another	1927	Par.
Only 38	1923	Par.
Our Leading Citizen *	1922	Par.
The Power of Silence	1928	US
The Prince Chap	1920	Par.
Shackled	1918	US
The Splendid Crime	1926	Par.
The Stranger *	1924	Par.
Tangled Threads	1919	US
The Tree of Knowledge	1920	Par.
The Trouble With Wives	1925	Par.
Two-Gun Betty	1918	US
The Turn of a Card	1918	US
What Every Woman Knows	1921	Par.
Wings *	1927	Par.
The Woman Michael Married	1919	US
The World's Applause		

684. IRVING WILLAT

Always in the Way	1915	Metro.
America *	1914	US
A Desert Wooing	1918	Par.
False Faces	1919	Par.
Spotlight Sadie	1919	Gold.
That Something	1921	US
Zeppelin's Last Raid	1918	US

685. BILLY WILLIAMS

Billion Dollar Brain	1967	UA
Boardwalk	1979	US
The Devil's Widow	1972	GB
Dreamchild	1985	GB--Univ.
Eagle's Wing	1979	GB--Rank
Eleni	1985	CBS/WB
Gandhi *	1982	GB--Col.
Going in Style	1979	WB
Just Ask for Diamond	1988	GB
Just Like a Woman	1966	GB
Kid Blue	1973	TCF
The Magus	1968	GB--TCF
The Manhattan Project	1986	TCF
The Mind of Mr. Soames	1970	GB--Col.
Monsignor	1982	TCF
Night Watch	1973	AE
On Golden Pond	1981	Univ.
Ordeal By Innocence	1984	GB--MGM-UA

Pope Joan	1972	GB--Col.
The Rainbow	1989	GB
Saturn Three	1980	US
The Silent Partner *	1978	Can.
Stella	1990	BV/Touch.
Sunday Bloody Sunday	1971	GB--UA
The Survivors	1983	Col.
Suspect	1987	Tri-S.
Thirty Is a Dangerous Age, Cynthia	1967	Col.
Two Gentlemen Sharing	1969	GB--AIP/Par.
Voyage of the Damned	1976	GB--AE
The Wind and the Lion	1975	MGM-UA
X, Y and Zee	1972	GB--Col.

686. CEDRIC WILLIAMS

Dick Barton Strikes Back	1949	GB
The Dynamiters	1956	GB
The Fake	1953	GB--UA
The Fatal Night	1948	GB--Col.
Meet Simon Cherry	1949	GB--Ham.
Third Time Lucky *	1949	GB
When Thief Meets Thief	1937	GB

687. DERICK WILLIAMS

Ask a Policeman	1938	GB--MGM
Beware of Pity	1946	GB
Flying Doctor	1936	Aus.
For Them That Trespass	1948	GB
The Ghost of St. Michael's	1941	GB--Eal.
High Fury	1947	GB--UA
Inspector Hornleigh *	1938	GB--TCF
Johnny in the Clouds	1945	GB--UA
My Brother Jonathan	1947	GB--AA

688. FRANK D. WILLIAMS

An Arabian Knight	1920	US
The Beggar Prince	1920	US
Black Roses	1921	US
Brand of Lopez	1920	US
The Devil's Claim	1920	US
The Dragon Painter	1919	US
The First Born	1921	US
His Debt	1919	US
The Illustrious Prince	1919	US
Li Tang Lang	1920	US

The Man Beneath	1919	US
Mickey	1918	US
The Poor Rich Man	1918	Metro.
Queen of the Sea	1918	Fox
Secret Strings	1918	Metro.
The Swamp	1921	US
Tillie's Punctured Romance	1914	US
Tong Man	1919	US
Where Lights Are Low	1921	US

689. LAWRENCE WILLIAMS

The Bishop's Emeralds	1919	Pathe
Crimes of Dr. Crespi	1936	US
Eve's Daughter	1918	Par.
The Family Closet	1921	US
Father Tom	1921	US
Follow the Leader	1930	Par.
Girl Habit	1931	Par.
His Wife	1915	US
The Idol of the North	1921	Par.
Impossible Catherine	1919	Pathe
Inspiration	1915	US
Lonely Heart	1921	US
The Man She Brought Back	1922	US
Marriage for Convenience	1919	US
Ramshackle House *	1924	US
The Sap from Syracuse	1930	Par.
The Struggle Everlasting	1918	US
Tarnished Lady	1931	Par.
Tevya	1939	US
The Wives of the Prophet	1926	US
Young Man of Manhattan	1930	Par.

690. WALTER WILLIAMS

Beware of the Bride	1922	Fox
Hearts of Youth	1921	Fox
Her Honor the Mayor	1920	Fox
The Husband Hunter	1920	Fox
The Iron Heart	1920	Fox
The Land of Jazz	1920	Fox
Lost Money	1919	Fox
Snares of Paris	1919	Fox
The Spirit of Good	1920	Fox
The Splendid Sin	1919	Fox
The Tattlers	1920	Fox
What Would You Do?	1920	Fox

691. GORDON WILLIS

All the President's Men	1976	WB
Annie Hall	1977	UA
Bad Company	1972	Par.
Bright Lights, Big City	1988	MGM-UA
Broadway Danny Rose	1984	Orion
Comes a Horseman	1978	UA
The Drowning Pool	1975	WB
End of the Road	1970	AA
The Godfather	1971	Par.
The Godfather Part Two	1974	Par.
The Godfather Part III	1990	Par.
Interiors	1978	UA
Klute	1971	WB
The Landlord	1970	UA
Little Murders	1971	TCF
Loving	1970	Col.
Manhattan	1979	UA
A Midsummer Night's Sex Comedy	1982	Orion/WB
The Money Pit	1986	Univ.
9/30/55	1978	Univ.
Paper Chase	1973	TCF
The Parallax View	1974	Par.
Pennies from Heaven	1982	MGM
The People Next Door	1970	AE
Perfect	1985	Col.
The Pick-Up Artist	1987	TCF
Presumed Innocent	1990	WB
Stardust Memories	1980	UA
Up the Sandbox *	1972	NG
Windows	1980	UA
Zelig	1983	Orion/WB

692. JAMES WILSON

Act of Murder	1964	GB--WB
The Agitator	1944	GB
Among Human Wolves	1939	GB
Appointment with Crime *	1945	GB
Arms and the Man *	1932	GB
Asking for Trouble	1941	GB
Balaclava *	1930	GB
Ball at Savoy	1936	GB
Candles at Nine *	1944	GB
The Common Touch	1941	GB
Counterblast	1948	GB
Crooks' Tour	1940	GB
The Crouching Beast	1935	GB--RKO
The Depraved	1947	GB

The Double	1963	GB
Dual Alibi	1947	GB
The Dummy Talks	1943	GB
The Gay Dog	1954	GB
Gay Intruders	1946	GB
Give Me the Stars	1944	GB
Heaven Is Around the Corner *	1943	GB
Incident at Midnight *	1966	GB
Invasion	1966	GB
Keepers of Youth *	1931	GB
Let the People Sing	1942	GB
The Living Dead	1936	GB
Lord Camber's Ladies	1932	GB
Love on the Dole	1941	GB
The Main Chance	1966	GB
Mrs. Fitzherbert *	1947	GB
No Room at the Inn	1948	GB
Old Mother Riley	1952	GB
Old Mother Riley at Home	1945	GB
Old Mother Riley Detective	1943	GB
Old Mother Riley in Business	1940	GB
Old Mother Riley in Society	1940	GB
Old Mother Riley Joins Up	1939	GB
Old Mother Riley MP	1939	GB
Old Mother Riley Overseas	1943	GB
Old Mother Riley's Circus	1941	GB
Old Mother Riley's Ghosts	1941	GB
Old Mother RIley's Jungle Treasure	1951	GB
On the Run	1967	GB
The Partner	1963	GB
Reluctant Heroes	1951	GB
Ricochet	1966	GB
Salute John Citizen	1942	GB
Satellite in the Sky *	1956	GB
2nd Bureau	1936	GB--RKO
The Secret of the Loch	1934	GB
The Shipbuilders	1943	GB
Strawberry Roan	1945	GB
The Tell-Tale Heart	1962	GB
Theatre Royal	1943	GB
Those Kids From Town	1941	GB
£20,000 Kiss	1964	GB
Twilight Hour	1944	GB
We'll Smile Again *	1942	GB
When We Are Married *	1942	GB
Wide Open Faces *	1938	Col.
Wings over Africa	1939	GB
Woman to Woman	1946	GB
Worm's Eye View	1951	GB

693. REX WIMPY

The Case of the Stuttering Bishop	1937	FN/WB
Challenge of the Range	1949	Col.
Desert Vigilante	1949	Col.
El Dorado Pass	1949	Col.
Laramie	1949	Col.
Only Saps Work	1930	Par.
Pointed Heels	1929	Par.
Quick on the Trigger	1949	Col.
The Reluctant Astronaut	1967	Univ.
Smoky Mountain Melody	1949	Col.
Stairs of Sand	1929	Par.
Talent Scout	1937	FN/WB

693a. OLIVER WOOD

The Adventures of Ford Fairlane	1990	TCF
Alphabet City	1984	US
Die Hard 2	1990	TCF
Don't Go in the House	1980	US
Feedback	1979	US
The Honeymoon Killers	1969	US
Joey	1985	US
Maya	1982	US
New Maniacs *	1986	US
Popdown	1968	GB
The Returning	1983	US
The Sex O'Clock News	1986	US

694. RALPH WOOLSEY

Black Eye	1974	WB
Black Spurs	1965	Par.
Claudelle Inglish	1961	WB
The Culpepper Cattle Company	1972	TCF
Deadhead Miles	1982	Par.
Dirty Little Billy	1972	Col.
Fire Sale	1977	TCF
The Great Santini	1979	Orion/WB
Honky	1971	US
The Iceman Cometh	1973	AFT
The Last Married Couple in America	1979	Univ.
The Lawyer	1970	Par.
Lifeguard	1976	Par.
Little Fauss and Big Halsey	1970	Par.
The Mack	1973	US
Mother, Jugs and Speed	1976	TCF
The New Centurions	1972	Col.

99 and 44/100 Per Cent Dead	1974	TCF
Oh God, Book II	1980	WB
The Pack	1977	WB
Persuader	1957	AA
The Promise	1978	Univ.
Rafferty and the Gold Dust Twins	1975	WB
The Strawberry Statement	1970	MGM
What Am I Bid?	1967	US
Wiretappers	1973	US

695. DAVID WORTH

Any Which Way You Can	1980	WB
Bloodsport	1988	Cannon
Bronco Billy	1980	WB
California Dreaming *	1979	AIp
China Cry	1990	US
Death Game	1977	US
Never Too Young To Die	1986	US
To Hell You Preach	1972	US

696. LATHROP WORTH

Battle Taxi	1954	UA
Billy the Kid vs. Dracula	1965	US
Fort Utah	1967	Par.
Gog	1954	UA
Hostile Guns	1967	Par.
I Was a Teenage Frankenstein	1957	AIP
Jesse James Meets Frankenstein's Daughter	1966	US
Shootout at Big Sag	1962	US
Unwed Mother	1958	AA

697. WALTER WOTTITZ (1911-1986)

Arm at the Left	1965	Fr.
La Cage	1975	Fr.
The Cat	1973	Fr.
A Cop	1973	Fr.
Dirty Money	1977	Fr.--AA
"Elite" Group	1974	Fr.
En Legitime Defense	1958	Fr.
From Hong Kong with Love	1975	Fr.
The Gardener of Argenteuil	1966	Fr.
Hoodlums' Sun	1967	Fr.
La Horse	1970	Fr.
Leather and Nylon	1969	Fr./It.

The Longest Day *	1962	TCF
Love Is at Stake	1957	Fr.
The Most Beautiful Life	1956	Fr.
The Passengers *	1977	Fr.--Col./WB
Those Daring Young Men in Their Jaunty Jalopies	1969	Fr./GB/It.--Par.
The Thunder of God	1965	Fr.
The Train *	1964	Fr./It.--UA
The Train	1973	Fr.--TCF
24 Hours in a Woman's Life	1968	Fr./Ger.
Under the Sign of the Bull	1969	Fr.
Up from the Beach	1965	TCF
The Upper Hand	1967	Fr./Ger./It.--Par.
Where Are You, Johnny?	1964	Fr.
Widow Couderc	1971	Fr.

698. DEWEY WRIGLEY

After Business Hours	1925	Col.
Before Midnight	1925	US
Blonde for a Night	1928	Pathe
The Danger Signal	1925	Col.
Fighting the Flames	1925	Col.
Girl in the Pullman	1927	Pathe
A Harp in Hock	1927	Pathe
Ladies of Leisure	1926	Col.
The Million Dollar Handicap *	1925	PDC
My Friend Flicka	1943	TCF
My Friend from India	1927	Pathe
Mystery Sea Raider *	1940	Par.
The Night Bride	1927	PDC
Paris at Midnight *	1927	PDC
Reap the Wild Wind *	1942	Par.
The Rush Hour	1927	Pathe
Shipwrecked *	1926	PDC
Steppin' Out	1925	Col.
Union Pacific *	1939	Par.
Wings in the Dark *	1935	Par.

699. ALVIN WYCKOFF

Adam's Rib *	1923	Par.
Affairs of Anatol *	1923	Par.
The Arab	1915	Par.
Blind Alleys	1927	Par.
Blood and Sand	1922	Par.
Bold Caballero *	1937	Rep.

The Border Legion	1924	Par.
Brewster's Millions	1914	FP
The Call of the North	1914	FP
The Canadian	1926	Par.
The Captive	1915	FP
Carmen	1915	FP
The Cheat	1915	Par.
Chimmie Fadden	1915	Par.
Chimmie Fadden Out West	1915	Par.
The Devil Stone	1917	US
Don't Change Your Husband	1919	US
The Dream Girl	1916	FP
Fires of Faith *	1919	Par.
Fool's Paradise *	1921	Par.
For Better, For Worse	1919	Par.
Forbidden Fruit	1921	Par.
The Girl of the Golden West	1915	FP
The Golden Chance	1916	Par.
The Heart of Nora Flynn	1916	FP
Irish Luck	1925	Par.
It's the Old Army Game	1926	Par.
Joan the Woman	1917	FP
Kindling	1915	FP
A Kiss in the Dark	1925	Par.
Lily of the Dust	1926	Par.
The Little American	1917	US
Lucky Devil	1925	Par.
Male and Female	1919	Par.
The Man from Home	1914	FP
The Man Who Found Himself	1925	Par.
The Man Who Saw Tomorrow	1922	Par.
Manslaughter *	1922	Par.
Maria Rosa	1916	FP
Men	1924	Par.
The New Klondike	1926	Par.
Night Ride	1930	Univ.
Old Home Week	1925	Par.
Old Wives for New	1918	US
Pleasure Mad *	1923	Metro.
A Romance of the Redwoods	1917	US
Rose of the Rancho	1914	FP
Saturday Night *	1922	Par.
Something To Think About *	1920	Par.
Spider Webs *	1927	US
The Spoilers *	1914	US
The Squaw Man	1918	US
The Storm	1930	Univ.
Strangers in the Night	1923	Metro.
The Swan	1925	Par.
Temptation	1916	Par.
Till I Come Back to You *	1918	Par.

Tin Gods	1926	Par.
The Trail of the Lonesome Pine	1916	FP
The Unafraid	1915	FP
The Virginian	1914	FP
The Warrens of Virginia	1915	FP
We Can't Have Everything	1918	US
What's His Name?	1914	FP
When a Girl Loves	1924	US
The Whispering Chorus	1918	US
Why Change Your Wife?	1920	Par.
The Wild Goose Chase	1915	FP
The Woman God Forgot	1917	US

700. REG WYER

Across the Bridge	1957	GB--Rank
An Alligator Named Daisy	1955	GB--Rank
All for Mary	1956	GB--Rank
Bad Sister	1947	GB--Rank
The Beachcomber	1954	GB--UA
Both Sides of the Law	1953	GB--Rank
The Brigand of Kandahar	1965	GB--WB
Burn, Witch, Burn	1962	GB--AIP
The Calendar *	1948	GB
Carry On Nurse	1959	GB
Carry On Teacher	1959	GB
Dancing with Crime	1947	GB--Par.
Daybreak	1946	GB
Dentist in the Chair	1961	GB
The Devils of Darkness	1964	GB--TCF
Diamond City *	1949	GB
Eyewitness	1956	GB--Rank
The Fast Lady	1962	GB--Rank
Father Came Too	1963	GB--Rank
Four Sided Triangle	1953	GB
A Girl in a Million *	1946	GB
The Happy Family	1952	GB
Heart of a Man	1959	GB--Rank
Here Come the Huggetts	1948	GB
Highly Dangerous *	1950	GB
Home to Danger	1951	GB
Island of Terror	1966	GB--Univ.
Island of the Burning Damned	1971	GB
The Kitchen	1961	GB
Mad Little Island	1958	GB--Rank
Make Mine Mink	1960	GB
Man in the Back Seat	1961	GB
Never Look Back	1952	GB--Ham.
Operation Amsterdam	1958	GB--Rank/TCF
Personal Affair	1953	GB--UA

A Place to Go	1963	GB
Play It Cool	1963	GB--AA
The Prisoner	1955	GB--Col.
Quartet *	1948	GB--EL/Rank
Rattle of a Simple Man	1964	GB
Sea Fury	1958	GB--Rank
The Seventh Veil 8	1945	GB--Univ.
So Long at the Fair	1950	GB--EL/Rank
Spaceways	1953	GB--Ham./Lip.
Those Fantastic Flying Fools	1967	GB--AIP
To Paris with Love	1954	GB
Trio *	1950	GB--Par.
True as a Turtle	1956	GB--Rank
Underworld Informers	1965	GB--Rank
The Unearthly Stranger	1963	GB--AIP
The Upturned Glass	1947	GB--Univ.
Violent Playground	1958	GB--Rank
The Weapon	1956	GB--Rep.
What a Whopper	1961	GB
The Years Between *	1946	GB--Univ.
You Know What Sailors Are	1954	GB--UA

701. EDWARD WYNARD

De Luxe Annie	1918	US
The Earl of Pawtucket	1915	Univ.
Fanchow the Cricket	1915	Par.
The Forbidden City *	1918	US
Her Only Way *	1918	US
The Man of Shame	1915	Univ.
Perjury	1921	Fox
The Red Viper	1919	US
The Safety Curtain	1918	US
The Tonopah Stampede of Gold	1913	US
The White Moll	1920	Fox
A Woman's Honor	1916	Fox

702. MANNY WYNN

Big Dig	1969	Isr.--US
Girl with Green Eyes	1963	GB
The Happiness Cage	1972	US
Having a Wild Weekend	1965	GB--WB
The Luck of Ginger Coffey	1964	Can.--US
A Nice Girl Like Me *	1969	AE
Smashing Time	1967	GB--Par.
Time Lost and Time Remembered	1966	GB--Rank
Tom Jones *	1963	GB
The Uncle	1966	GB

702a. ROBERT YEOMAN

Dead Heat	1988	US
Drugstore Cowboy	1989	US
Hero *	1985	US
Johnny Be Good	1988	Orion
Rampage	1987	US
Rented Lips	1988	US
Too Much Sun	1990	US
The Wizard	1989	Univ.

703. FREDERICK A. YOUNG (1902-   )

The Asphyx	1973	GB
Backstage *	1937	GB
The Barretts of Wimpole Street	1956	MGM
The Battle of Britain	1969	GB--UA
Bedelia	1946	GB
Bedevilled	1955	MGM
Beyond Mombasa	1957	Col.
Betrayed	1954	MGM
Bhowani Junction	1956	MGM
Bitter Sweet	1933	GB
Blackout	1940	GB
Bloodline	1979	Par.
The Blue Bird *	1976	TCF
Busman's Honeymoon	1940	GB
Caesar and Cleopatra *	1945	GB--EL/UA
Calling Bulldog Drummond	1951	GB--MGM
Come Out of the Pantry	1935	GB--UA
Conspirator	1949	GB--MGM
The Deadly Affair	1966	GB--Col.
Doctor Zhivago	1965	MGM
Edward My Son	1949	GB--MGM
Escape	1948	GB--TCF
Gideon's Day	1958	GB--Col.
Girl in the Street	1938	GB
Goodbye Mr. Chips	1939	GB--MGM
Gorgo	1960	GB--MGM
Great Expectations	1975	GB
Hand in Hand	1960	GB--Col.
I Accuse	1958	GB--MGM
Indiscreet	1958	WB
The Inn of the Sixth Happiness	1958	TCF
The Invaders	1941	GB--Col.
Invitation to the Dance *	1956	MGM
Invitation to the Wedding	1985	GB
Island in the Sun	1957	TCF
Knights of the Round Table *	1953	MGM
Lawrence of Arabia	1962	GB--Col.

The Little Damozel	1933	GB
The Little Hut	1957	MGM
Loss of Innocence	1961	GB--Col.
Lord Jim	1964	GB--Col.
Lust for Life *	1956	MGM
Luther	1973	AFT
Macbeth	1963	US
Magic Night	1933	GB--UA
Millions	1936	GB
Mogambo *	1953	MGM
Nell Gwyn	1934	GB--UA
Nicholas and Alexandra	1971	GB--Col.
A Night Like This	1932	GB
Night of the Garter	1933	GB--UA
Nurse Edith Cavell *	1939	RKO
On Approval	1930	GB
Peg of Old Drury	1935	GB--Par.
Permission To Kill	1975	Aus.--AE
Plunder	1930	GB
The Rat	1937	GB--RKO
Richard's Things	1981	GB
Rotten to the Core	1965	GB
Rough Cut	1980	GB--Par.
A Royal Divorce	1938	GB--Par.
Ryan's Daughter	1970	GB--MGM
The Seventh Dawn	1964	UA
The Show Goes On	1937	GB
Sinful Davey *	1968	GB--UA
Sixty Glorious Years	1938	GB--RKO
So Well Remembered	1947	GB--RKO
Solomon and Sheba	1959	UA
The Speckled Ban	1931	GB
Stevie	1978	GB
Suicide Legion	1940	GB
Sword of the Valiant *	1984	GB--Cannon
The Tamarind Seed	1974	GB--AE
Terror on a Train *	1952	MGM
Thark	1932	GB
That's a Good Girl	1933	GB--UA
Tilly of Bloomsbury	1931	GB--RKO
Treasure Island	1950	GB--Dis./RKO
Two's Company	1936	GB
Up for the Cup	1931	GB
Victoria the Great *	1937	GB--RKO
The "W" Plan 8	1930	GB--RKO
When Knights Were Bold	1936	GB
While I Live	1947	GB--TCF
The Winslow Boy	1948	GB--EL
You Only Live Twice *	1967	GB--UA
Young Mr. Pitt	1942	GB--TCF

704. HAL YOUNG

The Amateur Wife	1920	Par.
Anne of Green Gables	1919	US
Appearances	1921	GB--Par.
At the Mercy of Men	1918	US
Burn 'Em Up Barnes *	1921	US
The Call of Youth	1921	GB--Par.
Civilian Clothes	1920	Par.
Come Out of Kitchen	1919	Par.
The Common Law	1916	US
The Dark Silence	1916	US
Diplomacy	1920	FP
The Easiest Way	1917	Selz.
Easy To Get	1920	Par.
Fires of Faith *	1919	Par.
The Foolish Virgin	1917	Selz.
Girls *	1919	Par.
The Great Day	1921	GB--Par.
Heedless Moths	1921	US
Let's Elope	1919	Par.
The Lodger	1926	GB
Luck in Pawn	1919	Par.
Madame Butterfly	1915	FP
My Cousin	1918	US
Mystery Road	1921	GB--Par.
Princess of New York	1921	GB--Par.
Private Peat	1918	Par.
The Rat	1926	GB
Suspense *	1930	GB
The Two Brides	1919	Par.
Widow by Proxy *	1919	Par.
The Witness for the Defense *	1919	Par.
A Woman of Impulse	1918	par.

705. JACK YOUNG

Blue Blazes	1926	Univ.
Chasing Trouble	1926	Univ.
Drum Taps	1933	US
The Escape	1926	Univ.
A Little Girl in a Big City *	1925	US
My Lady of Whims	1925	US
The Nature Girl	1919	US
The Princess on Broadway	1927	Pathe
The Right Man	1925	US
Wanderers of the West	1941	Mon.

706. BERNARD ZITZERMANN

Alexina Mystery	1985	Fr.
La Balance	1983	Fr.
The Big Brother	1982	Fr.
The Big Pardon	1982	Fr.
Chouans!	1988	Fr.
Come to My Place...	1981	Fr.
The Devil in the Heart	1976	Fr.--Col.
The Falcon	1983	Fr.
The French Revolution: The Light Years/The Terrible Years *	1989	Can./Fr./Ger./It.
I Married a Shadow	1983	Fr.
If the Sun Never Returns	1987	Fr./Switz.
Journey to Paimpol	1985	Fr.
Man in Love	1987	Fr.
A Man Who Sleeps	1974	Fr.
Moliere	1978	Fr.--UA
My First Love	1978	Fr.
The Nark	1982	Fr.
No Man's Land	1985	Fr.
November Moon	1985	Fr.
Out of Whack	1980	Fr.
1789 *	1974	Fr.
Street of Departures	1986	Fr.
Tug of Love	1984	Fr.
Us Two	1979	Fr.
The Woman Banker	1980	Fr.

707. VILMOS ZSIGMOND (1930-   )

Blood of Ghastly Horror	1965	US
Blow Out	1981	US
The Bonfire of the Vanities	1990	WB
Cinderella Liberty	1974	TCF
Close Encounters of the Third Kind	1977	Col.
Dandy the All-American Girl	1976	MGM-UA
Deadwood '76	1965	US
Deer Hunter	1978	Col./EMI/WB
Deliverance	1972	WB
Fat Man and Little Boy	1989	Par.
Futz	1969	US
The Girl from Petrovka	1974	Univ.
The Gun Riders	1969	US
Heaven's Gate	1980	UA
The Hired Hand	1971	Univ.
Horror of the Blood Monsters *	1970	US
A Hot Summer Game	1965	US
Images	1972	Ire.--Col.

Incredible Strange Creatures...	1964	US
Jennie, Wife/Child	1968	US
Jinxed	1982	MGM-UA
Journey to Spirit Island	1988	US
Living between Two Worlds	1963	US
The Long Goodbye	1973	UA
McCabe and Mrs. Miller	1971	WB
The Monitors	1968	US
The Name of the Game Is Kill!	1968	US
The Nasty Rabbit	1964	US
Obsession	1976	Col.
Rat Fink	1965	US
Real Genius	1985	Tri-S.
Red Sky at Morning	1970	Univ.
The Rose	1979	TCF
The Sadist	1963	US
Scarecrow	1973	WB
The Sugarland Express	1974	Univ.
Table for Five	1983	WB
Tales of a Salesman	1965	US
The Time Travelers	1964	AIP
The Two Jakes	1990	Par.
What's Up Front	1964	US
Winter Kills	1977	AE
The Witches of Eastwick	1987	WB

708. FRANK ZUCKER

Broken Hearts	1926	US
Camille of the Barbary Caost	1925	US
The Cantor's Son	1937	US
East Side Sadie	1929	US
Faithless Lover	1928	US
Haldane of the Secret Service	1923	US
His Wife's Lover	1931	US
The Kick-Off	1926	US
Life Is Like That	1931	US
Lying Wives	1925	US
The Mad Marriage *	1925	US
The Man from Beyond *	1922	US
A Man of Quality	1926	US
Meddling Women	1924	US
The Silver Lining *	1921	Metro.

A Ay (1990: Turkey) — Ugur Eruzin
A Nos Amours (1984: Fr.) — Jacques Loiseleux
[A.W.O.L. (Lionheart)] (1990: Univ.) — Robert New
Abby (1974: US) — William Asman
About Last Night (1986: Tri.S.) — Andrew Dintenfass
Acceptable Levels (1983: GB) — Robert Smith
Accused (1936: GB--UA) — Victor Armenise
Ace High (1969: It.--Par.) — Marcello Mascoicchi
Across the Tracks (1990: US) — Michael Delahoussaye
The Act (1984: US) — Benjamin Davis
Act of Pain (1990: It.) — Romano Albani
An Actor's Revenge (1963: Jap.) — Setsuo Kobayashi
Adalen 31 (1969: Swed.) — Jorgen Perrson
L'Addition (1984: Fr.) — Robert Fraisse
Adios Amigo (1974: US) — Tony Palmieri
Adios Sabata (1971: It./Sp.--UA) — Sandro Mancori
Admiral Nakhimov (1948: USSR) — A. Golovna; T. Lobova
The Adolescent (1978: Fr./Ger.) — Pierre Gautard
Adolf Hitler--My Part in His Downfall (1973: GB) — Terry Maher
Adorable Julia (1964: Aust./Fr.) — Werner Krien
An Adventure of Salvator Rosa (1940: It.) — Scotti Berni
The Adventures of Frontier Fremont (1976: US) — George Stapleford
The Adventures of Gerard (1970: GB--UA) — Witold Sobocinski
The Adversary (1974: India) — Soumendu Ray; Purmendu Base

Aelita (1924: USSR) — Y. Jeliaboujski
Affair at Akitsu (1980: Jap.) — Toichiro Narushima
Affairs of a Model (1942: Swed.) — Ake Dahlquist
Affairs of Dr. Holl (1954: Ger.) — Franz Weihmayr
Affairs of Maupassant (1938: Aust.) — Willy Goldberger
After Dark, My Sweet (1990: US) — Mark Plummer
After the Fall of New York (1985: Fr./It.) — Giancarlo Ferrando

634

After the Storm (1990: Arg.)	Ricardo de Angelis
After the War (1989: Fr.)	Claude Lecomte
After You, Comrade (1967: S. Afr.)	Manie Botha
Against a Crooked Sky (1975: US)	Joe Jackman
L'Age d'Or (1930: Fr.)	Albert Duverger
Age of Consent (1969: Aus.--Col.)	Hannes Staudinger
Agency (1981: Can.)	Miklos Lente
Airborne (1978: US)	Larry Raimond
Alambrista (1977: US)	Robert M. Young
Alberto Express (1990: Fr.)	Philippe West
Alert in the South (1954: Fr.)	Lucien Joulin
Alias Big Shot (1962: Arg.)	Oscar Melly
Alibi (1931: GB)	Sydney Blythe
Alice Doesn't Live Here Anymore(1975:WB)	Kent Wakeford
Alice, Sweet Alice (1978: AA)	John Friberg; Chuck Hall
Alice's Restaurant (1969: UA)	Michael Nebbia
Alien (1979: TCF)	Derek Vanlint
The Alien Factor (1984: US)	Britt McDonough
Alien Predator (1987: US)	Tote Trenas
Alien Seed (1989: US)	Ken Carmack
Alien Thunder 1975: US)	Claude Fournier
Aliens (1986: TCF)	Adrian Biddle
Alissa in Concert (1990: Holl.)	Alejandro Agresti
All-Around Reduced Personality, The Outtakes (1978: Ger.)	Katia Forbert
All My Good Countrymen (1985: Czech.)	Jaroslav Kucera
All Nudity Shall Be Punished (1974: Braz.)	Lauro Escorel
All the Vermeers in New York (1990: US)	Jon Jost
Alley Cat (1984: US)	Howard Anderson
Alligator Eyes (1990: US)	Todd Crockett
The Allnighter (1987: Univ.)	Joseph Urbanczyk
All's Fair (1989: US)	Peter Lyons Collister
Almonds and Raisins (1985: US)	Jacek Laskus
Almost Angels (1962: Dis.)	Kurt Grigoleit
Almost Transparent Blue (1980: Jap.)	Shuya Schigawa
Almost You (1984: TCF)	Alexander Gruszynski
Alone on the Pacific (1964: Jap.)	Yoshihiro Yamazaki
Alpha Beta (1973: GB)	Charles Stewart
Alpine Fire (1987: Switz.)	Pio Corradi
Alsino and the Condor (1983: US)	Jorge Herrera; Pablo Martinez
Alvin Rides Again (1974: Aus.)	Robin Copping
Always a Bridesmaid (1943: Univ.)	Louis Da Pron
Amada (1985: Cuba)	Livio Delgado
Amateur Hour (1985: US)	Lisa Rinzler
The Amazing Dobermans (1976: US)	Jack Adams
Amazing Grace (1974: UA)	Ed Brown, Sr.; Sol Negrin

Amazing Grace and Chuck
(1987: Tri.S.) — Robert Elswit
Amazon Women on the Moon
(1987: Univ.) — Daniel Pearl
Amazons (1987: MGM-UA) — Leonard Solis
Ambush Bay (1966: UA) — Emmanuel Rojas
American Graffiti (1973: Univ.) — Ron Everslage
American Ninja 2: The Confrontation
(1987: Cannon) — Gideon Porath
American Ninja 3: Blood Hunt
(1989: Cannon) — George Bartels
The American Scream (1988: US) — Bryan England
American Stories (1989: Belg./Fr.) — Luc Ben Hamou
An American Summer (1990: US) — Bruce Dorfman
American Tattoo (1984: US) — Lee Nesbit; Steve Lustgarten
Eric Edwards; Mark
Whitney

Americana (1981: US) — Michael Stringer
Amigos (1985: Sp.) — Henry Vargas
Amityville II; The Possession
(1982: DeL./Orion) — Franco Digiacomo
Among the Cinders (1985: US) — Rory O'Shea
El Amor Brujo (1986: Sp.--Orion) — Teo Escamilla
Anatomy of a Marriage (1964: Fr.) — Roger Fellous
And Hope To Die (1972: Fr.--TCF) — Edmond Wilson
And Now My Love (1975: Fr.--AE) — Jean Collomb
Andrei Roublov (1973: USSR) — Vadim Youssov
Andy (1965: Univ.) — Ernesto Capparos
Angel (1984: US) — Andy Davis
Angel, Angel Down We Go (1969: AIP) — Jack Warren
An Angel at My Table (1990: Aus.) — Stuart Dryburgh
Angel III: The Final Chapter
(1988: US) — Howard Wexler
Angel Town (1990: US) — John LeBlanc
Angelina (1948: It.) — Paoli Craveri
Angelo (1951: It.) — Carlo Bellero
Angelo in the Crowd (1952: It.) — Carlo Bellero
Angelo My Love (1983: US) — Joseph Friedman
Angels Die Hard (1970: US) — Arch Archambault
Angels from Hell (1968: AIP) — Herman Knox
Angels of the City (1989: US) — Richard Pepin
Angi Vera (1980: Hung.) — Lajos Koltai
Angry Harvest (1986: Ger.) — Josef Ort-Snep
Angry Island (1960: Jap.) — Selichi Kizuka
Animal Behavior (1989: US) — David Spellvin
The Animals (1971: US) — Keith Smith
Anita-Dances of Vice (1987: Ger.) — Elfi Mikesch
Anna (1981: Fr./Hung.) — Tamas Andor
Anna (1987: US) — Bobby Bukowski
The Anna Cross (1954: USSR) — G. Reisgoff

The Annihilators (1985: US) — Henning Schellerup
The Anonymous Letter (1990: Sp.) — Gonzalo F. Berridi
Antigone (1962: Greece) — Dinos Katsourdis
Antoine (1917: Fr.) — P. Castanet
Antoine et Antoinette (1947: Fr.) — Pierre Montzel
Antonio Das Mortes (1970: Braz.) — Alfonso Beato
Antony and Cleopatra (1973: GB) — Rafael Pacheco
Apache Gold (1965: Ger.) — Ernest Kalinke
Apache Rifles (1964: TCF) — Arch Dalzell
Aparajito (1959: India) — Subrata Mitra
Apartment Zero (1988: GB) — Miguel Rodriguez
Apollo Goes on Holiday
  (1968: Greece/Swed.) — Tony Forsberg
The Apple Game (1980: Czech.) — Frantisel Vilcek
The Applegates (1990: Aus/US) — Mitchell Dubin
The Apprenticeship of Duddy Kravitz
  (1974: Can.) — Miklos Lente
April Fool's Day (1986: Par.) — Charles Minsky
Arabian Nights (1980: Fr./It.) — Giuseppe Ruzzolini
Archangel (1990: Can.) — Guy Maddin
The Arena (1973: US) — Aristide Massacessi
Ariane (1931: Ger) — Adolf Schlasy; Adolf Jansen
Arizona Heat (1988; US) — Howard Wexler
L'Armee des Ombres (1969: Fr./It.) — Pierre Lhomme
Arnold (1973: US) — William Jurgenson
Around the World in Eighty Ways
  (1987: Aus.) — Louis Irving
Arson, Inc. (1949: US) — Carl Berger
Arthur's Hallowed Ground (1986: GB) — Chick Anstiss
As the Devil Commands (1933: Col.) — Glen Rominger
As the Sea Rages (1960: Col.) — Kurt Hasse
Ascendancy (1983: GB) — Clive Tickner
The Assam Garden (1986: GB) — Bryan Loftus
The Assault (1986: Holl.--Cannon) — Theo Van De Sande
Assault of the Killer Bimbos (1988: US) — Thomas Calloway
Assault of the Party Nerds (1989: US) — Howard Wexler
Assault on Precinct 13 (1976: US) — Douglas Knapp
The Assistant (1982: Czech.) — Jozef Simoncic
The Associate (1982: Fr./Ger.) — Etienne Szabo
The Astounding She-Monster (1958: AIP) — William C. Thomas
Los Astronautas (1960: Mex.) — Manuel Gomez Urquiza
The Astro-Zombies (1969: US) — Robert Maxwell
At Close Range (1986: Orion) — Juan Ruiz Anchia
At Stalling Speed (1989: Cannon) — Fred Tammes
L'Atlantide (1921: Fr.) — G. Specht; V. Morin
Atragon (1965: Jap.) — Hajime Koizumi
Attack of the Killer Tomatoes
  (1978: US) — John K. Culley
Auntie Danielle (1990: Fr.) — Philippe West
Autumn Marathon (1982: USSR) — Sergei Vronsky
Autumn Moon (1990: Taiwan) — Kuo Musheng

The Avengers (1942: GB)	Cyril Knowles
The Avengers (1952: Rep.)	Pablo Tabernero
Avenging Angel (1985: US)	Peter Lyons Collister
Avenging Force (1986: Cannon)	Gideon Porath
The Aviator (1985: MGM-UA)	David Connell
The Aviator's Wife (1981: Fr.)	Bernard Lutic
L'Avventura (1960: It.)	Aldo Scavarda
Ay Carmela! (1990: It./Sp.)	Jose Luis Alcaine
Aya (1990: Aus.)	Geoff Burton
B. S. I Love You (1971: TCF)	David Dans
Baby Blood (1990: Fr.)	Bernard Decht
The Baby Maker (1970: NG)	Charles Rosher, Jr.
Baby Riasan'skie (1927: USSR)	K. Kouznetsov
Bachelor Party (1984: TCF)	Hal Trussel
Back to School (1986: Orion)	Thomas Ackerman
Bad Blood (1987: Fr.)	Jean-Yves Escoffier
Bad Dreams (1988: TCF)	Alexander Gruszynski
Bad Influence (1990: US)	Robert Elswit
Bad Jim (1990: US)	David Golia
Bad Man's River (1972: Sp.)	Alexander Ulloa
Bad Taste (1988: NZ)	Peter Jackson
The Badge of Marshal Brennan (1957: AA)	Charles Straumer
Bait (1954: Col.)	Edward P. Fitzgerald
Baker's Hawk (1976: US)	Bernie Abramson
Le Bal (1984: It./Sp.)	Ricardo Aronovich
Ballad of a Hussar (1963: USSR)	Leonid Kralnekov
Ballerina (1950: Fr.)	Robert Le Febvre
Banana Busters (1990: Holl.)	Lasse Spang Olsen
Bananas (1971: UA)	Andrew Costikyan
Band of Assassins (1971: Jap.)	Kozuo Yamdada
Bandits on the Wind (1964: Jap.)	Kozuo Yamdada
The Bang Bang Kid (1968: Sp.--US)	Antonio Macasoli
Bang Bang, You're Dead (1966: AIP)	John Von Kotze
Bang the Drum Slowly (1973: Par.)	Richard Shore
Bang! You're Dead (1954: GB)	Brendan Stafford
Banished (1978: Jap.)	Kazuo Miyagawa
Banned from Heaven (1990: Finland)	Timo Heinaenen
Banzai Runner (1987: US)	Howard Wexler
Barbarian Queen (1985: US)	Rudy Donovan
The Barbarians (1987: It.--Cannon)	Gianlorenzo Battaglia
The Barber of Seville (1973: Fr./Ger.)	Ernst Wild
Baron Blood (1972: AIP)	Emilio Varriano
Barrier (1966: Pol.)	Jan Laskowski
Basic Training (1985: US)	Steven Gray
Batman (1966: TCF)	Howard Schwartz
Batteries Not Included (1987: Univ.)	John McPherson

Battle beyond the Stars (1980: US)	Daniel Lacambre
Battle of the Worlds (1961: It.)	Raffaello Masciocchi
Bayou (1957: UA)	Ted Salzis; Vincent Salzis
Beach Ball (1965: Par.)	Alfred Taylor
Beach Girls (1982: US)	Michael Murphy
Beach Party (1963: AIP)	Kay Norton
Beach Red (1967: UA)	Cecil R. Cooney
The Beachcomber (1938: GB--Par.)	Jules Kruger; Gus Drisse
The Beads of the Rosary (1982: Pol.)	Wieslaw Zdort
The Bear (1963: Fr.)	Andre Villard
The Bear (1984: Emb.)	Laszlo George
The Bears and I (1974: Dis.)	Ted Landon
The Beast (1988: Col.)	Douglas Milsome
The Beast of Hollow Mountain (1956: UA)	Jorge Stahl, Jr.
The Beast with Five Fingers (1946: WB/FN)	Wesley Anderson
The Beast Within (1982: MGM-UA)	Jack L. Richards
The Beat (1987: US)	Tom DiCillo
The Beat Generation (1959: MGM)	Walter Castle
Beat Street (1984: Orion)	Tom Priestley
Le Beau Mariage (1982: Fr.--UA)	Bernard Lutic; Roman Winding; Nicholas Brunet
Beautiful Dreamers (1990: Can.)	Francois Protat
The Bees (1978: US)	Leon Sanchez
Beetlejuice (1988: WB)	Thomas Ackerman
Before Him All Rome Trembled (1947: It.)	Anchise Brizzi
Beginners Luck (1986: US)	Ayne Coffey
Behind Closed Shutters (1942: It.)	Antonio Belviso
The Being (1983: US)	Robert Ebinger
Belizaire the Cajun (1986: US)	Richard Bowen
Bella Donna (1934: GB)	Sydney Blythe
The Bellman (1947: Fr.)	Louis Page
Below the Belt (1980: US)	Alan Metzger
Benvenuta (1983: Fr.)	Charles Van Damme
Berlin Blues (1988: Sp.)	Teo Escamilla
Best of the Best (1989: US)	Doug Ryan
Betrayed (1988: MGM-UA)	Patrick Blossier
A Better Tomorrow (1987: HgKg.)	Wong Wing-hang
Betty Blue (1986: Fr.)	Jean-Francois Robin
Between the Lines (1977: US)	Kenneth Van Sickle
Beverly Hills Bodysnatchers (1990:US)	Zoran Hochstatter
Beverly Hills Brats (1989: US)	Harry Mathias
Beverly Hills Cop II (1987: Par.)	Jeffrey Kimball
Beverly Hills Vamp (1989: US)	Stephen Ashley Blake
Beware the Blob (1972: US)	Al Hamm
Beyond Evil (1980: US)	Ken Plotin
Beyond Reasonable Doubt (1980: NZ)	Alan Bollinger
Beyond the Law (1967: It.)	Enzo Serafin

Beyond the Law (1968: US)	D. A. Pennebaker; Nicholas Proferes; Jan Welt
Beyond the Limit (1983: Par.)	Phil Meheux
Beyond the Ocean (1990: It.)	Franco di Giacomo
Beyond the Reef (1981: Univ.)	Sam Martin
Beyond the Time Barrier (1960: AIP)	Meredith M. Nicholson
Beyond the Walls (1985: Isr.--WB)	Amnon Salomon
Big Bad Mama II (1987: US)	Robert New
The Big Bounce (1969: WB)	Howard Schwartz
The Big City (1963: India)	Subrata Mitra
The Big Dis (1989: US)	John O'Brien
The Big Easy (1987: Col.)	Alfonso Beato
The Big Frame (1953: RKO)	Monte Berman
The Big Game (1972: US)	Mario Fioretti
The Big Man (1990: GB)	Ian Wilson
The Big Operator (1959: MGM)	Walter Castle
The Big Picture (1989: Col.)	Jeff Jur
The Big Steal (1990: Aus.)	David Parker
A Bigger Splash (1984: US)	Jack Hazan
Billion Dollar Brain (1967: GB--UA)	David Harcourt
The Billion Dollar Hobo (1977: US)	Irv Goodnoff
Billy Galvin (1986: US)	Eugene Shlugleit
Bingo Bongo (1983: It.--Col.)	Aldo Contini
Biohazard (1985: US)	Paul Elliott; John McCoy
Biquefarre (1983: Fr.)	Andre Villard
Bird on a Wire (1990: Univ.)	Robert Primes
Birds Do It (1966: Col.)	Howard Winner
The Birds, the Bees and the Italians (1967: It.)	Aiace Parolin
The Biscuit Eater (1972: Dis.)	Richard A. Kelley
Bizarre Bizarre (1939: Fr.)	Roger Kahan
Black Belt Jones (1974: WB)	Kent Wakeford
Black Caesar (1973: AIP)	Fenton Hamilton
Black Eagle (1989: US)	George Koblasa
Black Girl (1972: US)	Glenwood Swanson
Black Jack (1951: Fr.--US)	Andre Thomas
Black Jack (1973: AIP)	Thomas Spaulding
Black Joy (1977: GB)	Phil Meheux
Black Like Me (1964: US)	Victor Lukens; Henry Mueller
Black Magic (1949: UA)	Ubaldo Arata; Anchise Brizzi
Black Milan (1989: Fr./Switz.)	Willy Kurant
Black Moon Rising (1986: US)	Misha Suslov
The Black Room (1984: US)	Robert Harmon
Black Sabbath (1963: It.)	Ubaldo Terzano
Black Samson (1974: WB)	Henning Schellerup
A Black Veil for Lisa (1969: Ger./It.)	Angelo Lotti
Blackeyes (1990: GB)	Andrew Duncan
Blackjack (1990: Swed.)	Jorgen Persson

Blackout (1954: GB--Ham./Lip.)	Jimmy Harvey
Blackout (1988: US)	Arledge Armenaki
Blackout Nights (1990: Turkey)	Colin Mounier
Blade (1973: US)	David Hoffman
Blanche (1971: Fr.)	Andre Dubreuil
Blast of Silence (1961: Univ.)	Erich Kollar
Bleak Moments (1972: GB)	Bahram Manoochehri
Bless Their Little Hearts (1984: US)	Charles Burnett
Blind Chance (1987: Pol.)	Krzysztof Pakulski
Blind Date (1984: US)	Andrew Bellis
The Blind Ear of Opera (1990: Ger.)	Denedict Nevenfels
Blind Fury (1989: Tri-S.)	Don Burgess
The Blind Goddess (1948: GB)	Ray Elton; Dudley Lovell
Bliss (1986: GB)	Paul Murphy
The Blob (1958: Par.)	Thomas Spaulding
The Blockhouse (1974: GB)	Keith Goddard
Blonde Comet (1941: PDC)	Mervyn Freeman
Blonde Nightingale (1931: Ger.--UFA)	Werner Brandes
Blood and Black Lace (1965: It.--AA)	Herman Tarzana
Blood Arrow (1958--TCF)	Fleet Southcott
Blood in the Streets (1975: Fr./It.)	Aldo Scavarda
The Blood of Fu Manchu (1968: GB)	Manuel Merino
Blood of the Vampire (1958: GB--Univ.)	Geoffrey Seahorn
Blood Red (1990: Hem.)	Toyomichi Kurita
Blood Salvage (1990: US)	Michael Karp
Blood Tide (1982: US)	Ari Stavrou
Blood Wedding (1981: Sp.)	Teo Escamilla
Bloodhounds of Broadway (1989: US)	Elliot Davis
Blow to the Heart (1983: It.)	Tonino Nardi
Blue Fin (1978: Aus.)	Geoff Burton
Blue Heaven (1985: US)	Kees Van Oostem
The Blue Iguana (1988: Par.)	Rodolfo Sanchez
Blue Monkey (1987: US)	Brenton Spencer
Blue Steel (1990: MGM/UA)	Amir Mokri
The Blue Veil (1947: Fr.)	Rene Caugau
Blueberry Hill (1988: US)	David Lewis
Blueberry Hill (1989: Belg.)	Jean Claude Neckelbrouck
The Boarding School (1970: Sp.)	Manuel Berenguer
Boardinghouse (1984: US)	Jan Lucas
The Boat Is Full (1981: Ger.)	Hans Liechti
Boat People (1983: China)	Chung Chi-man
Bobbie Jo and the Outlaw (1976: AIP)	Stanley Wright
Body and Soul (1981: Cannon)	James Forest
Body Chemistry (1990: US)	Phedon Papamichael
The Body Stealers (1969: AA)	Peter Henry
Boggy Creek (1985: US)	Shirah Kojayan
La Boheme (1965: It.--WB)	Werner Krien
Bolero (1984: Canon)	John Derek
Bombs Away (1985: US)	Marty Openheimer
Book of Love (1990: US)	Peter Deming

Boomerang (1960: Ger.--UFA)	Kurt Hasse
The Boost (1988: US)	Howard Atherton
Boots of Destiny (1937: GN)	Tom Galligan
Border Devils (1932: US)	William Dietz
Border Street (1950: Pol.)	Jaroslav Tuzar
Boris Godunov (1959: USSR)	V. Nikolayev
Born in Flames (1983: US)	Ed Bowes
Born Losers (1967: AIP)	Gregory Sandor
Boss Nigger (1974: US)	Robert Caramico
Boss of Bullion City (1941: Univ.)	Harry Sherman
The Boss's Son (1978: US)	Alfonso Beato
Boudu Saved from Drowning (1967: Fr.)	Marcel Lucien Asselin
Bountiful Summer (1951: USSR)	A. Mishurin
The Bounty Hunters (1970: It.)	Sandro Mancori
Boxer (1971: Pol.)	Miklaj Sprudin
Boy of the Terraces (1990: Fr./Tun.)	Georges Barsky
Boy Soldier (1987: Wales)	Roger Pugh Evans
The Boys in Company C (1978: Col.)	Godfrey A. Godar
Boys in the Island (1990: Aus.)	Andrew Lesnie
The Boys Next Door (1985: US)	Arthur Albert
The Boys of Paul Street (1969: Hung.--TCF)	Gyorgy Illes
Boys on the Outside (1990: It.)	Mauro Marchetti
Brady's Escape (1984: US)	Elemer Ragalyi
Brain Damage (1988: US)	Bruce Torbet
Brain Dead (1990: US)	Ronn Schmidt
The Brain Eaters (1958: AIP)	Larry Raimond
The Brain That Wouldn't Die (1959: US)	Stephen Hajinal
Brainstorm (1983: MGM-UA)	Richard Yurich
Brainwashed (1961: Fr.--AA)	Gunther Senftleben
Brainwaves (1983: US)	Jon Kranhouse
Branches of the Tree (1990: India)	Barun Raha
Brandy for the Parson (1952: GB)	Martin Curtis
Bread, Love and Tears (1953: It.)	Arturo Gallea
The Bread of Love (1954: Swed.)	Sven Thermaenius
Breaker! Breaker! (1977: AIP)	Mario Di Leo
Breaking In (1989: US)	Michael Coulter
Breaking the Sound Barrier (1952: GB)	Anthony Squire
A Breed Apart (1984: Orion)	Geoffrey Stephenson
The Bride (1973: US)	Geoffrey Stephenson
Bride of the Lake (1934: GB)	Sydney Blythe
Bride With a Dowry (1954: USSR)	N. Vlassov; S. Shenin
The Bridge (1961: Ger.--AA)	Gerd Von Bonin
Bridge to the Sun (1961: MGM)	Marcel Weiss; Selichi Kizuka Bill Kelly
Bright Angel (1990: Hem.)	Elliott Davis
Brink of Life (1960: Swed.)	Max Wilen

The Brink's Job (1978: Univ.)   Norman Leigh
Broken Journey (1948: GB)   David Harcourt
Broken Victory (1988: US)   Brett Webster
Bronx Warrior (1983: US)   Sergio Salvati
Brothers and Sisters (1980: GB)   Pascoe MacFarlane
Die Bruder Karamazov (1920: Ger.)   O. Tober
The Brute (1942: Mex.)   A. Jiminez
Buck Rogers in the 25th Century
   (1979: Univ.)   Frank Beascoschea
Bucktown (1975: AIP)   Robert Virchall
Buddha (1965: Jap.--UA)   Hiroshi Imai
Buddies (1983: US)   David Eggby
Buddies (1984: US)   Carl Teitelbaum
Bulldog Drummond Comes Back
   (1937: Par.)   Henry Mills
A Bullet for Pretty Boy (1970: AIP)   James R. Davidson
A Bullet for Sandoval
   (1970: It./Sp.--Univ.)   Francisco Sempere
A Bullet for the General (1967:
   It.--MGM)   Toni Secchi
A Bullet in the Head (1990: Can.)   Michael Lamothe
Bulletproof (1988: US)   Francis Grumann
Bum Rap (1988: US)   Kevin Lombard
The 'Burbs (1989: Univ.)   Robert Stevens
Burning an Illusion (1982: GB)   Roy Cornwall
Burning Secret (1988: Ger./GB--US)   Ernest Day
The Burning Years (1979: It.)   Safai Teherani
The Bus Is Coming (1971: US)   Mike Rhodes
Bush Christmas (1983: Aus.)   Malcolm Richards; Ross
    Berryman
The Bushbaby (1970: MGM)   Davis Boulton
The Bushido Blade (1982: GB)   Shoji Ueda
Bustin' Loose (1981: UA)   Dennis Dalzell
Busting (1974: UA)   Earl Rath
Buy and Cell (1988: US)   Danielle Nannuzzi
Bye Bye Barbara (1969: Fr.--Par.)   Claude Lecomte
Bye Bye Blues (1989: Can.)   Vic Sarin
Bye-Bye Brazil (1980: Braz.)   Lauro Escorel Filho

Cabiria (1914: It.)   S. de Chomon; G. Tomatis;
    A. Batagliotti
Cactus (1986: Aus.)   Yuri Sokol
Cactus in the Snow (1972: US)   Wilbur Grossman
Cafe Express (1980: It.)   Claudio Cirillo
Cage of Nightingales (1947: Fr.)   Paul Cotteret
Caged Fury (1990: US)   Kenneth Wiatrak
Cagliostro (1975: It.--TCF)   Giuseppe Pinori
California (1963: AIP)   Edward Fitzgerald
Call of the Wild (1972: Fr./Ger./
   It./Sp.--MGM)   John Cabrera

Calling Bulldog Drummond (1951: GB--MGM) — Graham Kelly

Calypso (1959: Fr./It.) — Pierludovici Pavoni

Came a Hot Friday (1985: NZ--Orion) — Alun Bollinger

Camela (1985: Arg.) — Fernando Arribas

Camille Claudel (1988: Fr.) — Pierre Lhomme

Camera Buff (1983: Pol.) — Jacek Petrycki

Cammina Cammina (1985: It.) — Ermanno Olmi

Campus Man (1987: Par./RKO) — Francis Kenny

Can She Bake a Cherry Pie? (1983: US) — Bob Fiore

Canaris (1955: Ger.) — Franz Welhmayr

Candidate for Murder (1966: GB) — Bert Mason

Candide (1962: Fr.) — Robert Lefebvre

Cannibal Girls (1973: AIP) — Robert Saad

Cannibal Women in the Avocado Jungle of Death (1989: US) — Robert G. Knouse

The Cannon and the Nightingale (1969: Greece) — S. Danillis; N. Kavoukidis

Cannon for Cordoba (1970: UA) — Antonio Macasoli

Can't Buy Me Love (1987: Dis.) — Peter Lyons Collister

Capetown Affair (1967: S. Afr.--US) — David Millin

Captain Apache (1971: GB) — John Cabrera

Captain from Koepenick (1933: Ger.) — Ewald Daub

The Captain from Koepenick (1956: Ger) — Albert Benitz

Captain Scarlet (1953: UA) — Charles Carbajal

Captain Sinbad (1963: MGM) — Gunther Senftleben

Caravaggio (1986: GB) — Gabriel Beristain

Caravan to Vaccaro (1974: Fr./GB-- Rank/TCF) — John Cabrera; David Bevan; Ted Deason

Carmen (1926: Fr.) — M. Desfassiaux; P. Parguel

Carmen (1946: It.) — Ubaldo Arata

Carmen (1949: Sp.) — Reimar Kuntze

Carmen (1983: Sp.--Orion) — Teo Escamilla

Carnival (1953: Fr.) — Andre Germain

Carnival of Souls (1962: US) — Maurice Prather

Caroline Cherie (1957: Fr.) — Maurice Barry

The Cars That Ate Paris (1974: Aus.) — John McLean

The Case against Ferro (1980: Fr.) — Etienne Becker

The Case of the Witch Who Wasn't (1990: Can.) — Eric Cayla

Case Van Geldern (1932: Ger.) — Emil Schuenemann

Casino de Paris (1957: Fr./Ger.) — Bruno Mondi

Casque D'Or (1956: Fr.) — Robert Lefebvre

The Castelan (1963: Sp.--WB) — Mario Pacheco

Castle of Blood (1964: Fr./It.) — Richard Kramer

Casual Sex? (1988: Univ.) — Rolf Kesterman

The Cat (1959: Fr.) — Pierre Montazel

Cat and Mouse (1978: Fr.)	Jean Collomb
The Cat Burglar (1961: UA)	Taylor Byars
Cat Girl (1957: AIP)	Paddy A-Hearne
Cat O'Nine Tails (1971: Fr./Ger. It.--NG)	Erico Menczer
The Catamount Killing (1975: Ger.)	Witold Sobocinski
Catch As Catch Can (1937: GB)	Stanley Grant
Catherine and Co. (1976: Fr.--WB)	Richard Suzuki
Cathy's Child (1979: Aus.)	Gary Hansen
Cauldron of Blood (1971: Sp.-- Cannon)	Francisco Sempere
The Cavalier of the Streets (1937: GB--Par.)	Francis Carver
Cavalry Command (1963: US)	Felipe Sacdalan
Cavegirl (1985: US)	David Oliver
Cease Fire (1985: US)	Henning Schellerup
Ceddo (1978: Nig.)	Georges Caristan
Celeste (1982: Ger.)	Jurgen Martin; Horst Becker; Helmo Sahliger; Hermann Ramelow
Celia (1989: Aus.)	Geoffrey Simpson
Celine and Julie Go Boating (1974: Fr.)	Jacques Renard; Michel Cenet
Cellar Dweller (1988: US)	Sergio Salvati
Cello (1990: GB)	Remi Adefarasian
The Census Taker (1981: US)	Tom Jewitt
Certain Fury (1985: US)	Kees Van Oostrum
Cesar (1936: Fr.)	Willy
Chafed Elbows (1967: US)	Stan Warnow
The Chair (1988: US)	Steven Ross
The Challenge (1982: Emb.)	Kozo Okazaki
Chan Is Missing (1982: US)	Michael Chin
Chanel Solitaire (1981: Fr.--US)	Ricardo Aronovich
Un Chapeau de Paille d'Italie (1927: Fr.)	N. Desfassiaux; N. Roudakoff
Charles and Lucie (1982: Fr.)	Gilbert Sanchez
Charles, Dead or Alive (1972: Switz.)	Renato Berta
Chastity (1969: AIP)	Ben Colman
Cheaper to Keep Her (1980: US)	Roland "Ozzie" Smith
The Cheater (1990: USSR)	Sergei Taraskin
Checking Out (1989: WB)	Ian Wilson
Cheech and Chong's The Corsican Brothers (1984: Orion)	Harvey Harrison
Cheetah (1989: BV)	Tom Burstyn
Cherez Ternii K. Svezdam (1981: USSR)	Alexander Rybin
The Cherry Blossom Ballad (1990: Den.)	Henning Bendtsen
The Chess Players (1978: India)	Soumendu Roy
Chesty Anderson (1984: US)	Henning Schellerup

Chicago 70 (1970: US) — Mogens Gander; Henri Fiks
Chief Zabu (1988: US) — Frank Prinzi
Chiji Tabinikki (1927: Jap.) — T. Okusaka
A Child Is a Wild Thing (1976: US) — Peter Sudarsky
Child Under a Leaf (1975: Can.) — Don Wilder
The Children (1949: Swed.) — O. Nordemar
Children of God's Earth (1983: Nor.) — Rolv Haan
Children of Hiroshima (1952: Jap.) — Takeo Itch
Children of the Damned (1963: GB--MGM) — David Boulton
Child's Play (1954: GB) — Denny Densham
China Girl (1987: US) — Bojan Bazelli
China Lake (1990: US) — Jasper Marquardt
Chinel (1926: USSR) — A. Moskvine; E. Mikhailov
Choose Me (1984: US) — Jan Kiesser
Choppy Chicks in Zombietown (1990: US) — Tom Fraser
A Chorus of Disapproval (1989: GB) — Alan Jones
The Chosen (1978: GB/It.--AIP) — Erico Menczer
Chosen Survivors (1974: Mex.--Col.) — Gabriel Torres
The Christian Licorice Store (1971: NG) — David Butler
Christian the Lion (1976: GB) — Simon Trevor
The Christine Keeler Affair (1964: GB) — Michel Rocca
The Christmas Kid (1968: Sp.--US) — Manolo Hernandez San Juan
Chronicle of Anna Magdalena Bach (1968: Ger./It.) — Ugo Piccone
Chushiungura (1963: Jap.) — Kazuo Yamada
Le Ciel est a Vous (1957: Fr.) — Louis Page
Circle of Power (1984: US) — Alfonso Beato
Circle of Two (1980: Can.) — Lazlo George
Circuitry Man (1990: US) — Jamie Thompson
City News (1983: US) — Jonathan Sinaiko
City of Fear (1965: GB--AA) — Martin Curtis
City of Secrets (1963: Ger.) — Albert Benitz; Dieter Bartels
Clair de Femme (1980: Fr.) — Ricardo Aronovich
The Clairvoyant (1935: GB) — Errol Hinds
Clarence and Angel (1981) — Doug Harris
Claretta and Ben (1983: It.) — Mario Vulpiani
Class Meeting (1989: Switz.) — Edwin Horak
Clay (1964: Aus.) — Giorgio Manglamele
Clean and Sober (1988: WB) — Jan Kiesser
Clean Cut (1989: Fr.) — Philippe Theaudiere
Cleaning Up (1933: GB) — Alex Bryce
Clear Skies (1963: USSR) — Sergey Poluyanov
Cleopatra's Daughter (1963: Fr./It.) — Anchise Brizzi
The Climax (1967: Fr./It.) — Aiace Parolin
The Clonus Horror (1979: US) — Max Beaufort
Cloportes (1966: Fr./It.) — Nicholas Hayer

Close-Up (1990: Iran) — Alireza Zarrindast
Closely Watched Trains (1967: Czech.) — Jaromir Sofr
Closer and Closer Apart (1990: Aus.) — Vladimir Osherov
Cloud Dancer (1980: US) — Travis Hill
Cloudburst (1952: GB--UA) — Jimmy Harvey
Clouds Over Israel (1966: Isr.) — Marko Yakovlevich
Club Life (1986: US) — Joel King
The Clue of the Missing Ape (1953: GB) — James Allen
The Clue of the New Pin (1929: GB) — Horace Wheddon
Clue of the Twisted Candle (1968: GB) — Brian Rhodes
C'mon Let's Live a Little (1967: Par.) — Carl Berger
Coach (1978: US) — Mike Murphy
Cocaine Wars (1985: US) — Victor Kavlev
The Cockeyed Cowboys of Calico County (1970: Univ.) — Richard L. Rawlings
Codename: Wild Geese (1986: It.--US) — Peter Baumgartner
Cold Feet (1984: US) — Benjamin Blake
Cold Feet (1989: US) — Bryan Duggan
Cold Front (1989: Can.) — Thomas Burstyn
Colonel March Investigates (1952: GB) — Jonah Jones
Colonel Redl (1985: Ger./Hung.--Orion) — Lajos Koltai
Color Me Dead (1969: Aus.) — Mike Borneman
The Color of Pomegranates (1980: Arm.) — A. Samvellian
Colorado Serenade (1946: PRC) — Robert Shackleford
The Colossus of Rhodes (1961: Fr./It./Sp.--MGM) — Antonio Ballesteros
Comanche (1956: UA) — Jorge Stahl, Jr.
Come On Rangers (1939: Rep.) — Al Wilson
Come Spy with Me (1967: TCF) — Zoli Vidor
Coming to America (1988: Par.) — Woody Omens
Communion (1989: US) — Louis Irvin
Companeros (1970: Ger./It./Sp.) — Alejandro Ulloa
The Company of Wolves (1985: GB) — Bryan Loftus
Complex World (1990: US) — Dennis Maloney
Computer Free-for-All (1969: Jap.) — Senchiki Nagai
Comrades (1987: GB) — Gale Tattersall
Conan the Barbarian (1982: Univ.) — John Cabrera
Concentration Camp (1939: USSR) — E. Andrikanis
Concerning Mr. Martin (1937: GB--TCF) — Stanley Grant
The Concrete Jungle (1982: US) — Andrew W. Friend
Condemned to Death (1932: GB) — Sydney Blythe
The Conductor (1981: Pol.) — Slawomir Idziak
The Conductor (1989: Belg./Fr.) — Acacio de Almeida
Confessions of a Police Captain (1971: It.) — Claudio Ragona
Confessions of a Rogue (1948: Fr.) — Jean Feyte

The Confessions of Aman (1977: US)   Gregory Nava
Confidence (1980: Hung.)   Lajos Koltai
The Consequence (1979: Ger.)   Joerg Michael Baldenius
The Constant Factor (1980: Pol.)   Slawomir Idziak
Constantine and the Cross (1962: It.)   Massimo Dallamano
The Consul (1989: Pol.)   Julian Szczerkowski
Continental Express (1939: GB--Mon.)   Bernard Browne
The Contract (1982: Pol.)   Slawomir Idziak
The Cool and the Crazy (1958: AIP)   Harry Birch
Cool Breeze (1972: MGM)   Andy David
The Cool World (1963: US)   Baird Bryant
Cooley High (1975: AIP)   Paul Von Brock
Cop Hater (1958: UA)   J. Burgi Contner
The Copper (1930: GB)   Heinrich Gartner
Cops and Robbers (1973: UA)   David Quaid
The Corpse of Beverly Hills (1965: Ger)   Ernst Wild
Corridor of Mirrors (1948: GB)   Andre Thomas
The Corrupt Ones (1967: Ger.--WB)   Heinz Pehlke
The Corruption of Chris Miller (1979: Sp.)   Juan Gelpi
The Cossacks (1960: It.--Univ.)   Massimo Dallamano
Couer Fidele (1923: Fr.)   P. Guichard; L. Donnot
Count Dracula (1971: Ger./GB/It./Sp.)   Manuel Marion
Count Yorga, Vampire (1970: AIP)   Arch Archambault
Countdown (1981: WB)   William W. Spencer
Counterfeit Commandos (1981: It.)   Gianfranco Bergamini
The Counterfeit Plan (1957: GB--WB)   Philip Grinwood
The Counterfeiters of Paris (1962: Fr./It.)   Louis Page
Country Music Holiday (1958: Par.)   William B. Kelly
Countryman (1982: Jam.)   Dominique Chapuis
Coup de Sirocco (1981: Fr.)   Jean-Francois Robin
Le Coupable (1916: Fr.)   P. Castanet
The Courier (1988: GB)   Gabriel Beristain
Courrier Sud (1937: Fr.)   Robert Lafevre
The Court Concert (1936: Ger.--UA)   Franz Weihmayr
Cousin Cousine (1976: Fr.)   Georges Lendl
Cowboy from Lonesome River (1944: Col.)   David Ragin
Cowboys Don't Cry (1988: Can.)   Brian Hebb
Crack in the Mirror (1988: US)   Neil Smith
Crack in the World (1965: Par.)   Manuel Berenguer
The Cranes Are Flying (1960: USSR)   Sergei Urussevsky
The Crawling Hand (1963: AIP)   William Van Der Leer
The Crazies (1973: US)   S. William Hinzman
Crazy Desire (1964: It.)   Erico Menczer
The Creature Called Man (1970: Jap.)   Kazutami Hara
Les Creatures (1969: Fr./Swed.)   Willy Kurant
Creepshow (1982: WB)   Michael Gornick

Creepshow 2 (1987: US) — Dick Hart; Tom Hurwitz
Crime and Passion (1976: AIP) — Dennis C. Lewiston
Crime and Punishment (1935: Fr.) — Rene Colas; Joseph-Louis Mundvillier
Crime at Porta Romana (1980: It.) — Giovanni Ciarlo
Crime over London (1936: GB) — Victor Armenise
Criminal Conversation (1980: Ire.) — Sean Corcoran
Criminal Law (1988: Tri-S.) — Phil Meheux
The Criminal Life of Archibaldo de La Cruz (1962: Mex.) — Augustin Jiminez
The Crimson Trail (1935: Univ.) — John Hickson
Critters 2: The Main Course (1988: US) — Russell Carpenter
The Crook (1971: Fr.--UA) — Jean Collomb
The Crooked Billet (1930: GB) — Claude McDonnell
The Crooked Sky (1957: GB) — Phil Grindrod
The Cross and the Switchblade (1970: US) — Julian C. Townsend
Cross Currents (1935: GB--Par.) — Francis Carver
Cross My Heart (1937: GB--Par.) — Francis Carver
Cross My Heart (1990: Fr.) — Jean-Claude Saillier
The Crossing (1990: Aus.) — Jeff Darling
Crossing Delancey (1988: WB) — Theo Van De Sande
Crossover Dreams (1985: US) — Claudio Chea
Crossplot (1969: GB--UA) — Brendan Stafford
Crow Hollow (1952: GB--AA) — Bob Lapresle
The Crowning Experience (1960: US) — Richard Tegstrom
Cry-Baby (1990: Univ.) — David Insley
Cry Blood, Apache (1970: US) — Bruce Scott
Cry Freedom (1961: Phil.) — Mike Accion
A Cry from the Street (1959: GB) — Harry Gilliam
Cry of Battle (1963: AA) — Felipe Sacdalan
Cry of the City (1948: TCF) — Fred Sersin
Crystal Heart (1987: US) — Alejandro Ulloa
Crystalstone (1988: US) — John Stephens
The Curse of the Doll People (1968: Mex.--AIP) — Enrique Wallace
The Curse of the Living Corpse (1964: TCF) — Richard L. Hilliard
Curucu, Beast of the Amazon (1956: Univ.) — Rudolf Icsey
Cutting Class (1989: US) — Avi Karpick
The Cycle (1979: Iran) — Houshang Bahariou
Cycle Savages (1969: AIP) — Frank Ruttencutter
Cyclone Ranger (1935: US) — Donald Keyes
Cyrano de Bergerac (1990: Fr.) — Pierre Lhomme

D.O.A. (1988: Dis./Touch.) — Yuri Neyman
Da (1988: US) — Alar Kivilo

Dad (1989: Univ.) — Jan Kiesser
Daddy Nostalgie (1990: Fr.) — Denis Lenoir
Daddy's Boys (1988: US) — David Stump
Daddy's Deadly Darling (1984: US) — Glenn Roland
Daddy's Dyin' ... Who's Got the Will? (1990: MGM/UA) — Paul Elliott
Dad's Army (1971: GB--Col.) — Terry Maher
Dakota (1988: US) — Jim Wrenn
The Dalton Gang (1949: Lip.) — Arch Dalzell
Dames Ahoy (1930: Univ.) — C. Allen Jones
Damned River (1990: MGM/UA) — George Tirl
Dance of the Polar Bears (1990: Den.) — Bjorn Blixt
Dancin' Thru the Dark (1990: GB) — Philip Bonham-Carter
Dancing in the Dark (1986: Can.--US) — Vic Sarin
Dancing Machine (1990: Fr.) — Jose Luis Alcaine
Dandin (1988: Fr.) — Bernard Lutic
Danger: Diabolik (1968: Fr./It.--Par.) — Antonio Rinaldi
Danger Zone II: Reaper's Revenge (1989: US) — Daniel Yarussi
Danger Zone III: Steel Horse War (1990: US) — Daniel Yarussi
Dangerous Game (1988: Aus.) — Peter Levy
Dangerously Close (1986: Cannon) — Walt Lloyd
Dangerously Yours (1937: TCF) — Harry Davis
Daniella by Night (1962: Fr.) — Andre Germain
Danton (1921: Ger.) — A. Viragh
Danton (1931: Ger.) — Nikolaus Farkas
Daredevil in the Castle (1969: Jap.) — Kazuo Yamada
Daredreamer (1990: US) — Christopher Tufty
Daring Game (1968: Par.) — Edmund Gibson
Dark Age (1988: Aus.) — Andrew Lesnie
Dark Are Nights on the Black Sea (1990: USSR) — Efrim Reznikov
Dark Eyes (1987: It.) — Franco Di Giacomo
Dark Eyes of London (1961: Ger.) — Karl Loeb
Dark Is the Night (1946: USSR) — Sergei Gevorkian
Dark Odyssey (1961: US) — Peter Erik Winkler
Dark of the Night (1986: NZ) — Alun Bollinger
Dark Red Roses (1930: GB) — A. Virago
Dark Star (1975: US) — Douglas Knapp
Dark Tower (1989: US) — Gordon Haymann
Darkman (1990: Univ.) — Bill Pope
Date with a Dream (1948: GB) — Monty Berman
Daughter of Deceit (1977: Mex.) — Jose Ortiz Ramos
Daughter of the Sands (1952: Fr.) — Andre Bac
Daughters of Satan (1972: UA) — Nonong Rasca
David (1979: Ger.) — Al Ruban
David and Lisa (1962: US) — Leonard Hirschfield

David Holzman's Diary (1968: US) — Michael Wadleigh; Paul Goldsmith; Paul Glickman

Dawn of the Dead (1979: US) — Michael Gornick

Dawn over Ireland (1938: Ire.) — James Lawler

The Dawning (1988: GB) — Shaun O'Dell

Day of Wrath (1948: Den.) — Carl Anderson

The Day That Shook the World (1977: Czech./Yugo.--AIP) — Jan Curik

The Day the Earth Froze (1959: Fin./USSR--AIP) — Sid Roth

The Day the Hotline Got Hot (Fr./Sp.--AIP) — Manuel Berenguer

The Day the War Ended (1961: USSR) — Boris Monastyrsky

The Daydreamer (1966: Emb.) — Daniel Cavelli; Tad Mochinaga

The Daydreamer (1975: Fr.) — Daniel Vogel

Days and Nights (1946: USSR) — Yevgeni Andrikanis

Days of the Dead (1985: US) — Michael Gornick

Days of 36 (1972: Greece) — George Arvanitis

Days of Thunder (1990: Par.) — Ward Russell; Charles Mills

De Sade (1969: Ger.--AIP) — Heinz Pahlke

Dead End Drive In (1986: GB--US) — Paul Murphy

Dead Kids (1981: Aus./NZ) — Louis Horvath

Dead Man's Float (1980: Aus.) — David Eggby

Dead Men Don't Die (1990: US) — Tom Fraser

The Dead Mountaineer Hotel (1979: USSR) — Yuri Sillart

Dead of Summer (1970: Fr./It.) — Giulio Albonico

Dead of Winter (1987: MGM-UA) — Jan Weincke

Dead Pigeon on Beethoven Street (1972: Ger.) — Jerzy Lipman

Dead Run (1961: Fr./Ger./It.--Univ.) — Pierre Petit

The Deadliest Sin (1956: GB--AA) — Philip Grindrod

The Deadly Game (1955: GB) — Jimmy Harvey

Deadly Reactor (1989: US) — David Hue

Deadly Spygames (1989: US) — Wayne Kohlar

Deadly Strangers (1974: GB) — Graham Edgar

Deadly Trackers (1973: WB) — Gabriel Torres

Dealing (1971: WB) — Ed Brown

Dear Detective (1978: Fr.) — Jean-Paul Schwartz

Dear John (1966: Swed.) — Rune Ericson

Dear Mr. Prohack (1949: GB) — H. E. Fowle; Nigel Huke

Dear Summer Sister (1985: Jap.) — Yasuhiro Yoshioka

Death before Dishonor (1987: US) — Don Burgess

Death Collector (1976: US) — Bob Bailan

Death Hunt (1981: TCF) — James Devis

Death in Brunswick (1990: Aus.) — Ellery Ryan

Death in the Garden (1977: Fr./Mex.) — Jorge Stahl, Jr.

Death Is a Number (1951: GB) — Philip Grindrod

Death Is Called Engelchen (1963: Czech.) — Rudolf Milic

Death of a Bureaucrat (1979: Cuba) — Ramon F. Suarez
Death of a Soldier (1986: Aus.) — Louis Irving
The Death of Mario Ricci
  (1985: Fr./Switz.) — Hans Liechti
The Death of Tarzan (1968: Czech.) — Josef Hanus
Death over My Shoulder (1958: GB) — Jimmy Harvey
Death Took Place Last Night
  (1970: Ger./It.) — Lamberto Galm
Death Vengeance (1982: EMI) — Franco Di Giacomo
Death Warrant (1990: MGM/UA) — Russell Carpenter
Death Wish 3 (1985: Cannon) — John Stainer
Death Wish 4: The Crackdown
  (1987: Cannon) — Gideon Porath
Deathstalker (1984: US) — Leonardo Rodriguez Solis
December (1990: It.) — Tonino Nardi
The Decks Ran Red (1958: MGM) — Meredith Nicholson
The Decline of the American Empire
  (1986: Can.) — Guy Dufaux
Deed Undone (1989: Holl.) — Bernd Woutliuysen
Deep End (1970: Ger.--Par.) — Charly Steinberger
Deep in the Heart (1983: EMI/WB) — Charles Stewart
Deep Sleep (1990: Can.) — Rene Ohashi
Def-Con (1985: Can.) — Doug Connell; Les Krizan
The Defense of Volotchayevsk
  (1938: USSR) — Alexander Sigayev; Apollinari
  Dudko

A Degree of Murder (1969: Ger.--
  Univ.) — Franz Rath
Dejavu (1985: GB--Cannon) — David Holmes
The Delavine Affair (1954: GB) — Jonah Jones
The Delinquents (1957: UA) — Charles Paddock; Harry
  Birch
The Delinquents (1989: Aus.) — Andrew Lesnie
The Delta Factor (1970: US) — Ted Saizis; Vincent Saizis
Delta Force Commando (1990: It.) — Al Bartholomew
Demented (1980: US) — Jim Tynes
Dementia 13 (1963: AIP) — Charles Hannawalt
Demon Pond (1980: Jap.) — N. Sakamoto
Demoniaque (1958: Fr.) — Henry Thibault
Demons in the Garden (1984: Sp.) — Jose Luis Alcaine
Demonstrator (1971: Aus.) — John McLean
Demonwarp (1988: US) — R. Michael Stringer
The Deputy (1985: Sp.) — Antonio Cuevas
Deputy Marshal (1949: Lip.) — Carl Berger
Deranged (1974: Can.--AIP) — Jack McGowan
Dersu Uzala (1976: Jap./USSR) — Asakadru Nakai; Yuri
  Gantman; Fyodor Dobrona

Desert Hearts (1986: US) — Robert Elswit
The Desert Raven (1965: AA) — Taylor Byars
Desert Warrior (1985: US) — Richard Remias

Deserter (1934: USSR) — Anatoli Golovnya; Yuli Fogelman

The Deserter and the Nomads (1969: Czech./It.) — Juro Jabubisko

Desire, the Interior Life (1980: Ger./It.) — Claudio Cirillo

The Desperado (1954: AA) — Joseph M. Novac

The Desperado Trail (1965: Ger./Yugo.--Col.) — Ernest Kalinke

Desperate Hours (1990: MGM/UA) — Douglas Milsome

Desperately Seeking Susan (1985: Orion) — Edward Lachman

Destination 60,000 (1957: AA) — Hal McAlpin

Destiny of a Man (1961: USSR) — Vladimir Monakhov

Destroy All Monsters (1969: Jap.--AIP) — Taiichi Kankura

Detective School Drop Outs (1986: Cannon) — G. Ferrando

The Detour (1968: Bulg.) — Todor Stoyanov

Detroit 9000 (1973: US) — Harry May

The Devil and Max Devlin (1981: Dis.) — Howard Schwartz

The Devil and the Ten Commandments (1962: Fr.) — Roger Fellous

Devil in Silk (1968: Ger.) — Franz Weihmayr

The Devil Is an Empress (1939: Fr.--Col.) — Rene Gaveau; Charles Gaveau

The Devil Made a Woman (1962: Sp.) — Antonio Ballesteros

The Devil Makes Three (1952: MGM) — Vaclav Vich

Devil on Horseback (1954: GB) — Denny Densham

The Devil's General (1957: Ger.) — Albert Benitz

Devil's Rock (1938: GB--Col.) — Germain Gerard Burger

The Devil's Trap (1964: Czech.) — Rudolf Milic

The Devil's Wanton (1962: Swed.) — Goran Strindberg

The Devonsville Terror (1983: US) — Ulli Lommel

Diagnosis Murder (1974: GB) — Bob Edwards

Diamond Safari (1958: TCF) — David Millin; Peter Lang

The Diamond Wizard (1954: GB--UA) — Arthur Grahame

Diamonds of the Night (1968: Czech.) — Jaroslav Kucera

Diary for Mother and Father (1990: Hung.) — Nyika Jansco

Diary for My Children (1984: Hung.) — Miklos Jansco

Diary of a Bachelor (1964: AIP) — Julian Townsend

Diary of a Chambermaid (1964: Fr./It.) — Roger Fellous

Diary of a Schizophrenic Girl (1970: It.--AA) — Franco Fornari

Diary of a Shinjuku Burglar (1969: Jap.) — Yasuhiro Yoshioka; Seizo Sengen

Diary of an Italian (1972: It.) — Antonio Piazza

Dick Barton At Bay (1950: GB--Ham.) — Stanley Clinton

Dick Barton-Special Agent (1948:
   GB--Ham.)   Stanley Clinton
Dillinger Is Dead (1969: It.)   Mario Vulpiani
Dim Sum: A Little Bit of Heart
   (1985: Orion)   Michael Chin
Dimboola (1979: Aus.)   Tom Cowan
Dimka (1964: USSR)   Mikhail Kirillov
Diner (1982: MGM-UA)   Peter Sova
Dingaka (1965: S. Afr.)   Manie Botha; Judex Vijoen
The Diplomatic Corpse (1958: GB)   Philip Grindrod
The Dirt Bike Kid (1985: US)   Daniel Lacambre
Dirty Dancing (1987: US)   Jeff Jur
Dirty Heroes (1971: Fr./Ger./It.)   Gianni Bergamini
Dirty Mary, Crazy Larry (1974: TCF) Mark Margulies
The Dirty Outlaws (1971: It.)   Angelo Filippini
Dirtymouth (1970: US)   Bert Spielvogel
The Discreet (1990: Fr.)   Romain Winding
Disorderlies (1987: WB)   Rolf Kesterman
Disorganized Crime (1989: Dis.)   Ron Garcia
Distant Trumpet (1952: GB)   Gordon Lang
Distant Voices, Still Lives (1988: GB) William Diver
Django (1966: It./Sp.)   Enzo Barboni
Do Not Throw Cushions into the Ring
   (1970: US)   Louis Teague; Basil Bradbury
                                 Arch Archambault

Do You Keep a Lion at Home?
   (1966: Czech.)   Jiri Vojta
The Doberman Gang (1972: US)   Robert Caramico
Doctor Beware (1951: It.)   Vincenzo Seratrice
Doctor Crimen (1953: Mex.)   Victor Herrera
Dr. Goldfoot and the Girl Bombs
   (1966: It.--AIP)   A. Rinaldi
Dr. Hackenstein (1989: US)   Jens Sturup
Dr. Heckyl and Mr. Hype (1980:
   Cannon)   Robert Carras
Doctor of Doom (1962: Mex.)   Enrique Wallace
Dr. Petiot (1990: Fr.)   Patrick Blossier
Dodeska-Den (1970: Jap.)   Tako Saito
Dodge City Trail (1937: Col.)   Goerge Cooper
The Dog and the Diamonds (1962:
   GB--Lip.)   Gordon Lang
Dog's Feast (1990: USSR)   Vladimir Kouzel
Dogs in Space (1987: Aus.)   Andrew De Groot
Doin' Time (1986: WB)   Ronald Garcia
The Doll (1964: Swed.)   Ake Dahlquist
The Doll (1990: USSR)   Vladimir Nakhabtsev
Dollar (1938: Swed.)   Ake Dahlquist
$ [Dollars] (1971: Col.)   Petrus Schloemp
Dolores (1949: Sp.)   Antonio Merayo
Dominick and Eugene (1988: Orion) Curtis Clark
Don Juan, My Dear Ghost (1990: Sp.) Carlos Suarez

Don Quixote (1935: Fr.--UA)	Nicholas Farkas
Don Quixote (1961: USSR)	Andrey Moskvin; Appollinariy Dudko
Dona Flor and Her Two Husbands (1977: Braz.)	Maurilo Salles
Don't Call Me a Con Man (1966: Jap.)	Tadashi Iimura
Don't Cry with Your Mouth Full (1974: Fr.)	Christian Rachman
Don't Drink the Water (1969: AE)	Harvey Genkins
Don't Let the Angels Fall (1969: Can.)	Paul Leach
Don't Panic Chaps! (1959: GB--Col.)	Arthur Graham
Don't Play Us Cheap (1973: US)	Bob Maxwell
Don't Tell Her It's Me (1990: US)	Reed Smoot
Don't Touch White Women (1974: Fr.)	Etienne Becker
Don't Turn the Other Cheek (1974: Ger./It./Sp.)	Jose Aguayo
Door to Door (1985: US)	Reed Smoot
The Dorm That Dripped Blood (1984: US)	Stephen Carpenter
Dossier 51 (1979: Fr.)	Claude Lecomte
The Double-Barrelled Detective Story (1965: US)	Graeme Ferguson; Karl Bissinger
Double Exposure (1989: US)	Cliff Ralke
Double Stop (1968: US)	Flemming Olsen
Double Suicide (1970: Jap.)	Toichiro Narushima
Doubles (1978: US)	P. Kip Anderson
Down and Dirty (1979: It.)	Dario Di Palma
The Dozens (1981: US)	Joe Vitagliano
Dracula and Son (1976: Fr.)	Alain Levent
Dracula's Widow (1989: Del.)	Giuseppe Macari
Dragon Sky (1964: Fr.)	Raymond Le Moigne
The Dragonfly (1955: USSR)	T. Lobova
Dragonslayer (1981: Dis./Par.)	Derek Vanlint
A Dream Come True (1963: USSR)	Aleksei Gerasimov
Dream of a Cossack (1982: USSR)	S. Urusevsky
A Dream of Passion (1978: Greece)	Geroge Arvanitis
Dream of Schonbrunn (1933: Aust.)	Karl Drews
Dreaming Lips (1937: GB--UA)	Roy Clark
Dreams (1960: Swed.)	Hilding Bladh
Dreams (1990: Jap.)	Takao Saito
Dreams Come True (1985: US)	John Drake
Dreams of Glass (1969: Univ.)	Michael Murphy
Dreamscape (1984: TCF)	Brian Tufano
The Dressmaker (1988: GB)	Michael Coulter
The Drifter (1966: US)	Steve Winsten
Drifter (1975: US)	Pat Rocco
The Drifter (1988: US)	David Sperling
Drive-In Massacre (1976: US)	Kenneth Lloyd Gibb
Drunken Angel (1948: Jap.)	Takeo Ito

Dry Summer (1967: Turk.) — Ali Ugur
Duck in Orange Sauce (1976: It.) — Franco Di Giacomo
The Duck Rings at Half Past Seven
(1969: Ger./It.) — Wolf Wirth
Duck, You Sucker! (1972: It.--UA) — Giuseppe Ruzzolini
The Duel (1964: USSR) — Antonina Egina
Duel at Ezo (1970: Jap.) — Hiroshi Murai
Duel in the Jungle (1954: GB--WB) — Edwin Miller
Duet for Cannibals (1969: Swed.) — Lars Swanberg
Dulcinea (1962: Sp.) — Gofferdo Pacheco
The Dybbuk (1989: Pol.) — A. Wymerka

Eagle in a Cage (1971: Yugo.--US) — Franco Vodopivec
Eagle over London (1973: It.) — Alejandro Ulloa
The Ear (1990: Czech.) — Josef Illik
Early Autumn (1962: Jap.) — Asakazu Nakai
Early Works (1970: Yugo.) — Karpo Acimovic Godina
The Earth Dies Screaming (1964:
GB--TCF) — Arthur Lowis
Earth Entranced (1970: Braz.) — Luis Carlos Barreto
Earthbound (1990: Ger.) — Ludolph Weyer
East China Sea (1969: Jap.) — Masahisa Himeda
East of Kilimanjaro (1962: GB/It.) — Edwin E. Olsen
The Easy Life (1963: It.--Emb.) — Alfio Contini
The Easy Life (1971: Fr.) — Georges Strouve
Easy Wheels (1989: US) — James Lemmo
Eat the Peach (1988: GB) — Arthur Wooster
The Eavesdropper (1966: Arg.--US) — Alberto Etchebehere
The Echo (1964: Pol.) — Jerzy Wojcik
Echo Park (1986: US) — Karl Kofler
Echoes of Silence (1966: US) — Peter Emmanuel Goldman
Ecstasy (1933: Czech.) — Jan Stallich; Hans Androsch
The Edge (1968: US) — Robert Machover
Edge of Hell (1956: Univ.) — Edward Fitzgerald
Edge of Sanity (1989: GB) — Tony Spratling
The Education of Sonny Carson
(1974: Par.) — Ed Brown
Edvard Munch (1976: Nor./Swed.) — Odd Geir Saether
Edward and Caroline (1952: Fr.) — Robert Lefebvre
Eglantine (1972: Fr.) — Alain Derobe
Egon Schiele--Excess and Punishment
(1981: Ger.) — Rudolf Blahacek
Egypt by Three (1953: US) — Nicholas Hayer
Eight Men Out (1988: Orion) — Robert Richardson
Eight O'Clock Walk (1954: GB) — Brendan Stafford
Eight Tales of Gold (1990: Hg.Kg.) — Bill Wong; Tony Ducchiari
1871 (1990: GB) — Elso Roque
1812 (1944: USSR) — Mikhail Gindin
The Eighth Day of the Week
(1959: Ger./Pol.) — Jerzy Lipman

The Eighties (1985: Fr.)   Michel Hossiau
84 Charlie Mopic (1989: US)   Alan Caso
El Dorado (1988: Fr./Sp.)   Teo Escamilla
The Electronic Monster (1960: GB)   Bert Mason
An Elephant Called Slowly (1970: GB)   Simon Trevor
Elisabeth of Austria (1931: Ger.)   Frederik Fugslang
Eliza Fraser (1976: Aus.)   Robin Copping; Dan Burstall
Ellie (1984: US)   George Tirl
The Elusive Corporal (1963: Fr.)   Georges Leclerc
Elvira Madigan (1967: Swed.)   Jorgen Persson
Embezzled Heaven (1959: Ger.--UFA)   Bruno Mondi
Emil and the Detective (1931: Ger.)   Werner Brandes
Emil and the Detectives (1964: Dis.)   Gunther Senftleben
Eminent Domain (1990: Can./Fr./Isr.)   Witold Adamek
Emmanuelle 4 (1985: Fr.--Cannon)   Jean-Francis Gondre
The Emperor and a General (1968: Jap.)   Hiroshi Murai
The Emperor and the Golem (1955: Czech.)   Jan Stallich; Bohumil Haba
The Emperor and the Nightingale (1949: Czech.)   Ferdinand Pecenka
Enchanted Island (1958: WB)   Jorge Stahl, Jr.
The Enchanting Shadow (1965 Hg.Kg.)   Ho Lu-ying
End of a Priest (1970: Czech.)   Jaromir Sofr
The End of August (1982: US)   Bob Elswit
The End of August at the Hotel Ozone (1967: Czech.)   Jiri Macak
End of Innocence (1960: Arg.)   Anibal Gonzalez Paz
The End of Innocence (1990: US)   Alex Nepomniaschy
End of Mrs. Cheney (1963: Ger.)   Gunther Anders
End of the Line (1988: Orion)   George Tirl
End Play (1975: Aus.)   Robin Copping
The Endless Night (1963: Ger.)   Hans Jura
Enemy of the People (1989: India)   Barun Raha
The Enforcer (1976: WB)   Charles Short
Engagement Italiano (1966: Fr./It.)   Enzo Serafin
England Made Me (1973: GB)   Ray Parslow
Enid Is Sleeping (1990: US)   Affonso Beato
Enigma (1983: US)   Jean Louis Picavet
Enjo (1959: Jap.)   Kazuo Miyagawa
Enormous Changes at the Last Minute (1985: US)   Thomas McDonough
Enough Rope (1966: Fr./Ger./It.)   Jacques Natteau
Entr'acte (1924: Fr.)   J. Berliet
Entre Nous (1983: Fr.--MGM-UA)   Bernard Lutic
Epilogue (1967: Den.)   Henning Kristiansen
Equinox (1970: US)   Mike Hoover
Erendira (1984: Sp.)   Denys Clerval
Eric Soya's "17" (1967: Den.)   Ole Lytken
Erik the Viking (1989: GB--Orion)   Ian Wilson

Ernest Goes to Camp (1987:
    Dis./Touch.)   Harvey Mathias;   Jim May
Ernesto (1983: It.)   Camillo Bazzoni
Eroica (1966: Pol.)   Jerzy Wojcik
Escape by Night (1954: GB)   Monty Berman
Escape from Paradise (1990: It.)   Alfio Contini
Escape from the Bronx (1985: It.)   Blasco Giurato
Escape from Yesterday (1939: Fr.)   Jules Kruger; Marc Fossard
Escape in the Sun (1956: GB--Par.)   Bernard Davies
Escape to Berlin (1962: Ger./Switz.--
    US)   Gunter Haase; Gerd von Bor
Escape 2000 (1983: Aus.)   John McLean
Escaped from Dartmoor (1930:
    GB)   S. Rodwell; M. Lindblom
Esquilache (1989: Sp.)   Juan Amoros
The Eternal Husband (1946: Fr.)   Nicolas Toporkoff
The Eternal Mask (1937: Switz.)   Oscar Schnirch
Eternity (1990: US)   John Lambert
Eternity of Love (1961: Jap.)   Asakazu Nakai
Eve Wants To Sleep (1961: Pol.)   Stevan Matyjaszkiewicz;
                                             Josef Stawiski
Evenings (1990: Holl.)   Willy Stassen
Every Man for Himself and God against
    All (1975: Ger.)   Jorge Schmidt-Reitwein
Every Time We Say Goodbye (1986:
    Tri-S.)   Giuseppe Lanci
Everybody Go Home! (1962: Fr./It.--
    Del.)   Carlo Carlini; Gastone Di
                                             Giovanni
Everybody's Fine (1990: Fr./It.)   Blasco Giurato
The Evictors (1979: AIP)   Chuck Bryant
The Evil (1978: US)   Mario Di Leo
The Evil Dead (1983: US)   Tim Philo; Joshua Becker
Evil Dead 2: Dead by Dawn (1987:
    US)   Peter Deming; Eugene Shug
Evils of the Night (1985: US)   Don Stern
Excess Baggage (1933: GB)   Sydney Blythe
The Exiles (1966: US)   Erik Daarstad; John Merril;
                                             Robert Kaufman
Experience Preferred--But Not
    Essential (1983: GB)   Phil Meheux
The Exterminator (1980: AE)   Robert Baldwin
The Exterminator of the Year 3000
    (1985: It./Sp.)   Alejandro Ulloa
The Eye Creatures (1965: AIP)   Ralph Johnson
An Eye for an Eye (1981: AE)   Roger Shearman
The Eye of the Needle (1965: Fr./It.)   Riccardo Pallottini
Eyes of a Stranger (1980: WB)   Mini Rojas
The Eyes of Annie Jones (1963:
    GB--TCF)   Peter Hennessy

The Eyes, the Mouth (1982: Fr./It.) — Giuseppe Lanci
Eyes, the Sea and a Ball (1968: Jap.) — Hiroyuki Kusuda

F. P. 1 (1933: GB--Fox) — Fritz Thiery
Fabian of the Yard (1954: GB) — Hilton Craig
Fabiola (1951: It.--UA) — Osvaldo Civirani
The Fabulous World of Jules Verne (1961: Czech.--WB) — George Taran; B. S. Piccard; Anthony Hora
Face of Fire (1959: GB--AA) — Edward Vorkapich
Face to Face (1967: It.) — Rafael Pacheco
Faces (1968: US) — Al Ruban
The Falcon Fighters (1970: Jap.) — Kimio Watanabe
The Fall of Rome (1963: It.) — Riccardo Pallottini
Fallada--The Last Chapter (1989: Ger.) — Roland Dressel
Falling Over Backwards (1990: Can.) — Savas Kalogeras
False Identity (1990: US) — Bernard Aurox
Family Life (1971: GB--EMI/MGM — Charles Stewart
Fandango (1985: WB) — Peter Lansdown
A Fantastic Comedy (1975: Rom) — Grigoire Ionescu; Stefan Horvath

The Fantastic Three (1967: Fr./Ger./It./Yugo.) — Franscesco Izzarelli
Fantomas (1913: Fr.) — G. Guerin
Fantomas Strikes Back (1965: Fr./It.) — Raymond Lemoigne
Far from Dallas (1972: Fr.) — Jean Bourdelon
Far from Poland (1984: US) — Jack Laskus
Far Out Men (1990: US) — Greg Gardiner; Erik Woster
Farewell, My Beloved (1969: Jap.) — Hiroyuki Nagaoka
Farewell, Street Urchins (1989: USSR) — Boris Novoselov
The Farmer (1977: Col.) — Irv Goodnoff
The Fascist (1965: It.) — Erico Menczer
Fast Charlie ... The Moonbeam Rider (1979: Univ.) — William Birch
Die Fastnachtsbeichte (1962: Ger.--UFA) — Heinz Pehlke
Fatal Attraction (1987: Par.) — Howard Atherton
Father (1967: Hung.) — Sandor Sara
Father (1990: Aus.) — Dan Burstal
Father of a Soldier (1966: USSR) — Lev Sukhov; A. Filipashvili; L. Namgalashvili
Father Sergius (1918: USSR) — Fedot Burgason; Nikolai Rudakov
Father's Dilemma (1952: It.) — Mario Craveri
Fatso (1980: TCF) — Brianne Murphy
Faust (1963: Ger.) — Gunther Anders
The Favorite (1989: Switz.--TCF) — Howard Wexler; Giorgio Tonti

Favorites of the Moon (1985: Fr.)　　Philippe Theaudiere
FBI Code 98 (1964: WB)　　Robert Hoffman
Fear (1956: Ger.)　　Peter Heller
The Fear (1967: Greece)　　Nikos Gardelis
Fear and Desire (1953: US)　　Stanley Kubrick
Fear City (1985: US)　　James Lemmo
Fear Eats the Soul (1974: Ger.)　　Jurgen Jurges
Fear No Evil (1981: AE)　　Fred Goodlich
Federal Man (1950: EL)　　Clark Ramsey
Fedora (1946: It.)　　Giuseppe La Torre
Fellow Traveler (1990: GB/US)　　John Kenway
Female Fiends (1958: GB)　　Philip Grindrod
La Femme Enfant (1982: Fr.)　　Alain Derobe
Femmina (1968: Fr./Ger./It.)　　Maurice Fellous
Fernandel the Dressmaker (1947: Fr.)　　Charles Suin
La Fete Espagnole (1919: Fr.)　　P. Parguel
Feu Mathias Pascal (1925: Fr.)　　P. Guichard; J. Letort
The Feud (1989: US)　　John Beymer
Fever Heat (1968: Par.)　　Gary Young
A Few Bullets More (1968: It./Sp.)　　Miguel Mila
The Fiances (1964: It.)　　Lamberto Caimi
The Fickle Finger of Fate (1967: Sp.)　　Antonio Macasoli
Fidelio (1961: Aust.)　　Nicholas Hayer; Hannes
　　　　Fuchs; Viktor Meihsl;
　　　　Walter Tuch

Fidelio (1970: Ger)　　Hannes Schindler
The Field (1990: GB)　　Jack Conroy
The Fifth Horseman Is Fear (1968:
　Czech.)　　Jan Kalis
The Fifth Monkey (1990: US)　　Gideon Porath
Fight for Us (1989: Fr./Phil.)　　Rody Lacap
Fighting Hero (1934: US)　　J. Henry Kruse
Fighting Mad (1976: TCF)　　Michael Watkins
The Fighting Stallion (1950: EL)　　Clark Ramsey
The Fighting Wildcats (1957: GB--Rep.)　Jimmy Harvey
Film without a Name (1950: Ger.)　　Igor Oberberg
The Final Chord (1936: Ger.--UFA)　　Robert Baberske
The Final Comedown (1972: US)　　William B. Caplan
The Final Cut (1980: Aus.)　　Ron Johanson
The Final Option (1983: GB--MGM)　　Phil Meheux
The Final Terror (1984: US)　　Andreas Davidescu
The Final Test (1953: GB)　　Bill McLeod
The Final War (1960: Jap.)　　Tadashi Arakami
Find the Lady (1936: GB--TCF)　　Stanley Grant
Find the Lady (1956: GB)　　Brendan Stafford
A Fine Pair (1969: It.--NG)　　Alfio Contini
Finger on the Trigger (1965: Sp.--AA)　Antonio Macasoli; Miguel
　　　　Barquero
The Fingerman (1963: Fr.)　　Nicholas Hayer
Finnegans Wake (1965: US)　　Ted Nemeth

Finney (1969: US)   Jack Richards
Fino a Farti Male (1969: Fr./It.)   Patrice Pouget
A Fire Has Been Arranged (1935: GB)   Sydney Blythe
Fire in the Flesh (1964: Fr.)   Jean Isnard
The Fire in the Stone (1983: Aus.)   Ross Berryman
Fire in the Straw (1943: Fr.)   Marcel Lucien
Fire Maidens from Outer Space (1956:
  GB)   Ian Struthers
Fire with Fire (1986: Par.)   Hiro Narita
Fireball Jungle (1968: US)   Clifford Poland
Fires on the Plain (1962: Jap.)   Setsuo Kobayashi
Firestarter (1984: Univ.)   Giuseppe Ruzzolini
The Firm Man (1975: Aus.)   Sasha Trikojus
First Contact (1984: US)   Dennis O'Rourke
The First Nudie Musical (1976: Par.)   Douglas Knapp
The First Power (1990: Orion)   Theo Van De Sande
First Spaceship on Venus (1960:
  Ger./Pol.)   Joachim Hasler
First Start (1953: Pol.)   Felike Srednicki
First Taste of Love (1962: Fr.)   Roger Duculot
The First Time (1978: Fr.)   Jean Cesar Chiabaut
The First Time (1983: US)   Steve Fierberg
The First Turn On (1984: US)   Lloyd Kaufman
Fist Fighter (1989: US)   Hans Burman
Fist in His Pocket (1968: It.)   Alberto Marrama
A Fistful of Dollars
  (1964: Ger./It./Sp.--UA)   Massimo Dallamano
Fists of Fury (1973: China)   Chen Ching-Cchu
Five (1951: Col.)   Louis Clyde Stoumen; Sid
                                                         Lubow
Five Days from Home (1978: Univ.)   Harvey Genkins
Five Days in June (1989: Fr.)   Jean-Yves Le Mener
Five Giants from Texas (1966: It./
  Sp.)   Victor Montreal
Five Golden Dragons (1967: GB--WB)   John von Kotze
5 Sinners (1961: Ger.)   Walter Tuch
Five the Hard Way (1969: US)   Jon Hall
The Flag Lieutenant (1932: GB)   Stanley Rodwell
Flagrante Delicto (1988: Can./Fr.)   Francois Protat
Flame over Vietnam (1967: Ger./Sp.)   Miguel Mila
Flaming Frontier (1958: Can.--TCF)   Frederick Ford
Flanagan (1985: US)   Ivan Strasburg
Flareup (1969: MGM)   Andrew McIntyre
A Flash of Green (1985: US)   Victor Nunez
Flashpoint (1984: Tri-S.)   Peter Moss
The Flaxfield (1985: Holl.)   Ben Tenniglo
Die Fledermaus (1964: Aust.)   Willy Winterstein
The Flesh Eaters (1964: US)   Carson Davidson
Flesh Feast (1970: US)   Thomas Casey
Fleshburn (1984: US)   Bill Pecchi

Fletch Lives (1989: Univ.) — John McPherson
Flex (1990: US) — Dan Swietlik
Flight from Vienna (1956: GB) — Hal Morey
Flight of the Navigator (1986: Dis.) — James Glennon
Flight to Fury (1966: Phil.--TCF) — Mike Accion
The Floating Dutchman (1953: GB--AA) — Joe Ambor
Floating Weeds (1970: Jap.) — Kazuo Miyagawa
Flowers for the Man in the Moon
   (1975: Ger.) — Helmut Grewald
Flowers in the Attic (1987: US) — Frank Byers; Gil Hubbs
Flowing (1985: Jap.) — Masao Tamai
Flunkey Time (1990: Czech.) — S. A. Brabec
Fly Away Peter (1948: GB) — Roy Fogwell
Flying Fox in a Freedom Tree
   (1989: Aus.) — Allen Guilford
The Flying Guillotine (1975: China) — Tsao Hui-chi
The Flying Matchmaker (1970: Isr.) — Romolo Garroni
The Flying Saucer (1964: It.) — Bruno Barcarol
Folies Bergere (1958: Fr.) — Pierre Montazel
Follow Your Star (1938: GB) — Cyril Bristow
Fond Memories (1982: Can.) — Guy Dufaux
The Fool and the Princess (1948: GB) — A. T. Dinsdale
Fools of Fortune (1990: GB) — Jerry Zielinski
For a Few Dollars More
   (1967: Ger./It./Sp.--UA) — Massimo Dallamano
For Love of Ivy (1968: US) — Joseph Coffey
For Queen and Country (1988: GB) — Richard Greatrex
The Forbidden Dance (1990: Col.) — R. Michael Stringer
Forbidden Journey (1950: Can.--UA) — Roger Racine
Forbidden Jungle (1950: EL) — Clark Ramsey
Forbidden Relations (1983: Hung.) — Janos Kende
Forbidden Sun (1989: GB) — Richard Greatrex
Forbidden Territory (1938: GB) — R. Goldenberg
Force Majeure (1989: Fr.) — Bertrand Chantry
A Force of One (1979: US) — Roger Shearman
Forced Entry (1984: US) — Aaron Kleinman
Foreign Intrigue (1956: UA) — Bertil Palmgren
Forever My Love (1962: AUst.--Par.) — Bruno Mondi
Forever Young (1986: GB) — Norman Langley
Forever Yours (1937: GB--UA) — Hans Schneeberg
Forgery and the Use of Forgeries
   (1990: Fr.) — Robert Alazraki
Forget About Me (1990: GB/Hung.) — Ray Orton
Fort Graveyard (1966: Jap.) — Rokuro Nishigaki
The Fortress (1979: Hung.) — Miklos Biro
Fortune and Men's Eyes (1971:
   Can.--MGM) — Georges Dufaux
Fortune Lane (1947: GB) — Jo Jago; Brendan Stafford
Forty Deuce (1982: US) — Francois Reichenbach;
   Stefan Stapasik; Steven
   Fierberg

48 Hours to Acapulco (1968: Ger.)	Hubs Hagen; Niklas Schilling
Forty-Nine Days (1964: USSR)	Arkadiy Koltsatyy
The Fountain of Love (1968: Aust.)	Franz Lederle
Four Bags Full (1957: Fr./It.)	Jacques Natteau
Four Boys and a Gun (1957: UA)	J. Burgi Contner
Four Days (1951: GB)	Ray Elton
Four Days Leave (1950: Switz.)	Emil Berna
Four in a Jeep (1951: Switz.)	Emil Berna
Four Masked Men (1934: GB--Univ.)	Sydney Blythe
Four Nights of a Dreamer (1972: Fr.)	Pierre Lhomme
The Fourth Protocol (1987: GB--Lor.)	Phil Meheux
The Fox with Nine Tails (1969: Jap.)	Masayoshi Kishimoto
Foxes (1980: UA)	Leon Bijou
Francesco (1989: Ger./It.)	Giuseppe Lanci
Frankenstein Conquers the World (1964: Jap.--AIP)	Hajime Koizumi
Frankenstein Meets the Space Monster (1965 AA)	Saul Midwall
Frankenstein Unbound (1990: TCF)	Michael Scott
Frantic (1988: WB)	Witold Sobocinski
Frasier, The Sensuous Lion (1973: US)	David Butler
Fraternity Row (1977: Par.)	Peter Gibbons
Fraternity Vacation (1985: US)	Paul Ryan
Free, White and 21 (1963: AIP)	Ralph Johnson
Freedom (1985: GB)	Ron Johnson
Freeze-Die-Come to Life (1990: USSR)	Vladimir Bryliakov
Der Freischutz (1970: Ger.)	Hannes Schindler
The French Detective (1979: Fr.)	Jean Collomb
French Lesson (1986: Fr./WB)	Clive Tickner
French Quarter (1978: US)	Jerry Kalogeratos
The French Revolution: The Light Years/The Terrible Years (1989: Can./Fr./Ger./It.)	Francois Catonne
The French Touch (1954: Fr.)	Charles Suin
Friday Foster (1975: AIP)	Harry May
Friday the 13th (1980: Par.)	Barry Abrams
Friday the 13th Part III (1982: Par.)	Gerald Feil
Friday the 13th Part VI: Jason Lives (1986: Par.)	Jon Kranhouse
Friday the 13th Part VII--The New Blood (1988: Par.)	Paul Elliott
Friday the 13th Part VIII: Jason Takes Manhattan (1989: Par.)	Bryan England
Friend of the Family (1965: Fr./It.)	Robert Lefebvre
A Friend Will Come Tonight (1948: Fr.)	Robert Lefebvre
The Friendly Killer (1970: Jap.)	Sei Kitaizumi
Friends, Comrades (1990: Fin.)	Kjell Lageroos
Fright Night (1985: Col.)	Jan Kiesser
The Frightened Man (1952: GB)	Monty Berman

From Hell to Victory (1979:
    Fr./It./Sp.)   Jose Luis Alcaine
Front Woman (1989: Fr.)   Ramon Suarez
Frontier Hellcat (1966:
    Fr./Ger./It./Yugo.--Col.)   Karl Loeb
The Fruit Is Ripe (1961: Fr./It.)   Paul Coteret
Full Metal Jacket (1987: WB)   Douglas Milsome
Full Moon High (1986: Orion)   Daniel Pearl
Full Speed Ahead (1936: GB--Par.)   Stanley Grant
Full Speed Ahead (1939: GB)   W. Winterton
Funeral Ceremony (1969: Czech.)   Jiri Machane
Funnyman (1967: US)   John Korty
Further Up the Creek (1958:
    GB--Col.)   Len Harris
Fury of the Pagans (1963: It.--Col.)   Vincenzo Seratrice
Future Hunters (1989: US)   Ricardo Remias
Future Zone (1990: US)   Voya Mikulic

Gaby--A True Story (1987: Tri-S.)   Lajos Koltai
Le Gai Savoir (1968: Fr.)   Georges Leclerc
Gal Young Un (1979: US)   Victor Nunez
The Galaxy Invader (1985: US)   Paul Loeschke
Galia (1966: Fr./It.)   Maurice Fellous
Galileo (1968: Bulg./It.)   Alfio Contini
The Gallant One (1964: Peru--US)   J. Carlos Carbajal
The Gambling Samurai (1966: Jap.)   Rokuro Nishigaki
The Game (1989: US)   Paul Gibson
A Game for Six Lovers (1962: Fr.)   Roger Fellous
The Game of Death (1979: Col.)   Godfrey A. Godar
The Game of Love (1954: Fr.)   Robert Lefebvre
Die Gans Von Sedan (1962:
    Fr./Ger.--UFA)   Jacques Leteiller
The Garbage Pail Kids (1987: US)   Harvey Genkins
The Garnet Bracelet (1966: USSR)   Leonid Kraynenkov
Gas-s-s-s! (1970: AIP)   Ron Dexter
The Gate (1987: Can.)   Thomas Vamos
Gate of Hell (1954: Jap.)   Kohei Sugiyama
Gates of Paris (1958: Fr./It.)   Robert Lefebvre
Gates to Paradise (1968: Ger./GB)   Wieczyslaw Jahoda
Les Gauloises Bleues (1969: Fr.)   Alain Levent
The Gay Adventure (1953: GB--UA)   Guy Drisse
Gay Love (1936: GB)   Alex Bryce
A Geisha (1978: Jap.)   Kazuo Miyagawa
General John Regan (1933: GB--UA)   Cyril Bristow
General Massacre (1973: Belg./US)   Herman Wuyts
General Suvorov (1941: USSR)   A. Golovnya; T. Lobova
The Genius (1976: Fr./Ger./It.)   Giuseppe Ruzzolini
Gentle Giant (1967: Par.)   Howard Winner
The Gentle Rain (1966: Braz.--AA)   Mario Di Leo

Genuine Risk (1990: US) — Dean Lent
Georg (1964: US) — Detlev Wiede
George (1973: Switz.--US) — Peter Rohe
George in Civvy Street (1946: GB--Col.) — Philip Grindrod
George Washington Carver (1940: US) — Ernest St. George
George's Island (1989: Can.) — Les Kriszan
Georgia (1988: Aus.) — Yuri Sokol
The German Sisters (1982: Ger.) — Franz Rath
Gertrud (1966: Den.) — Henning Bendtsen; Arne Abrahamsen

Getting Even (1986: US) — Peter Lyons Collister
Getting It Right (1989: GB) — Clive Tickner
Ghidrah, The Three-Headed Monster (1965: Jap.) — Hajime Koizumi
Ghost Ship (1953: GB) — Stanley Grant
Ghost Story (1974: GB) — Peter Hurst
The Ghost Train (1930: GB) — Leslie Rowson
Ghosts Can Do It (1990: US) — John Derek
Ghoulies II (1988: US) — Sergio Salvati
The Gift (1983: Fr./It.) — Daniel Gaudry
The Gig (1985: US) — Jeri Sopanen
Gigantis (1959: Jap.--US) — Seichi Endo
The Gilded Cage (1954: GB) — Monty Berman
Gina (1961: Fr./Mex.) — Jorge Stahl, Jr.
The Girl and the Burglar (1967: USSR) — A. Panasyuk
Girl from Hong Kong (1966: Ger.) — Klaus von Rautenfeld
The Girl from the Marsh Croft (1935: Ger.--UFA) — Willie Winterstein
The Girl from Trieste (1983: It.) — Alfio Contini
Girl in the Picture (1956: GB) — Ian Struthers
The Girl in the Picture (1986: GB--US) — Dick Pope
The Girl in the Swing (1988: GB--US) — Claus Loof
The Girl Is Mine (1950: GB) — Ben Hart
The Girl of the Moors (1961: Ger.) — Albert Benitz
Girl with a Suitcase (1961: Fr./It.) — Tino Santoni
The Girl with Red Hair (1983: Hol.) — Theo Van De Sande
The Girl with Three Camels (1968: Czech.) — Rudolf Stahl
The Girls (1972: Swed.) — Rune Ericson
Girls Just Want to Have Fun (1985: US) — Thomas Ackerman
Girls Night Out (1984: US) — Joe Rivers
Girls on the Beach (1965: Par.) — Arch Dalzell
Give 'Em Hell, Harry! (1975: US) — Ken Palius
Give Me My Chance (1958: Fr.) — Maurice Barry
Give My Regards to Broad Street (1984: TCF) — Ian McMillan
Give Us the Moon (1944: GB) — Philip Grindrod
The Given Word (1964: Braz.) — Chick Fowle

Gladiators 7 (1964: It./Sp.) — Adalberto Albertini; Eloy Mella

The Glass Cage (1964: US) — Jean-Philippe Carson

A Glass of Water (1962: Ger.) — Gunther Anders

The Glass Sphinx (1968: Egypt/It./Sp.) — Felix Miron Martinez

Gleaming the Cube (1989: TCF) — Reed Smoot

The Glitterball (1977: GB) — Alan Hall

Glowing Autumn (1981; Jap.) — Kozo Okazaki

Go, Johnny, Go! (1959: US) — Edward Fitzgerald

Go, Man, Go! (1954: UA) — Phil Steiner

The Go Masters (1986: China/Jap.) — Shoehei Ando; Luo De-an

Go Tell It on the Mountain (1984: US) — Hiro Narita

God Forgives--I Don't (1969: It./Sp.) — Alfio Contini

The Goddess (1962: India) — Subrata Mitra

The Gods Must Be Crazy (1984: TCF) — Buster Reynolds; Robert Lewis

The Gods Must Be Crazy 2 (1989: Botswana) — Buster Reynolds

God's Witness (1990: Yugo.) — Aleksandar Petkovic

Godspell (1973: Col.) — Richard G. Heimann

Godzilla 85 (1985: Jap.) — Kazutami Hara

Goin' Home (1976: US) — Chris Prentiss

Goin' to Chicago (1990: US) — Francis Grumman

Gold Fever (1952: Mon.) — Clark Ramsey; Glen Gano

Gold for the Caesars (1964: MGM) — Raffaele Masciocchi

The Golden Arrow (1964: It.--MGM) — Mario Capriotti

Golden Braid (1990: Aus.) — Nino Martinetti

Golden Demon (1956: Jap.) — Michio Takahashi

Golden Gate Girl (1941: US) — J. Sunn

The Golden Head (1965: Hung.--US) — Istvan Hildebrand

Golden Mountains (1958: Den.) — Joergen Skov

Goldstein (1964: US) — Jean-Philippe Carson

The Golem (1937: Czech.) — Jan Stallich; Vaclav Vich

Golem (1980: Pol.) — Zygmunt Samosiuk

Golgotha (1937: Fr.) — G. J. Kruger

Goliath and the Sins of Babylon (1964: It.--AIP) — Mario Sbrenna

Goliath and the Vampires (1964: It.--AIP) — Alvaro Mancori

Gone in 60 Seconds (1964: US) — John Vacek

Good Evening, Mr. Wallenberg (1990: Swed.) — Esa Vuorinen

Good Morning, Vietnam (1987: Dis./Touch.) — Peter Sova

The Good Old Days (1989: Ger.) — Marian Czura

Good People (1990: Swed.) — Per Kallberg; Stefan Henez

Good Riddance (1981: Fr.) — Michel Brault

Good Times (1967: Col.) — Robert Wyckoff

The Good Wife (1987: Aus.) — James Bartle

Goodbye, Moscow (1968: Jap.)	Yasumichi Fukuzawa
Goodbye Pork Pie (1981: NZ)	Alun Bollinger
Goodnight, Ladies and Gentlemen (1977: It.)	Claudio Ragona
Goodnight, Sweet Marilyn (1989: US)	Miles Anderson
The Goose Girl (1967: Ger.)	Gerhard Huttula
The Gordeyev Family (1961: USSR)	Margarita Pilikhina
The Gorilla Greets You (1958: Fr.)	Louis Page
The Gospel Road (1973: TCF)	Robert Elfstrom; Tom McDonough
Gothic (1987: US)	Mike Southron
Goyokin (1969: Jap.)	Kozo Okazaki
Gran Varieta (1955: It.)	Carlo Carlini
The Grand Escapade (1946: GB)	Jo Jago
Grand Slam (1968: Ger./It./Sp.-- Par.)	Antonio Macasoli
The Grand Substitution (1965: HgKg.)	Yu Tsang-shan
Granddad Rudd (1935: Aus.)	Frank Hurley
La Grande Bouffe (1973: Fr.)	Mario Vulpiani; Paschale Rachini
Grandmother's House (1989: US)	Peter Jensen
The Grass Is Singing (1982: GB/Swed.)	Bille August
Grayeagle (1977: AIP)	Jim Roberson
Greased Lightning (1977: WB)	George Bouillet
Greaser's Palace (1972: US)	Peter Powell
The Great Adventure (1955: Swed.)	Arne Sucksdorff
Great Balls of Fire! (1989: Orion)	Alfonso Beato
The Great Big World and Little Children (1962: Pol.)	Kazimierz Vavrzyniak; Jacik Korcelli
The Great Game (1953: GB)	Philip Grindrod
The Great Macarthy (1975: Aus.)	Bruce MacNaughton
The Great St. Louis Bank Robbery (1959: UA)	Victor Duncan
The Great Smokey Roadblock (1978: US)	Ed Brown
The Great Spy Chase (1966: Fr.-- AIP)	Maurice Fellous
The Great Texas Dynamite Chase (1976: US)	Jamie Anderson
The Great Wall (1965: Jap.)	Michio Takahashi
The Great Waltz (1972: MGM)	Dave Boulton
The Greed of William Hart (1948: GB)	D. P. Cooper
Green Card (1990: Aus./Fr.--BV/ Touch.)	Geoffrey Simpson
The Green Mare (1961: Fr./It.)	Jacques Natteau
The Green Pack (1934: GB)	Alex Bryce
The Green Slime (1969: Jap.--MGM)	Yoshikazu Yamasawa

The Green Tree (1965: It.)	A. Grasso; Joseph Sacchi
The Green-Eyed Blonde (1957: WB)	Edward Fitzgerald
Greenwich Village Story (1963: US)	Baird Bryant
Gregory's Girl (1982: GB)	Michael Coulter
Greh (1962: Ger./Yugo.)	Bruno Stephan
Grievous Bodily Harm (1988: Aus.)	Ellery Ryan
Grim Prairie Tales (1990: US)	Janusz Minski
Gringo (1963: It./Sp.)	Massimo Dallamano
Grizzly (1976: US)	William Anderson
The Groove Tube (1974: US)	Bob Bailin
Gross Anatomy (1989: BV/Touch.)	Steven Yaconelli
Grown-Up Children (1963: USSR)	Sergey Zaytsev; Vladimir Meybom
The Guard (1990: USSR)	Valeri Martynov
The Guardian Angel (1990: Swed.)	Goran Nilsson
Guardian of the Wilderness (1977: US)	Henning Schellerup
Guerrilla Girl (1953: UA)	Charles Wecker; George Stoetzel; Sidney Zucker
The Guest (1984: GB)	Rod Stewart
Guests Are Coming (1965: Pol.)	Stanislaw Loth
The Guide (1965: India--US)	Fali Mistry
Guilt (1967: Swed.)	Lars Goran Bjorne
Guilt Is My Shadow (1950: GB)	William McLeod
Guinguette (1959: Fr.)	Pierre Montazel
The Gumshoe Kid (1990: US)	Harvey Genkins
Gunfighters of Casa Grande (1965: Sp.--MGM)	Jose Aguayo
Gunmen of the Rio Grande (1965: Fr./It./Sp.--AA)	Gugliemo Mancori; Mario Capriotti
The Gunrunner (1989: US)	Alain Dostie
Guns (1980: Fr.)	Richard Kopans; Louis Bihi; Eric Pittard; Claude Michaud
Guns (1990: US)	Howard Wexler
Guns of the Black Watch (1961: Fr./It.)	Carlo Bellero
Guns of the Magnificent Seven (1969: UA)	Antonio Macasoli
The Guru (1969: India--TCF)	Subrata Mitra
A Guy, a Gal and a Pal (1945: Col.)	Glen Gano
Guyana, Cult of the Damned (1980: Mex./Panama/Sp.--Univ.)	Leopoldo Villasenor
Gymkata (1985: MGM-UA)	Godfrey Godar
H (1990: Can.)	Gerald Parker
The H-Man (1959: Jap.--Col.)	Hajime Koizumi
La Habanera (1937: Ger.--UFA)	Franz Weihmayr

Hagbard and Signe (1968: Den./
  Ice./Nor.)
Hail (1983: US) — Henning Bendsten
Hail Mary (1985: Fr.) — William Storz

Jean-Bernard Menoud;
  Jacques Firmann
The Hairdresser's Husband (1990: Fr.) — Edouardo Serra
Hairspray (1988: US) — David Insley
Haixan (1921: Swed.) — J. Ankerstjerne
Hallelujah the Hills (1963: US) — Ed Emshviller
Halloween 4: The Return of Michael
  Myers (1988: US) — Peter Lyons Collister
Halloween 5 (1989: US) — Robert Draper
Hambone and Hillie (1984: US) — Jon Kranhouse
Hamburger (1986: US) — Karen Grossman
Hamburger Hill (1987: Par./RKO) — Peter MacDonald
Hamlet (1962: Ger.) — Kurt Geweissen
Hamlet (1964: WB) — Bill Colleran
Hamlet (1966: USSR) — Ionas Gritsyus
Hamlet (1976: GB) — Robina Rose; Dick Perrin;
  A. Humphreys
Hammer (1972: UA) — Robert Steadman
The Hand (1960: GB--AIP) — Jimmy Harvey
The Hand in the Trap (1963: Arg./
  Sp.) — Alberto Etchebehere; Juan
  Julion Baena
The Hand of Night (1968: GB) — William Jordan
Handcuffs, London (1955: GB) — Brendan Stafford
Handle with Care (1932: Fox) — John Schmitz
Handle with Care (1964: US) — William Troiano
Hang Your Hat on the Wind (1969:
  Dis.) — Edward Hughes
Hank Williams: The Show He Never
  Gave (1982: Can.) — Albert Dunk
Hannah K (1983: Fr.--Univ.) — Ricardo Aronovich
Hanna's War (1988: Cannon) — Elemer Ragalyi
Hannibal (1960: It.--WB) — R. Masciocchi
Hansel and Gretel (1954: Ger.) — Wolf Schwan
Hanusen (1988: Ger./Hung.) — Lajos Koltai
Happily Ever After (1986: Braz.) — Alfonso Beato
Happiness of Us Alone (1962: Jap.) — Masao Tamai
Happy Birthday, Gemini (1980: UA) — James B. Kelly
Happy Birthday to Me (1981: Col.) — Miklos Lente
Happy End (1968: Czech.) — Vladimir Novotny
The Happy Hooker Goes to Hollywood
  (1980: Cannon) — Stephen Gray
The Happy Hooker Goes to Washington
  (1977: Cannon) — Robert Caramico
Harakiri (1963: Jap.) — Toshio Miyajima
Harbor Light Yokohama (1970: Jap.) — Kazumi Hamazaki
Harbour Beat (1990: Aus./GB) — Ellery Ryan
Hard Act to Follow (1990: US) — Emiko Omori

Hard Choices (1986: Lor.) — Tom Hurwitz
Hard Country (1981: Univ.) — Dennis Dalzell
Hard Knocks (1980: Aus.) — Zbigniew Friedrich
The Hard Part Begins (1973: Can.) — Robert Saad
The Hard Ride (1971: AIP) — Robert Sparks
Hard Traveling (1986: US) — David Myers
Hardware (1990: GB/US) — Steven Chivers
Harlem Nights (1989: Par.) — Woody Omens
Harlow (1965: US) — Jim Kilgore
Harp of Burma (1967: Jap.) — Minoru Yokoyama
Harper Valley P.T.A. (1978: US) — Willy Kurant
Harry's Machine (1986: Cannon) — Gideon Porath
Harry's War (1981: US) — Reed Smoot
Harvest (1939: Fr.) — Willy Ledru; Roger Ledru
Hate for Hate (1967: IT.) — Alejandro Ulloa
The Haunting (1963: MGM) — Davis Boulton
The Haunting of M (1979: US) — Gregory Nava
Have Rocket, Will Travel (1959: Col.) — Ray Cory
Hawks (1988: GB) — Douglas Milsome
He Knows You're Alone (1980: MGM-UA) — Gerald Fell
He Snoops To Conquer (1944: GB--Col.) — Roy Fogwell
Head Office (1936: GB--WB) — William Luff
The Headless Ghost (1959: GB--AIP) — John Wiles
Health (1980: TCF) — Edmond Koons
Heart Condition (1990: US) — Arthur Albert
The Heart of a Nation (1943: Fr.) — Jules Kruger
Heart of Dixie (1989: Orion) — Robert Elswit
Heart of Midnight (1988: US) — Ray Rivas
Heart to Heart (1981: Fr.) — Renan Polles
Heartaches (1981: Can.) — Vic Sarin
Heartbreak Hotel (1988: Dis.) — Stephen Dobson
Heartbreaker (1983: US) — Michael Lonzo
Heat of Desire (1984: Fr.) — Bernard Lutic
Heat of the Summer (1961: Fr.) — Marcel Combes; Arthur Raimondo

Heathers (1989: US) — Francis Kenney
Heatwave (1954: GB--Ham./Lip.) — Jimmy Harvey
Heaven and Earth (1990: Jap.) — Yonezo Maeda
Heaven Tonight (1990: Aus.) — David Connell
Heavenly Bodies (1985: MGM-UA) — Thomas Burstyn
Heidi (1954: Switz.--UA) — Emil Berna
Heidi and Peter (1955: Switz--UA) — Emil Berna
Heldinnen (1962: Ger.--UFA) — Werner Krien
Hell on Earth (1934: Ger.) — Alexander Lagorio
Hell Ship Mutiny (1957: Rep.) — Robert H. Cummings; Bill Judd

Hell Up in Harlem (1973: AIP) — Fenton Hamilton
The Hellfire Club (1963: GB) — Robert S. Baker; Monty Berman

Hello Again (1987: Dis./Touch.)	Jan Weincke
Hello Down There (1969: Par.)	Cliff Poland
Hello Mary Lou, Prom Night II (1987: Can.)	John Herzog
Henry ... Portrait of a Serial Killer (1989: US)	Charlie Lieberman
Henry V (1989: GB)	Kenneth MacMillan
Henry IV (1985: It.--Orion)	Giuseppe Lanci
Her Last Affaire (1935: GB: PDC)	Harry Gilliam; Leslie Rowson
Hercules' Pills (1960: It.)	Enrico Menczer
Here Come the Tigers (1978: AIP)	Barry Abrams
Hero (1982: GB)	Adam Baker-Mill
Hero (1985: US)	Robert Yeomans
Hero and the Terror (1988: Cannon)	Eric Van Haren Noman
Herod the Great (1960: It.--AA)	Massamo Dallamano
Heroes Are Made (1944: USSR)	R. Monsatirsky
Heroes Die Young (1960: AA)	Glen R. Smith
Heroes of the Sea (1941: USSR)	Michael Kaplan
Heroina (1965: US)	Luis A. Maisonet
Herzlich Wilkommen (1990: Ger.)	Hermann Fahr
He's My Girl (1987: US)	Peter Lyons Collister
Hester Street (1975: US)	Kenneth Van Sickle
Hex (1973: TCF)	Charles Rosher, Jr.
Hey Boy! Hey Girl! (1959: Col.)	Ray Cory
Hey, Let's Twist (1961: Par.)	George Jacobson
Hi, Mom! (1970: US)	Robert Elfstrom
Hidden Agenda (1990: GB)	Clive Tickner
The Hidden Fortress (1959: Jap.)	Kuzuo Yamazaki
Hidden Guns (1956: Rep.)	Clark Ramsey
Hidden Pleasures (1986: Sp.)	Carlos Suarez
The Hideout (1956: GB)	Brendan Stafford
Hider in the House (1989: US)	Jeff Jur
Hiding Out (1987: DeL.)	Daniel Pearl
High (1968: Can.)	Paul van der Linden
High and Low (1963: Jap.)	Choichi Nakai, Takao Sakai
High Rolling (1977: Aus.)	Dan Burstall
High School Caesar (1960: US)	Harry Birch
High Seas (1929: GB--FN)	Claude MacDonnell
High Treason (1937: GB)	Sydney Blythe
Highland Fling (1936: GB--TCF)	Stanley Grant
Highly Dangerous (1950: GB--Lip.)	David Harcourt
Highpoint (1984: US)	Bert Dunk
Highway 13 (1948: Lip.)	Carl Berger
Hiken Yaburi (1969: Jap.)	Chishi Makiura
Hildur and the Magician (1969: US)	Larry Jordan
A Hill on the Dark Side of the Moon (1984: Swed.)	Sten Holmberg; Rolf Lindstrom
The Hills Run Red (1967: It.-- DeL./UA)	Toni Secchi
Himatsuri (1985: Jap.)	Masaki Tamura

Hinotori (1980: Jap.) — Kiyoshi Hasegawa
Hippodrome (1961: Aust./Ger.) — Gunther Anders
Hippolyt, the Lackey (1932: Hung.) — Istvan Eiben
The Hired Killer (1967: Fr./It.) — Erico Menczer
His Majesty, King Ballyhoo
  (1931: Ger.) — Karl Sander; Willy Goldberger
Histoire d'Un Perriot (1913: Fr.) — G. Ricci
History of the World, Part I (1981:
  TCF) — Woody Omens
Hit and Run (1982: US) — Tony Mitchell
Hit List (1989: US) — James Lemmo
Hit Man (1972: MGM) — Andrew Davis
A Hitch in Time (1978: GB) — Tommy Fletcher
Hoa Binh (1971: Fr.) — Georges Liron
Hollywood Boulevard (1976: US) — Jamie Anderson
Hollywood Chainsaw Hookers (1988: US) Scott Rensler
Hollywood Cop (1988: US) — Peter Palian
Hollywood Hot Tubs 2: Educating
  Crystal (1990: US) — Areni Milo
Hollywood Shuffle (1987: US) — Peter Deming
Holy Blood (1989: It.) — Daniele Nannuzzi
The Holy Innocents (1984: Sp.) — Hans Burmann
The Holy Mountain (1973: Mex.--US) — Rafael Corkidi
Home Alone (1990: TCF) — Julio Macat
The Home and the World (1985: India) — Soumendu Roy
A Home for Tanya (1961: USSR) — P. Katayev
Home Free All (1983) — Robert Levi
Home Movies (1979: UA) — James Carter
Home Sweet Home (1981: Fr.) — Michel Baudour
Homeboy (1988: US) — Gale Tattersall
Homer (1970: NG) — Lazlo George
Homer and Eddie (1989: US) — Lajos Koltai
Homework (1990: Mex.) — Tony Kuhn
L'Homme Blesse (1985: Fr.) — Renata Berta
Honey, I Shrunk the Kids (1989: BV) — Hiro Narita
Honeymoon Academy (1990: US) — John Cabrera
Hong Kong Affair (1958: AA) — S. T. Chow
The Hoodlum (1951: UA) — Clark Ramsey
The Hooked Generation (1969: AA) — Gregory Sandor
The Horrible Dr. Hitchcock
  (1964: It.) — Raffaele Masciocchi
Horror Castle (1965: It.) — Riccardo Pallotini
Horror Express (1972: GB/Sp.) — Alejandro Ulloa
Horror House (1970: GB--AIP) — Jack Atcheler
The Horror of Frankenstein
  (1970: EMI/Ham.) — Moray Grant
The Horror of It All
  (1964: GB--Lip./TCF) — Arthur Lavis
The Horror of Party Beach (1964:
  TCF) — Richard L. Hilliard

Horror Planet (1982)	John Metcalfe
Horse (1986: Jap.)	Hiromitsu Kararsawa
The Horseplayer (1990: US)	Dean Lent
The Hostage (1966: US)	Ted Mikels
Hot and Deadly (1984: US)	Stephen Kim
The Hot Box (1972: Phil.--US)	Felipe Sacdalan
Hot Dog (1984: MGM-UA)	Paul Ryan
Hot Hours (1963: Fr.)	Arthur Raimondo
Hot Ice (1952: GB)	Ted Lloyd
Hot Moves (1984: US)	Eugene Shugleit
Hot News (1936: GB--Col.)	Jack Barker
Hot Potato (1976: WB)	Ronald Garcia
Hot Resort (1985: Cannon)	Frank Flynn
The Hot Rock (1972: TCF)	Ed Brown
Hot Rod Hullabaloo (1966: AA)	Thomas Spalding
The Hot Spot (1990: Orion)	Veli Steiger
Hotel New York (1985: US)	Babette Mangolte
Hotel Sahara (1951: GB--UA)	David Harcourt
Hotsprings Holiday (1970: Jap.)	Masao Kosugi
The Hounds ... of Notre Dame (1980: Can.)	Ron Orieux
The Hours of Love (1965: It.)	Erico Menczer
House Broken (1936: GB--Par.)	Francis Carver
The House by the Lake (1977: Can.--AIP)	Robert Saad
House of Blackmail (1953: GB)	Philip Grindrod
House of Darkness (1948: GB)	Cyril Bristow
House of Evil (1968: Mex.--US)	Austin McKinney
House of Games (1987: Orion)	Juan Ruiz Anchia
The House of Long Shadows (1983: GB--Cannon)	Norman Langley
House of 1,000 Dolls (1967: GB/Ger./Sp.--AIP)	Manuel Merino
The House of the Three Girls (1961: Aust.)	Bruno Mondi
House on the Edge of the Park (1985: It.--US)	Sergio d'Offizi
The House on the Front Line (1963: USSR)	Vyacheslav Shumsky
House Party (1990: US)	Peter Deming
The House That Dripped Blood (1971: GB)	Ray Parslow
The House That Screamed (1970: sp.--AIP)	Manuel Berenguer
The House With an Attic (1964: USSR)	A. Tybin
Housekeeping (1987: Col.)	Michael Coulter
How I Got into College (1989: TCF)	Robert Elswit
How Willingly You Sing (1975: Aus.)	Peter Tammer
Howling II ... Your Sister's a Werewolf (1986: EMI)	G. Stephenson

The Howling III (1987: Aus.) — Louis Irving

Hugs and Kisses (1968: Swed.--AE) — Lars Swanberg

Hu-Man (1975: Fr.) — Jimmy Glasberg

The Human Condition (1959: Jap.) — Yoshio Miyajima

Humanoids from the Deep (1980: US) — Daniel Lacambre

Humongous (1982: Can.) — Brian Hebb

Hungarians (1981: Hung.) — Gyorgy Illes

Hunger (1968: Den./Nor./Swed.) — Henning Kristiansen

Hungry Wives (1973: US) — Geroge Romero; Bill Hinzman

Hunk (1987: US) — Bryan England

The Hunt (1967: Sp.) — Luis Cuadrado

Hunter's Blood (1987: US) — Tom Denobe

Hunting (1990: Aus.) — David Connell; Dan Burstall

Hunting in Siberia (1962: USSR) — Georghy Kholnyy

Hurry Up or I'll Be 30 (1973: AE) — Burleigh Wartes

Hush-a-Bye-Baby (1990: GB) — Breffni Byrne

Hyde Park Corner (1935: GB) — Cyril Bristow

The Hyperboloid of Engineer Garin (1965: USSR) — Alexander Rybin

The Hypnotic Eye (1960: AA) — Arch Dalzell

I Am the Cheese (1983: US) — David Quaid

I Bombed Pearl Harbor (1961: Jap.) — Kazuo Yamada

I Didn't Do It (1945: GB--Col.) — Roy Fogwell

I Escaped from Devil's Island (1973: UA) — Rosalio Solano

I Killed Einstein, Gentlemen (1970: Czech.) — Ivan Slapeta

I Live in Fear (1967: Jap.) — Asakazu Nakai

I Lived with You (1933: GB) — Sydney Blythe

I Love You, I Kill You (1972: Ger.) — Andre Debreuil

I Miss You, Hugs and Kisses (1978: Can.) — Don Wilder

I, Monster (1971: GB--Cannon) — Moray Grant

I Never Sang for My Father (1970: Col.) — Morris Hartzband; George Stoetzel

I Spit on Your Grave (1983: US) — Yuri Haviv

I, the Worst of All (1990: Arg.) — Felix Monti

I Was a Teenage Zombie (1987: US) — Peter Lewnes

Ice House (1989: US) — Brown Cooper

Identification Marks: None (1969: Pol.) — Witold Mickiewicz

The Idiot (1960: USSR) — V. Pavlov

The Idiot (1963: Jap.) — Toshio Ubukata; Choichi Nakai

If He Hollers, Let Him Go (1968: US) — William Spencer

Igor and the Lunatics (1985: US) — John Ragulis

Igoroata, the Legend of the Tree
  of Life (1970: Phil.)   Loreto Isleta
Ikiru (1960: Jap.)   Asakazu Nakai
Illuminations (1976: Aus.)   Wolfgang Beliharz
Illusion of Blood (1966: Jap.)   Hiroshi Murai
The Illusion Travels by Streetcar
  (1977: Mex.)   Raul Martinez Solares
The Illusionist (1985: Holl.)   Theo Van De Sande
I'm Going to Get You--Elliot Boy
  (1971: Can.--Col.)   Peter Reusch
An Imaginary Tale (1990: Can.) Georges Dufaux
The Immoral Moment (1967: Fr.) Henri Raichi
The Immortal Story (1969: Fr.) Willy Kurant
L'Immortelle (1969: Fr./It./Turk.--
  DeL.)   Maurice Barry
Impasse (1969: UA)   Mars B. Rasca
Imperative (1985: Ger.)   Slawomir Idziak
Impulse (1955: GB)   Jonah Jones
In a Pig's Eye (1989: US)   Jim Hayman
In a Shallow Grave (1988: US)   Jerzy Zielinski
In Praise of Older Women (1978:
  Can.--AE)   Miklos Lente
In the Country (1967: US)   Robert Machover
In the Name of Life (1947: USSR) Vladimir Gardanov
In the Soup (1936: GB)   Sydney Blythe
In the Spirit (1990: US)   Dick Quinlan
In the White City (1983: Port./Switz.) Acacio de Almeida
Incident in Shanghai (1937: GB--
  Par.)   Francis Carver
The Incredible Invasion
  (1971: Mex.--Col.)   Austin McKinney; Raul
                           Dominguez
The Incredible Melting Man (1978:
  AIP)   Willy Curtis
Indecent (1962: Ger.)   Karl Schroeder
Independence Day (1976: US)   Elliot Davis
Indian Nocturnal (1989: Fr.)   Yves Angelo
Indiana Jones and the
  Last Crusade * (1989: Par.)   Rexford Metz; Robert Stevens
Inferno (1980: It.--TCF)   Romano Albani
Inferno (1986: TCF)   Romano Albani
Ingagi (1931: RKO)   Harold Williams; Ed Joyce;
                           George Summerton; Fred
                           Webster; L. Gillingham
The Inheritance (1964: Jap.)   Ko Kawamata
The Inheritors (1985: Aust.)   Hanua Polak
L'Inhumaine (1924: Fr.)   G. Specht
Injun Fender (1973: US)   Deidi Von Schaewen
Inner State (1990: Pol.)   Jan Mogilnicki
Innocence Unprotected (1971: Yugo.) Branko Perak; Stevan Miskovic

Film	Credit
Inquest (1939: GB--GN)	D. P. Cooper
The Insect Woman (1964: Jap.)	Masahisa Himeda
Inside Looking Out (1977: Aus.)	Paul Cox; Peter Tammer; Bryan Gracey
Inside the Room (1935: GB)	William Luff
The Inspector General (1937: Czech.)	Jan Stallich
Instant Karma (1990: MGM)	Thomas Jewett
Intermezzo (1937: Swed.)	Ake Dahlquist
Intimacy (1966: US)	Ted Saizis; Vincent Saizis
Intimacy (1990: Mex.)	Carlos Markowich
The Intruder (1962: US)	Taylor Byars
Invaders from Mars (1986: Cannon)	Daniel Pearl
Invasion 1700 (1965: Fr./It./Yugo.)	Pier Ludovico Pavoni
Investigation (1984: Fr.)	Jean Charvein
The Invisible Avenger (1958: Rep.)	Willis Winford; Joseph Wheeler
The Invisible Dr. Mabuse (1965: Ger.)	Ernest Kalinke
The Invisible Kid (1988: US)	Michael Barnard
The Invisible Man (1963: Ger.)	Michael Marszalek
The Invitation (1975: Fr./Switz.)	Jean Zeller
Iphigenia (1977: Greece)	Georges Arvanitis
Iron Eagle II (1988: Can./Isr.-- Tri-S.)	Alain Dostie
The Iron Triangle (1989: US)	Irv Goodnoff
Ironweed (1987: Tri-S.)	Lauro Escorel
Is Your Honeymoon Really Necessary? (1953: GB)	Philip Grindrod
Isabel (1968: Can.)	Georges Dufaux
The Island (1962: Jap.)	Kiyoshi Kuroda
Island (1989: Aus.)	Mike Edols
Island of Doom (1933: USSR)	Yuri Utekin
Island of the Damned (1976: Sp.--AIP)	Jose Luis Alcaine
It! (1967: GB--WB)	Davis Boulton
It Had to Be You (1989: US)	Bert Lau
It Happened at the Inn (1945: Fr.)	Pierre Montazel
It Happened in Canada (1962: Can.)	Luigi Petrucci
It Lives Again (1978: WB)	Fenton Hamilton
It Takes All Kinds (1969: Aus.-- MGM)	Mick Bornemann
It Takes Two (1988: MGM-UA)	Peter Deming
The Italian Connection (1973: Ger./It.--AIP)	Franco Villa
Italiano Brava Gente (1965: It./USSR)	Antonio Secchi; V.
It's Alive (1974: WB)	Fenton Hamilton
It's All Right Comrades (1990: Czech.)	Joseph Vanis
It's Hard to Be Good (1950: GB)	Laurie Friedman

J. D.'s Revenge (1976: AIP)	Harry May
Jabberwocky (1977: GB)	Terry Bedford
Jack Frost (1966: USSR)	Dmitriy Surenskiy
The Jack of Diamonds (1949: GB)	Moray Grant
The Jack of Diamonds (1967: Ger.--MGM)	Ernst Wild
Jack the Giant Killer (1962: UA)	David S. Horsley
Jack the Ripper (1959: GB--Par.)	Monty Berman
Jacob Two-Two Meets the Hooded Fang (1979: Can.)	Francois Protat
Jacob's Ladder (1990: Tri-S.)	Jeffrey Kimball
Jaguar (1980: Phil.)	Conrado Balthazar
Jaguar Lives (1979: AIP)	John Cabrera
Jake Speed (1986: US)	Bryan Loftus
Jamboree (1957: WB)	Jack Etra
James Joyce's Women (1985: Univ.)	John Metcalfe
Jaws: The Revenge (1987: Univ.)	John McPherson
The Jazzband Five (1932: Ger.--UFA)	Reimer Kuntze
Jedda, the Uncivilized (1956: Aus.)	Carl Kayser
Jenifer Hale (1937: GB--TCF)	Stanley Grant
Jennifer (1978: AIP)	Irv Goodnoff
Jenny (1969: US)	David Quaid
Jeremy (1973: UA)	Paul Goldsmith
Jesse and Lester, Two Brothers in a Place Called Trinity (1972: It.)	Antonio Modica
Jesus Christ's Horoscope (1989: Hung.)	Janos Kende
Jesus of Montreal (1989: Can.)	Guy Dufaux
Jet over the Atlantic (1960: US)	Jorge Stahl, Jr.
Jetlag (1981: Sp.--US)	Al Ruban
Jezebel's Kiss (1990: US)	Brian Reynolds
Jigsaw (1990: Aus.)	James Grant
Joan of the Angels (1962: Pol.)	Jerzy Wojcik
Joe Hill (1971: Swed.--Par.)	Jorgen Persson
Joe Panther (1976: US)	Robert Morrison; Jordan Klein
John of the Fair (1962: GB)	Joe Ambor
Johnny Be Good (1988: Orion)	Robert Yeoman
Johnny Steals Europe (1932: Ger.)	Ewald Daub
Johnny the Giant Killer (1953: Fr.)	Kostia Tchikine
Johnny Tiger (1966: Univ.)	Charles Straumer
Johnny Vik (1973: US)	Marcel Shain
A Joke of Destiny (1984: It.--US)	Camillo Bazzoni
Jonah--Who Will Be 25 in the Year 2000 (1976: Switz.)	Renato Berta
Jonathan Livingston Seagul (1973: Par.)	Jack Couffer
Joni (1980: US)	Frank Raymond
Joniko and the Kush Ta Ka (1969: US)	Chuck D. Keen

Jory (1972: AE)	Jorge Stahl, Jr.
Joshua Then and Now (1985: Can.--TCF)	Francois Protat
Jour de Fete (1952: Fr.)	Jean Mercanton
Journey among Women (1977: Aus.)	Tom Cowan
Journey beneath the Desert (1967: Fr./It.)	Enzo Serafin
Journey into Nowhere (1963: GB)	Vaclav Vich
Journey of Hope (1990: Switz.)	Elemer Ragalyi
Journey through Rosebud (1972: US)	Minervino Rojas
Journey to Love (1953: It.)	Augusto Tiezzi
Journey to Shiloh (1968: Univ.)	Enzo Martinelli
Journey to the Beginning of Time (1966: Czech.)	Vaclav Pazdernik; Antonin Horak; Anthony Huston
Journey to the Center of Time (1967: US)	Robert Caramico
Journey to the Far Side of the Sun (1969: GB--Univ.)	John Read
Journey to the Seventh Planet (1969: Swed.--AIP)	Aage Wiltrup
Journeys from Berlin--1971 (1980: US)	Carl Teitelbaum; Michael Steinke; Wolfgang Senn; Jon Else; Shinichi Tajiri
Jovita (1970: Pol.)	Jan Laskowski
Ju Dun (1990: China/Jap.)	Gu Chang-Wei; Yang Lun
Jubilee (1978: GB)	Peter Middleton
Judex (1916: Fr.)	G. Guerin
Judex (1966: Fr./It.)	Marcel Fradetal
The Judge and the Sinner (1964: Ger.)	Erich Claunick
Judo Showdown (1966: Jap.)	Shozo Honda
Juggernaut (1937: GB--GN)	Sydney Blythe; William Luff
Juliana (1989: Peru)	Danny Gavidia
Julie (1956: MGM)	Fred Jackman, Jr.
Julie the Redhead (1963: Fr.)	Roger Fellous
Jump (1971: Cannon)	Greg Sandor
Jungle Goddess (1948: Lip.)	Carl Berger
Jungle Man (1941: PRC)	Mervyn Freeman
Jungle of Chang (1940: Swed--RKO)	Gustaf Boge
Jungle Raiders (1985: It.--Cannon)	Gugliemo Mancori
Jupiter (1952: Fr.)	Marc Fossard
Just a Big Simple Girl (1949: Fr.--UA)	M. Kruger
Just a Gigolo (1979: Ger.--UA)	Charley Steinberger
Just Like at Home (1979: Hung.)	Lajos Koltai
Just Like in the Movies (1990: US)	Peter Fernberger
Just Once More (1963: Swed.)	Martin Bodin
Just One of the Guys (1983: Col.)	John McPherson

Just the Way You Are (1984: MGM-UA) Claude Lecomte
Just William's Luck (1948: GB--UA) Leslie Rowson

Kadoyng (1974: GB) Mark McDonald
Kagemusha (1980: Jap.--TCF) Takao Saito; Shoji Ueda;
  Kazuo Miyagawa; Asaichi
  Nakai
Kamouraska (1973: Can./Fr.) Michel Brault
Kanal (1961: Pol.) Jerzy Lipman
Kanchenjunga (1966: India) Subrata Mitra
Kansas (1988: US) David Eggby
Kapo (1964: Fr./It./Yugo.) Goffredo Bellisario; Alexander
  Sekulovic

The Karate Kid Part III (1989: Col.) Stephen Yaconelli
Karate, the Hand of Death (1961: AA) Minoru Miki
Karla (1965: E. Ger.) Gunther Ost
Katerina Izmailova (1969: USSR) Rostislav Davydov;
  Vladimir Ponomaryov

Kaya, I'll Kill You (1969: Fr./Yugo.) France Vodopivec
Keaton's Cop (1990: Cannon) Roland "Ozzie" Smith
Kenner (1969: MGM) Dieter Liphardt
Kenny and Co. (1976: TCF) Don Coscarelli
The Key (1990: Iran) Mohammad Aladpoush
The Kid from Canada (1957: GB) Paddy Carey
Kid Rodelo (1966: Sp.--Par.) Manuel Merino
The Kidnappers (1964: Phil.--US) Felipe Sacdalan
A Kiev Comedy (1963: USSR) V. Ilyenko
Kill (1968: Jap.) Rokuro Nishigaki
Kill a Dragon (1967: UA) Emmanuel Rojas
Kill and Kill Again (1981: US) Tai Krige
Kill Baby Kill (1966: It.) Antonio Rinaldi
Kill Me Again (1989: MGM-UA) Jacques Steyn
Kill or Be Killed (1967: It.) Aldo Giordani
Kill or Be Killed (1980: US) Mane Eotha
Kill Them All and Come Back Alone
  (1970: It./Sp.) Alejandro Ulloa
Killer Force (1975: Ire./Switz.--
  AIP) David Millin; Ken Eddy
The Killers (1964: Univ.) Richard L. Rawlings
Killer's Kiss (1955: UA) Stanley Kubrick
Killers Three (1968: AIP) J. Burgi Contner
A Killing Affair (1988: US) Dominique Chapuis
The Killing Game (1968: Fr.) Jacques Robin; Guy Peelaert;
  Bandes Dessinees
The Killing of a Chinese Bookie
  (1976: US) Mike Farris; Michael Stringer
Killzone (1985: US) Victor Alexander
Kimberley Jim (1965: S. Afr.--Emb.) Judex Viljoen
The Kindred (1987: US) Stephen Carpenter

King in Shadow (1961: Ger.) — Goran Strindberg
King Kong Escapes (1968: Jap.
  --Univ.) — Hajime Koizumi
King Kong vs. Godzilla
  (1963: Jap.--Univ.) — Hajime Koizumi
King Lear (1971: Den./GB) — Henning Kristiansen
King, Murray (1969: US) — David Hoffman
King of Hearts (1967: Fr./It.--UA) — Pierre Lhomme
King of New York (1990: US) — Bojan Bazelli
King of the Coral Sea (1956:
  Aus.--AA) — Ross Wood; Keith Loone
King, Queen, Knave (1972: Ger.--
  AE) — Charly Steinberger
The King's Jester (1947: It.) — Ubaldo Arata
The King's Trial (1990: Fr./Port.) — Edouardo Serra
The King's Whore (1990:
  Aust./Fr./GB/It.) — Gernot Roll
Kinjite (Forbidden Subjects)
  (1989: Cannon) — Gideon Porath
The Kiss (1988: Tri-S.) — Francois Protat
Kiss Me (1989: Fr.) — Darius Khondji
Kiss Me Goodbye (1935: GB) — Willy Goldberger
The Kiss of Fire (1940: Fr.) — Robert Lefebvre
Kiss of the Spider Woman (1985:
  Braz.) — Rodolfo Sanchez
Knife in the Head (1980: Ger.) — Frank Bruhne
Knife in the Water (1963: Pol.) — Jerzy Lipman
Knightriders (1981: US) — Michael Gornick
Knights and Emeralds (1986: GB--WB) — Richard Greatrex
Knights of the City (1986: US) — Rolf Kesterman
The Knights of the Teutonic Order
  (1962: Pol.) — Mieczyslaw Jahoda
Knives of the Avenger (1967: It.) — Antonio Rinaldi
Kojira (1967: Jap.) — Takao Saito
Konets Sankt-Peterbourga (1927:
  USSR) — A. Golovnia
Kongi's Harvest (1971: Nig.--US) — Ake Lindqvist
Krakatit (1948: Czech.) — Vaclav Hanus
Krakatoa, East of Java (1969: US) — Manuel Berenguer
Kuragejima--Legends from a Southern
  Island (1970: Jap.) — Masao Tochizawa
Kuroenko (1968: Jap.) — Kiyomi Kuroda
Kurutta Ippeji (1926: Jap.) — K. Sugiyama
Kwaidan (1965: Jap.) — Yoshio Miyajima

L.A. Heat (1989: US) — Richard Pepin
Lacenaire (1990: Fr.) — Bruno de Keyzer
The Lad (1935: GB--Univ.) — Sydney Blythe
Lad from Our Town (1941: USSR) — S. Uralov

Ladies on the Rocks (1985: Den.)	Dirk Bruel
Lady Chatterley's Lover (1981: Fr./GB)	Robert Fraisse
The Lady in Red (1979: US)	Daniel Lacambre
Lady in White (1988: US)	Russell Carpenter
The Lady Is Fickle (1948: It.)	Alverto Fusi
Lady Liberty (1972: Fr./It.--UA)	Alfio Contini
Lady of the Camelias (1987: Ger.)	Ingo Hamer
Lady of Vengeance (1947: GB--UA)	Ian Struthers
The Lady with the Dog (1962: USSR)	Andrey Moskvin; Dmitry Meskhiyev
The Lady without Camellias (1981: It.)	Enzo Serafin
Ladybug Ladybug (1963: UA)	Leonard Hirschfield
Lambada (1990: WB)	Roberto d'Ettore Piazzoli
The Lambeth Walk (1940: GB--MGM)	Francis Carver
Lancashire Luck (1937: GB--Par.)	Francis Carver
Landscape after Battle (1978: Pol.)	Zygmunt Samosiak
Landscape with a Woman (1990: Yugo.)	Karpo Acimovic Godina
Larks on a String (1969: Czech.)	Jaromir Sofr
Laser Mission (1989: Ger.)	Hans Kuhle, Jr.
Lassie's Great Adventure (1963: TCF)	Edward Fitzgerald
The Last American Hero (1973: TCF)	George Silano
The Last Barricade (1938: GB--TCF)	Stanley Grant
The Last Bridge (1957: Aust.)	Fred Kollhanck
The Last Chance (1945: Switz.--MGM)	Emil Berna
The Last Chase (1981: US)	Paul Van Der Linden
The Last Curtain (1937: GB--Par.)	Francis Carver
The Last Day of the War (1969: It./Sp.--US)	Romolo Garoni
The Last Days of Pompeii (1960: It.--UA)	Antonio Ballesteros
The Last Escape (1970: GB--UA)	Gernot Roll
The Last Ferry (1990: Pol.)	Dariusz Kuc
The Last Game (1964: USSR)	Sergey Zaytsev
The Last Hill (1945: USSR)	Arcady Kalzaty
Last Holiday (1950: GB)	Ray Elton
Last House on the Left (1972: AIP)	Victor Hurwitz
The Last Island (1990: Holl.)	Marc Felperlaan
The Last Load (1948: GB)	Jo Jago
The Last Man (1968: Fr.)	Pierre Lhomme
The Last Mercenary (1969: It./Ger./Sp.)	Juan Gelpi
Last Night at the Alamo (1984: US)	Brian Huberman
The Last of the Finest (1990: Orion)	Juan Ruiz-Anchia
The Last of the Knucklemen (1981: Aust.)	Dan Burstall
Last of the Renegades (1966: Fr./Ger./It./Sp.--Col.)	Ernst Kalinke
The Last Rebel (1961: Mex.)	Jose Luis Crtiz
The Last Rebel (1971: Col.)	Carlo Carlini

Last Romantic Lover (1979: Fr.) — Robert Fraisse
The Last Shot You Hear (1969: Lip./TCF) — David Holmes
The Last Stop (1949: Pol.) — Borys Monastryski
The Last Ten Days (1956: Ger.--Col.) — Gunther Anders
The Last Tomahawk (1965: Ger./It./Sp.) — Ernst Kalinke
The Last War (1962: Jap.) — Rokuro Nishigaki
The Last Winter (1984: Tri-S.) — Amnon Salomon
The Last Winter (1990: Can.) — Ian Elkin
The Last Woman of Shang (1964: HgKg.) — Ho Lan-shan
Late Autumn (1973: Jap.) — Ushun Atsuta
Late Chrysanthemums (1985: Jap.) — Masao Tamai
Late Extra (1935: GB--Fox) — Alex Bryce
Latino (1986: US) — Tom Sigel
Latitude Zero (1969: Jap.--US) — Taiichi Kankura
Laughter in Paradise (1951: GB) — William McLeod
Lava (1989: Pol.) — Piotr Sobocinski
The Law (1990: Borkino Faso) — Alix Comte; Dominique Hennequin

Law and Lead (1937: Rep.) — Charles Henkel
Lean on Me (1989: WB) — Victor Hammer
Leap into the Void (1982: It.) — Beppe Lanci
Leap of Faith (1931: GB) — T. B. Lynch
Leatherface: Texas Chainsaw Massacre III (1990: US) — James L. Carter
The Legacy of the 500,000 (1964: Jap.) — Takao Saito
The Legend of Billie Jean (1985: Tri-S.) — Jeffrey Kimball
The Legend of Boggy Creek (1973: US) — Charles Pierce
Legend of Cougar Canyon (1974: US) — David E. Jackson
The Legend of Nigger Charley (1972: Par.) — Peter Eco
Legions of the Nile (1960: It.--TCF) — Mario Pacheco
Lemonade Joe (1966: Czech.) — Vladimir Novotny
Lenz (1985: US) — Alexandre Rockwell
Leo and Loree (1980: UA) — Costa Petals
Leopard in the Snow (1979: Can./GB) — Alfie Hicks
Lepke (1975: Isr.--WB) — Andrew Davis
Less Than Zero (1987: TCF) — Edward Lachman
A Lesson in Love (1960: Swed.) — Martin Bodin
Let It Ride (1989: Par.) — Curtis J. Wehr
Let's Rock (1958: Col.) — Jack Etra
Let's Scare Jessica to Death (1971: Par.) — Bob Baldwin
The Letter That Was Never Sent (1962: USSR) — Sergey Urusevskiy

Letters from Alou (1990: Sp.)   Alfredo Mayo
Letters from My Windmill (1955: Fr.)   Willy Factorouitch
Leviathan (1961: Fr.)   Nicolas Hayer
Lianna (1983: UA)   Austin de Beche
Liar's Dice (1980: US)   Douglas Murray
Libido (1973: Aus.--MGM)   Robin Copping; Bruce MacNaughton

Lies My Father Told Me (1975: Can.)   Paul Van Der Linden
The Life and Loves of Beethoven
   (1937: Fr.)   Robert Lefebvre; Marc Fossard

The Life and Loves of Mozart (1959:
   Ger.)   Oskar Snirch
Life and Nothing But (1989: Fr.)   Bruno de Keyzer
The Life and Times of Chester Angus
   Ramsgood (1971: Can.)   David Curnick
The Life and Times of Grizzly Adams
   (1974: US)   George Stapleford
Life Begins Anew (1938: Ger.--UFA)   Franz Weihmayr
Life Begins Tomorrow (1952: Fr.)   Fred Langenfeld
Life in Her Hands (1951: GB--UA)   Fred Gamage
A Life in the Balance (1955: TCF)   J. Gomez Urquiza
Life Is a Circus (1962: GB)   Arthur Graham
Life Is Cheap (1989: US)   Amir Mokri
Life Is Sweet (1990: GB)   Dick Pope
Life of a Country Doctor (1961: Jap.)   Kazuo Yamada
Life of Oharu (1964: Jap.)   Yoshimi Kono; Yoshimi Hirano
Life Study (1973: US)   Michael Nebbia
Life Upside Down (1965: Fr.--AA)   Jacques Robin
The Lift (1983: Holl.--WB)   Marc Felperlaan
The Lift (1985: Holl.)   Andre Sjouerman
The Light across the Street (1957:
   Fr.)   Louis Page
Light Fantastic (1964: US)   J. Burgi Contner
Light Years Away (1982: Fr./Switz.)   Jean-Francois Robin
Lightning Bolt (1967: It./Sp.)   Riccardo Pallotini
Lightning Conductor (1938: GB)   Francis Carver
Lightning--The White Stallion (1986:
   Cannon)   Steven Shaw
The Lightship (1986: US)   Charly Steinberger
Lilies of the Field (1934: GB--UA)   Cyril Bristow
The Limit (1972: Cannon)   Fenton Hamilton
The Limping Man (1936: GB)   Cyril Bristow
Line 1 (1988: Ger.)   Frank Bruhne
Lion of St. Mark (1967: It.)   Alvaro Mancori
Lipstick (1965: Fr./It.)   Pier Ludovico Pavoni
Liquid Sky (1982: US)   Yuri Neyman
Lisa (1990: MGM/UA)   Alex Nepomniaschy; Stanley Lazan

Little Australians (1940: Aus.--Univ.)   George D. Malcolm
The Little Ballerina (1951: GB--Univ.)   Frank North
Little Darlings (1980: Par.)   Fred Batka
Little Dorrit (1987: GB)   Bruno de Keyzer
The Little Fugitive (1953: US)   Morris Engel
The Little Humpbacked Horse (1962: USSR)   Mikhail Silenko; Yevgeniy Yatsun
The Little Martyr (1947: It.)   Mario Benotti
Little Melody from Vienna (1948: AUst.)   Fritz Wodlitzke
The Little Nuns (1965: It.--Emb.)   Erico Menczer
The Little Ones (1965: GB--Col.)   David Holmes
Little Red Riding Hood and Her Friends (1964: Mex.)   Jose Ortiz Ramos
Little Red Riding Hood and the Monsters (1965: Mex.)   Rosalio Solano
The Little Savage (1959: TCF)   Jorge Stahl, Jr.
Little Shop of Horrors (1961: US)   Archie Dalzell
The Little Sister (1985: US)   Edward Lachman
Little Sweetheart (1988: GB)   John Hooper
The Little Thief (1989: Fr.)   Dominique Chapuis
Live Your Own Way (1970: Jap.)   Yoshio Miyajima
The Living Corpse (1928: Ger./ USSR)   Anatoly Golounya; Pier Jutzi
Lobster Man from Mars (1989: US)   Gerry Lively
Lodgers (1990: USSR)   Leri Machaidze
Lollipop (1966: Braz.)   Toni Rabatoni
The Lone Climber (1950: Aust./GB)   Walter Riml
Lone Wolf McQuade (1983: Orion)   Roger Shearman
Lonely Hearts (1983: Aus.)   Yuri Sokol
Lonely in America (1990: US)   Phil Katzman
Lonely Lane (1963: Jap.)   Jun Yasamoto
The Long Absence (1962: Fr./It.)   Marcel Weiss
A Long and Happy Life (1967: USSR)   D. Meshev
The Long Good Friday (1982: GB-- Emb.)   Phil Meheux
Long Is the Road (1948: Ger.)   Franz Koch
The Long Night (1976: US)   James Malloy
A Long Ride from Hell (1970: It.)   Enzo Barboni
The Long Rope (1961: TCF)   Kay Norton
Long Shot (1981: GB)   Michael Davis
Longing for Love (1966: Jap.)   Yoshio Mimiya
Longtime Companion (1990: US)   Tony Jennelli
Look Out Sister (1948: US)   Carl Berger
Looking Up (1977: US)   Arpad Makay; Lloyd Friedas
Loose Screws (1985: US)   Brian Foley
Loose Shoes (1980: US)   John P. Beckett
Lord Babs (1932: GB)   Leslie Rowson
Lord Edgeware Dies (1934: GB--RKO)   Sydney Blythe

Lord of the Flies (1963: GB)	Tom Hollyman
Lord of the Flies (1990: Col.)	Martin Fuhrer
Lord of the Manor (1933: GB--Par.)	Henry Harris
Lord Shango (1975: US)	Edward Brown
The Lords of Discipline (1983: Par.)	Brian Tufano
Lords of the Deep (1989: US)	Austin McKinney
Loss of Feeling (1935: USSR)	M. Magidson
Lost Angels (1989: Orion)	Juan Ruiz-Anchia
Lost Battalion (1961: Phil.--AIP)	Felipe Sacdalan
The Lost Face (1965: Czech.)	Jiri Vojta
Lost Lagoon (1958: UA)	Harry W. Smith
Lost on the Western Front (1940: GB)	William Luff
The Lost One (1951: Ger.)	Vaclav Vich
Lost Sex (1968: Jap.)	Kiyomi Kuroda
Lost Time (1990: Iran)	Hossein Jafarian
The Lost World of Sinbad (1965: Jap.--AIP)	Shinichi Sekizawa
Lotna (1966: Pol.)	Jerzy Lipman
Louisiana Story (1948: US)	Richard Leacock
Louisiana Territory (1953: RKO)	Harry W. Smith
Loutch Smerti (1925: USSR)	A. Levitski
Love (1972: Hung.)	Janos Toth
Love (1990: Fr.)	Bernard Tiphine
Love Affair or the Case of the Missing Switchboard Operator (1968: Yugo.)	Aleksandar Petkovic
Love and Kisses (1965: Univ.)	Robert Moreno
Love and Larceny (1963: Fr./It.)	Massamano Dallamano
Love and Learn (1947: WB)	Wesley Anderson
Love and Marriage (1966: It.--Emb.)	Luciano Trasatti; Alfio Contini; Riccardo Pallotini
Love and the Frenchwoman (1961: Fr.)	Robert Lefebvre
Love at First Bite (1979: AIP)	Edward Rosson
Love at Large (1990: Orion)	Elliot Davis
Love at Sea (1936: GB--Par.)	Francis Carver
Love Cycles (1969: Greece)	Andrea Anastassatos
The Love Eterne (1964: Hg.Kg.)	Ho Lan-shan
Love Has Lied (1988: Fr.)	Gernot Roll
Love in a Hot Climate (1958: Fr./Sp.)	Maurice Barry
Love In Pawn (1953: GB)	Monty Berman
Love Is My Profession (1959: Fr.)	Jacques Natteau
Love Letters (1983: US)	Alec Hirschfeld
Love Me Not (1989: Greece)	George Panoussopoulos
Love Now ... Pay Later (1966: It.)	Romolo Garroni
Love on the Riviera (1964: Fr./It.)	Enzo Serafin
Love or Money (1990: Hem.)	Igor Sunara
Love Problems (1970: It.)	Antonio Borghesi
Love Slaves of the Amazon (1957: Univ.)	Mario Page
Love Songs (1986: Can./Fr.)	Robert Alazraki

Love Streams (1984: Cannon) — Al Ruban
Love, the Italian Way (1964: It.) — Tino Santoni
Love under the Crucifix (1965: Jap.) — Yoshio Miyajima
Love under the Date Tree (1990: Greece) — Vassilis Kapsoupos
The Love Waltz (1930: Ger.--UFA) — Werner Brandes
The Loveless (1982: US) — Doyle Smith
A Lovely Way to Die (1968: Univ.) — Morris Hartzband
Lovers and Lollipops (1956: US) — Morris Engel
Lovers on a Tightrope (1962: Fr.) — Pierre Gueguen
Lovers' Rock (1966: Taiwan) — Hung Ching-yun
The Loves and Times of Scaramouche (1976: It.--AE) — Giovanni Bergamini
The Loves of Kafka (1989: Argen.) — Frantisek Uldrich
Lovin' Molly (1974: Col.) — Edward Brown
The Lower Depths (1937: Fr.) — F. Bourgas
The Lower Depths (1962: Jap.) — Ichio Yamazaki
Loyalty of Love (1937: It.) — Anchise Brizzi
The Luckiest Man in the World (1989: US) — Jeri Sopanen
The Lucky Bride (1948: USSR) — Eugene Andrikanis
Lucky Days (1935: GB--Par.) — Francis Carver
Lucky Jade (1937: GB--Par.) — Horace Wheddon
The Lucky Mascot (1951: GB--AA) — Bert Mason
Luggage of the Gods (1974: US) — Steven Ross
Lullaby (1961: USSR) — Vadim Derbenyov
Lumiere (1976: Fr.) — Ricardo Aronovich
Lumiere d'Ete (1943: Fr.) — Louis Page
Lunch Wagon (1981: US) — Fred Lemler
The Lure of the Jungle (1970: Den.) — Henning Bendtsen; Niels Carsten; Arthur Christiansen
Lure of the Wasteland (1939: Mon.) — Francis Corby
Lust for a Vampire (1971: GB--EMI/Ham.) — David Muir
Lydia (1964: Can.) — Julius Rascheff
The Lyons in Paris (1955: GB--Ham.) — Jimmy Harvey

Ma Barker's Killer Brood (1960: US) — Clark Ramsey
Macaroni (1985: Par.) — Claudio Ragona
MacArthur's Children (1985: Jap.) — Kazuo Miyagawa
Machine Gun McCain (1970: It.--Col.) — Erico Menczer
Machismo--40 Graves for 40 Guns (1975: US) — Richmond Aguilar; Ron Garcia
Mack the Knife (1989: US) — Elemer Ragalyi
Mackintosh & T. J. (1975: US) — Terry Mead
Macon County Line (1974: AIP) — Daniel Lacambre
Macumba Love (1960: UA) — Rudolpho Lesey
Macushla (1937: GB--TCF) — Stanley Grant

The Mad Atlantic (1967: Jap.)	Takao Saito
The Mad Bomber (1973: US)	Bert I. Gordon
The Mad Hatters (1935: GB--Par.)	Francis Carver
Mad Max (1979: Aus.--AIP)	David Eggby
The Mad Monkey (1989: Fr./Sp.)	Jose Luis Alcaine
The Mad Queen (1950: Sp.)	Jose Aguayo
Madame Aki (1963: Jap.)	Kozo Okazaki
Madame Sousatzka (1988: GB--Univ.)	Nat Crosby
Madame White Snake (1963: Hg.Kg.)	T. Nishimoto
Made (1972: GB--EMI)	Ernest Day
Made for Each Other (1971: TCF)	William Storz
Made in Heaven (1987: Lor.)	Jan Kiesser
Madeline Is (1971: Can.)	Doug McKay
Madhouse (1974: GB--AIP)	Ray Parslow
Madhouse (1990: Orion)	Dennis Lewiston
Madigan's Millions (1970: It./Sp. --AIP)	Manola Rojas
The Madman of Lab 4 (1967: Fr.)	Raymond Lemoigne
Maedchen in Uniform (1965: Fr./Ger.)	Werner Krien
Maeva (1961: US)	Alberto Baldecchi
The Mafia (1972: Arg.)	Anibal Di Salvo
Magic Boy (1960: Jap.)	Segio Otsuka; Mitsuaki Ishikawa
The Magic Face (1951: Aust.--Col.)	Tony Braun
The Magic Fountain (1961: US)	Wolf Schneider
The Magic Voyage of Sinbad (1962: USSR)	F. Provorov
The Magic Weaver (1965: USSR--AA)	Dmitriy Surenskiy
The Magic World of Topo Gigo (1961: It.)	Giorgio Battilana
The Magiochi Saga (1970: Jap.)	Kazuo Miyagawa
The Magnificent Concubine (1964: Hg.Kg.)	T. Nishimoto
The Magnificent One (1974: Fr./It.)	Rene Mathelin
The Magnificent Seven Deadly Sins (1971: GB)	Harvey Harrison, Jr.
The Magnificent Tramp (1962: Fr./It.)	Louis Page
Maicol (1989: It.)	Fabricio Borelli
Maid to Order (1987: US)	Shelly Johnson
The Maiden (1961: Fr.)	Marc Fossard
The Main Thing Is To Love (1975: Fr./It.)	Ricardo Aronovich
Mais Ou et Donc Ornicar (1979: Fr.)	Nurith Aviv; Jean-Louis Melun; Thierry Jault
Majin (1968: Jap.)	Fujio Morita
Make a Face (1971: US)	Jeri Sopanen; Ken Van Sickle
Make Like a Thief (1966: Fin.)	Kalle Peronkoski; Reijo Hassinen
Make-Up (1985: Jap.)	Noritaka Sakamoto
Making Mr. Right (1987: Orion)	Edward Lachman

The Makioka Sisters (1985: Jap.) — Kiyoshi Hasegawa
Malcolm (1986: Aus.) — David Parker
Male Hunt (1965: Fr./It.) — Andreas Winding
Malpractice (1989: Aus.) — Steve Arnold
Mamma Dracula (1980: Belg./Fr.) — Willy Kurant
The Man (1972: ABC/Par.) — Edward Rosson
A Man, a Woman and a Killer (1975: US) — Richard R. Schmidt
Man Against Man (1961: Jap.) — Rokuro Nishigaki
A Man and a Woman: 20 Years Later (1986: Fr./WB) — Jean-Yves LeMener
The Man and the Beast (1951: Arg.) — Antonio Merayo; Alberto Munoz

The Man behind the Mask (1936: GB--MGM) — Francis Carver
The Man Called Noon (1973: GB--NG) — John Cabrera
The Man from Cairo (1953: Lip.) — Mario Abutelli
Man from Cocody (1966: Fr./It.--AIP) — Pierre Petit
Man from Headquarters (1942: Mon.) — William Strohbach
The Man from the East (1961: Jap.) — Kozo Okazaki
A Man from the East (1974: Fr./It.--UA) — Aldo Giordani
The Man from Toronto (1933: GB) — Leslie Rowson
The Man Inside (1990: US) — Ricardo Aronovich
A Man Like Eva (1985: Ger.) — Horst Schier
Man of Iron (1981: Pol.) — Edward Klosinski; Janusz Kalicinski

Man of Marble (1979: Pol.) — Edward Klosinski
A Man of Passion (1989: Sp.) — Tote Trenas
Man Stolen (1934: Fr.--Fox) — Rene Colas
Man under Suspicion (1985: Ger.) — Jurgen Jurges; Renato Fortunato

The Man Upstairs (1959: GB) — Gerald Massie-Collier
The Man Who Came for Coffee (1970: It.) — Lamberto Caimi
The Man Who Couldn't Walk (1964: GB) — James Harvey
The Man Who Envied Women (1985: US) — Mark Daniels
The Man Who Haunted Himself (1970: GB) — Tony Spratling
The Man Who Laughs (1966: It.--MGM) — Enzo Barboni
The Man Who Stole the Sun (1980: Jap.) — Tatsuo Suzuki
The Man Who Wagged His Tail (1961: It./Sp.) — Enrique Guerner
The Man Who Walked through the Wall (1961: Ger.) — Bruno Mondi
The Man Who Wasn't There (1983: Par.) — Frederick Moore
The Man Who Would Be Guilty (1990: Den./Fr.) — Peter Roos
Man with a Gun (1958: GB) — John Wiles

The Man with Connections (1970: Fr.--Col.) — Alain Derobe

The Man with the Transplanted Brain (1972: Fr./Ger./It.--Orion/Par.) — Etienne Becker

Mandabi (1970: Fr./Senegal) — Paul Soulignac

Manfish (1956: UA) — Charles S. Wellborn

Manganinnie (1982: Aus.) — Gary Hansen

Mangeclous (1989: Fr.) — Patrick Blossier

Manhunt in the Jungle (1958: WB) — Robert Brooker

Mania (1961: GB) — Monty Berman

Maniac Cop 2 (1990: US) — James Lemmo

Maniacs on Wheels (1951: GB) — H. E. Fowle; L. Cave-Chinn

Mankurts (1990: Turk./USSR) — Nurtay Borviev

Manolete (1950: Sp.) — Enrique Guerner

A Man's Affair (1949: GB) — Douglas Ransome; Norman Johnson

Man's Hope (1937: Sp.) — Louis Page

The Manster (1962: Jap.--UA) — David Mason

March on Paris 1914-Of Generaloberst Alexander Von Kluck-and His Memory of Jessie Holladay (1977: US) — Walter Gutman; Mike Cuchar

Marco (1973: US) — Richard R. Nishigaki

Marco Polo (1962: Fr./It.) — Riccardo Pallotini

Margarit & Margarita (1990: USSR) — Krassimir Kostov

The Margin (1969: Braz.) — Belarmino Mancini

Marianne and Julian (1982: Ger.) — Franz Rath

Maria's Lovers (1985: Cannon) — Gary Remal

Marie in the City (1988: Can.) — Daniel Jobin

Marie of the Isles (1960: Fr.) — Pierre Petit

Marigolds in August (1980: S. Afr.) — Michael Davis

Marketa Lazarova (1968: Czech.) — Bedich Batka

Marrakesh Express (1989: It.) — Italo Petriccione

A Marriage (1983: US) — Benjamin Davis

The Marriage Came Tumbling Down (1968: Fr.) — Jean-Marc Ripart

The Marriage of Balzaminov (1966: USSR) — G. Kupriyanov

Marriage of Convenience (1970: GB) — Brian Rhodes

The Marriage of Figaro (1970: Ger.) — Hannes Schindler

Marry Me! (1949: GB) — Ray Elton; David Harcourt

La Marseillaise (1938: Fr.) — Jean-Serge Bourgoin; Alain Douarinou; Jean-Marie Maillols; Jean-Paul Alphen

Martha and I (1990: Fr./Ger.) — Viktor Rozicka

Martians Go Home (1990: US) — Peter Deming

Martin (1979: US) — Michael Gornick

The Martyr (1976: Ger./Isr.) — Jerzy Lipman

Mascara (1987: Belg./Holl.--Cannon) — Gilberto Azevado

Masculine Feminine (1966: Fr./Swed.) — Willy Kurant

The Mask (1961: Can) — Herbert S. Alpert
Masoch (1980: It.) — Angelo Bevilacqua
Massacre at Central High (1976: US) — Burt Van Munster
Massive Retaliation (1984: US) — Richard Derner
Master of Dragonard Hill (1990: Cannon) — Gerard Loubeau
The Master Plan (1955: GB) — Jonah Jones
Mat' (1926: Ussr) — A. Golovnia
The Matchmaking of Anna (1972: Greece) — Nicos Kavoukides
Matilda (1978: AIP) — Jack Woolf
Matinee (1989: Can.) — Cyrus Block
A Matter of Days (1969: Czech./Fr.) — Vladimir Novotny; Claude Saunier

Maurice (1987: GB) — Pierre Lhomme
Max & Laura & Henk & Willie (1989: Holl.) — Frans Bromet
Maya (1966: MGM) — Gunter Senftleben
Mc Vicar (1982: GB) — Vernon Layton
Me (1970: Fr.) — Claude Beausoleil
Me and Him (1989: Ger.) — Helge Weindler
The Meadow (1982: It.) — Franco Di Giacomo
Mean Johnny Barrows (1976: US) — Robert Caramico
Mean Streets (1973: WB) — Kent Wakeford
Meatballs (1979: Can.--Par.) — Don Wilder
Meatballs III (1987: US) — Peter Benison
The Medium (1951: US) — Enzo Serafin
Meet Me in Moscow (1966: USSR) — Vadim Yusov
Megaville (1990: US) — Zoltan David
The Melody of Love (1928: Univ.) — Walter Scott
Member of the Jury (1937: GB--TCF) — Stanley Grant
Memories of Me (1988: MGM-UA) — Andrew Dintenfass
Memory of Us (1974: US) — Hiro Morakawa
Men (1986: Ger.) — Helge Weindler
Men against the Sun (1953: GB) — Brendan Stafford
Men of Ireland (1938: Ire.) — Sidney Eaton
Men of Respect (1990: US) — Bobby Bukowski
Men of San Quentin (1942: PRC) — Clark Ramsey
Men of Sherwood Forest (1957: GB--Ham.) — Jimmy Harvey
Men of Tomorrow (1935: GB) — Bernard Browne
Men Prefer Fat Girls (1981: Fr.) — Bernard Lutic
Menace in the Night (1958: GB--UA) — Arthur Graham
The Men's Club (1986: US) — John Fleckenstein
Mephisto (1981: Ger.) — Lajos Koltai
The Mephisto Waltz (1971: TCF) — William W. Spencer
The Mercenary (1970: It./Sp.--UA) — Alejandro Ulloa
Mercenary Fighters (1988: Cannon) — Daniel Schneor
The Mermaid (1966: Hg.Kg.) — Tung Shao-yung
Mermaids (1990: Orion) — Howard Atherton

Film	Director
Merry Christmas Mr. Lawrence (1983: GB/Jap.--Univ.)	Toichiro Narushima
The Merry Wives (1940: Czech.)	Jan Roth
The Merry Wives of Tobias Rouke (1972: Can.)	Paul Van Der Linden
The Merry Wives of Windsor (1952: Ger.)	Eugen Klagemann
The Merry Wives of Windsor (1966: Aust.)	Hannes Staudinger
Message from Space (1978: Jap.--UA)	Toro Nakajima
Messaline (1952: Fr./It.)	Anchise Brizzi
Messenger of Death (1988: Cannon)	Gideon Porath
Metropolitan (1990: US)	John Thomas
Michael and Mary (1932: GB--Univ)	Leslie Rowson
Michael Strogoff (1960: Fr./It./Yugo.)	Robert Lefebvre
Middle Age Spread (1979: NZ)	Alun Bollinger
Midnight (1983: US)	Paul McCollough
Midnight (1989: US)	David Golia
Midnight at the Wax Museum (1936: GB--Par.)	Jan Stallich
Midnight Crossing (1988: US)	Henry Vargas
Midnight Folly (1962: Fr.)	Gilbert Sarthre
Mignon Has Left (1988: Fr./It.)	Luigi Verga
The Mighty Quinn (1989: MGM-UA)	Jacques Steyn
Mighty Ursus (1962: It./Sp.--UA)	Eloy Mella
Miles from Home (1988: US)	Elliot Davis
Milestones (1975: US)	Douglas Kramer
Military Secret (1945: USSR)	Sergei Uruseysky
Mill of the Stone Women (1963: Fr./It.)	Pier Ludovico Pavoni
The Million Dollar Collar (1929: WB)	Nelson Laraby
The Million Eyes of Su-Muru (1967: GB--AIP)	John Kotze
Mindwalk (1990: US)	Karl Kases
The Mini-Skirt Mob (1968: AIP)	Arch Dalzell
Ministry of Vengeance (1989: US)	Mark Harris
Minnesota Clay (1966: Fr./It./Sp.)	Jose Fernandez Aguayo
The Minotaur (1961: It.--UA)	Aldo Giordani
A Minute To Pray, a Second To Die (1968: It.)	Aiace Parolin
Miracle in Milan (1951: It.)	Aldo Graziati
Miracle Mile (1988: Tri-S.)	Theo Van De Sande
Miracle of the White Stallions (1963: Dis.)	Gunther Anders
The Miracle Worker (1962: UA)	Ernesto Caparros
Mirage (1972: Peru)	Mario Robles Godoy
Miranda (1949: GB--EL)	Ray Elton
Mirror Mirror (1990: US)	Robert Brinkman
Mirrors (1984: US)	Michael Murphy
Les Miserables (1936: Fr.)	Jules Kruger

Miss Arizona (1988: Hung./It.) — Elemer Ragalyi
Miss Firecracker (1989: US) — Arthur Albert
Miss Jessica Is Pregnant (1970: US) — David Prince; Brian Blauser; Art Stifel

Miss Mary (1986: Arg.--US) — Miguel Rodriguez
Miss Pilgrim's Progress (1950: GB) — Bert Mason
Miss Right (1988: It.) — Franco Di Giacomo
Missile to the Moon (1959: US) — Meredith Nicholson
Missing, Believed Married (1937: GB--Par.) — Francis Carver
Mission Bloody Mary (1967: Fr./It./Sp.) — Juan Julio Baena
Mission Galactica: The Cyclon Attack (1979: US) — Frank Thackery; H. John Penner
Mission Mars (1967: AA) — Cliff Poland
Mississippi Mermaid (1970: Fr./It.--UA) — Denys Clerval
Mister Brown (1972: US) — Roger Andrieux
Mr. Cantor and Lady Rose (1989: Hg.Kg.) — Wong Ngok-tai
Mister Freedom (1970: Fr.) — Pierre Lhomme
Mister Frost (1990: Fr./GB) — Dominique Brenguier
Mr. Hulot's Holiday (1954: Fr.) — Jacques Mercanton; Jean Mouselle

Mr. Love (1986: GB--WB) — John Davey
Mr. Peek-A-Boo (1951: Fr.--UA) — Charles Suin
Mister Rock and Roll (1957: Par.) — Morris Hartzband
Mr. Satan (1938: GB--WB-FN) — Robert La Presle
Mr. Smith Carries On (1937: GB--Par.) — Francis Carver
Mr. Superinvisible (1974: Ger./It./Sp.) — Alejandro Ulloa
Mrs. Warren's Profession (1960: Ger.) — Albert Benitz
Mixed Blood (1985: US) — Stefan Zapasnik
Mixed Company (1974: UA) — Stan Lazan
Modern Love (1990: US) — Christopher Tufty
Modern Problems (1981: TCF) — Edmund Koons
The Moderns (1988: US) — Toyomichi Kurita
Moment of Terror (1969: Jap.) — Rokuro Nishigaki
Le Monde Tremblera (1939: Fr.) — Robert Lefebvre
The Money (1975: US) — Burleigh Wartes
Money on the Street (1930: Aust.) — Nicolas Farkas
The Mongols (1966: Fr./It.) — Aldo Giordani
Monkey Grip (1983: Aus.) — David Gribble
The Monkey Hustle (1976: AIP) — Jack L. Richards
A Monkey in Winter (1962: Fr.--MGM) — Louis Page
Monsieur (1964: Fr.) — Louis Page
Monsieur (1990: Belg./Fr.) — Jean-Francois Robin

Monster in the Closet (1986: US)	Ronald McLeish
The Monster of Highgate Ponds (1961: GB)	Frank North
The Monster Squad (1987: Tri-S.)	Bradford May
Monster Zero (1970: Jap.)	Hajime Koizumi
Monsters from the Unknown Planet (1975: Jap.)	Motoyoshi Tomioka
Monty Python and the Holy Grail (1975: GB)	Terry Bedford
Moonchild (1972: US)	Emmett Alston
Moonlight Sonata (1938: GB--UA)	Jan Stallich
The Moonlight Sonata (1989: Fin.)	Kari Sohlberg
Moonrunners (1975: UA)	Brian Roy
Moonwolf (1966: Fin./Ger.--AA)	Herbert Korner; Anton Markic; Esko Toyri
The Moralist (1964: It.)	Alvaro Mancori
The Morals of Marcus (1936: GB)	Sydney Blythe
More Deadly Than the Male (1961: GB)	Robert Bucknell
Morgan's Marauders (1929: US)	Fred S. Fitzgerald
Morning Star (1962: USSR)	Apollinariy Dudko
The Moro Affair (1987: It.)	Camillo Bazzoni
Moro Witch Doctor (1964: Phil.--TCF)	Felipe Sacdalan
Morons from Outer Space (1985: EMI/Univ.)	Phil Meheux
Morphine and Dolly Mixtures (1990: GB)	Russ Walker
Mortal Passions (1989: US)	Christian Sebaldt
Moscow-Cassiopeia (1974: USSR)	Andrei Kirilov
Moscow Does Not Believe in Tears	Igor Slabnjewitsch
Moscow Shanghai (1936: Ger.)	Franz Weihmayr
Moses and Aaron (1975: Fr./Ger./It.)	Ugo Piccone; Saverio Diamanti; Gianni Canfarelli; Renato Berta
The Most Beautiful Age (1970: Czech.)	Josef Ort-Snep
The Most Dangerous Man Alive (1961: Col.)	Carl Carvahal
The Most Wonderful Evening of My Life (1972: Fr./It.--DeL.)	Claudio Cirillo
The Mother (1990: USSR)	Mikael Agranovich
Mother and Daughter (1965: USSR)	V. Tyshkovets
The Mother and the Whore (1973: Fr.)	Pierre Lhomme; Jacques Renard; Michel Cenet
Mothra (1962: Jap.--Col.)	Hajime Koizumi
Mountain Family Robinson (1979: US)	James W. Roberson
Mountaintop Motel Massacre (1986: US)	John Wilcots
The Mourning Suit (1975: Can.)	Henry Fiks
The Mouse and the Woman (1981: GB)	Nick Gifford
Mouth to Mouth (1978: Aus.)	Tom Cowan
Movie Star, American Style, or LSD I Hate You (1966: US)	Robert Caramico

The Moving Finger (1963: US)	Max Glenn
Moving Violations (1985: TCF)	Robert Elswit
Ms. 45 (1981: US)	James Momel
Muddy River (1982: Jap.)	Shohei Ando
The Mugger (1958: UA)	J. Burgi Contner
Mumu (1961: USSR)	Konstantin Petrichenko
Munchies (1987: MGM-UA)	Jonathan West
Murder at 45 R.P.M. (1965: Fr.--MGM)	Marcel Weiss
Murder at the Baskervilles (1941: GB)	Sydney Blythe
Murder at the Cabaret (1936: GB--Par.)	Roy Fogwell
Murder Czech Style (1968: Czech.)	Jan Nemecek
Murder in the Cathedral (1952: GB)	David Kosky
Murder on Approval (1956: GB--RKO)	Monty Berman
Murder Reported (1958: GB--Col.)	Brendan Stafford
Murder Story (1989: GB/Holl.)	Marc Felperlaan
Murder Will Out (1953: GB)	Monty Berman
Murders in the Rue Morgue (1971: AIP)	Manuel Berenguer
Murieta (1965: Sp.--WB)	Miguel Mila
Murmur of the Heart (1971: Fr./Ger./It.)	Ricardo Aronovich
Museum Mystery (1937: GB--Par.)	Francis Carver
The Mushroom Eater (1976: Mex.)	Raul Perez Cubero; Miguel Arana
Music Box (1989: Tri-S.)	Patrick Blossier
The Music Room (1963: India)	Subrata Mitra
Mustang Country (1976: Univ.)	J. Barry Herron
The Mutilator (1985: US)	Peter Schnall
Mutiny in Outer Space (1965: AA)	Arch Dalzell
My Ain Folk (1974: GB)	Gale Tattersall
My Baby Is Black (1965: Fr.)	Jean Collomb
My Bloody Valentine (1981: Can.--Par.)	Rodney Gibbons
My Brother, the Outlaw (1951: EL)	Jose Ortiz Ramos
My Brother's Wedding (1983: US)	Charles Burnett
My Chauffeur (1986: US)	Henry Mathias
My Childhood (1972: GB)	Mick Campbell
My Cinema (1990: Turk.)	Ertuno Senkay
My Death Is a Mockery (1952: GB)	Philip Grindrod
My Dinner With Andre (1981: US)	Jeri Sopanen
My Dog, Buddy (1960: Col.)	Ralph Hammeras
My Father Lives in Rio (1989: Holl.)	Jules van de Steenhoven
My Father's Glory (1990: Fr.)	Robert Alazraki
My First Wife (1985: Aus.)	Yuri Sokol
My Friends Need Killing (1984: US)	Parker Bartlett
My Geisha (1962: Par.)	Shunichiro Nakao
My Hobo (1963: Jap.)	Hiroshi Murai
My Life as a Dog (1987: Swed.)	Jorgen Persson; Rolf Lindströ

My Lover, My Son (1970: GB--MGM) David Muir
My Margo (1969: Isr.) Ya'acov Kalach
My Mom's a Werewolf (1989: US) Bryan England
My Name Is Ivan (1963: USSR) Vadim Yusov
My Old Dutch (1934: GB) Leslie Rowson
My Seven Little Sins (1956: Fr./It.) Charles Suin
My Son, the Hero (1963: Fr./It.) Alfio Contini
My Third Wife George (1968: US) Tom Barnett
My 20th Century (1989: Hung.) Tibor Mathe
My Uncle Antoine (1971: Can.) Michel Brault
My Widow and I (1950: It.) Arturo Gallea
My Wife's Lodger (1952: GB) Len Harris
The Mysterians (1959: Jap.--MGM) Hajime Kozumi
Mysterious Island (1941: USSR) M. B. Belskin
The Mysterious Island of Captain Nemo
   (1973: Cameroons/Fr./It./Sp.) Enzo Serafin; Guy Decleuse;
                                         Julio Ortaz
The Mysterious Satellite (1956: Jap.) Kimio Watanabe
Mystery at the Burlesque (1950:
   GB--Mon.) Bert Mason
Mystery at the Villa Rosa (1930: GB) Sydney Blythe
Mystery Mansion (1984: US) Milas Hinshaw
Mystery of the Black Jungle (1955:
   Rep.) Massimo Dallamano
The Mystery of Thug Island (1966:
   Ger./It.--Col.) Gugliemo Mancori
Mystery on Bird Island (1954: GB) William Pollard
The Myth (1965: It.) Franco Villa

N. P. (1971: It.) Nicola Dimitri
Naked among the Wolves (1967: Ger.) Gunther Manszinkowsky
The Naked Brigade (1965: Greece--
   Univ.) Aristedes Karides-Fuchs
The Naked Cage (1986: Cannon) Hal Trussell
The Naked General (1964: Jap.) Asaichi Nakai
The Naked Gun (1988: Par.) Robert Stevens
Naked in the Sun (1957: AA) Charles T. O'Rork
Naked Obsession (1990: US) Dick Buckley
The Naked Prey (1966: S. Afr.--Par.) H. A. R. Thomson
Naked Youth (1961: Jap.) Ko Kawamata
Napoleon (1955: Fr.) Pierre Montazel
The Narco Men (1969: It./Sp.) Oberdan Trojani
Narrow Margin (1990: Tri-S.) Peter Hyams
The Narrowing Circle (1956: GB) Jonah Jones
Nashville Rebel (1966: AIP) John Eisenbach
The Nasty Girl (1990: Ger.) Axel de Roche
Nathalie (1958: Fr.) Robert Lefebvre
Nathalie, Secret Agent (1960: Fr.) Robert Lefebvre
National Lampoon's Christmas
   Vacation (1989: WB) Thomas Ackerman

Native Son (1951: Arg.--US) A. U. Meray
Natural Enemies (1979: US) Richard E. Brooks
Navajo Run (1966: AIP) Gregory Sandor
The Navigator (1988: NZ) Geoffrey Simpson
Nea: A New Woman (1978: Fr.) Andreas Winding
Negatives (1968: GB) George Minassian
Neither by Day Nor by Night
    (1972: Isr.--US) Amnon Salomon
Neither the Sea nor the Sand
    (1974: GB) David Muir
The Neon Palace (1970: Can.) Jim Lewis
The Nest (1982: Sp.) Teo Escamilla
The Nest (1988: US) Richard Jacques Gale
A Nest of Gentry (1982: USSR) Giorgi Rerberg
Never Cry Wolf (1983: Dis.) Hiro Narita
Never on Sunday (1960: Greece) Jacques Natteau
Never on Tuesday (1989: US) Alan Jones
Never Put It in Writing (1964: AA) Martin Curtis
Never Say Die (1988: NZ) Rory O'Shea
The Neverending Story II: The Next
    Chapter (1990: Ger.--WB) Davis Connell
The New Adventures of Pippi
    Longstocking (1988: Col.) Roland "Ozzie" Smith
New Girl in Town (1977: US) Irv Goodnoff
New Orleans after Dark (1958: AA) Willis Winford
New Year's Day * (1989: US) Nesya Blue
New York Confidential (1955: WB) Edward Fitzgerald
New York Nights (1984: US) Alan Doberman
Night Affair (1961: Fr.) Louis Page
Night and Fog in Japan (1985: Jap.) Takashi Kawamuta
Night Angel (1990: US) David Lewis
The Night Before (1988: US) Ronald Garcia
A Night before Christmas (1963:
    USSR) Dmitriy Surenskiy
Night Comes Too Soon (1948: GB) Ray Densham
Night Encounter (1963: Fr./It.) Jacques Robin
Night Games (1966: Swed.) Rune Ericson
Night Games (1980: AE) Dennis Lewiston
Night in Bangkok (1966: Jap.) Taiichi Kankura
A Night in Heaven (1983: TCF) David Quaid
A Night in Hong Kong (1961: Jap.) Rokuro Nishigaki
A Night in June (1940: Swed.) Ake Dahlquist
A Night in the Life of Jimmy Reardon
    (1988: TCF) John Connor
Night Is My Future (1962: Swed.) Goran Strindberg
Night of Dark Shadows (1971: MGM) Richard Shore
A Night of Magic (1944: GB) W. Richards
Night of the Comet (1984: US) Arthur Albert
Night of the Creeps (1986: Tri-S.) Robert New
Night of the Demons (1988: US) David Lewis

Night of the Following Day (1969: GB--UA)	Willy Kurant
Night of the Lepus (1972: MGM)	Ted Voigtlander
Night of the Living Dead (1968: US)	George Romero
Night of the Living Dead (1990: Col.)	Frank Prinzi
The Night of the Seagull (1970: Jap.)	Choichi Nakai
The Night of the Shooting Stars (1982: It.--UA)	Franco di Giacomo
Night of the Zombies (1984: US)	John Cabrera
Night Patrol (1984: US)	Jug Walthers
The Night Porter (1974: It.--US)	Alfio Contini
Night Ride (1937: GB--Par.)	Francis Carver
Night Shadows (1984: US)	Al Taylor
The Night They Killed Rasputin (1962: Fr./It.)	Adalberto Albertini
Night Train to Paris (1964: GB-- Lip./TCF)	Arthur Lavis
Night Train to Terror (1985: US)	Susan Malijan
The Night Visitor (1970: Swed.)	Henning Kristiansen
Night Visitor (1989: MGM-UA)	Peter Jensen
The Night Won't Talk (1952: GB)	Brendan Stafford
Nightfall (1988: US)	Dariusz Wolski
Nighthawks (1978: GB)	Joanna Davis
Nightmare at Noon (1990: US)	Cliff Ralke
Nightmare Castle (1966: It.--AA)	Enzo Barboni
A Nightmare on Elm Street 3: Dream Warriors (1987: US)	Roy Wagner
A Nightmare on Elm Street 4: The Dream Master (1988: US)	Steven Fierberg
A Nightmare on Elm Street 5: The Dream Child (1989: US)	Peter Levy
The Nights of Lucretia Borgia (1960: It.--Col.)	Massimo Dallamano
The Nights of Prague (1968: Czech.)	Jan Kallis; Frantisek Uldrych
Nights of Shame (1961: Fr.)	Roger Fellous
Nikki, Wild Dog of the North (1961: Can.--Dis.)	Lloyd Beebe; Jack Couffer; Ray Jewell; William Bacon
Nine Days of One Year (1964: USSR)	German Lavrov
9 Deaths of the Ninja (1985: US)	Roy Wagner
976-Evil (1989: US)	Paul Elliot
1918 (1985: US)	George Tirl
Nineteen Nineteen (1986: GB)	Ivan Strasburg
1990: The Bronx Warriors (1983: It.)	Sergio Salvati
1939 (1989: Swed.)	Jens Fischer
90 Days (1986: Can.)	Andrew Kitzanuk
90 Degrees in the Shade (1966: Czech.)	Bedrich Batka
The Ninth Circle (1961: Yugo.)	Ivan Marincek
The Ninth Heart (1980: Czech.)	Jiri Machane
Nirvana Street Murder (1990: Aus.)	Mark Lane

No Blade of Grass (1970: GB--MGM)	H. A. R. Thomson
No Drums, No Bugles (1971: US)	Richard McCarthy; Parker Bartlett
No Exit (1962: Arg.--US)	Ricardo Younis
No Funny Business (1934: GB--UA)	W. Blakeley; D. Langley
No Greater Love (1944: USSR)	V. Rappaport; A. Zavalov
No Greater Love Than This (1969: Jap.	Kenji Hagiwara
No Harvest but a Thorn (1985: Malayia)	Johan Braham
No Haunt for a Gentleman (1952: GB)	Ted Lloyd
No Man Is an Island (1962: MGM)	Carl Kayser
No Man's Land (1964: US)	James Houston
No Man's Land (1987: Orion)	Hiro Narita
No Mercy (1986: Tri-S.)	Michel Brault
No Parking (1938: GB)	Francis Carver
No Place for Jennifer (1950: GB)	William McLeod
No Retreat, No Surrender (1986: US)	David Golia
No Room To Die (1969: It.)	Franco Villa
No Surrender (1986: GB)	Michael Coulter
No Time for Ecstasy (1963: Fr.)	Raymond Lemoigne
No Time for Flowers (1952: RKO)	Tony Braun
No Time To Kill (1963: Ger./GB/ Swed.)	Bengt Lindstrom
No Trace (1950: GB)	Eric Befche
No Way Back (1949: GB)	Robert Navarro
Nobody Waved Goodbye (1965: Can.)	John Spotton
Nobody's Fool (1986: US)	Mikhail Suslov
Nobody's Perfect (1968: Univ.)	Robert Wyckoff
Nobody's Perfect (1989: US)	Claus Loof
Nomads (1986: US)	Stephen Ramsey
None but the Brave (1963: US)	Ronald Perryman
Noose for a Gunman (1960: UA)	Al Cline
Noose for a Lady (1953: GB)	Jimmy Harvey
Norman's Awesome Experience (1989: Can.)	Vic Sarin
The Norseman (1978: AIP)	Robert Bethard
El Norte (1984: Sp.)	James Glennon
Northern Lights (1978: US)	Judy Irola
Nosferatu, the Vampire (1979: Fr./Ger.--TCF)	Jorg Schmidt-Reitwein
Nostalghia (1984: It.)	Giuseppe Lanci
Not for Publication (1984: US)	George Tirl
Not of This Earth (1988: US)	Zoran Hochstatter
Not Reconciled (1969: Ger.)	Wendelin Sachtler
Not So Quiet on the Western Front (1930: GB)	James Rogers
Nothing but a Man (1964: US)	Robert Young
Nothing Venture (1948: GB)	Jo Jago
Nous Irons a Paris (1949: Fr.)	Charles Suin

Nowhere to Hide (1987: Can.)	Victor Sarin
The Nude Bomb (1980: Univ.)	Henry L. Wolf
The Nun (1971: Fr.)	Alain Levent
Nuns on the Run (1990: GB--TCF)	Michael Garfath
Nunzio (1978: Univ.)	Edward Brown
Nutcracker Fantasy (1979: US)	Fumio Otani; Aguri Sugita; Ryoji Takamori

Objective 500 Million (1966: Fr.)	Alain Levent
Oblomov (1981: USSR)	Pavel Lebechev
The Obscure Illness (1990: It.)	Carlo Tafani
Obsession (1968: Swed.)	Bertil Wiktorsson
Odd Jobs (1986: Tri-S.)	Peter Lyons Collister; Arthur Albert
Odd Obsession (1961: Jap.)	Kazuo Miyagawa
Oedipus Rex (1957: Can.)	Roger Barlow
Oedipus Rex (1984: It.)	Giuseppe Ruzzolini
Of Flesh and Blood (1964: Fr./It.)	Andreas Winding
Of Wayward Love (1964: Ger./It.)	Erico Menczer
The Offering (1966: Can.)	Stanley Lipinski
The Office Picnic (1974: Aus.)	Michael Edols
The Official Story (1985: Sp.)	Felix Monti
Oh, Boris (1990: Aust.)	Hanus Polak
Ohayo (1962: Jap.)	Yushin Atsuta
Old Explorers (1990: US)	Jeffrey Laszlo
Old Gringo (1989: Col.)	Felix Monti
Old Roses (1935: GB--Fox)	Alex Bryce
Old Shatterhand (1968: Fr./Ger./It./Yugo.)	Siegfried Hold
The Oldest Profession (1968: Fr./Ger./It.)	Pierre Lhomme; Heinz Holscher
The Olive Trees of Justice (1967: Fr.)	Julius Rascheff
On a Moonlit Night (1989: Fr./It.)	Carlo Tafani
On Probation (1935: US)	Henry Kurse
On the Air (1934: GB)	Alex Bryce
On the Buses (1972: GB--EMI)	Mark McDonald
On the Comet (1970: Czech.)	Rudolf Stahl
On the Edge (1986: US)	Stefan Czapsky
On the Right Track (1981: TCF)	Jack Richards
On the Run (1983: Aus.)	Paul Onorato
On the Sunnyside (1936: Swed.)	Ake Dahlquist
On the Wire (1990: GB)	Yoshi Tezuka
On the Yard (1978: US)	Alan Metzer
Once a Rainy Day (1968: Jap.)	Aizawa Yuzuru
Once in Paris (1978: US)	Claude Saunier
Once There Was a Girl (1945: USSR)	George Gariblan
One Big Affair (1952: UA)	Jose Ortiz Ramos
One Body Too Many (1944: Par.)	Fred Jackman, Jr.
One Dark Night (1983: US)	Hal Trussel

One Deadly Summer (1984: Fr./UA) — Etienne Becker

One-Eyed Soldiers (1967: GB/Yugo. --US) — Branko Ivatovic

$100 a Night (1968: Ger.) — Walter Tuch

102 Boulevard Hausmann (1990: GB) — John Hooper

One Jump Ahead (1955: GB) — Brendan Stafford

One Man (1979: Can.) — Douglas Kiefer

One More Saturday Night (1986: Col.) — James Glennon

One More Train to Rob (1971: Univ.) — Alric Edens

One Night Stand (1976: Fr.) — Alain Derobe

One Sings, the Other Doesn't (1977: Fr.) — Charlie Van Damme; Nurith Aviv; Elisabeth Prouvost

1,000 Convicts and a Woman (1971: AIP) — Gerald Moss

The 1,000 Plane Raid (1969: UA) — William Spencer

1 2 3 Monster Express (1977: Thai.) — Pisan Prasingh

The One Way Trail (1931: Col.) — John Hickson

One Wild Night (1938: TCF) — Harry Davis

One Wild Oat (1951: GB) — Robert Navarro

One Wish Too Many (1956: GB) — Adrian Jeakins

Onimasa (1983: Jap.) — Fujio Morita

The Only Thing You Know (1971: Can.) — Paul Lang

The Only Way (1970: Den./Pan.-- US) — Henning Kristiansen

The Only Way Home (1972: US) — Henning Schellerup

Open City (1946: It.) — Ubaldo Arata

Open Doors (1990: It.) — Tonino Nardi

Open Season (1974: Sp.--Col.) — Fernando Arribas

Opening Night (1977: US) — Al Ruban

Opera Prima (1982: Sp.) — Angel Luis Fernandez

Operation Camel (1961: Den.--AIP) — Aage Wiltrup; Ole Lytken

Operation Cross Eagles (1969: Yugo. --US) — Nenad Jovicic

Operation Cupid (1960: GB--Rank) — Jimmy Harvey

Operation Dames (1959: AIP) — Edward Martin

Operation Diamond (1948: GB) — Ronnie Pilgrim

Operation Ganymed (1977: Ger.) — Wolfgang Grasser

Operation Kid Brother (1967: Iy. --UA) — Alejandro Ulloa

Operation Manhunt (1954: UA) — Akos Farkis; Benoit Jobin

Operation St. Peter's (1968: It. --Par.) — Erico Menczer

Operation X (1963: Jap.) — Yuzuru Aizawa

Operetta (1949: Ger.) — Hans Schneeberger

Opiate 67 (1967: Fr./It.) — Alfio Contini

Opposing Force (1987: Orion) — Michael Jones

Options (1989: US) — James Robb; Leo Napolitano

Ordered To Love (1963: Ger.) — Igor Oberberg

The Orders (1977: Can.)	Michael Brault
Ordet (1957: Den.)	Henning Bendtsen
The Oregon Trail (1959: TCF)	Kay Norton
Orphans of the North (1940: Mon.)	Norman Dawn
Orpheus (1950: Fr.)	Nicholas Hayer
Otets Sergei (1917: Russ.)	N. Roudakoff; F. Bourgassov
Othello (1955: Fr./It.--UA)	Anchise Brizzi
Othello (1955: USSR)	E. Andrikanis
Othello (1989: US)	James Swain
The Other Woman (1954: TCF)	Edward Fitzgerald
Our Daily Bread (1950: Ger.)	Robert Baberakd
Our Silent Love (1969: Jap.)	Kozo Okazaki
Out (1982: US)	Robert Ball
Out of the Dark (1989: US)	Julio Macat
Out of the Tiger's Mouth (1962: US)	Emmanuel Rojas
Outback (1989: Aus.)	Ross Berryman
Outlaw Force (1988: US)	David Huey; James Mathers
Outlaw: The Saga of Gisli (1982: Ice.)	Sigurdur Sverrir Palsson
Outlaw Treasure (1955: AIP)	Clark Ramsey
Outlaws of the Rockies (1945: Col.)	George Kelley
Outpost of Hell (1966: Jap.)	Kazuo Yamada
Outrageous! (1977: Can.)	James B. Kelly
The Outsider (1980: Par.)	Ricardo Aronovich
Outsider in Amsterdam (1983: Holl.)	Marc Felperlaan
Over the Edge (1979: Orion/WB)	Andrew Davis
The Overcoat (1965: USSR)	G. Marandzhyan
Overseas (1990: Fr.)	Dominique Chapuis
The P.O.W. (1973: US)	Benjamin Gruberg
P.O.W.: The Escape (1986: Cannon)	Yechel Ne'eman
Pacific Destiny (1956: GB)	Martin Curtis
Pacific Heights (1990: TCF)	Dennis Jones
Paddy (1970: Ire.--AA)	Daniel Lacambre
Padre Padrone (1977: It.)	Mario Masini
Pagan Island (1961: US)	Mark Dennis
Paganini (1989: It.)	Pier Luigi Santi
Paid To Kill (1954: GB--Ham.)	Jimmy Harvey
Palm Beach (1979: Aus.)	Oscar Scherl
Panama Sugar (1990: It.)	Roberto Benevenuti
Pandemonium (1988: Aus.)	David Sanderson
Panic Button (1964: US)	Enzo Serafin
Panique (1947: Fr.)	Nicholas Hayer
The Panisperna Street Boys (1989: It.)	Tonino Nardi
Paper Lion (1968: UA)	Morris Hartzband
Paper Mask (1990: GB)	Nat Crosby
Paper Peter (1990: Iceland)	Tony Forsberg
Paper Tiger (1975: GB)	John Cabrera; Charley Steinberger; Tony Braun
A Paper Wedding (1990: Can.)	Sylvain Brault

Paperback Hero (1973: Can.)	Don Wilder
Paperhouse (1988: GB)	Mike Southron
Parades (1972: US)	Sol Negrin
Parades pour Tous (1982: Fr.)	Jacques Robin
Parallels (1980: Can.)	Douglas Cole
Parents (1989: US)	Ernest Day
Paris Belongs to Us (1962: Fr.)	Charles Bitsch
Paris Ooh-La-La (1963: Fr.--US)	Alain Derobe
Paris Pick-Up (1963: Fr./It.--Par.)	Andre Bac
The Parisian (1931: Fr.)	P. J. Faulener
The Parson and the Outlaw (1957: Col.)	Clark Ramsey
Parting Glances (1986: US)	Jacek Laskus
Partings (1962: Pol.)	Mieczyslaw Jahoda
The Party Animal (1985: US)	Bryan England
The Party Crashers (1958: Par.)	Edward Fitzgerald
Party Line (1988: US)	John Hunnel
Party Party (1983: GB--TCF)	Sydney Macartney
A Passage to India (1984: Col.)	Ernest Day
La Passante (1983: Fr./Ger.)	Jean-Jacques Cazoit
The Passenger (1970: Pol.)	Krzysztof Winiewicz
Passenger to London (1937: GB--TCF)	Stanley Grant
The Passing (1985: US)	Jochi Melero; Richard Chisol
Passing Shadows (1934: GB--Fox)	Alex Bryce
Passing Through (1977: US)	Roderick Young; George Geddis
Passion (1968: Jap.)	Setsuo Kobayashi
Passion for Life (1951: Fr.)	Andre Dumaitre; Marc Fossard; Maurice Pecqueu
Passion of Love (1982: Fr./It.)	Claudio Ragona
The Passion of Slow Fire (1962: Fr.)	Jean-Louis Picavet
The Passionate Demons (1962: Nor.)	Ragnar Sorensen
Passport (1990: Fr./Isr./USSR)	Vadim Youssov
The Password Is Courage (1962: GB--MGM)	David Boulton
Patakin (1985: Cuba)	Luis Garcia Mesa
Pather Panchali (1958: India)	Subrata Mitra
Pathos (1989: It.)	Romano Albani
Patience Is a Virtue (1989: USSR)	Yuri Vorontsov
Patty Hearst (1988: US)	Bojan Bazelli
A Paucity of Flying Dreams (1990: Jap.)	Shinsaku Himeda
Pawnee (1957: Rep.)	Hal McAlpin
Payment in Blood (1968: It.--Col.)	Aldo Pennelli
Peace to Him Who Enters (1963: USSR)	Anatoliy Kuznetsov
Peacemaker (1990: US)	Thomas Jewett
The Peach Thief (1969: Bulg.)	Todor Stoyanov
The Pearl of Tlayucan (1964: Mex.)	Rosalio Solano
Pearls of the Crown (1938: Fr.)	Jules Kruger

Peeper (1975: TCF) — Earl Rath
Penitentiary (1979: US) — Marty Ollstein
Penitentiary III (1987: Cannon) — Marty Ollstein
Penn & Teller Get Killed (1989: Lor./WB) — Jan Weincke
The Penny Pool (1937: GB) — Germaine Berger
Le Penseur (1920: Fr.) — G. Specht
The Penthouse (1967: GB--Par.) — Arthur Lavis
Pentimento (1990: Fr.) — Pascal Lebeque
People Meet and Sweet Music Fills the Heart (1969: Den./Swed.) — Henning Kristiansen
Pepe Le Moko (1937: Fr.) — Jules Kruger ; Marc Fossard
Pepi, Luci, Born and the Other Girls (1980: Spain) — Palo Femenia
A Perfect Couple (1979: TCF) — Edmond Koons
Perfect Strangers (1984: US) — Paul Glickman
The Performers (1970: Jap.) — Keiji Maruyama
Peril (1985: Fr.) — Martial Thury
Peril for the Guy (1956: GB) — James Allen
The Perils of Gwendoline in the Land of Yik Yak (1985: Fr.--US) — Andre Domage
Permanent Vacation (1982: US) — James A. Lebovitz; Thomas DiCillo
Personal Choice (1989: US) — John Bartley
Personal Column (1939: Fr.) — R. Voinquel
The Personals (1982: US) — Peter Markle; Greg Cummins
Petersen (1974: Aus.) — Robin Copping
Le Petit Theatre de Jean Renoir (1974: Fr.) — Georges Leclerc
Phaedra (1962: Fr./Greece-US) — Jacques Natteau
Phantasm (1979: AE) — Don Coscarelli
Phantasm II (1988: Univ.) — Daryn Okada
Phantom of Death (1989: It.) — Giorgio Di Battista
The Phantom of the Opera (1989: US) — Elemer Ragalyi
The Phantom Planet (1961: AIP) — Elwood Nicholson
The Pharaoh's Woman (1961: It.--Univ.) — Pier Ludovico Pavoni
The Phony American (1964: Ger.) — Ernst Kalinke
Picasso Tiger (1988: US) — Howard Wexler
Picnic on the Grass (1960: Fr.) — Georges Leclerc
The Picture Show Man (1980: Aus.) — Geoff Burton
Pictures (1982: NZ) — Rory O'Shea
Pilgrim, Farewell (1980: US) — Franz Rath
The Pillar of Fire (1963: Isr.) — Haim Shreiber
Pillars of Society (1936: Ger.--UFA) — Carl Drews
Pillow to Post (1945: WB) — Wesley Anderson
Pinocchio (1969: E. Ger.) — Gunter Haubold
Pippi in the South Seas (1974: Ger./Swed.) — Kalle Bergholm
Piranha (1978: US) — Jamie Anderson

Piranha II: The Spawning (1981: Holl.--Col.) — Roberto D'Etore Piazzoli
The Pirate Movie (1982: Aus.--TCF) — Robin Copping
The Pirate of the Black Hawk (1961: Fr./It.) — Vincenzo Seratrice
Pirates (1986: Cannon) — Witold Sobocinski
The Pirates of Capri (1949: US) — Anchise Brizzi
A Pistol for Ringo (1966: It./Sp.) — Francisco Marin
Pixote (1981: Braz.) — Rodolfo Sanches
A Place Called Glory (1966: Ger./Sp.) — Federico Larraya
Place of Weeping (1986: S. Afr.) — Paul Witte
Plain Clothes (1988: Par.) — Daniel Hainey
Plainsong (1981: US) — Joe Ritter
Planet of the Vampires (1965: It./Sp. --AIP) — Antonio Rinaldi
The Planets against Us (1961: Fr./It.) — Pier Ludovico Pavoni
The Plank (1967: GB) — Arthur Wooster
Platoon (1986: Orion) — Robert Richardson
Play It Cool (1970: Jap.) — Setsuo Kobayashi
The Playboy (1942: GB) — Francis Carver
Playing for Keeps (1986: Univ.) — Eric Van Halen Norman
Playmates (1969: Fr./It.) — Jacques Robin
Please, Not Now! (1963: Fr./It.-- TCF) — Robert Lefebvre
The Pleasure Lovers (1964: GB) — Jimmy Harvey
Pleasures and Vices (1962: Fr.) — Jean Isnard
The Pleasures of the Flesh (1965: Jap.) — Akira Takada
The Plot against Harry (1989: US) — Robert Young
The Ploughman's Lunch (1984: GB--US) — Clive Tickner
Plucked (1969: Fr./It.) — Dario Di Palma
The Plumber (1980: Aus.) — David Sanderson
Pocomania (1939: US) — Jay Rescher
Point of View (1990: Isr.) — Ilan Rosenberg
Poitin (1979: Ire.) — Seamus Deasy
Police Academy (1984: WB) — Michael Margulies
Police Academy 3: Back in Training (1986: WB) — Robert Saad
Police Academy 4: Citizens on Patrol (1987: WB) — Robert Saad
Police Academy 6: City under Siege (1989: WB) — Charles Rosher, Jr.
Police Python 357 (1976: Fr.) — Etienne Becker
Polikouchka (1919: Russ.) — Y. Jeliabouvski
Political Asylum (1975: Mex.) — Juan Manuel Herrera
Polonaise (1989: Holl.) — Goert Giltay
Poltergeist III (1988: MGM-UA) — Alex Nepomniaschy
Polyester (1981: US) — David Insley
Pontius Pilate (1967: Fr./It.) — Massimo Dallamano
Pony Express Rider (1976: US) — Bernie Abramson

Por Mis Pistolas (1969: Mex.--Col.)	Jose Ramos
Port of Escape (1955: GB)	Philip Grindrod
Portland Expose (1957: AA)	Carl Berger
Portrait of a Woman (1946: Fr.)	Jacques Mercanton; Adrien Porchet
Portrait of Chielko (1968: Jap.)	Hiroshi Takamura
Portrait of Hell (1969: Jap.)	Kazuo Yamada
Portrait of Lenin (1967: Pol./USSR)	Jan Laskowski
Portrait of the Artist as a Young Man (1979: Ire.)	Stuart Hetherington
Postman's Knock (1962: GB--MGM)	Gerald Moss
Potomok Tchinghiz Khana (1928: USSR)	A. Golovnia
Pourquoi Pas! (1979: Fr.)	Jean-Francois Robin
The Power (1984: US)	Stephen Carpenter
Practice Makes Perfect (1980: Fr.)	Jean-Paul Schwartz
Praise Marx and Pass the Ammunition (1970: GB)	Charles Stewart
Prancer (1989: Orion)	Misha Suslov
Pray for Death (1985: US)	Roy Wagner
A Prayer for the Dying (1987: US)	Mike Garfath
Predator 2 (1990: TCF)	Peter Levy
Prelude to Ecstasy (1963: Fin.)	Olavi Tuomi
The Premonition (1976: AE)	Victor C. Milt
The Presidio (1988: Par.)	Peter Hyams
Pressure (1976: GB)	Mike Davis
Pressure of Guilt (1964: Jap.)	Hiroshi Murai
Pretty Boy Floyd (1960: US)	Chuck Austin
Pretty Poison (1968: TCF)	David Quaid
Pretty Woman (1990: BV/Touch.)	Charles Minsky
The Prey (1984: US)	Teru Hayashi
The Price of Power (1969: It./Sp.)	Stelvio Massi
The Priest of St. Pauli (1970: Ger.)	Franz Lederle
The Priest's Wife (1971: Fr./It.--WB)	Alfio Contini
Prime Evil (1988: US)	Roberta Findlay
Prince Jack (1985: US)	Hiro Narita
Prince of Darkness (1987: Univ.)	Gary Kibbe
The Prince of Pennsylvania (1988: US)	Frank Prinzi
The Princess and the Magic Frog (1965: US)	Donald Gundrey
The Princess Bride (1987: TCF)	Adrian Biddle
The Principal (1987: Tri-S.)	Arthur Albert
Prism (1971: US)	Jay Freund
The Prisoner of St. Petersburg (1989: Aus./Ger.)	Ray Argall
Prisoner of the Desert (1990: Fr.)	Raymond Depardon
Prisoner of the Iron Mask (1962: Fr./It.)	Raffaele Masciocchi

Prisoners of Inertia (1989: US)	James McCalmont
La Prisonniere (1969: Fr./It.)	Andreas Winding
Private Collection (1972: Aus.)	David Gribble
Private Duty Nurses (1972: US)	John McNichol
The Private Files of J. Edgar Hoover (1978: AIP)	Paul Glickman
Private Life (1983: USSR)	Nikolai Olonovsky
A Private Life (1989: GB)	Nat Crosby
Private Life of Louis XIV (1936: Ger.)	Reimar Kuntze
Private Parts (1972: MGM)	Andrew Davis
Private Pooley (1962: E. Ger./GB)	Rolf Sohre
Private Potter (1963: GB--MGM)	Arthur Lavis
The Private Secretary (1935: GB)	Sydney Blythe; William Luff
Private War (1990: US)	Karpo Godina
Privates on Parade (1984: GB--Orion)	Ian Wilson
The Prize (1952: Fr.)	Charles Suin
Problem Child (1990: Univ.)	Peter Lyons Collister
The Prodigal Son (1935: Univ.)	Albert Benitz
The Prodigal Son (1964: Jap.)	Asaichi Nakai
The Producers (1967: US)	Joseph Coffey
The Projectionist (1970: US)	Victor Petrashevic
Prologue (1970: Can.)	Douglas Kiefer
Prom Night (1980: AE)	Robert New
Prom Night III: The Last Kiss (1990: Can.)	Rhett Morita
Promised Land (1987: US)	Ueli Steiger; Alexander Gruszynski
Property (1979: US)	Eric Edwards
Prophecies of Nostradamus (1974: Jap.)	Rokuro Nishigaki
Prostitute (1980: GB)	Charles Stewart
Prostitution (1965: Fr.)	Quinto Albicocco; Paul Fabian Enzo Riccioni; Jacques Mercanton
The Proud and the Damned (1972: Col.)	Remegio Young
The Proud Rider (1971: Can.)	Walter Wasik
Providence (1977: Fr.)	Ricardo Aronovich
Psychic Killer (1975: AE)	Herb Pearl
Psychout for Murder (1971: Arg./It.)	Luciano Trasatti
Psycosissimo (1962: It.)	Tino Santoni
A Public Affair (1962: US)	Howard Schwartz
Pulse (1988: Col.)	Peter Lyons Collister
Pump Up the Volume (1990: Can./US)	Walt Lloyd
Pumpkinhead (1988: US)	Bojan Bazelli
Punishment Park (1971: US)	Joan Churchill
Puppet Master (1989: US)	Sergio Salvati
Pure S (1976: Aus.)	Tom Cowan
Purgatory (1989: US)	Tom Fraser
Purple Haze (1982: US)	Richard Gibb

Purple Hearts (1984: WB)	Jan Kiesser
Purse Strings (1933: GB--Par.)	Henry Harris
Puss in Boots (1989: Cannon)	Avi Karpick
Puss 'N' Boots (1964: Mex.)	Rosalio Solano
Puss 'N'Boots (1967: Ger.)	Ted Kornowicz
Putney Swope (1969: US)	Gerald Cotts
Pyro (1964: Sp.--AIP)	Manuel Berenguer

Quadrophenia (1979: GB)	Brian Tufano
The Quare Fellow (1962: GB)	Peter Hennessy
Quartet (1949: GB--EL/Rank)	Ray Elton
Quartet (1981: Fr./GB)	Pierre Lhomme
Quatrevingt-Treize (1914: Fr.)	G. Specht
Queen of Hearts (1989: GB)	Mike Southron
The Queen of Spades (1916: Russia)	Evgeny Slavinsky
Queen of Spades (1961: USSR)	N. Shifirn
Queen of the Nile (1964: It.)	Massimo Dallamano
Queen of the Pirates (1961: Ger./It.--Col.)	Raffaele Masciocchi
Quest for Love (1989: S. Afr.)	Roy MacGregor
The Question (1977: Fr.)	Alain Levent
Question 7 (1961: Ger.--US)	Gunter Senftleben
A Quiet Day in Belfast (1974: Can.)	Harry Makin
A Quiet Woman (1951: GB)	Monty Berman
Quigley Down Under (1990: MGM/UA)	David Eggby

The Rabbi and the Shikse (1976: Isr.)	Nissim Leon
The Rabbit Man (1990: Swed.)	Andra Lasmanis
The Rabble (1965: Jap.)	Kazuo Yamada
Rabid Grannies (1989: US)	Hugh Labye
A Race for Life (1955: GB--Ham./Lip.)	Jimmy Harvey
Racing Fever (1964: AA)	Julio Chavez
Radio Follies (1936: GB)	Cyril Bristow; Philip Grindrod
Radio On (1980: Ger./GB)	Martin Schafer
Radio Stars on Parade (1945: RKO)	Harry Walker
Rage (1966: Mex.--Col.)	Rosalio Solano
Raid on Rommel (1971: Univ.)	Earth Rath
Raiders of Old California (1957: Rep.)	Charles Straumer
Railroad Workers (1948: Swed.)	Martin Bodin
Rain and Shine (1978: Hung.)	Lajos Koltai
The Rainbow (1944: USSR)	Boris Monastirsky
The Rainbow Boys (1973: Can.)	Robert Saad
Rambo III (1988: Tri-S.)	John Stainer
Rampage at Apache Wells (1966: Ger./Yugo.--Col.)	Heinz Holscher
Ran (1985: Jap.)	Takio Saito; Masaharu Ueda; Asakazu Nakai

Rangle River (1939: Aus.--Col.)	Errol Hinds
Rango (1931: Par.)	Alfred Williams
The Rape (1965: Greece)	Nikos Kavoudikis
Rapture (1950: It.)	Rudolf Icsey
Rashomon (1951: Jap.--RKO)	Kazuo Miyagawa
Raspad (1990: Ukraine/US)	Alexander Shigayev; Piotr Trashevski
Raspoutine (1954: Fr.--WB)	Pierre Petit
Rasputin (1985: USSR)	Leonid Kalashnikov
Raspy & Dolly (1990: Fin.)	Travho Hirvonen
Rat (1960: Yugo.)	Kresko Grcevic
Rat Pfink and Boo Boo (1966: US)	Dennis Steckler
The Rat Saviour (1977: Yugo.)	Iveco Rajkovic
Ratataplan (1979: It.)	Mario Battistoni
The Rats (1955: Ger.)	Goran Strindberg
The Ravagers (1979: Col.)	Vincent Saizis
The Raven (1948: Fr.)	Nicholas Hayer
Raven's End (1970: Swed.)	Jan Lindestrom
A Ravishing Idiot (1966: Fr./It.)	Andreas Winding
Raw Wind in Eden (1958: Univ.)	Enzo Serafin
The Rebel (1933: Ger.--Univ.)	Sepp Algeier; Albert Benitz; Willy Goldberger
The Rebel Gladiators (1963: It.)	Carlo Bellero
Rebel Love (1985: US)	Joseph Whigham
Rebellion (1967: Jap.)	Kazuo Yamada
Recess (1967: US)	George Silano
Recoil (1953: GB)	Monty Berman
Recollections of the Yellow House (1989: Port.)	Jose Antonio Loureiro
Reconstruction of a Crime (1970: Ger.)	George Arvanitis
Record City (1978: AIP)	William Klages
Red (1970: Can.)	Bernard Chentrier
The Red and the White (1969: Hung./USSR)	Tamas Somlo
Red Beard (1966: Jap.)	Asaichi Nakai; Takao Saito
Red Blooded American Girl (1990: Can.)	Ludek Bogner
The Red Cloak (1961: Fr./It.--AA)	Adalberto Albertini
Red-Dragon (1967: Ger./It.--US)	Werner Lenz
Red Headed Stranger (1986: US)	Neil Roach
The Red Inn (1954: Fr.)	Andre Bac
Red Kiss (1986: Fr.)	Ramon Suarez
Red Lanterns (1965: Ger.)	Nikos Gardelis
Red Lion (1971: Jap.)	Takao Saito
Red Lob (1989: It.)	Giuseppe Lanci
The Red Sheik (1963: It.)	Gianni Narzisi; Angelo Lotti
The Red Tent (1971: It./USSR--Par.)	Leonid Kalashnikov
The Red, White and Black (1970: US)	Lewis Guinn
The Reflecting Skin (1990: GB)	Dick Pope
Reform School Girls (1986: US)	Howard Wexler

Relentless (1989: US)	James Lemmo
Remembrance (1982: GB)	John Metcalfe
The Removalists (1975: Aus.)	Graham Lind
Rendezvous on the Docks (1953: Fr.)	Paul Carpita
Renegades (1989: Univ.)	Phil Meheux
Renfrew of the Royal Mounted (1937: GN)	Francis Corby
Rent Control (1981: US)	Benito Frattari
A Report on the Party and the Guests (1968: Czech.)	Jaromir Sofr
Repossessed (1990: US)	Michael Margulies
Reptilicus (1962: Den.--AIP)	Aage Wiltrup
Requiem for Dominic (1990: Aust.)	Hans Selikovsky
Resurrected (1989: GB)	Ivan Strasburg
Resurrection (1963: USSR)	Era Savelyeva; Sergey Poluyanov
The Resurrection of Zachary Wheeler (1971: US)	Bob Boatman
Return from the River Kwai (1989: GB)	Arthur Wooster
Return Home (1990: Aus.)	Mandy Walker
The Return of Dr. Mabuse (1961: Fr./Ger./It.)	Karl Lob
The Return of Martin Guerre (1983: Fr.)	Andre Neau
The Return of Rin Tin Tin (1947: EL)	Carl Berger
Return of Sabata (1972: Fr./Ger./It.--UA)	Francisco Marin
The Return of Superfly (1990: US)	Anghel Decca
Return of the Black Eagle (1949: It.)	Rodolfo Lombardi
Return of the Dragon (1974: China)	Ho Lang Shang
The Return of the Musketeers (1989: Fr./GB/SP.--Univ.)	Bernard Lutic
Return of the Secaucus Seven (1980: US)	Austin de Besche
Return to Horror High (1987: US)	Roy Wagner
Return to Waterloo (1985: GB)	Roger Deakins
Reunion (1989: Fr./GB/Ger.)	Bruno de Keyzer
Revenge (1990: Col.)	Jeffrey Kimball
Revenge at El Paso (1968: It.)	Marcello Masciocchi
Revenge of the Creature (1955: Univ.)	Charles Welbourne
Revenge of the Gladiators (1965: It.--Par.)	Gugliemo Mancori
Revenge of the Pink Panther (1978: UA)	Ernest Day
The Revengers (1972: Mex.--NG)	Gabriel Torres
The Reverse Be My Lot (1938: GB--Col.)	John Silver
The Revolt of Job (1984: Hung.)	Gabor Szabo

Revolt of the Mercenaries (1964:
   It./Sp.--WB)   Godofredo Pacheco
Revolution (1985: GB/Nor.--WB)   Bernard Lutic
Rhinestone (1984: TCF)   Timothy Galfas
Rice Girl (1963: Fr./It.)   Luciano Trasatti
Richard (1972: US)   Victor Petrashevic
The Rickshaw Man (1960: Jap.)   Kazuo Yamada
Ride a Northbound Horse (1969: Dis.) Robert Hoffman
Ride in the Whirlwind (1966: US)   Gregory Sandor
Ride the High Iron (1965: Col.)   Joe Novak
The Rider in the Night (1968:
   S. Afr.)   John Brown
Rider on the Rain (1970: Fr./It.--AE) Andreas Winding
Riders of the North (1931: US)   Carl Himm
Riff Raff Girls (1962: Fr./It.)   Pierre Montazel
Rififi in Tokyo (1963: Fr./It.)   Tadashi Arakami
Rigoletto (1949: US)   Anchise Brizzi
Rikky and Pete (1988: Aus.--MGM-UA) David Parker
Ring of Spies (1964: GB)   Arthur Lavis
Ringo and His Golden Pistol (1966:
   It.)   Riccardo Pallotini
Rise against the Sword (1966: Jap.) Kazuo Yamada
The Rise of Louis XIV (1970: Fr.)   Georges Leclerc
Rising Storm (1989: US)   Robb Hinds
Rita, Sue and Bob Too (1987: GB--
   Orion)   Ivan Strasburg
Rituelen (1989: Holl.)   Marc Felperlaan
The Ritz (1976: WB)   Paul Wilson
Rivals (1972: AE)   Harvey Goodman
The River House Mystery (1935: GB--
   Univ.)   Alex Bryce
The River Niger (1976: US)   Michael Margulies
River of Death (1989: Cannon)   Avi Karpick
The River Rat (1984: Par.)   Jan Kiesser
Riverbend (1989: US)   Ken Lamkin
Riverrun (1968: Col.)   John Korty
The Road Home (1947: USSR)   Ivan Goldberg; Alexander
                        Zavialov
The Road Hustlers (1978: AIP)   Gerhard Maser
Road Movie (1974: US)   Don Lenzer
Road to Eternity (1962: Jap.)   Yoshio Miyajima
Road to Life (1932: USSR)   Vasili Pronin
Road to Salina (1971: Fr./It.--AE) Maurice Fellous
Roadhouse 66 (1984: US)   Thomas Ackerman
Robert et Robert (1979: Fr.)   Jacques Le Francois
Rock and Rule (1985: MGM-UA)   Lenora Hume
Rock Around the World (1957: GB--
   AIP)   Peter Hennessy
Rock, Rock, Rock! (1956: US)   Morris Hartzband
Rockers (1980: US)   Peter Sova

Rocket to Nowhere (1962: Czech.)	Jan Kallis
Rocky V (1990: MGM/UA)	Victor Hammer
Rodan (1958: Jap.)	Isamu Ashida
Rogue's Yarn (1956: GB)	Hal Morey
Rollin' Plains (1938: GN)	Francis Corby
Rome Wants Another Caesar (1974: It.)	Janos Kende
Romeo (1990: Holl.)	Theo Birkens
Romeo and Juliet (1955: USSR)	A. Chelenov; Tehen-You-Lin
Romeo--Juliet (1990: US)	Armando Acosta
Romero (1989: US)	Geoff Burton
Rooftops (1989: US)	Theo van de Sande
Roogie's Bump (1954: Rep.)	J. Burgi Contner
Rosa Rosa (1990: Holl.)	Piotr Kukla
The Rosary Murders (1987: US)	David Golia
A Rose for Everyone (1967: It.)	Alfio Contini
The Rose Garden (1989: Ger./US)	Gernot Roll
Roselyne and the Lions (1989: Fr.)	Jean-Francois Robin
Roses for the Prosecutor (1961: Ger.)	Erich Claunigk
Rossini (1948: It.)	Mario Albertelli
The Rossiter Case (1950: GB--Ham.)	Jimmy Harvey
Rothschild (1938: Fr.)	Gaston Nrun
Round Midnight (1986: WB)	Brune de Keyzer
The Round Up (1969: Hung.)	Tamas Somlo
The Rowdyman (1973: Can.)	Edmund Long
A Royal Affair (1950: Fr.)	Robert Lefebvre
Royal Affairs in Versailles (1957: Fr.)	Pierre Montazel
The Royal Hunt of the Sun (1969: GB--NG)	Roger Barlow; Francisco Sempere
The Rubber Gun (1977: Can.)	Frank Vitale; Jim Lawrence
Ruby (1971: US)	Dick Bartlett
Rude Awakening (1989: Orion)	Tom Sigel
Rude Boy (1980: GB)	Jack Hazan
The Rugged O'Riordans (1949: Aus.--Univ.)	Bert Nicholas; Carl Kayser
Rumpelstiltskin (1965: Ger.)	Ted Kornowicz
The Runaway (1964: GB--Col.)	Jimmy Harvey
Runaway Girl (1966: US)	Edward Fitzgerald
Running (1979: Can.--Univ.)	Laszlo George
Running Brave (1983: Can.--Dis.)	Francois Protat
Running Scared (1972: GB--Par.)	Ernest Day
Running Scared (1986: MGM)	Peter Hyams
Russkies (1987: US)	Reed Smoot
Rustlers' Rhapsody (1985: Par.)	Jose Luis Alcaine
The Ruthless Four (1969: Ger./It.)	Sergio D'Offizi
SOS--Swedes at Sea (1989: Swed.)	Rune Ericson
Sabata (1969: It.--UA)	Sandro Mancori

Sabra (1970: Fr./Isr./It.) — Alain Levent
Sacred Ground (1984:US) — Charles Pierce
Sacred Knives of Vengeance (1974: HgKg.--WB) — Wu Cho-hua
Saga of the Vagabonds (1964: Jap.) — Akira Suzuki
Sail Into Danger (1957: GB) — Philip Grindrod
Sally Bishop (1932: GB) — Alex Bryce
Salome's Last Dance (1988: US) — Harvey Harrison
Salt of the Earth (1954: US) — Leonard Stark; Stanley Meredith

Salto (1966: Pol) — Kurt Weber
The Salute of the Juggler (1989: Aus.) — David Eggby
The Salvage Gang (1958: GB) — James Allen
Sam Whiskey (1969: UA) — Robert Moreno
Samar (1962: WB) — Emmanuel Rojas
Sam's Son (1984: US) — Ted Voightlander
Samson and the Seven Miracles of the World (1963: Fr./It.--AIP) — Riccardo Pallotini
Samson and the Slave Queen (1963: It.--AIP) — Augusto Tiezzi
Samurai (1955: Jap.) — Yun Yasumoto
Samurai Assassin (1965: Jap.) — Hiroshi Murai
Samurai from Nowhere (1964: Jap.) — Yoshiharu Ota
Samurai (Part II) (1967: Jap.) — Asushi Atumoto
Samurai (Part III) (1967: Jap.) — Kazuo Yamada
San Francisco Docks(1941: Univ.) — Art Lasky
Sandokan The Great (1964: Fr./It./Sp.--MGM) — Angelo Lotti; Giovanni Scarpellini; Aurelio Guitierrez Laraya

Sandu Follows the Sun (1965: USSR) — Vadim Derbenev
Sanjuro (1962: Jap.) — Fukuzo Koizumi; Kozo Saito
Sansho the Bailiff (1969: Jap.) — Kazuo Miyagawa
Santa Claus Conquers the Martians (1964: Emb.) — David Quaid
The Saragossa Manuscript (1972: Pol.) — Mieczyslaw Jahoda
Sardinia: Ransom (1968: It.) — Ugo Piccone
The Satin Mushroom (1969: PRC) — Ray Nadeau
Saturday,Sunday and Monday (1990: It.) — Carlo Tapani
Saturday the 14th (1981: US) — Daniel Lacambre
Saul and David (1968: It./Sp.) — Marcello Masciocchi; Juan Ruiz Romero

The Savage (1975: Fr.) — Pierre Lhomme
Savage Beach (1989: US) — Howard Wexler
The Savage Eye (1960: US) — Jack Couffer
Savage Gold (1933: US) — George Dyott
The Savage Guns (1962: Sp.--MGM) — Alfredo Fraille
Savage Pampas (1967: Arg./Sp.) — Manuel Berenguer
Savage Sisters (1974: AIP) — Justo Paulino
Savage Weekend (1983: Cannon) — Zoli Vidor
The Savage Wild (1970: AIP) — Gordon Eastman

Savannah Smiles (1983: Gold Cst.)	Stephen Gray
Saxo (1988: Fr.)	Bruno de Keyzer
Say It with Flowers (1934: GB--RKO)	Sydney Blythe
Scalpel (1976: US)	Edward Lacheman, Jr.
Scandal (1964: Jap.)	Toshio Ubukata
Scandal (1989: GB)	Mike Molloy
The Scandalous Adventures of	
Buraikan (1970: Jap.)	Kozo Okazaki
Scandals of Paris (1935: GB)	Jack Beaver
Scarab (1982: Sp.--US)	Fernando Arribas
The Scarecrow (1982: NZ)	Jim Bartle
Scarecrow in a Garden of Cucumbers	
(1972: US)	Paul Glickman
The Scarface Mob (1962: US)	Charles Straumer
The Scarlet Camellia (1965: Jap.)	Ko Kawamata
The Scarlet Spear (1954: GB--UA)	Bernard Davies
Scarred (1984: US)	Michael Miner
The Scars of Dracula (1970: GB--	
EMI/Ham.)	Moray Grant
Scavenger Hunt (1979: TCF)	Ken Lamkin
The Scavengers (1959: Phil.--US)	Felipe Sacdalan
Scenes from the Class Struggle in	
Beverly Hills (1989: US	Steven Fierberg
Scent of a Woman (1976: It.--UA)	Claudio Cirillo
Scent of Mystery (1960: US)	John Von Kotze
Scherben (1921: Ger.)	F. Weinmann
Schizoid (1980: Cannon)	Norman Leigh
Schlock (1973: US)	Bob Collins
School for Brides (1952: GB)	Ray Elton
School for Sex (1966: Jap.)	Jo Aizawa
School Spirit (1985: US)	Robert Ebinger
Schoolgirl Diary (1947: It.)	Jan Stallich
Schoolmates (1989: It.)	Danilo Desideri
Schweitzer (1990: US)	Buster Reynolds
The Scientific Cardplayer (1972: It.)	Giuseppe Ruzzolini
Scobie Malone (1975: Aus.)	Keith Lambert
Scorchy (1976: AIP)	Laszlo Pal
Scotland Yard Commands (1937:GB--GN)	Jan Stallich
Scotland Yard Dragnet (1957:GB--Rep.)	Philip Grindrod
Scotland Yard Hunts Dr. Mabuse	
(1963: Ger.)	Nenad Jovicic
Scotland Yard Inspector	
(1952: GB--Ham./Lip.)	Jimmy Harvey
Scratch Harry (1969: Cannon)	Alex Matter; Stephen Winsten
Scream (1985: US)	Rick Pepin
Screamplay (1985: US)	Dennis Piana
Scrooge (1935: GB--Par.)	Sydney Blythe; William Luff
Scum (1979: GB)	Phil Meheux
The Sea Gypsies (1978: WB)	Thomas McHugh
The Sea Pirate (1967: Fr./It./	
Sp.--Par.)	Juan Gelpi
The Search (1948: MGM)	Emil Berna

Seated at His Right (1968: It.) — Aiace Parolin

Second Best Secret Agent in the Whole Wide World (1965: GB--Emb.) — Terry Maher

Second Bureau (1936: Fr.) — Marcel Lucien; Robert Asselin; Raymond Clumy

A Second Chance (1981: Fr.--UA) — Jacques Le Francois

The Second Circle (1990: USSR) — Alexander Burov

Second Fiddle (1957: GB) — Arthur Graham

Second Fiddle to a Steel Guitar (1965: US) — Gary Galbraith

Second Sight (1989: WB) — Dana Christiaansen

A Second Wind (1978: Fr.) — Emmanuel Machuel

The Secret (1979: Hg.Kg.) — C. M. Chung

Secret Agent (1933: GB) — Cyril Bristow; Jack Parker

Secret Agent Fireball (1965: Fr./It.--AIP) — Riccardo Pallotini

The Secret Brigade (1951: USSR) — A. Gintsburg

Secret Document--Vienna (1954: Fr.) — Charles Bauer

The Secret Door (1964: AA) — Robert Moss; Aurelio Rodriguez

The Secret Mark of D'Artagnan (1963: Fr./It.) — Alvaro Mancori

Secret Mission (1949: USSR) — D. Demutsky

Secret Obsession (1989: Fr./Tun.) — Pierre Lhomme

The Secret of Monte Cristo (1961: GB--MGM) — Robert Baker; Monty Berman

The Secret of My Success (1965: GB--MGM) — David Boulton

The Secret of the Forest (1955: GB) — Sydney Samuelson

The Secret of the Purple Reef (1960: TCF) — Kay Norton

The Secret of the Telegian (1961:Jap.) — Kazuo Yamada

Secret Places (1985: GB--TCF) — Peter McDonald

Secret Scrolls (Part I) (1968: Jap.) — Tadashi Iimura

Secret Scrolls (Part II) (1968: Jap.) — Tadashi Iimura

The Secret Seven (1966:It.?Sp.--MGM) — Eloy Mella

Secrets of a Woman's Temple (1969: Jap.) — Chishi Makiura

Seduced and Abandoned (1964:Fr./It.) — Aiace Parolin

The Seed of Man (1970: It.) — Mario Vulpiani

La Segura (1985: CR) — Mario Cardona

Seizure (1974: AIP) — Roger Racine

Sellers of Girls (1967: Fr.) — Jacques Mercanton

Ser (1989: USSR) — Youri Skirtladze

Serafino (1970: Fr./It.) — Aiace Parolin

Serenade for Two Spies (1966: Ger./It.) — Ernest Wild

Sergeant Berry (1938: Ger.) — Franz Koch

Sergeant Jim (1962: Yugo.) — Rudi Vavpotic

The Sergeant Was a Lady (1961: Univ.) — Hal McAlpin

The Serpents of the Pirate Moon (1973: US)	David Garcia
The Servant (1989: USSR)	Denis Evstigneev
Seven Alone (1975: US)	Robert Stumm
The Seven Dwarfs to the Rescue (1965: It.)	Aldo Giordani
Seven Guns for the MacGregors (1968: It./Sp.)	Alejandro Ulloa
The Seven Minutes (1971: TCF)	Fred Mandl
Seven Minutes (1990: Ger./US)	Lajos Koltai
Seven Minutes in Heaven (1986: WB)	Steven Fierberg
The Seven Revenges (1967: It.--AE)	Adalberto Albertini
The Seven Samurai (1956: Jap.--Col.)	Akasaku Nakai
Seven Slaves against the World (1965: It.)	Gugliemo Mancori
The Seven Tasks of Ali Baba (1963: It.)	Mario Paradetti
The Seventh Continent (1968: Czech./Yugo.)	Karol Krska
The Seventh Juror (1964: Fr.)	Maurice Fellous
The Seventh Sign (1988: Tri-S.)	Juan Ruiz Anchia
Sex, Lies and Videotape (1989: US)	Walt Lloyd
Sexton Blake and the Mademoiselle (1935: GB--Fox/MGM)	Alex Bryce
Shades of Silk (1979: Can.)	John Cressy
The Shadow (1936: GB--UA)	Sydney Blythe
Shadow Man (1953: GB--Lip.)	Philip Grindrod
Shadow of Evil (1967: Fr./It.)	Raymond Lemoigne
The Shadow on the Window (1957: Col.)	Kit Carson
Shadow Play (1986: US)	Ron Orieux
Shadowman (1974: Fr./It.)	Guido Bertoni
Shadows (1960: US)	Erich Kollmar
The Shadows Grow Longer (1962: Ger./Switz.)	Enrique Gartner
Shadows in the Storm (1988: US)	John Connor
Shadows of Forgotten Ancestors (1967: USSR)	V. Ilyenko
The Shakedown (1960: GB)	Brendan Stafford
Shakespeare Wallah (1966: India)	Subrata Mitra
Shakma (1990: US)	Andrew Bieber
Shallow Grave (1988: US)	Orson Ochoa
The Shameless Old Lady (1966: Fr.)	Denys Clerval
The Share Out (1966: GB)	Bert Mason
Shark (1970: Mex.--US)	Raul Martinez Solares
The Shark Woman (1941: US)	John C. Cook
Shark's Treasure (1975: UA)	Jack Atcheler
She and He (1967: Jap.)	Juichi Nagano
The She Beast (1966: GB/It./Yugo.)	Amerigo Gengarelli

She Dances Alone (1981: Aust.)	Karl Kofler
She Shall Have Music (1935: GB)	Sydney Blythe; William Luff
The She-Wolf (1963: USSR)	A. Maslennikov
Sheba Baby (1975: AIP)	William Asman
Sheepdog of the Hills (1941: GB)	Germain Burger
She'll Be Wearing Pink Pajamas (1986: GB)	Clive Tickner
Sherlock Holmes' Fatal Hour (1931: GB)	Sydney Blythe
She's Back (1989: US)	Arthur Marks
She's Been Away (1989: GB)	Philip Bonham-Carter
Shipwrecked (1990: Nor.)	Erling Thurmann-Andersen
Shirley Thompson Versus the Aliens (1968: Aus.)	David Sanderson
Shivers (1984: Pol.)	Jerzy Zielinski
A Shock to the System (1990: US)	Paul Goldsmith
Shock Treatment (1973: Fr.)	Jacques Robinson
Shock Waves (1977: US)	Reuben Trane
Shoe Shine (1947: It.)	Anchise Brizzi
The Shoemaker and the Elves (1967: Ger.)	Wolf Schwan
Shogun Assassin (1980: Jap.)	Chriski Makiura
Shoot (1976: Can.--AE)	Zale Magder
Shoot First, Laugh Last (1967: Ger./It.)	Marcello Masciocchi
Shoot It: Black, Shoot It: Blue (1974: US)	Bob Bailin
Shoot Loud, Louder ... I Don't Understand (1966: It.)	Aiace Parolin; Danilo Desideri
Shoot Out (1971: Univ.)	Earl Rath
Shoot the Moon (1982: US)	Michael Seresin
The Shooting (1971: US)	Gregory Sandor
The Shooting Party (1981: USSR)	Anatoly Petritsky
The Shooting Party (1985: GB)	Fred Tammes
The Shop on Main Street (1966: Czech.)	Vladimir Novotny
Short Circuit 2 (1988: Tri-S.)	John McPherson
The Short Cut (1989: Fr./It.)	Blasco Giurato
Short Eyes (1977: Par.)	Peter Sova
Short Time (1990: TCF)	John Connor
A Shot at Dawn (1934: Ger.--UFA)	Konstantin Tschet; Werner Bohne
The Show Goes On (1937: GB)	Jan Stallich
A Show of Force (1990: Par.)	James Glennon
Showdown for Zatoichi (1968: Jap.)	Chishi Makiura
Shuttlecock (1989: US)	Hiro Narita
Siberiade (1982: USSR)	Levan Paatashvili
Side Out (1990: Tri-S.)	Ron Garcia
Sidecar Racers (1975: Aus.--Univ.)	Paul Onorato
Sidewalks of London (1940: GB--Par.)	Jules Kruger
Sidewinder One (1977: AE)	Dennis Dalzell

Siege (1983: Can.) — Les Krizsan
Siege of Fort Bismark (1966: Jap.) — Fukuzo Koizumi
The Siege of Sidney Street (1960: GB) — Robert Baker; Monty Berman
Siege of Syracuse (1962: Fr./It.
  --Par.) — Carlo Carlini
Sign of Aquarius (1970: US) — Paul Rubenstein
Sign of the Gladiator
  (1959: Fr./Ger./It.--AIP) — Luciano Trasatti
Sign of the Virgin (1969: Czech.) — Jan Kalis
Signals--An Adventure in Space
  (1970: E. Ger./Pol.) — Otto Hainisch
Signs of Life (1989: US) — Elliot Davis
Sigurd the Dragon Slayer (1990:
  Nor.) — Kjell Vassdal
Silence (1974: US) — Hiro Morikawa
Silence Has No Wings (1971: Jap.) — Tatsuo Suzuki
The Silence of Dean Maitland (1934:
  Aus.) — Frank Hurley
The Silence of Dr. Evans (1973:
  USSR) — Yuri Sokol; Vladimir Bondarev
The Silent Call (1961: TCF) — Kay Norton
Silent Madness (1984: US) — Gerald Feil
Silent Night, Deadly Night Part II
  (1987: US) — Harvey Genkins
Silent Night, Deadly Night III:
  Better Watch Out (1989: US) — Joseph Civit
Silent Night, Lonely Night (1984:
  Tri-S.) — Henning Schellerup
The Silent Passenger (1935: GB) — Jan Stallich
The Silent Playground (1964: GB) — Martin Curtis
Silent Scream (1980: US) — Michael Murphy; David Short
Silent Scream(1990: GB) — Denis Crossan
The Silent Witness (1962: US) — Richard Cunha
The Silver Darlings (1947: GB) — Francis Carver
The Simchon Family (1969: Isr.) — Marco Ya'acobi
Simon the Dreamer (1990: Can.) — Michael Caron
Simple Justice (1990: US) — Rob Draper
The Simple-Minded Murderer (1985:
  Swed.) — Jorgen Persson; Rolf Lindstrom
Simply Terrific (1938: GB--WB) — Robert Lapresle
The Sin of Mona Kent (1961: US) — James Lillis
Sin on the Beach (1964: Fr.) — Marcel Combes
Sinai Commandos: The Story of the
  Six Day War (1968: Ger./Isr.) — Benno Bellenbaum
Sincerely Charlotte (1986: Fr.) — Bruno de Keyzer
Singapore, Singapore (1969: Fr./It.) — Jean Charvein
The Singing Buckaroo (1937: US) — Robert Doran
The Singing Princess (1967: It.) — Cesare Pelizzari
The Sins of Rose Bernd (1959: Ger.) — Klaus von Rautenfeld
Sir Henry at Rawlinson End (1980:
  GB) — Martin Bell

Sir, You Are a Widower (1971: Czech.)   Vaclav Hanus
The Sister-In-Law (1975: US)   Bruce Sparks
A Sister to Assister (1948: GB)   Reggie Pilgrim
The Sisters (1969: Greece)   Demetris Papakonstantis
Sisters (1973: AIP)   Gregory Sandor
Sisters, or The Balance of Happiness
   (1982: Ger.)   Franz Raht; Rhomas Schwan
Sisters under the Skin (1934: Col.)   Joseph Black
Sitting Ducks (1979: US)   Paul Glickman
Situation Hopeless-But Not Serious
   (1965: Par.)   Kurt Hasse
Six P. M. (1946: USSR)   Valentin Paulov
Six Pack Annie (1975: AIP)   Daniel Lacambre
6.5 Special (1958: GB)   Leo Rogers
Six Weeks (1982: Univ.)   Michael Margulies
Sixth and Main (1977: US)   Hilyard John Brown
Skateboard (1978: Univ.)   Ross Kelsay
Skeleton Coast (1989: US)   Hanro Mohr
Ski Battalion (1938: USSR)   V. Velichko
Ski Fever (1969: Aust./Czech.--AA)   Jan Stallich
Ski Troop Attack (1960: US)   Andy Costikyan
Skin Deep (1978: NZ)   Leon Narby
The Skin Game (1965: GB)   Stanley Long
Skinner Steps Out (1929: Univ.)   R. Allyn Jones
The Skip Tracer (1979: Can.)   Ron Oreiux
Skullduggery (1970: Univ.)   Robert Moreno
Skullduggery (1989: GB)   Barry McCann
The Sky Calls (1959: USSR)   Nikolai Kulchitsky
Sky Liner (1949: Lip.)   Carl Berger
The Skydivers (1963: US)   Austin McKinney; Lee
     Strosnider

Skyline (1984: Sp.)   Angel Luis Fernandez
Slamdance (1987: GB--US)   Amir Mokri
The Slams (1973: MGM)   Andrew Davis
Slaughter (1972: AIP)   Rosalio Solano
The Slave (1963: It.--MGM)   Enzo Barboni
A Slave of Love (1978: USSR)   Pavel Lebeshev
Slayground (1984: Univ.)   Stephen Smith
The Sleazy Uncle (1989: It.)   Romano Albani
Sleeping Beauty (1965: Ger.)   Gerhard Huttula
The Sleeping Beauty (1966: USSR)   Anatoliy Nazartov
The Sleeping Car (1990: US)   David Lewis
Sleeping Dogs (1977: NZ)   Michael Sarasin
The Slipper Episode (1938: Fr.)   F. Bourgas
Slipstream (1974: Can.)   Marc Champion
Slogan (1970: Fr.)   Jean-Louis Maligne; Claude
     Beausoleil

Slumber Party Massacre II (1987:
   Emb.)   Thomas Calloway
Slumber Party Massacre 3 (1990: US)   Jurgen Baum

Smash Palace (1982: NZ)	Graeme Cowley
Smile Orange (1976: Jam.)	David McDonald
Smith (1969: Dis.)	Robert Moreno
Smithereens (1982: US)	Chririne El Khadem
Smoky (1966: TCF)	Jack Swain
Smooth Talk (1985: US)	James Glennon
The Snake People (1968: Mex.--Col.)	Austin McKinney; Raul Dominguez
Snow Country (1969: Jap.)	Toichiro Narushima
The Snow Devils (1965: It.)	Riccardo Pallotini
Snow in the South Seas (1963: Jap.)	Tokuzo Kuroda
Snow Treasure (1968: AA)	Sverre Bergli
Snow White (1965: Ger.)	Wolf Schwan
Snow White and Rose Red (1966: Ger.)	Wolf Schwan
So Long, Blue Boy (1973: US)	James A. Larson
Soapbox Derby (1958: GB)	Douglas Ransom
Sofi (1967: US)	Alfred Taylor
Solar Crisis (1990: Jap.)	Russ Carpenter
Solaris (1972: USSR)	Vadim Jusov
Solarbabies (1986: MGM-UA)	Peter McDonald
The Soldier (1982: Emb.)	Robert Baldwin
Soldier, Sailor (1944: GB--UA)	A. E. Jeakins; Ray Elton
A Soldier's Prayer (1970: Jap.)	Yoshio Miyajima
The Soldier's Tale (1964: GB)	Dennis Miller
A Soldier's Tale (1988: NZ)	Alun Bollinger
Sole Survivor (1984: US)	Russell Carpenter
The Solitary Child (1958: GB)	Peter Hennessey
Solo (1970: Fr.)	Marcel Weiss
Solo (1978: NZ)	John Blick
Solo for Sparrow (1966: GB)	Bert Mason
Some Girls (1988: MGM-UA)	Ueli Steiger
Some Kind of Wonderful (1987: Par.)	Jan Kiesser
Some May Live (1967: GB--RKO)	Ray Parslow
Some of My Best Friends Are (1971: AIP)	Tony Mitchell
Something in the City (1950: GB)	Brendan Stafford
Somewhere in Berlin (1949: E. Ger.)	Werner Krien
Son of a Gunfighter (1966: Sp.--MGM)	Manuel Berenguer
The Son of Captain Blood (1964: It./Sp.--Par.)	Alejandro Ulloa
Son of Mongolia (1936: USSR)	M. Kaplan; V. Levitin; E. Shtirtskober
The Song from My Heart (1970: Jap.)	Hiroshi Takemura
The Song of Life (1931: Ger.)	Victor Tinkler; Heinrich Belasch
Song of Norway (1970: US)	Davis Boulton
Song of the Buckaroo (1939: Mon.)	Francis Corby
Song of the Forest (1963: USSR)	A. Prokopenko
Song of the Loon (1970: US)	Robert Maxwell

Song over Moscow (1964: USSR) — Anatoliy Nazarov
Sonny Boy (1990: US) — Roberto d'Ettore Piazzoli
Sons and Mothers (1967: USSR) — Mikhail Yakovich
Sons of Satan(1969: Fr./Ger./It.--WB) — Carlo Carlini
Sophie's Ways (1970: Fr.) — Jean-Marc Ripert
The Sorcerers (1967: GB--AA) — Stanley Long
Sorrell and Son (1934: GB--UA) — Cyril Bristow
Soul Man (1986: US) — Jeffrey Jur
Soultaker (1990: US) — James Rosenthal
The Sound of Life (1962: USSR) — V. Masevich
The Sound of Trumpets (1963: It.) — Lamberto Caimi
La Sourinate de Madame Beudet (1922: Fr.) — A. Morrin
South Bronx Heroes (1985: US) — Eric Schmitz
Souvenir (1988: GB) — Fred Tammes
Space Monster (1965: AIP) — Robert Tobey
The Space Ship (1935: USSR) — A. Galperin
Spaced Invaders (1990: BV) — James L. Carter
Special Edition (1938: GB--Par.) — Roy Fogwell
Speedtrap (1978: US) — Dennis Dalzell
The Spell (1989: Iran) — Ali-Reza Zarrindast
Sperduti Nel Buio (1914: It.) — L. Romagnoli
Spermula (1976: Fr.) — Jean-Jacques Flori
Sphinx (1981: Orion/WB) — Ernest Day
Spike of Bensonhurst (1988: US) — Steven Fierberg
The Spirit and the Flesh (1948: It.) — Anchise Brizzi
The Spirit of the Beehive (1976: Sp.) — Luis Cuadrado
Spirit of the Wind (1979: US) — John Logue
Spiritism (1965: Mex.) — Enrique Wallace
Splatter University (1984: US) — Fred Cohen; Jim Grib
Splitting Up (1981: Holl.) — Ralf Boumans
Spoils of the Night (1969: Jap.) — Hanjiro Nakazawa
The Sporting Club (1971: AE) — John Courtland
A Spot of Bother (1938: GB) — Francis Carver
The Spots on My Leopard (1974: S. Afr.) — Ivo Pelligrini
Spring Symphony (1986: E. Ger./Ger.--Col./WB) — Gerard Vandenberg
Spring Tide (1990: Den.) — Dirk Bruel
Springtime on the Volga (1961: USSR) — Vyacheslav Shumskiy
Spy in the Sky (1958: AA) — Jimmy Harvey
Spy in Your Eye (1966: It.--AIP) — Fausto Zuccoli
Square Dance (1987: US) — Jacek Laskus
Square of Violence (1963: Yugo.--MGM) — Aleksandar Sekulovic
Squares (1972: US) — John Koester
Squatter's Daughter (1933: Aus.) — Frank Hurley
The Squeaker (1930: GB) — Horace Wheddon
The Squeeze (1977: GB--WB) — Dennis Lewiston

The Squeeze (1987: Tri-S.)	Arthur Albert
Stacking (1987: US)	Richard Bowen
Stagecoach to Dancer's Park (1962: Univ.)	Edward Fitzgerald
Stages (1990: US)	William Brooks
Stakeout (1962: US)	Jack Specht
Stakeout On Dope Street (1958: WB)	Mark Jeffrey
Stalker (1982: USSR)	Aleksandr Knyazhinsky
Stallion Canyon (1949: US)	Jack McCluskey
Stand Off (1989: Hung.)	Elemer Ragalyi
The Star Chamber (1983: TCF)	Richard Hannah
Star of Hong Kong (1962: Jap.)	Rokuro Nishigaki
Stardumb (1990: US)	Bryan Duggan
Starlight over Texas (1938: Mon.)	Francis Corby
Stars and Bars (1988: Col.)	Jerzy Zielinski
The Station (1990: It.)	Alessio Gelsini
Stay As You Are (1979: It./Sp.)	Jose Luis Alcaine
Stealing Heaven (1988: GB--Yugo.)	Mikael Salomon
Steel (1980: US)	Roger Shearman
Steel & Lace (1990: US)	Thomas Calloway
The Steel Claw (1961: WB)	Manuel Rojas
Stefania (1968: Greece)	Nikos Kavoudikis
The Steppe (1963: Fr./It.)	Enzo Serafin
Steps to the Moon (1963: Rom.)	Stefan Horvath
Stereo (1969: Can.)	David Cronenberg
Still Smokin' (1983: Par.)	Harvey Harrison
Stir (1980: Aus.)	Geoffrey Burton
Stitches (1985: US)	Hector Figueroa
The Stolen Airliner (1962: GB)	Jo Jago
The Stolen Dirigible (1966: Czech.)	Josef Novotny; Bohuslav Pikhart
Stolen Identity (1953: US)	Helmut Ashley
Stolen Kisses (1969: Fr.)	Denys Clerval
Stone (1974: Aus.)	Graham Lind
The Stone Boy (1984: TCF)	Juan Ruiz Anchia
Stop That Cab (1951: Lip.)	Carl Berger
Stop Train 349 (1964: Fr./Ger./It.-- AA)	Roger Fellous
Stork (1971: Aus.)	Robin Copping
Storm Boy (1976: Aus.)	Geoff Burton
Storm Planet (1962: USSR)	Arkady Klimov
Stormy Summer (1989: Fr.)	Willy Kurant
The Story of a Cheat (1938: Fr.)	Marcel Lucien
A Story of Girls and Boys (1989: It.)	Pasquale Rachnini
The Story of the Count of Monte Cristo (1962: Fr./It.--WB)	Jacques Natteau; Jean Isnard
The Story of Vickie (1958: Aus.)	Bruno Mondi
Story Without Words (1981: It.)	Alfio Contini
Stowaway in the Sky (1962: Fr.)	Maurice Fellous; Guy Tabary
Stranded (1965: US)	Demos Sakeyyariose

The Strange Case of Dr. Manning (1958: GB--Rep.)	Jimmy Harvey
Strange Invaders (1983: EMI/Orion)	Louis Horvath
Strange Masquerade (1980: Hung.)	Elemer Ragalyi
Strange Shadows in an Empty Room (1977: Can./It.--AIP)	Anthony Ford
The Strange Vengeance of Rosalie (1972: TCF)	Ray Parslow
Strange World (1952: UA)	Edgar Eichhorn
The Stranger (1987: Arg.--Col.)	Horacio Maira
Stranger at My Door (1950: GB)	Brendan Stafford
A Stranger in Town (1968: It.--MGM)	Marcello Masciocchi
A Stranger Is Watching (1982: MGM-UA)	Barry Abrams
A Stranger Knocks (1963: Den.)	Ake Borglund; Johan Jacobse
The Stranger Returns (1968: Ger./It./Sp.--MGM)	Marcello Masciocchi
Stranger Than Paradise (1984: US)	Tom DiCillo
The Strangers (1955: It.)	Enzo Serafin
Strangers (1990: Aus.)	Steve Arnold
The Stranger's Hand (1955: GB)	Enzo Serafin
Strangers in the City (1962: Emb.)	Rick Carrier
Strangers in the House (1949: Fr.)	Jules Kruger
Stranger's Kiss (1984: Orion)	Mikhail Suslov
Strapless (1989: GB)	Andrew Dunn
Die Strasse (1923: Ger.)	C. Hasselmann
Stray Dog (1963: Jap.)	Asakazu Kakai
Street Hunter (1990: US)	Phil Parmet
Street Justice (1989: Lor.)	Roland "Ozzie" Smith
Street Music (1982: US)	Richard Bowen
Streets (1990: US)	Phedon Papamichael
Streets of Gold (1986: TCF)	Arthur Albert
Streetwalkin' (1985: US)	Steven Fierberg
Strength (1990: Holl.)	Theo Birkens
Strictly Confidential (1959: GB--Rank)	Jimmy Harvey
Strike! (1934: GB)	Leslie Rowson
Striker (1989: It.)	Sandro Mancori
Stripper (1986: TCF)	Edward Lachman
The Stronger Sex (1931: GB)	William Shenton
Stronger Than the Sun (1980: GB)	Elmer Cossey
Struck by Lightning (1990: Aus.)	Yuri Sokol
Student Bodies (1981: Par.)	Robert Ebinger
The Stuff (1985: US)	Paul Glickman
The Subversives (1967: It.)	Gianni Nazisi; Giuseppe Ruzzolini
Subway (1985: Fr.)	Carlo Varini
Subway Riders (1981: US)	Johanna Heer
Sudden Death (1985: US)	Benjamin Davis

Sudden Fury (1975: Can.)	James Kelly
Sudden Terror (1970: GB--EMI)	David Holmes; Ernest Robinson
Suddenly, a Woman! (1967: Den.)	Henning Bendtsen
Suffering Bastards (1990: US)	Neil Hodges
Sugar Cane Alley (1984: Fr.--Orion)	Dominique Chapuis
Suicide Mission (1956: GB--Col.)	Per Johnson; Mattia Mathiesen
The Suitor (1963: Fr.)	Pierre Levent
Sullivan's Empire (1967: Univ.)	Hal McAlpin
Summer (1986: Fr.--Orion)	Sophie Maintigneux
Summer Camp Nightmare (1987: US)	Don Burgess
Summer Lovers (1982: US)	Peter Lyons Collister; Dimitri Papacostandis; Tim Galfas
Summer of the Falcon (1989: Ger.)	Jurgen Jurges
Summer Paradise (1978: Swed.)	Tony Forsberg
Summer Run (1974: US)	Klaus Konig
Summer Soldiers (1972: Jap.)	Hiroshi Teshigahara
A Summer Story (1988: GB--US)	Kenneth MacMillan
A Summer To Remember (1961: USSR)	Anatoliy Nitochkin
Summerdog (1977: US)	Bill Godsey
Summerskin (1962: Arg.)	Oscar Melli
Summerspell (1983: US)	Robert Elswit
Summertime Killer (1973: AE)	Juan Gelpi
Sun Above, Death Below (1969: Jap.)	Kiyoshi Hasegawa
The Sun Also Shines at Night (1990: Fr./Ger./It.)	Giuseppe Lanci
The Sun Shines for All (1961: USSR)	Anatoliy Kuznetsov
Sunday in the Country (1975: Can.-- AIP)	Marc Champion
A Sunday in the Country (1984: Fr.--MGM-UA)	Bruno de Keyzer
Sunday Too Far Away (1974: Aus.)	Geoff Burton
Sundown: The Vampire in Retreat (1990: US)	Levie Isaacs
The Sun's Burial (1985: Jap.)	Takashi Kawamata
Sunscorched (1966: Ger./Sp.)	Francisco Marin
Sunshine Ahead (1936: GB--Univ.)	Jack Barker
El Super (1979: Sp.)	Orlando Jiminez-Leal
Super Spook (1975: US)	Jim Walker
Superargo (1968: It./Sp.)	Godofredo Pacheco
Superargo Versus Diabolicus (1966: It./Sp.--Col.)	Francisco Marin
Superbeast (1972: UA)	Nonong Rasca
Superfly (1972: WB)	James Signorelli
Superfly T.N.T. (1973: Par.)	Robert Gaffney
Superman and the Mole Men (1951: Lip.)	Clark Ramsey
Superman IV: The Quest for Peace (1987: Cannon/WB)	Ernest Day

Superstition (1985: US) — Lee Madden
Superzan and the Space Boy (1972: Mex.) — Antonio Ruiz
The Supreme Kid (1976: Can.) — Tony Westman
Sure Death (1985: Jap.) — Ko Ishihara
Sure Fire (1990: US) — Jon Jost
The Sure Thing (1985: Emb.) — Robert Elswit
Surf Party (1964: TCF) — Kay Norton
Surrender (1987: Cannon/WB) — Juan Ruiz Anchia
Surrender--Hell! (1959: AA) — Miguel Acion
Suspended Alibi (1957: GB) — Peter Hennessey
Swallows and Amazons (1977: GB--EMI) — Dennis Lewiston
Swamp Thing (1982: Emb.) — Robin Goodwin
The Swan Lake (1967: US) — Gunther Anders
Swan Lake--The Zone (1990: USSR) — Yuri Illienko
Swedenhielms (1935: Swed.) — Ake Dahlquist
The Swedish Mistress (1964: Swed.) — Lars Bjorne
Swedish Wedding Night (1965: Swed.) — Rune Ericson
Sweeney (1977: GB--EMI) — Dusty Miller
Sweeney 2 (1978: GB--EMI) — Dusty Miller
The Sweet Body of Deborah (1969: Fr./It.--WB) — Marcello Masciocchi
Sweet Country (1987: US) — Andreas Bellis
Sweet Ecstasy (1962: Fr.) — Marc Fossard
Sweet Hours (1982: Sp.) — Teo Escamilla
Sweet Hunters (1969: Panama) — Ricardo Aronovitch
Sweet Kitty Bellairs (1930: WB) — Watkins McDonald
Sweet Lies (1989: US) — Dominique Chapuis
Sweet Light in a Dark Room (1966: Czech.) — Vaclav Hanus
Sweet Love, Bitter (1967: US) — Victor Solow
Sweet Revenge (1987: US) — Shane Kelly
Sweet Revenge (1990: Fr/US) — Olivier Gueneau
Sweet Skin (1965: Fr./It.) — Raymond Lemoigne
Sweet Substitute (1964: Can.) — Richard Bellamy
Sweet William (1980: GB) — Les Young
Sweetie (1989: Aus.) — Sally Bongers
Swept Away--By an Unusual Destiny in Blue Sea of August (1975: It.) — Giulio Battiferri; Giuseppe Fornari; Stefano Ricciotti
The Swimmer (1968: Col.) — David Quaid
Swing It Sailor (1937: GN) — Richard Fryer
A Swingin' Summer (1965: US) — Ray Fernstrom
Switching Channels (1988: Tri-S.) — Francois Protat
The Sword of Doom (1967: Jap.) — Hiroshi Murai
The Sword of El Cid (1965: It./SP.) — Francisco Marin
Sword of Heaven (1985: US) — Gil Hubbs
Sword of the Conqueror (1962: It.) — Raffaele Masciocchi
Sylvester (1985: Col.) — Hiro Narita

Sylvia (1985: NZ) — Ian Paul
Symphony of Life (1949: USSR) — Valentine Pavlov
The Syndicate (1968: GB) — George Stevens
Syrup (1990: Den.) — Dirk Bruel

THX 1138 (1971: WB) — Dave Meyers; Albert Kihn
Take a Hard Ride (1975: It.--TCF) — Riccardo Pallotini
Take Down (1979: Dis.) — Reed Smoot
Take Her by Surprise (1967: Can.--Cannon) — Gerhard Alsen
Take It All (1966: Can.) — Michel Brault; Jean-Claude Lebrecque; Bernard Gosselin

Take This Job and Shove It (1981: AE) — James Davis
Taking Tiger Mountain (1983: Wales--US) — Kent Smith
A Tale of Springtime (1990: Fr.) — Luc Pages
Tales from the Dark Side; The Movie (1990: Par.) — Robert Draper
Tales from the Vienna Woods (1981: Aust./Ger.) — Klaus Konig
Tales of the Uncanny (1932: Ger.) — Heinrich Gaertner
Talk of the Devil (1937: GB--UA) — Francis Carver
The Tall Blonde Man with One Black Shoe (1973: Fr.) — Rene Mathelin
The Tall Guy (1989: US) — Adrian Biddle
Tanga-Tika (1953: US) — Dwight Long
Tangos: The Exile of Gardel (1986: Fr./Sp.) — Felix Monti
Tank (1984: Univ.) — Don Birnkrant
Tapeheads (1988: NBC) — Bojan Bazelli
The Taras Family (1946: USSR) — Boris Monastrisky
Target Harry (1980: US) — Patrice Pouget
The Tartars (1962: It./Yugo.--MGM) — Amerigo Gengarelli; Elios Vercelloni

Tarzan and the Jungle Boy (1968: Switz.--Par.) — Ozen Sermet
Tarzan's Jungle Rebellion (1970: NG) — Abraham Vialla
A Taste of Life (1989: Fr./It.) — Giuseppe Ruzzolini
A Taste of Sin (1983: US) — Ulli Lommel
Tatsu (1962: Jap.) — Kazuo Yamada
Taxi Blues (1990: Fr./USSR) — Denis Evstigneev
Taxi to Heaven (1944: USSR) — A. Halpern
Taxi to the John (1981: Pol.) — Horst Schier
Tea and Rice (1964: Jap.) — Yushun Atsuta
Tea in the Harem (1986: Fr.) — Dominique Chapuis
The Teacher and the Miracle (1961: It./Sp.) — Antonio Macasoli

Teenage Mutant Ninja Turtles (1990: US)	John Fenner
Teenagers from Outer Space (1959: WB)	Tom Graeff
Teenagers in Space (1975: USSR)	Andrei Kirillov
The Telephone (1988: US)	David Claesson
Tell Me in the Sunlight (1967: GB)	Rod Yould
The Temptation (1988: Aust.)	Frank Bruhne
The Tempter (1974: GB)	Mario Vulpiani
The Tempter (1978: It.--AE)	Aristide Massaccesi
The Temptress and the Monk (1963: Jap.)	Minoru Yokoyama
The Ten Commandments (1989: Pol.)	Wieslaw Zdort; Edward Klosinski; Piotr Sobocinski; Krzysztof Pakulski; Slawomir Idziak; Witold Adamek; Dariusz Kuc; Andrzej Jarosiewicz
Ten Little Indians (1975: Fr./Ger./It./Sp.--AE)	Fernando Arribas
Ten Little Indians (1989: Cannon)	Arthur Lavis
10 Violent Women (1982: US)	Yuval Shousterman
Tenchu! (1970: Jap.)	Fujio Mokita
Tender Hearts (1955: US)	Edward Fitzgerald
The Tender Warrior (1971: US)	Gerardo Wenziner
Tentacles (1977: It.--AIP/TCF)	Robert D'Ettore
Teorama (1969: It.)	Giuseppe Ruzzolini
Teresa the Thief (1979: It.)	Dario Di Palma
Terminal Bliss (1990: US)	Gregory Smith
Terminal Choice (1985: US)	Zane Magruder
Terminal Entry (1988: US)	James Carter
Terminal Island (1973: US)	Daniel Lacambre
Termini Station (1989: Can.)	Brian Hebb
The Terra-Cotta Warrior (1990: Hg.Kg.)	Peter Pau
The Terrace (1964: Arg.)	Ignacio Souto
Terror after Midnight (1965: Ger.)	Klaus Von Rautenfeld
Terror from the Year 5,000 (1958: AIP)	Arthur Florman
Terror in the Wax Museum (1973: US)	William Jurgensen
Terror Is a Man (1959: Phil.--US)	Emmanuel Rojas
The Terror of Dr. Mabuse (1965: Ger.)	Albert Benitz
Terror Ship (1954: GB)	Joe Ambor
Terror Squad (1988: US)	Peter Jensen
Terror Street (1953--Ham./Lip.)	Jimmy Harvey
Terror Vision (1986: US)	Romano Albani
Tesha (1929: GB)	Werner Brandes
A Test of Love (1985: Univ.)	Mick Van Bornemann
The Test of Pilot Pirx (1978: Pol./USSR)	Janusz Pavlovksi

The Testament of Orpheus (1962: Fr.)	Roland Pontoiseau
The Texas Chain Saw Massacre (1974: US)	Daniel Pearl
Texas Chain Saw Massacre 2 (1986: Cannon)	Richard Kooris
The Texican (1966: Sp.--Col.)	Francisco Marin
Thank You, Aunt (1969: It.--AE)	Aldo Scavarda
That Certain Something (1941: Aus.)	Frank Coffey
That House in the Outskirts (1980: Sp.)	Manuel Rojas
That Man George! (1967: Fr./It./Sp. --AA)	Henri Raichi
That Man in Istanbul (1966: Fr./It./Sp.--Col.)	Juan Gelpi
That Night (1957: RKO/Univ.)	Morris Hartzband
That Sinking Feeling (1979: GB)	Michael Coulter
That Tennessee Brat (1966: Lip./TCF)	Jack Steeley
That Was Then ... This Is Now (1985: Par.)	Juan Ruiz Anchia
That Woman (1968: Ger.)	Wolfgang Luhrse
That's the Way of the World (1975: UA)	Alan Metzger
There Was a Young Man (1937: GB--TCF)	Stanley Grant
There Was An Old Couple (1967: USSR)	Sergei Poluya
There Were Days and Moons (1990: Fr.)	Jean-Yves Le Mener
There Were Times, Dear (1985: US)	Brian Murphy
There's Always a Thursday (1957: GB--Rank)	Brendan Stafford
Therese and Isabelle (1968: Ger.-- US)	Hans Jura
Therese Raquin (1915: It.)	A. Carta; L. Romagnoli
Therese Raquin (1927: Ger.)	F. Fugslang; H. Scheib
These Thirty Years (1934: US)	Jules Sindic
They Are Not Angels (1948: Fr.)	Nicholas Hayer
They Call Me Robert (1967: USSR)	Edgar Shtyrskober
They Came from Within (1976: Can.-- AIP)	Robert Saad
They Came To Rob Las Vegas (1969: Fr./Ger./It./Sp.--WB)	Juan Gelpi
They Can't Hang Me (1955: GB)	Michael Brandt
They Live (1988: Univ.)	Gary Kibbe
They Never Slept (1990: GB)	Chris Seager
They Were Five (1938: Fr.)	Jules Kruger; Marc Fossard
They Were Giants (1989: Fr.--TCF)	Jean Francois Gondre
They Were So Young (1955: Lip.)	Ekkehard Kyrath
The Thief of Venice (1952: TCF)	Anchise Brizzi

The Thin Line (1967: Jap.)	Yasumichi Fukuzawa
The Thin Line (1981: Isr.)	Nurith Aviv
The Thin Red Line (1964: AA)	Manuel Berenguer
The Thing with Two Heads (1972: AIP)	Jack Steeley
Things Change (1988: Col.)	Juan Ruiz Anchia
Think Big (1990: US)	Mark Morris
The Third Clue (1934: GB--Fox)	Alex Bryce
The Third Solution (1990: It.)	Mario Cimini
Third Time Lucky (1931: GB)	William Shenton
The Third Walker (1978: Can.)	Robert Fiore
The Thirteen (1937: USSR)	Boris Volchek
13 Easy Street (1952: GB)	Monty Berman
The Thirty Foot Bride of Candy Rock (1959: Col.)	Frank Carson
This Is Spinal Tap (1984: Emb.)	Peter Smokler
This Madding Crowd (1964: Jap.)	Kozo Okazaki
This Man Can't Die (1970: It.)	Claudio Cirillo
This Man in Paris (1939: GB--Par.)	Henry Harris
This Man Is Mine (1946: GB--Col.)	Philip Grindrod
This Man Is News (1939: GB--Par.)	Henry Harris
This Savage Land (1969: Univ.)	Ray Flin
This Week of Grace (1933: GB--RKO)	Sydney Blythe
Those Glory, Glory Days (1986: GB)	Philip Meheux
Thousand Cranes (1969: Jap.)	Setsuo Kobayashi
The Thousand Eyes of Dr. Mabuse (1960: Fr./Ger./It.)	Karl Lob
Thousand Pieces of Gold (1990: US)	Bobby Bukowski
Three (1969: GB--UA)	Etienne Becker
Three Amigos (1986: Orion)	Ronald Browne
Three Card Monte (1978: Can.)	Henry Fiks
Three Days of Viktor Tschernikoff (1968: USSR)	M. Jakowitsch
Three for Jamie Dawn (1956: AA)	Duke Green
Three Hours (1944: Fr.)	Robert Lefebvre
300 Miles to Heaven (1989: Den./Pol.)	Krzysztof Ptak
Three in One (1956: Aus.)	Ross Wood
Three in the Attic (1968: AIP)	J. Burgi Contner
3 Men and a Cradle (1986: Fr.)	Jean-Yves Escoffier
Three Moves to Freedom (1960: Ger.--Rank)	Gunther Senftleben
Three Penny Opera (1963: Fr./Ger.)	Roger Fellous
The Three Sisters (1969: USSR)	Fyodor Dobronravov
Three Steps North (1951: UA)	Aldo Giordani
The Three Stooges Meet Hercules (1962: Col.)	Charles Wellborn
Three Tales of Chekhov (1961: USSR)	Nicolai Olonovski
Three to Go (1971: Aus.)	Kerry Brown
Three Years (1990: Fr.)	Pierre-Laurent Chenieux

Threshold (1983: Can.--TCF)	Michael Brault
Throne of Blood (1961: Jap.)	Asaichi Nakai
The Throne of Fire (1986: It.-- Cannon)	Gugliemo Mancori
Through Days and Months (1969: Jap.)	Hiroshi Takemura
Thumbelina (1970: US)	Bill Tobin
Thunder Alley (1985: Cannon)	Karen Grossman
Thunder at the Border (1966: Ger./Yugo.--Col.)	Karl Lob
Thunder in the Blood (1962: Fr.)	Lucien Joulin
Thunder in the Pines (1949: Lip.)	Carl Berger
A Thunder of Drums (1961: MGM)	William Spencer
Thunderbird 6 (1968: GB--UA)	Harry Oakes
Thunderstorm (1956: AA)	Manuel Berenguer
Ticket of Leave (1936: GB--Par.)	Francis Carver
Tie Me Up! Tie Me Down! (1990: Sp.)	Jose Luis Alcaine
Tiger Girl (1955: USSR)	A. Dudko
Tiger of the Seven Seas (1964: Fr./It.)	Alvaro Mancori
Tiger Town (1984: Dis.)	Robert Elswit
Tiger Warsaw (1988: US)	Robert Draper
Tight Skirts, Loose Pleasures (1966: Fr.)	Roger Fellous
Tiko and the Shark (1966: Fr./It. --MGM)	Pier Ludovico Pavoni
Till Tomorrow Comes (1962: Jap.)	Kozo Okazaki
Tilly of Bloomsbury (1940: GB--RKO)	Bernard Browne
Tim (1981: Aus.)	Paul Onorato
A Time for Loving (1971: GB)	Andreas Winding
Time Lock (1959: GB)	Peter Hennessey
A Time of Destiny (1988: Col.)	James Glennon
Time of Miracles (1990: Yugo.)	Radoslav Vladic
Time of Roses (1970: Fin.)	Antti Peippo
Time of the Gypsies (1989: Yugo.)	Vilko Filac
Time of the Wolves (1970: Fr.)	Daniel Diot
Time Slip (1981: Jap.)	Iwao Isayama
Time Stands Still (1982: Hung.)	Lajos Koltai
Time Trackers (1989: US)	Ronn Schmidt
The Tin Girl (1970: It.)	Gastone de Giovanni
Tin Man (1983: US)	Virgil Harper
Tin Men (1987: Dis./Touch.)	Peter Sova
The Tinder Box (1966: E. Ger.)	Erich Gusko
To Be a Crook (1967: Fr.)	Jean Collomb
To Begin Again (1982: Sp.--TCF)	Manuel Rojas
To Commit a Murder (1970: Fr./Ger./It.)	Raymond Lemoigne
To Forget Venice (1980: It.)	Romano Albani
To Sleep With Anger (1990: US)	Walt Lloyd

To the Shores of Hell (1966: US)	Leif Rise
Today It's Me ... Tomorrow You (1968: It.)	Sergio d'Offizi
Toffee or Mint (1990: Chile)	Gaston Roca
Toilers of the Sea (1936: GB--Col.)	D. P. Cooper
Tokyo File 212 (1951: RKO)	Herman Schopp
Tokyo Story (1972: Jap.)	Yuhara Atsuta
Tomboy (1985: US)	Daniel Yarussi
Tomorrow (1972: US)	Allan Green
Tomorrow Is My Turn (1962: Fr./Ger./It.)	Roger Fellous
Tomorrow Never Comes (1978: Can./GB--Rank)	Francois Protat
Tonight a Town Dies (1961: Pol.)	Boguslaw Lambach
Too Bad She's Bad (1954: It.)	Aldo Giordani
Too Outrageous (1987: Can.)	Fred Guthe
Top Gun (1986: Par.)	Jeffrey Kimball
Topsy-Turvy Journey (1970: Jap.)	T. Takaha
Torment (1947: Swed.)	Martin Bodin
Torment (1986: US)	Stephen Carpenter
The Touch of Flesh (1960: US)	Charles O'Rork
Tout Va Bien (1973: Fr.)	Armand Marco
Tower of London (1962: UA)	Arch Dalzell
The Town That Dreaded Sundown (1977: AIP)	Jim Roberson
Town without Pity (1961: Ger./Switz. --US)	Kurt Hasse
Toxi (1952: Ger.)	Igor Oberberg
The Toxic Avenger (1985: US)	James London; Lloyd Kaufman
The Toxic Avenger, Part III (1989: US)	James London
The Toy (1979: Fr.)	Etienne Becker
Traces of the Stones (1990: E. Ger.)	Gunter Marczinskowsky
Tracks (1977: US)	Paul Glickman
Trader Horn (1973: MGM)	Ronald Browne
Trading Hearts (1988: US)	Karen Grossman
The Train Goes East (1949: USSR)	L. Geleya; A. Kolsaty
The Train Goes to Kiev (1961: USSR)	A. Gerasimov
Train Robbery Confidential (1965: Braz.)	Amleto Daisse
Transport from Paradise (1967: Czech.)	Jan Curik
Transylvania Twist (1990: US)	Zoran Hochstatter
The Trapp Family (1961: Ger.)	Werner Krien
Trapper County War (1989: US)	Iri Dixon
Treachery on the High Seas (1939: GB)	Roy Fogwell
Treasure at the Mill (1957: GB)	Jimmy Ewins
The Treasure of Makuba (1967: Sp. --US)	Alfonso Nieva; Pablo Ripoll

Treasure of Silver Lake (1965:
    Fr./Ger./Yugo.--Col.)   Ernst Kalinke
Treasure of the Four Crowns
    (1983: Sp.--Cannon)   Marcello Masciocchi; Giuseppe
                                 Ruzzolini
Tree of Hands (1989: GB)   Kenneth MacMillan
The Tree of Wooden Clogs (1979: It.)   Ermanno Olmi
A Tremendously Rich Man (1932:
    Ger.--Univ.)   Reimar Kuntze
Tremors (1990: Univ.)   Alexander Gruszynski
The Trial (1948: Aust.)   Oskar Schuirch; Helmut
                                 Fisher-Ashely
Trick or Treat (1986: DeL.)   Robert Elswit
Trinity Is Still My Name
    (1971: It.--AE)   Aldo Giordani
The Trip (1967: AIP)   Arch Dalzell
Tripwire (1990: US)   Igor Sunara
Tristana (1970: It./Sp.)   Jose Aguayo
The Triumph of Sherlock Holmes
    (1935: GB)   William Luff
Triumph of the Spirit (1989: US)   Curtis Clark
Troika (1969: US)   William Heick
The Trojan Horse (1962: Fr./It.)   Rino Filippini
The Trojan Women (1971: US)   Alfio Contini
Tromba, the Tiger Man (1952:
    Ger.--Lip.)   Werner Krien
Tropics (1969: It.)   Giorgio Pelloni
Trouble-Fete (1964: Can.)   Jean Roy
Trouble in Mind (1985: US)   Toyomichi Kurita
True Stories (1986: WB)   Edward Lachman
Trunk to Cairo (1966: Ger./Isr.
    --AIP)   Itzhak Herbst
The Trunks of Mr. O. F. (1932:
    Ger.)   Reimar Kuntze; Heinrich
                                 Balasch
The Tsar's Bride (1966: USSR)   Kh. Kukels
Tulips (1981: Can.--AE)   Francois Protat
Tune in Tomorrow (1990: US)   Robert Stevens
Tunnel to the Sun (1968: Jap.)   Mitsuji Kanu
The Turners of Prospect Road
    (1947: GB)   Frederick Ford
Twelfth Night (1956: USSR)   E. Shapiro
The Twelve Chairs (1970: US)   Djorde Nikolic
The Twelve-Handed Men of Mars
    (1964: It./Sp.)   Alfio Contini
Twelve Plus One (1970: Fr./It.)   Giuseppe Ruzzolini
20th Century Oz (1977: Aus.)   Dan Burstall
The 25th Hour (1967: Fr./It./Yugo.
    --MGM)   Andreas Winding
24-Hour Lover (1970: Ger.--AIP) Hubs Hagen; Niklas Schilling

Twenty-One Days Together (1940: GB--Col.) — Jan Stallich
Twice a Man (1964: US) — Gregory Markopolous
Twilight Path (1965: Jap.) — Hiroyuki Nagaoka
Twin Sisters of Kyoto (1964: Jap.) — Toichiro Narushima
Twist and Shout (1986: Den.) — Jan Weincke
Twisted Justice (1990: US) — David Hue
Twister (1989: US) — Renato Berta
Two Are Guilty (1964: Fr.--MGM) — Roger Fellous
The Two Colonels (1963: It.) — Tino Santoni
Two Daughters (1963: India) — Soumendu Roy
Two Evil Eyes (1990: It.) — Peter Reniers
Two Eyes, Twelve Hands (1958: India) — G. Balkrishna
Two for the Money (1985: US) — David Insley
Two Grooms for a Bride (1957: TCF) — Monty Berman
Two Guns and a Badge (1954: AA) — Joseph Novac
Two Hundred Motels (1971: GB--UA) — Tony Palmer
Two in a Sleeping Bag (1964: Ger.) — Klaus Von Rautenfeld
Two in the Shadow (1968: Jap.) — Jo Aizawa
Two-Lane Blacktop (1971: Univ.) — Jackson Deerson
Two Moon Junction (1988: Lor.) — Mark Plummer
Two Super Cops (1978: It.--Col./WB) — Claudio Cirillo
2010 (1984: MGM-UA) — Peter Hyams
2,000 Weeks (1970: Aus.--Col.) — Robin Copping
2,000 Years Later (1969: WB) — Mario Di Leo

U-Boat 29 (1939: GB--Col.) — Bernard Browne
UHF (1989: Orion) — David Lewis
Ugetsu (1954: Jap.) — Kazuo Miyagawa
The Ugly Ones (1968: It./Sp.--UA) — Enzo Barboni; Jose Herrero
Uncle Vanya (1972: USSR) — Georgy Rerberg; Yevgeny Guslinsky

An Uncommon Thief (1967: USSR) — Anatoliy Mukasey
Under Age (1964: AIP) — Henry Kokojan
Under Proof (1936: GB--TCF) — Stanley Grant
Under Texas Skies (1931: US) — Otto Himm
Under the Banner of Samurai (1969: Jap.) — Kazuo Yamada
Under the Sheets, the Stars (1989: Can.) — Pierre Letarte
Under the Sun of Rome (1949: It.--UA) — Domenico Scala
The Underachievers (1988: US) — Chuck Colwell
Undercover Agent (1935: GB--Lip.) — A. T. Dinsdale
Underground U.S.A. (1980: US) — Tom DiCillo
Underneath the Arches (1937: GB) — Sydney Blythe
Undersea Girl (1957: AA) — Hal McAlpin; Edwin Gillette
The Unearthly (1957: Rep.) — Merle Connell

The Unforgettable Director of Love
    Movies (1990: Turk.)   Orhan Oguz
The Unholy (1988: US)   Henry Vargas
Unholy Desire (1964: Jap.)   Masahisa Himeda
Unholy Rollers (1972: AIP)   Mike Shea
Union City (1980: US)   Edward Lachman
University of Life (1941: USSR)   Pyotr Yermolov
An Unremarkable Life (1989: US)   Alan Hall
An Unsuitable Job for a Woman (1982:
    GB)   Martin Schafer
Untamed Women (1952: UA)   Glen Gano
Until September (1984: MGM-UA)   Philippe Weit
Unwilling Agent (1968: Ger.)   Gunther Senftleben
Up for the Cup (1950: GB)   Henry Harris
Up in the Cellar (1970: AIP)   Earl Rath
Up the Creek (1984: Orion)   James Glennon
Up the Down Staircase (1967: WB)   Joseph Coffey
Up the Front (1972: GB--EMI)   Tony Spratling
Up the Junction (1968: GB--Par.)   Arthur Lavis
Up the MacGregors (1967: It./Sp.--
    Col.)   Alejandro Ulloa
Up to a Certain Point (1985: Cuba)   Mario Garciajoya
Up to the Neck (1933: GB--UA)   Cyril Bristow
Uphill All the Way (1986: US)   Roland "Ozzie" Smith
Uprising in Damascus (1989: Ger.)   Oskar Schnirch; Paul
    Rischke

Vagabond (1986: Fr.)   Patrick Blossier
Valentina (1983: Sp.)   Juan Ruiz Anchia
Valley of the Redwoods (1960: TCF)   Kay Norton
Vamp (1986: US)   Elliot Davis
Vamping (1984: US)   Skip Roessel
The Vampire and the Ballerina
    (1962: It.--UA)   Angelo Baistrocchi
Vampire Circus (1972: GB--TCF)   Moray Grant
The Vampire Lovers (1970:
    GB--AIP/Ham.)   Moray Grant
Les Vampires (1915: Fr.)   G. Guerin
The Vampires (1969: Mex.--Col.)   Alfredo Uriba
Vanina (1922: Ger.)   F. Fugslang
Variety (1985: US)   Tom DiCillo
Vassa (1983: USSR)   Leonid Kalashnikov
Vengeance (1968: It./Ger.)   Riccardo Pallotini
Vengeance Is Mine (1980: Jap.)   Shinsaku Himeda
The Vengeance of Fu Manchu
    (1968: Ger./GB/Hg.Kg./Ire.--WB)   John Von Kotze
Venus in Furs (1970: Ger./GB/It.
    --AIP)   Angelo Lotti
Verginita (1953: It.)   Giuseppe La Torre

Vermilion Door (1969: Hg.Kg.)	Liu Chi
Very Happy Alexander (1969: Fr.)	Rene Mathelin
A Very Natural Thing (1974: US)	C. H. Douglass
The Vicar of Bray (1937: GB)	William Luff
La Vie Continue (1982: Fr.--Col.)	Yves Lafaye
La Vie de Chateau (1967: Fr.)	Pierre Lhomme
La Vie Telle Qu'elle East (1911: Fr.)	G. Guerin
Vienna Waltzes (1961: Aust.)	Gunther Anders
The Village (1953: GB/Switz.--UA)	Emil Berna
The Villiers Diamond (1938: GB--TCF)	Stanley Grant
Vincent and Me (1990: Can.)	Andreas Poulsson
Vincent and Theo (1990: Fr./GB)	Jean Lepine
Vintage Wine (1935: GB)	Sydney Blythe
La Viol (1968: Fr./Swed.)	Rune Ericson
Violated Love (1966: Arg.)	Anibal Gonzalez Paz
The Violators (1957: RKO/Univ.)	Morris Hartzband
The Violent and the Damned (1962: Braz.)	Mario Pages
The Violent Four (1968: It.)	Otello Spila; Giuseppe Ruzzolini
Violent Summer (1961: Fr./It.)	Tino Santoni
Violin and Roller (1962: USSR)	Vadim Yusov
Viper (1988: US)	Gerald Wolfe
The Virgin of Charity (1930: Cuba)	Ricardo Delgado
Virus (1980: Jap.)	Daisaku Kimura
The Viscount (1967: Fr./Ger./It./Sp--WB)	Henri Raichi
Visit to a Chief's Son (1974: UA)	Ernest Day; James Wells
The Visitor (1973: Can.)	Doug McKay
The Visitors (1972: UA)	Nick Proferes
Visitors from the Galaxy (1981: Yugo.)	Jiri Macak
Vixen (1970; Jap.)	Setsuo Kobayashi
Voice in the Wind (1944: UA)	Dick Fryer
Voice of the Hurricane (1964: US)	Richard Tegstrom
Voices (1979: MGM-UA)	Alan Metzger
Volcano (1953; It.--UA)	Arturo Gallea
Vor Sonnenuntergang (1961: Ger.)	Kurt Hasse
The Vow (1947: USSR)	A. Kesmatov
Voyage en Douce (1981: Fr.)	Claude Lecomte
Voyage of Silence (1968: Fr.)	Alain Derobe
Voyage to the End of the Universe (1963: Czech.)	Jan Kalis
The Vulture (1982: Isr.)	Ilan Rosenberg
Das Wachstigurekabinett (1924: Ger.)	H. Lerski
Wait Until the Spring, Bandini (1989: Belg./Fr./It./US	Jean-Francois Robin

Waiting (1990: Aus.)	Steve Mason
Waiting for Caroline (1969: Can.)	Dennis Gillson
Waiting for the Light (1990: US)	Gabriel Beristain
Waiting for the Moon (1987: US)	Andre Neau; Michael Sahl
Walk into Hell (1957: Aus.)	Carl Kayser
Walker (1987: Univ.)	David Bridges
Walking Tall, Part II (1975: AIP)	Keith Smith
Walking the Edge (1985: US)	Ernie Poulos
Walkover (1969: Pol.)	Antoni Nurzynski
Wall-Eyed Nippon (1963: Jap.)	Taiichi Kankura
The Wallet (1952: GB)	Brendan Stafford
The Walls of Hell (1964: Phil.--US)	Felipe Sacdalan
The Walls of Malapaga (1950: Fr./It.)	Louis Page
Walpurgis Night (1941: Swed.)	Martin Bodin
Waltz across Texas (1982: US)	Ernest Day
Wanda (1971: US)	Nicholas Proferes
The Wanderer (1969: Fr.)	Quinto Albicocco
Wanderers of the West (1941: Mon.)	Jack Young
The Wandering Jew (1935: GB)	Sydney Blythe
The Wandering Jew (1948: It.)	Vaclav Vich
Wanted: Dead or Alive (1987: US)	Alex Nepomniaschy
War and Peace (1968: USSR)	Anatoliy Petriaskiy
War Italian Style (1967: AIP)	Fausto Zuccoli
War of the Buttons (1963: Fr.)	Andre Bac
War of the Monsters (1972: Jap.)	Koyoshi Hasegawa
The War of the Worlds--Next Century (1981: Pol.)	Zygmunt Samosiak
War Party (1988: Tri-S.)	Brian Tufano
War Requiem (1988: GB)	Richard Greatrex
Warkill (1968: Phil.--Univ.)	Remegio Uoung
Warlords (1989: US)	Laslo Regos
Warn London (1934: GB)	Alex Bryce
The Warrior and the Sorceress (1984: US)	Leonard Solis
The Warrior Empress (1961: It.--Col.)	Carlo Carlini
Warrior of the Lost World (1985: US)	Giancarlo Ferrando
Warriors Five (1962: Fr./It.--AIP)	Claudio Racca
Wartime Romance (1985: USSR)	Valery Blinov
Watched (1974: US)	Hart Perry; Ed Lynch; Kevin Keating; Jack Wright
Watchers II (1990: US)	Edward Pei
Wavelength (1983: US)	Paul Goldsmith
The Way Out (1956: GB--RKO)	Philip Grindrod
The Way We Live (1946: GB)	Laurie Friedman
The Way We Live Now (1970: UA)	Barry Brown
Ways in the Night (1983: Ger.)	Witold Sobocinski
The Wayside Pebble (1962: Jap.)	Shojiro Sugimoto
We Have Only One Life (1963: Greece)	Dinos Katsouridis
We of the Never Never (1983: Aus.)	Gary Hansen
We Shall Return (1963: US)	Ted Saizis; Vincent Saizis

We The Living (1942: It.)   Giuseppe Caracciolo
We Think the World of You (1988:
    GB)   Mike Garfath
We Will Remember (1966: Jap.)   Asaichi Nakai
The Weakness Syndrome (1990: USSR)   Vladimir Pankov
Web of Fear (1966: Fr./Sp.)   Manuel Berenguer
Web of the Spider (1972:
    Fr./Ger./It.)   Sandro Mancori
Web of Violence (1966: It./Sp.)   Emilio Foriscot
Wedding Night (1970: Ire.--AIP)   Ray Sturgess
Wedding Rehearsal (1932: GB)   Leslie Rowson
Weddings and Babies (1960: TCF)   Morris Engel
Weeds (1987: DeL.)   Jan Weincke
Weekend (1964: Den.)   Georg Oddner
Weekend at Bernie's (1989: TCF)   Francois Protat
The Weekend Murders (1972: It.--
    MGM)   Gugliemo Mancori
Weekend of Shadows (1978: Aus.)   Richard Wallace
Weekend Pass (1984: US)   Bryan England
Weekend with Kate (1990: Aus.)   Dan Burstall
Welcome Home, Roxy Carmichael
    (1990: Par.)   Paul Elliott
Welcome Kostya! (1965: USSR)   Anatoliy Kuznetsov
Welcome to Germany (1988: Ger.)   Axel Block
Wendy Cracked a Walnut (1990: Aust.)   Jeffrey Maloof
Werewolf in a Girl's Dormitory
    (1961: Aust./It.--MGM)   George Patrick
West Indies (1985: Fr.)   Francois Cartonne
Western Caravans (1939: Col.)   George Cooper
Wetherby (1985: GB--MGM-UA)   Stuart Harris
The Whales of August (1987: US)   Mike Fash
What! (1965: Fr./GB/It.)   Ubaldo Terzano
What a Carve Up! (1962: GB)   Monty Berman
What Have I Done to Deserve This?
    (1985: Sp.)   Angel Luis Fernandez
What Women Dream (1933: Ger.)   Willy Goldberger
What Would You Say to Some Spinach
    (1976: Czech.)   Frantisek Uldrich
What You Take for Granted (1984:
    US)   Francis Reid
What's Next? (1975: GB)   Ray Orton
What's So Bad About Feeling Good?
    (1968: Univ.)   Ernesto Caparros
What's Up, Hideous Sun Demon
    (1989: US)   John Lambert; Steve Dubin
What's Up, Tiger Lily? (1966: AIP)   Kazuo Yamada
The Wheel (1985: Korea)   Lee Sung-choon
When a Woman Ascends the Stairs
    (1963: Jap.)   Masao Tami
When Hell Broke Loose (1958: Par.)   Hal McAlpin

When Nature Calls (1984: US)	Mike Spera
When Our Father Was Away on Business (1985: Yugo.--Cannon)	Vilko Filac
When the Raven Flies (1985: Ice.)	Tony Forsberg
When the Trees Were Tall (1965: USSR)	Valeriy Ginzburg
Where the Buffalo Roam (1938: Mon.)	Francis Corby
Where the Bullets Fly (1966: GB--Emb.)	David Holmes
Where the Green Ants Dream (1985: Aus.)	Jorg Schmidt-Reitwein
Where the River Runs Black (1986: MGM)	Juan Ruiz Anchia
Where's Picone? (1985: It.)	Claudio Cirillo
Whirlpool of Woman (1966: Jap.)	Yoshihiro Yamazaki
Whirlwind (1968: Jap.)	Kazuo Yamada
A Whisper to a Scream (1989: Can.)	Paul Witte
Whispering Joe (1969: Jap.)	Koichi Saito
The Whistle Blower (1987: GB)	Fred Tammes
The White Devil (1948: It.)	Rodolfo Lombardi
White Fire (1953: GB--Lip.)	Monty Berman
The White Horse Inn (1959: Ger.)	Gunther Anders
White Lies (1989: Mex.)	Carlos Fuentes
White Lightning (1973: UA)	Edward Rosson
White Lilac (1935: GB--Fox)	Alex Bryce
White Palace (1990: Univ.)	Lajos Koltai
The White Rose (1983: Ger.)	Axel DeRoche
White Rose of Hong Kong (1965: Jap.)	Shinsaku Uno
The White Sheik (1956: It.)	Arturo Gallea
White Sister (1973: Fr./It./Sp.--Col./WB)	Alfio Contini
White Slave Ship (1962: Fr./It.--AIP)	Aldo Giordani
Who? (1975: Ger./GB)	Petrus Schloemp
Who Fears the Devil (1972: US)	Flemming Olsen
Who Killed Jessie? (1975: Czech.)	Jan Nemecek
Who Killed Mary What'ser Name? (1971: Cannon)	Gregory Sandor
Who Shot Patarango? (1990: US)	Robert Brooks
The Whole Shootin' Match (1979: US)	Eagle Pennell
Who's That Knocking at My Door? (1968: US)	Michael Wadleigh; Richard Coll; Max Fisher
Why Me? (1990: US)	Peter Deming
Why Rock the Boat? (1974: Can.--Col.)	Savos Kalogeras
Why Shoot the Teacher? (1977: Can.)	Marc Champion
The Wicked Die Slow (1968: Cannon)	Amin Chaudhri
Wicked Stepmother (1989: MGM-UA)	Bryan England
Wicked Woman (1953: UA)	Edward Fitzgerald

Widow's Nest (1977: Sp.--US)	John Cabrera
The Wild Duck (1983: Aus.)	Peter James
The Wild Eye (1968: It.--AIP)	Raffaele Masciocchi; Marcello Masciocchi
The Wild Life (1984: Univ.)	James Glennon
Wild Orchid (1990: It./US)	Gale Tattersall
The Wild Pack (1972: AIP)	Ricardo Aronovich
Wild Season (1968: S. Afr.--Univ.)	Vincent Cox
The Wild, Wild Planet (1967: It.--MGM)	Riccardo Pallotini
William Comes To Town (1948: GB--UA)	Bert Mason
Willow (1988: MGM-UA)	Adrian Biddle
Willy (1963: Ger.--US)	Ludwig Berger
Windfall (1955: GB)	Monty Berman
Windwalker (1980: US)	Reed Smoot
Wings of Chance (1961: Can.--Univ.)	Leonard Claremont
Wings of Victory (1941: USSR)	A. Ginsburg
Wink of an Eye (1958: UA)	Winston Jones
Winter of Our Dreams (1982: Aus.)	Tom Cowan
Winter People (1989: Col.)	Francois Protat
The Winter War (1989: Fin.)	Kari Sohlberg
Winter Wind (1970: Fr./Hung.)	Janos Kende
Wire Service (1942: Mon.)	Hilton Hall
Wise Guys (1937: GB--TCF)	Stanley Grant
Wiser Age (1962: Jap.)	Atsushi Yasumoto
Wishing Machine (1971: Czech.)	Jiri Kolin
A Witch without a Broom (1967: Sp.--US)	Alfonso Nieva
Witchcraft (1964: GB--Lip./TCF)	Arthur Lavis
Witchery (1989: It.)	Lorenzo Battaglia
The Witches (1990: WB)	Harvey Harrison
With Love and Tenderness (1978: Bulg.)	Dimko Minov
Without You (1934: GB--Fox)	Alex Bryce
The Witness (1959: GB)	John Wiles
The Witness (1982: Hung.)	Janos Zsombalyi
Witness in the Dark (1959: GB--Rank)	Brendan Stafford
Witness Out of Hell (1967: Ger./Yugo.)	Milored Markovic
The Wizard of Loneliness (1988: US)	Richard Bowen
The Wizard of Speed and Time (1988: US)	Russell Carpenter
WIzards of the Lost Kingdom (1985: Arg.--US)	Leonard Solis
Wizards of the Lost Kingdom II (1990: US)	Geza Sinkovics
Wolf Dog (1958: Can.--TCF)	Frederick Ford
The Wolfpen Principle (1974: Can.)	Hans Klardie

Woman, Demon, Human (1990: China)	Xia Lixing; J. Hongsheng
Woman Hater (1949: GB--Univ.)	Andre Thomas
A Woman in Flames (1984: Ger.)	Jurgen Jurges
Woman in the Dunes (1964: Jap.)	Hiroshi Segawa
The Woman Inside (1981: TCF)	Ron Johnson
Woman of Darkness (1968: Swed.)	Lars Bjorne
Woman of Sin (1961: Fr.)	Maurice Barry
The Woman on the Roof (1989: Swed.)	Ulf Brantas; Jorgen Persson
A Woman under the Influence (1974: US)	Mitch Breif
The Woman Who Wouldn't Die (1965: GB--WB)	Arthur Lavis
The Woman with Red Boots (1977: Fr./Sp.)	L. Vilasenor
Womanlight (1979: Fr./Ger./It.)	Ricardo Aronovich
A Woman's Devotion (1956: Rep.)	Jorge Stahl, Jr.
A Woman's Face (1939: Swed.)	Ake Dahlquist
A Woman's Life (1964: Jap.)	Asaichi Nakai
Women and War (1965: Fr.)	Maurice Fellous
Women in Prison (1957: Jap.)	Joji Ohara
Women of the Prehistoric Planet (1966: US)	Arch Dalzell
World Gone Wild (1988: Lor.)	Don Burgess
The World in My Pocket (1962: Fr./Ger./It.--MGM)	Vaclav Vich
The World of Apu (1960: India)	Subrata Mitra
The World without a Mask (1934: Ger.)	Ewald Daub
Woyzeck (1979: Ger.)	Jorg Schmidt-Reitwein
The Wrong Guys (1988: US)	Frank Byers
Wrong Number (1959: GB)	Josef Ambor
Xica (1982: Braz.)	Jose Medeiros
Xtro 11 (1990: Can.)	Nathaniel Massey
A Yank in Viet-Nam (1964: AA)	Emmanuel Rojas
The Year of the Horse (1966: US)	Morton Heilig
A Year of the Quiet Sun (1985: Ger./Pol.)	Slawomir Idziak
Yearning (1964: Jap.)	Jun Yasumoto
Yellow Dust (1936: RKO)	Earl Wolcott
Yellow Hair and the Fortress of Gold (1984: US)	John Cabrera
The Yellow Slippers (1965: Pol.)	Kazimierz Konrad
Yellowneck (1955: Rep.)	Charles O'Rork
Yog-Monster from Space (1970: Jap. --AIP)	Taiichi Kankura
Yojimbo (1961: Jap.)	Kazuo Miyagawa

Yol (1982: Turkey)   Erdogan Engin
Yolanta (1964: USSR)   Vadim Mass
You Are the World for Me (1964:
    Aust.)   Sepp Ketterer
You Better Watch Out (1980: US)   Ricardo Aronovich
You Can't Hurry Love (1988: US)   Peter Lyons Collister; John
                                                           Schwartzman
You Only Live Once (1969: Fr.)   Roger Duculot
Young and Evil (1962: Mex.)   Raul Martinez Solares
The Young and the Brave (1963: MGM)   Emmett Bergholz
Young Aphrodites (1966: Greece)   Giovanni Variano
Young Dynamite (1937: US)   John Kline
Young Einstein (1988: Aus.)   Jeff Darling
The Young Girls of Wilko (1979:
    Fr./Pol.)   Edward Klosinski
The Young Go Wild (1962: Ger.)   Kurt Hasse
Young Guy Graduates (1969: Jap.)   Yuzuri Aizawa
Young Guy on Mt. Cook (1969: Jap.)   Shinsaku Uno
Young Jesse James (1960: TCF)   Carl Berger
The Young Lord (1970: Ger.)   Ernst Wild
The Young Monk (1978: Ger.)   Joerg Jeshel
The Young Nurses (1973: US)   Sam Clement
The Young, the Evil and the Savage
    (1968: It.--AIP)   Fausto Zuccoli
Young Torless (1968: Fr./Ger.)   Franz Rath
Young Toscanini (1988: Fr./It.)   Daniele Nannuzzi
Young Woodley (1930: GB)   A. F. Birch
Your Number's Up (1931: US)   Henry Kohler
The Youth and His Amulet (1963:
    Jap.)   Kuzuo Yamada
Youth in Fury (1961: Jap.)   Masao Kosugi

Zabriskie Point (1970: MGM)   Alfio Contini
Zachariah (1971: US)   Jorge Stahl, Jr.
Zappa (1984: Den.)   Jan Weincke
Zapped! (1982: Emb.)   Daniel Pearl
Zatoichi (1968: Jap.)   Shozo Honda
Zatoichi Challenged (1970: Jap.)   Chishi Makiura
Zatoichi Meets Yojimbo (1970: Jap.)   Kazuo Miyagawa
Zatoichi's Conspiracy (1974: Jap.)   Shozo Honda
Zazie (1961: Fr.)   Henri Raichi
Zelly and Me (1988: Col.)   Mikael Salomon
Zig-Zag (1975: Fr./It.)   Jean-Pierre Baux
Zombie Brigade (1988: Aus.)   Alex McPhee
Zombie Island Massacre (1985: US)   Robert Baldwin
The Zoo Gang (1985: US)   Robert New
Zvenigora (1928: USSR)   B. Zavelev

ACADEMY AWARDS

1927-1928

George Barnes: Devil Dancer; Magic Flame; Sadie Thompson
Charles Rosher: My Best Girl; The Tempest
Karl Struss: Drums of Love
CHARLES ROSHER AND KARL STRUSS: SUNRISE

1928-1929

George Barnes: Our Dancing Daughters
CLYDE DeVINNA: WHITE SHADOWS IN THE SOUTH SEAS
Arthur Edeson: In Old Arizona
Ernest Palmer: Four Devils; Street Angel
John Seitz: The Divine Lady

1929-1930

William Daniels: Anna Christie
Arthur Edeson: All Quiet on the Western Front
Tony Gaudio and Harry Perry: Hell's Angels
Victor Milner: The Love Parade
JOSEPH T. RUCKER AND WILLARD VAN DER VEER: WITH BYRD
    AT THE SOUTH POLE

1930-1931

Edward Cronjager: Cimarron
FLOYD CROSBY: TABU
Lee Garmes: Morocco
Charles Lang: The Right to Love
Barney McGill: Svengali

1931-1932

LEE GARMES: SHANGHAI EXPRESS
Ray June: Arrowsmith
Karl Struss: Dr. Jekyll and Mr. Hyde

1932-1933

George Folsey: Reunion in Vienna
CHARLES LANG: A FAREWELL TO ARMS
Karl Struss: Sign of the Cross

1934

George Folsey: Operator 13
VICTOR MILNER: CLEOPATRA
Charles Rosher: Affairs of Cellini

1935

Ray June: Barbary Coast
Victor Milner: The Crusades
HAL MOHR: A MIDSUMMER NIGHT'S DREAM
Gregg Toland: Les Miserables

1936

George Folsey: The Gorgeous Hussy
TONY GAUDIO: ANTHONY ADVERSE
Victor Milner: The General Died at Dawn

1937

KARL FREUND: THE GOOD EARTH
Gregg Toland: Dead End
Joseph Valentine: Wings over Honolulu

1938

Norbert Brodine: Merrily We Live
Robert De Grasse: Vivacious Lady
Ernest Haller: Jezebel
James Wong Howe: Algiers
J. Peverel Marley: Suez
Ernest Miller and Harry Wild: Army Girl

Victor Milner: The Buccaneer
JOSEPH RUTTENBERG: THE GREAT WALTZ
Leon Shamroy: The Young in Heart
Joseph Valentine: Mad about Music
Joseph Walker: You Can't Take It With You

1939

(B&W):

Joseph August: Gunga Din
Norbert Brodine: Lady of the Tropics
Tony Gaudio: Juarez
Bert Glennon: Stagecoach
Arthur Miller: The Rains Came
Victor Milner: The Great Victor Herbert
Gregg Toland: Intermezzo: A Love Story
GREGG TOLAND: WUTHERING HEIGHTS
Joseph Valentine: First Love
Joseph Walker: Only Angels Have Wings

(Color):

Bert Glennon and Ray Rennahan: Drums along the Mohawk
ERNEST HALLER AND RAY RENNAHAN: GONE WITH THE WIND
Georges Perinal and Osmond Borrodaile: Four Feathers
Sol Polito and W. Howard Greene: The Private Lives of Elizabeth
    and Essex
Hal Rosson: The Wizard of Oz
William Skall: The Mikado

1940

(B&W):

GEORGE BARNES: REBECCA
Tony Gaudio: The Letter
Ernest Haller: All This and Heaven Too
James Wong Howe: Abe Lincoln in Illinois
Charles Lang: Arise, My Love
Rudolph Mate: Foreign Correspondent
Harold Rosson: Boom Town
Joseph Ruttenberg: Waterloo Bridge
Gregg Toland: The Long Voyage Home
Joseph Valentine: Spring Parade

(Color):

Oliver Marsh and Allen Davey: Bittersweet
Arthur Miller and Ray Rennahan: The Blue Bird
Victor Milner and W. Howard Greene: North West Mounted Police
GEORGES PERINAL: THE THIEF OF BAGDAD

Leon Shamroy and Ray Rennahan: Down Argentine Way
Sidney Wagner and William Skall: Northwest Passage

1941

(B&W):

Edward Cronjager: Sun Valley Serenade
Karl Freund: The Chocolate Soldier
Charles Lang: Sundown
Rudolph Mate: That Hamilton Woman
ARTHUR MILLER: HOW GREEN WAS MY VALLEY
Sol Polito: Sergeant York
Joseph Ruttenberg: Dr. Jekyll and Mr. Hyde
Gregg Toland: Citizen Kane
Leo Tover: Hold Back the Dawn
Joseph Walker: Here Comes Mr. Jordan

(C):

Karl Freund and W. Howard Greene: Blossoms in the Dust
Bert Glennon: Dive Bomber
Harry Hallenberger and Ray Rennahan: Louisiana Purchase
ERNEST PALMER AND RAY RENNAHAN: BLOOD AND SAND
William Skall and Leonard Smith: Billy the Kid
Karl Struss, Wilfrid Cline and William Snyder: Aloma of the South
    Seas

1942

(B&W):

Charles Clarke: Moontide
Stanley Cortez: The Magnificent Ambersons
Edward Cronjager: The Pied Piper
James Wong Howe: Kings Row
Rudolph Mate: the Pride of the Yankees
John Mescall: Take a Letter, Darling
Arthur Miller: This above All
JOSEPH RUTTENBERG: MRS. MINIVER
Leon Shamroy: Ten Gentlemen from West Point
Ted Tetzlaff: The Talk of the Town

(C):

Edward Cronjager and William Skall: To the Shores of Tripoli
W. Howard Greene: The Jungle Book
Milton Krasner: William Skall and W. Howard Greene, Arabian
    Nights
Victor Milner and William Skall, Reap the Wild Wind
Sol Polito, Captains of the Clouds
LEON SHAMROY, THE BLACK SWAN

1943

(B&W)

Arthur Edeson, Casablanca
Tony Gaudio, Corvette K-225
James Wong Howe, Elmer Dyer and Charles Marshall, Air Force
James Wong Howe, The North Star
Charles Lang, So Proudly We Hail
Rudolph Mate, Sahara
ARTHUR MILLER, THE SONG OF BERNADETTE
Joseph Ruttenberg, Madame Curie
John Seitz, Five Graves to Cairo
Harry Stradling, The Human Comedy

(C)

Charles Clarke and Allen Davey, Hello, Frisco, Hello
Edward Cronjager, Heaven Can Wait
George Folsey, Thousands Cheer
HAL MOHR AND W. HOWARD GREENE, THE PHANTOM OF THE
    OPERA
Ray Rennahan, For Whom the Bell Tolls
Leonard Smith, Lassie Come Home

1944

(B&W)

Stanley Cortez and Lee Garmes, Since You Went Away
George Folsey, The White Cliffs of Dover
Charles Lang, The Uninvited
JOSEPH LA SHELLE, LAURA
Lionel Lindon, Going My Way
Glen MacWilliams, Lifeboat
Joseph Ruttenberg, Gaslight
John Seitz, Double Indemnity
Robert Surtees and Hal Rosson, Thirty Seconds over Tokyo
Sidney Wagner, Dragon Seed

(C)

Edward Cronjager, Home in Indiana
George Folsey, Meet Me in St. Louis
Rudolph Mate and Allen Davey, Cover Girl
Ray Rennahan, Lady in the Dark
Charles Rosher, Kismet
LEON SHAMROY, WILSON

<u>1945</u>

(B&W)

Ernest Haller, Mildred Pierce
Arthur Miller, The Keys to the Kingdom
John Seitz, The Lost Weekend
HARRY STRADLING, THE PICTURE OF DORIAN GRAY

(C)

George Barnes, The Spanish Main
Tony Gaudio and Allen Davey, A Song To Remember
Robert Planck and Charles Boyle, Anchors Aweigh
LEON SHAMROY, LEAVE HER TO HEAVEN
Leonard Smith, National Velvet

<u>1946</u>

(B&W)

George Folsey, The Green Years
ARTHUR MILLER, ANNA AND THE KING OF SIAM

(C)

CHARLES ROSHER, LEONARD SMITH AND ART ARLING, THE
    YEARLING
Joseph Walker, The Jolson Story

<u>1947</u>

(B&W)

George Folsey, Green Dolphin Street
GUY GREEN, GREAT EXPECTATIONS
Charles Lang, The Ghost and Mrs. Muir

(C)

JACK CARDIFF, BLACK NARCISSUS
Harry Jackson, Mother Wore Tights
J. Peverel Marley and William Skall, Life with Father

<u>1948</u>

(B&W)

Joseph August, Portrait of Jennie
WILLIAM DANIELS, THE NAKED CITY
Charles Lang, A Foreign Affair
Ted McCord, Johnny Belinda
Nicholas Musuraca, I Remember Mama

(C)

Charles Clarke, Green Grass of Wyoming
Robert Planck, The Three Musketeers
William Snyder, The Loves of Carmen
JOSEPH VALENTINE, WILLIAM SKALL AND WINTON HOCH, JOAN
   OF ARC

1949

(B&W)

Joseph LaShelle, Come to the Stable
Franz Planer, Champion
Leon Shamroy, Prince of Foxes
Leo Tover, The Heiress
PAUL VOGEL, BATTLEGROUND

(C)

Charles Clarke, Sand
WINTON HOCH, SHE WORE A YELLOW RIBBON
Robert Planck and Charles Schoenbaum, Little Women
William Snyder, Jolson Sings Again
Harry Stradling, The Barkeleys of Broadway

1950

(B&W)

ROBERT KRASKER, THE THIRD MAN
Milton Krasner, All About Eve
Victor Milner, The Furies
Hal Rosson, The Asphalt Jungle
John Seitz, Sunset Boulevard

(C)

George Barnes, Samson and Delilah
Ernest Haller, The Flame and the Arrow
Ernest Palmer, Broken Arrow
Charles Rosher, Annie Get Your Gun
ROBERT SURTEES, KING SOLOMON'S MINES

1951

(B&W)

Norbert Brodine, The Frogmen
Robert Burks, Strangers on a Train
WILLIAM MELLOR, A PLACE IN THE SUN
Franz Planer, Death of a Salesman
Harry Stradling, A Streetcar Named Desire

(C)

JOHN ALTON AND AL GILKS, AN AMERICAN IN PARIS
Charles Rosher, Show Boat
John Seitz and W. Howard Greene, When Worlds Collide
Leon Shamroy, David and Bathsheba
Robert Surtees and William Skall, Quo Vadis

1952

(B&W)

Russell Harlan, The Big Sky
Charles Lang, Sudden Fear
Joseph LaShelle, My Cousin Rachel
Virgil Miller, Navajo
ROBERT SURTEES, THE BAD AND THE BEAUTIFUL

(C)

George Folsey, Million Dollar Mermaid
WINTON HOCH AND ARCHIE STOUT, THE QUIET MAN
Leon Shamroy, The Snows of Kilimanjaro
Harry Stradling, Hans Christian Andersen
Frederick Young, Ivanhoe

1953

(B&W)

Joseph Brun, Martin Luther
BURNETT GUFFEY, FROM HERE TO ETERNITY
Hal Mohr, The Four Poster
Franz Planer and Henri Alekan, Roman Holiday
Joseph Ruttenberg, Julius Caesar

(C)

Edward Cronjager, Beneath the 12 Mile Reef
George Folsey, All the Brothers Were Valiant
LOYAL GRIGGS, SHANE
Robert Planck, Lili
Leon Shamroy, The Robe

1954

(B&W)

George Folsey, Executive Suite
BORIS KAUFMAN, ON THE WATERFRONT
Charles Lang, Sabrina
John Seitz, Rogue Cop
John Warren, The Country Girl

(C)

Robert Burks, Rear Window
George Folsey, Seven Brides for Seven Brothers
MILTON KRASNER, THREE COINS IN THE FOUNTAIN
Leon Shamroy, The Egyptian
William Skall, The Silver Chalice

1955

(B&W)

Art Arling, I'll Cry Tomorrow
Russell Harlan, Blackboard Jungle
JAMES WONG HOWE, THE ROSE TATTOO
Charles Lang, Queen Bee
Joseph LaShelle, Marty

(C)

ROBERT BURKS, TO CATCH A THIEF
Harold Lipstein, A Man Called Peter
Leon Shamroy, Love Is a Many-Splendored Thing
Harry Stradling, Guys and Dolls
Robert Surtees, Oklahoma!

1956

(B&W)

Burnett Guffey, The Harder They Fall
Boris Kaufman, Baby Doll
Hal Rosson, The Bad Seed
JOSEPH RUTTENBERG, SOMEBODY UP THERE LIKES ME
Walter Strenge, Stagecoach to Fury

(C)

Jack Cardiff, War and Peace
Loyal Griggs, The Ten Commandments
LIONEL LINDON, AROUND THE WORLD IN 80 DAYS
Leon Shamroy, The King and I
Harry Stradling, The Eddy Duchin Story

1957

Ellsworth Fredericks, Sayonara
JACK HILDYARD, THE BRIDGE ON THE RIVER KWAI
Ray June, Funny Face
Milton Krasner, An Affair To Remember
William Mellor, Peyton Place

1958

(B&W)

Daniel Fapp, Desire under the Elms
Charles Lang, Separate Tables
SAM LEAVITT, THE DEFIANT ONES
Lionel Lindon, I Want To Live!
Joe MacDonald, The Young Lions

(C)

William Daniels, Cat On a Hot Tin Roof
James Wong Howe, The Old Man and the Sea
JOSEPH RUTTENBERG, GIGI
Leon Shamroy, South Pacific
Harry Stradling, Auntie Mame

1959

(B&W)

Charles Lang, Some Like It Hot
Joseph LaShelle, Career
Sam Leavitt, Anatomy of a Murder
WILLIAM MELLOR, THE DIARY OF ANNE FRANK
Harry Stradling, The Young Philadelphians

(C)

Daniel Fapp, The Five Pennies
Lee Garmes, The Big Fisherman
Franz Planer, The Nun's Story
Leon Shamroy, Porgy and Bess
ROBERT SURTEES, BEN-HUR

1960

(B&W)

FREDDIE FRANCIS, SONS AND LOVERS
Charles Lang, The Facts of Life
Joseph LaShelle, The Apartment
Ernest Laszlo, Inherit the Wind
John Russell, Psycho

(C)

William Clothier, The Alamo
Sam Leavitt, Exodus
Joe MacDonald, Pepe
RUSSELL METTY, SPARTACUS
Joseph Ruttenberg and Charles Harten, Butterfield 8

1961

(B&W)

Edward Colman, The Absent-Minded Professor
Daniel Fapp, One, Two, THree
Ernest Laszlo, Judgment at Nuremberg
Franz Planer, The Children's Hour
EUGENE SCHUFFTAN, THE HUSTLER

(C)

Jack Cardiff, Fanny
DANIEL FAPP, WEST SIDE STORY
Charles Lang, One-Eyed Jacks
Russell Metty, Flower Drum Song
Harry Stradling, A Majority of One

1962

(B&W)

JEAN BOURGOIN AND WALTER WOTTITZ, THE LONGEST DAY
Burnett Guffey, Bird Man of Alcatraz
Ernest Haller, What Ever Happened to Baby Jane?
Russell Harlan, To Kill a Mockingbird
Ted McCord, Two for the Seesaw

(C)

Russell Harlan, Hatari!
Harry Stradling, Gypsy
Robert Surtees, Mutiny on the Bounty
Paul Vogel, The Wonderful World of the Brothers Grimm
FREDERICK YOUNG, LAWRENCE OF ARABIA

1963

(B&W)

Lucien Ballard, The Caretakers
George Folsey, The Balcony
Ernest Haller, Lilies of the Field
JAMES WONG HOWE, HUD
Milton Krasner, Love With the Proper Stranger

(C)

William Daniels, Milton Krasner, Charles Lang, Joseph LaShelle,
    How The West Was Won
Joseph LaShelle, Irma La Douce
Ernest Laszlo, It's a Mad, Mad, Mad, Mad World
Leon Shamroy, The Cardinal
LEON SHAMROY, CLEOPATRA

1964

(B&W)

Joseph Biroc, Hush ... Hush, Sweet Charlotte
Gabriel Figueroa, The Night of the Iguana
Philip Lathrop, The Americanization of Emily
WALTER LASSALLY, ZORBA THE GREEK
Milton Krasner, Fate Is the Hunter

(C)

William Clothier, Cheyenne Autumn
Edward Colman, Mary Poppins
Daniel Fapp, The Unsinkable Molly Brown
HARRY STRADLING, MY FAIR LADY
Geoffrey Unsworth, Becket

1965

(B&W)

Robert Burks, A Patch of Blue
Loyal Griggs, In Harm's Way
Burnett Guffey, King Rat
Conrad Hall, Morituri
ERNEST LASZLO, SHIP OF FOOLS

(C)

Russell Harlan, The Great Race
Ted McCord, The Sound of Music
William Mellor and Loyal Griggs, The Greatest Story Ever Told
Leon Shamroy, The Agony and the Ecstasy
FREDERICK YOUNG, DOCTOR ZHIVAGO

1966

(B&W)

Marcel Grignon, Is Paris Burning?
Ken Higgins, Georgy Girl
James Wong Howe, Seconds
Joseph LaShelle, The Fortune Cookie
HASKELL WEXLER, WHO'S AFRAID OF VIRGINIA WOOLF?

(C)

Conrad Hall, The Professionals
Russell Harlan, Hawaii
Ernest Laszlo, Fantastic Voyage
Joe MacDonald, The Sand Pebbles
TED MOORE, A MAN FOR ALL SEASONS

1967

BURNETT GUFFEY, BONNIE AND CLYDE
Conrad Hall, In Cold Blood
Richard Kline, Camelot
Robert Surtees, Doctor Doolittle
Robert Surtees, The Graduate

1968

PASQUALE DE SANTIS, ROMEO AND JULIET
Daniel Fapp, Ice Station Zebra
Ernest Laszlo, Star!
Oswald Morris, Oliver!
Harry Stradling, Funny Girl

1969

Daniel Fapp, Marooned
CONRAD HALL, BUTCH CASSIDY AND THE SUNDANCE KID
Arthur Ibbetson, Anne of the Thousand Days
Charles Lang, Bob & Carol & Ted & Alice
Harry Stradling, Hello, Dolly!

1970

Fred Koenekamp, Patton
Ernest Laszlo, Airport
Jack Martin Smith, et al., Tora! Tora! Tora!
Billy Williams, Women In Love
FREDERICK YOUNG, RYAN'S DAUGHTER

1971

OSWALD MORRIS, FIDDLER ON THE ROOF
Owen Roizman, The French Connection
Robert Surtees, The Last Picture SHow
Robert Surtees, Summer of '42
Frederick Young, Nicholas and Alexandra

1972

Charles Lang, Butterflies Are Free
Douglas Slocombe, Travels with My Aunt
Harold Stine, The Poseidon Adventure
Harry Stradling, Jr., 1776
GEOFFREY UNSWORTH, CABARET

1973

Jack Couffer, Jonathan Livingston Seagull
SVEN NYKVIST, CRIES AND WHISPERS
Owen Roizman, The Exorcist
Harry Stradling, Jr., The Way We Were
Robert Surtees, The Sting

1974

John A. Alonzo, Chinatown
FRED KOENEKAMP AND JOSEPH BIROC, THE TOWERING INFERNO
Philip Lathrop, Earthquake
Bruce Surtees, Lenny
Geoffrey Unsworth, Murder on the Orient Express

1975

JOHN ALCOTT, BARRY LYNDON
Conrad Hall, The Day of the Locust
James Wong Howe, Funny Lady
Robert Surtees, The Hindenburg
Haskell Wexler and Bill Butler, One Flew Over the Cuckoo's Nest

1976

Richard Kline, King Kong
Ernest Laszlo, Logan's Run
Owen Roizman, Network
Robert Surtees, A Star Is Born
HASKELL WEXLER, BOUND FOR GLORY

1977

William Fraker, Looking for Mr. Goodbar
Fred Koenekamp, Islands in the Stream
Douglas Slocombe, Julia
Robert Surtees, The Turning Point
VILMOS ZSIGMOND, CLOSE ENCOUNTERS OF THE THIRD KIND

1978

NESTOR ALMENDROS, DAYS OF HEAVEN
William Fraker, Heaven Can Wait
Oswald Morris, The Wiz
Robert Surtees, Same Time, Next Year
Vilmos Zsigmond, The Deer Hunter

1979

    Nestor Almendros, Kramer vs. Kramer
    William Fraker, 1941
    Frank Phillips, The Black Hole
    Giuseppe Rotunno, All That Jazz
    VITTORIO STORARO, APOCALPYSE NOW

1980

    Nestor Almendros, The Blue Lagoon
    Ralf Bode, Coal Miner's Daughter
    Michael Chapman, Raging Bull
    James Crabbe, The Formula
    GEOFFREY UNSWORTH AND GHISLAIN CLOQUET, TESS

1981

    Miroslav Ondricek, Ragtime
    Douglas Slocombe, Raiders of the Lost Ark
    VITTORIO STORARO, REDS
    Alex Thomson, Excalibur
    Billy Williams, On Golden Pond

1982

    Nestor Almendros, Sophie's Choice
    Allen Daviau, E.T.--The Extra Terrestrial
    Owen Roizman, Tootsie
    Jost Vacano, Das Boot
    BILLY WILLIAMS AND RONNIE TAYLOR, GANDHI

1983

    Caleb Deschanel, The Right Stuff
    William Fraker, Wargames
    SVEN NYKVIST, FANNY AND ALEXANDER
    Don Peterman, Flashdance
    Gordon Willis, Zelig

1984

    Ernest Day, A Passage to India
    Caleb Deschanel, The Natural
    CHRIS MENGES, THE KILLING FIELDS
    Miroslav Ondricek, Amadeus
    Vilmos Zsigmond, The River

1985

Allen Daviau, the Color Purple
William Fraker, Murphy's Romance
Takio Saito, Masaharu Ueda and Asakazu Nakai, Ran
John Seale, Witness
DAVID WATKIN, OUT OF AFRICA

1986

Jordan Cronenweth, Peggy Sue Got Married
CHRIS MENGES, THE MISSION
Don Peterman, Star Trek IV: The Voyage Home
Tony Pierce-Roberts, A Room with a View
Robert Richardson, Platoon

1987

Michael Ballhaus, Broadcast News
Allen Daviau, Empire of the Sun
Philippe Rousselot, Hope and Glory
VITTORIO STORARO, THE LAST EMPEROR
Haskell Wexler, Matewan

1988

PETER BIZIOU, MISSISSIPPI BURNING
Dean Cundey, Who Framed Roger Rabbit
Conrad Hall, Tequila Sunrise
Sven Nykvist, The Unbearable Lightness of Being
John Seale, Rain Man

1989

FREDDIE FRANCIS: GLORY
Robert Richardson: Born on the Fourth of July
Mikael Salomon: The Abyss
Haskell Wexler: Blaze

1990

Allen Daviau: Avalon
DEAN SEMLER: DANCES WITH WOLVES
Vittorio Storaro: Dick Tracy
Gordon Willis: The Godfather, Part III
Philippe Rousselot: Henry and June

BRITISH ACADEMY AWARDS

1963

Douglas Slocombe: The Servant (B&W)
Ted Moore: From Russia With Love (C)

1964

Oswald Morris: The Pumpkin Eater (B&W)
Geoffrey Unsworth: Becket (C)

1965

Oswald Morris: The Hill (B&W)
Otto Heller: The Ipcress File (C)

1966

Oswald Morris: The Spy Who Came in from the Cold (B&W)
Christopher Challis: Arabesque (C)

1967

Gerry Turpin: The Whisperers (B&W)
Ted Moore A Man for All Seasons (C)

1968

Geoffrey Unsworth: 2001: A Space Odyssey

1969

Gerry Turpin: Oh, What a Lovely War

1970

Conrad Hall: Butch Cassidy and the Sundance Kid

1971

Pasquale De Santis: Death in Venice

1972

Geoffrey Unsworth: Alice's Adventures in Wonderland and Cabaret

1973

Anthony Richmond: Don't Look Now

1974

Douglas Slocombe: The Great Gatsby

1975

John Alcott: Barry Lyndon

1976

Russell Boyd: Picnic at Hanging Rock

1977

Geoffrey Unsworth: A Bridge Too Far

1978

Douglas Slocomobe: Julia

1979

Vilmos Zsigmond: The Deer Hunter

1980

Giuseppe Rotunno: All That Jazz

1981

Geoffrey Unsworth and Ghislain Cloquet: Tess

1982

Jordan Cronenweth: Blade Runner

1983

Sven Nykvist: Fanny and Alexander

1984

Chris Menges: The Killing Fields

1985

Miroslav Ondricek: Amadeus

1986

Chris Menges: The Mission

AMERICAN SOCIETY OF CINEMATOGRAPHERS

1986

Jordan Cronenweth: Peggy Sue Got Married

1987

Allen Daviau: Empire of the Sun

1988

Conrad Hall: Tequila Sunrise

1989

Mikael Salomon: The Abyss

Titles are keyed to citation numbers unless preceded by "p." for page.

Captain Alvarez 587
Captain Apache p. 644
Captain Applejack 429
Captain Bill 644
Captain Blood (1924) 566
Captain Blood (1935) 420
Captain Boycott 114
Captain Calamity 575
Captain Carey USA 552
Captain Caution 71
Captain China 12
Captain Clegg 228
Captain Courtesy 103
Captain Cowboy 9
Captain Eddie 378
Captain Fly-by-Night 14
Captain Fracassa's Journey 627
Captain Fracasse 240
Captain from Castile 16, 102
Captain from Koepenick (1933)
  p. 644
The Captain from Koepenick
  (1956) p. 644
Captain Fury 71
The Captain Hates the Sea 20
Captain Horatio Hornblower RN
  232
Captain Hurricane 14
The Captain Is a Lady 565
Captain January (1924) 380
Captain January (1936) 552
Captain John Smith and Pocahontas
  95
Captain Kidd 584
Captain Kidd, Jr. 526
Captain Lash 673
Captain Lightfoot 218
Captain Lust 383
Captain Macklin 254
Captain Nemo and the Underwater
  City 286
Captain Newman MD 411
Captain of the Guard 666
Captain Pirate 350
Captain Salvation 133
Captain Scarlet p. 644
Captain Sinbad 544; p. 644
Captain Swift 136
Captain Thunder 645
Captain Tugboat Annie 439
The Captain's Captain 557
Captains Courageous 528
The Captain's Kid 249
Captains of the Clouds 106, 488
The Captain's Paradise 537
The Captain's Table 97
The Captive 699

The Captive City (1951) 204
The Captive City (1963) 39
Captive Girl 429
The Captive God 151
The Captive Heart 38, 564
Captive of Billy the Kid 377
Captive Wild Women 520
Captive Women 293
The Capture 125
Capture That Capsule 343
The Car 272
Car 99 408
Car of Dreams 235
Car Wash 572
Les Carabiniers 120
Caravaggio p. 644
Caravan (1934) 455, 570
Caravan (1946) 131
Caravan to Vaccaro p. 644
Caravan Trail 357
Caravans 564
Carbine Williams 408
Carbon Copy 326
The Card 431
Cardboard Cavalier 268
The Cardboard Lover 17
Cardigan 640
The Cardinal 555
Cardinal Messias 622
Cardinal Richelieu 386
Career (1939) 502
Career (1959) 345
Career Girl 473
Career Woman 483, 645
Carefree 143
Careful, Soft Shoulders 102
Careless (1928) 417
Careless (1982) 437
Careless Lady 552
The Careless Years 352
The Caretakers 36
The Carey Treatment 572
Cargo to Capetown 350
Caribbean 361
The Caribbean Mystery 151
The Cariboo Trail 295
Carleton Browne of the FO 235
Carmela 486
Carmen (1915) 48, 540, 699
Carmen (1918) 570
Carmen (1926) p. 644
Carmen (1946) p. 644
Carmen (1949) p. 644
Carmen (1983) p. 644
Carmen Jones 352
Carnaby M.D. 580
Carnage 44

Charlie Chan in Honolulu 102
Charlie Chan in London 447
Charlie Chan in Panama 417
Charlie Chan in Paris 455
Charlie Chan in Reno 417
Charlie Chan in Rio 378
Charlie Chan in Secret Service
    429
Charlie Chan in Shanghai 405
Charlie Chan on Broadway 297
Charlie Chan's Chance 20
Charlie Chan's Courage 420
Charlie Chan's Greatest Case
    455
Charlie Chan's Murder Cruise 417
Charlie Chan's Secret 398
Charlie McCarthy Detective 520
Charly 450
Charm of La Boheme 484
The Charm School 542
The Charmer 281
Charro! 191
Charter Pilot 14
The Chase (1947) 484
The Chase (1966) 345
Chase a Crooked Shadow 270
The Chaser (1928) 358
The Chaser (1938) 350
Chasing Danger 417
Chasing Rainbows (1919) 31
Chasing Rainbows (1929) 429
Chasing the Moon 322
Chasing Trouble (1926) 705
Chasing Trouble (1940) 439
Chasing Yesterday 14
Chastity (1923) 74, 416
Chastity (1969) p. 645
Chastity Belt 156
Chato's Land 461
Chatterbox (1936) 143
Chatterbox (1943) 416
Chatter-Box (1977) 197
Che! (1969) 678
Che? (1973) 206
The Cheap Detective 11
Cheap Kisses 127
Cheaper by the Dozen 555
Cheaper To Keep Her p. 645
Cheaper To Marry 40
The Cheat (1915) 699
The Cheat (1923) 415
The Cheat (1931) 185
Cheated Hearts 417
Cheated Love 221
The Cheater p. 645
The Cheater Reformed 151
Cheaters (1927) 161

The Cheaters (1945) 342
The Cheaters (1961) 510
The Cheaters (1984) 433
Cheaters at Play 455
Cheating Blondes 75
Cheating Cheaters (1919) 166
Cheating Cheaters (1927) 524
Cheating Cheaters (1934) 520
Cheating Herself 231
Cheating the Public 301
The Chechako 473
Check Your Guns 416
The Checkered Coat 524
Checkers (1913) 600
Checkers (1919) 485
Checkers (1937) 101
Checking Out p. 645
Checkmate 45
Checkpoint 580
Cheech and Chong's Next Movie 27
Cheech and Chong's The Corsican
    Brothers p. 645
Cheer Boys Cheer 438
Cheer Up and Smile 637
The Cheerful Fraud 620
Cheerful Givers 353
The Cheerleader 214
Cheers for Miss Bishop 420
Cheers of the Crowd 331, 439
Cheetah p. 645
The Chelsea Girls 663
Chelsea 7750 72
Chen-Bibi 424
Cherez Ternii K Svezdam p. 645
The Cherokee Flash 342
The Cherokee Kid 435
Cherokee Strip (1937) 403, 447
Cherokee Strip (1940) 253
Cherokee Uprising 666
The Cherry Blossom Ballad p. 645
Cherry, Harry and Raquel 413
Cherry 2000 246
The Chess Players p. 645
Chesty Anderson p. 645
Chetan, Indian Boy 37
Chetniks 380
Chevalier de La Nuit 283
Cheyenne (1929) 225
Cheyenne (1947) 262
Cheyenne Autumn 108
The Cheyenne Kid 334
Cheyenne Rides Again 288
Cheyenne Roundup 560
The Cheyenne Social Club 108
Cheyenne Takes Over 416
Cheyenne Trails 9
Cheyenne's Pal 513

Companys, Catalonia on Trial 456

Compassion 199

Competition (1968) 448

The Competition (1980) 323

Complex World p. 647

Compliments of Mr. Flow 23

Compromise 1

Compromising Positions 567a

Compulsion 408

The Compulsory Husband 570

Computer-Free-For-All p. 647

The Computer Wore Tennis Shoes 476

Comrade John 45

Comrade X 533

Comrades (1934) 607

Comrades (1987) p. 647

Comrades of 1918 653

Conan the Barbarian 89; p. 647

Conan the Destroyer 91

Conceit 201

The Concentratin' Kid 439

Concentration Camp p. 647

Concerning Mr. Martin p. 647

The Concert 671

Concert Magic 293

Concorde: Airport 79 349

The Concrete Jungle p. 647

Condemned (1930) 41, 621

The Condemned (1975) 547

The Condemned of Altona 209

Condemned to Death p. 647

Condemned to Live 13

Condemned Women 435

El Condor 470

Condorman 678

Conduct Unbecoming 285

The Conductor (1981) p. 647

The Conductor (1989) p. 647

Conductor 1492 217

Cone of Silence 228

Coney Island (1928) 605

Coney Island (1943) 455

Confession 262

The Confessions 120

Confessions from a Holiday Camp 274

Confessions of a Co-Ed 204

Confessions of a Driving Instructor 274

Confessions of a Nazi Spy 488

Confessions of a Police Captain p. 647

Confessions of a Pop Performer 286

Confessions of a Queen 267

Confessions of a Rogue p. 647

Confessions of a Wife 13

Confessions of a Window Cleaner 667

The Confessions of Aman p. 648

Confessions of an Opium Eater 51

The Confessions of Boston Blackie 602

The Confessions of the Swindler Felix Krull 47

Confidence p. 648

Confidence Girl 108

The Confidence Man 126

Confidential 391, 416

Confidential Agent 281

Confidentially Connie 363

Confidentially Yours 10

Confirm or Deny 555

The Conflict (1921) 299

Conflict (1936) 584

Conflict (1939) 454

Conflict (1945) 211

Conflict of Wings 228

The Conformist 583

Congo Crossing 411

Congo Maisie 350

Congress Dances 275

The Conjugal Bed 241

A Connecticut Yankee (1931) 455

A Connecticut Yankee in King Arthur's Court (1921) 14

A Connecticut Yankee in King Arthur's Court (1949) 509

Connecting Rooms 681

The Connection 450

Conquered Hearts 357

The Conquering Horde 584

The Conquering Power 552

Conquering the Woman 41

The Conqueror (1917) 103

The Conqueror (1956) 345,567, 626, 682

The Conquerors 125

Conquest 193

The Conquest of Canaan 468

Conquest of Cochise 192

Conquest of Space 361

Conquest of the Air 114, 204

Conquest of the Citadel 372

Conquest of the Planet of the Apes 596

Conrack 11

Conrad in Quest of His Youth 683

Consequence (1977) 37

The Consequence (1979) p. 648

Consider All Risks 107

Consolation Marriage 287

The Conspiracy (1914) 72

Conspiracy (1939) 502

Conspiracy of Hearts 580

Conspirator 703

The Conspirators 166

Cyclone of the Range 435
Cyclone on Horseback 682
Cyclone Ranger p. 649
The Cyclone Rider 654
Cyclops (1956) 429
Cyclops (1982) 480
Cynara 306
Cynthia 542
Cynthia of the Minute 538
Cyrano and D'Artagnan 392
Cyrano de Bergerac (1950) 484
Cyrano de Bergerac (1990) p. 649
Cytherea 415

- D -

D.C. Cab 130
D-Day: The Sixth of June 204
The DI 109
DOA (1949) 348
D.O.A. (1988) p. 649
Da p. 649
Dad p. 650
Dad and Dave Come to Town 259
Dad Rudd, M.P. 259
Daddies 594
Daddy 225
Daddy Long Legs (1919) 126, 526
Daddy Long Legs (1938) 341
Daddy Longlegs (1931) 14
Daddy Longlegs (1955) 555
Daddy Nostalgie p. 650
Daddy's Boys p. 650
Daddy's Deadly Darling p. 650
Daddy's Dyin' ... Who's Got the
    Will? p. 650
Daddy's Gone A-Hunting (1925)
    374
Daddy's Gone A-Hunting (1969)
    348
Dad's Army p. 650
Daisy Kenyon 555
Daisy Miller 569
Dakota (1945) 391
Dakota (1974) 141
Dakota (1988) p. 650
Dakota Incident 249
The Dakota Kid 377
Dakota Lil 237
Daleks--Invasion Earth 681
Dalia and the Sailors 670
Dallas 249
The Dalton Gang p. 650
The Dalton Girls 245
The Daltons Ride Again 644
The Dam Busters 270

Damaged Hearts 543
Damaged Lives 561
Dame Chance 238
Dames (1934) 41, 262
Dames Ahoy p. 650
Les Dames du Bois de Boulogne 3
Damien: Omen Two 84
Damn Citizen 95
Damn the Defiant! 97
Damn Yankees 363
Damnation Alley 586
Damned (1947) 8
The Damned (1961) 228
The Damned (1969) 148, 437
The Damned Don't Cry 403
Damned River p. 650
Damon and Pythias 622
A Damsel in Distress (1919) 600
A Damsel in Distress (1937) 660
Dan Matthews 561
Dance Band 341
Dance Fools Dance 526
Dance, Girl, Dance (1933) 13
Dance, Girl, Dance (1940) 411
Dance Goes On 262
Dance Hall (1929) 379
Dance Hall (1942) 14
Dance Hall (1950) 564
Dance Little Lady 114
Dance Madness 17, 133
Dance Magic 249
Dance of Death 634
The Dance of Life 287
Dance of the Herons 647
Dance of the Polar Bears p. 650
Dance Pretty Lady 457
Dance Program 312
Dance Team 281
Dance with a Stranger 252
Dance with Me, Henry 520
The Dancer of Paris 249
Dancer of Sansoucci 47
The Dancer of the Nile 127
The Dancers (1925) 455
The Dancers (1930) 620
Dancers (1987) 241
Dancers in the Dark 591
Dances with Wolves 553
The Dancin' Fool 216
Dancin' Thru the Dark p. 650
The Dancing Cheat 616
Dancing Co-Ed 216
Dancing Days 72
Dancing Feet 391, 416
Dancing Girl 72
Dancing in Manhattan 447
Dancing in the Dark (1949) 297

Daniel Boone, Trail Blazer 159
Daniella by Night p. 650
Danny Boy (1941) 131
Danny Boy (1946) 237
Dante's Inferno (1924) 20
Dante's Inferno (1935) 398
Danton (1921) p. 650
Danton (1931) p. 650
Danton (1983) 372
Darby O'Gill and the Little People
  273
Darby's Rangers 108
Dare Devil's Time 480
Daredevil 301
Daredevil Drivers 403
Daredevil in the Castle p. 650
Daredevil's Reward 101
Daredevils of the Clouds 377
Daredreamer p. 650
The Daring Caballero 679
Daring Chances 439
Daring Danger 322
Daring Daughters 186
Daring Days 322
Daring Game p. 650
Daring Hearts 527
Daring Love 153, 389
The Daring Young Man 211
Daring Youth 644
The Dark 430
Dark Age p. 650
Dark Alibi 560
Dark Angel (1925) 41
The Dark Angel (1935) 621
Dark Are Nights on the Black Sea
  p. 650
Dark at the Top of the Stairs
  585
The Dark Avenger 232
Dark City 419
The Dark Command 391
The Dark Corner 378
The Dark Crystal 431
Dark Delusion 526
Dark Eyes (1938) 610
Dark Eyes (1987) p. 650
Dark Eyes of London (1939) 341
Dark Eyes of London (1961)
  p. 650
Dark Hazard 488
The Dark Horse 293
The Dark Hour 13
The Dark House 488
Dark Intruder 665
Dark Is the Night p. 650
Dark Journey 467, 585
A Dark Lantern 453

The Dark Man 129
Dark Manhattan 503
The Dark Mirror (1920 594
The Dark Mirror (1946) 331
Dark Mountain 295
Dark Odyssey p. 650
Dark of the Night p. 650
Dark of the Sun 537
Dark Passage 262
The Dark Past 659
Dark Places 580
Dark Purpose 486
Dark Red Roses p. 650
The Dark Room of Damocles 120
Dark Sands 65
Dark Secrets 528
The Dark Silence 704
Dark Skies 508
The Dark Star (1919) 72
Dark Star (1975) p. 650
Dark Streets 249
Dark Streets of Cairo 68
Dark Sun 448
The Dark Swan 1
The Dark Tower (1943) 260
Dark Tower (1989) p. 650
Dark Victory 249
Dark Waters 410, 584
Darkened Rooms 584
Darker Than Amber 476
The Darkest Hour 527
Darkman p. 650
Darling 265
Darling, How Could You? 172
Darling Lili 253, 672
The Darling of New York 594
The Darling of Paris 525
Darling of the Gods 518
The Darling of the Rich 459
The Darwin Adventure 112
D.A.R.Y.L 669
Date with a Dream p. 650
Date with an Angel 614
A Date with Judy 597
A Date with the Falcon 143
Dateline Diamonds 131
Daughter: I a Woman III 5
Daughter Angele 358
Daughter of Darkness 460
Daughter of Deceit p. 650
Daughter of Dr. Jekyll 665
Daughter of Evil 329
A Daughter of Luxury 34
A Daughter of MacGregor 359
Daughter of Mine 357
The Daughter of Rosie O'Grady 106
Daughter of Shanghai 542
Daughter of the Dragon 419

De Sade (1969)   15; p. 651
The Dead   434
Dead and Buried   493
Dead-Bang   182
Dead Calm   553
The Dead Don't Dream   575
Dead End   621
Dead End Drive In   p. 651
Dead End Kids on Dress Parade
   620
Dead Game   310
Dead Heat   702a
Dead Heat on a Merry Go Round
   361
Dead Kids   p. 651
The Dead Line (1920)   217
The Dead Line (1926)   506
Dead Man's Evidence   274
Dead Man's Eyes   293
Dead Man's Float   p. 651
Dead Man's Gulch   342, 416
Dead Men Don't Die   p. 651
Dead Men Don't Wear Plaid   99
Dead Men Tell   102
Dead Men Tell No Tales (1920
   249
Dead Men Tell No Tales (1938)
   341
Dead Men Walk   237
Dead Men's Shoes   329
The Dead Mountaineer Hotel
   p. 651
Dead of Night   460, 564
Dead of Summer   p. 651
Dead of Winter   p. 651
Dead People   308
Dead Pigeon on Beethoven Street
   p. 651
Dead Poets Society   549
The Dead Pool   232a
Dead Reckoning   626
Dead Ringer   249
Dead Ringers   598
Dead Run   p. 651
The Dead Season of Loves   647
The Dead Woman's Hand   145
The Dead Zone   292
Deadfall   632
Deadhead Miles   694
The Deadlier Sex   310
Deadlier Than the Male (1957)   610
Deadlier Than the Male (1967)   580
The Deadliest Sin   p. 651
The Deadline (1932)   256
Deadline (1987)   400
Deadline at Dawn   435
Deadline at Eleven   527

Deadline for Murder   322
Deadline USA   331
The Deadly Affair   703
Deadly Blessing   302
The Deadly Companions   108
Deadly Duo   21
Deadly Eyes   646
Deadly Friend   349
The Deadly Game   p. 651
Deadly Hero   43
Deadly Mantis   95
Deadly Passion   121a
Deadly Reactor   p. 651
Deadly Spygames   p. 651
Deadly Strangers   p. 651
Deadly Sweet   291
Deadly Trackers   p. 651
The Deadwood Coach   101
Deadwood '76   707
Deaf Smith and Johnny Ears   145
Deal of the Century   323
Dealing   p. 651
Dear Brat   552
Dear Brigette   36
Dear Detective   p. 651
Dear Fatherland Be at Peace   636
Dear Heart   253
Dear John   p. 651
Dear Michael   145
Dear Mr. Prohack   p. 651
Dear Mr. Wonderful   37
Dear Murderer   131
Dear Octopus   123
Dear Papa   145
Dear Ruth   348
Dear Summer Sister   p. 651
Dear Wife   612
Dearie   1
Death at Broadcast House   329
Death before Dishonor   p. 651
Death Collector   p. 651
The Death Dance   72
Death Flies East   561
Death from a Distance   13
Death Game   695
Death Goes North   186
Death Hunt   p. 651
Death in Brunswick   p. 651
Death in Small Doses   245
Death in the Garden   p. 651
Death in the Sky   153, 503
Death in Venice   148
Death Is a Number   p. 651
Death Is Called Engelchen   p. 651
The Death Kiss   71
Death of a Bureaucrat   p. 652
Death of a Champion   612

Delta Pi 367
Deluge 71
Delusions of Grandeur 142
Demented p. 652
Dementia 613
Dementia 13 p. 652
Demetrius and the Gladiators 331
The Demi-Bride 267
The Demi-Paradise 325
Democracy 262
The Demon (1926) 443
The Demon (1981) 121a
Demon Des Meeres 335
Demon Pond p. 652
The Demon Rider 118
Demon Seed 84
Demoniaque p. 652
Demonoid 475
Demons in the Garden p. 652
Demons of the Mind 228
Demons of the Swamp 442
Demonstrator p. 652
Demonwarp p. 652
The Denial 513
Dentist in the Chair 700
Denver and the Rio Grande 509
The Denver Dude 439
Deo Gratias 80
Deported 133
The Depraved 692
The Deputy p. 652
Deputy Marshal p. 652
Deranged (1974) p. 652
Deranged! (1987) 512
Derby Day 235
Derek and Clive Get the Horn 324
The Derelict (1917) 48
Derelict (1930) 584
Le Dernier Milliardaire 398
Les Derniers Vacances 3
Dersu Uzala p. 652
Desert Attack 604
Desert Bandit 443
Desert Bloom 648
Desert Blossoms 183
The Desert Bride 306
The Desert Demon 508
Desert Desperadoes 132
Desert Driven 143, 616
Desert Dust 70
The Desert Flower 403
The Desert Fox 71
Desert Fury 125, 340
Desert Gold (1919) 620
Desert Gold (1926) 542

Desert Gold (1936) 104
The Desert Hawk 411
Desert Hearts p. 652
Desert Hell 442
Desert Legion 552
Desert Love 225
The Desert Man 20
Desert Mice 274
Desert Nights 281
Desert of Lost Men 377
The Desert of the Lost 508
The Desert of the Tartars 627
The Desert Outlaw 74
Desert Patrol 114
Desert Phantom 369
Desert Pursuit 560
The Desert Rats 36
The Desert Raven p. 652
Desert Rider (1923) 369
The Desert Rider (1929) 503
Desert Sands 21
Desert Song (1929) 405
Desert Song (1943) 221
The Desert Song (1953) 81
Desert Trail 584
Desert Valley 376
Desert Vengeance 403
Desert Vigilante 693
Desert Warrior p. 652
A Desert Wooing 684
Deserted at the Altar 380
Deserter (1934) p. 653
The Deserter (1970) 622
The Deserter and the Nomads p. 653
The Desert's Price 376
The Desert's Toll 578
Design for Living 419
Design for Scandal 133, 565
Designing Woman 12
Desirable 249
Desire (1923) 41
Desire (1936) 340, 419
Desire (1984) 529
Desire in the Dust 36
Desire Me 533
Desire, the Interior Life p. 653
Desire under the Elms 172
The Desired Woman 673
Desiree 331
Desk Set 555
Despair 37
The Desperado p. 653
Desperado City 400
The Desperado Trail p. 653
The Desperadoes (1943) 407
The Desperadoes Are in Town 410
Desperadoes of Dodge City 377

The Enemy (1927) 389
Enemy (1953) 423
Enemy Agent 18
Enemy Agent against Ellery
  Queen 75
The Enemy Below 528
The Enemy General 168
An Enemy of Man 225
An Enemy of the People (1977)
  367
Enemy of the People (1989)
  p. 657
Enemy of Women 12
The Enemy Sex 77
Enemy Territory 153a
The Enemy Within 42
L'Enfant Sauvage 10
Les Enfants du Paradis 283
Les Enfants Terribles 142
The Enforcer (1950) 81
Enforcer (1976) 222; p. 657
Engagement Italiano p. 657
England Made Me 458; p. 657
English without Tears 325
An Englishman's Home 235
Enid Is Sleeping p. 657
Enigma p. 657
L'Enigmatique Monsieur Parkes 561
Enjo p. 657
Enlighten Thy Daughter 357
Enoch Arden 178
Enormous Changes at the Last
  Minute p. 657
Enough Rope p. 657
Enrapture 512
The Enrico Mattei Affair 148
Ensign Pulver 350
Entente Cordiale 454
Enter Laughing 51
Enter Madame (1922) 447
Enter Madame (1935) 408, 570
Enter the Dragon 282
Enter the Ninja 244
The Entertainer (1960) 431
The Entertainer (1975) 122
Entertaining Mr. Sloane 599
Enticement 556
Entire Days in the Trees 10
The Entity 82
Entr'acte p. 657
Entre Nous p. 657
Envy 339
Epilogue p. 657
Episode 585
Equinox p. 657
L'Equipage 80
Equus 431

Eraserhead 167
Erblinka 614
Erendira p. 657
Eric Soya's "17" p. 657
Erik the Conqueror 44
Erik the Viking p. 657
Erika/One 383
Erika's Hot Summer 230
Erika's Passions 400
Ernest Goes to Camp p. 658
Ernest Goes to Jail 573a
Ernest Saves Christmas 573a
Ernesto p. 658
Eroica p. 658
The Errand Boy 315
Erstwhile Susan 453
Escalation 336
Escapade (1935) 249
Escapade (1955) 129
Escapade in Japan 567
The Escape (1914) 52
The Escape (1926) 705
The Escape (1928) 393
Escape (1930) 379
Escape (1939) 125
Escape (1940) 483
Escape (1948) 703
The Escape Artist 82
Escape by Night (1937) 567
Escape by Night (1954) p. 658
Escape by Night (1963) 171
Escape from Alcatraz 596
Escape from Crime 645
Escape from Devil's Island 594
Escape from East Berlin 333
Escape from Fort Bravo 597
Escape from Hong Kong 68
Escape from New York 130
Escape from Paradise p. 658
Escape from Red Rock 30
Escape from San Quentin 322
Escape from the Bronx p. 658
Escape from the Dark 46
Escape from the Planet of the Apes 51
Escape from Yesterday p. 658
Escape from Zahrain 191
Escape in the Desert 81
Escape in the Fog 407
Escape in the Sun p. 658
Escape Me Never (1935) 467
Escape Me Never (1947) 488
Escape to Athena 604
Escape to Berlin p. 658
Escape to Burma 12
Escape to Danger 235
Escape to Glory 484
Escape to Paradise 542

Fabian of the Yard   p. 659
Fabiola   p. 659
The Fabulous Baker Boys   37
The Fabulous Bastard from
   Chicago   230
The Fabulous Dorseys   645
The Fabulous Joe   65
The Fabulous Senorita   391
The Fabulous Suzanne   556
The Fabulous Texan   342
The Fabulous World of Jules
   Verne   p. 659
The Face   181
The Face at the Window   465
The Face behind the Mask   484
The Face Between   396
A Face in the Crowd   511, 585
Face in the Dark   53
The Face in the Fog   429, 674
The Face in the Moonlight   14
A Face in the Rain   677
Face in the Sky   204
Face of a Fugitive   106
Face of Fire   p. 659
The Face of Fu Manchu   580
The Face of Marble   439
Face of the World   151
The Face on the Barroom Floor
   (1923)   540
The Face on the Barroom Floor
   (1932)   322
The Face That Launched a
   Thousand Ships   154
Face to Face (1952)   157
Face to Face (1967)   p. 659
Face Value   320
Faces   p. 659
Faces in the Dark   274
Faces in the Fog   342
The Facts of Life   340
Facts of Love   455
The Facts of Murder   39
Fade to Black   475
Fagasa   13
Fahrenheit   451   522
Fail Safe   272
The Failure   178
Faint Perfume   561
The Fair   333
Fair and Warmer   396
The Fair Cheat   451
The Fair Co-Ed   552
Fair Lady   585
Fair Play   416
Fair Warning   654
Fair Week   34
Fair Wind to Java   391

The Fairy and the Waif   421
Faith   335
Faith and Endurin'   530
The Faith Healer   468
Faithful City   215
Faithful in My Fashion   535
A Faithful Woman   510
Faithless   389
Faithless Lover   708
The Fake   686
Fake-Out   642
The Faker   607
The Falcon   706
The Falcon and the Coeds   287
The Falcon Fighters   p. 659
The Falcon in Danger   502
The Falcon in Hollywood   435
The Falcon in Mexico   502
The Falcon in San Francisco   417
The Falcon Out West   682
Falcon Strikes Back   502
The Falcon Takes Over   520
The Falcon's Adventure   502, 682
The Falcon's Alibi   502
The Falcon's Brother   411
The Fall   366
The Fall Guy (1930)   626
Fall Guy (1947)   575
Fall In   481
The Fall of a Nation (1916)   65, 613
The Fall of Eve   607
The Fall of Rome   p. 659
Fall of the Roman Empire   330
Fallada--The Last Chapter   p. 659
Fallen Angel   345
A Fallen Idol (1919)   533
The Fallen Idol (1948)   467
The Fallen Sparrow   435
Fallguy (1962)   343
Falling for You   325
Falling in Love   598
Falling in Love Again   83, 599
Falling Over Backwards   p. 659
The False Alarm   140
False Ambition   379
The False Code   310
False Colors   253
False Evidence   17
False Faces (1919)   684
False Faces (1943)   66
False Feathers   439
False Friends   227
False Husband   275
False Identity   p. 659
False Kisses   513
The False Madonna   556
False Paradise   575

Fast Companions 166
Fast Company (1929) 125
Fast Company (1938) 151
Fast Company (1953) 363
Fast Company (1979) 292
Fast Fightin' 508
The Fast Lady 700
Fast Life (1929) 140
Fast Life (1932) 674
The Fast Mail 540, 559
Fast on the Draw 416
The Fast Set 683
Fast Talking 237a
Fast Times at Ridgemont High
  356
Fast Walking 27
The Fast Worker 513
Fast Workers 386
The Fastest Guitar Alive 315
The Fastest Gun Alive 185
Die Fastnachtsbeichte p. 659
Fat City 247
The Fat Man 218
Fat Man and Little Boy 707
Fat Spy 79
Fatal Attraction p. 659
Fatal Beauty 662
Fatal Desire 591
The Fatal Hour 439
Fatal Lady 555
The Fatal Mistake 611
The Fatal Night 686
The Fatal Witness 608
 Fate Is the Hunter 331
The Fate of a Flirt 338
Father (1967) P. 659
Father (1990) p. 659
Father and Son 607
Father and the Boys 633
Father Brown Detective 570
Father Came Too 700
Father Dear Father 286
Father Goose 340
Father Is a Bachelor 242
Father Is a Prince 403
Father of a Soldier p. 659
Father of the Bride 12
The Father of the Girl 305
Father Sergius p. 659
Father Takes a Wife 143
Father Takes the Air 560
Father Tom 689
Father Was a Fullback 4
Fatherland 409
Fathers and Sons 39
Father's Dilemma p. 659
Father's Doing Fine 270

Father's Little Dividend 12
Father's Son (1931) 415
Father's Son (1941) 561
The Father's Trip 625
Fathom 564
Fatso p. 659
Fatty Finn 549
Faust (1924) 193
Faust (1926) 275
Faust (1963) p. 659
Faustina 209
Faustine and the Beautiful Summer 107
A Favor to a Friend 396
The Favorite p. 659
Favorites of the Moon p. 660
Fazil 447
Fear (1946) 524
Fear (1956) p. 660
The Fear (1967) p. 660
Fear (1975) 480
Fear and Desire p. 660
Fear, Anxiety and Depression 130a
Fear City p. 660
Fear Eats the Soul p. 660
The Fear Fighter 183
Fear in the City 464
Fear in the Night (1947) 237
Fear in the Night (1972) 228
Fear Is the Key 614
The Fear Market 185
Fear No Evil p. 660
Fear No More 249
Fear Not, Jacob! 372
Fear of Falling 547
Fear Strikes Out 59
Fearless Fagin 363
Fearless Frank 84
The Fearless Lover 611
Fearless Vampire Killers 564
The Fearmakers 352
Feast of Life 14
A Feather in Her Hat 659
Feather Your Nest 438
The Feathered Serpent 560
Federal Agent 186
Federal Agent at Large 377
Federal Bullets 666
Federal Fugitives 396
Federal Man p. 660
Federico Fellini's Intervista 145
Fedora (1918) 640
Fedora (1946) p. 660
Fedora (1978) 182
Feds 595
Feedback 693a
Feel My Pulse 287
Feelings 274

Finian's Rainbow 349
Finishing School 287
Finnegan's Ball 652
Finnegans Wake p. 660
Finney p. 661
Fino a Farti Male p. 661
Fire and Steel 659
Fire at Will 625
Fire Birds 290
The Fire Brigade (1922) 527
Fire Brigade (1926) 17
The Fire Cat 499
Fire Down Below 154
Fire Flingers 280
A Fire Has Been Arranged p. 661
Fire in the Flesh p. 661
FIre in the Opera 653
The Fire in the Stone p. 661
Fire in the Straw p. 661
Fire Maidens from Outer Space
    p. 661
Fire over Africa 97
Fire over England 281
The Fire Patrol 33
Fire Sale 694
Fire with Fire p. 661
The Fire Within 107
The Fireball 679
Fireball 500 128
Fireball Jungle p. 661
The Firebird 249
The Firebrand (1922) 375
The Firebrand (1962) 128
Firebrand Jordan 443
Firebrand Trevision 660
Firecreek 108
Firefighters 290
The Firefly 389
Firefox 596
Fireman, Save My Child (1927)
    393
Fireman Save My Child (1932)
    488
Fireman Save My Child (1959)
    581
The Fireman's Ball 448
The Firemen of Viggin 622
Firepower 332, 461
FIres of Faith 542, 699, 704
Fires on the Plain p. 661
Firestarter p. 661
Firewalker 475
The Firing Line 359
The Firm Man p. 661
First a Girl 380
First Aid 127
The First Auto 1

First Baby 405
First Blood 347
The First Born 688
First Comes Courage 659
First Contact p. 661
The First Deadly Sin 495
The First Degree 322
First Family 326
The First Gentleman 268
The First Great Train Robbery 634
The First Kiss 216
First Lady 262
The First Legion 143
First Love (1921) 393
First Love (1939) 637
First Love (1970) 446
First Love (1977) 86
First Love (1979) 145
First Man into Space 171
First Monday in October 326
First Name Carmen 120
The First Night 575
The First Nudie Musical p. 661
The First of the Few 268, 467
First Offenders 192
First 100 Years 533
The First Polka 37
The First Power p. 661
The First Season 354
First Spaceship on Venus p. 661
First Start p. 661
First Taste of Love p. 661
The First Texan 106
First Time (1968) 348
The First Time (1978) p. 661
The First Time (1983) p. 661
The First Time on the Grass 206
First To Fight 672
The First Traveling Saleslday 567
The First Turn On p. 661
First Voyage 370
First Yank into Tokyo 682
The First Year (1926) 374
The First Year (1932) 420
A Fish Called Wanda 286
Fish, Football and Girls 244
Fish Hawk 646
The Fish That Saved Pittsburgh 572
Fisherman's Wharf 542
Fisher's Ghost 263
F.I.S.T. 328
Fist Fighter p. 661
Fist in His Pocket p. 661
A Fistful of Dollars 132
Fists of Fury p. 661
Fit for a King 650
Fitzcarraldo 400

For the Defense (1930) 340
For the First Time 622
For the Love O' Lil 607
For the Love of Ada 286
For the Love of Benji 501
For the Love of Mary 133
For the Love of Mike (1927) 249
For the Love of Mike (1960) 474
For the Love of Rusty 173
For the Service 320, 611
For the Soul of Rafael 166
For Them That Trespass 687
For Those Who Think Young 582
For Valour 602
For Whom the Bell Tolls 509
For Wives Only 528
For Woman's Favor 357
For You Alone 455
For You I Die 108
For You My Boy 196
For Your Eyes Only 286
Forbidden (1919) 103, 321
Forbidden (1932) 659
Forbidden (1949) 219
Forbidden (1953) 133
Forbidden (1955) 622
Forbidden (1984) 628
Forbidden Cargo (1925) 33
Forbidden Cargo (1954) 463
The Forbidden City 701
Forbidden Company 13
The Forbidden Dance p. 662
Forbidden Fire 593
Forbidden Fruit (1921) 699
Forbidden Fruit (1952) 8
Forbidden Grass 13
Forbidden Heaven 331
Forbidden Hours 211
Forbidden Island 666
Forbidden Journey p. 662
Forbidden Jungle p. 662
Forbidden Love 196
Forbidden Music 65
Forbidden Paradise 644
Forbidden Paths 469
Forbidden Planet 185
The Forbidden Range 574
Forbidden Relations p. 662
The Forbidden Room (1919) 301
The Forbidden Room (1977) 145
Forbidden Sun p. 662
Forbidden Territory p. 662
The Forbidden Thing 208
Forbidden To Know 370
The Forbidden Trail (1923) 76
Forbidden Trail (1936) 447
Forbidden Trails (1920) 660
Forbidden Trails (1928) 159

Forbidden Trails (1941) 439
Forbidden Valley (1920) 2
Forbidden Valley (1938) 68
Forbidden Waters 48
The Forbidden Woman (1920) 166
The Forbidden Woman (1927) 1
Forbidden World 595
Force Five 282
Force Majeure p. 662
Force of Arms 403
Force of Evil 41
A Force of One p. 662
Force Ten from Navarone 97
Forced Entry p. 662
Forced Landing (1936) 439
Forced Landing (1941) 12, 295
Forced Vengeance 412
A Foreign Affair 340
Foreign Affairs 316
Foreign Agent 575
Foreign Body 606
Foreign Correspondent 398
Foreign Devils 151
Foreign Intrigue p. 662
The Foreign Legion 524
The Foreman Went to France 114
Foreplay 57
Forest Havoc 631
The Forest Rangers 340, 563
Forest Rivals 279
Forester's Daughter (1931) 235
The Forester's Daughter (1952) 47
Forester's Sons 366
Forever 415
Forever After 591
Forever Amber 555
Forever and a Day 143, 204, 411, 435
Forever Darling 363
Forever Female 585
Forever My Love p. 662
Forever Young p. 662
Forever Young, Forever Free 450
Forever Yours (1937) p. 662
Forever Yours (1945) 439
Forged Passport 391
Forgery and the Use of Forgeries p. 662
Forget about Me p. 662
Forget-Me-Not 620
Forgive and Forget 231
Forgotten Commandments 591
Forgotten Faces (1928) 287
Forgotten Faces (1936) 570
Forgotten Girls 416
The Forgotten Law 594
The Forgotten Woman 117
Forgotten Women (1932) 584
Forgotten Women (1949) 357
Forlorn River (1926) 542
Forlorn River (1937) 248

- G -

Gun the Man Down 108
Gun Town 213
The Gun Woman 280
Gun Wound 8
A Gunfight (1970) 662
Gunfight at Comanche Creek 51
Gunfight at Dodge City 245
Gunfight at the O.K. Corral
 340
Gunfight in Abilene 213
The Gunfighter (1917) 20
The Gunfighter (1923) 301
The Gunfighter (1950) 415
The Gunfighters 295
Gunfighters of Abilene 213
Gunfighters of Casa Grande
 p. 668
A Gun-Fightin' Gentleman 76
Gunfire 416
Gung Ho! (1943) 331
Gung Ho! (1986) 471
Gunga Din 20
The Gunman from Bodie 439
Gunman's Walk 350
Gunmen of Abilene 95
Gunmen of Laredo 362
Gunmen of the Rio Grande
 p. 668
Gunn 349
Gunnar Hede's Saga 298
Gunplay (1951) 287
Gunpoint 385
The Gunrunner p. 668
Guns (1980) p. 668
Guns (1990) p. 668
Guns and Guitars 416
Guns at Batasi 564
Guns for San Sebastian 610
Guns, Girls and Gangsters 462
Guns in the Heather 504
Guns of Darkness 330
Guns of Diablo 442
Guns of Fort Petticoat 509
Guns of Hate 157
The Guns of Navarone 431
Guns of the Black Watch p. 668
Guns of the Magnificent Seven
 p. 668
Guns of the Pecos 403
Guns of the Timberland 552
Gunsight Ridge 348
Gunslinger 676
Gunslingers 439
Gunsmoke (1953) 64
Gunsmoke in Tucson 680
Gunsmoke Mesa 429
Gunsmoke Range 473

The Guru p. 668
Gus 476
Gutter Girls 440
The Guttersnipe 425
The Guvnor 235
A Guy, a Gal and a Pal 202
A Guy Could Change 12
Guy De Maupassant 531
A Guy Named Joe 185, 193
The Guy Who Came Back 345
Guyana, Cult of the Damned p. 668
Guys and Dolls 585
Gymkata p. 668
Gypsy (1962) 585
The Gypsy (1975) 603
The Gypsy and the Gentleman 268
Gypsy Colt 363
Gypsy Fury 399
Gypsy Law 24
Gypsy Melody 195
The Gypsy Moths 349
Gypsy of the North 147
The Gypsy Trail 203
Gypsy Wildcat 236, 520

- H -

H p. 668
H. M. Pulham, Esquire 306
The H-Man p. 668
La Habanera p. 668
The Habit of Happiness 184
Hagbard and Signe p. 669
Hail p. 669
A Hail Fellow Well Met 120
Hail Hero! 258
Hail! Mafia 120
Hail Mary p. 669
Hail the Artist 464
Hail the Conquering Hero 552
Hail the Woman 556
Hail to the Rangers 322
Hair 332, 448
Hair Trigger Baxter 249, 416
The Hairdresser's Husband p. 669
Hairpins 41
Hairspray p. 669
The Hairy Ape 14
Haixan p. 669
Halbblut 275
Haldane of the Secret Service 708
Half a Bride 419
Half-a-Dollar Bill 40
Half a Hero 650
Half a Sinner (1934) 520
Half a Sinner (1940) 644

The Heat's On 484
Heatwave (1954) p. 670
Heatwave (1982) 422
Heaven and Earth p. 670
Heaven Can Wait (1943) 125
Heaven Can Wait (1978) 189
Heaven Is around the Corner
 228, 692
Heaven Knows Mr. Allison 431
Heaven on Earth 17
Heaven on One's Head 550
Heaven Only Knows 591
Heaven Over the Marshes 7
Heaven Tonight p. 670
Heaven with a Barbed Wire
 Fence 125
Heaven with a Gun 326
Heavenly Bodies (1963) 413
Heavenly Bodies (1985) p. 670
The Heavenly Body 483
Heavenly Days 287
The Heavenly Kid 493
Heavens Above! 235
Heaven's Gate 707
Hedda 564
Heedless Moths 704
Heels Go to Hell 312
Heidi (1937) 415
Heidi (1954) p. 670
Heidi (1968) 15
Heidi and Peter p. 670
Heimkehr 518
Heinrich 400
The Heir 464
Heir to Trouble 320
The Heiress 626
Heiress for a Day 444
The Heist 475
Held by the Enemy 542
Held by the Law 524
Held to Answer 519
Heldinnen p. 670
Heldorado 66
The Helen Morgan Story 403
Helen of Troy 585
Helene of the North 72
Helen's Babies 133, 380
The Helicopter Spies 326
Heliotrope 528
Hell and High Water (1933) 216
Hell and High Water (1954) 378
Hell Below Zero 681
Hell Bent 513
Hell Bent for Heaven 435
Hell Bent for Leather 581
Hell Bent for Love 322
Hell Boats 46
Hell Bound 245

The Hell Cat (1918) 267
The Hell Cat (1934) 322
The Hell Diggers 542
Hell Divers 674
Hell Drivers 634
Hell Fire Austin 403
Hell Harbor 198, 575
Hell in the City 39
Hell in the Heavens 221
Hell in the Pacific 247
Hell Is a City 228
Hell Is for Heroes 363
Hell Night 5
Hell on Devil's Island 249
Hell on Earth p. 670
Hell on Frisco Bay 552
Hell Raiders of the Deep 622
Hell Roarin' Reform 31
The Hell Ship 540
Hell Ship Mutiny p. 670
Hell to Eternity 242
"Hell to Pay" Austen 353
Hell Train 464
Hell Up in Harlem p. 670
The Hell with Heroes 608
Hellbent for Frisco 127
Hellbound: Hellraiser II 646a
The Hellcats 282
Hellcats of the Navy 362
Helldorado 552
Helle 510
Heller in Pink Tights 363
Hellfighters 108
Hellfire 391
The Hellfire Club p. 670
Hellgate 416
The Hellions 427
Hello Again p. 671
Hello Annapolis 602
Hello Anxiety 625
Hello Cheyenne 101
Hello Dolly! 585
Hello Down There p. 671
Hello Elephant 622
Hello Everybody 666
Hello Frisco Hello 102
Hello God 192, 293
Hello Goodbye 142
Hello Mary Lou, Prom Night II p. 671
Hello Sister (1930) 528
Hello Sister (1933) 281
Hello Sucker 644
Hello Trouble 322
Hellraiser 646a
Hell's Angels (1930) 208, 468, 164,
 698
Hell's Angels (1969) 367
Hell's Angels on Wheels 328

- I -

Jenny Be Good   645
Jenny Lamour   610
Jens Monson in America   575
Jeopardy   419
Jeremiah Johnson   89
Jeremy   p. 677
The Jerk (1965)   142
The Jerk (1979)   317
The Jerusalem File   120, 496
Jes' Call Me Jim   357
Jesse and Lester, Two Brothers
   in a Place Called Trinity
   p. 677
Jesse James (1927)   561
Jesse James (1939)   41
Jesse James at Bay   443
Jesse James, Jr.   377
Jesse James Meets Frankenstein's
   Daughter   696
Jesse James vs. The Daltons
   679
Jesse James' Women   462
Jessica   489
Jessie's Girls   230
Jesus Christ Superstar   564
Jesus Christ's Horoscope   p. 677
Jesus of Montreal   p. 677
Jet Attack   676
Jet Job   357
Jet over the Atlantic   p. 677
Jet Pilot   273
Jet Storm   268
Jetlag   p. 677
Les Jeux Interdits   305
Jew Suss   325
The Jewel of the Nile   141
Jewel Robbery   335
Jeweled Nights   266
The Jewelers of Midnight   610
Jewels of Brandenberg   322
Jewels of Desire   48
Jezebel   249
Jezebel's Kiss   p. 677
Jiggs and Maggie in Society   447
Jiggs and Maggie Out West   447
Jigsaw (1949)   381
Jigsaw (1962)   228
Jigszw (1968)   532
Jigsaw (1990)   p. 677
The Jilt   390
Jim Hanvey Detective   391
Jim the Conqueror   528
Jim the Penman   585
Jim, the World's Greatest   412
Jim Thorpe--All American   249
Jimmie's Millions   390
Jimmy the Gent   429

Jimmy Valentine   443
Jinx   671
Jinx Money   357
Jinxed   707
Jitterbugs   14
Jivaro   361
Jive Junction   429
Jo   142
Jo Jo Dancer, Your Life Is Calling   11
Joan at the Stake   486
Joan of Arc   637
The Joan of Arc of Loos   42
Joan of Ozark   416
Joan of Paris   411
Joan of Plattsburg   389
Joan of the Angels   p. 677
Joan the Woman   699
Joanna (1925)   335
Joanna (1968)   346
Joao   141
Jocks   233
Joe (1924)   465
Joe (1970)   22
Joe and Ethel Turp Call on the
   President   565
Joe Butterfly   218
Joe Dakota   520
Joe Hill   p. 677
Joe Kidd   596
The Joe Louis Story   79
Joe Macbeth   168
Joe Palooka   166
Joe Palooka, Champ   322
Joe Palooka in Fighting Mad   560
Joe Palooka in the Big Fight   575
Joe Palooka in the Squared Circle   357
Joe Palooka in Winner Takes All   560
Joe Palooka Meets Humphrey   560
Joe Panther   p. 677
Joe Smith American   350
Joey   693a
Johan   298
Johanna Enlists   526
John and Julie   228
John and Mary   511
John and the Missus   618
John Goldfarb, Please Come Home!
   555
John Loves Mary   386
John Meade's Woman   180
John of the Fair   p. 677
John Paul Jones   312
John Petticoats   20
John Smith   127
John Wesley   219
Johnny Allegro   51
Johnny Angel   682

- K -

Kentucky Pride 540
Kerby Gow 277
La Kermesse Herique 585
Kes 409
The Kettles in the Ozarks 520
The Kettles on Old MacDonald's
   Farm 16
The Key (1934) 249
The Key (1958) 431
The Key (1983) 291
The Key (1990) p. 679
Key Exchange 434
Key Largo 193
Key to the City 528
The Key to Yesterday 548
Key Witness (1946) 602
Key Witness (1960) 672
The Keyhole 405
The Keys of the Kingdom 415
Khartoum 537, 670
Khyber Patrol 644
Kibitzer 216
Kick Back 143
Kick In (1922) 415
Kick-In (1931) 419
The Kick-Off 708
The Kid 624
Kid Blue 685
Kid Boots 419
The Kid Brother 371
The Kid Comes Back 166
The Kid from Amarillo 78
The Kid from Arizona 127
The Kid from Broken Gun 78
The Kid from Brooklyn 621
The Kid from Canada p. 679
The Kid from Cleveland 391
Kid from Kansas 65
The Kid from Kokomo 262
The Kid from Left Field 297
The Kid from Santa Fe 288
The Kid from Spain 621
The Kid from Texas (1939) 654
The Kid from Texas (1950) 644
A Kid for Two Farthings 537
Kid Galahad (1937) 208
Kid Galahad (1962) 242
Kid Glove Killer 650
Kid Gloves 513
The Kid Is Clever 353
Kid Millions 509, 621
Kid Monk Baroni 644
Kid Nightingale 166
The Kid Rides Again 237
Kid Rodelo p. 679
The Kid Sister (1927) 605
The Kid Sister (1945) 75

The Kid Stakes 263
Kidnapped (1938) 221, 621
Kidnapped (1948) 560
Kidnapped (1959) 46
Kidnapped (1971) 46
The Kidnappers p. 679
The Kid's Clever 303
The Kid's Last Ride 105
A Kiev Comedy p. 679
Kiki 389
Kildare of Storm 396
The Kill (1966) 510
Kill (1968) p. 679
Kill (1971) 514
Kill a Dragon p. 679
Kill and Kill Again p. 679
Kill Baby Kill p. 679
Kill Her Gently 255
Kill Me Again p. 679
Kill or Be Killed (1950) 287
Kill or Be Killed (1967) p. 679
Kill or Be Killed (1980) p. 679
Kill or Cure 171
Kill Me Tomorrow 171
Kill the Referee 514
Kill the Umpire 350
Kill Them All and Come Back Alone
   p. 679
The Killer (1921) 638
The Killer (1972) 510
Killer Ape 680
Killer at Large (1935) 561
Killer at Large (1947) 75
Killer Dill 560
The Killer Elite 349
Killer Fish 569
Killer Force 121a; p. 679
The Killer Inside Me 189
The Killer Is Loose 36
Killer Leopard 439
Killer McCoy 533
Killer Party 360a
Killer Shark 560
The Killer Shrews 106
The Killer That Stalked New York 51
The Killers (1946) 68
The Killers (1964) p. 679
Killers from Space 108
Killer's Kiss p. 679
The Killers of Kilimanjaro 427
Killers Three p. 679
The Killing 36
A Killing Affair p. 679
The Killing Fields 409
The Killing Game p. 679
Killing Hour 482
Killing Me Softly 372

Lucky Boy 297
The Lucky Bride p. 686
Lucky Cisco Kid 14
Lucky Days p. 686
Lucky Devil 699
Lucky Devils (1933) 287
Lucky Devils (1941) 644
Lucky Horeshoe 101
Lucky in Love 585, 602
Lucky Jade p. 686
Lucky Jim 235
Lucky Jordan 552
Lucky Lady (1926) 419
Lucky Lady (1975) 634
Lucky Larkin 403
Lucky Larrigan 584
Lucky Legs 602
Lucky Losers 357
The Lucky Mascot p. 686
Lucky Me 106
Lucky Night 306
The Lucky Number 329
Lucky Partners 143
Lucky Star (1929) 374
The Lucky Star (1980) 618
The Lucky Stiff (1948) 348
Lucky Stiff (1989) 246
Lucky Terror 503
The Lucky Texan 584
Lucky To Be a Woman 392
Lucky Gallant 361
Lucretia Borgia 399
Ludwig 437
Ludwig II 564
Luggage of the Gods p. 686
The Lullaby (1924) 379
Lullaby (1961) p. 686
Lullaby of Broadway 106
Lulu 312
Lulu Belle 348
Lumberjack 253
Lumiere p. 686
Lumiere d'Ete p. 686
Lummox 591
Luna 583
The Lunatic at Large 447
Lunch Wagon p. 686
Lure of Ambition 351
The Lure of Egypt 638
Lure of Gold 25
The Lure of Jade 301
The Lure of Luxury 334
The Lure of the Bush 42
The Lure of the Jungle p. 686
The Lure of the Night Club 441
Lure of the Swamp 588
Lure of the Wasteland p. 686

Lure of the Wild 407
Lure of the Wilderness 125
The Lure of Youth 335
Lured 133
Luring Lips 417
Lust for a Vampire p. 686
Lust for Gold 584
Lust for Life 253, 703
The Lusty Men 204
Luther 703
Luv 348
Luxury Girls 489
Luxury Liner (1933) 419
Luxury Liner (1948) 348, 483
Lydia (1941) 204
Lydia (1964) p. 686
Lydia Bailey 297
Lying Lips 556, 593
The Lying Truth 243
Lying Wives 708
The Lyons in Paris p. 686

– M –

M (1931) 653
M (1951) 348
Ma and Pa Kettle 213
Ma and Pa Kettle at Home 245
Ma and Pa Kettle at the Fair 213, 644
Ma and Pa Kettle at Waikiki 581
Ma and Pa Kettle Back on the Farm
  644
Ma and Pa Kettle at Waikiki 581
Ma and Pa Kettle Back on the Farm
  644
Ma and Pa Kettle Go to Town 644
Ma and Pa Kettle on Vacation 520
Ma Barker's Killer Brood p. 686
Ma, He's Making Eyes at Me 68
Ma Nuit Chez Maude 10
Mac and Me 406
Macabre 245
Macao 682
Macario 177
Macaroni p. 686
MacArthur 623
MacArthur's Children p. 686
Macbeth (1948) 532
Macbeth (1963) 703
Macbeth (1971) 604
Machete 591
Machine Gun Kelly 128
Machine Gun Mama 473
Machine Gun McCain p. 686
Machismo--40 Graves for 40 Guns p. 686
Macho Callahan 182

Madonna of the Desert 377
Madonna of the Seven Moons 121
Madonna of the Streets (1924) 335
Madonna of the Streets (1930) 488
Madonnas and Men 87
The Madonna's Secret 12
Madron 233, 240
The Madwoman of Chaillot 242, 510
Maedchen in Uniform p. 687
Maeva p. 687
Mafia (1969) 145
The Mafia (1972) p. 687
Mafioso 437
Mafu Cage 29
A Magdalene of the Hills 92
The Maggie 155
Maggie Pepper 1
Magic 317
Magic Boy p. 687
The Magic Bow 121
The Magic Box 91
The Magic Carpet 95
The Magic Christian 634
The Magic Cup 453
The Magic Face p. 687
Magic Fire 249
The Magic Flame 41
The Magic Fountain p. 687
The Magic Garden (1927) 561
The Magic Garden (1952) 463
The Magic Garden of Stanley
  Sweetheart 317
The Magic Mountain 37
Magic Night 703
The Magic of Lassie 385
Magic Spectacles 343
The Magic Sword 650
Magic Town 51
The Magic Voyage of Sinbad
  p. 687
The Magic Weaver p. 687
The Magic World of Topo Gigo
  p. 687
The Magician (1926) 552
The Magician (1959) 181
The Magician of Lublin 244
The Magiochi Saga p. 687
The Magistrate 486
Magliari 158
The Magnet 38
Magnet of Doom 142
The Magnetic Monster 644
The Magnificent Ambersons 117
The Magnificent Brute (1921) 178
The Magnificent Brute (1936) 211
The Magnificent Concubine p. 687
The Magnificent Cuckold 437

Magnificent Doll 637
The Magnificent Dope 386
The Magnificent Flirt 210
The Magnificent Fraud 408
The Magnificent Lie 340
The Magnificent Matador 36
Magnificent Obsession (1935) 410
Magnificent Obsession (1954) 411
The Magnificent One p. 687
Magnificent Roughnecks 644
The Magnificent Seven 340
The Magnificent Seven Deadly Sins
  p. 687
The Magnificent Seven Ride 326
Magnificent Sinner 312
The Magnificent Tramp p. 687
The Magnificent Two 580
The Magnificent Yankee 533
Magnum Force 572
The Magus 685
The Mahabharata 370
Mahler 83
Mahoghany 668
Maicol p. 687
The Maid of Belgium 257
Maid of Salem 626
Maid of the West 67
Maid to Order p. 687
The Maiden p. 687
A Maiden for a Prince 209
The Maidens' War 366
The Maids 564
Maid's Night Out 502
Mail Order Bride 650
The Mailman 183
The Main Attraction 634
The Main Chance 692
The Main Event (1938) 561
The Main Event (1979) 623
Main Street (1923) 162
Main Street (1956) 312
Main Street after Dark 524
The Main Street Kid 377
Main Street Lawyer 391
Main Street to Broadway 281
The Main Thing Is To Love p. 687
Main Sales 23
Mais Ou et Donc Ornicar p. 687
Maisie 565
Maisie Gets Her Man 585
Maisie Goes to Reno 483
Maisie Was a Lady 350
Maj la Male 446
Majin p. 687
The Major and the Minor 626
Major Barbara 438
Major Dundee 352

Man-Eater of Kumaon 408
A Man Escaped 80
Man Friday 474
A Man for All Seasons 427
A Man Four Square 376
The Man from Beyond 180, 708
The Man from Bitter Ridge 411
The Man from Blankley's 645
The Man from Cairo p. 688
Man from Cheyenne 342
Man from Cocody p. 688
The Man from Colorado 567
Man from Dakota 306
Man from Del Rio 117
The Man from Down Under 654
Man from Frisco 391
The Man from Funeral Ridge 645
The Man from Galveston 221
Man from God's Country (1924)
  494
Man from God's Country (1958)
  439
The Man from Guntown 153
The Man from Hardpan 660
Man from Headquarters (1928)
  147
Man from Headquarters (1942)
  p. 688
The Man from Hell 443
The Man from Hell's River 194
The Man from Home (1914) 699
The Man from Home (1922) 453
The Man from Hong Kong 63
The Man from Laramie 340
The Man from Lost River 71
Man from Montana 644
The Man from Monterey 403
The Man from Montreal 331
The Man from Morocco 168
Man from Music Mountain (1938)
  391
Man from Music Mountain (1943)
  66
The Man from Nevada 147
The Man from New Mexico 334
A Man from Nowhere (1920) 443
The Man from Nowhere (1930
  147
Man From Nowhere (1953) 154
Man From Oklahoma 66
The Man from Painted Post 184
The Man from Planet X 532
The Man from Rainbow Valley 608
The Man from Red Gulch 48
The Man from Rio Grande 377
Man from Snowy River 656
The Man from Sundown 322

Man from Texas (1938) 357
The Man from Texas (1948) 524
The Man from the Alamo 411
The Man from the Black Hills 416
The Man from the Diner's Club 420
A Man from the East p. 688
The Man from the East p. 688
The Man from the Niger 80
The Man from the West 360
The Man from Toronto p. 688
The Man from Tumbleweeds 407
The Man from Utah 584
The Man from Wyoming (1924) 211
The Man from Wyoming (1930) 180
Man from Yesterday 591
Man Hunt (1936) 533
Man Hunt (1941) 415
The Man Hunter (1919) 187
The Man Hunter (1930) 645
The Man I Love (1929) 210
The Man I Love (1946) 262
The Man I Killed 419
The Man I Married 386
The Man I Marry 198, 637
The Man in Blue (1925) 151
The Man in Blue (1937) 520
The Man in Grey 123
Man in Half Moon Street 556
The Man in Hobbles 297
Man in Love 706
Man in Possession 389
Man in the Attic 626
Man in the Back Seat 700
Man in the Dark (1953) 128
Man in the Dark (1965) 168
Man in the Dinghy 235
The Man in the Glass Booth 352
The Man in the Gray Flannel Suit 102
Man in the Iron Mask 483
Man in the Middle 114
The Man in the Mirror 119
Man in the Moon 670
The Man in the Net 552
A Man in the Open 441
The Man in the Raincoat 283
Man in the Rough 602
The Man in the Saddle (1926) 360
Man in the Saddle (1951) 350
Man in the Shadow (1926) 238
Man in the Shadow (1957) 16
Man in the Trunk 380
Man in the Vault 108
Man in the White Suit 564
Man in the Wilderness 182
The Man Inside (1958) 427
The Man Inside p. 688
The Man Life Passed By 374

994 / Film Title Index

That Night (1958--Fr.) 80
That Night in Rio 555
That Night with You 68, 644
That Obscure Object of Desire
  514
That Other Woman 378
That Riviera Touch 260
"That Royle Girl" (1925) 180,
  562
That Sinking Feeling p. 727
That Something 684
That Summer 668
That Summer of White Roses 480
That Tennessee Brat p. 727
That Touch of Mink 411
That Uncertain Feeling 41
That Was Then ... This Is Now
  p. 727
That Way with Women 403
That Wild West 494
That Woman p. 727
That Woman Opposite 38
That Wonderful Urge 102
That'll Be the Day 598
That's a Good Girl 703
That's Adequate 176
That's Carry On 290
That's Good 396
That's Gratitude 192
That's Life 515
That's My Baby (1926) 379
That's My Baby (1944) 481
That's My Boy (1932) 20
That's My Boy (1951) 204
That's My Daddy 620
That's My Gal 608
That's My Man 208
That's My Story 68
That's Right, You're Wrong 411
That's the Spirit 644
That's the Ticket 168
That's the Way of the World p. 727
Theatre of Blood 599
Theatre of Death 604
Theatre Royal 692
Their Big Moment 674
Their Last Night 3
Their Mutual Child 519
Their Own Desire 133
Thelma 379
Them! 262
Then Came the Woman 238
Theodora Goes Wild 659
There Ain't No Justice 235
There Are No Villains 17
There Goes Kelly 560
There Goes My Girl 20

There Goes My Heart 71
There Goes the Groom 331
There Is No 13 57
There Was a Crooked Man (1960) 289
There Was a Crooked Man (1970) 586
There Was a Young Man p. 727
There Was an Old Couple p. 727
There Were Days and Moons p. 727
There Were Times, Dear p. 727
There You Are! 513
There's a Girl in My Heart 602
There's a Girl in My Soup 670
There's Always a Thursday p. 727
There's Always a Way To Find a Way
  646
There's Always a Woman 192
There's Always Tomorrow 411
There's No Business Like Show
  Business 555
There's One Born Every Minute 65
There's Something about a Soldier
  407, 602
There's That Woman Again 659
Therese 531
Therese and Isabelle p. 727
Therese Desqueroux 399
Therese Raquin (1915) p. 727
Therese Raquin (1927) p. 727
Therese Raquin (1953) 283
These Dangerous Years 155
These Glamour Girls 216
These Sorcerers Are Mad 142
These Thirty Years p. 727
These Thousand Hills 102
These Three 621
These Wilder Years 185
They All Came Out 151, 650
They All Kissed the Bride 659
They All Laughed 433
They Are Not Angels p. 727
They Asked for It 117
They Call It Sin 645
They Call Me Mister Tibbs 179
They Call Me Robert p. 727
They Came by Night 121
They Came from beyond Space 667
They Came from Within p. 727
They Came To a City 460
They Came To Blow Up America 14
They Came To Cordura 242
They Came To Rob Las Vegas p. 727
They Can't Hang Me p. 727
They Dare Not Love 484
They Died with Their Boots On 221
They Drive by Night (1938) 168
They Drive by Night (1940) 166
They Flew Alone 235

The Thirteenth Chair (1919)   451
The Thirteenth Chair (1929)   211
The Thirteenth Chair (1937)   102
The Thirteenth Commandment   645
The Thirteenth Guest   439
The Thirteenth Hour   170
The Thirteenth Juror   513
The Thirteenth Letter   345
The 13th Man   293
--30--   109
Thirty a Week   671
30 below Zero   376
Thirty Day Princess   555
Thirty Days   77
The Thirty Foot Bride of Candy
   Rock   p. 728
Thirty Is a Dangerous Age,
   Cynthia   685
39 East   453
The Thirty Nine Steps (1935)
   325
The Thirty Nine Steps (1960)   580
The Thirty-Nine Steps (1978)   115
30 Seconds of Love   423
Thirty Seconds over Tokyo   528,
   597
Thirty Six Hours   349
36 Hours To Kill   415
$30,000   620
This above All   415
This Angry Age   392
This Could Be the Night   253
This Day and Age   386
This Earth Is Mine   273, 411
This England   235
This Gun for Hire   552
This Happy Breed   438
This Happy Feeling   16
This Hero Stuff   519
This Is a Hijack   365
This Is Elvis   282
This Is Heaven   41, 621
This Is Life   101
This Is My Affair   483
This Is My Love   306
This Is My Street   286
This Is Spinal Tap   p. 728
This Is the Army   221, 488
This Is the Life   420
This Island Earth   581
This Kind of Love   209
This Land Is Mine   502
This Love of Ours   36
This Mad World   386, 528
This Madding Crowd   p. 728
This Man Can't Die   p. 728
This Man in Paris   p. 728

This Man Is Mine (1934)   1
This Man Is Mine (1946)   p. 728
This Man Is News   p. 728
This Man Must Die   498
This Man's Navy   654
This Marriage Business   20
This Modern Age   526
This One or None   119
This Property Is Condemned   281
This Rebel Breed   19
This Reckless Age   556
This Savage Land   p. 728
This Side of Heaven   528
This Side of the Law   245
This Special Friendship   399
This Sporting Age   607
This Sporting Life   112
This Thing Called Love (1929)   71
This Thing Called Love (1941)   659
This Time for Keeps (1947)   193
This Time for Keeps (1954)   350
This Was a Woman   329
This Was Paris   168
This Way, Please   180
This Week of Grace   p. 728
This Wine of Love   44
This Woman   72
This Woman Is Dangerous   403
This Woman Is Mine   331
Thomas   370
The Thomas Crown Affair   677
Thomasine and Bushrod   36
Thorns and Apple Blossoms   591
The Thoroughbred (1925)   494
The Thoroughbred (1930)   163
Thoroughbred (1936)   259
Thoroughbreds   66
Thoroughbreds Don't Cry   565
Thoroughly Modern Millie   411
Those Calloways   109
Those Daring Young Men in Their
   Jaunty Jalopies   486, 697
Those Endearing Young Charms   607
Those Fantastic Flying Fools   700
Those Glory, Glory Days   p. 728
Those High, Grey Walls   594
Those Kids from Town   692
Those Lips, Those Eyes   86
Those Magnificent Men in Their
   Flying Machines   97
Those of the Side Show   260
Those Redheads from Seattle   361
Those Three French Girls   211
Those We Love   166
Those Were the Days (1934)   307
Those Were the Days (1940)   419
Those Who Dance   262

Tomorrow It Will Be Better 260
Tomorrow Never Comes p. 730
Tomorrow the World 556
Tomorrow We Live 237
Tomorrow's Love 221
Tom's Gang 435
Tong Man 688
Tongues of Flame 140
Tongues of Scandal 555
Toni 510
Tonight a Town Dies p. 730
Tonight and Every Night 398
Tonight at Twelve 18
Tonight Is Ours 591
Tonight or Never 621
Tonight We Raid Calais 36
Tonight We Sing 555
Tonight's the Night (1954) 460
Tonight's the Night (1966) 437
Tonio, Son of the Sierras 227
Tonka 239
The Tonopah Stampede of Gold 701
Tonto Basin Outlaws 105
Tony America 658
Tony Rome 51
Tony Runs Wild 101
Too Bad She's Bad p. 730
Too Beautiful for You 531
Too Busy To Work 102, 125
Too Far To Go 346
Too Fat To Fight 87
Too Hot To Handle (1938) 528
Too Hot To Handle (1960) 260
Too Late Blues 361
Too Late for Tears 408
Too Late the Hero 51
Too Many Blondes 331
Too Many Cooks 435
Too Many Crooks (1919) 127
Too Many Crooks (1958) 460
Too Many Girls 502
Too Many Husbands 659
Too Many Kisses 528
Too Many Millions 526
Too Many Parents 591
Too Many Winners 237
Too Many Wives 435
Too Much Business 517
Too Much Johnson 542
Too Much Married 444
Too Much Money 185
Too Much Speed 542
Too Much Sun 702a
Too Much, Too Soon 245, 435
Too Outrageous p. 730
Too Small, My Friend 603

Too Soon To Die 437
Too Tough To Kill 407
Too WIse Wives 187
Too Young To Kiss 533
Too Young To Know 245
Too Young To Love 215
Too Young To Marry 262
The Toolbox Murders 230
Toomorrow (1970) 83
Tootsie 523
Top Banana 66
Top Gun (1955) 679
Top Gun (1986) p. 730
Top Hat (1935) 1, 660
Top Hat (1977) 372
Top Man 420
The Top O' the Morning (1922) 593
Top 'O the Morning (1949) 361
The Top of New York 645
Top of the Town 637
Top of the World (1925) 102
Top of the World (1955) 682
Top Secret! 97
Top Secret Affair 117
Top Sergeant 520
Top Sergeant Mulligan (1928) 105
Top Sergeant Mulligan (1941) 575
Top Speed 262
Topaz 268
Topaze 14
Topeka 416
Topkapi 8
Topper 71
Topper Returns 71
Topper Takes a Trip 71
Topsy and Eva 65
Topsy-Turvy Journey p. 730
Tora! Tora! Tora! 678
The Torch 177
Torch Singer 591
Torch Song 483
Torch Song Trilogy 535a
Torchlight 475
Torchy Blaine in Chinatown 373
Torchy Blaine in Panama 208
Torchy Gets Her Man 620
Torchy Plays with Dynamite 620
Torchy Runs for Mayor 373
Torment (1924) 620
Torment (1947) p. 730
Torment (1986) p. 730
Torn Curtain 665
The Tornado (1924) 594
Tornado (1943) 295
Tornado Range 75
Torpedo Alley 560
Torpedo Bay 486
Torpedo Boat 295

- X -

- Y -

- Z -